MEN, WOMEN, AND CHANGE

A SOCIOLOGY OF MARRIAGE AND FAMILY

MEN, WOMEN, AND CHANGE

A SOCIOLOGY OF MARRIAGE AND FAMILY

THIRD EDITION

Letha Dawson Scanzoni

John Scanzoni
University of Florida-Gainesville

McGRAW-HILL BOOK COMPANY

New York   St. Louis   San Francisco   Auckland   Bogotá   Hamburg
London   Madrid   Mexico   Milan   Montreal   New Delhi
Panama   Paris   São Paulo   Singapore   Sydney   Tokyo   Toronto

MEN, WOMEN, AND CHANGE

A Sociology of Marriage and Family

2 3 4 5 6 7 8 9 0 DOCDOC 8 9 3 2 1 0 9 8

ISBN 0-07-055063-8

This book was set in Caslon 224 Book by the College Composition Unit
in cooperation with University Graphics, Inc.
The editors were Stephanie K. Happer and David Dunham;
the designer was Joan E. O'Connor;
the production supervisor was Denise L. Puryear.
R. R. Donnelley & Sons Company was printer and binder.

Credits for part-opening and chapter-opening photos are on pages 668 and 669.

Library of Congress Cataloging-in-Publication Data

Scanzoni, Letha.
    Men, women, and change.
    Bibliography: p.
    Includes index.
    1. Marriage.   2. Family.   3. Sex role.   4. Sociali-
zation.   I. Scanzoni, John H., (date).   II. Title.
HQ734.S3764   1988   306.8   87-3802
          ISBN 0-07-055063-8

TO
DAVE SCANZONI
AND
TO
STEVE, KAREN, AND BRYAN SCANZONI

C·O·N·T·E·N·T·S

IN BRIEF

P·A·R·T F·I·V·E
STRUCTURE AND PROCESS IN MARRIAGE

P·A·R·T S·I·X
CONTINUING PROCESSES OF THE FAMILY EXPERIENCE

C·O·N·T·E·N·T·S

P·R·E·F·A·C·E

In the first edition of *Men, Women, and Change* (1976), we stated that our aim was "to write a marriage and family textbook that could utilize the best in recent sociological theory, presented not in some abstract way but in terms of issues that students care about most." That goal has been kept in mind in writing subsequent editions as well. We are interested, as are students, in the concerns of real people living in the real world. In this third edition, we again have made every effort to treat topics not only scientifically and systematically but humanely and practically as well.

We've tried to present concepts such as social exchange, conflict, gender roles, power, and decision-making in ways that make sociology come alive. To aid in this, we've interwoven throughout the text numerous case studies, photos, drawings, cartoons, and boxed inserts designed to relate the material to life all around us.

Tables and graphs, in which statistics "tell a story," have also been used abundantly to show how patterns and trends are spotted. Contrary to their unfortunate stereotype, statistics are far more than cold, boring, impersonal numbers. The statistics in this book provide information on matters of interest to most students: for example, the upward trend in age at marriage, premarital sexual behavior, cohabitation patterns, singleness, employment, racial and gender income differences, mothers' labor-force participation, childcare arrangements, contraceptive usage, abortion, birth rates, divorce and remarriage, issues surrounding aging, and so on. Great pains have been taken to obtain the latest available statistics at the time of writing. (Students need to be aware, however, of the time lag that occurs between the gathering and the presentation of statistical information. For example, a census publication may present a statistical picture that shows something about the population at a point in time two or more years before the date the publication is issued. Not only does it take time for researchers to conduct surveys and collect data, but more time must be spent sorting out and analyzing the findings and putting them in a form that will be most useful to those needing the information. Only then does the material enter the publishing process and move toward its appearance in print. At this point, the published material becomes accessible to scholars who then integrate it into their own studies and writings, and it then enters another publishing process, which again takes more time! In the case of this book, new data has become available from the Census Bureau just as we are going to press; and we are including it to ensure that the material presented herein is as current as possible.)

The combination of a professional writer who specializes in the study and communication of sociology (Letha Dawson Scanzoni) working with a sociologist involved in sociological research, teaching, and theory-building (John Scanzoni) helps information and theory come to life in an intellectually stimulating manner with maximum personal involvement on the part of the reader. Our aim has been to present research and *explain* research findings—especially through exchange or cost/reward theory, but through other approaches as well—so that students can see what sociology is all about. It's about nothing less than the essentials of daily living—human beings in relationships with or in conflicts with other human beings, whether in conventional or emerging marriage and family arrangements or in alternative lifestyles.

Incidentally, in using the word *family,* we don't consider it synonymous with "white, middle-class, nuclear family." In all three editions of this book, the information presented has been presented with *all* families in mind, and the theoretical explanations should help shed light on all types of marriage and family situations. Material on marriages and families that vary according to socioeconomic status or race is interwoven throughout rather than being treated in isolated fashion as has often been the custom. For example, while this book abounds with material on black families of both higher and lower socioeconomic status, there is no separate chapter on "the black family." We believe students are interested in learning about similarities and differences among racial and socioeconomic groupings *with re-*

spect to each subject area treated: dating, cohabitation, premarital sex, reproduction, employment, gender role, marital satisfaction, divorce, and so on.

WHAT'S DIFFERENT IN THE THIRD EDITION?

Some changes have been made in the organization of this edition. For example, the material on premarital sex (two chapters in the second edition) is now combined into one chapter. The chapter on the extended kin has been moved to Part Six, "Continuing Processes of the Family Experience," which seemed a more logical placement. Some of the chapter titles have been changed, and a new chapter on women's employment and its impact on marriage has been added.

Each chapter contains new material as well as an updating of subjects treated in the earlier editions. Some chapters have been overhauled and changed considerably; others (often at the request of reviewers who liked the material in previous editions) have been revised only slightly.

Part One briefly lays the groundwork for understanding how marriage and family can be studied scientifically and introduces students to some key concepts and theoretical approaches used by family scholars.

As in the two previous editions, societally assigned gender roles and the current questioning of those roles constitute a major focus. The two chapters in Part Two present discussions of gender-role socialization and the male-female equality question in historical and cross-cultural perspective. New material on gender roles in Cuba has been added, and the material on the kibbutz has been updated.

In Part Three, "Before Marriage," the chapter on dating and choosing a marriage partner provides a historical and cross-cultural perspective on dating and courtship customs, new material on innovative, nontraditional practices in meeting potential dating and marriage partners, new material on gender-role ideology and dating practices, more material on black singles and dating, an expanded section on interracial and interreligious marriages, and a look at dating and mate selection in a context of social change. The other chapter in Part Three provides a detailed discussion of sex before marriage and includes updated statistics on premarital sex and premarital pregnancies; it also shows the greater convergence between the premarital sexual behavior of blacks and whites in recent years.

Part Four, "Alternatives to Traditional Marriage and Family," examines other lifestyles and ways of "being family" to one another that considerable numbers of persons are experiencing today. Chapter 6 provides updated cohabitation statistics and gives further attention to research indicating who cohabits, types of cohabitation relationships, trends in cohabitation, and whether prior cohabitation has an effect on marriage. The second section of Chapter 6 contains an expanded discussion of gay parenthood, what same-sex couples and heterosexual couples share in common, and more material on everyday living among lesbian and gay male couples, as well as detailed material carried over from the second edition.

Chapter 7 presents new material on the likelihood of marriage for women and men at various age and education levels; why greater numbers of people today are living alone; both chosen and circumstantial singleness; the male-female ratio among blacks and the limitations in marriage prospects among college-educated black women; expanded material on motherhood outside of marriage; unwed fathers and legitimacy/custody issues; single parenthood through adoption, divorce, or the death of a spouse; and new material on combined households and substitute kin through shared living arrangements.

Part Five, "Structure and Process in Marriage," contains what many instructors tell us they consider to be the core of the book—an analysis of the structure and dynamics of marriage using a uniquely developed typology of marriage patterns and what goes on in each form. In this new edition, all four basic patterns are now brought together and explained in a single chapter (Chapter 8), along with a new discussion of an alternative pattern, "wives as senior partners."

Chapter 9 is a new chapter pulling together certain material from several chapters in the earlier editions along with vast amounts of completely new material on past and present women's employment and its impact on marriage and family. Special attention is given to the effects that societal gender-role ideology has had historically on women in the workforce. Changing attitudes toward women's employment are also discussed.

In Chapter 10, the treatment of marital expressiveness is updated and enhanced with more material on economic factors in marital expressiveness, the contribution of a wife's occupation to her own and her family's social status, extramarital sex, dual earner couples and work overload, and sexual expression in marriage.

Chapters 11 and 12, on power, decision-making, and conflict, retain much of the material that was so well received in the two previous editions, including a description of the marital dynamics of a hypothetical couple, Bob and Julie. There is also an expansion of the material on economic factors and the balance of power in marriage and alternative relationships, gender roles and decision-making, written contracts, and more material on communication and its part in negotiation and conflict resolution. The section on marital violence has also been updated and enlarged.

Part Six, the final section of the book, "Continuing Processes of the Family Experience," deals with childbearing decisions, childrearing, the extended kin, the middle and later years of marriage, and divorce, remarriage, and stepfamilies.

Chapter 13 contains updated statistics and other research findings on contraception, sterilization, and abortion. In addition to the discussion of voluntary childlessness carried over from the earlier editions, a discussion of *involuntary* childlessness and alternative routes to parenthood (including new reproductive technologies) has been included in this edition. Material on intentionally delayed motherhood has also been added. The updated macro view of reproduction has been expanded to give a picture of world trends in population control today.

Chapter 14 in this edition contains more material on both motherhood and fatherhood, an expanded and updated discussion of child abuse, and a new section on the sexual abuse of children.

Chapter 15, "The Extended Kin," has been considerably revised and given a different placement in the book's sequence. Additions include a new section on adult adoptees' search for their biological roots and an examination of the changing and more complex kinship structure associated with longer life expectancies of family members along with the multiple relationships resulting from divorce, remarriage, and blended families.

The focus on the middle and later years of marriage in Chapter 16 provides a new look at the increased fluidity of life events over the life span. New material has also been added on a variety of topics, including adult

children who return to live with their parents, gender roles and caregiving responsibilities toward frail elderly parents, and elder abuse. The discussions of retirement and grandparenthood have also been expanded.

Chapter 17 includes an expanded discussion of divorce as a process and of the period after divorce, updated statistics on divorce and solo parenting after divorce, and a new section on the unexpected consequences of divorce law reforms. The treatment of the process of remarrying and establishing a stepfamily has also been enlarged.

Throughout this third edition, as in the previous editions, we have tried to provide students not only with factual information but also with learning tools to aid them in their ongoing out-of-class understanding of gender-role issues, marriage, and family. Analytical tools include the theoretical approaches presented in the text (especially cost/reward theory and conflict theory). The extensive references are another valuable tool to acquaint students with the broad range of materials available on the various subjects discussed, thus providing a useful resource for further study and research in areas of particular interest.

We send out this third edition with the same hope with which we launched its predecessors, namely, that it will help equip students with the kind of accurate insight and understanding necessary to make rational decisions and sound judgments. We also hope that it will provide a solid basis for the choices they will have to make about themselves, their present and future families, and for the social policy decisions they may wish to support, influence, or oppose as part of this world of men, women, and *change*.

I would like to express my thanks for the many useful comments and suggestions provided by colleagues who reviewed this text during the course of its development, especially to: Benigro Aquirre, Texas A&M University; Rose Marie Arnhold, Fort Hays State University; James L. Bull; Gerard A. Brandmeyer, University of South Florida; William Egelman, Iona College; Ann Goetting, Western Kentucky University; James Gruber, University of Michigan, Dearborn; Charles S. Henderson, Memphis State University; Raymond Kennedy, John Jay College of Criminal Justice, C.U.N.Y.; David E. Olday, Moorhead State University; Jeffrey P. Rosenfeld, Nassau Community College; Robert T. Russell, SUNY, Agricultural and Technical College; Hanna C. Selvin, SUNY at Stony Brook; R. N. Singh, East Texas State University and Kenrick S. Thompson, Northern Michigan University. Thanks also go to Rebecca S. Bowers for her assistance in library research and indexing.

Letha Dawson Scanzoni
John Scanzoni

P·A·R·T O·N·E

· 1 ·

A BRIEF INTRODUCTION TO STUDYING MARRIAGE AND FAMILY

Most of us live out a large share of our lives in some form of family or another. And we can easily see that families can't be ignored if we want to understand the societal patterns and processes all around us. Why? Because the social relationships called *family* are such an important part of society. In fact, no society has ever existed without some sort of social arrangements that may be labeled *kinship* or *familial*.

What people do in their families makes a difference in the larger society. For example, if people have large families, crowded schools may be a problem. On the other hand, what happens in the larger society can have considerable impact on families. Changing economic conditions may make it necessary for a family to alter its plans for financing the children's college education or may force a move to another location and means of livelihood (as happened to many farm families in the mid-1980s). Income tax laws and governmental policies in such areas as Social Security, Medicare, Medicaid, child care, dual-earner couples, and so on all affect families and the decisions they make. Occupational demands may have a profound effect on home life. The world of the family and the broader world beyond the home are interacting constantly.

The U.S. Bureau of the Census (1986, *Current Population Reports*, Series P-20, No. 411, p. 116) defines the term *family* as "a group of two persons or more (one of whom is the householder) related by birth, marriage, or adoption and residing together." Such a definition of *family* limits the term to members of an immediate household and doesn't take into account the extended family of relatives; nor does it fit some of the "quasi-kin" and alternative family forms that some persons may choose instead of conventional family living arrangements. Neverthe-less, the Census Bureau's definition provides us with a starting point.

A SOCIOLOGICAL APPROACH IS A SCIENTIFIC APPROACH

Since families are so much a part of our lives, it may seem strange to look at them in the way sociologists do. Won't something of the wonder and "mystery" of love, marriage, and family be lost if we try to analyze them? Not really—no more than the wonder of plant life is lost through the studies of biologists. And no more than our marvel at the vastness of the universe is lost through the efforts of astronomers. In fact, the work of such scientists *enhances* our experience and appreciation of plants and the universe by increasing our understanding of them. And so it is with the study of marriage and family.

Modern sociology originated in the nineteenth century. It rests on the notion that the basic principles and methods of science can be applied to the study of human societies in much the same way that they are applied to the biological and physical sciences. Science is a way of thinking, a way of discovering why things happen as they do, how things work, and how such knowledge can be used for humanity's benefit.

Sociologists, in their particular area of scientific study, focus on *associations*—that is, two or more persons in some kind of relationship to one another, whether it be a marriage, a labor union, or an entire society. They are looking for answers to four basic questions: (1) How did this association come into being? (2) What holds it together? (3) How and why does it change? (4) How and why does such an association break up?

A sociological study of marriage and family can be understood very simply as an attempt

In studying marriage and family, sociologists seek to understand how families form, why they stay together, how they change, and why some break apart. (© Erika Stone, 1986)

to understand how families form, why they stay together, how and why they change, and why some of them break apart.

HOW SOCIOLOGISTS STUDY MARRIAGE AND FAMILY

In seeking answers to these questions, sociologists gather data in a variety of ways. They may use surveys in which one or more family members answer questions about some aspect of family life. They may conduct in-depth interviews. They may analyze data from census reports to ascertain trends in family-related issues. They may conduct participant-observation studies or use videotapes to study families up close in everyday living situations. Sometimes they design experimental studies to observe the ways couples or family groups interact with one another. But regardless of the particular research method used, the goal is to study marriage and family *scientifically*. An important aspect of the scientific method is the measurement of concepts. A *concept* is a general idea or notion about something that is arrived at by mentally combining its various particulars into one overall picture. Education is a concept, as is fertility. When we begin measuring a concept, it is also called a *variable*. The emphasis is on how something varies.

For example, counting the number of years spent in school is a way to measure education. Years in school could vary anywhere from zero to ten or twelve or more. Thus we may speak of education (number of years in school) as a variable. Or, to take another example, the number of children born to a woman is a way to measure her fertility. Again, that too could vary—anywhere from zero to six to twenty.

Scientists are vitally interested in the relationships between variables. Therefore, they often make use of statistics to examine relationships. Here, for instance, it has been found that the more years of schooling a woman has completed, the fewer children she is likely to have. In other words, there is an *inverse relationship* between education and fertility. As education goes up, fertility goes down. On the other hand, there is a *direct relationship* between education and the age at which persons marry. The lower the level of education, the lower the marriage age tends to be; the higher the education, the higher the marriage age tends to be.

The procedure of selecting concepts, measuring them, and examining their interrelationships is part of theory building. *Theory* involves explanation; it is an effort to help us understand the *why* of things. By seeking answers to "why" questions, we can better understand what marriage and family are all about. While sociological research provides facts (for example, statistics on births out of wedlock, data on marriages and divorces, and so on), facts don't always speak for themselves. The vast store of information on mar-

riage and family needs to be analyzed, compared, and explained; this procedure, too, is part of sociological research and is essential not only for present understanding but for predicting future trends as well. We'll be seeing how this works throughout this book.

KEY CONCEPTS IN STUDYING MARRIAGE AND FAMILY

As part of their scientific study of marriage and family, including theory building, sociologists have tended to organize their thinking around three key concepts: time, structure, and interaction. Some sociologists stress one or another of these primarily; others stress all three to some degree.

Time

With the passage of time, one generation follows another and one family leads to the formation of another family. Children grow up under their parents' care in one *nuclear family* (the term sociologists use for the basic unit of a husband and wife and their children because this unit forms the *nucleus*, or core grouping, for what is meant by the term *family*). This first nuclear family is a child's *family of orientation*, the family from which he or she originates. The word *orientation* comes from a Latin root meaning "the east" or "sunrise." Sometimes the family of orientation is spoken of as the *family of origin*. Upon reaching adulthood, persons continue to remain members of their families of orientation; but they are also likely to become members of other families as well—the new families that come into being when these persons marry and have children of their own. Such a nuclear family, in which a person is a spouse and parent rather than a

Social scientists use the term *nuclear family* for the social unit comprised of a husband and wife and their children. (© Erika Stone, 1986)

daughter or son, is called the *family of procreation.*

In that family of procreation, changes also take place with the passage of time. We see a cycle in which a person goes from being single to being one of a pair (through marriage), to being one of a group (as children join the family), then back to being one of a pair (as children leave home), and finally to a single existence once again (after the death of a spouse). This sequence in which a family first expands and then contracts is often called the *family life cycle* (Duvall, 1962). Some sociologists prefer the term *family career* and have various ways of dividing up its stages (Hill, 1964; Rodgers, 1964, 1973; Hill and Rodgers, 1964).

A focus on these cycles and the changes in relationships and patterns that occur in families with the passage of time is often referred to as the *developmental approach* to studying families. Responsibilities attached to different stages of the family career are called *developmental tasks* and range from toddlers' learning to feed themselves to aging persons' adjustments to retirement (Havighurst, 1953; Rodgers, 1973; Duvall, 1962; Aldous, 1978).

Of course, everyone doesn't fit neatly into the conventional family life-cycle pattern. Some persons never marry; others marry but never have children. Some marry but become divorced or widowed at some stage in the family life cycle. Some remarry, while others do not. Some persons rear children as single parents (never-married, divorced, or widowed). And some persons marry for the first time in old age. Thus, a number of sociologists and others with an interest in family research have sounded a call for recycling,

NEVER TOO LATE!

101-YEAR-OLD BACHELOR TO WED

Stockholm, Sweden (AP)—No date has been set for the wedding, but at age 101, Artur Jonsson has become engaged.

"After 100 years as a bachelor I've got a lot to catch up on," said Jonsson, who recently marked his 101st birthday. "Never say never," he added with a chuckle.

Jonsson has spent his life as a bachelor, working as a farmer and a horse dealer from his home town of Askersund, some 110 miles southwest of Stockholm. But last spring he started to feel his age, and placed an advertisement for a housekeeper.

He hired 55-year-old Ingrid Engdal, who moved in this spring. This week, they celebrated their engagement—helped out by the future bride's four grown children.

"This is the best old-age care you can get," Jonsson said.

SOURCE: *Greensboro (NC) News and Record,* Oct. 6, 1984, p. A-5.

rethinking, or updating the traditional life-cycle concept to accommodate today's reality (Feldman and Feldman, 1975; Glick, 1977; Nock, 1979; Aldous, 1978; Rodgers, 1973; Spanier and Sauer, 1979; Murphy and Staples, 1979; Trost, 1974, 1977; Spanier and Glick, 1980a; Norton, 1983; Scanzoni, 1983a).

An alternative perspective is provided by sociologist Glen Elder, Jr., (1975) whose preferred term is the *life course* (p. 165). Elder sees three different time dimensions involved in the course of our lives. First, there is *individual time*—a person's own life span from birth to death. Second, there is *social time*—the timetable marked by important social events and transitions, such as marriage, becoming a parent, or entering retirement. And third, there is *historical time*—the era in which a person lives. Sociologists need to take all three into account.

For example, by emphasizing the need to look at historical time as well as individual and social time, Elder is alerting us to the differing life chances and experiences that characterize persons born in a particular year or decade as compared with persons born at some other point in time. An individual's life course and a family's life cycle are affected by changing social conditions. A war or changing economic conditions, for instance, could affect age at marriage, the number of children a couple chooses to have, when children will be born, where the family will live, what lifestyle they'll be able to attain or maintain, whether the children will go to college, and so on.

To take another example: a person born during a year when the birthrate was especially high can expect more crowded schools and more limited occupational opportunities. That person may therefore settle into a particular job or family pattern that would have been quite different had she or he been born at another time with a less competitive job market.

A group of persons who experience a specific event at the same point in time is called a *cohort*. The word comes from a Latin term for a certain military unit, one of the ten divisions of the Roman legion. The word was later used for any band of soldiers and even-

THE FLUID LIFE CYCLE

What Hirschhorn (1977) has called the "fluid" life cycle [is] one marked by an increasing number of role transitions and by the disappearance of traditional timetables, or what may also be described as the proliferation of timetables and the lack of synchrony among age-related roles. Some observers are impressed with other idiosyncrasies in timing: with the "renewal" activities represented, for example, by the middle-aged or old person who becomes a college freshman or the persons who enter May-December marriages and begin new families, with the occasional result that a man may become a father again at the same time he becomes a grandfather.

While there are few studies in which this social change has actually been measured, our society is becoming accustomed to the 28-year-old mayor, the 30-year-old college president, the 35-year-old grandmother, the 50-year-old retiree, the 65-year-old father of a preschooler, and the 70-year-old student, and even the 85-year-old mother caring for a 65-year-old son.

SOURCE: Bernice L. Neugarten, "Time, Age, and the Life Cycle," *The American Journal of Psychiatry* 136 (July 1979), p. 889.

---

tually came to be used to designate any group or company of persons.

A *birth cohort* consists of persons born in a particular year (or other designated period of time), a *marriage cohort* consists of persons married at the same point in time, a *graduation cohort* would be a group that graduated from high school or college during a certain year, and so on. Elder (1975) especially urges more sociological studies of birth cohorts so that the life course of a group of persons born at one point in time can be compared with the life course of another group born at a different point. Such research can yield a great deal of knowledge about social change, including social change within the specific areas of marriage and family.

Structure

In addition to focusing on time and the changes time brings, sociologists like to look at how a certain social arrangement is put to-gether—in other words, how is it *structured*, what are its various parts, and how do they work together? To think of structure this way leads us to the idea of social systems. Dictionaries define the word *system* as a combination of parts that work together to form a complex, unified whole. We're all familiar with terms like transportation system, heating system, reproductive system, system of government, and so on.

Sociologists who utilize what is called the *structural-functional approach* emphasize that the family is a system. They sometimes borrow from the biological sciences and view the family as an organism with a structural arrangement of interdependent parts, each having a function to perform, just as is true of the human body. They also point out the functions performed by the family in relation to the larger society: replacing society's members through bringing children into the world, socializing children, producing and consuming goods and services, maintaining the physical and emotional well-being of its

As a structure, the family is characterized by persons in various positions (spouse, parent, child, sibling) whose behavior affects one another because the parts are interdependent. (© Ellis Herwig/ The Picture Cube)

members, and performing specified tasks within the home and community.

As a structure, the family is characterized by persons in various positions (spouse, parent, child, sibling), each of whose behavior affects the others because the parts are interdependent. The system works best when all parts are functioning properly. From the structural-functional point of view in sociology, anything that would be considered unfavorable to the smooth working of the system is termed *dysfunctional.* The emphasis is on *order,* or keeping the system "in equilibrium" (Parsons, 1951; Abrahamson, 1978).

Interaction

In addition to time and structure, sociologists place great importance on a third key concept—the process of human interaction.

Put very simply, *interaction* is the back-and-forth interplay that goes on between persons, whether in society as a whole or in a group within society (such as a family). On another level, what goes on inside our minds is also important because various thought processes constitute a kind of "interaction with oneself" (Meltzer et al., 1975:vii). This inner interaction both affects and is affected by our outer interaction with people. For example, a young couple may be trying to decide whether or not to continue their relationship. Each looks at what is liked about the other (what seems rewarding in the relationship) and weighs that against what isn't liked (what seems costly in the relationship). The way the relationship goes is affected by such thought processes; but on the other hand, such thought processes are being affected by how the relationship goes!

Some sociologists emphasize a *symbolic interaction approach,* pointing out that humans interact with one another through symbols (words, gestures, or pictures that stand for something else). And we must be able to interpret the symbols (a smile, a clenched fist, a traffic sign, a spoken word) or meaningful communication and interaction can't take place effectively. Symbolic interactionists stress that *shared meanings* are what hold society together (Meltzer et al., 1975:50).

As applied to the sociology of marriage and family, a symbolic-interactional perspective gives special attention to communication processes through observing "the world of everyday experience" and developing theory out of that experience (Stryker, 1964: 135–136). Furthermore, it isn't enough to observe what family members *do;* our understanding is incomplete unless we try to find out how they *feel* about what they do and why.

Furthermore, how we feel or what we do depends to a great extent upon how we define a particular situation (Thomas, 1923). The key word is *define*. It's not what a situation is in any objective sense, but what persons perceive it to be that matters. If persons "define situations as real, they are real in their consequences" said one of the early pioneers in symbolic interaction theory, W. I. Thomas (1928; quoted in Truzzi, 1971:275). Thomas's notion of the *definition of the situation* is important to keep in mind in understanding human interaction.

To Georg Simmel, a turn-of-the-century pioneer in sociological theory, *reciprocity* was the stuff of everyday life. He observed how people give to each other, receive from each other, and take from each other. One person acts, the other reacts; and the actions and attitudes of each affect the other. Sociologists who have devoted much attention to Simmel's insights point out that he was hammering home one central idea—namely, that "all human interactions should be viewed as kinds of exchanges" (Levine et al., 1976:823). He thus laid the groundwork for the sociological approach that has come to be known as *exchange theory* (Simmel, 1950).

Exchanges both cost us and reward us. That's why we may just as easily speak of exchange theory as cost/reward (or reward/cost) theory. When in the process of human interaction we are giving, it costs us something—time, energy, money or material goods, comfort and convenience, or perhaps something else, depending upon the situation. And when we receive, somebody else is experiencing cost so that we may receive the reward or benefit that comes to us through the particular interaction.

Simmel (1955) makes another important point by stressing that both conflict and cooperation are ways human beings relate to each other. And that statement applies to male-female relationships and family rela-

tionships as well as to other kinds of social interaction. To say that cooperation is the essence of human relationship and that *conflict* means the absence of relationship is, according to Simmel, nothing short of erroneous.

In other words, Simmel saw conflict as nothing more nor less than a form of human interaction—a kind of exchange in itself. There couldn't *be* a conflict without at least two persons, Simmel stressed; so why not admit that conflict is a form of exchanging something between the parties involved? If it takes two to tango, it also takes two (or more) to engage in conflict; and when parties are involved directly in something of concern to both sides, some kind of interchange is occurring. True, the exchange may be of grievances, punishments, force, or resistance—quite a contrast from the exchange of favors and benefits most persons think about in connection with the idea of reciprocity. But it's an exchange nevertheless.

Human beings interact with one another through symbols that have shared meanings. (Seghers/Monkmeyer)

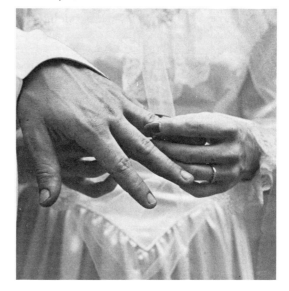

In speaking of interaction, then, as a key sociological concept, we're thinking about symbols and shared meanings in communication, how situations are defined by the individuals involved, and all that is involved in exchange processes—including both cooperation and conflict. Especially important is an emphasis on rewards and costs because this emphasis is receiving widespread attention in all the social sciences today. In fact, it is becoming an increasingly dominant way of thinking about society. But all of the other key concepts relating to time, structure, and interaction have important parts to play as well.

That's why some social scientists are suggesting that a multiple theoretical approach may provide the most complete understanding of marriage and family processes. Among these scientists are Mark Rank and Craig LeCroy (1983), who would like to see more use of a combined approach based particularly on the complementarity of *exchange theory,* which emphasizes investments and returns on investments; *symbolic interaction theory,* which helps us understand how persons define what is costly or rewarding to them over time; and *conflict theory,* which helps us understand the conflict that arises when family members perceive exchanges to be unequal. (See Scanzoni [1978] and Blalock and Wilken [1979] for a similarly eclectic theoretical approach.)

CHAPTER HIGHLIGHTS

What happens in families affects the larger society, and what happens in the larger society affects families. That's why a sociological study of marriage and family is so important. Sociology utilizes the basic principles and methods of science in studying human societies, focusing especially on associations—how and why they form, change, hold together, and break apart. Families are associations that may be studied in this way. As part of their scientific study of marriage and family, sociologists conduct research, measure and compare variables, seek explanations of findings through theory building, and tend to organize their thinking around three key concepts: time, structure, and interaction.

P·A·R·T T·W·O

GENDER ROLES

·2·

BECOMING WOMEN AND MEN

A baby boy survived a highway crash in which both his parents died. The baby's aunt, an unmarried middle-aged woman, took the child to rear. This was the theme of a strange and eerie television drama that unwittingly presented a lesson in *role socialization* (how a person is trained to play a particular part in society).

The infant's aunt was obsessed with an intense hatred of men. Unable to bear the thought that this tiny baby would grow to be a noisy, irksome boy, she determined to rear him as a girl. Moving to a remote area where her situation would not be known, she gave the boy a girl's name, kept him isolated and virtually housebound, and dressed him in frilly clothes. The child contentedly played with dolls and in other ways acted as girls were expected to act, never suspecting he was a male. Only after several years, when an outsider happened upon the scene, was the shocking secret discovered.

Farfetched? Perhaps. The drama was, after all, fiction. Yet John Money and Anke Ehrhardt, authorities on psychohormonal research, report the real-life case of a baby boy, who, through a tragic accident, lost his penis. The misfortune took place during the performance of a circumcision by means of electrocautery. A sudden surge of too-powerful electrical current burned the penis so severely it sloughed off not long afterward. The distraught parents sought help for many months and were eventually directed to the Johns Hopkins Hospital and School of Medicine. There, they were counseled to rear the child as a girl; and, with the help of further surgery and hormonal treatment, this is being done quite successfully (Money and Ehrhardt, 1972, chap. 7; Money and Tucker, 1975, chap. 4).

Money and Ehrhardt tell of similar child-rearing stories in cases of *hermaphroditism*—a congenital condition in which a baby's sexual anatomy is not clearly differentiated. The infant may appear as neither distinctly male nor distinctly female. And in some cases, the baby appears to be of the opposite sex from what she or he actually is.

In one such case, the parents thought they had a son when, in reality, they had a daughter. As puberty approached, the "boy" loved motorbike racing with male companions, had a girl friend, enjoyed hunting and fishing with his father, and, in general, followed a traditional masculine behavior pattern. Imagine his dismay when breasts began to develop! If more time had elapsed, he would have begun menstruating as well. However, after expert counseling, a decision was made that he should continue through life as a male. His female reproductive organs were surgically removed, and he was given hormones which would make possible the development of secondary sexual characteristics such as a deepened voice and facial hair (Money and Ehrhardt, 1972, chaps. 8 and 10).

Such stories are unusual and may seem strange to us. Most of us take the ideas of masculinity and femininity for granted. We tend to think that what we are by birth (either male or female) will determine what we become (either masculine or feminine). Don't boys grow up to be *masculine* (defined as active, courageous, assertive, and rational), while girls grow up to be *feminine* (defined as passive, dependent, emotional, and nurturant)? How then can we explain what happened in the stories we examined?

In both the fictional and true-life stories, what mattered was not the infant's biological sexual makeup but, rather, how the child was brought up by adults. That's why Money and Ehrhardt (1972, chap. 8) stress the importance of what they call the "sex of assignment." In the case of the circumcision accident, for example, the sex assigned to the baby boy was female. In other words, *gender identity* (awareness of oneself as either male or female) is more dependent upon social learning than upon genetic makeup.

Of course, for most persons, the biological sexual makeup (chromosomal pattern, sex glands, and internal and external sex organs) and the sex of assignment are one and the same. A male child is reared as a boy, a female child as a girl. But we're talking about social learning nevertheless. To be reared as a boy means *learning* to act as males are expected to act in our society. To be reared as a girl means *learning* to act as females are expected to act in our society. When a girl is told to "act like a lady," it's expected that she has in mind some image of how a "lady" is expected to act—an image learned from others. And when a boy is encouraged to be a "man's man," he is expected to have learned what that expression means and to act accordingly.

FIGURE 2-1 Gender roles: The "packages" of social expectations carried around by males and females.

UNDERSTANDING GENDER ROLES

These expectations of how a person should act because she is female or he is male are called *gender-related norms. Norms* are the "supposed to's" of life—the behaviors our society lays down for us and expects us to carry out. Certain norms are attached to various social positions. For example, attached to the social position of parent is the norm that parents should take care of their children. If we think of the whole cluster of norms attached to a social position, we have what sociologists call a *role*. We're accustomed to the theater's usage of this term. An actor takes a certain part and then speaks and conducts himself or herself according to a prewritten script, thus "playing the role" of, for instance, Macbeth or Lady Macbeth.

Gender roles or *sex roles* are the parts society assigns us to play in the drama of life according to whether we entered this life as a baby girl or a baby boy. To state it another way, a gender role consists of the cluster of shared norms attached to the differing social positions of male and female. Figure 2-1 shows how we carry these roles around with us—although in reality, of course, we carry the norms in our heads, not in boxes!

The norms for each sex relate to both temperaments (what females and males are supposed to be like) and tasks (what males and females are supposed to do). But by no means is there universal agreement on how each sex is expected to act or on how labor should be shared or divided up between men

Gender roles vary considerably among different cultures. This Senoufu tribe weaver in Ivory Coast, Africa, is performing a task often assigned to women in other cultures. (© Marc and Evelyne Bernheim/ Woodfin Camp & Associates)

and women. Gender roles vary considerably among different cultures.

Take the matter of temperament, for example. In Margaret Mead's (1935) anthropological study of New Guinea tribes, she found that one tribe considered a gentle temperament the ideal for both sexes. But in another tribe, an aggressive temperament was the ideal for both sexes. In yet another tribe, the cultural ideal was aggressiveness for women and gentleness and sensitivity for men. In the familiar pattern of our own culture, we have the reverse of this third tribe.

Besides such variations in ideal *temperaments* encouraged for each sex, there are also variations in the *tasks* that are labeled "men's work" or "women's work" in different societies. Such variations (as illustrated by Table 2-A) seem to show that gender roles do not spring from natural, biological traits or "instincts" which cause men the world over to "act like men" and women to "act like women." What it means to "act like a woman" or "act like a man" depends mainly upon the expectations of one's society.

THE SOCIALIZATION PROCESS

We learn our society's expectations and requirements through a process called *socialization*. In other words, we are taught to be social beings. How? Think of it this way: We're born into a particular social world. That social world—or *culture*—is already there when we arrive on the scene. It consists of customs, values, and rules that need to be transmitted to us so that we can fit into that world and become a part of it.

Our parents are usually (but not always) the first *transmitters*, or agents, of socialization. But as time goes by, many others also play a part in the process—for example, brothers and sisters, friends, teachers, and religious leaders. Reading materials, radio, television, and movies may also play an important part in our socialization.

Theories of Childhood Gender-Role Learning

Gender-role socialization is a major component of our overall socialization. Children may grow up to either challenge or conform to the societal expectations for male and fe-

TABLE 2-A Cross-cultural data from 224 societies on division of labor by sex

ACTIVITY	NUMBER OF SOCIETIES IN WHICH ACTIVITY IS PERFORMED BY				
	MEN ALWAYS	MEN USUALLY	EITHER SEX	WOMAN USUALLY	WOMEN ALWAYS
Subsistence Activities					
Pursuit of sea mammals	34	1	0	0	0
Hunting	166	13	0	0	0
Trapping small animals	128	13	4	1	2
Herding	38	8	4	0	5
Fishing	98	34	19	3	4
Clearing land for agriculture	73	22	17	5	13
Dairy operations	17	4	3	1	13
Preparing and planting soil	31	23	33	20	37
Erecting and dismantling shelter	14	2	5	6	22
Tending fowl and small animals	21	4	8	1	39
Tending and harvesting crops	10	15	35	39	44
Gathering shellfish	9	4	8	7	25
Making and tending fires	18	6	25	22	62
Bearing burdens	12	6	35	20	57
Preparing drinks and narcotics	20	1	13	8	57
Gathering fruits, berries, nuts	12	3	15	13	63
Gathering fuel	22	1	10	19	89
Preservation of meat and fish	8	2	10	14	74
Gathering herbs, roots, seeds	8	1	11	7	74
Cooking	5	1	9	28	158
Carrying water	7	0	5	7	119
Grinding grain	2	4	5	13	114
Manufacture of Objects					
Metalworking	78	0	0	0	0
Weapon making	121	1	0	0	0
Boatbuilding	91	4	4	0	1
Manufacture of musical instruments	45	2	0	0	1
Work in wood and bark	113	9	5	1	1
Work in stone	68	3	2	0	2
Work in bone, horn, shell	67	4	3	0	3
Manufacture of ceremonial objects	37	1	13	0	1
House building	86	32	25	3	14
Net making	44	6	4	2	11
Manufacture of ornaments	24	3	40	6	18
Manufacture of leather products	29	3	9	3	32
Hide preparation	31	2	4	4	49
Manufacture of nontextile fabrics	14	0	9	2	32
Manufacture of thread and cordage	23	2	11	10	73
Basket making	25	3	10	6	82
Mat making	16	2	6	4	61
Weaving	19	2	2	6	67
Pottery making	13	2	6	8	77
Manufacture and repair of clothing	12	3	8	9	95

SOURCE: Roy G. D'Andrade, "Sex Differences and Cultural Institutions," in *The Development of Sex Differences*, ed. Eleanor E. Maccoby (Stanford, CA: Stanford University Press, 1966), pp. 177–178.

male behavior they learned in childhood. And they will find that their gender-role preferences will profoundly affect virtually all aspects of their lives and relationships. That's why we will be giving attention to gender roles throughout this book. Understanding the shifts in gender roles that have been taking place is crucial to exploring the topic of "men, women, and change."

But first we need to ask how children learn in the first place that boys are to behave one way and girls another. Psychologists Eleanor Maccoby and Carol Jacklin (1974:1) have examined the many behavioral science studies that have been undertaken to answer that question. They found that theories explaining sex differences fall into three basic categories: imitation, self-socialization, and reinforcement.

Imitation *Imitation theories* emphasize a child's early identification with the same-sex parent. The little girl wants to model herself after Mommy and other female figures who are important in her life. The little boy wants to model himself after Daddy and other male figures who are important in his life. Mimicking adults in all aspects of life—not only gender roles—is common during a child's early years. Such behavior is a way of forming

Imitation theories of gender-role learning emphasize a child's early identification with the same-sex parent. (© Leonard Freed/Magnum Photos)

what George Herbert Mead, a pioneering symbolic interactionist theorist, called the *social self*—a sense of self in relation to others (Meltzer, 1967; Strauss, 1956).

Self-Socialization The theoretical approach that Maccoby and Jacklin label *self-socialization* comes from the work of cognitive developmental theorists such as Lawrence Kohlberg (1966). Such theorists focus on a child's early personal development of a gender-related self-concept ("I'm a girl," or "I'm a boy"), which includes an understanding of what behavior is considered appropriate for each sex. ("I'm a girl, and girls do this." "Girls don't do that! That's what boys do!" "I'm a boy, and this is how boys act.") In other words, children are grasping societal rules of the game for males and females as part of their overall growing awareness of how the world is organized and how people fit into it.

Reinforcement In the third category of theories attempting to explain sex-related differences, the focus is on adult efforts to shape children's gender-role preferences. Through the use of rewards and punishments, parents and others encourage children to behave in ways considered appropriate for their particular sex.

Norwegian sociologist Harriet Holter (1970) contrasts cognitive development and reinforcement theories by pointing out the different sequence of a child's experience in the two. In cognitive development theory, the pattern seems to be this: "I am a boy, therefore I want to do boy things, therefore the opportunity to do boy things (and to gain approval for doing them) is rewarding." However, says Holter, in reinforcement theory, the pattern is more like this: "I want rewards, I am rewarded for doing boy things, therefore I want to be a boy" (p. 191). The

same would hold true of a girl who might reason similarly about being rewarded for doing "girl things." Note that in cognitive development theory, gender identity precedes reinforcement. In reinforcement theories, gender identity is a consequence of reinforcement.

Imitation, self-socialization, and reinforcement theories all support the idea that gender roles are learned, not innate, and that they are learned at a very young age. Furthermore, explains Holter, children are learning much more than the fact that two social categories—women and men—exist. Children are also learning social evaluations of these categories. Even during their preschool years, they begin to realize that "males are defined as powerholders, women as the opposite" (p. 196). (See also Bem, 1983.)

How and Why Gender-Role Learning Takes Place

The stage is set with the announcement: "It's a girl!" or "You have a son!" Studies have shown that adults describe a baby differently according to whether they have been told the baby is a girl or a boy. If they think a baby is a girl, they describe her as "cuddly." But the very same baby is described as "active and aggressive," if they think the baby is a boy (Meyer and Sobieszek, 1972; see also Chafetz, 1978, chap. 3).

Parents, of course, *know* whether they have a boy or a girl. And that makes a difference in how they treat their infant. The tradition of dressing girls in pink and boys in blue has been one way of making a distinction between the sexes—although such rigid color coding is less common today. Parents also interact differently with baby girls and baby boys. They tend to talk more to their infant daughter. But if they have an infant son, they are more likely to pick him up often and enjoy playing roughly with him. Barbara Lusk Forisha (1978:323–324), a specialist in the study of gender roles, has summarized much of the research on adult-infant interaction. She points out that parents evidently expect boys to be more active and girls to be more gentle and verbal and thus interact with their infant children accordingly. Without realizing it, they are probably helping bring about the very behaviors they expected! Sociologists call this a *self-fulfilling prophecy.*

Sanctions Animal trainers elicit desired behaviors by offering rewards. A porpoise learns that jumping through the hoop will bring a tasty morsel of food, but failing to follow the trainer's instructions will mean that the choice prize will be withheld. The porpoise who chooses to misbehave and not cooperate at all may be taken out of the game and set aside for a while. Through the use of sanctions, both positive ones and negative

Traditional gender-role socialization uses positive sanctions to reward little girls for behavior considered appropriate to their sex. (© Erika Stone, 1986)

ones, the creature is learning to act as the trainer wishes.

As human beings interact with each other, sanctions also come into the picture. This is particularly true in gender-role socialization. *Positive sanctions* are the rewards people give us for behavior that they consider appropriate for persons of our gender. *Negative sanctions* are punishments for behavior considered inappropriate.

For example, if a little girl announces that she wants to be a nurse when she grows up, adults may pat her on the head and smile approvingly. Parents will buy her a toy nursing kit and cap and encourage her to practice on her dolls. But if the girl says she plans to be a brain surgeon, adult encouragement may not be so quickly forthcoming. She is likely to feel that she isn't being taken seriously. "What? A pretty little girl like you? Brain surgeons have to work long, hard hours. Don't you want to be a mommy? You wait and see; some handsome young man will come along someday and want to take care of you, and you can forget about such ideas. Let *him* be the brain surgeon, not you!"

But suppose a small boy were to announce he plans to be a nurse when he grows up. With few exceptions, adults would voice disapproval and would tell him his aspirations are "too low" or that nursing is "woman's work" and not at all a man's job. His parents would buy him a play doctor's kit, not a nurse's kit. Even the pictures on the toy boxes would reinforce the stereotype of male physicians and female nurses.

Sanctions are related to the power parents hold in controlling resources that a child needs or desires. Some of these resources are tangible and include money spent or withheld for certain toys or hobbies or for education, enrichment programs, travel opportunities, and the like. But beyond such obvious material aspects of parental power, there are intangible aspects which exert a tremendous influence. The desire of children to know that their parents approve of their conduct, feel warmly toward them, and are proud of them makes children very conscious of any sanctions—whether positive or negative.

In such a social exchange process, the attitude and actions of parents seem to be saying, "If you give me what I want from you, I'll give you what you'd like to have from me. But if you don't act the way I want you to, you'll be sorry. I'll show my displeasure, and I'll withhold the rewards you want. Or there will be penalties of some other sort. Then you'll learn how important it is that you shape up to my expectations." Of course, this is never stated in such bald terms! But it provides a description of the underlying dynamics taking place between parents and children.

During the early years, children have few resources of their own that could make it possible for them to challenge their parents' power. However, the power of one person over another decreases when the second person finds alternative sources or rewards. Thus, as children are increasingly exposed to influences beyond those of their parents, they may not respond quite so readily to parental sanctions. Outside sources may provide the benefits once largely sought from parents alone. Pleasing one's peers may become more important than pleasing one's parents on certain issues. New ideas learned in school or through the media may cause children to challenge their parents' views on politics, religion, or social customs. Also, as children grow older, they become more aware of their own part in the exchange process between them and their parents. Children obtain more bargaining leverage as they awaken to the potential power they have through being able to give or withhold the positive reinforcement desired by their parents. If children feel they are not being rewarded for certain behaviors for which they feel they deserve to be rewarded, they may in turn not reward their parents with the approval and role-model identification that matters so much to the parents.

Adolescents in particular may identify with role models who provide benefits they consider more worthwhile than those provided by their parents. These alternative role models may markedly influence the gender-role norms the young person chooses to follow. For example, Bill's father may be a truck driver and part-time auto racer and have little interest in the world of ideas. His hobbies may be mechanics and hunting. Bill's interests may lie in books and music. Of a gentle, sensitive temperament, he cringes at the thought of killing animals for sport and refuses to accompany his father on hunting trips. Bill prefers to attend the nature-study club sponsored by the public library. He likes to write poetry and play the piano. Bill's father worries about his son and fears he is a "sissy," not living up to the father's stereotyped notions of masculinity. But Bill has found a friend in Mr. Peterson, the English teacher at his junior high school. Mr. Peterson provides Bill with books and articles to read, gives him the encouragement and approval the boy yearns for, and provides Bill with a sounding board for the discussion of his ideas and poetry. Already Bill is planning to major in literature in college and someday to be a teacher like Mr. Peterson.

Similarly, an adolescent girl might be influenced by the example of a woman by whom she is employed during the summer. Even though the girl's parents may have reinforced traditional gender-role patterns, she begins admiring other qualities in her employer—assertiveness, independence, strength, and leadership. Realizing that such qualities are necessary for advancement in the business or professional world, and impressed with her employer's exciting life, the adolescent begins to reject her mother's traditional life as an example of what a woman should be and chooses to follow her employer as a role model instead. The rewards offered in this setting appear far more compelling than anything provided at home, regardless of the positive and negative sanctions the girl's parents have been using.

Parents desire the gratification that comes with having their children identify with them and look up to them for guidance and support. (© Carol Palmer/The Picture Cube)

Concerns of Parents It is said that imitation is the sincerest form of flattery. It means a great deal to any one of us to know that somebody looks up to us and wants to be like us. And parents especially, having had the primary task of molding their children from infancy, desire to have their task rewarded by producing human beings who admire them enough to want to identify with them. When children don't identify with their parents and reject them as role models, the parents feel punished—not only by their children's repudiation of their example but also by the disapproval of the parents' peers (their reference group). The parents then are experiencing *costs* rather than rewards in the process of social exchange, and the sense of "net profit" in the parent-child relationship is diminished.

Let's take some hypothetical examples to see how this works. Alice Grey has two daughters and a son. The son is established in a business and is happily married to a young woman who reminds Alice of herself as a young bride years ago. The daughter-in-law holds traditional gender-role norms and regards her greatest responsibility and joy in life to lie in "being a good wife and mother." This outlook on life is precisely that which Alice has always held. She and her husband feel rewarded: not only has their son followed the pattern of his father in developing qualities suited to achievement in the business world but also he has chosen a wife who fulfills the gender-role norms his parents held up for females during his childhood socialization. Alice's younger daughter's aspirations also are rewarding to Alice and make her feel a success in having socialized her for an appropriate role in adult life. The young woman is presently working as a secretary but hopes to marry and settle down to raising a family soon.

It's the older daughter, Susan, who worries Alice. Susan is working on a Ph.D. in marine biology and is not at all concerned about marriage. If she does marry at some point in life, she tells Alice, the marriage will be egalitarian, and there will be no sacrifice of career commitment on Susan's part. Furthermore, Susan has no desire to have children and says that if she were to marry, either she or her husband would have sterilization surgery. Alice cannot understand Susan and feels she is rejecting all that Alice has lived for and held dear. Susan has no desire to be the kind of woman her mother is; in fact, Susan thinks of her mother as a *negative role model*—an example of what she doesn't want to be, a pattern of the kind of life she doesn't want to lead. By not identifying with her mother, Susan is calling into question her mother's self-identity and the values her mother upholds. Alice Grey finds this threatening and is deeply hurt. She feels that her daughter is not only failing to reward her but is actually punishing her.

In another case, the hard-driving businessman who lives for money and buries himself in his work may find that his son turns completely away from such a lifestyle. Instead, the son devotes himself to some humanitarian project and calls into question his father's materialistic values, shattering his father's dreams for him.

Of course, children may also take *nontraditional* parents as negative role models. Instead of following their parents' way of life, they follow the conventional societal patterns that their parents have rejected. For example, a mother who has emphasized intellectual excellence, independence, achievement, mastery, and career commitment for her daughter and has provided her with a living example of professional accomplishment will likely experience deep disap-

Parent-child companionship in sharing tasks is an important part of socialization. (© Erika Stone, 1981)

pointment if the daughter organizes her life around traditional gender-role norms. It's as though the daughter is saying, "I want to be just the opposite of what you are." One mother who went to medical school when her youngest daughter was 4 years old could not understand why, ten years later, the girl refused to share her mother's joy upon opening a new clinic. The girl talked only about becoming a full-time housewife and expressed no interest in either college or career.

In so many words, parents themselves are seeking reinforcement in the gender-role norms they have chosen to follow. They desire the gratification that comes with having their children identify with them and look up to them as role models. They want to be rewarded by their children's choice of them as living examples of what it means to be a man or woman, and therefore they reward their children in ways that will reinforce such gender-role identification.

Companionship, as well as identification, may be concern of parents—especially in many mother-daughter relationships. Social psychologist Ralph Turner (1970) points out that in homes where gender roles are traditional, deep comradeship between a mother and daughter is most likely to occur if "the daughter forms a somewhat traditional self-conception. The common interest in domestic activities permits a collaboration that can continue into adulthood, so long as the daughter's self-conception does not move toward a repudiation of traditional feminine activity" (p. 387). Mothers who socialize their daughters to delight in work traditionally considered *women's work* (sewing, decorating, cooking, making beds, washing dishes, doing laundry, and so on) are essentially working to build a lifelong friendship based on shared interests—a friendship that mothers anticipate as being very rewarding. Daughters who choose not to follow such a pattern may also wish for a close relationship with their mothers but may have little hope that it will be experienced. Poet Adrienne Rich (1976) explains: "The woman activist or artist born of a family-centered mother may in any case feel that her mother cannot understand or sympathize with the imperatives of her life; or that her mother has preferred and valued a more conventional daughter, or a son" (chap. 9).

In contrast to mother-daughter comradeship built around task bonds, according to Turner, father-son collaboration has been made more difficult through traditional gender-role norms which assign fathers the breadwinning responsibility. Thus, while during their growing-up years boys may ex-perience comradeship and task bonding through working together with their fathers in certain household chores, hobbies, and sports, sons are not actually involved in a father's occupational career in the way that daughters are involved in the mother's major activity, homemaking. What sons learn from this arrangement, says Turner (1970), is that "the work that is crucial to the male identity is usually removed from the home" (p. 388).

Other concerns of parents in socializing their children may relate to religious beliefs, a concern for societal order, and a concern for what parents believe to be their children's best interests.

Some parents believe that traditional gender roles have been ordained by God and are not open to questioning. Thus, sons are to be socialized for a strong leadership role and daughters for a supportive, subordinate role. Other parents, however, may be equally religious but may view matters quite differently. Such persons may see the teachings of their faith as upholding female-male equality—especially when those teachings are understood in the light of current theological studies (Driver, 1976:434–442; Mollenkott, 1977; Ruether and McLaughlin, 1979; Fiorenza, 1983; Trible, 1978; Ruether, 1983; Heschel, 1983; Bilezikian, 1985; Scanzoni and Hardesty, 1986).

Why Has Traditional Gender-Role Socialization Persisted?

Many parents may give little thought to the "why" behind their childrearing practices because traditional gender-role patterns have had such strong support in the larger society outside the home. Such parents may simply accept traditional gender roles as the given *order of things* ("that's just the way life is."). The sanctions they use to reinforce those roles are seen as being in their *children's best interests*—a way of fitting sons and daughters into the parts society expects them to play in adulthood, including gender-role specialization in marriage.

Such a view has been common in the *structural-functional approach* to a sociology of marriage and family. The emphasis is on keeping a system in equilibrium. One sociologist from this school of thought, Talcott Parsons (1955), has been quite explicit in claiming that gender-role specialization benefits the nuclear family by functioning to maintain that system. The roles of the spouses are viewed as complementary from Parsons' vantage point. If the husband attends to his occupation and the wife attends to her role as the family's center of nurturance, there is less chance for competitiveness to develop between husband and wife—a rivalry that could lead to marital dissolution. Such a functionalist perspective suggests that serious conflict and system disruption could occur if a woman chooses to be as active and achievement-oriented as her husband in pursuing an occupation. Therefore, the functionalist might argue, parents socialize their children in traditional gender roles so that such system disruption can be avoided.

On the other hand, writers who think in *conflict* terms tend to view such a functionalist perspective as a freezing of the status quo. Those who take a Marxist position and look upon male-female relations as an illustration of class struggle would say that present socialization practices simply reflect the domination of women by men (Engels, 1884; Rowbotham, 1972; Mitchell, 1971). Some would argue that, out of self-interest, men want to limit the participation of women in the occupational opportunity system. In this way, one-half the population can be kept from its rewards so that the other half can have them for itself. One method of accomplishing this would be to socialize boys for such access to the opportunity system but to socialize girls to behave in precisely the opposite manner necessary to achieve society's economic and power benefits.

Other sociologists who take a different conflict perspective from that taken by Marxist theorists also disagree with the functionalist emphasis on gender-role specialization in the family. These sociologists would point out that persons in a relationship can work out a negotiated arrangement of "who does what" in a way that is agreeable to each and which does not produce feelings of rivalry. Furthermore, from this perspective, conflict can be healthy for a husband-wife relationship and strengthen it rather than lead to dissolution.

Parents, of course, are not usually rearing their children with such sociological analyses in mind! Rather, they are trying to prepare their children for life as they, the parents, see it. They want what they think will be good for their children. Included in their concern may be a desire to protect their children from societal criticism and pressures that are sometimes directed toward those who don't fit the conventional mold for their gender. For example, we spoke earlier of a little girl who would like to be a brain surgeon and of a little boy who would like to be a nurse. Because of gender-role stereotyping, persons in both situations are likely to encounter problems directly associated with their being nontraditional—in spite of changes in recent years which have meant more men in nursing schools and more women in medical schools (Schoenmaker and Radosevich, 1976; Fitzpatrick, 1977; Bourne and Wikler, 1976).

Studies have shown that for a male nurse, both his professional identity and other persons' perceptions of his sexual identity become problems (Etzkowitz, 1971). He is constantly mistaken for either an orderly (lower status) or a physician (higher status). And because of another kind of stereotyping, his sexual orientation is sometimes called into question: "There is a set of mental equations which go: Female + Nursing role = Nurse; Male + Nursing role = homosexual" (p. 432).

Sociologists Patricia Bourne and Norma Wikler (1976) write similarly of the "double binds" of women in medical school: "When women do demonstrate the characteristics and traits of the 'ideal' professional, they violate the expectations of the female role. This role violation tends to engender anger and hostility from others. . . . But if [the female physician] exhibits traits appropriate to her role as female, she will jeopardize her standing in her role as professional."

MOVING BEYOND GENDER ROLES

Many persons believe that traditional gender roles are *not* in children's best interests—not if they keep both males and females from realizing their full human potential by forcing them to be something they don't wish to be or to do something they don't wish to do. An increasing number of persons are convinced that traditional gender roles need to be critically examined and many childhood socialization practices changed.

For example, various researchers have called attention to the way gender-role stereotypes are reinforced through the design, display, and promotion of toys (Chafetz, 1978:80–85; Kutner and Levinson, 1976). And some studies suggest that differences in girls' and boys' childhood games may prevent girls from developing certain skills, at-

titudes, and work styles that are so important later on for achievement in the business world (Hennig and Jardim, 1977 edition, chap. 2; Lever, 1978).

Even traditional differences in dress have affected the relative freedom of the sexes (Chafetz, 1978:88). In the Victorian period, women's activities were curtailed through such encumbrances as tightly laced corsets and long, heavy skirts. The freedom of movement offered by more realistic garments seemed exhilarating. One ecstatic woman wrote in 1894 of the "delightful sense of independence and power" she experienced when she put on a pair of knickers to ride her bicycle (Roberts, 1977). And in our own day, say social scientists Marcia Guttentag and Helen Bray (1977), "teachers have reported that recent changes in dress codes which allow girls to wear slacks are the most important factors in erasing distinctions in activities, since the elementary school girls can now climb and jump and run as fast as the boys without the hindrance of a skirt" (p. 397).

Traditional gender-role socialization limits the options and opportunities open to males as well as females. The notion that being tender or giving way to tears is "unmasculine" and that one must always live up to an image of toughness and control can have negative consequences. Psychologist Herb Goldberg was so concerned about this that he entitled one of his books *The Hazards of Being Male* (1976). He points out the countless ways males are socialized to hold back their feelings and to deny needs—and the toll this takes on mental and physical health.

Why do we need gender roles at all? some persons are asking. Such a point was raised in a short story by Lois Gould (1972, 1978) that appeared first in *Ms.* magazine and later grew into a book. "X: A Fabulous Child's

Story'' told of a fictitious scientific experiment in which a couple agreed to rear their child completely apart from gender roles. They told no one else their child's sex—friends and relatives found it infuriating to be told only, "It's an X"—and reared the child according to the Official Instruction Manual for Project Baby X. There, they read that their infant should receive "plenty of bouncing and plenty of cuddling, *both.* X ought to be strong and sweet and active. Forget about *dainty* altogether." The child was given both "girl toys" and "boy toys," including a "boy doll that made pee-pee and cried, 'Pa-Pa,' and a girl doll that talked in three languages and said, 'I am the Pres-i-dent of Gen-er-al Motors.' " The child's hairstyle and clothing were suited to both sexes and didn't give away X's secret. And the guidebook instructed the parents never to make little X feel embarrassed or ashamed about any play activities. If X got dirty, they were not to say, "Nice little Xes don't get dirty climbing rocks." Or "If X falls down and cries," said the book, "never say, 'brave little Xes don't cry.' Because, of course, nice little Xes *do* get dirty, and brave little Xes *do* cry. No matter how dirty X gets, or how hard it cries, don't worry. It's all part of the Xperiment." The story goes on to tell of the joys, problems, and challenges associated with X's entrance into school with all its gender-related rules and customs and the expectations of teachers, other children, and their parents.

Some behavioral scientists point out the greater flexibility that characterizes persons not bound by traditional gender roles (Forisha, 1978). One of the leading researchers in this area is psychology professor Sandra Bem (1975, 1976). Her special interest has been in a combining of qualities traditionally viewed as "masculine" or "feminine" and thus closed off to one or the other sex. She

speaks instead of "psychological androgyny," which gets its name from the Greek words for male (*andros*) and female (*gyne*). Bem (1977) explains that *psychological androgyny* "allows men and women to be *both* independent and tender, *both* assertive and yielding, *both* masculine and feminine. In other words, psychological androgyny expands the range of behaviors available to everyone" (p. 319).

Some behavioral scientists prefer to go beyond the concept of androgyny. They would rather not think in terms of a combination of so-called masculine and feminine qualities because such terminology could still suggest that various traits *are* gender-related. Instead, they propose transcending gender roles altogether and reformulating masculinity/femininity measurement scales in research and theory (summarized in Harrison, 1978, p. 328). In other words, a person who displays a high degree of nurturance would not be said to rank high in "femininity" but

Personal attributes, interests, and activities need not be linked to gender. (© Suzanne Szasz, 1981/Photo Researchers, Inc.)

simply characterized by warmth and caring. And if that same person also displays a high degree of assertiveness, that doesn't mean his or her "masculine" side is being shown. The problem is in the terminology. Perhaps some sociological concepts can help us here.

Two Dimensions of Life: Expressive and Instrumental

We can begin by thinking of life as having two basic *dimensions,* or sides. There is the "people" side of life (called *expressive* by sociologists) and the "work and activities" side (which sociologists call *instrumental*). The terms were popularized by structural-functionalist theorists Talcott Parsons and Robert Bales (1955), but the expressive-instrumental concept can be used in other schools of thought as well.

Behaviors associated with the *expressive dimension of life* include nurturance, tenderness, warmth, caring, empathy, showing affection through words and gestures, and everything else concerned with interpersonal relationships. Behaviors associated with the *instrumental dimension of life,* on the other hand, include such qualities as autonomy, activity, creativity, drive, ambition, courage, assertiveness, leadership abilities, mastery—qualities associated with getting a job done. Instrumental behaviors are task-oriented, whereas expressive behaviors are person-oriented.

Some people are quick to label expressive behaviors *feminine.* However, caring about other human beings and putting forth effort to establish and maintain human relationships is as appropriate for males as for females. Similarly, instrumental behaviors aren't "masculine." A woman who achieves is not trying to be—or performing—"like a man," as is sometimes asserted. The word *instrumental* is derived from a Latin word

meaning "equipment." Instrumental qualities such as drive, assertiveness, mastery, and self-sufficiency are nothing more nor less than tools or equipment necessary for obtaining society's economic benefits; and they can be utilized by persons of either sex.

In sum, *both* females and males can develop qualities associated with *both* dimensions of life: expressive and instrumental. Many persons may, in fact, feel more comfortable thinking simply in terms of desirable *human* qualities to be utilized according to the situation rather than insisting that each individual must be a rigidly balanced combination of "femaleness" and "maleness." Bem (1983:616) herself has begun raising questions about an overemphasis on androgyny that has sometimes had the effect of replacing "a prescription to be masculine *or* feminine with the doubly incarcerating prescription to be masculine *and* feminine" (italics supplied). As a result, "the individual now has not one but two potential sources of inadequacy with which to contend." She, too, advocates moving beyond traditional categories. "Human behaviors and personality attributes should no longer be linked with gender," she writes, "and society should stop projecting gender into situations irrelevant to genitalia."

Fears About Changes in Gender Roles

While many people view a movement away from traditional gender roles as being expansive, liberating, and more fully in accord with human potential, many other people find the idea threatening. They fear that "unisex" tendencies are emerging that will blur virtually all sex differences. Some persons fear that homosexuality will increase—although there is no evidence of a causal connection between gender-role preference and *sexual* (erotic) orientation. Furthermore, many homosexual persons are very traditional in terms of gender roles ("macho" men and "feminine" women). Gender roles, whether traditional or nontraditional, do not make people either homosexual or heterosexual.

An overlapping fear is that children will become confused about their own gender identities and will grow up not knowing what is expected of them as women and men. These various fears were probably behind the decision of television censors to turn down a proposed television dramatization of the story of Baby X described earlier (*Newsday* syndicated report, *The Greensboro (NC) Record*, August 2, 1978).

Professors Money and Ehrhardt (1972, chap. 1) offer the reassurance that a growing child can recognize that there are two distinguishable sexes no matter how much culturally prescribed behaviors may overlap at any given time or place. Why? Because "nature herself supplies the basic irreducible elements of sex difference which no culture can eradicate, at least not on a large scale." These basic elements of sex difference include the differing sexual organs and the fact that women menstruate, have babies, and

produce milk for their infants. Men cannot do these things but can produce sperm and impregnate. Other reminders that the bodies of the two sexes differ are seen in such secondary sexual characteristics as differences in voice pitch and in the presence or absence of facial hair. What is really important, say Money and Ehrhardt, is that a child grow up "to know that sex differences are primarily defined by the reproductive capacity of the sex organs, and to have a positive feeling of pride in his or her own genitalia and their ultimate reproductive use." If such is the case, it doesn't matter how interchangeable activities may be between mother and father. In fact, they emphasize, "it does not even matter if mother is a bus driver and daddy a cook."

However, throughout history, societies all over the world have tended to add to the obvious physical distinctions and have insisted upon other kinds of differences between the sexes—differences that are socially created. In Chapter 3, we'll look at some of these differences and what they have meant in various times and places.

CHAPTER HIGHLIGHTS

In this chapter, we have considered how males are trained (socialized) to be *masculine* and females are trained to be *feminine* according to their particular society's definitions of those terms. Gender roles encompass both *temperaments* (what males and females are expected to be like) and *tasks* (what females and males are expected to do). In gender-role socialization, *positive sanctions* are the rewards people give us for behavior they consider appropriate for persons of our sex; and *negative sanctions* are the punishments and disapproval directed our way when our behavior is considered inappropriate for our sex. Many persons today are questioning the wisdom in rearing children according to gender-role stereotypes. Some behavioral scientists point out that greater flexibility characterizes persons not bound by traditional gender roles. Such persons feel they have more options and opportunities and can simply be themselves rather than feeling they must conform to societal expectations of masculinity or femininity. *Psychological androgyny* is the combination in one person (of either sex) of those qualities that have usually been associated with masculinity (strength, rationality, independence) and those qualities that have usually been associated with femininity (tenderness, intuitiveness, dependence). Some behavioral scientists suggest getting away from the terms *masculine* and *feminine* altogether. One way would be to think in terms of two basic dimensions of life: the "people" or "interpersonal relationships" side (called *expressive* by sociologists) and the "work and activities" side (called *instrumental*), with all human beings encouraged to develop both sides as not gender-linked but human qualities.

· 3 ·

THE MALE-FEMALE EQUALITY QUESTION

don't want to do that. That's *boys' work!*''
a middle-aged woman remembers telling her
mother years ago. The mother quickly saw
through the child's chore-avoidance strategy
and replied simply, "Work doesn't know
whether a boy or girl is doing it. Now get
busy!"

Perhaps work doesn't know, but societies
do. And as we saw in Chapter 2, males and
females have been expected to fulfill different societal roles that include both work activities and personal characteristics. "Boys'
work" has been geared toward keeping the
world running, "girls' work" toward keeping
the home running. Why should this pattern
be so widespread? And why has greater prestige generally been associated with the male
role?

WHAT ACCOUNTS FOR THE
PREVALENCE OF MALE-FEMALE
INEQUALITY?

Careful observation of the society around us
should alert us to an important realization:
the economic-opportunity system bestows
its rewards of prestige, power, and material
gain not on those who perform expressively
but on those who perform instrumentally.
(The term *economic-opportunity system* can
serve as a kind of shorthand to sum up all
that is involved in the network of means and
ends associated with work and achievement.) And it is this unequal reward distribution that provides a key to understanding
the male-female inequality we see in most societies. We've already seen that female socialization has concentrated more on the expressive side of life than on the instrumental,
thereby putting women at a disadvantage in
the economic-opportunity system as compared to men.

Before exploring this topic further, we
need first to give critical attention to other
explanations sometimes put forth.

BIOLOGY ISN'T DESTINY

Some persons argue that women are just naturally less endowed with instrumental qualities; and if that means they are thereby cut
off from equal achievement opportunities, no
one is to blame except nature. Such a thesis
is expressed, for example, even in the title of
anthropologist Steven Goldberg's book, *The
Inevitability of Patriarchy* (1974), and is
summed up in a statement on the book
jacket: "Why the biological difference between men and women always produces male
domination." Goldberg (1974:210–212) sees
a "biologically based male superiority" that
includes aggression and dominance and extends to reasoning abilities and achievements in the arts and sciences. *Ignoring the
societal constraints that have limited opportunities for women,* and arguing chiefly
from a biological base centered in male hormones, Goldberg attempts to prove his point
by claiming that "there is not a single woman
whose genius has approached that of any
number of men in philosophy, mathematics,
composing, theorizing of any kind, or even
painting."

Hormones and Gender Roles

One person who has reacted strongly to such
assumptions about male and female potential
is Estelle Ramey, a professor of physiology
and biophysics who specializes in hormonal
research. Referring to an old religious dictum
that asserts that "the devil can quote Scrip-

ture for his own purposes," Ramey (1973) charges that "the Devil can quote endocrinology as well as Scripture" (p. 237). She is disturbed that some persons have attempted to "keep woman in her place" by referring to hormonal studies without taking into account the complexity of the topic. She compares such efforts to the way in which the "anatomy is destiny" ideas of Sigmund Freud were once used. In the society of his day, says Ramey, "Freud's distorted view of female psychology" was the most easily received of all his theories. Why? "Because it appeared to give a physiological basis to the prevailing theological and cultural attitudes toward women."

Ramey doesn't deny that hormones have a part to play in certain sex-related differences. Some of her own research, for example, indicates that females might be better suited physiologically than males to serve as astronauts. And her concern about the shorter life span of males has prompted her to study the part hormones may play in the development of heart disease (Kolbenschlag, 1976).

However, she cautions against reading *too much* into certain research findings—especially about the effects of prenatal hormones on the developing brain and any influence on later behavior. She refers to one study that compared a control group with fifteen girls who had been exposed before birth to excess androgens (sometimes called *male hormones* because males produce androgens in greater amounts than females do). The "masculinized" girls were characterized by more "tomboyism," higher energy levels, more career interest, and less interest in babies and motherhood (Ehrhardt, Epstein, and Money, 1968). Ramey (1973:240–41) points out that a close look at the data should forestall any conclusion that hormones themselve *cause*

females to be either traditional or nontraditional in gender roles. The parents of the masculinized girls knew their daughters were different in certain respects; in fact, some of the girls were thought to be boys at birth. Ramey wonders if parents in such cases might not treat their children differently, and she cautions that certain other environmental factors need to be taken into account as well.

Other researchers, including Money and Ehrhardt themselves (1972) likewise call for a measure of caution in the conclusions drawn from such studies (Weitz, 1977). Research psychologist Anke Ehrhardt (1977), who was one of the investigators in this particular study, suggests that the influence of hormones versus environmental factors might not be a matter of either/or but rather both/and—in other words, an interaction between the two. One possibility she raises is that exposure to excessive androgen before birth may *predispose* such girls to be more energetic and less maternal but a certain environment is required in order for that predisposition to show up in actual behavior patterns.

At the same time, sociologist Alice Rossi (1977; 1985), who is a feminist and by no means interested in "keeping women in their place," has come to the position that social scientists need to take the human biological heritage more seriously. This includes not dismissing out of hand the possibility that hormonal factors may enter into differing male and female attitudes and behaviors concerning parenthood. She calls for a "biosocial perspective on parenting" that stresses "the influence of physiological factors on women as a consequence of hormonal cyclicity, pregnancy, and birth" (1977:24).

The problem is that so many complexities surround this topic (Gross et al., 1979). Take the matter of testosterone, for example. Testosterone is produced in much greater amounts in male bodies than in female bodies and is therefore considered one of the "male" hormones. Yet, Estelle Ramey (1973:242) points out that when researcher A. E. Fisher injected testosterone into one part of the brain of both male and female rats, the rats of both sexes acted like mothers! When Fisher injected it into another part of the brain, both sexes began showing male sexual behavior. Commenting on this same research, Money and Ehrhardt (1972) write:

> Fisher's experiment clearly demonstrates not only that testosterone might release parental behavior of the type usually designated as maternal [such as nest-building and grooming the young], but also that males carry in their brains the capacity for this behavior. Maternalism should, therefore, more accurately be designated parentalism. (p. 268)

Ramey (1973:243) also shows that it is overly simplistic to call testosterone the "take charge" hormone while ignoring social factors. She is aware of research that has shown an association between high testosterone levels and aggressiveness and leadership, but she points out that the *situation* might affect the amount of testosterone produced rather than the other way around. She tells of an experiment in which a monkey was considered "top monkey" in his social world; and, along with his high position, he was found to have a high level of testosterone. But, when he was placed in a lower position on the social ladder of the monkey world, his testosterone level dropped along with his status! Thus, one cannot make the assumption that greater levels of testosterone mean greater leadership abilities and that therefore men are more likely to be leaders than women. It doesn't work out quite so neatly.

Perhaps the only thing that can be said about hormones and sex differences is that while hormonal factors both before and after birth cannot be ignored, they should not be viewed as a basis for a fatalistic determinism that seals the destinies of females and males. We must pay attention to the social environment and how human beings of both sexes respond to that environment. And we must keep in mind a point emphasized by Ramey, namely, that the differences that may be seen between one man and another man or one woman and another woman are as great as any differences that may be seen between women as a group and men as a group. In other words, it's a matter of *individual* differences between human beings for the most part, as well as different life circumstances. As Ramey (1973) concludes:

> In all this miasma of claims and counter claims about the role of sex hormones in determining human behavior, there are no data to show that males as a group are more intelligent than females, or that there is any area of psychic response unique to either sex. . . . To the question: Which has the best hormonal basis for leadership and achievement, man or woman? The meaningful answer can only be: Which man and which woman? (p. 244)

Animal Studies and Gender Roles

Just as Ramey cautions against drawing unwarranted conclusions from hormone research, other scientists warn against overgeneralizing from animal studies to human beings.

Psychology professor Annette Ehrlich, who specializes in the study of primates, emphasizes that even those primates most closely related to human beings show great variation in social organization, roles, traditions, and rituals. Some social patterns fit with stereotypical male-female behavioral differences in humans, others are opposite, and still others show amazing flexibility. Attempts to prove that any particular kind of human behavior stems directly from our primate ancestry are nothing more than "an interesting form of game playing" that provide no help in solving social problems such as sex discrimination, Ehrlich (1976) asserts. She elaborates further:

> The behavior of each species needs to be viewed in relation to its own environment. Thus, if we want to resolve specifically human problems such as war, then we have to look closely at such specifically human environmental factors as the military-industrial complex, nationalism, poverty, and racism—none of which has any counterpart among the nonhuman primates. (p. 30)

Psychologist Naomi Weisstein (1971) points out another problem related to claims that certain gender-role patterns are rooted in the very fabric of nature. Writers who make such claims tend to be very selective in the studies they cite. They ignore examples from among certain primates where female aggressiveness and competitive behaviors exceed those of males, just as they ignore studies of those primates where males are greatly involved in parenting. "In marmosets, for instance, the male carries the infant at all times except when the infant is feeding," writes Weisstein (p. 154). "In summary," she goes on, "primate arguments can tell us very little about our 'innate' sex-role behavior; if they tell us anything at all, they tell us that there is no one biologically 'natural' female or male behavior, and that sex-role behavior in non-human primates is much more varied than has previously been thought" (p. 156; see also Stack et al., 1975).

GENDER ROLES IN PRELITERATE AND DEVELOPING SOCIETIES

Having seen that neither hormonal studies nor animal studies provide answers to the sex-stratification system we see among humans, we next turn our attention to other societies. Are men ranked higher than women everywhere in terms of prestige, power, and wealth? And if so, why?

Preliterate Societies

In trying to answer these questions, anthropologists, social theorists, and others have taken three basic positions. Some have said, "In the beginning, women ranked higher than men." Others have argued, "In the beginning, women and men were equal to each other." And still others have asserted, "In the beginning and ever since, men have always outranked women." Let's briefly examine each of these viewpoints.

Idea 1: "In the Beginning, Women Ranked Higher Than Men" During the nineteenth century, drawing upon ancient myths and folklore, various persons proposed that in early evolutionary stages women held the power. Friedrich Engels was one of the supporters of this view (Tavris and Offir, 1977:16–17). Interest in the idea of a matriarchal era was revived in recent years by some spokespersons in the women's movement (for example, Davis, 1971).

However, unable to find convincing evidence for such matriarchal systems, whether of the past or present, most anthropologists tend to doubt their existence. "We now know," writes anthropologist Ernestine Friedl (1975), "that even in societies with matrilineal descent-reckoning, that is, those in which eligibility for marriage, the holding of property, inheritance, and succession to office all depend on a person's kin relationships through females . . . , it is the men who hold the most prized offices and exercise basic control over resources" (p. 4). Although matrilineal systems *do* provide certain advantages for women, they assuredly do not put women in the top position. Take the Iroquois, for example. Women of this group could exercise considerable power. But, say social scientists Carol Tavris and Carole Offir (1977), "even Iroquois women, who played an important role in village politics and lineage, could not join the Council of Elders, the ruling body" (p. 17).

For some scholars, a major problem in relying on legends to prove a former era of female dominance is that "the link which would explain how the rule of men succeeded that of women has always been missing" (Sullerot, 1971, p. 20). At the same time, certain other scholars specializing in the history of women's status—including some anthropologists—have endeavored to supply theories to answer that riddle. Some scholars are persuaded that, if not matriarchy, then at least a kind of "primitive egalitarianism" existed in the beginning; and their theories have generated considerable discussion and debate among both supporters and those who disagree (Reed, 1975; Leacock, 1976; Rohrlich-Leavitt, 1976; Friedlander, 1976; Whitehead, 1976a, 1976b). These debates lead us to the next point.

Idea 2: "In the Beginning, Women and Men Were Equal" Many Marxists today believe that women started out not *above* men but rather as men's equals. However, that equality was eroded as class societies developed, along with private property and the nuclear family system. Likewise, colonial conquests played a part in destroying the

original equality. The model is one of oppression and conflict. Eleanor Leacock (1977:497) is one anthropologist who believes such ideas make sense. She points out that in simple societies childbearing and childrearing did not keep women from making other contributions to society as well; women provided food supplies for their families and enjoyed autonomy. Yet, she asserts, the situation changed with the coming of conquerors, missionaries, traders, and colonial officials. In view of this change, Leacock wonders why women's role *in reproduction* should be considered the reason for their subordination when that was not true at the beginning.

In hunting and gathering societies, the simplest societies of all, groups move about seeking food rather than remaining in one location and cultivating it. Both men and women work together in finding food; they are *co-providers*. And the more the sexes work together in subsistence endeavors, the greater the measure of equality between them (Friedl, 1975). An awareness of this pattern no doubt lies behind sociologist Joyce McCarl Nielsen's (1978) assertion that "all evidence suggests that at the very beginning of human civilization, women and men were roughly equal in status; at least the status gap between them was not as great as it is in more technologically developed societies. . . . women's status, relative to men's, seems to be decreasing over time" (pp. 22, 39).

Friedl (1975), on the other hand, is convinced that some degree of male dominance may be found in all societies. By male dominance, she means that although men may not always have *exclusive* rights, they do have "highly preferential access . . . to those activities to which the society accords the greatest value"—activities that give them some measure of power or control over others. And that brings us to the third point of our discussion on the relative ranking of the sexes.

Idea 3: "Men Have Always Outranked Women in Status"

Most hunting and gathering societies divide up labor in a certain way between males and females (Friedl, 1975:12–16; Nielsen, 1978:24–25). Men usually do the hunting or fishing while women gather small plants, certain small land creatures, and some small creatures of the sea, such as clams or mussels. However, the prestige food is meat; and since men bring home the meat, men have the greater prestige. Still, women's contributions are highly valued, too; and women are viewed as nearly—though not necessarily fully—equal partners.

On the other hand, male dominance is greatest where the food supply is entirely dependent upon hunting—as is true among the Eskimos. If obtaining and controlling the distribution of meat gives men power and prestige even where meat makes up only a small part of the diet, it isn't surprising that such prestige and power are magnified enormously when meat becomes the whole diet! Friedl emphasizes a point we shall see again and again in attempting to understand the differing roles of the sexes, namely, that "the

Male dominance has been greatest where the food supply is entirely dependent upon hunting, as has been the tradition among the Eskimos. (© George Gerster/Photo Researchers, Inc.)

generous distribution of scarce or irregularly available resources is a source of power, and that men and women differ with respect to their opportunities" (p. 32) in this regard.

But why do "men and women differ with respect to their opportunities"? Peggy Sanday (1973), another anthropologist interested in gender roles, suggests that human survival requires an investment of energy in three basic tasks: reproduction, defense, and subsistence. Reproduction has been assigned to women through biology. And the demands associated with bearing and rearing children may limit the energy and attention a woman can give to the other two tasks. Even if a woman makes a major contribution to subsistence in hunting and gathering societies, which is what Leacock referred to previously, she is often carrying an infant within her body or else outside of it, nursing at her breasts. Thus, she is not free to engage in the prestige activity of hunting, which requires traveling unencumbered by burdens while tracking down animals (Friedl, 1975:16–18). And just as a "male monopoly" on hunting exists among the simple societies of hunters and gatherers, a "male monopoly" on the clearing and allocation of land exists among the more technologically advanced societies of *horticultural peoples*—those using hoes and digging sticks to cultivate food (Friedl, 1975). Friedl emphasizes that by controlling land allocation and warfare, men in such societies "are more deeply involved than women in economic and political alliances which are extradomestic" (p. 135)—alliances that are maintained through an exchange of goods and services.

It becomes clear at this point that the differing statuses of the sexes may somehow be related to economic factors, even in simple societies. It's an idea worth examining more fully.

Factors Affecting the Status of Women and Men Some anthropologists suggest that the key to explaining male-female differences in prestige and power is quite simple: traditionally, women have been assigned to the *domestic* sphere of life whereas men have been assigned to the *public* sphere (Rosaldo, 1974). And it is the public sphere that seems to count in terms of prestige and power (Lamphere, 1977:626).

For example, in a hunter-gatherer society, women may play an important part in providing for their families through the fruits and vegetables they gather. But the products of their labors are not for distribution and exchange *outside* their own families—in contrast to the male hunters who control the distribution of big game to the entire community. Friedl (1975) stresses that greater value is attached to that which is produced for extradomestic exchanges than to that which is produced for immediate household use. A similar principle seems to be at work in urban, industrialized societies where the work of homemakers is seldom granted the same social value as paid employment in the public world.

Marx and Engels argued that as long as women were restricted to work within private households and excluded from a society's productive labor, the sexes could never be equal (Sanday, 1973:1685). Therefore, some social scientists assert that the movement away from hunting and gathering societies toward horticultural and agricultural societies, and later industrialization, has meant a gradual decrease in women's status over time. In this view, technological advances such as the invention of the plow—and, thousands of years later, the industrial revolution—have resulted in a greater separation between men in the public world, engaged in market-value work, and women in the private world, engaged in care and maintenance work for their families (Nielsen, 1978:9–10).

May we assume, then, that the more women contribute to subsistence through their productive labor, the higher will be their status in a particular society? Sanday (1973) sought an answer to this question by examining data from 748 societies. Surprisingly, she found that although it was *necessary* for women to be engaged in productive labor in order to have higher status, productive labor in itself did not *guarantee* higher status. Other factors entered in.

Sanday defined *female status* in terms of "the number of economic and political rights which accrue to women" (p. 1682). She found societies in which such rights were extremely few even though women contributed as much as 75 percent of what such societies required in order to survive! Why should this be? "In many societies," explains Sanday, "it appears that females are used as slave labor and are rigidly prohibited from access to control over what they produce" (p. 1697). If a woman is considered her husband's property, both she and the fruits of her labor are under his control—which is one reason some anthropologists say that we must study marriage exchange customs in relation to women's subordinate position (Lamphere, 1977:621).

Not only must a woman *control* what she produces if she is to have higher status, says Sanday, but her product must be something that has a *high prestige or market value.* Rosaldo (1974:19), for example, speaks of parts of New Guinea where women grow sweet potatoes for daily consumption. But men grow yams. And yams are the food distributed at the special feasts of the society, which means yams have the greater prestige value, just as was true of the socially distributed meat of the hunter-gatherer societies.

In some societies, male power stems from contributing to the society something considered of high value; however, in other societies, power is simply *ascribed* to men, not because of what they do but because of what they are—men. They are considered to have a right to control on the basis of beliefs associated with religion or magic. How women may gain power in these two different situations is described by Sanday (1973):

> In societies where control and production are linked and a competitive market exists, female power is likely to develop *if* females are actively engaged in producing valued market goods. In societies where control is based on a magical or religious title, female power is unlikely to develop unless some exogenous influence (such as the introduction of cash cropping, famine, etc.) creates a new demand or results in a revaluation of female produce. (p. 1695)

Developing Societies

Developing societies are those societies in which vast changes are taking place through technological advances in agriculture and a movement toward industrialization and urbanization. Whether such changes raise or lower the status of women has been a matter of some dispute. No doubt, depending on the particular situation, women's status can move in either direction.

Greater Opportunities for Female Independence Sanday spoke of outside influences creating new demands for what women can produce. The Afikpo Ibo women of Nigeria illustrate her point well.

Before European contact, these women made and traded pottery (although their mobility was hindered because of frequent war-

Women in West Africa have been market vendors for generations and, with their earnings, have supported their entire families. (© Marc and Evelyne Bernheim, 1980/Woodfin Camp & Associates)

fare) and also cultivated crops. But the control of income was in the hands of the men, who also carried on such prestige activities as yam cultivation. With the cessation of war, women began traveling more freely, which meant increased trade opportunities. Contact with the outside world also had an impact on the farming activities of the women because the *cassava plant* (the source of tapioca and other food products) was introduced.

The Afikpo Ibo men treated the cassava plant with contempt. *They* would stick with their ritually esteemed yams. However, they said, the women could grow cassava in between the men's heaps of yams if they wished. And any profits the women earned could be kept by the women. The crop proved to be successful beyond everyone's wildest dreams, making it possible for the women to become quite self-sufficient. They were now capable of providing both for themselves and their children. As a result, "Afikpo husbands have found it increasingly difficult to keep their wives at home in their

formerly subordinate position" (Levine, 1970:178, as quoted in Sanday, 1973:1696).

Decreased Opportunities for Female Independence Contact with other cultures and movement toward modernization, while increasing opportunities for women in some cases, can reduce them in others. (See Strobel, 1982; Kelly, 1981.) For example, the demand for their small handicrafts may diminish as manufactured goods become more available. Or work loads for women may increase without compensation, as in cases where men migrate to urban centers to find work while their wives remain behind to cultivate crops. Only rarely do the women share in the wages their husbands earn, although the men may invest a considerable portion of those earnings in purchasing more farmland that the women are expected to work. Such work is considered a woman's duty and is not regarded as productive labor with cash value (Boulding, 1976:104).

One sociologist (Papanek, 1977) faults governments for insensitivity and wrong assumptions. "As long as women are considered the dependents of men, in the economic and legal sense," she writes, "it will be difficult to consider women's needs *directly* in development planning" (p. 16). She is critical of the way official government records list women in the statistical category of "unpaid family worker," as though men are supporting their families rather than recognizing that women and men are doing so together. To illustrate, she cites the women who work as carpet weavers in the Middle East. The product is marketed by male family members, but the women who make the carpets receive no monetary payment, only food, shelter, and clothing.

Problems of Both Sexes in Developing Societies Living and working in societies undergoing change is sometimes painful for men as well as women. For example, one writer from a university in Kenya provides examples of men who, under colonialism, left their African villages expecting great gain by working as soldiers or plantation workers. But pay was low, and they returned to find themselves "no better off than their wives, who had to till the land to feed their children" (Pala, 1977, p. 11).

Anthropologist Ann Stoler (1977) speaks of the "Green Revolution" in Indonesia, where "as in other countries, the introduction of new high-yielding rice varieties, hulling machines, expensive pesticides, and fertilizers to increase agricultural production has primarily benefited the already secure members of rural society and has increased rural income inequalities" (p. 87). Women from poor families who once relied on daily employment as rice pounders now find their work done by hulling machines. Even so, they are better off than their male counterparts because the women have a tradition of alternative ways to earn income, such as through handicraft and small-scale trade. For the men, the options are more limited. In some societies, the solution is thought to lie in leaving rural areas and seeking employment in urban centers. In such cases, men usually find better employment opportunities than do migrant women, a large portion of whom can find no employment in the cities except domestic service at low pay (de Miranda, 1977; Arizpe, 1977).

At this point, it should be clear that the impact of modernization on women's and men's roles in developing societies is complex and varies greatly by economic conditions, social class, and other factors (Chinchilla, 1977). For example, religious beliefs about the roles of the sexes may have to undergo change in some societies. One sociologist (Mernissi, 1975) who specializes in a study of Muslim societies points out the tension between a tradition that segregates the sexes, on the one hand, and a recognition, on the other hand, that full economic development and national advancement will mean using all the talent available—including the talent of women—in the production process. "But to achieve that aim," Mernissi writes, "Muslim society would have to grant the women . . . all the other rights which have until now been male privileges" (p. viii), which would mean vast changes throughout all areas of social life.

Summing up the general impact of the development process in Third World countries, economist Ester Boserup (1977) reports that although some societal groups gain and other groups lose through the replacement of their goods or services by something new, women are especially likely to find themselves among the losers. She explains:

> Although both men and women may become victims of development, it is more difficult for women to adapt to new conditions, because (1) family obligations make them less mobile than men, (2) their occupational choice is more narrowly limited by custom, (3) they usually have less education and training, and (4) even without these handicaps they often face sex discrimination in recruitment. (p. xii)

She also stresses that the work force of these developing countries has a higher percentage of females than of males who are "engaged in traditional occupations, which are precisely those gradually replaced by modern enterprises in economic development."

GENDER ROLES IN INDUSTRIALIZED SOCIETIES

Sociologist Michael Gordon (1978:71–92) has shown how industrialization separates the home from the place of work and transforms the family from a *unit of production* (making and growing things) to a *unit of consumption* (buying things with money earned outside the home rather than manufacturing items directly). Having already examined gender roles in societies that are beginning to industrialize, we now turn to several societies that have already achieved a significant degree of industrialization.

The United States

In the United States, as well as in England, the early stages of industrialization were characterized by the employment of whole families together in the mills and factories— much as whole families had once worked together on the farm or in family-run cottage industries (Kanter, 1977:10; Gordon, 1978:76). But over the course of the nineteenth century, a variety of factors combined to edge women out of the labor force. The emergence of a middle class made it possible for married women to enjoy the "luxury" of remaining at home, supported by their husbands who were now expected to carry the entire breadwinning burden alone. A spate of "female-culture" books were published, admonishing women to be dependent, pious, domestic, and entirely centered in home and family (Welter, 1966). At the same time, industrialization was also producing an urban working class whose lifestyle was quite different, out of necessity. Many of its members were immigrants. Both single and married working-class women found that the stay-at-home cultural ideal was impossible for them to attain. Their families couldn't live on the husband's paycheck alone; they needed any earnings wives and children could bring in, too.

Social Status and Gender-Role Socialization *Social stratification* is an important concept to sociologists because class position bears upon how persons think and act with regard to most matters—including gender roles.

Just as a geologist examines various layers, or strata, of rock that make up a cliff, so the sociologist notes the characteristics of different strata of society. However, we need to keep in mind that when sociologists speak of higher and lower statuses, they aren't saying that one group of persons is *better* than another group. But they are saying that one group is *better off* than another group. One group holds a more advantageous position than another in relation to the economic-opportunity system, and that makes a big difference in a society that values persons according to where they fit into that system.

The Census Bureau measures social status by looking at three indicators: education, occupation, and income. Since occupation and income depend to a great extent upon education, many sociologists consider education itself to be a good indicator of social status.

Research shows that the less education parents have, the more likely they are to have different expectations for sons and daughters and to treat the two sexes differently. Parents with more education, on the other hand, tend to be less traditional in the gender-role training they give their children. Stated another way: the lower the social status, the greater the gender differentiation; the higher the social status, the less the gender differentiation (Scanzoni, 1975b).

Persons with limited educational opportunities are less likely to raise questions about traditional values and customs. In addition, the realistic conditions under which working-class persons live affect their outlooks on life. For example, the restrictive natures of their jobs usually permit little creative thought and independent judgment. "The essence of lower class position is the belief that one is at the mercy of forces and people beyond one's control," writes sociologist Melvin Kohn (1969). In contrast, he suggests that "the essence of higher class position is the expectation that one's decisions and actions can be consequential" (p. 189). Because of differing expectations related to both educational and occupational opportunities, persons of higher status are more likely to be characterized by *self-direction;* they are accustomed to acting on the basis of their own judgment.

But persons of lower status, having had limited educational opportunities, tend to be characterized by *conformity.* They are concerned with obedience, not rocking the boat, and following the dictates of authority. Such behavior is required of them on the job; and so they socialize their children accordingly, thus perpetuating the pattern.

Conformity to what is expected of one can even bring a sense of security. One sociologist suggests that lower-status persons, having been unable to attain a high *achieved status* through education and accomplishments, tend to attach great importance to *ascribed status* (a status assigned by others so that one fits into what is considered one's "proper" place in life). Gender roles are in the ascribed category. Thus, a lower-status person's feelings of "anxious vulnerability" seem to be "soothed by rigidly defined social relationships" (McKinley, 1964).

For such persons, who feel so little control over the circumstances that govern their lives, clearly spelled-out gender roles may seem one way of providing some sense of order, predictability, and certainty. "And you knew who you were then," sang the blue-collar Bunkers of television's *All in the Family.* What was it in those bygone days that made you know "who you were then"? Archie regularly crooned out the answer: "Girls were girls, and men were men."

Earlier, we spoke of *instrumental* (task-oriented) behaviors and *expressive* (person-

The early stages of industrialization were characterized by the employment of whole families together in the mills and factories much as families had once worked together on the farm or in family-run cottage industries. (The Granger Collection)

oriented) behaviors, pointing out that instrumentality has traditionally been emphasized in the socialization of boys and expressiveness in the socialization of girls. However, the degree to which either expressiveness or instrumentality is stressed for either sex varies by social class. Middle-class parents, more than blue-collar parents, are interested in seeing their children develop to some extent along *both* instrumental and expressive lines. Working-class parents, on the other hand, are more interested in seeing their sons develop instrumental qualities and their daughters expressive qualities.

Both middle-class and working-class parents socialize their sons to be active, aggressive, competitive, independent, adventuresome, strong, and courageous. But there is a difference in the degree of *expressiveness* emphasized at these different status levels. Middle-class parents tend to strive for more nurturance and tenderness in their sons than do blue-collar parents (Komarovsky, 1962; Balswick and Peek, 1971). And, although both classes stress instrumental behaviors, there are differences in what instrumentality *means* among boys at different status levels, one indication being a lower regard for scholastic achievement among adolescent boys at lower status levels (Chafetz, 1978:92–93). In contrast, in homes where the parents have higher levels of education, instrumentality does not mean great emphasis on physical strength and demonstrations of macho but, rather, on mastery, competency, aspirations for academic excellence, and working toward achievement within higher-status occupations.

When it comes to daughters, middle-class parents encourage behaviors considered traditionally "feminine," such as nurturance and gentleness; but at the same time, they want their daughters to develop a considerable degree of independence and assertiveness. In other words, middle-class parents desire that their daughters be somewhat instrumental as well as expressive—though not quite so instrumental as their sons. Working-class parents, for their part, tend to consider instrumental behaviors "masculine" and don't encourage such behaviors in their daughters. As a result, girls from these homes are likely to be more passive and subordinate than girls at higher status levels. This is true in spite of the likelihood that the circumstances of life will make it necessary for many of these girls to enter the labor force when they reach adulthood, and thus they could have benefited from more emphasis on developing instrumental skills.

Race and Gender-Role Socialization The purpose of gender-role socialization is to prepare persons for their adult functioning in relation to the economic-opportunity system.

Historically in the United States, white males have been socialized for direct participation in that system, while white females have been socialized primarily for indirect participation, the expectation being that the economic-opportunity system's rewards would come to them through their husbands' accomplishments.

Of course, history shows that not all persons had equal access to economic opportunity—either directly or indirectly. Numerous men were disappointed to find that despite the rags-to-riches theme of the Horatio Alger stories, hard work did not always bring wealth and success. And numerous women were very much involved in providing for their families, working side by side with the men in carving out the wilderness, running family farms, and laboring for long, hard hours in factories. They were anything but the weak, passive, dependent, genteel ladies of leisure described in the female advice books. Yet, for both white women and white men, as evasive as financial success might have seemed at times, there was still the American dream to drive them onward. There was still hope.

For black persons, the story was different. Even when socialized to *want* the American dream and to aspire toward it, they were hindered constantly by obstacles placed in their way by the dominant white society. The door to opportunity might appear open, but as soon as blacks ran up to it, they would find it slammed in their faces. Black men and black women had to develop together strength, perseverance, and resiliency in order to survive.

Cut off from the economic opportunities open to whites, black males found that socialization for mastery, achievement, and competition counted for nothing if a person was going to be judged on the basis of skin color rather than ability. Both under slavery and later during the period of Jim Crow (when segregation was legal and encouraged), the black male's self-concept was dealt heavy blows. He was told both directly and indirectly that he was inferior because he was black. But at the same time, he was a man. And societal gender norms stressed proving one's manhood through achievement. Yet the white-controlled occupational structure blocked his chances for the very thing societal norms demanded! It was a no-win situation. First, there had been the degradation of slavery; later, there was the degradation of being given only the lowest-paying, unskilled service jobs—or no jobs at all. For some black males in the agricultural South, sharecropping opportunities opened up so that husbands, wives, and children could work together on farms under former slave owners. But conditions were far from ideal.

Often black males couldn't find any work, and their families had to rely on the efforts of their wives, sometimes being forced to depend on incomes that meant bare subsistence (Lerner, 1972). Under slavery, black females had learned from earliest childhood that being female did not mean being docile, weak, passive, and dependent. Black women worked right alongside men—cutting wood, building fences, driving ox carts, and working in the fields in the blazing heat. Gender made no difference.

Sojourner Truth, a tall black woman with no formal education who traveled around speaking and singing for the antislavery cause, underscored that point. At the second National Woman's Suffrage Convention held

"I have plowed and planted and gathered into barns and no man could head me. And ain't I a woman?"—Sojourner Truth. (Library of Congress)

in Akron, Ohio, in 1852, a group of clergymen invaded the gathering and monopolized the convention floor with endless discourses on woman's supposed "inferior nature" and "proper place in life." When one speaker stressed that woman was innately helpless and dependent, Sojourner Truth could stand it no longer. She rose and dramatically put such myths to rest by recounting her days as a slave. It took strength to bear the lash. It took strength to keep going and not be utterly crushed in spirit as one by one her children were sold. And it took strength to perform the hard work imposed on her. What was all this foolish talk about woman's need to be treated as a fragile object? Nobody had ever helped *her* into carriages or lifted *her* over mud puddles! And nobody had ever given *her* the best place, Sojourner Truth declared. "And ain't I a woman?" she asked. Holding up her strong arm, she told the audience to look at it as she continued: "I have plowed and planted and gathered into barns, and no man could head me! And ain't I a woman?" (Quoted in Brawley, 1921). Sojourner Truth provided the delegates with a living example of the way black women refused to be confined to the gender-role stereotypes held up by white society. Circumstances had forced them to be active, assertive, and independent in spirit.

After slavery ended, black women frequently found it easier than did black men to find employment. According to anthropologist Diane K. Lewis (1977), the laws that segregated blacks and whites and limited black opportunities were mainly concerned with defining the black *man's* place and making sure he stayed in it. "Since slavery coexisted with male dominance in the wider society," says Lewis, "black men, as men, constituted a potential threat to the established order of white superiority. Laws were formulated that specifically denied black men normal adult

prerogatives" (p. 341). She refers to the powerlessness black males were made to feel in view of lynchings and the sexual exploitation of black women by whites—acts which were "covertly sanctioned" by the dominant society. And for nearly a century after slavery, Lewis continues, "stringent institutionalized barriers" blocked black men from membership in trade unions (and thus from the job market), prevented full participation in the political process, and undermined their status as husbands and fathers, such as through certain welfare laws.

Although racial discrimination was experienced by women and men alike, black women had certain limited access to the opportunity structure. They could usually find employment in domestic and service occupations, working as maids, cooks, laundresses, or day laborers—occupations where there was little competition from whites. Factory jobs, except for the most menial tasks, however, were usually closed off from black persons of both sexes (Lerner, 1972).

For all these reasons, over the course of American history, socialization patterns for blacks were in some ways similar and in some ways different from those of whites. Black males learned the dominant society's values with regard to achievement but found they were blocked from economic opportunities in adulthood. Young black women learned that having been born female did not destine them to fulfill the dominant society's gender-role stereotypes. By force of circumstance, black women found themselves participating directly in the economic system and bringing home the meager rewards that system permitted to persons with black skin.

Contrary to myths about the black family, the majority of husbands and wives put great effort into keeping their families together—often against incredible odds (Genovese, 1974; Gutman, 1976). In spite of the difficulties placed in their paths, both partners did everything they could to help one another and their children. "We read of exhausted black men tending plots of land and going hunting and fishing to obtain food for their families," writes Lewis (1978), "just as we read of overburdened women having to cook and sew after a full day's work in the fields" (p. 737).

The widespread employment of black women which resulted from whites' determination to keep black men out of the labor force had an unintended consequence that continues today: less rigid gender roles for black children (Noble, 1966; Steinmann, Fox, and Farkas, 1968; Scanzoni, 1977). Black daughters tend to be socialized in ways that emphasize strength, drive, mastery, individualism, and independence. And black sons, living in a subculture where female employment has been a long tradition, tend to grow up to be husbands who, more than white men, are likely to hold egalitarian gender-role norms (Scanzoni, 1975a, 1975b; Lewis, 1975, 1977, 1978).

Lewis (1975) points out that research on child rearing in black families is limited. But what research does exist has led her to conclude that there may be a distinctive Afro-American cultural heritage that helps de-emphasize the gender polarity found in white culture. For example, a small black child of either sex learns to fondle and care for babies and toddlers—the child's younger siblings. And these nurturance behaviors carry over into adult life. In other words, not only do both women and men in black culture display "behavior considered appropriate for males in white culture," comments Lewis (1975), "but behavior which is associated with females in white culture is characteristic of both men and women in black culture."

Although her emphasis is on gender-role egalitarianism among blacks, Lewis

A small black child of either sex learns to fondle and care for babies and toddlers—the child's younger siblings—and these nurturant behaviors carry over into adult life. (© Suzanne Szasz/Photo Researchers, Inc.)

(1977:345) is not unaware of problems that arise in certain situations—particularly where male unemployment is high. Some black men, having been severely beaten down by white injustices in the economic system, may sometimes react to the bread-winning role and aspirations of black women with bitterness rather than appreciation. And the resentment may show up in efforts to dominate women (Wallace, 1979). The feeling seems to be that the degree of autonomy that black women have gained by earning necessary income has actually come about because of racist policies that have kept down black men from slavery onward—thus keeping them from the leadership role society says males should enjoy. Not feeling that they could strike back at the society and the structural conditions that caused the problem, some angry black men have reacted against black women. A number of black women have written of the harm done to *both* black women and black men by society's unquestioning acceptance of the stereotype of "domineering matriarchs" out to "emasculate" and dominate men and its lack of recognition that black women were often *forced* into taking primary responsibility for their families and did so out of concern for the entire family's well-being (Lerner, 1972, chap. 10).

In one study of 155 middle-class black men, sociologist Noel Cazenave (1983:349) found evidence that a "feeling of strained relationships, and antagonism between black men and black women, is not limited to lower-class black men." According to this researcher, "there may be attitudes and issues that are peculiar to the highly ambitious, upwardly mobile, and often occupationally stressed black middle-class." Interestingly, the men most pessimistic about the state of male-female relationships among blacks were found to be the men who indicated more traditional gender-role preferences. The *majority* of men in Cazenave's sample, however, felt that poor communication was the chief problem in the relationships between black men and black women. They did not feel black women had too much control in the family, but they were convinced that black women have more opportunities than do black men today in the larger society.

Socialist Societies

Because Marx and Engels deplored the social system in which men dominated women, the socialist and communist countries have made a special effort to promote equality for women and men in their social roles (Holter, 1970; Sedugin, 1973; Nazzari, 1983). We shall, at various points throughout this book, be examining some of these efforts to see how successful they have been in certain aspects of life. Here we want to look briefly at general attitudes toward gender roles in several select societies.

Eastern European Countries Observers have pointed out that gender-role emancipation is considerably more advanced in East Germany than in West Germany (Katzenstein, 1970) because women in East Germany have received greater encouragement to pursue occupational achievements (Geiger, 1968; Field and Flynn, 1970)—just as has been true of the Soviet Union for an even longer period of time.

Women are represented in large numbers in the industrial, professional, and agricultural sectors of the Soviet economy; and official ideology stresses the equality of the sexes and the abolishment of gender-linked roles. Nevertheless, a great deal of inequality remains (Croll, 1981).

Studies have consistently shown that Soviet women remain responsible for maintaining the home, no matter how heavily involved they are in occupational achievements (Field and Flynn, 1970; Morgan, 1984). Tatyana Mamonova (1984), exiled from the Soviet Union in 1980 for publishing an underground feminist journal, has made available an insightful collection of writings by Soviet women. A major complaint of these women is the exhaustion they feel because of the menial, time-consuming housework that falls to them and drains their creative energies after their daily official working hours have ended. Yet, marriage and motherhood continue to be extolled in the Soviet Union, and women are conscious of the social approval and benefits attached to the married status. At the same time, as the boxed insert shows, some women are beginning to reject the notion that marriage is necessary or desirable. They are disenchanted with the attitudes of many Russian men who refuse to be actively involved in home responsibilities.

Some leaders of the Communist party have expressed concern. They are aware of the chidings of Lenin, who once wrote: "So few men—even among the proletariat—realize how much effort and trouble they could save women, even quite do away with, if they were to lend a hand in 'women's work.' But no. . . . They want their peace and comfort" (Zetken, 1934). A journal of the Communist Party, U.S.A., has called attention to the problem in several articles, suggesting collective child-care arrangements and the socialization of housework as possible solutions. In the meantime, writes Alva Buxenbaum (1973), "we have had to take into our account the fact that the double burden of house and job (or in the case of housewives with young children, being tied down to the household) is a major obstacle to their consistent participation in activity. . . . A sharing of household chores by conscious Communist husbands and wives can free Communist Women for political activity."

Hilda Scott (1974), in dealing with the question raised in the title of her book, *Does Socialism Liberate Women?* points up similar problems in Czechoslovakia, where household and child-care responsibilities fall to women disproportionately and where men have greater work opportunities and receive higher pay in spite of the socialist ideology of equality of the sexes. Gender-role stereotypes continue, and the weight of tradition hinders change.

Cuba Such gender-based specialization in household work has been outlawed in Cuba. According to the official Family Code of 1974, if both spouses are in the labor force, they must share equally all household and childrearing tasks. "Theoretically at least, a woman may now take her husband to the People's Court or ultimately divorce him on the grounds that his behavior and nonparticipation in domestic labor prevented her from either studying or entering employment," writes Elisabeth Croll (1981:391), a researcher with the United Nations Research Institute for Social Development. This law is read at all marriage services and is considered to have had some effect on male *attitudes*, if not on actual practice. "In one recent survey," Croll points out, "almost 80 percent of a sample comprising both sexes thought that men and women should share housework, but there is no evidence yet that any widespread sharing has actually occurred or greatly reconciled the conflicting demands of production and reproduction on the time and energies of women."

Muriel Nazzari (1983), a specialist in Latin American history, calls attention to Fidel Castro's 1959 "Speech to the Women" and his efforts over the next two decades to improve women's status and promote the equality of the sexes. "Many Cuban women have claimed that women were the greatest beneficiaries of the Revolution," writes Nazzari (p. 250), pointing out however that social class position determines that assessment to a great extent. Most Cuban women were not wage earners at the time of the Revolution. Upper- and middle-class women, except for those who were professionals themselves, enjoyed a status and income provided by their husbands, along with leisurely comfort made possible through an inexpensive labor pool of domestic servants. All this changed when the Revolution redistributed wealth and altered upper- and middle-class living standards drastically. In exchange-theory terms, upper- and middle-class women

RUSSIAN WOMEN CHANGE, BUT THE MENFOLKS DON'T

Moscow (AP)—Galina is a university professor with her own apartment and two privileges much prized in the Soviet Union—trips abroad and her own car.

But she is unhappy because she can't find a suitable husband.

Galina's problem is not unique. More and more women in the Soviet Union, which celebrates International Women's Day on Thursday, appear to be chafing against ingrained male chauvinism, staying single and pursuing careers rather than marrying for marriage's sake.

Their changing attitudes, as reflected in a recent newspaper article and the published responses from readers, have given rise to social problems which are increasingly worrying Soviet authorities. A declining birthrate is one of the chief concerns.

The Communist Party last year called for more meticulous studies on the changing society.

"What do you need a man for?" is one of the most frequent utterances of young Moscow women. "They all drink, they are lazy, good for nothing. It is very difficult to find a good man."

"How can I marry a man and have his children if I don't respect him?" a Moscow woman asked recently. "It's better to be alone, although to be alone is terrible."

Although Soviet women make up 50 percent of the labor force, they rarely hold senior posts. Promotion is blocked by traditional prejudice and hampered by women taking time off for children.

The typical Russian husband doesn't help at home. His wife shops, queuing for hours for scarce goods. She cooks, cleans and cares for the children.

Younger, mostly Russian women are beginning to rebel. They are forging ahead in education, with statistics showing that 59 percent of those with secondary and higher education are women.

Women's greater independence has spawned a rocketing divorce rate—3 percent 30 years ago, 30 percent nationwide now and as high as 50 percent in Russian cities such as Leningrad.

A decade ago, most divorcees quickly remarried. Now, says journalist Tatyana Panina, a writer on women's affairs, "the picture is changing."

The problem of liberated women rebelling against their men is almost exclusive to Russians, the dominant nationality in the Soviet Union. . . .

The main newspaper of the Russian federation. Sovietskaya Rossiya, recently carried a reader discussion of Galina's fruitless search for a good husband and the antagonism between sexes.

"For many years, I have lived alone," a Moscow divorcee, S. Romanova, wrote in response to Galina's story.

She has had marriage proposals, she said, "but I have had enough. I have no desire to link my life with a drunkard or a loafer puffed up with the mere realization that he is a man. I haven't met one man on whom I could rely, who could be my helpmate and my friend, not just an egoistic consumer. I have no confidence I will marry again . . . Live again under one roof with a stranger who is just called a husband. What for?"

Male anger with modern women was no less great. Galina's tale drew a rebuttal from V. Sysenko, an academic who accused modern women of being selfish and unfeminine.

"You certainly can't apply the words dear or sweet to them," he wrote. . . .

Ms. Panina, who summarized the letters in a long article, said the response was so overwhelming that her newspaper would continue the discussion of male-female problems.

SOURCE: Alison Smale, *(Salt Lake City) Deseret News*, March 8–9, 1984, pp. A-13, 14.

experienced the Revolution as *costly* while lower-class women experienced the Revolution as *rewarding.* The literacy campaign, free health care, better housing, slashed rents and utility rates, educational opportunities, and the generally improved standard of living made possible a life poor families had never known. Efforts were made to ensure full employment for males at first, with a call for women to enlist in the labor force coming only later on. However, women already employed were provided with day care and other services to aid them in combining work and family responsibilities. In addition, women who had worked as domestic servants or who had turned to prostitution to support themselves and their children were retrained at special schools to equip them for new jobs.

"Though the Revolution did not immediately incorporate all women into paid work," Nazzari points out, "it created the Federation of Cuban Women to mobilize them for building the new society." Day-care centers and schools for training day-care workers came about through the voluntary work of this federation. But something else began to happen as well. As women participated in voluntary organizations to help build the new society, they began to question traditional gender roles and the norms of male dominance and female subordination that had confined them to the home. The *way* women saw themselves began to change, and many

men were not happy with these new perceptions. "It was husbands who were most limiting," said one woman quoted by Nazzari (p. 254), "and the rest of the family, too, because they were used to seeing woman as the center of the home, the one who solved all problems, and they didn't understand that women could solve problems outside the home, too."

After the goal of full male employment had been reached, Castro issued a call for a million women to join the paid labor force. At the same time, other demands on the economy made it increasingly difficult to keep up with the need for more nurseries, school cafeterias, and other services necessary for employed mothers. In 1969, more than three-quarters of the women who had previously joined the labor force dropped out. Home responsibilities made employment too difficult.

After careful study of the problem, the Federation of Cuban Women presented suggestions for easing the lives of employed women—for example, giving their children priority at boarding schools and day-care centers, extending business hours so that they could shop after work, providing laundry services at places of employment, and so on. But although such measures helped, "they did not eliminate women's double work shift," Nazzari reports. At this point, a change in thinking occurred and the Family Code was enacted; equal *male* participation

A Cuban day-care center—one effort toward easing the difficulty of combining home and employment responsibilities. (© Roberto Marinez/Photo Researchers, Inc.)

in household tasks now became law. The government's early solution, attempting to "move women toward equality by transferring family duties to social institutions without disturbing men's lives or roles," had deflected resources from other areas of economic development. "The Family Code, on the other hand, provided a solution to the woman question that did not need to come out of the national budget," says Nazzari (p. 257). "It would take place within the home without affecting the rest of society. It did, nevertheless, require a change in individual men's lives, and men resisted."

Nazzari is persuaded that the continuing inequality between the sexes in Cuba, in spite of *ideological* commitment to nondiscrimination, is tied to changes in the economic system that (1) eliminated free day care and other services, (2) treat women as a reserve labor supply, and (3) foster dependency on husbands as primary breadwinners in view of a move toward distributing re-

sources increasingly on the basis of wages rather than need. "Since they constitute a labor reserve and cannot always find employment, individual women who realize they may not be economically self-sufficient all their lives will rely primarily on relationships with men for financial support," Nazzari concludes (p. 263). Thus, traditional gender roles are reinforced.

People's Republic of China Mainland China is of particular interest in this regard because, up to the time of the 1949 Revolution, traditional male-female roles were deeply imbedded within the rigid norms of Confucianism. Yet the Chinese Communist party remains determined to accomplish a blurring of gender-role differences.

Long before the Communists came to power, certain voices were raised against a number of practices that severely oppressed women: foot binding, female infanticide, the sale of young girls, prostitution, concubinage, the expectation that widows and betrothed women who had lost fiancés should commit suicide, and various cruel marriage and divorce customs. However, the Communists led an all-out campaign to elevate the status of women—although, as psychologist Joyce Jennings [Walstedt] (1978) observes, the intensity and seriousness of that campaign had its ups and downs over the years. Even so, she points out, "given that all factions in the Chinese struggle grew up in a country that was one of the least advanced in terms of sexual equality, the extent of change in 28 years is without precedent in modern times." Whereas only a few decades ago the position of women in the Chinese family was one of "virtual serfdom," it is now "one of economic independence in relatively egalitarian marriage relationships" (pp. 379–80).

At the same time, enough remnants of

older thought patterns have remained to cause Jennings [Walstedt] to conclude that "despite gains made under socialism, the revolution has fallen short of its goal of a classless society in which women have coequality" (p. 379). Service work, traditionally viewed as "women's work," is downgraded whether done in or out of the home. And a certain amount of job discrimination that favors men and limits women is still present. Furthermore, women continue to have the greater responsibility for child care, although, says Jennings, "women are not as overburdened by their parenting role as they are in some countries" (p. 390) because the whole community helps in the rearing of children. However, the custom of assigning to women such chores as cooking, cleaning, mending, shopping, and laundering persists—even though women are also actively engaged in the labor force as full-time workers. Such practices occur in spite of the fact that official propaganda associated with the new Marriage Law of 1950 encourages husbands and wives to share household tasks (Kristeva, 1975:61; Lu, 1984:153).

Irene Eber, a specialist in Asian studies, shows how the literature of the Chinese people also reveals more than a trace of traditional values regardless of the official commitment to male-female equality. Although recent literature in the People's Republic emphasizes such themes as free choice in marriage partners, equal work and educational opportunities for both sexes, and economic independence for women, the stories are honest about the struggles involved. Such tensions show that change doesn't come easily or instantly.

Traditional "feminine" virtues—such as tact, resourcefulness, gentleness, and modesty—are extolled in women. But at the same time, women are expected to be strong and independent, capable of making wise decisions on their own. "Women's difficulty in working with men derives in large part from the latter's fear of losing face and being humiliated," writes Eber (1976). "Thus women must be unobtrusively competent, firm, but not aggressive—a difficult situation, especially when one is the only woman among men" (p. 34).

Eber illustrates by citing a 1973 story in which the only woman on board ship is second in command to the captain. Knowing of the captain's displeasure in working with women, the woman modestly declines opportunities to display her skills—until an emergency forces her to take over the ship. Even in her heroism, it is made clear in the story that she must continue to "behave modestly and tactfully throughout, in order not to embarrass the captain" (p. 34).

In another story recounted by Eber, three boys and a girl are coworkers at a hydroelectric-station construction site. When the boys' hand-sewn shoes wear out, they decide to place them by the side of the road, hoping that the girl will notice them and mend them. Exceeding their expectations, the girl instead sews *new* pairs of shoes for each boy and at the same time keeps up her occupational endeavors.

And in yet another story, a wife prides herself on her contributions as a behind-the-scenes helpmate to her husband. She says that because he works in the collective all day, she is serving the people best indirectly, by helping her husband so that he can perform his work better. She views this as a more important duty than concentrating on her own achievements. Eber explains why Chinese fiction presents such ideas:

> Women's increased role in production and their insistence that they be allowed to perform other than traditional women's work clearly produced uncomfortable visions of competition between

the sexes. Because the prospect of wives abandoning housework and children as well as their submissive role was not easily accepted, a number of stories show women fulfilling their various roles with equal competency—and dutifully taking second place to men. (p. 30)

Some observers believe the yin-yang philosophy of old China may foster what Walstedt calls "nonconscious sexism." Yin is the passive "feminine principle" believed to exist throughout the universe, and yang is the active "masculine principle." The two are viewed as complementary opposites in all of nature. Thus, it is possible that some persons are fearful of upsetting an assumed natural balance by the introduction of drastic changes in gender roles; and so they resist (Walstedt, 1978:389; Hong, 1976; Lu, 1984).

Israeli Kibbutzim The Israeli *kibbutzim* (plural for *kibbutz*) represent one of the most dramatic attempts anywhere to experiment with alternative lifestyles and variations in family forms. A *kibbutz* is an agricultural commune. Strictly speaking, a discussion of such communes does not fit with our focus on industrialized societies. Yet, such a discussion is appropriate at this point in line with our consideration of socialist experiments because the kibbutzim are based on Engels' notion that all social differences between the sexes should be done away with.

In the kibbutz, an infant is housed with other infants in a "baby house" separate from the parents. (Ken Heyman)

How can this be done? The conventional pattern based on the original ideology involves rather elaborate steps to assure that children of the kibbutz learn undifferentiated gender roles from their earliest days. The process begins at birth by housing the infant with other infants in a "baby house" (*créche*) separate from the parents. From birth to 9 months, infants interact progressively less with their biological parents. At 9 months, contacts are restricted to two or three hours daily after the parents complete their workday, with longer periods permitted on holidays. Until children are 18 years old, virtually all their socialization is transmitted by a *metapelet*, a female caretaker in charge of each small group of children, as well as by schoolteachers and peers (Rabin, 1970:292–95).

When parents and children get together during this period, parents reinforce what the children have learned from their other role models. The entire system was designed to eliminate traditional gender-role images among kibbutz children and had a record of working relatively well over the years. When kibbutz and American children of 10 years of age were compared, kibbutz children were found to be much less aware of sex differences in social roles (Rabin, 1970:294). Summarizing a number of studies, including their own, psychologists Benjamin Beit-Hallahmi and Albert Rabin (1977) report no negative clinical or psychological effects stemming from kibbutz childrearing patterns. Follow-up studies show kibbutz-born young adults "to be remarkably effective, productive, and well-adjusted" in their overall functioning (Beit-Hallahmi and Rabin, 1977; Rabin and Beit-Hallahmi, 1982).

However, something has been happening in the kibbutzim in recent years. Certain changes have begun showing up which indicate a return to some degree of gender-role traditionalism—the very thing the founders of the kibbutzim had worked so hard to abandon (Schlesinger, 1977). In view of that early commitment to sexual equality, such a turn of events surprised many observers. Some even claim that the renewed emphasis on the nuclear family and a more stereotypical division of labor proves that a woman's "natural bent" is toward domestic concerns after all.

But as sociologist Helen Mayer Hacker (1975) stresses, what has happened in some kibbutzim isn't really "a female retreat from equality" but, rather, "a retreat from the ideal of women doing 'masculine' work." And there are structural reasons for this which are associated with how the kibbutz is set up. Hacker points out that total commitment to role *interchangeability* never existed. "Rather," she writes, "the emphasis was on changing women's roles without any corresponding change in men's roles" (p. 189).

Joseph Blasi (1981:452) of Harvard University's Project for Kibbutz Studies also underscores the point that "the ideology was one sided." Males did not define *equality be-*

tween the sexes as something requiring changes in their own behavior. Furthermore, the kibbutz arrangement itself has promoted a traditional division of labor along gender lines. Blasi calls attention to the assignment of child care and childrearing to *female* members of the kibbutz. True, such work is collectivized rather than privatized; but it is considered "women's work" nonetheless. Women are also found predominantly in the laundry house, kitchen, and other areas of communal service, whereas the men of the kibbutz are found in the higher status occupations in the productive sector of the economy. Blasi believes that the efforts to erase traditional gender roles were only half-hearted because so many persons involved in the kibbutz movement were there for reasons other than single-minded commitment to the original ideology. Historical evidence, he emphasizes, "proves there was never any affirmative attempts to provide education in economic planning, management, engineering, or agricultural science to the kibbutz women nor education for men in the arts and sciences of child, kitchen, and clothing" (p. 454).

ROLE INTERCHANGEABILITY

The observations of Hacker and Blasi have come up again and again in discussing gender roles throughout the world. Most efforts at change have been in one direction only. But, to be effective, change must move in two directions: men must share in domestic and childrearing tasks even as women share in the world of outside work (Rosaldo and Lamphere, 1974:14). Sociologist Elise Boulding (1976) says this is something "Marxist analysis failed to put its finger on," assuming instead that state-supported services would solve the problem. In Boulding's opinion, "there is no way out for men but to confront parenthood, and no way out for women but to confront sharing their centuries-old monopoly on the breeder-feeder role" (p. 116). Rosaldo (1974) makes the same point when she asserts that "the most egalitarian societies are not those in which male and female are opposed or are even competitors, but those in which men value and participate in the domestic life of the home. Correspondingly, they are societies in which women can readily participate in important public events" (p. 41). In this way of thinking, the roles of women and men are not reversed but interchangeable.

CHAPTER HIGHLIGHTS

Traditionally, males have been socialized to concentrate on the instrumental side of life and females on the expressive. Some persons have ignored societal factors and argued that biology determines the relative status of the sexes. However, the part hormones may play in certain behavioral differences between females and males is extremely complex. Also, animal studies indicate great variation in male-female behaviors in the primate world so that no particular pattern can be assumed to be "naturally" male or "naturally" female. Some anthropologists suggest that the traditional assignment of women to the domestic sphere and men to the public sphere explains male-female differences in prestige and power. At the same time, cross-cultural studies indicate that the amount of labor a woman does won't in itself enhance her status unless she has *control* over what she produces and thus has some degree of economic independence. In addition, what she produces must rank high in prestige or market value. Historically in the United States, white males have been socialized for direct, and white females for indirect, participation in the economic-opportunity system. Widespread employment of black women that resulted from whites' determination to keep black men out of the labor force has had unintended consequences: less rigid gender roles for black children; a tradition of strength, independence, and occupational endeavors on the part of black women; and a willingness on the part of black men to hold egalitarian gender-role norms.

Among industrialized nations, the communist and socialist countries have made special attempts to eliminate inequalities between the sexes; yet vestiges of traditional gender-role patterns remain. Some social scientists are persuaded that efforts toward full equality for women and men are doomed to failure unless men develop expressive qualities and share in domestic and child-care responsibilities at the same time that women develop instrumental qualities and aim toward achievement in the economic-opportunity system. Thus, *all* of life would be shared by both sexes, without disproportionate loads or privileges assigned to either.

P·A·R·T T·H·R·E·E

BEFORE MARRIAGE

· 4 ·

DATING AND MATE SELECTION

For the most part, the right to choose one's mate has been a freedom taken for granted throughout the history of the United States. The early immigrants often left behind parents and other relatives (the *extended kin*). Thus, finding a marriage partner was up to the *individual* rather than to his or her family. The fact that a *woman* had such free choice in finding a marriage partner seemed surprising to a French traveler who visited America in the mid-nineteenth century. "While still quite young," he wrote, "ignorant of herself, life not yet a lesson, when circumstances the most frivolous, appearances the most deceptive, and errors of judgment may blind her reason—she makes the most important decision of her life" (Carlier, 1867:33–34).

In many times and places, however, *parents* were the ones who chose marriage partners for their sons and daughters. Kin involvement and economic considerations have played a large part in marriage customs the world over. In China, for example, before sweeping reforms were launched following the 1949 Revolution, traditional marriage customs were based on bargaining between two sets of parents and often involved an intermediary who negotiated the "bride price." Many of the marriages were "blind marriages," so named because the man and woman had never seen each other before the wedding. In some cases, parents arranged the marriages of their offspring while the boy and girl were yet small children, although the couple would not live together as husband and wife until they were older. The Chinese elders claimed that the old god in the moon bound together the feet of males and females destined for each other, and parents and intermediaries merely acted as instruments to carry out his will (Macciocchi, 1972:356–357).

Historically and cross-culturally, financial bargaining has been an important facet of mate selection. Some cultures require a bridegroom to pay a *bride price,* or *bride wealth*—in the form of money, livestock, or other goods—to the bride's parents as compensation for their loss of their daughter's domestic services. The payment of the bride price also symbolizes the linkage between the groom's family and the bride's family. Similarly, in some societies, the family of the bride contributes a *dowry* (money, goods, or other property that the bride brings into the marriage). The persistence of such practices in China in spite of the government's 1950 attempt to make major changes in marriage customs prompted the enactment, in 1980, of a much stronger law, part of which specifically *prohibits* "the extraction of money or gifts in connection with marriage" (Engel, 1984:956).

PARENTAL INFLUENCE IN MATE SELECTION

Like parents elsewhere, American parents have been concerned about their children's marriages and have done everything they could to keep their sons and daughters from striking poor bargains in the marriage market. The seventeenth-century Puritans who settled in New England, for example, considered it their duty before God, not only to make sure their children found their "particular calling" in the vocational realm, but to make certain their grown sons and daughters were settled in proper marriages. But this sense of responsibility did not mean that the wishes of the young couple were disregarded. Ministers admonished parents not to impose their wills on their children, pointing out that "we know by long Experience that forc'd Matches any way seldome do well." Historian Edmund Morgan (1966) writes that usually "the Puritan fathers must have confined the exercise of their power to haggling over the financial agreement after the children had chosen for themselves—provided of course that they had chosen within the proper economic and religious limitations" (p. 85).

Deciding on financial agreements involved a great deal of bickering and bargaining between the two sets of parents, although the normal ratio was for the woman's parents to furnish half as much as was furnished by the man's parents. Sometimes the settlements included lands and other times money; but in any case, once the bargaining ended, a legal contract was drawn up binding the parties to the financial agreement. Only then could the marriage take place.

The bargaining between families was rooted in a concern that the newlyweds have sufficient goods to set up housekeeping rather than a concern that the families make a profit or strike a good deal in uniting two kinship lines. "What shall these young beginners do for household stuff?" asked one worried Puritan father who had given a sum of money toward his daughter's marriage but realized the father of her future husband had given only a tract of land. On the advice of a third party, both fathers agreed to add more money so that the young couple could purchase supplies needed for their new home (Morgan, 1966:82). Such concerns are not remote from the concerns of loving parents today.

Although the Puritans did not *arrange* their children's marriages, they supervised and gave advice. Today in the United States, parents continue to influence their children's marriage choices in a variety of ways—by socializing them during their growing-up years

A YOUNG LADY'S DOWER HER WEIGHT IN PINE TREE SHILLINGS

Economic factors, such as dowries (money, goods, or property contributed by the bride's family), were important in seventeenth-century marriage bargaining. (New York Public Library Picture Collection)

and by choosing the neighborhoods in which they live, the people with whom they associate, the schools they attend, and so on. One function of sororities and fraternities has been to serve in the parents' stead, assuring that young men and women away from home supervision would mix with the "right" kind of persons in the parents' eyes—persons considered suitable as potential marriage partners (Rubin, 1973:201–203; Scott, 1965).

Except in highly unusual cases of coercion, however, the degree of parental control over marital choice in the United States today simply reflects the degree of resource-based

EXTREME EXAMPLE OF PARENTAL CONTROL OVER YOUNG PERSON'S LOVE LIFE

Lamia, Greece (AP)—A 47-year old Greek woman was held captive for 29 years in a basement dungeon because her family was scandalized by a love affair she had when she was a teen-ager, police said today.

The discovery was made after one of the villagers "could no longer bear the woman's screams and decided to speak," police said.

Police said an investigation was underway against local authorities because they knew of the captivity but pledged themselves to secrecy for the family's sake.

The woman, Helen Karioti, was hospitalized suffering from malnutrition, anemia, partial mental derangement and other ailments, police said.

Her brother and two sisters, who kept her captive, were arrested and charged with illegal detention.

They testified that Miss Karioti was kept in the dungeon on their parents' orders because she had fallen in love and had an affair with another teen-ager. The parents died two years ago.

"Because of the scandal in the village and the family dishonor, our parents decided to lock her up," the oldest brother, Efthimios 59, testifies.

Police said the woman was dressed in rags, slept on a mud floor, and was fed scraps through a grate. Her fingernails were several inches long, and she had not seen the light of day since her captivity.

The woman was held captive at the village of Kostalexi, just outside Lamia.

SOURCE: "Family Imprisons Woman 29 Years over Love Affair," *Greensboro (NC) Record,* Nov. 8, 1978.

power held by the parents. Sociologist Richard Emerson (1962) has spelled out the ways in which resources and power are linked together. Perhaps it would be helpful to rephrase some of his basic principles.

"What I Can Offer You Gives Me Power over You."

(See Figure 4-1.) When A gives more benefits to B than B gives to A, A has the greater power. B needs the resources of A more than A needs the resources that B has to offer. In the past, parents obviously had more resources to hold out to their offspring than vice versa, and thus parents could choose or else strongly influence the selection of mates. Parents could offer to pass on farms, lands, and family businesses to those offspring who conformed to their wishes with regard to marriage and could threaten to withhold such benefits from children who refused to comply.

"If You Can Get as Good or Better Rewards Elsewhere, I Lose Power."

A's high degree of power decreases as B finds other sources of benefits. (See Figure 4-2.) As societies modernize and business and industrial enterprises develop, young persons have opportunities to obtain both tangible and intangible benefits apart from their parents. Thus the power of parents over their children is diminished, with subsequent loss of influence in mate selection.

"If You Don't Want What I Have to Offer, I Lose Power."

Another way that A's power can be limited occurs if B *renounces* the rewards that A can give. (See Figure 4-3.) Even in premodern times, if a young person decided to become a priest or nun, for example, both the material benefits offered by parents and the prospect of marriage benefits became meaningless. Church power totally replaced parental power. Or to take another example of renouncing rewards, a young person might be willing to finance his or her own college education rather than accept parental money known to have "strings attached" as to college choice and career and/or marriage decisions. Similarly, persons have been known to renounce family inheritances in order to marry someone their parents disapprove of, and with the renunciation of these financial rewards comes a freedom from the parents' control.

"If You Can Get Me to Change My Mind, My Power Decreases."

Finally, power is limited on the part of parents if their children have the ability to persuade them to change their minds about marital choice. The process of persuasion can take the form of discussion, a bargaining session, blackmail, or various types of coercion, including actual physical force. Young people might threaten to elope if their parents withhold consent to marry, or they might use a premarital pregnancy to force their parents to go along with their wishes. There has been speculation that such may have been the case with Lord and Lady Randolph Churchill, the parents of Winston. Both families had op-

FIGURE 4-1 Party A has a high degree of power because of the resources A is able to hold out to party B.

FIGURE 4-2 Party A has limited power because party B has alternative sources of rewards.

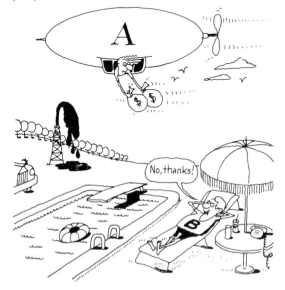

FIGURE 4-3 Party A has limited power if party B renounces the kinds of rewards party A can give.

posed the marriage, and there had been interminable negotiations about financial arrangements and legal matters. Yet, rather suddenly, a surprisingly small, simple wedding took place; and Randolph's parents did not even attend. These factors, combined with the birth of Winston Churchill seven months later, raised in some people's minds a question about whether the marriage may have been forced by the young couple (Martin, 1969, chap. 4).

Power Is Related to Social Class

The ability to persuade or bargain with one's parents so they will accept one's choice of a mate depends in great measure on the outside resources a young person has access to *as compared to the parents' resources*. In an upper-class family, for example, a son or daughter knows that the wealth his or her parents have available for their offspring is vastly greater than any material resources

the offspring could expect to find elsewhere. In such cases, young persons hesitate to run the risk of being cut off from the family assets. Overall, however, in the United States and in Western society generally, young persons have considerable power and autonomy in selecting whom they wish to marry.

DATING

Bargaining in the marriage market begins with the custom conventionally known as dating. For a time, the term *dating* was largely discarded because many young persons felt it was too formal to describe the kind of social interaction that takes place between the sexes—especially the pattern that became common in the 1960s and 1970s: informal get-togethers, group activities, and spur-of-the-moment mutual decisions to go out for a pizza. To a great extent, this more relaxed style replaced the older pattern in which a man phoned a woman days or even weeks in advance to arrange to take her to a special dance or movie on some specific evening (hence, the term *date*—in the calendar sense of a set-apart time).

With the newer pattern that emerged in the sixties and seventies, terms like "getting together" and "going out" came to be preferred (Hoult, Henze, and Hudson, 1978:114–120). By the late 1970s, however, there was some indication of a return to the term *dating*, broadening it to include both the formal sense and the more casual arrangements. Some sociologists suggested the coexistence of "two separate streams . . . one closely allied with the pattern of formal dates typical of the 1950s and early 1960s, and the other characterized by a spirit of 'comradeship' and more continuous interaction with no formal dates" (Krain, Cannon, and Bagford, 1977:664).

COURTSHIP IN THE ZULU SOCIAL SYSTEM

Poverty and enforced migratory labor among the indigenous peoples of South Africa are part of an ideology of apartheid. . . . This paper is about those women who live in the countryside while their husbands work in the city as migrant laborers.

The Zulu social system is organized on patrilineal lines; descent is through males organized into lineages—the most important group being a lineage segment whose members trace descent to a common grandfather. In order to perpetuate these lineages and maintain continuity while the men, the most important members of the corporate group, are away, women have devised various ways of coping with the men's absenteeism. For instance, young men now find it very difficult to meet and court young women. Courtship in my society is, by tradition, quite different from the Western manner of courtship. A Zulu young man makes no dates but, instead, surprises a young woman by waiting for her at a waterhole, on the road to a store, or wherever she is likely to be on her own, away from her parents. On these occasions, using the best phrases and oratory he can master, he tells her of his love for her. The woman responds by ignoring or deprecating him. To demonstrate his sincerity, he persists by trying to get further opportunities to speak to her and to win her heart. Only after several attempts, if it becomes obvious that all his efforts are futile, does he give up. Now that young men do not find time to pursue a girl in this way, their sisters often take over and woo other girls on their behalf, while the brothers always put in an appearance whenever they have an opportunity to return to the countryside. Thus a young woman finds herself acting the role of her brother while simultaneously seeking for herself a suitable husband, who is most of the time represented by his sister.

On marriage a woman joins her husband's family. Marriage in Zulu is not a contractual union between the spouses. A Zulu woman goes on a long journey (*enda*); a man receives her into his patrilineage (*thatha*), where she is expected to continue the descent line of her husband. She gradually becomes incorporated into her husband's group, and in her old age she is a full member. As an ancestress she is considered the mother of her descendants rather than a daughter of her parents in the spirit world. Conceptually she has indeed made a long journey—from her natal family to full membership in her family of procreation.

SOURCE: Harriet Sibisi, "Migrants and Women Who Wait: How African Women Cope with Migrant Labor in South Africa," *Signs: Journal of Women in Culture and Society* 3 (Autumn 1977), pp. 167–168.

Rating and Dating, and Dating and Rating

The late sociologist Willard Waller (1937) was probably the first to study seriously the phenomenon of dating. He viewed it as an end in itself—something distinct from traditional *courtship*, which had marriage as its aim.

Waller's research focused on the dating system among fraternity and sorority members at Penn State during the 1929–1930 school year. The picture that emerged at that time was one that some sociologists have called "an almost ruthless competition for dates" (Krain, Cannon, and Bagford, 1977:665). The persons one dated and the frequency of dates could either enhance or hinder one's social status, and that's what all the competition was about.

Waller called this status-seeking process the "rating-dating complex." Persons who *rated* dated, and persons who *dated* rated. The more dates a person had with different individuals who were ranked prestigious and desirable, the greater the person's own prestige. To be popular—or at least to *appear* popular by pretending to be greatly sought after—was the goal of young women under this system. The young men who rated were those who had abundant material resources—money, a car, good clothes—and were recognized for their accomplishments in campus activities. They were the ones who dated the popular women. Women and men who didn't have dates or who dated less prestigious persons found themselves lower on the prestige hierarchy. The social pressures were intense. Thrill seeking and exploitiveness were key elements, and older understandings of the courtship process were disregarded (Gordon, 1981).

Update on the "Rating-Dating Complex"

Forty years after Waller's study was published, researchers Mark Krain, Drew Cannon, and Jeffery Bagford (1977) studied fraternity and sorority members at the University of Iowa. Although they found that Greek organizations were still ranked by prestige, just as had been the case on the campus Waller studied, and although students continued to date persons at the same prestige level as themselves, Waller's rating-dating complex did not hold in other re-

spects. The researchers took this finding, along with studies by other sociologists, as indicative of a trend toward a "more relaxed and humanistic pattern of dating," which had been gradually replacing "the more competitive and materialistic aspects of dating" that Waller had observed.

Michael Gordon (1981), who specializes in the social history of male-female relationships, asserts that even though Waller's 1937 article "has provided three generations of family sociologists with a benchmark against which change in courtship customs can be compared," the rating-and-dating pattern in its pure form was never the *predominant* form of cross-sex socializing. According to Gordon, rating and dating found most widespread acceptance on college campuses dominated by fraternities and sororities during the 1920s and was already on the decline by the late 1930s and early 1940s even among the members of these groups. Both the Depression and World War II contributed to a seriousness of outlook among college students and a desire for more depth and meaning in relationships. The gradual movement away from the competitive and pluralistic dating system described by Waller and toward the pairing-off and "going-steady" patterns of the 1950s reflects a trend toward more meaningful relationships. In Gordon's view, "rating and dating represented a brief, albeit important, episode in American courtship whose persistence was exaggerated by the too-ready acceptance of Waller's 1937 paper." He points out that in the half century between 1930 and 1980, the rating-and-dating complex virtually disappeared "as a significant aspect of adolescent socializing" and gave way to group socializing as "the path that ultimately leads to exclusive, though not necessarily mate choice-oriented, relationships" (p. 75).

"Game Playing" and Dating among Blacks

However, sociologist Robert Staples (1978) states that "because of the differential socialization of men and women in our society, dating is often laden with conflict. Once dating ceased to be a means to marriage, it became more exploitative." As a result, says Staples, there has arisen "a dating game in which individuals attempt to maximize their gains while minimizing their efforts" (p. 59). While pointing out that game playing goes on among both blacks and whites, Staples has given special attention to what he calls "the black dating game."

Staples (1973) cites a number of problems reported by black single adults: the insensitivity some women have shown in declining date invitations and the resultant hostility and ego deflation many men feel, differing expectations between dating partners as to the place and meaning of sex in dating, and the failure of dating partners (either sex) to show up for agreed upon dates.

The main complaint of black women, according to Staples, is that they feel it's unfair for a man to insist that a woman refrain from dating anyone but him at the same time that he sees no need for such exclusiveness on his own part. Women in such situations feel they are considered a man's property. "The Black male's justification for his behavior," writes Staples, "is that he will lose face if his main woman is known to be dating other men."

Black men, for their part, often complain that many black women are "gold diggers," trading sex for economic and material rewards. Staples describes the feelings of some men who charge that some black women are actively "looking for men with money and then helping them spend all of it as soon as possible." "Sex for such purposes, however," he comments, "leads Black men to view women as enemies and allows them to justify their own exploitative behavior." At the same time, inasmuch as many black women have high incomes of their own, cases abound in which black men turn to women for financial benefits—including the subsidization of a man's artistic endeavors or graduate education. "In Washington, D.C., where black men are in large demand," writes Staples (1981a:56), "there are examples of men requesting and often getting at least the payment of their car note." The "gaming for material rewards" isn't confined to one sex.

Speaking as a black himself, Staples (1981a:46–47) has voiced concern over the "distrust, negative conceptions, and hostility that characterize many relationships between the two sexes"—the problem of a "silent war between black men and women." He points out that negative experiences in the "dating game" have often served to reinforce remnants of a "collective self-hatred" felt by many blacks because of the dominant society's labeling and treatment of blacks as inferior. As a result, black women and men have learned to use various defense and avoidance mechanisms in their dealings with one another. "Black people cannot afford such internal tensions," writes Staples (1978:66–67). "We have to accept responsibility for eliminating the sources of these male-female conflicts," he asserts, "and, the best place to begin is at home." At the same time, Staples emphasizes that there exist regional, historical, and social-class variations in black dating practices, and "lack of information limits the generalizations that we can make" about such practices. What *is* clear is that certain problems related to bargaining and "game playing" exist among black men and women.

Male-Female Dating Trade-offs

Similar patterns can be observed among whites as well. Whether we're talking about "rating and dating" or dating "games," at the root of such practices are traditional assumptions about male-female inequality and the very real differential bargaining resources of the sexes.

One sociological study that tapped into this was Judith Richman's 1972 participant-observation study of a New York City dating service. Although caution must be exercised with regard to generalizing from findings based on such a select group—those persons who decide to phone a dating service to arrange for a dating partner—the study nevertheless provides some interesting information. Richman's small sample consisted of twenty-seven women (median age: mid-thirties) and thirty-two men (median age: mid-twenties). "The responses of the majority of males and females in this sample were consistent with the sociological conceptualization of the traditional bargaining relationship between the sexes," writes Richman (1977). When respondents were asked to describe the "ideal date" and tell what qualities in a man or woman were most important to them, "the majority of women consistently cited and placed greatest emphasis on the achieved occupational-economic statuses of men, while the majority of men placed greatest emphasis on the ascribed physical qualities of women" (p. 162).

However, when Richman endeavored to find out if respondents' attitudes toward gender roles made any difference in qualities desired in a dating partner, as well as respondents' own self-image, she found the following: Females holding traditional attitudes toward gender roles wanted to date males who were up to fifteen years older than they themselves were. Females who were more open to feminism, on the other hand, stated that the age of their dating partners was unimportant or that they assumed they would date men their own age. Some stated a willingness to date men younger than themselves. Males open to feminism also felt age was unimportant in a dating partner or preferred to date females the same age as themselves. (None, however, indicated a willingness to date women older than themselves.) Traditionalist males, for their part, preferred to date females younger than themselves.

On the matter of self-identity, traditionalist women thought of themselves chiefly in terms of physical attributes and *expressive qualities* (such as being friendly and understanding). More feminist-minded women saw their identity as encompassing their own "achievements, interests, and intelligence in addition to physical and expressive characteristics" (p. 164). The self-concepts of traditionalist males in Richman's sample centered almost totally around their *achieved statuses* (education, income, career accomplishments, and prospects), whereas men more favorable to feminist ideology stressed other factors as well, including their own physical and expressive qualities.

What did traditionalist males look for in a dating partner? Richman found they placed "great emphasis on physical characteristics and secondarily on expressive qualities." Some men emphasized a permissive attitude toward sex as well. Men more open to equality in gender roles "were generally the individuals seeking intellectual and expressive qualities in women rather than focusing chiefly on physical qualities or sexual behavior" (p. 161). Women who supported the goals of the women's movement also were nontraditional in what they looked for in a dating partner, just as was true of their male counterparts. These women "desired to meet men with certain expressive qualities or similar interests instead of those of high-class statuses" (p. 160). In contrast, traditionalist women were most concerned about the achievement and social status of their potential dates and were only secondarily concerned about their expressive and intellectual characteristics.

Richman concludes that traditional expectations about male-female trade-offs in dating will continue so long as women are primarily defined in terms of their wife-mother roles and men are defined through their occupational roles. "When the economy ceases to discriminate between the sexes," she asserts, "we may also see the beginning of a bargaining situation in the dating institution that is not differentiated by sex" (p. 165).

In another study of dating trade-offs conducted more than a decade after the Richman study, three researchers performed a content analysis on self-advertisements placed in a singles magazine (Bolig, Stein, and McKenry, 1984). "One rather paradoxical conclusion of this analysis," they wrote, "is that the men who placed profiles in this magazine were not looking for the women who placed profiles (nor were the women looking for these men)" (p. 592). The classified ads (or "profiles") placed by *both* men and women were emphasizing very similar exchange desires! Men offered their career status and attractiveness and wanted to meet women who could offer the men expressssiveness and attractiveness in return. But the women who advertised also emphasized their own careers, education, and expressive qualities as valued resources to exchange and wanted to meet men who could offer them various expressive qualities and attractiveness *rather* than a high occupational status. The researchers concluded that "consistent with other research on changing gender roles, men in this sample did not appear to have changed as much as women" (p. 591).

Dating: A Recent American Custom

Dating is taken for granted in modern America, but actually the custom is relatively new. Prior to around the time of World War I, a young woman and man could plan on getting together on a regular basis only if they had marriage in mind—and then only under the watchful eyes of their elders. In 1913, a newspaper editorial sounded an alarm: "Sex o'clock" had struck in America. Young men and women were enjoying one another's company as they tried out the newest dances and went off on other "dangerous" recreational pursuits such as unchaperoned swimming, buggy rides, and picnics (Feline, 1975, chap. 3). The editorial was in reaction to the increasing incidence of what we now know as *dating* (cross-sex interaction for its own sake) in contrast to the then more acceptable pattern of *courtship* (cross-sex interaction with marriage as its goal).

However, a growing body of recent work by social historians indicates that unescorted young persons in rural America during the early nineteenth century also participated in group activities such as dances, sleigh rides, and parties without pursuing marriage goals at the same time—practices anticipating and resembling, in certain respects, the dating patterns that emerged a century later (Gordon, 1981). By the early twentieth century, the impact of industrialization was being felt as young men and women left the farms and small towns and moved to the cities. Parental supervision and control over male-female relationships was lessening. During the World War I period and on through the 1920s, a dating system of cross-sex pairing off without marriage as its goal was gathering momentum. One could go out on different occasions with many different dating partners, even following the prestige-seeking "rating-and-dating" patterns which reached their highest

By the early part of the twentieth century, young people were getting together for recreational times without necessarily having marriage in mind. (The Staten Island Historical Society)

prominence in sororities and fraternities at that time, as discussed earlier. Or one could settle down in a special "steady" (though not necessarily exclusive) relationship with one primary person without thinking at all in terms of marriage (Gordon, 1981:70–73). As we'll see in the next chapter, this same time period marked the beginning of other changes in male-female relationships, most notably increases in sexual intimacy.

Purposes of Dating

So far we've implied at least two purposes of dating. Dating provides a way of getting to know a number of persons out of whom a po-

tential mate *may* be chosen. And dating can be a recreational end in itself—a way of having a good time. Sociologists James Skipper and Gilbert Nass (1966) suggest that, along with these purposes, dating can be a way of status-seeking; and it can also have a socialization function. In other words, dating can be a way of socializing persons into the "how" of getting along with persons of the other sex—a way of learning and trying out social skills.

Sometimes one partner may have one motivation in mind, whereas the other partner may have an altogether different reason for dating. Skipper and Nass provide several illustrations. For example, a woman may date a wealthy sports-car owner in order to impress her friends as she rides around with him (status seeking on her part). However, the man she is dating may be interested in learning to feel more at ease with women (socialization purposes on his part). "In another case," write Skipper and Nass, "a boy may date an attractive girl because he desires a sexual experience with her (recreation). The girl may be dating the boy because she views him as a potential husband (courtship)" (p. 413).

Skipper and Nass studied some of the problems that may occur when dating partners have differing dating motivations—especially when one partner is thinking in terms of a serious commitment leading to marriage while the other cares only about having a good time or is looking for a sexual experience. Assuming only the four basic motivations for dating that these sociologists list—*courtship* (mate selection), *recreation, socialization,* and *status seeking*—Skipper and Nass suggest that future research could examine ten possible dating-motivation combinations: "courtship-courtship, courtship-recreation, courtship—status seeking, courtship-socialization, recreation-recreation, recreation—status seeking, recreation-socialization, status seeking—status seeking, status seeking—socialization, and socialization-socialization" (p. 420). Such research, according to these sociologists, might also show variations in the importance attached to certain motivations and also how motivations might change over the course of dating.

Trends

One of the most noticeable trends in recent years is a movement away from rigid gender roles in dating. Evidence of this trend is seen in such matters as asking for dates and paying for dates (either sex may do either, or the costs may be shared) and in uncertainty about some aspects of *dating etiquette* (opening doors, putting on coats, handling the check at a restaurant, and so on). Some of these matters are now being discussed in books and articles; meanwhile, dating partners have been making their own rules.

Some research indicates that the degree to which young women adhere to feminist ideology determines the degree to which they take a nontraditional approach to high school and college dating. Sociologist Sheila Korman (1983) found that young women holding egalitarian gender-role preferences were more likely than were traditionally minded women to initiate dates and to share date expenses. At the same time, she found that even women who hold traditional gender-role beliefs were becoming more open to initiating dates and sharing expenses. She attributes these signs of change to the cultural influence of feminist ideology with its emphasis on the equality of women and men.

In his study of black singles, Staples (1981a:60–61) found that frequently it was the *men* who expected women to share expenses and didn't hesitate to ask women to "dutch treat." Women who thought of dating in more traditional terms tended to complain of the "stinginess" of such men. Some women also complained that the men they dated were becoming increasingly passive and leaving the initiative up to the women. "I've noticed that many (not all) black males are expecting more and more from women," one female educator in Staple's sample told him. "Many expect the women to be the aggressor, expect them to phone them and to invite them out. They have been spoiled by the fact that there are more available women than men. Most women aren't accustomed to being on their own and men know how to manipulate women around their needs." Staples explains that we are in a transition period in which the older dating patterns, with their implied sexual and economic bargaining based on prescribed gender roles, are giving way to newer patterns that require changes in the attitudes of both men and women.

Sociologist Michael Gordon points out that friendship and companionship are what many persons are now seeking in the dating experience. Commenting on the "going-steady" pattern of dating that became especially noticeable in the years after World War II, Gordon (1978:183) suggests that not only a desire for commitment but a desire for *convenience* may have come into play. (A great deal of anxiety can be avoided if you know one special person is always available to go out with you!) Exclusive dating also provides relief from the competition and stress associated with rating and dating. Under that older pattern, writes Gordon, "one was essentially putting oneself and one's self image on the auction block and continually being fed messages concerning self-worth. For those who did not rate high, the psychic costs of such a system must have been very high indeed."

The Mate-Selection Marketplace: An Exchange-Theory Perspective

Emerging patterns may make their own demands and have their own costs, as well. "It is obvious that today's mate-selection is no longer a period of determining the best bargain and sealing that bargain in marriage," writes sociologist Michal McCall (1966:197). Marriage is not necessarily considered for life and may be but one of many involvements with a person of the opposite sex. Speaking in terms of weighing costs and benefits and making a worthwhile exchange in the mate-selection marketplace, McCall asserts that the modern courtship system serves as a training school in bargaining. "In

other words, 'courtship' teaches the individual how to bargain—how to form, maintain, and leave relationships," says McCall. "The emphasis in modern life is on keeping up one's bargaining skills, for one never entirely leaves the market."

McCall uses quotation marks around the word *courtship* because she is trying to show that the "contemporary pattern" differs from the mate-selection patterns of two other historical periods. In what she calls the "traditional pattern," parents and kin groups did the marriage bargaining. In the "'intermediary pattern," both the parents and the young persons themselves were involved; and it was under this pattern that true courtship took place. One courted or was courted by a prospective mate, a person selected from among many other suitors or young women. This person was believed to be the one "for whom one was destined," the "one true love," the "one and only with whom one would go through life." Having found another and having sought parental approval, the woman and man made a "permanent contract of exchange"—the *marriage contract*. From the time the marriage vows were spoken until "death did them part," these persons were expected to exchange their personal resources *only* with each other. "This contract," says McCall, "was a bargain to end any further cross-sex bargaining" (p. 196).

However, McCall observes a different bargaining system taking place in what she terms the "contemporary pattern." Under the traditional and intermediary patterns, the bargaining (whether conducted by the kin or the courting couple primarily) concentrated on *marriage* as the end goal. That was what the bargaining was all about; with marriage, the bargaining was over for all practical purposes. In the contemporary pattern, on the other hand, it is not unusual for a person to enter many close relationships in succession, with each involvement supposed to be appreciated for its own uniqueness. Individuals are expected to be deeply committed to the current serious relationship—whether the relationship is an exclusive dating partnership, a living-together arrangement, or a socially recognized marriage. Bargaining takes place within these relationships and can be a training ground for further relationships, but it is not necessarily bargaining directly aimed toward marriage. (See also Swidler, 1980.)

According to McCall, no longer is the emphasis on finding the "one and only" for a lifetime because few people any longer believe in a "one and only" for whom each person is destined. Persons have the potential of relating to many other persons. Furthermore, relationships break up, even after marriage, and new relationships are formed—or at least *can* be—throughout life. That is why McCall, drawing upon the "permanent availability model" of sociologist Bernard Farber (1964, chaps. 4–5), claims that individuals are never out of the marriage market. The whole modern dating system, therefore, is "*set up* to give individuals training and experience in 'getting along with others' in intimate relationships." McCall explains further:

> [In the sense of the contemporary pattern], involvements (including the marriage involvement) are not contracts but restrictive trade agreements. The two individuals agree to exchange only with one another, at least until such time as the balance of trade becomes unfavorable in terms of broader market considerations. They agree to exchange exclusively for so long as the rewards in *this* involvement exceed the costs of continuing it in the face of chances for other rewards elsewhere. The individual, by forming numerous such exclusive and reciprocal trade agreements at various times, gets some idea of his [or her] overall worth as a product and of the market conditions, as well as learning bargaining skills, as mentioned above. (pp. 197–198)

SELECTING A MARRIAGE PARTNER

Although McCall claims that "marriage is merely one kind (though perhaps a more stable and lasting kind) of involvement" (p. 198), in the minds of most people marriage is considered a *unique* relationship.

What Is Marriage?

During the 1960s and 1970s, a great deal of discussion centered about when a "relationship" becomes a "marriage." Some argued that the whole idea of legal marriage should be discarded because legal bonds suffocate freedom and spontaneity, causing persons to stay together because they "ought to" or "must" rather than because they want to. Such critics suggested that the relationship of a man and woman should be regarded as a private matter, concerning only the individuals involved. They saw no need for the regulations and forms set up by society. "How can a piece of paper or reciting some words make us married?" some asked. "We feel we're already married in our own hearts—perhaps even in the eyes of God. We can't see why some sort of ceremony is necessary."

But even though such persons may feel married, are they really? What *does* make people married? Is it sex? Are two persons married who have coitus with each other twice a week? What if, in addition, each has sexual intercourse with another person? Does a group marriage then exist? Few people would be willing to define marriage on the basis of sex relations alone. Could it be the license then that makes a marriage? No, not really. However, there have been cases of poorly informed and often illiterate persons who have mistakenly thought that obtaining the license was all that was required of them, only to find out after many years of living together that they were never legally married.

If it isn't sex and it isn't a license that makes a couple married, then it must be the wedding ceremony—right? Not really. There isn't anything magic in the words themselves that transports two people from one state (singleness) into another state (marriage). Furthermore, there is a wide variation in wedding ceremonies in various cultures. In ancient biblical times, Isaac and Rebekah's wedding ceremony consisted of nothing more than an exchange of gifts and entering a tent together (Genesis 24); but in our culture, a man and woman who enter a house together after a gift exchange could hardly argue that these acts made them married.

Or to take another example, anthropologists have written of the marriage ritual practiced by the Kwoma of New Guinea. A prospective bride is brought to live with a young man's family for a time of observation by his mother. If the mother feels the young woman is a suitable future daughter-in-law, she asks her to cook some food for the young man. Unsuspectingly, he eats it, without realizing it has been cooked by his future wife. At that moment, the mother announces that the young man is now married because he is eating food prepared by his betrothed. Upon hearing this announcement, the new husband is supposed to rush out shouting that the food tastes awful. This is the public declaration to the tribe that the couple is now considered to be married (Stephens, 1963:221–222). Needless to say, no man in our society would consider himself married because he ate dinner at a woman friend's apartment and then told his friends that she

is a terrible cook. It is not the ceremony itself that makes a marriage but rather what it signifies in a particular culture.

What we need is a definition of marriage that is applicable historically and cross-culturally but yet able to fit new varieties of marriage patterns that are emerging. Anthropologist George Murdock (1949) provides us with the basis of just such a definition. From his studies, he concludes that there are two essential dimensions to marriage—the economic and the sexual. When a man and woman are interdependent both economically and sexually, they may be said to be married.

We can broaden the scope of the definition and say that marriage exists when two (or more) persons maintain ongoing instrumental and expressive exchanges. The *expressive*, or person-oriented, dimension includes sexual gratification, but it may also include other elements, such as companionship (someone to do things with, joint participation in leisure activities) and empathy (someone to listen and talk to, someone who understands and cares). The *instrumental*, or task-oriented, dimension of marriage includes economic behaviors (earning and spending income) and the performance of necessary household tasks.

Furthermore, for marriage to be valid from a societal point of view, there must be some sort of *public disclosure*. Therefore, societies require rituals, ceremonies, licenses, and the like to symbolize that a legal bond between a particular man and woman exists, a bond recognized by the society in which they live. The arrangement of mutual sexual access and economic sharing between the two persons is of concern not only to the individuals but to others, as well (parents and other relatives, friends, and society as a whole).

If we ask *why* people get married, the answer now becomes clear. People enter marriage because they believe it to be a rewarding situation in terms of both the instrumental and expressive sides of life. And that's where bargaining comes in. Before marriage, and afterward as well, the processes of social exchange go on as each partner endeavors to find ways of giving and receiving both expressively and instrumentally to the satisfaction of the other and for the overall benefit of the relationship.

Who Marries Whom?

Anthropologists and sociologists use the term *endogamy* to describe marriages between persons within the same social group. When a person marries someone outside his or her own social group, the practice is called *exogamy*. (The terms are easily remembered by thinking of their roots. The ending comes from the Greek *gamia*, meaning "act of marrying." *Endo* means "within," and *ex* means "out of.") Thus, endogamy occurs when blacks marry blacks or Jews marry Jews. Exogamy occurs when blacks marry whites or when Jews marry Gentiles.

Persons who choose marriage partners who are higher or lower in socioeconomic status than themselves are said to be "marrying up" (*hypergamy*) or "marrying down" (*hypogamy*). A more commonly used term in discussions of who marries whom is *homogamy* (from the Greek term *homos*, meaning "the same"), which refers to the tendency of persons to marry persons with characteristics similar to their own—particularly in terms of age, intelligence, education, and social background. The physician's daughter marries the lawyer's son. The college graduate marries a fellow college graduate. The waitress marries the factory worker—and so

on. There is some evidence that *remarriages* are somewhat less likely than first marriages to be homogamous in age, religion, and educational attainments (Dean and Gurak, 1978).

Education One area where the principle of homogamy is clearly at work is education. Most people marry those whose amount of education is similar to their own.

Education is a resource persons may offer in marriage bargaining, and it is also an indication of social status. Persons with the same or similar education levels are more likely to perceive the marriage bargain to be a just and fair one than are spouses with vast differences in education (where there would be an imbalance in resources brought to the marriage). And of course, it goes without saying that persons with similar education are likely to hold similar values, goals, and outlooks on life and, thus, have more in common than is generally true where wide gaps exist in educational background. Thus, nearly two-thirds of husbands with four years of college have wives with at least some college. And four out of five wives with four years of college are married to husbands who have also attended college (Rawlings, 1978:13).

One study of currently married dual-career couples showed not only that educational incompatibility is associated with marital dissatisfaction, but also that disparities in levels of education may call forth different reactions from husbands and wives. Using survey data from the National Opinion Research Center, the researchers found that husbands tended to define their marriages as "stressful" if educational incompatibility resulted from their wives being "overeducated" in comparison to themselves. Achievement-oriented wives, on the other hand, tended to

In 1983, actress Mary Tyler Moore married Dr. Robert Levine, a cardiologist sixteen years her junior. (AP/Wide World Photos)

"find marriage to an 'overeducated' husband to be satisfying" (Hornung and McCullough, 1981:138). Such findings show the pervasive influence of traditional gender-role expectations.

Age Just as wide gaps in education are rare, so, too, are wide differences in the ages of marriage partners. Such *age heterogamy* (marriage to someone in a different age group) was more common in the early part of the present century than it is today, as may be seen in Table 4-A. At the time of the 1980 census, about 70 percent of married couples were characterized by *age homogamy* (similarities in the ages of the spouses, defined in the table as a difference of no more than four years). Wide differences between the ages of husbands and wives are more common at lower socioeconomic levels than at higher levels, are more common among blacks than among whites, and are more common in second marriages than in first marriages (Vera, Berardo, and Berardo, 1985; Atkinson and Glass, 1985; Spanier and Glick, 1980b). There is also evidence that marriages char-

TABLE 4-A Proportion of wives in 5 categories of marital age homogamy/heterogamy, by year

	1900		1960		1980	
	N	%	N	%	N	%
Husband older (5–9 years)	3,285	20.1	9,021	23.0	7,822	19.5
Husband older (10+ years)	4,409	27.0	3,952	10.0	2,968	7.4
Total husband older	7,694	47.1	12,973	33.0	10,790	26.9
Husband and wife same age (±4 years)	6,039	37.1	24,875	63.3	28,040	69.9
Husband younger (5–9 years)	865	5.3	1,100	2.8	1,003	2.5
Husband younger (10+ years)	1,736	10.5	361	0.9	241	0.6
Total husband younger	2,601	15.8	1,461	3.7	1,244	3.1
Total	16,344	100.0	39,309	100.0	40,115	100.0

SOURCE: Maxine P. Atkinson and Becky L. Glass, "Marital Age Heterogamy and Homogamy, 1900 to 1980," *Journal of Marriage and the Family* 47 (August 1985), p. 687. Based upon data from the 1900, 1960, and 1980 population surveys conducted by the U.S. Bureau of the Census.

acterized by dissimilarities in the ages of spouses do not have a lower marital quality than marriages in which spouses' ages are similar (Vera, Berardo, and Berardo, 1985).

Even in age-similar marriages, it is more common for the husband to be older than the wife than for the wife to be older than the husband—just as persons tend to expect that the husband will be taller, better educated, and have a better occupation than the wife. All of this is symbolic of a phenomenon sociologists call the *marriage gradient* (Bernard, 1972, chap. 3), the expectation that the male partner will have slightly superior status as compared to the female partner when marriage choices are made. This pattern stems from traditional notions of gender roles in which men are considered leaders and protectors and women followers who look up to men.

Earlier we saw Richman's study of dating that showed that persons holding more egalitarian gender-role norms are less likely to hold traditional attitudes about male-female age differences. Having a younger husband is also more common among women over age 65. "Since women generally live longer than men," explains sociologist Stephens Rawlings (1978:4), "one would expect that widows who remarry would tend to choose a man younger than themselves."

Religion   Data on religious intermarriage is not as complete as social scientists would like it to be—one reason being that questions on religious identification are not included in the census or on many other public registrations. However, the limited data on trends in interfaith marriages seem to indicate an increase in such marriages (Barron, 1972; Mueller, 1971). Particularly among Roman Catholics and Protestants, a great deal of exogamy occurs. The religious climate of greater openness, tolerance, and co-operation between Catholics and Protestants since Vatican II may be one explanation for more persons feeling free to marry outside their particular church group (Mueller, 1971:21; Besanceney, 1970:162–167).

Exogamy is rarest of all among the third major religious grouping, Jews, where persons are strongly encouraged to select mates from within their own group. Loyal Jews are expected by parents and religious leaders alike to marry endogamously. Such a stance has been taken by the Jewish community throughout their history. The popular musical *Fiddler on the Roof* made clear the agony that Jewish parents have traditionally undergone when one of their offspring marries a Gentile. The Hebrew Scriptures provide warnings against marriages between Jews and non-Jews. The prophet Ezra, for example, counseled his people to divorce their foreign wives. On the other hand, the two Old Testament books named after women both contain stories of Jewish-Gentile marriages. Esther, a Jew, by her influence as the wife of a Persian king, saved her people from destruction. And the Gentile Ruth had Jewish husbands in both her first and second marriages. Ruth, however, was willing to say, "Thy people shall be my people, and thy God my God" (Ruth 1:16). Such conversion to Judaism by a non-Jew has traditionally been the one way in which he or she becomes acceptable as a potential marriage partner for a Jew (Gordon, 1964). In about one-third of marriages between Jews and non-Jews, the non-Jewish partner converts to Judaism (Mayer, 1983:34).

At the same time, as journalist Kenneth Briggs (1976) points out in a report on an American Jewish Committee study of intermarriage, "religious law forbids conversion solely for the purpose of marriage. It must be based on personal, religious grounds." But he goes on to say that "even some Orthodox rabbis are re-examining their attitudes toward this practice to make it easier for the non-Jewish person to be taken into the faith." It is the Orthodox branch of Judaism that traditionally has been most opposed to religious intermarriage, whereas the Conservative and Reform branches have become somewhat more accepting. "Much of this reassessment seems to reflect a conviction that condemning intermarriage or declaring the Jewish partner 'dead' in the eyes of his religion have been counterproductive," writes Briggs. He refers to a comment by one of the researchers involved in the Committee's study: "If there is going to be intermarriage, what is the most creative way of responding to make sure that there is no loss of Jewishness by the Jewish partner?"

And because of the modern emphasis on free choice in mate selection, there *is* going to be intermarriage. Several studies, in fact, indicate an upsurge in marriages between Jews and Gentiles in recent decades (Gordon, 1964; Mueller, 1971; Mayer and Sheingold, 1979), with the rate of intermarriage among American Jews currently estimated to stand between 24 percent (Silberman, 1985:295-296) and 40 percent (Mayer, 1983). Many Jewish leaders have expressed alarm over this upsurge, viewing it as symptomatic of a "weakening of Jewish religious ties and the lack of empathy for their own people that has characterized Jews in the past (Gordon, 1964:213). Some are convinced that intermarriage actually "jeopardizes Jewish survival" by causing further decreases in the proportion of the population clearly identified as Jewish (Gittelsohn, 1980:272–273). Some Jewish leaders go so far as to call interfaith marriage "treason against the Jewish people" (Lamm, 1980:64).

Others take a more moderate stance, seeking constructive and creative ways to deal with the undeniable reality of religious exogamy. They do not believe intermarriage will result in the death of Judaism (Silberman, 1985). One study showed that where Jewish involvement on the part of mixed-marriage couples is lacking, it is likely to stem "from the disinterest of the Jewish-born spouses rather than from opposition by the born-Gentile spouses, or the latter's desire to raise their children in another religion." Furthermore, "where conversion takes place," write sociologists Egon Mayer and Carl Sheingold (1979:31), "the fact that one of the spouses was not born Jewish is no obstacle to a Jewish family life." Their data indicated that most non-Jewish spouses do not convert to Judaism; but in cases where they do, "Jewish identity is not merely asserted; it is acted upon." Religious affiliation and observance are matters of choice and commitment. "Thus, in some ways, there is more reason for optimism about Jewish continuity in families where the born-Gentile spouse has converted to Judaism than there is in the typical endogamous family" (p. 30).

Children of both *conversionary marriages* (those in which the Gentile spouse had converted to Judaism) and *mixed marriages* (where the non-Jewish spouse had not converted) were *not* found to experience stress and discomfort from feelings of *marginality*—a sense of being part of two different cultures and not quite belonging to either. Children in the conversionary category tended more than did those of mixed marriages to consider themselves Jewish and to receive Jewish educations and actively participate in Jewish rites and holidays. But many children from both groups reported observing both Hanukkah and Christmas, Passover and Easter. Adult children from Jewish-Gentile marriages in which the Gentile parent had not converted to Judaism were more likely to marry outside Judaism than were children from conversionary marriages. But neither group said they would discourage their own children from marrying persons not of the Jewish faith (Mayer, 1983). On the other side, among Gentiles, acceptance of Gentile-Jewish marital unions has shown signs of increasing over recent decades (Stember, 1966:104–107; Silberman, 1985:287)—another reason to expect the number of such marriages to grow.

Some studies indicate that greater marital satisfaction is associated with religious homogamy (Glenn, 1982; Heaton, 1984). However, as sociologist Norval Glenn (1982:564) emphasizes, "As interreligious marriages become more frequent and socially accepted, any negative effects they have on marital quality are likely to diminish." He points out that some problems in interreligious marriages stem from the disapproval of friends and relatives and speculates that "as such disapproval diminishes, so should some of the disruptive influences on interreligious marriages."

Race With rare exceptions, people tend to marry within their own racial grouping. In other words, racial endogamy seems to be the strongest of all.

By examining Table 4-B, we see that 96 percent of black husbands have black wives, and over 99 percent of white husbands have white wives. Among husbands of other races, about 1 out of 6 has a white wife and less than 1 out of 100 has a black wife; the vast majority are married to women in the "other races" category. If we add up the appropriate numbers in the table, we see that out of the nearly 50.7 million married couples in the United States in 1983, only 719,000 couples (less than 1.5 percent) were in interracial marriages—marriages between blacks and whites, whites and other races, or blacks and other races. In black-white and black-

TABLE 4-B Interracial marriages and racially endogamous marriages—March, 1983

	BLACK HUSBAND	WITH WHITE WIFE	WITH BLACK WIFE	WITH WIFE OF OTHER RACE
Number	3,577,000	118,000	3,434,000	24,000
Percent	100%	3.3%	96%	0.7%

	WHITE HUSBAND	WITH WHITE WIFE	WITH BLACK WIFE	WITH WIFE OF OTHER RACE
Number	45,858,000	45,500,000	46,000	312,000
Percent	100%	99.2%	0.1%	0.7%

	HUSBAND OF OTHER RACE	WITH WHITE WIFE	WITH BLACK WIFE	WITH WIFE OF OTHER RACE
Number	1,231,000	210,000	9,000	1,012,000
Percent	100%	17%	0.8%	82.2%

NOTE: Racially endogamous marriages (those with both spouses in same racial category) are shaded. "Other" races include Japanese, Chinese, Indian, and all other races except black and white.
SOURCE: Compiled from figures in U.S. Bureau of the Census, *Current Population Reports*, Series P-20, no. 388, *Household and Family Characteristics: March 1983* (Washington, D.C.: U.S. Government Printing Office, 1984), pp. 165–166.

Tyne Daly, who plays Mary Beth Lacey of the New York City Police Department in the television series *Cagney and Lacey,* married actor-director George Stanford Brown in 1966. They are the parents of three daughters. (Ralph Dominquez/Globe Photos)

other marriages, the black partner is more often the husband. In white-other marriages, the white partner is more apt to be the husband; but in white-black marriages, the white partner is more likely to be the wife.

Some states had laws against interracial marriage up until the 1967 United States Supreme Court decision which declared such laws unconstitutional. In recent years, the number of interracial marriages of all kinds has been growing. Between 1970 and 1977, there was a 92 percent increase in marriages between blacks and whites, the number of such marriages growing from 65,000 to 125,000 (U.S. Bureau of the Census, *Current Population Reports,* P-23, No. 77, 1978, p. 8). By 1983, as the figures in Table 4-B show, 164,000 marriages consisted of a black-white couple.

A number of sociologists have pointed out that much more research must be done in the area of interracial marriage before we can

clearly ascertain trends and understand their meaning (Monahan, 1973; Aldridge, 1973; Heer, 1974). Past explanations for the low incidence of white-black marriages have focused on evidence that in a color-caste society, the dominant group rates the characteristics of the less-dominant group as being of less worth than the characteristics of the dominant group (Washington, 1970; Sickels, 1972; Barron, 1972; Gordon, 1964). Thus, in a white-dominated society, whites have defined blackness as of less value than whiteness and therefore have tended not to strike a marriage bargain that seemed unfavorable. Not only did the exchange of rewards in interracial marriage seem unequal according to this line of reasoning, but there were also costs to consider. Whites who marry blacks have traditionally suffered severe disapproval from other whites, with especially negative sanctions from relatives and close friends.

Blacks, too, often negatively sanction those of their number who marry outside their race. Many are strongly against such marriages for reasons similar to the traditional views of Jews cited earlier. Pride in one's own group and loyalty to that group are expected to be reinforced by endogamy. (See Staples, 1981a, chap. 7.) Many blacks look upon marriage to a white person as not only undesirable but almost an act of treason against the black race and black culture. To enter such a marriage is viewed by some as acquiescence to a society that has held blacks down, an alliance with the oppressor. Many black women, especially, feel a sense of rejection and betrayal when black men choose white women as dating and marriage partners because the supply of eligible and suitable black men is limited (Staples, 1981a, 1985)—a topic we'll be discussing more fully in Chapter 7.

One way sociologists over the years have

PINK IS FROM MAMA

"Daddy is brown and Mama is pink," says my young son Ricky. "I get my dimple and curly hair from Daddy and my pink from Mama."

We are an interracial family with three sons. . . .

Some people may feel that Kermit and I have denied our sons an identity, a sense of stability in a particular community or race. But I think that in the future people will have to overcome the narrow boundaries of race and nationality if true harmony among the world's peoples is ever to be achieved. . . .[Our sons] have a race to belong to—the human race.

SOURCE: Marion Booker, "A Young Mother's Story: Pink Is from Mama," *Redbook* (October 1969), p. 12.

attempted to explain what happens in black-white marriages has been in terms of a theory of racial-caste hypogamy coupled with social-class hypergamy. First suggested by sociologists Kingsley Davis (1941) and Robert Merton (1941), the theory states that a woman from a higher racial caste may be willing to marry a man from a lower racial caste if to do so will raise her from a lower to a higher *social* class. What is "marrying down" on the one hand (*hypogamy*) is "marrying up" on the other (*hypergamy*). David Heer (1974), a sociologist who has given much attention to the study of black-white marriages, suggests caution with regard to such an explanation, although he points out that the theory may have some validity if other considerations are taken into account.

The Merton-Davis theory has been widely accepted because of evidence from government studies that has shown a tendency for black men who marry white women to have a higher level of education than black men who marry black women. White women who marry black men have tended to have a lower level of education than white women who marry white men (Carter and Glick 1970:126–129). Sociologist Zick Rubin (1973) sums up what has sometimes been

called the *compensation principle* in terms of exchange theory. He writes: "These interracial marriages can be seen as exchanges on the interpersonal marketplace, in which the higher educational status of the black husband (and the earning power that may go along with it) is exchanged for the higher social status of the white wife (which accrues to her simply by virtue of her skin color)" (p. 196).

Jessie Bernard (1966), another sociologist, was one of the first to take issue with this notion. Bernard's analysis of the 1960 census data did not show a tendency for wives of black men to have less education if they were white rather than black. The idea that interracial marriage involves an exchange of status based on skin color for status based on educational and occupational achievement may be increasingly questionable (Monahan, 1973; Staples, 1981a:140).

Perhaps what may be occurring is a tendency for marriages between blacks and whites to involve other kinds of exchanges, with persons being attracted to one another on the basis of rewards which make the consideration of racial differences less important than was once the case. Education, exposure to persons of other races in travel, work, and school, and ideological concerns based on humanistic and religious values may all play a part in de-emphasizing skin color as a basis for evaluating persons.

Among highly educated persons with a common universe of values, for example, partners in cross-national marriages have been known to consider themselves as belonging to a kind of international community or lifestyle that transcends national boundaries. In one study of Western nationals who married persons from India, it was found that spouses considered the culture they shared in common (for example, the scientific community) to be far more important than the cultures of their countries of origin. As one Indian respondent summed it up: "I would have so little in common with a parochial Indian." Sociologist Ann Baker Cottrell (1973) concludes that such Indian-Western marriages are inaccurately called mixed marriages. Perhaps a similar statement might be made about many black-white marriages, as well.

But at the same time, idealism must not be allowed to blind us to the realistic problems faced by interracial couples. Social pressures and disapproval can take their toll, one evidence being the greater likelihood of marital dissolution in black-white marriages as compared to marriages where both spouses are black or both are white (Glick, 1981:119; Staples, 1981a:140). "As long as racial groups have selfstyled definitions of superior and inferior, and the oppressor and oppressed, biracial unions cannot occur as natural events in the dating marketplace," writes Robert Staples (1981a:161). He urges couples contemplating racial intermarriage to do a "cost-benefit analysis before proceeding with all deliberate speed." Concurrently, he expresses a wish "that these factors did not have to be taken into consideration; that people could meet, date, and marry with no concern for the color of their skin but only the content of their character" (p. 162). But in the present social climate, according to Staples, "those biracial couples who do effect a merger will find the going rough."

Somewhat more common than marriages between persons of different races are marriages in which one partner is of Spanish origin and the other is not. Under "Spanish origin," the Census Bureau includes persons who indicate their origins as: "Mexican, Puerto Rican, Cuban, Central or South American, or some other Spanish origin." Persons may be of any race and yet be considered of Spanish origin as well. In 1983, 842,000 couples were comprised of a Spanish-origin spouse and a spouse of some other origin. Out of the nearly 2.6 million married men of Spanish origin, 374,000 (almost 15 percent) had wives who were not of Spanish origin. And out of the more than 2.6 million married women of Spanish origin, 468,000 (about 18 percent) had husbands of some other origin than Spanish (U.S. Bureau of the Census, *Current Population Reports,* Series P-20, no. 388, 1984:165–166).

The Incest Taboo The question may arise: If persons tend to marry within their own group (e.g., the same race or religion), why don't persons marry within the most basic group of all—their own family? Wouldn't that be endogamy of the purest type? This brings us to the matter of *incest,* or sexual intercourse between persons who are closely related. The *incest taboo* is an institutionalized norm, found almost universally, that prohibits sex relations between parents and their children, between brothers and sisters, and (with some variations in the degree of kinship) between members of the nuclear family and relatives outside the nuclear family (for example, with in-laws, aunts and uncles, cousins, and so on).

There have been many attempts to explain the existence of the incest taboo. Some scholars have pointed out the complexity of family relationships and roles if incest were the norm. For example, a boy born of a father-daughter union would be both the son and grandson of the father and both the brother and son of the daughter (Davis, 1960). Others have suggested that the prohibition of incest helps children to learn the necessity of controlling their erotic desires and to prepare them not only for marriage outside the family but also for the nonfamilial roles so essential to society (Parsons, 1954).

The usual rationale for the existence of the incest taboo today relates to genetics, namely, a concern that marriages between closely related persons might increase the likelihood of defective offspring (since both spouses might be carriers of the same inherited genetic weakness). However, although this rationale has provided support for the incest taboo, it does not explain its *origin* because there is no evidence that a concern about genetic abnormalities guided the ancients in forming their prohibitions. Nor does the genetic explanation always seem logical even today (for example, in cases where elderly first cousins, long past the age of childbearing, are forbidden to marry by certain state laws). (See also Chapter 15, p. 508.)

Some scholars believe that economic factors may lie behind the origin of the incest taboo. Once again, it may be useful to think in terms of exchange theory. For example, anthropologist Claude Lévi-Strauss (1956) has written of the way the incest taboo reinforces the interdependency of families. "For incest-prohibition simply states that families

(however they should be defined) can only marry between each other and that they cannot marry inside themselves." Furthermore, "the prohibition of incest is a rule of reciprocity. It means: I will only give up my daughter or my sister if my neighbor will give up his also. . . . The fact that I can obtain a wife is, in the last analysis, the consequence of the fact that a brother or a father has given up a woman" (Lévi-Strauss, 1949).

The emphasis in these statements is upon an exchange of women in traditional cultures, and we are again reminded of the customs surrounding the *bride wealth,* or bride price, and of the economic gains and social linkages which are associated with marriage. Building upon the ideas of Lévi-Strauss, we might suggest that the incest prohibition originally served as a means of ensuring an institutionalized pattern of gains through exchanges. Couples who married within their own families would only be sharing what they already possessed; it would be a closed arrangement with no bride prices, dowries, greater social linkages, and so on. But to marry *outside* one's family opened the way to bringing other resources in.

Exceptions to keeping the incest taboo may be similarly explained. If persons married outside their families in order to bring in additional resources, there might also be cases where persons married inside their families in order to keep resources. Marrying out of the family could bring gains; but marrying in the family could prevent loss. This is likely the reason for the father-daughter and brother-sister marriages during the time of the Pharaohs. In fact, Egyptologists have uncovered evidence of brother-sister marriages in many periods of Egypt's history, not only within the royalty but also among the commoners. Sociologist Russell Middleton (1962) suggests that the most plausible explanation is that such unions "served to maintain the property of the family intact and to prevent the splintering of the estate through the operation of the laws of inheritance. Since daughters usually inherited a share of the estate, the device of brother-sister marriage would have served to preserve intact the material resources of the family as a unit." Often these were "marriages of convenience" so that property could be transmitted which would otherwise have fallen to the state.

It should be noted that in this discussion of the incest taboo as possibly having originated because of economic-exchange considerations, we are exploring only the question of societally legitimized sexual unions, or intermarriage between family members. We are not at this point addressing a subject receiving widespread attention today—adult-child incest, as a social problem in which the more powerful adult figure seeks sexual gratification by exploiting a child's trust, dependence, and obedience to parental or other adult authority. This topic will be examined under the section on child abuse in Chapter 14.

WHY DO PEOPLE CHOOSE PARTICULAR MATES?

"I can't for the life of me figure out how those two got together!" "I wonder what she sees in *him?*" "That guy could have married any woman he pleased, and yet he picked her. I can't understand it."

We've all heard statements like these, and perhaps we've made similar remarks ourselves. Most people are interested in how particular persons got together and decided to form a marriage partnership. All sorts of questions arise: Why do persons tend to choose mates with similar social character-

istics? How can we explain mate selection in terms of our earlier discussion about male-female exchanges prior to marriage? And what is the place of love in all of this?

Field of Potential Mates

Men and women view each other through an initial screening or filtering process which is represented by a potential field of eligibles. Screened out are persons not defined as eligible, perhaps because they are not within the same race, religion, educational level, or age group. We have seen, for example, that the percentage of black-white marriages is small. Or to take another illustration, a devout Catholic is unlikely to consider an atheist as a potential marriage partner. A woman with a Ph.D. in psychology is not likely to marry the auto mechanic who services her car—no matter what movies and soap operas may say. The 30-year-old single woman who is introduced to her friend's 70-year-old bachelor uncle will in all probability think of him as only an acquaintance and not as a possible marriage partner. There are, of course, exceptions to every one of these patterns; but in general, as we have seen from the statistics, they hold true.

Narrowing the Choice

When persons have passed through the filtering process and have been defined as belonging to a category that makes a marriage bargain seem equitable, the question of which one to marry still remains (Becker, 1973). Obviously, no one can marry all of them; he or she is faced with the task of selecting just one potential mate out of the total field of eligibles. How is that selection made? And why do some people cross these lines to marry persons from somewhat different backgrounds?

Again we see the part that exchange and bargaining play in the mate-selection process. Clearly, there are numerous kinds of resources that men and women can offer each other in addition to those benefits represented by the broad categories of race, religion, and educational groupings. Particularly important are those resources that cluster around gender-role definitions.

The *traditional form of marriage* places the husband in the role of breadwinner and the wife in the role of nurturant sustainer of the home. Persons who want this form of marriage will gravitate toward those who hold similar views, and again it is a matter of reward seeking. Women who hold traditional gender-role patterns will be attracted to men who appear able to provide them with the status and material comfort they define as acceptable. Sociologist Willard Waller had this in mind when he wrote in 1938 that "a man, when he marries, chooses a companion and perhaps a helpmate, but a woman chooses a companion and at the same time a standard of living. It is necessary for a woman to be mercenary" (Waller, 1938:243 as quoted in Rubin, 1973:205).

At the same time, men who hold traditional views of gender roles are attracted to women who feel the same way. Such men desire wives who will provide the nurturance, support, and respect that husbands have traditionally deemed essential in a good homemaker. They are looking for women who will center their lives around husbands and children and for whom all other interests are secondary.

Persons who hold modern, egalitarian notions of marriage also seek out like-minded partners. Women who are persuaded that they have the right to self-determination and an individual identity are certainly not interested in joining themselves in marriage to men who believe that females should be pas-

"In 1953, Horton was considered a real catch."
(Drawing by Henry Martin, © 1978 The New Yorker Magazine, Inc.)

sive, dependent, and subordinate to male leadership. Instead such women are attracted to men who give promise of granting them the rewards of acceptance, recognition, free choice, affirmation of talents, and encouragement to achieve.

Similarly, some men highly value and admire achievement-oriented women and are drawn toward them, finding what they have to offer rewarding rather than threatening. In answer to the question often put to men married to successful women, "How does it feel to be the husband of. . . . ?" Bertrand B. Pogrebin (1972) writes, "In a word—terrific." Pogrebin, a lawyer, is married to the writer Letty Cottin Pogrebin. "I could go on at this point with all the superlatives that describe the pleasures of living with someone who likes what she is doing and is recognized for doing it well," he writes. "I could describe the people I've met and the places I've been because of her. Or the genuine interest and respect I have for her activities." Pogrebin is clearly speaking here in terms of rewards.

One study of college students showed that although both blacks and whites valued expressive qualities in a prospective mate, black males especially placed a high value on instrumental qualities such as a mate's having a good job, being willing to share financial responsibilities, and desiring to "move ahead" and improve economic status. "Black college males, influenced by the possibility of restricted economic opportunity, may be particularly sensitive to the economic demands of family life," write researchers Willie Melton and Darwin L. Thomas (1976). "Hence, qualities of a wife which make her agreeable to, and capable of, sharing with him the role of provider are highly valued" (p. 516).

Gender-role patterns are important parts of the exchange process prior to marriage because they set the stage for what is likely to occur later in marriage. The partners are either implicitly or explicitly anticipating their *future* roles.

WHAT PART DOES LOVE PLAY?

We say that persons "marry for love," but already we have seen that love isn't some mysterious force that strikes indiscriminately. Rather, love seems to be sparked among persons of similar social characteristics and resources. Whatever love is, it is clear that persons do not "fall in love" with just anybody; only certain ones will do.

Romantic Love

Love has many meanings, but one of the first meanings that comes to mind in connection with man-woman relationships is the notion of romantic love. Such love has its roots in the Greek idea of *eros,* or what the ancient Greeks saw as "diseased hysteria," an overwhelming force that irresistibly draws two persons together and makes them helpless under its power. All that matters is that the two are together, and all other considerations become secondary. Smitten, overcome, engulfed, the star-crossed lovers try to explain what has happened to them and conclude that it must have been moon glow or fate or the season or a magic potion of the gods or some other strange power which brought them straight to one another.

The idea is as recent as current love songs, and as ancient as the dramas of Euripides, whose Phaedra "groans in bitterness of heart and the goads of love prick her cruelly, and she is like to die." The goddess Aphrodite had stricken Phaedra with an uncontrollable seizure of desire for the chaste young man, Hippolytus, Phaedra's husband's illegitimate son. Aphrodite did this out of spite, desiring to punish Hippolytus for ignoring her, the goddess of love, and worshiping another goddess instead. Poor Phaedra in her suffering tries to fight off the lovesickness, believing she can conquer love "with discretion and good sense," but when that fails, she concludes that death is the only answer. Her faithful nurse provides comfort, telling Phaedra that it is futile to think that her puny swimming can provide an escape from the great sea of love into which she has fallen. "Give up your railing," counsels the old woman. "It's only insolent pride to wish to be superior to the gods. Endure your love. The gods have willed it so. You are sick" (Euripides, *Hippolytus,* Prologue, lines 395–400, 470–475).

The ballads of the twelfth-century troubadours with their themes of knights who pledged undying devotion to their ladies went a step further and exalted romantic love as the noblest emotion of which the human heart is capable. This courtly love of which the troubadours sang reinforces traditional male-female images. The man is the pursuer and protector, and the woman is the pure, beautiful prize to be pursued and adored. The gentleman is to *serve* his lady—to perform significant deeds for her that will make her justly proud of him, dependent on him, and in his debt.

Love Isn't Only a Feeling

The "diseased hysteria" and courtly "*amor*" notions of romantic love do not exhaust the meanings of the word *love*. Denis de Rougemont (1940) distinguishes between "an obsession which is undergone and a destiny that we shoulder." "*To be in love*," he writes, "is not necessarily *to love*. To be in love is a state; to love, an act. A state is suffered or undergone; but an act has to be decided upon."

Social psychologists Elaine Hatfield and G. William Walster (1978) put it another way:

> Love can appear in two very different forms: passionate love and companionate love. Passionate love is a wildly emotional state, a confusion of feelings: tenderness and sexuality, elation and pain, anxiety and relief, altruism and jealousy. Companionate love, on the other hand, is a lower-key emotion. It's friendly affection and deep attachment to someone. (p. 2)

Developing Love after the Mate-Selection Process

Even where mates are selected by parents, the mates are expected to develop feelings of affection for each other (Goode, 1959; Rubin, 1973). The Bible speaks of Isaac, who watched the arrival of a special camel caravan. It was bringing the bride whom he had never met but who had been chosen by his father's trusted servant. "Then Isaac brought her into the tent, and took Rebekah, and she became his wife; and he loved her" (Gen.

24:67). In such situations, factors other than love are considered the basis for marriage. "Love does not lead to marriage but marriage leads to love," goes a Korean saying, which continues rather cynically, "if such a thing as 'love' exists."

Sociologist Choong Soon Kim (1974) points out that many Korean young people are exposed to this and other teachings that de-emphasize the notion of love. For example: "I never knew what love was/I don't know what love is/I don't care what love is/I don't intend to be told what love is." Through such teachings, parents—especially in rural villages—have sought to justify the practice of having their children's marriages arranged by a go-between in charge of matchmaking.

The old Korean custom of arranged marriages has been incorporated into the contemporary teachings of the Unification Church (or "Moonies"), a controversial religious sect founded by Sun Myung Moon. The group, which has alarmed many parents, is active in the United States and elsewhere. Surprisingly, a number of American young people who have joined the group are willing to have their mates chosen for them by Moon, even though arranged marriages are very out of keeping with the usual pattern of mate selection in the United States today.

Most persons in contemporary American society, however, prefer choosing for themselves those they will marry. And they don't want to wait until after the wedding to get to know and love that person.

What Makes Certain Persons Love Each Other?

Attractions between persons may be either extrinsic or intrinsic. In an *extrinsic relationship*, the emphasis is on something outward and tangible. Some firms advertise very bluntly: "We want your business." But in an *intrinsic relationship,* the emphasis is on the inward and intangible. It is not a case of "wanting someone's business," but rather of wanting the *someone*—and wanting that person for his or her own sake. (The military may, of course, say, "We want *you!*" in their recruiting advertisements; but there the emphasis is on something extrinsic—the service a person can give.)

In an extrinsic relationship, one person treats the other as a means to some end. We might think of philosopher Martin Buber's (1958) description of an "I-it" relationship, in which a subject is relating to an object. Thus, a sales representative takes a client out to dinner, hoping to make a sale. Their being together has only this end in view.

In contrast, the intrinsic relationship corresponds to Buber's notion of an "I-Thou" encounter, where the relationship is one of subject to subject rather than one of subject to object. The two persons are attracted because of each other and because of the relationship itself. Friends or lovers go out for dinner simply because they enjoy each other and like to be together. There is an exchange of listening and speaking in which each person's self is revealed to the other. There are inputs on both sides that shape and mold the relationship itself. The two persons are associating with one another for their own sakes and not for the sake of some expected external benefit.

This does not mean, however, that no benefits are desired or expected at all. Throughout this book, we have observed the general sociological principle of reward-exchange in the formation and maintenance of associations. Love does not mean that a relationship is exempted from this principle (Blau, 1964:36, 76). But different dynamics are at work in a love relationship. In an extrinsic re-

lationship (the sales representative with a client), the exchange of specific rewards is the very reason that the association exists; the rewards themselves are the aim. But in an intrinsic association, the supreme value is the *association* in and of itself, with the mutual exchange of rewards taking place *in order to sustain the relationship.*

Although we usually think of love in altruistic terms, Blau makes the point that "selfless devotion generally rests on an interest in maintaining the other's love." Persons in love furnish benefits to each other to show commitment to the partner and to their relationship and to induce the partner to enlarge his or her commitment and inputs as well. Love, therefore, is the extreme example of a deep, strong, intrinsic attraction between persons; yet it is based on the norm of reciprocity. To love is to expect love in return. Love unrequited becomes love unkindled. "Men and women who insist that they are capable of dispensing love with no thought of return are simply deceiving themselves," write Hatfield and Walster (1978). "Those who expect such selfless love from their partners most assuredly are" (p. 134).

Desire for Equity

Hatfield and Walster are not merely expressing an opinion but speak from their scientific research on love. In fact, Elaine Hatfield (Walster) and another social psychologist, Ellen Berscheid, unexpectedly found themselves in the news when in 1975 Senator William Proxmire alerted taxpayers that the National Science Foundation had awarded these researchers an $84,000 grant for continuing work on passionate and companionate love. Proxmire was against such research because he felt no amount of money could provide an answer to the "why" of love. But there was another reason. "I'm also against it because I don't want the answer," he said in a press release. "I believe that 200 million other Americans want to leave some things in life a mystery, and right at the top of things we don't want to know is why a man falls in love with a woman and vice versa" (quoted in Hatfield and Walster, 1978, viii).

Columnist James Reston (*New York Times,* March 14, 1975) retorted that although it may be true that many persons prefer to leave love a mystery and "don't want the answer," "if the sociologists and psychologists can get even a suggestion of the answer to our pattern of romantic love, marriage, disillusion, divorce—and the children left behind—it could be the best investment of federal money since Jefferson made the Louisiana Purchase." In the years since the Hatfield, Walster, and Berscheid research, increasing numbers of social scientific studies have been devoted to the topics of attraction, affiliation, liking, and love. (See summaries in Hendrick and Hendrick, 1983; Murstein, 1980.)

One way to understand what goes on in intimate relationships is to think in terms of what Hatfield (Walster), Walster, and Berscheid (1978) call *"equity theory."* They define *intimate relationships* as "relationships between loving persons whose lives are deeply intertwined" (p. 146). Among other characteristics of such relationships, persons have a deep liking or love for one another, expect the relationship to endure, and have the capability of highly rewarding each other. By the same token, they also have the capability of deeply hurting one another.

Equity theory deals with costs and rewards and combines exchange theory with a number of psychological theories (Hatfield [Walster], Walster, and Berscheid, 1978:2). It is concerned with judgments about what is fair or unfair in a situation or relationship. One of the basic propositions of equity theory is stated and explained by Hatfield and Walster (1978):

> People feel most comfortable when they're getting exactly what they feel they deserve in a relationship. *Everyone* in an inequitable relationship feels uneasy. While it's not surprising that deprived partners (who are, after all, getting less than they deserve) should feel resentful and angry about their inequitable treatment, it's perhaps not so obvious why their *overbenefited* mates (who are getting more than they deserve) feel uneasy too. But they do. They feel guilty and fearful of losing their favored position. (p. 135)

Hatfield and Walster (1978:135; Hatfield [Walster], et al. 1978) have observed that if two persons are in a relationship that turns out to be inequitable, they experience distress and try to relieve that distress in one of three ways: they try to do something to restore equity to the relationship, or they try to convince themselves that the relationship is equitable even though it isn't (so that equity exists in their heads if not in actuality). Or third, they simply decide to break up.

"It appears, then," say Hatfield and Walster (1978), "that just falling in love is *not enough for most of us.... Implication: We all want a lot more out of our relationships than we think we do*" (p. 133; italics in the original).

Rewards of Love

But what do we want out of our relationships? For one thing, we want to be appreciated.

Gratitude Some sociologists point out that gratitude is an important component in social bonding and can be a crucial factor in bringing and holding persons together (Nisbet, 1970). We're disappointed if our gifts and good deeds aren't recognized by those who benefit from them. Suppose, for example, we see someone drop an armload of books and papers. We rush to help, not even thinking about recognition or reward. However, if our efforts are met with only cold indifference or, worse yet, a brusque directive to get out of the way and mind our own business, we feel disappointment. Even a simple "thank you" would have been enough. But as it is, a potential bond between two persons has been slashed.

Being loved by someone means you have a confidant to whom you can express your innermost feelings. (© Chip Henderson, 1985/Woodfin Camp & Associates)

If gratitude is so important in social bonding in general, it is especially important in the interactions associated with a love relationship. Such a point is being made by the wife who complains, "You just take me for granted. I never hear a word of thanks for all the things I do for you." Or the husband who laments, "Nag, nag, nag. That's all you ever do! Does it occur to you that a man might like to hear a word of appreciation once in a while?" Interactions that call forth admiration, recognition, and gratitude go on before marriage as well—whether in the exchange of tangible gifts or in the exchange of intangible benefits such as compliments and loving gestures.

Self-Disclosure Of course, the development of love as an exchange involves more than gratitude. Social psychologists have been giving much attention to what they call the *social-penetration process*, or how persons in a sense "get into" one another so that interpersonal relationships can develop (Taylor, 1968). If true intimacy is to come about, the interaction between persons must include self-disclosure. In other words, we reveal information about ourselves (our feelings, ambitions, fears, attitudes, anxieties, incidents from our past, and so on)—information that otherwise would not be known by the other person. The other person, in turn, looks on our intentional self-disclosure as a social reward. It shows that person that we like and trust her or him. And it also frees that person to make similar disclosures about herself or himself (Worthy, Gary, and Kahn, 1969; Taylor, Altman, and Sorrentino, 1969).

At the same time, an element of risk is always involved in self-disclosure. The person to whom we open ourselves up may react negatively to the information revealed and lower his or her regard for us. Maybe that person will even use that information to hurt us in some way. These are some of the reasons that self-disclosure is difficult for many people (Rubin, 1973:160–162).

However, in a relationship involving commitment and love, a high degree of self-disclosure comes to be expected as an element of reward in the social-exchange process. Being loved by someone means that person accepts you as you are—even when the secrets of your heart are laid bare. Thus you have a confidant to whom you can unload your heartaches and expose your innermost feelings. And loving someone in return means that likewise you are rewarded by that person's trust and confidence through self-disclosure on his or her part.

Reiss's "Wheel Theory" of Love Sociologist Ira Reiss (1960b) sees self-disclosure as a crucial second step in his "wheel theory" of love and its development. Reiss conceptualizes love as an ongoing cycle that begins with a sense of rapport between two individuals. This rapport then turns toward mutual self-revelation; and as the "wheel" turns further, the persons develop a mutual dependency on one another. Reiss notes that the more technical term for such mutual dependencies is "interdependent habit systems." He explains: "One becomes dependent on the other person to fulfill one's own habits: e.g., one needs the other person to tell one's ideas or feelings; . . . to joke with; . . . to fulfill one's sexual desires. When such habitual expectations are not fulfilled, loneliness and frustration are experienced. Thus, such habits tend to perpetuate a relationship." From mutual dependencies, the wheel turns to personality-need fulfillment. The harmonious connection between the persons (*rapport*) is increased, the self-revelation continues, and so on, as the wheel keeps turning. (See Figure 4-4.)

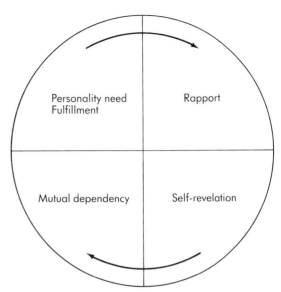

FIGURE 4-4 Graphic presentation of the wheel theory of the development of love. (Source: Ira L. Reiss, "Toward a Sociology of the Heterosexual Love Relationship." *Journal of Marriage and Family Living, 22* [May, 1960]: 143.)

At the same time, says Reiss, the wheel could hit a snare at some point and the relationship could begin to unwind. An argument or competing interest might lessen rapport between the persons, which in turn would block the self-disclosure, disturb the interdependent habit systems, and frustrate fulfillment of personality needs.

Reinforcement and Feelings of Self-Worth Akin to the notion of mutual dependency is the emphasis two psychologists place on the part reinforcement plays in building self-esteem in persons who are loved. "Through reinforcement, lovers mutually enhance each other's self-concept," write Howard Miller and Paul Siegel (1972:14–22). Pointing out that in an ongoing love relationship, reinforcement efforts often need to be *intentional,* they write: "By 'conscious and deliberate' we mean that each partner can deliberately choose to help satisfy the other's needs, to bolster the other's feelings of self-worth and attractiveness. The fading of the original thrill of mutual discovery and infatuation can be replaced by consciously learning how to make the other person feel attractive, adequate, and simply good about himself. This can be as obvious as praise, or as subtle as paying attention at appropriate moments." However, unless this reinforcement springs from honesty, it has little value. When compliments and expressed interest are not genuine, "that person will lose his power to reward you."

Should Love Be beyond Reward-Seeking? Many people are reluctant to admit that an exchange of rewards occurs in love. They feel that such a notion somehow devalues the ideal of love as intrinsically selfless and sacrificial, without any expectation of anything in return. However, a little reflection on the kinds of rewards sought in a love relationship might make the notions of exchange, bargaining, and benefits a bit easier to accept. After all, why else would persons

enter into love relationships and marriage than out of an expectation that they would gain something from such relationships?

We have already talked about two parts of marriage: the instrumental side being concerned with economic factors and task performance and the expressive side having to do with the affectionate-companionate dimension. To speak of love is to speak of the *expressive rewards* persons seek from a marriage partner—rewards such as *companionship* (someone to do things with, go places with, spend leisure hours with), *empathy* (someone to talk things over with, someone to bring reinforcement of one's self-concept, someone to understand and care), and *physical affection* (hugging, kissing, the squeeze of a hand, caressing, sexual gratifications). Prior to marriage, these same three elements in one degree or another are sought after as valued rewards in a developing relationship. Though it is often unconscious, a type of bargaining is going on between the partners as they reach out to receive these benefits from one another. The decision to continue the relationship and later to enter into marriage hinges in large part on this reward exchange.

Earlier, we quoted Hatfield and Walster's statement that "we all want a lot more out of our relationships than we think we do." That statement was based on a study they and their colleagues Jane Traupmann and Mary Utne conducted in which several hundred dating couples and married couples were asked what they expected to give and get in relationships (Hatfield and Walster, 1978:130–133; Hatfield [Walster], Walster, and Berscheid, 1978:236–242). Among the assets considered "critically important in a date or mate" were the ability to be friendly and relaxed in social settings, being intelligent and informed, being physically attractive and practicing good health habits, show-

(Drawing by Wm. Hamilton, © 1978 The New Yorker Magazine, Inc.)

"I got what I wanted, but it wasn't what I expected."

ing and expressing love to the partner, understanding and responding to the partner's emotional needs and personal concerns, providing security in the relationship at the same time the partner's individuality and freedom are respected, a willingness to work on a mutually satisfying sexual relationship, sexual fidelity, sharing in day-to-day household and financial responsibilities, being a good companion, sharing the load of decision-making, remembering special occasions such as birthdays and anniversaries, and being appreciative. There's no denying that people want their most intimate associations to be nothing short of rewarding.

RATIONALITY IN LOVE AND MATE SELECTION

For years, critics have charged that romantic love by its very nature inhibits rational discussion of elements beyond the couple's relationship itself—elements such as finances, status, education, occupation, and lifestyle. Added to these older criticisms are some new challenges to romantic love emerging on several fronts. Essentially, the goal is to make the mate-selection process more rational so that persons will become more aware of the realities (actual costs and rewards) involved.

Premarital Contraceptive Attitudes and Practices

For example, the introduction of contraceptive usage in premarital sexual relations is based upon rational considerations. Through the efforts of organizations such as Planned Parenthood, sexually active unmarried men and women have been urged to take precautions against conceiving children. Even some religious groups and spokespersons have suggested that despite traditional prohibitions against sex outside marriage, a realistic approach should take into account that many persons do engage in premarital sex and therefore need guidance in avoiding undesirable consequences, such as pregnancy and sexually transmitted diseases. One minister (Shedd, 1968) has suggested that an unmarried couple who are engaging in sexual intercourse should have a "deep-think" discussion, considering every angle of what they are doing; and if they feel they cannot quit, they should determine to use contraceptives. "Since you can't be as good as you wish," he writes, "will you at least be as smart as you can?" (p. 78). The essence of the advice is rationality.

Persons of both sexes who hold egalitarian gender-role attitudes are especially likely to take a rational approach to premarital contraception because they want to avoid costs such as interrupted educational and career plans. Egalitarian gender roles have been found to be associated with both more frequent and more effective use of contraception in premarital sexual relationships (MacCorquodale, 1984).

Later Age at First Marriage

Rationality—realistically assessing rewards and costs—also enters into the *timing* of marriage. In fact, it isn't difficult to see important connections between gender roles, contraception, pregnancy, and the age at first marriage. The teenager who expects only to be a wife and mother some day, who begins dating early, engages in premarital sex, does not use contraceptives, and becomes pregnant before she finishes high school quite likely will marry young. Moreover, age at marriage has important consequences for the future. The adolescent girl in the example just mentioned has a high chance of becoming divorced. If she and her husband remain married, they are likely to have a greater number of children than if they had married later. And their income can be expected to be lower than that of persons who marry later.

The more education persons have, the older they are when they marry (U.S. Bureau of Census, 1973, PC (2)-4D, p. 266). We have already seen the association between education and gender roles. The more a woman seeks individualistic rewards for herself, the greater her autonomy and independence as a person, the later she is likely to marry. Men who favor such female reward seeking are also likely to marry later, choosing women who have taken time to complete their education and perhaps already embarked on careers. One researcher suggests, on the other hand, that an opposite explanation may fit in some cases in which men choose to remain single longer. "Perhaps some men, unable to adjust to the changing situation of women, are less actively seeking marriage partners," writes Andrew Cherlin (1980:364). For some men, changes in gender roles may be perceived as making marriage less rewarding and more costly—or even less necessary.

Women who are less educated marry younger because fewer alternative rewards are open to them. When such women become pregnant out of wedlock, their marriage age is often lowered still further. Regardless of class background, however, premarital conceptions tend to have a lowering effect on age at marriage.

In compiling statistics on the ages at which people marry, the Census Bureau records the median age at first marriage in a given year. In speaking of *median age,* demographers mean the dividing point—the point at which half the persons in a particular category are above that age and half are below. For example, the latest available statistics show us that in 1986, the median age at which men

married was 25.7. This means that half the men entering their first marriage were older than age 25.7 and half were younger. The median age for women entering their first marriage that year was 23.1.

Between 1890 and 1956, the median age at first marriage kept dropping. Both women and men were marrying at younger ages. (See Table 4-C) During that same period, the gap between the sexes at the age of first marriage narrowed. In 1890, there was a four-year difference between the age at which women married and the age at which men married; but beginning in 1956, that difference shrank to about 2½ years.

Beginning in 1957, there was a new trend for both sexes to wait longer to marry. Between 1970 and 1978, the median age increased one full year. And by 1986, it was up nearly another 1 1/2 years for both sexes.

We can also examine marriage trends by looking at proportions of age categories who have or have never married. In 1970, nearly two-thirds of women in their early twenties were already married, as were 45 percent of men. But by 1986, only about 1 out of 4 men in that age range was married. Among 20- to 24-year-old women, only about 4 out of 10 had married. Figure 4-5 makes clear that the postponement of marriage extends to other age categories as well.

The phenomenon of later marriage today is no doubt related to changes in gender-role norms and shifts in lifestyles, a topic to be explored more fully in Part 4 of this book. One reason social scientists find the trend to postpone marriage of such great interest is because later marriage has been found to be associated with a number of other phenomena—for example, a lower probability of divorce, later childbearing, and fewer children (U.S. Bureau of the Census, *Special Demographic Analyses,* CDS-80-8, 1983). The connection between later marriage and fewer

TABLE 4-C *Median age at first marriage, by sex: 1890–1986*

YEAR	MEN	WOMEN	YEAR	MEN	WOMEN
1986	25.7	23.1	1962	22.7	20.3
1985	25.5	23.3	1961	22.8	20.3
1984	25.4	23.0	1960	22.8	20.3
1983	25.4	22.8	1959	22.5	20.2
1982	25.2	22.5	1958	22.6	20.2
1981	24.8	22.3	1957	22.6	20.3
1980	24.7	22.0	1956	22.5	20.1
1979	24.4	22.1	1955	22.6	20.2
1978	24.2	21.8	1954	23.0	20.3
1977	24.0	21.6	1953	22.8	20.2
1976	23.8	21.3	1952	23.0	20.2
1975	23.5	21.1	1951	22.9	20.4
1974	23.1	21.1	1950	22.8	20.3
1973	23.2	21.0	1949	22.7	20.3
1972	23.3	20.9	1948	23.3	20.4
1971	23.1	20.9	1947	23.7	20.5
1970	23.2	20.8	1940	24.3	21.5
1969	23.2	20.8	1930	24.3	21.3
1968	23.1	20.8	1920	24.6	21.2
1967	23.1	20.6	1910	25.1	21.6
1966	22.8	20.5	1900	25.9	21.9
1965	22.8	20.6	1890	26.1	22.0
1964	23.1	20.5			
1963	22.8	20.5			

SOURCE: U.S. Bureau of the Census, *Current Population Reports,* Series P-20, no. 412, *Households, Families, Marital Status, and Living Arrangements: March 1986 (Advance Report)* (Washington, D.C.: U.S. Government Printing Office, 1986), p. 4.

children also lies behind Article 5 of the 1980 marriage law of the People's Republic of China, which requires that men be at least 22 years old and women 20 years old before they marry. The law encourages even later marriage and later childbirth as part of the government's population-control efforts (Engel, 1984).

Innovative Approaches to Meeting Eligible Dating and Marriage Partners

Two basic issues a person faces in the mate-selection process are (1) how to meet eligible

persons and (2) how to present oneself as *desirable* (rewarding) to the other person.

In traditional societies, as we saw earlier, such matters are left up to parents, who arrange their children's marriages. Japan was a prime example of such a society until recent decades. Even now, arranged marriages (usually in modified form, with considerable input from the man and woman involved) continue in many Japanese families—although the general movement has been toward the "love-match" system of free choice (Mochizuki, 1981; Murstein, 1980). Under the older system, as one sociologist points out, "concern on both sides created a bargaining situation in which each party exag-

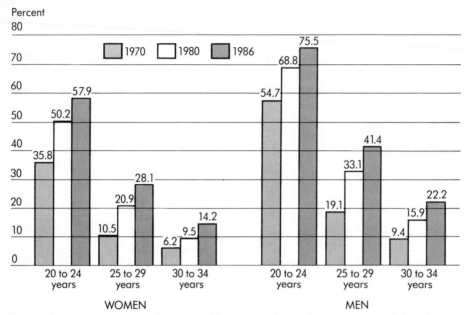

FIGURE 4-5   Percentages of the United States population that never married, by age and sex, for the years 1970, 1980, and 1986. (Source: U.S. Bureau of the Census, Current Population Reports, Series P-23, No. 130, *Population Profile of the United States, 1982* (Washington, D.C.: U.S. Government Printing Office, 1983). p. 14. Percentages for 1986 (latest available statistics) are from U.S. Bureau of the Census, Current Population Reports, Series P-20, No. 412, Households, Families, Marital Status, and Living Arrangements: March 1986 (Advance Report) (Washington, D.C.: U.S. Government Printing Office, Nov. 1986), p. 4.

gerated its assets and hid its liabilities, worrying lest the antagonist succeed in doing the same'' (Blood, 1967:5). To avoid the problems and feuds this caused and to save face in cases where offers were rejected, families engaged the services of a matchmaker, who acted as a go-between in negotiations between the two families.

Some family scholars see similar logic in some of the less conventional approaches to dating and mate selection that have been emerging in the United States and Europe. Davor Jedlicka (1980:199), for example, calls attention to "formal mate selection networks including agencies, clubs, go-betweens, name-list brokers, and others who try to improve their clients' chances for con-

tacts with the opposite sex." Video mate-selection services, computer dating services, and the use of newspaper and magazine classified advertisements are some of the methods used to bring together persons interested in meeting other available persons in the dating and marriage market. A 1984 television program introduced viewers to one of the most novel approaches yet: the California-based "Freeway Singles" club. Persons who pay a membership fee are given a decal with the club's name and their identification numbers which they can place in the rear windows of their cars. If another member driving along a highway sees the decal and would like to meet that particular person, he or she can write to the club headquarters and ex-

LOVE AMONG THE CLASSIFIEDS

Well, good news: there is a way, if not to find a guaranteed soulmate, to at least improve your odds. Get out your checklist—and take out an ad.

If you haven't looked at the fine print in the personals column of late, your associations with them probably hover between the historical (immigrants ordering mail-order brides) and the hysterical (either the back pages of *Screw* magazine or the Miss Lonelyhearts syndrome: "Pathetic loser, 35, seeks same").

Not to worry. The personals have quietly but steadily become the province of people who are probably pretty much like you. . . .

If you take a look, you'll probably be surprised at how *few* ads seem even remotely kinky. The stigma of loser-dom in part remains, which is why people who've met this way might not tell you they did. And yet it's precisely *because* they allow you to let your fingers do the walking and ask outright for a particular sort of person that the personals are more than just another stop on the "respectable" bars/parties/Club Med/night school circuit. They represent a wholly alternative approach to dating, best exemplified in the Californian phrase "Go for it!"

SOURCE: Excerpted from Lindsy Van Gelder, "Love Among the Classifieds: A Take-Charge Way to Meet People," *Ms.* 12 (August 1983):39–43.

press interest in being contacted by the person whose identifying number was observed on the decal.

All such attempts reflect a take-charge attitude toward dating and mate selection rather than waiting passively for random chance to bring some eligible and compatible person into one's life. Taking issue with the widely held view that "both the increase in singles and singles' services [are] symbolic of the loneliness and alienation of society in general," social scientists Rosemary Bolig, Peter Stein, and Patrick McKenry (1984:587) assert that the development of singles' services more accurately reflects "a healthy and innovative adaption to rapid social change." They go on to say that "use of diverse and unique means to find persons with whom to relate, date, and possibly mate, may indicate a more purposive and rational approach as opposed to the game playing of romantic love."

Once again we see rationality. The self-advertisement approach to dating that Bolig,

Stein, and McKenry examined simply makes explicit that the parties involved are engaging in *bargaining*—a system of exchanges. The man and woman are doing for themselves (or hiring a third party such as a dating service to do for them) what matchmakers have done in traditional societies. Even in the People's Republic of China, where the 1980 marriage law forbids the interference of third parties and the government has denounced professional matchmaking ever since the cultural revolution got underway many years earlier, there have arisen "marriage introduction services" to help eligible young adults meet each other, even though actual marriages are not arranged (Engel, 1984).

TRENDS

Up until recent years, most marriages started out on a traditional footing, with the husband designated as the *unique provider* and the marriage centering around his job and all the demands and rewards associated with it. Decisions about where to live, the family's lifestyle, employment or educational plans for the wife, and the number and spacing of children were expected to be determined by the husband and his occupational role.

In preparation for this, women were trained from childhood to develop what sociologist Shirley Angrist (1969) has called a "contingency orientation." They learned to be flexible and prepared to adapt to whatever contingencies life might bring their way. And, of course, long-range goals, mastery, and self-determination cannot hold a high place in the lives of persons who know plans may be disrupted at any point. Marriage was looked upon as the first contingency that would probably come into a woman's life. But at the same time, she was to realize that she must be prepared for an occupation— just in case marriage wasn't in the picture for her or in case she became divorced or widowed. Within marriage, she was expected to be her husband's adjunct, always ready to adapt to his needs and wishes. Pregnancy and child care were viewed as further contingencies for which she must be prepared to adjust at any point.

Today, as more and more women move away from "contingency-orientation" thinking, they are viewing their life course differently and seeing marriage as less central to their lives. Many are making long-range plans and pursuing educational and career goals as alternatives to marriage—or at least as reasons to delay marriage (U.S. Bureau of the Census, *Special Demographic Analyses,* CDS-80-8, 1983; Allen and Kalish, 1984). In one study of late marriage among highly educated professional women, the researchers found "that willingness to participate in intimate personal and sexual relationships outside of marriage [also] reduces the attractiveness of the marriage role" (Allen and Kalish, 1984:381). Men, too, are apparently finding alternative rewards (in singleness and cohabitation, for example).

The evidence suggests that young adults of traditional marriage age have been weighing the costs and rewards of marriage to a greater degree perhaps than ever before. And changes in mate-selection patterns are reflecting this examination and evaluation the world over. As Bernard Murstein (1980:63) points out, having specialized in years of study of marital-choice patterns, "Cross-culturally, there seems to be a movement towards individual determination in marriage, though its pace varies considerably from country to country. One of the choices is the right to avoid marriage altogether." He goes on to observe that the traditional reasons for marriage, such as cementing family alliances and providing opportunities for regular, societally approved sexual gratification and procreation, are considered less valid today.

An understanding of dating and mate selection must therefore be seen in the context of social change. Marriage patterns have not stood still for the past 200 years, and they are not standing still today. What persons are seeking from marriage is changing, and mate-selection patterns may be expected to reflect that change as perceptions of what is costly and what is rewarding in marriage, singleness, and other arrangements are sorted out.

CHAPTER HIGHLIGHTS

Historically and cross-culturally, kin have influenced or controlled the choice of a marital partner. However, for the most part, the right to choose one's own mate has been a freedom taken for granted in the United States. At the same time, *dating* (getting together for a good time, without intending the relationship to lead toward marriage) is a relatively new custom; and over the years, both the term *dating* and the patterns of social interaction between the sexes have undergone changes. When it comes to selecting a mate, men and women view each other through an initial screening or filtering process represented by a potential "field of eligibles." Persons tend at first to screen out those whose educational level, age, race, and religion are very different from their own—although there are, of course, exceptions in all these areas. In general, we may say that persons are attracted to each other and maintain a relationship on the basis of the rewards they give one another. To speak of love is to speak of the *expressive rewards* persons seek from a partner—companionship, empathy, and physical affection. When two (or more) persons maintain ongoing instrumental and expressive exchanges, we may say a marriage exists; the basic elements are sexual and economic interdependency. But to be valid from a societal point of view, some form of public disclosure is also necessary. Marriage patterns are coming under close scrutiny today, and there appears to be a move toward making the mate-selection process more rational (in contrast to romantic love notions of being helplessly "swept off one's feet"). Frank questions are being asked as persons become more aware of the realities of marriage—the costs and rewards—and are weighing decisions about whether, when, and whom to marry with those realities in mind. Crucial to the bargaining process taking place between a woman and man before marriage are gender-role patterns because they set the stage for what is likely to occur later within the marriage.

·5·

SEX BEFORE MARRIAGE

I f a virgin happens to walk by, the statue of the pioneer mother over there will rise up in surprise!'' So goes the campus folklore at one university. Other colleges have similar legends. Maybe a cannon will spontaneously fire or the stone lions will roar. Of course, no one expects this to happen. After all, there aren't any virgins any more. Or are there? To find some answers, let's look at what's been happening in the present century as well as during earlier times.

In view of traditional norms decreeing that sexual intercourse belongs only in marriage, many Americans were shocked and outraged by the publication of what were popularly known as the ''Kinsey Reports,'' published in 1948 and 1953. Dr. Alfred Kinsey (1953, chap. 8) and his associates at the Institute for Sex Research at Indiana University found that of the married women in their sample who had been born after 1900, nearly half had engaged in sex before marriage.

Americans who were accustomed to the double standard that maintained that ''boys will be boys but girls will be angels'' found it a bit easier to accept the Kinsey findings on *male* sexual behavior. Among men with a high school education in Kinsey's sample, 85 percent had experienced sexual intercourse before marriage; and among men with some college, the figure was 68 percent.

Although, at first, many questions were raised about the reliability of the Kinsey sampling procedures, studies by others verified his findings. Sociologist Ira Reiss (1960a, chap. 3) points out that studies by Terman (published in 1938), Burgess and Wallin (1953), and Kinsey (1948 and 1953) included couples from California, Chicago, and the Northeast, yet the results were strikingly similar. Each of these major studies indicated that about 50 percent of the women born in this century were not virgins at the time of marriage.

Another point of agreement in these studies was the finding that women tended to link sex with love and affection. Their premarital sexual activity did not necessarily indicate *promiscuity*, engaging in sex with a variety of partners. The Terman, Burgess and Wallin, and Kinsey studies taken together showed that of the women studied who reported having had premarital intercourse, from one-half to two-thirds reported that their only partner was the man they later married.

Up until the late 1960s, the incidence of premarital sex appeared to remain much the same as the Kinsey research revealed. To be sure, many people *believed* that rates of premarital intercourse were soaring, and the popular press kept referring to a ''sexual revolution.'' However, the word *revolution* implies an abrupt and radical change; and scholars could find no evidence that any such thing had occurred since the period around World War I. At that time, it was true, there had been a sudden upsurge in rates of premarital sex, as shown in Kinsey's finding that only 25 percent of women born before 1900 entered marriage nonvirginal in contrast to 50 percent of the women born between 1900 and 1910 (Kinsey et al., 1953, chap. 8). This doubling of the rate of nonvirginity among women in just one decade could be called, with some justification, a sexual revolution. But since that time, any changes have been gradual and the continuation of a trend rather than something abrupt. Some scholars have suggested that it might be more accurate to speak of an *evolution* in sexual permissiveness rather than a revolution.

CHANGING ATTITUDES

According to Reiss (1972, p. 169) and other researchers, the changes that occurred after the 1920s were mainly changes in *attitudes*.

MEN ARRESTED FOR TOPLESS BATHING

As recently as 1936, it was illegal for men to wear topless bathing suits in New York.

U.S. men won topless rights after a decade of controversy. In the '30s, male bathers began discarding the shoulders-to-thighs tank suits for new swimming trunks.

In 1934, eight men were fined $1 each for topless bathing at Coney Island. "All of you fellows may be Adonises," said the presiding magistrate, a woman, "but there are many people who object to seeing so much of the human body exposed." A year later, a mass arrest of 42 topless males in Atlantic City, N.J., fattened the municipal coffers by $84. The city fathers declared: "We'll have no gorillas on our beaches."

Gradually, the guardians of national decency relented, and local ordinances were revised to allow topless bathing for men. In 1936, it was economy rather than morality that finally induced the Westchester, N.Y., County Park Commission to allow swimming trunks. The commission, which purchased suits for rental at county beaches and pools, found that the trunks were substantially cheaper.

SOURCE: Irving Wallace, David Wallechinsky, and Amy Wallace, "Significa." *Parade*, Oct. 3, 1982, p. 19.

The evolution of women's bathing suit styles from 1900 to 1920 reflects the changes in sex attitudes and behavior during that same period. (The Bettmann Archive, Inc.)

People began feeling more free to discuss sex openly. Regrets and guilt feelings about premarital sex—particularly in a stable, affectionate relationship—were reduced. Other changes related to both the timing of premarital sex (nearness to marriage being less important than was once the case) and the meaning of premarital sex (a move toward what Reiss calls *person-centered sex* rather than body-centered sex).

Petting

Another significant change that took place had to do with petting. Kinsey and associates used the term *petting* to refer to "physical contacts which involve a deliberate attempt to effect erotic arousal," that is, sexual contacts that do not involve an actual union of the male and female genitals. Petting might involve manual or oral stimulation of the breasts and genitals, or it might include the placing of the genitals close together without any effort toward penetration. Sometimes petting is a prelude to actual sexual union, but in other cases, petting (especially to the point of orgasm) is an end in itself—a substitute for sexual intercourse. Kinsey (1953, chap. 7) pointed out that although premarital petting certainly existed among Americans in earlier times, the practice was more widespread among those born after 1900 and its incidence had increased steadily down to the time of his studies.

Robert R. Bell (1966) spoke of this increase in premarital petting as "the greatest behavioral change in premarital sexual experience since the 1920s" (p. 58), a point that had also been stressed by Winston Ehrmann (1957). In a similar vein, Reiss (1960a, chap. 10) found in his research on sexual attitudes that among those who believed in abstinence from sexual intercourse before marriage, there was nevertheless a great increase

in the number who felt petting was permissible. Petting provided a way to engage in considerable sexual intimacies while at the same time preserving one's virginity since actual *coitus* (sexual intercourse) did not occur.

Reiss's Categories of Premarital Sexual Standards

Sociologists are interested both in what people believe and in how people behave. Concentrating primarily on beliefs or attitudes, Ira Reiss has added significantly to the body of sociological studies on premarital sex by differentiating and labeling four main sexual standards. His research showed that in the United States between 1920 and 1965, "young people increasingly came to see the selection of a sexual code and sexual behavior itself as a private choice similar to that made in politics and religion" (1973).

Attitudes toward premarital sex, according to Reiss (1960a), fall into these four categories: abstinence, the double standard, permissiveness with affection, and permissiveness without affection. Persons who hold the *abstinence standard* believe that sexual intercourse before marriage is wrong for both males and females. The *double standard*, on the other hand, is in essence two standards—one for males and one for females. Persons who hold the double standard believe that males have the right to engage in sexual intercourse before marriage but that premarital sexual intercourse is not permissible for females. Traditionally, the abstinence standard and the double standard have existed side by side, with abstinence being viewed as almost a kind of "official" standard while covertly the double standard was widely practiced.

Reiss found that young men and women were no longer willing to limit their notions about premarital sex to choice between these two standards alone. They added to abstinence and the double standard two new standards, both of which were basically egalitarian. Reiss labeled these standards *permissiveness with affection* and *permissiveness without affection.* Persons who hold the permissiveness-with-affection standard believe that a man and woman who are in a stable relationship such as engagement or who love each other or have strong affection for one another have the right to express their feelings through coitus. In other words, premarital sex is not wrong for either males or females if deep affection is present.

The remaining standard, permissiveness without affection, also makes no distinctions between male and female privileges. Those who hold this standard believe that both women and men may engage in premarital sexual intercourse regardless of how stable the relationship is or how much affection the partners feel toward each other. Sex is viewed as primarily a giving and receiving of sexual pleasure, a part of the good time two persons may have in going out together. It's sex for fun—casual, hedonistic, without any feeling that love is necessary to justify it.

Two other researchers found evidence of a fifth standard, which they call *nonexploitive permission without affection* (Jurich and Jurich, 1974). The emphasis is on an agreed-upon meaning before sexual intercourse takes place so that exploitation will not occur. According to this standard, "if one party desires both sex and commitment and the other wants just sex, any sexuality would be exploitive and is, therefore, immoral" (pp. 736–37).

HISTORICAL BACKGROUND

Most of the so-called sex revolution or evolution has centered around female autonomy. *Autonomy* has to do with self-government, independence, being free to carry out one's own will and being responsible for one's own actions, in contrast to being under the control of another. Traditionally, women have been under the control of men—first their fathers, later their husbands. This means that female sexuality has usually been subject to stricter regulations than has been true of men, who throughout history have been given freedom by parents and the larger society to "sow their wild oats" with prostitutes or women of low social position.

Sexual intercourse before marriage is not a new phenomenon. If one takes a historical perspective, it must be remembered that prior to modernization and the rise of the dominant Puritan ethic regarding sex, most Western societies consisted largely of lower-class, uneducated masses, with the remainder being upper-class aristocrats and gentry. Literature of the times indicates that premarital sex was very widespread among the masses and among much of the upper strata as well. However, with the rise of the middle classes and the influences of Lutheranism and especially Calvinism (in which both the Protestant work ethic and the Puritan sex ethic are rooted), sexual permissiveness came to be less acceptable.

Puritan Influence

Puritan theology took seriously biblical warnings against both pre- and extramarital sex. Sanctions against sex outside of marriage were rigidly enforced, as is clearly seen both in the Puritans' own writings and in such fictionalized accounts as Hawthorne's *The Scarlet Letter.* Both men and women were expected to be chaste, abstaining from coitus until after wedding vows had been exchanged and remaining completely faithful to each other from that time forward.

Rationality and self-discipline were important virtues in Puritan thinking, and they were expected to be demonstrated in sexual conduct as well as in affairs of business. Over time, rational control meant financial and occupational success as the Protestant work ethic took root and blossomed into the middle-class lifestyle. And to be "of good character" meant steering clear of irrational and irresponsible sexual behavior that might disgrace the family, bring about an unwise "forced" marriage, or dishonor one's reputation through the birth of an illegitimate child. Because women were the childbearers, it was they who faced greater restrictions and tighter controls.

Revivalism

The great eighteenth-century Wesleyan revivals in England and similar movements in America converted large numbers of the lower-class masses into lives that involved frugality, hard work, and respectability. Historians have pointed out that although revivalism did not fully accept the Calvinist theology of the Puritans, the movement was in thorough agreement with "the Puritan concern for a rigorous public and private moral code" (Gaer and Siegel, 1964:190; see also Cowing, 1968:641–42). Any indication of sexual permissiveness was attacked in the interests of protecting the sanctity of marriage and the home. The religious groups that grew out of revivalism as well as those that descended from Puritanism greatly influenced the moral tone of the United States. One reflection of this was in the materials people read. As Joseph Gaer and Ben Siegel (1964), authorities on religion and literature, have pointed out, "So successfully did evangelical Protestantism impose its views on literature that nineteenth-century American fiction was almost totally devoid of illicit love at a time when Europe's romantic writers were making it a central theme" (p. 190).

Historian Edmund S. Morgan (1966) cautions, however, against the popular assumption that the Puritans were ascetics or prudes. They viewed human sexuality in a positive way as a creation of God to be enjoyed within marriage according to God's law. But they urged watchfulness so that human love would not be permitted to assume greater importance than divine love. And although one result of the later revivalist movements was increasingly stricter control over sexuality—especially female sexuality—there was no attempt to desexualize women totally. It was left to nineteenth-century Victorianism to try something like that.

The Victorian Period

During the Victorian period, women were taught that no decent woman had sexual desires; only "loose" women enjoyed sex. Married women were expected to tolerate coitus as a wifely duty and a necessary indulgence of their husbands' "animal nature." As much as possible, respectable women were protected from all that might add to their knowledge of sex; they were to be kept innocent. Newspapers in some cases refused to publish news of births (though marriages and deaths were published), and pregnant women were ashamed to be seen publicly in what was euphemistically called "a delicate condition." Female physicians were rare, and many women delayed essential medical examinations and treatment rather than endure the embarrassment of having their bodies seen and touched by a male. Some doctors tried to help the situation by having dummies in their offices so that a woman could point to the corresponding areas that were troubling her in her own body (Graham-Murray, 1966:153).

America's first female physician, Dr. Elizabeth Blackwell, was one person who spoke out against the misconceptions of women's sexuality and urged women to have a positive regard for their bodies, including their sexual functioning. She pointed out that the notion that women did not feel sexual passion came about because women of higher social status had been taught that sexual passion was "lust" and "sin." Therefore, they tended to *deny* their natural feelings because of a sense of shame. In contrast, she argued, women of lesser privilege who were not restrained by social conventions showed themselves capable of the same unbridled sexual impulses as the men to whom they related, proving sexual disinterest was *not* something innate to women. Blackwell expressed concern that the woman of her day had "not been taught that sexual passion is love, even more than lust." "The growth and indications of her own nature she is taught to condemn," Blackwell continued, "instead of to respect them as foreshadowing that mighty impulse towards maternity which will place her nearest to the Creator if reverently accepted" (1894, reprinted in Cott, 1972:303).

As guardians of virtue, women of the Victorian era were also expected to be characterized by refined speech. References to anything related to sex or parts of the human body must be expurgated from their vocabularies or spoken of in euphemisms. For example, respectable women substituted words such as *lower extremities* or *limbs* in speaking of legs—even if they were referring to table legs or the legs of a piano. The word *breast* was also taboo; in the presence of ladies, it was proper to refer to a *bosom* of chicken at the dinner table. Both the clothing styles and furniture styles of the period showed a desire to cover up any hint of nakedness, with even the "limbs" of furniture often wearing ruffles and skirts.

Censors abounded. Eager to save society, such crusaders even sought to remove all earthy or sexual references from great works of art. Noah Webster in 1833 issued a special edition of the Bible in which offensive words (such as *womb, belly,* or *teat*) were removed or changed and all sexual references were blurred and made as inexplicit as possible. For example, the testicles were referred to as "peculiar members" or "secrets." Thomas Bowdler's nineteenth-century *Family Shakespeare* was another attempt to take great writings and make them tame and decent enough for women and children. With abandonment, he mutilated the great plays of Shakespeare, cutting out all that in Bowdler's opinion was offensive and coarse (Rugoff, 1971).

There seemed no end to prudery. The first museum in the United States endeavored to protect modesty by having separate visiting days for ladies so that they would be spared the embarrassment of viewing nude statues and paintings in the presence of men. And in England, Lady Gough in her 1863 *Etiquette* wrote that the perfect hostess should make sure that "the works of male and female authors be properly separated on her bookshelves." It was considered indecent for books by male and female authors to rest side by side unless the authors happened to be married to each other (Rugoff, 1971:61, 111).

However, scholars are quick to point out that the notion of Victorian prudery was nothing but a myth if one considers society as a *whole.* The congested conditions of the cities in the wake of the industrial revolution, in which working-class families were crowded together in deplorable, subhuman conditions, constantly threw persons of both sexes together in such a way that sexual relations were difficult to avoid. James Graham-Murray in his book *A History of Morals* refers to the communal dormitories of nineteenth-century England in which there was no segregation by sex. Men, women, boys,

With large numbers of young women laboring for meager wages, factory owners took full advantage of the situation. (The Bettmann Archive, Inc.)

and girls who worked together in the factories also slept together at night on piles of dirty straw in hovels called "padding kens." Graham-Murray also points out that it was legal at that time to have intercourse with any girl over 12 years of age. With large numbers of young girls and women laboring for meager wages in their factories, factory owners and managers took full advantage of the situation. Prostitution flourished. "During the Victorian age the supply of prostitutes in proportion to the size of the population was greater than ever before or since," writes Graham-Murray (1966:149, 152). Pornographic materials were also widely distributed in Victorian England, especially pornography that featured bizarre acts and torture.

How could all this occur in a society so obsessed with sexual morality and prudery? The Victorian middle and upper classes were concerned about one aspect of sexual morality only—female chastity. Perhaps never in history did the double standard enjoy wider acceptance. Wives tolerated their husbands' extramarital affairs and visits to prostitutes as a necessary evil in view of men's supposedly greater sexual needs and stronger passions. For unmarried men, prostitution was even considered a positive good; it provided a means of sexual outlet. Single young men could thereby satisfy their sexual urges without degrading respectable women who were in the pool of eligible marriage prospects. At the same time, there were cases of moralists who advised men to "test the virtue" of young women they courted; and if a woman responded to amorous advances, she was to be spurned as unworthy (Rugoff, 1971:49).

Changes in Female Sexual Behavior

In view of this historical perspective, it is easy to see that the major place for change (whether in the "sex revolution" around the 1920s or the "sex evolution" afterward) would likely be in the area of female sexuality. And this is exactly what various sociological studies have shown. We are not saying that changes have not also occurred among males because there *are* certain changes—for example, a lowering in the percentage of males who have their first experience of sexual intercourse with a prostitute. However, the *greatest* changes in premarital sexual behavior have been changes among females.

Sociological studies that focus on such changes have *not* been attempts to "count virgins" in order to demonstrate that things are getting either better or worse (depending on one's personal value position). Rather, sociologists are interested in studying current social phenomena, contrasting them with the past and then trying to find out *why* changes occur and what they *mean*.

PREMARITAL SEX TODAY

Some sociologists have suggested that the term *premarital sex* implies sexual intercourse between two persons who will eventually wed one another or who at least will marry someone eventually. They suggest that the general notion of sexual behavior outside of marriage might be better described as *nonmarital sex*. However, since most studies of the sex behavior of nonmarried persons use the term *premarital* without assuming that marriage is in everybody's future, we

will use the same terminology as we examine some of the research on this topic.

Signs of Change During the 1960s

We've already seen that the incidence of premarital sexual intercourse remained much the same from around the time of World War I through the 1950s. But by the late sixties and early seventies, sociologists were beginning to find evidence of a rise in the incidence of premarital sex and a lowering of the age at which sexual intercourse first occurred (Kantner and Zelnik, 1972; Bell and Chaskes, 1970; Christensen and Gregg, 1970; Clayton and Bokemeier, 1980). A marked reduction in the age at which first coitus occurred was found in a study of West German adolescents, with a particularly big jump in the percentage of both male and female 16-year-olds who had experienced sexual intercourse.

Especially striking to German sociologists Gunter Schmidt and Volkmar Sigusch (1972) were the parallel changes in sexual behavior in the United States and Germany during both the 1920s and the 1960s. Furthermore, there was a corresponding rise in premarital coitus during those two time periods in other industrialized countries, such as England and France (Schmidt and Sigusch, 1972; Chesser, 1957; French Institute of Public Opinion, 1961). Were these happenings mere coincidences, or do they show us something?

A number of sociologists suggest that such patterns do indeed have something to say to us. They can help us to see that social factors are involved even in such personal matters as sexual intercourse. The times and places in which we live and the persons with whom we associate have much to do with how we think about premarital sex and what we do about it. It is not simply an individual, private decision.

Comparing Two Periods of Significant Change

There is some debate about exactly when the first period of increased sexual permissiveness began, with some sociologists saying the 1920s and others suggesting several years earlier (Smith, 1973), but there is general agreement that it occurred sometime around World War I. Ira Reiss (1973) singles out the period 1915–1920 to be compared with the years 1965–1970. Both five-year periods were times of rapid social change, and both were *starting times* for increases in sexual permissiveness that would continue for at least another five years.

World War I marked the end of one era and the beginning of another. As Reiss points out, "Historically, this period appeared as a culmination of trends toward making the United States a modern, industrial nation," adding that the increase in female nonvirginity at this time "seemingly was part and parcel of an overall societal change occurring in all major social institutions." Similarly, in the mid-1960s, the United States was again involved in another major war, Vietnam, and in addition was undergoing another change into a different kind of society, a postindustrial society. Reiss writes: "the postindustrial society is usually distinguished by its concern for the equitable distribution of rights and privileges whereas the industrial society is primarily concerned with the production of goods and services." During both the 1915–1920 and the 1965–1970 periods, doubts and questions were raised about society, its values, and its morals. Some sociologists viewed this as a rebellion on the part of youth and a rejection of norms imposed upon them by adults, including sexual norms. It was a movement away from the traditional roles assigned to youth as "dependent and inexperienced learners," with emphasis instead on a new self-definition in which young people came to view themselves as a social and political force in their own right. "The result was a radical rejection of the societal infantilization of youth and an emphasis on a new autonomy," write Schmidt and Sigusch (1972:42–43).

They suggest that at least in West Germany, there were probably two reasons that sexuality played such a key role in this process: (1) the conflict between restrictive sexual norms and the strong sexual desires of youth and (2) a feeling that sexual prohibitions are demonstrative and symbolic of overall "societal tendencies toward the infantilization of youth." Demanding sexual freedom is a way of demanding other freedoms as well. Schmidt and Sigusch write: "A society which denies legal sexuality to those of its members who have the strongest sexual desire creates the preconditions for making sexuality the central problem in generation conflict and for instrumentalizing sexuality as a weapon and provocative challenge in the conflict."

At the same time, from the vantage point of the United States, Ira Reiss (1973) suggests that what may appear to be a rebellion against adult values is, in reality, "an actualization of rather traditional American values . . . equalitarianism, openness, honesty, legitimation of choice, autonomy, happiness, pleasure, love, affection, and experimentation." These values, including attempts to implement them in the sexual realm, have deep roots in the past. Historian William O'-Neill (1967), for example, has suggested that the late-nineteenth-century debates over divorce and the victory of the prodivorce forces in the early years of the present century meant a triumph for an individualistic approach to marriage. This triumph was on the cutting edge of a new outlook on morality.

In comparing the commonly called "sexual revolutions" beginning during the two time periods under discussion (around the time of World War I and in the latter half of the sixties), we should keep in mind that there have been other periods with a high incidence of premarital sexual activity and there will doubtless be others, with periods of lower incidence in between. This raises the possibility of a cyclical pattern over history (with highs and lows of premarital sexual intercourse) rather than a linear pattern (a continually increasing incidence of premarital sexual intercourse over time).

Some evidence of such a cyclical pattern showed up when social historian Daniel Scott Smith (1973) examined historical records to compare the percentage of white American first births that occurred within nine months of marriage during different periods of history. He found that prior to our own century, the peak period of premarital pregnancy occurred in the late 1700s, with lows occurring in the mid-seventeenth and mid-nineteenth centuries. With certain variations, a similar cycle was found in Western European premarital pregnancy and illegitimacy data as well.

Much more research needs to be done to explain what the probable upsurge in premarital sex meant during earlier periods; but, for the two time periods highlighted in our own century, the desire for *autonomy*—for control over one's own sexual destiny—stands out as a major factor.

Moving Away from the Double Standard

Having focused on the quest for autonomy among youth, both around the time of World War I and again in the 1960s, we cannot pass over that other segment of the population which also made new demands for autonomy during these same two time periods—*women.*

Women began to insist on their right to control their own lives rather than being dependent upon and subordinate to men. The feminist movement of the early decades of the twentieth century and the women's movement which received much of its impetus from the 1963 publication of Betty Friedan's book *The Feminine Mystique* coincide with the two periods of a greater incidence of premarital sexual intercourse. In saying this, we are not implying that feminism "causes" premarital sexual acitivity to increase, nor that conversely an increase in premarital sex will "cause" feminism to emerge. (In fact, women active in the early suffrage movement tended themselves to be quite conservative on the topic of sexuality.) The link between feminism and sexual freedom is simply that cluster of values mentioned earlier, particularly the *quest for autonomy* (the right to individual choice and self-direction for all persons) and *egalitarianism,* which insists that women and men deserve equal treatment and which, therefore, demolishes the arguments for the old double standard.

Continuing Changes

A movement toward a single standard does not *necessarily* mean a movement toward greater sexual permissiveness. It simply means that women and men are expected to hold the same standard, whether that standard is total abstinence, total permissiveness, or something in between.

However, during the 1970s, the movement already evident during the 1960s continued in the same direction: toward greater permissiveness for women. This is particularly evident in the research findings of sociologists John Kantner and Melvin Zelnik. As authorities on the dynamics of population growth and change, they were interested in finding out the extent to which adolescent women were engaging in sexual intercourse, practicing contraception, and experiencing pregnancy. In their 1971 study, the first of three, they found that 46 percent of young women were no longer virgins at age 19. In contrast, Kinsey's 1953 volume had indicated that only 20 percent of the women in his sample had experienced sexual intercourse by age 20.

Zelnik and Kantner found that the proportion of unmarried women who had experienced sexual intercourse by age 19 continued to climb through the decade of the seventies—from the 1971 figure of 46 percent to 59.5 percent in 1976 to 69 percent in 1979. Based on national probability samples, their three studies showed that taken as a whole, young women in the 15- to 19-years-of-age category at the end of the decade were much more sexually active than were young women in this same age range at the begin-

TABLE 5-A Percentage of women aged 15–19 who ever had intercourse before marriage, by marital status and race, United States, 1979, 1976, and 1971

MARITAL STATUS AND AGE	1979			1976			1971		
	TOTAL	WHITE	BLACK	TOTAL	WHITE	BLACK	TOTAL	WHITE	BLACK
All									
%	49.8	46.6	66.2	43.4	38.3	66.3	30.4	26.4	53.7
(N)	(1,717)	(1,034)	(683)	(1,452)	(881)	(571)	(2,739)	(1,758)	(981)
Ever-married									
%	86.7	86.2	91.2	86.3	85.0	93.9	55.0	53.2	72.7
(N)	(146)	(106)	(40)	(154)	(121)	(33)	(227)	(174)	(53)
Never-married*									
Total	46.0	42.3	64.8	39.2	33.6	64.3	27.6	23.2	52.4
15	22.5	18.3	41.4	18.6	13.8	38.9	14.4	11.3	31.2
16	37.8	35.4	50.4	28.9	23.7	55.1	20.9	17.0	44.4
17	48.5	44.1	73.3	42.9	36.1	71.0	26.1	20.2	58.9
18	56.9	52.6	76.3	51.4	46.0	76.2	39.7	35.6	60.2
19	69.0	64.9	88.5	59.5	53.6	83.9	46.4	40.7	78.3
Age at First Intercourse (All)									
Mean	16.2	16.4	15.5	16.1	16.3	15.6	16.4	16.6	15.9
(N)	(933)	(478)	(455)	(726)	(350)	(376)	(936)	(435)	(501)

*Ns are not shown for each single year of age in order to simplify the presentation; N≥ 87 for each age-race cell among the never-married.
NOTE: In this table, figures refer to the household population of standard metropolitan statistical areas (SMSAs). Base excludes those for whom no information was obtained on premarital intercourse. Percentages are computed from weighted data. "White" includes the relatively small number of women of races other than black. Except where indicated, the base excludes those who did not respond to the question analyzed in the table. Absolute numbers shown in parentheses are unweighted sample Ns.
SOURCE: Melvin Zelnik and John F. Kantner, "Sexual Activity, Contraceptive Use and Pregnancy Among Metropolitan-Area Teenagers: 1971–1979," *Family Planning Perspectives*, 12, September/October 1980, p. 231.

ning of the decade (Kantner and Zelnik, 1972; Zelnik and Kantner, 1977, 1980; Zelnik, Kantner, and Ford, 1981). In 1971, less than 1 out of 3 had experienced sexual intercourse during this period of adolescence; but by 1979, half of the young women aged 15 to 19 were no longer virgins. The average age of first intercourse in 1979 was 16. (See Table 5-A.)

In their 1979 survey, Zelnik and Kantner also interviewed 17- to 21-year-old men (an age category chosen because their earlier surveys had shown that the sexual partners of young women tended to be about two years older than the women themselves). As Table 5-B shows, 70 percent of these young men reported having experienced sexual intercourse. Among the unmarried 17-year-olds, just under 56 percent reported having engaged in sexual intercourse.

Contrary to what many parents and other adults believe about the association of adolescent sexual activity with automobile usage, Zelnik and Kantner (1977:60) found that "more than three out of four white and black respondents report that they have had intercourse in their own or their partner's home, or in the home of a friend or relative, regardless of whether it was the first, most recent, or only time that they have had intercourse." If the sexual activity took place outside a home, it was for blacks most likely to have occurred in a hotel or motel; for whites, automobiles and out-of-doors were other favorite spots. First intercourse was most likely to occur in the summer.

Studies of college students have also indicated a rise in premarital sexual experience—particularly among women (King, Balswick, and Robinson, 1977). Table 5-C shows the results of four comparative studies of students at a large Southern state university conducted between 1965 and 1980. Notice that slightly more than 1 out of 4 college

TABLE 5-B Percentage of men aged 17–21 who ever had intercourse before marriage, by marital status and race, 1979

MARITAL STATUS AND AGE	TOTAL	WHITE	BLACK
All			
%	70.3	69.6	74.6
(N)	(917)	(567)	(350)
Ever-married			
%	82.7	83.3	72.8
(N)	(74)	(58)	(16)
Never-married*			
Total	68.9	67.8	74.7
17	55.7	54.5	60.3
18	66.0	63.6	79.8
19	77.5	77.1	79.9
20	81.2	80.7	85.7
21	71.2	68.0	89.4

*N > 33 for each age-race cell among the never-married.
SOURCE: Melvin Zelnik and John F. Kantner, "Sexual Activity, Contraceptive Use and Pregnancy Among Metropolitan-Area Teenagers: 1971–1979," *Family Planning Perspectives*, 12, September/October 1980, p. 233.

TABLE 5-C Percentage of 1965, 1970, 1975 and 1980 college students having pre-marital intercourse

YEAR	MALES		FEMALES	
	%	N	%	N
1965	65.1	129	28.7	115
1970	65.0	136	37.3	158
1975	73.9	115	57.1	275
1980	77.4	168	63.5	230

SOURCE: Ira E. Robinson and Davor Jedlicka, "Change in Sexual Attitudes and Behavior of College Students from 1965 to 1980: A Research Note," *Journal of Marriage and the Family* 44 (February 1982):238.

women in the 1965 sample had engaged in premarital sexual intercourse; but by 1980, that figure had jumped to 2 out of 3.

Nonintercourse behaviors also increased during this time period, with 73 percent of female students in the 1975 and 1980 samples reporting they engaged in heavy petting, compared to 34 percent in 1965. Among male students, the percentage was already high in 1965 (71 percent) but had jumped to 85 percent by 1980 (Robinson and Jedlicka, 1982).

Another study, which compared the premarital sexual behaviors of both students and nonstudents in the age range of 18 to 23 years, was conducted at the University of Wisconsin and the surrounding community. The research included an examination of the prevalence of nine kinds of sexual behavior and the ages at which males and females began each activity (DeLamater and Mac-Corquodale, 1979). Findings from this research may be seen in Table 5-D.

Data from national studies conducted during the 1980s also provide evidence of changes in women's premarital sexual experience over recent decades. The 1982 National Survey of Family Growth revealed that two-thirds of married women in the United States in the age range of 15 to 44 years had had sexual intercourse before marriage. Women who married between 1960 and 1964 were considerably more likely to have entered marriage as virgins (48 percent) than were women who married between 1970 and 1974 (28 percent). Among women who married between 1975 and 1979, just over 1 out of 5 reported not having engaged in sexual intercourse before marriage. The research also indicated than women who married dur-

TABLE 5-D Lifetime sexual behavior by gender and educational status and average age at which each premarital behavior began

| | MALE | | | | FEMALE | | | |
| | STUDENT | | NONSTUDENT | | STUDENT | | NONSTUDENT | |
Behavior	%	Age*	%	Age*	%	Age*	%	Age*
Necking	97	14.2	98	13.9	99	14.8	99	14.9
French kissing	93	15.3	95	15.1	95	15.8	95	16.0
Breast fondling	92	15.8	92	15.5	93	16.6	93	16.6
Male fondling of female genitals	86	16.6	87	16.3	82	17.2	86	17.5
Female fondling of male genitals	82	16.8	84	16.7	78	17.4	81	17.8
Genital apposition	77	17.1	81	16.8	72	17.6	78	17.9
Intercourse	75	17.5	79	17.2	60	17.9	72	18.3
Male oral contact with female genitals	60	18.2	68	17.7	59	18.1	67	18.6
Female oral contact with male genitals	61	18.1	70	17.8	54	18.1	63	18.8

*Includes only those who have engaged in the behavior
SOURCE: John DeLamater and Patricia MacCorquodale, *Premarital Sexuality: Attitudes, Relationships, Behavior* (Madison: University of Wisconsin Press, 1979), p. 59.

CHANGES IN PREMARITAL SEXUAL IDEOLOGY

In the contemporary period the ideal of sexual restraint has weakened, and the possibilities for sexual expression have been broadened. The ideology of individual development has entered the sexual sphere, condemning relationships that limit individual growth or possibilities for exploring new experiences. In this view jealousy is bad, a possessive attempt to own another person and limit that person's freedom to grow. Sexual restraints are rejected as artificial restrictions on experience, and sexual experimentation is valued because it opens the self to new experiences.

SOURCE: Ann Swidler, "Love and Adulthood in American Culture," in *Themes of Work and Love in Adulthood,* Neil J. Smelser and Erik H. Erikson eds. (Cambridge: Harvard University Press, 1980), p. 139.

---

ing the 1975–1979 period were far more likely than were women who married in the early 1960s to have had their first experience of sexual intercourse *three or more years* before their marriage. This finding is indicative of both the later median age of marriage that has been occurring and the drop in the average age of first intercourse that has also been taking place (Bachrach and Horn, 1985).

In another study, the 1983 National Survey of Unmarried Women, which focused on single women in their twenties, it was found that 82 percent had experienced sexual intercourse (Tanfer and Horn, 1985a).

Attitudes about the *morality* of premarital sexual behavior has also undergone considerable change over recent decades. Data from five national surveys conducted between 1972 and 1978 by the National Opinion Research Center indicate that the percentage of respondents believing there is nothing wrong with premarital intercourse increased from 27 percent to nearly 39 percent over the six-year time span (Singh, 1980). And in a 1985 Gallup poll of adults aged 18 and older, only 1 out of 10 had no opinion when asked if it was wrong for persons to have sexual relations before mar-

riage. Of those with an opinion, 58 percent said they did not believe premarital sex was wrong. In 1969, only 24 percent held that opinion (*The Gallup Report*, June 1985, no. 237, p. 28).

PREMARITAL SEX, PREGNANCY, AND CONTRACEPTION

Along with the increase in premarital sexual experience has come an increase in the likelihood of premarital pregnancy. In their three national studies of unmarried young women, Zelnik and Kantner (1980:230) found that "the proportion of all teenage women who have ever been premaritally pregnant rose from nine percent in 1971 to 13 percent in 1976 and to 16 percent in 1979." The percentage of these women whose pregnancy ended with an abortion rose from 23 percent in 1971 to 37 percent in 1979, while the percentage who experienced a live birth dropped from 67 percent to 49 percent over that same time period. (See Table 5-E.) According to government statistics, 686,605 births to unmarried women took place in 1981 (*Monthly Vital Statistics Report*, vol. 32, no. 9, December,

TABLE 5-E Percentage distribution of women aged 15–19 who ever experienced a premarital first pregnancy and were unmarried at the time the pregnancy was resolved, by pregnancy outcome, according to race, 1979, 1976 and 1971*

PREGNANCY OUTCOME	1979			1976			1971		
	TOTAL (N = 291)	WHITE (N = 111)	BLACK (N = 180)	TOTAL (N = 178)	WHITE (N = 52)	BLACK (N = 126)	TOTAL (N = 224)	WHITE (N = 39)	BLACK (N = 185)
Live birth	49.4	38.6	71.4	55.8	32.4	84.9	67.1	44.0	83.5
Stillbirth or miscarriage	14.0	16.4	9.0	11.7	15.9	6.5	9.5	8.1	10.4
Induced abortion	36.6	45.0	19.6	32.5	51.7	8.6	23.4	47.9	6.1
Total	100.0	100.0	100.0	100.0	100.0	100.0	100.0	100.0	100.0

*Excludes respondents pregnant at time of interview
SOURCE: Melvin Zelnik and John F. Kantner, "Sexual Activity, Contraceptive Use and Pregnancy Among Metropolitan-Area Teenagers: 1971–1979," *Family Planning Perspectives* 12 (September/October 1980):234.

1983). Teenage pregnancy rates in the United States are considerably higher than those in most other developed countries (Jones et al., 1985).

Zelnik and Kantner (1980) found that premarital pregnancies among the young women in their studies had increased in spite of the finding that more young persons were using some method of birth control and doing so more consistently. They attributed this increase in pregnancies at least partially to a decline in usage of the most effective methods of contraception, the pill and IUD (probably because of the concern over their side effects), and an increase in the usage of the least effective methods, such as withdrawal (Zelnik, Kantner, and Ford, 1981:177–178).

Deciding About Contraception

A team of sociologists who studied a sample of unmarried university women found that young women who sought contraceptive advice were likely to be those who (1) believed in the right of sexual choice, (2) felt assured they could make such a choice, and (3) were involved in a relationship with some degree

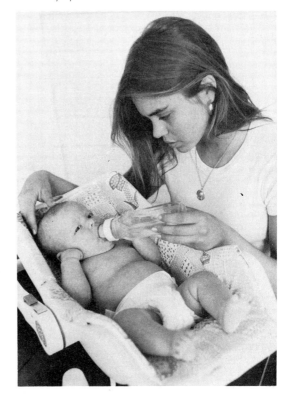

Despite an increased use of contraceptives, the number of teenage pregnancies is still high. (© Rhoda Sidney/Monkmeyer)

NOT TOO SOON

Concerned about the rising level of premarital pregnancies, some agencies and educators have not only urged sexually active young people to use effective contraceptive methods but have also urged adolescents to see the advantages in sexual abstinence. The following material—prepared by the education department of Planned Parenthood of Santa Cruz County (California)—is excerpted from an information sheet that also stresses that "everyone" is not having sexual intercourse and that many who have engaged in premarital sex wish they had delayed having their initial experiences.

GOOD REASONS TO CHOOSE ABSTINENCE

Medical Reasons

• Abstinence is the only method of birth control that is 100% effective and 100% free of side effects.

• Abstinence reduces the risk of unwanted pregnancy. ("Reduces" because pregnancy can occur without sexual intercourse if sperm is ejaculated near the entrance to the vagina during heavy petting.)

• Abstinence reduces the risk of contracting herpes, gonorrhea and other sexually transmissible diseases. (STDs can be passed by sexual contact with an infected person through contact of any mucous membranes or saliva.)

• Abstinence reduces the risk of cervical cancer. Cancer researchers are now suggesting a connection between early sexual activity, multiple sexual partners and increased incidence of cervical cancer in women under 25.

Relationship Reasons
A couple may find that delaying sexual intercourse contributes in a positive way to their relationship.

• Abstaining may allow a couple time to develop a deeper friendship. They may spend more time talking, building mutual interests, sharing their good times with other friends and establishing an intimacy that is other than sexual.

• Abstaining can be a test of love. Counter to the old line "you would if you loved me," abstinence can allow time to test the endurance of love beyond the first attraction and before having sexual intercourse.

• Abstaining may contribute to teaching people to be better lovers; to explore a wide range of ways to express love and sexual feelings.

Personal Reasons

• Abstinence can be a sign of real emotional maturity and integrity. Many young women and men report feeling pressured into having sexual intercourse before they are ready. It requires maturity and honesty to be able to resist the pressure of someone you love in order to make a decision that is consistent with personal values and needs.

SOURCE: *Family Life Educator* 3, no. 1 (Fall, 1984):33.

of serious commitment. In this model, the starting point is one's own mental attitude (acceptance of sexuality), which is *then* applied to sexual behavior with a dating partner. (Reiss, Banwart, and Foreman, 1975:628).

Sociologist Prudence Rains (1971) suggests a different sequence in which the relationship itself is the starting point, and this in turn shapes attitudes and behavior. Rains also recognizes the part "moral ambivalence" plays in the decision to use or not to use contraception. In studying a sample of unwed mothers, she found that those young women who engage in premarital intercourse even though such behavior goes against their moral convictions are the ones tending not to use contraception or to use it only inconsistently. Thus, this model, like that of Reiss and his colleagues, emphasizes the part played by an *acceptance* of sexual activity and one's own sexuality. However, Rains suggests a pattern that with some variation seems to go like this: In the first stage, the young woman experiences feelings of love for someone that "provides a rationale for sexual intimacy" (DeLamater and Mac-Corquodale, 1978:235). Second, she enters an exclusive dating relationship. Third, she begins rethinking her sexual standards to the point of concluding that sexual intercourse with her partner would be right for her. And fourth, she accepts the possibility of sexual involvement in future relationships. When her thinking reaches this fourth stage, according to Rains, the woman is most likely to become a consistent user of contraceptives.

On the basis of their own study of sexually active young women, sociologists John De-Lamater and Patricia MacCorquodale (1978) found moderate support for the Rains model with its emphasis on how a young woman reformulates her sexual standards to line up with her experience. They found somewhat less support for the other model (Reiss et al., 1975) with its focus on the way prior-held sexual standards influence sexual activity and contraception. Yet, since neither model appears to tell the whole story, DeLamater and MacCorquodale conclude that further research is likely to show that "premarital contraceptive use is influenced by both of the

Seeking contraceptive advice appears to be influenced by two factors: an accepting attitude toward premarital sexual activity and one's actual experience with a partner. (Sybil Shelton/Monkmeyer)

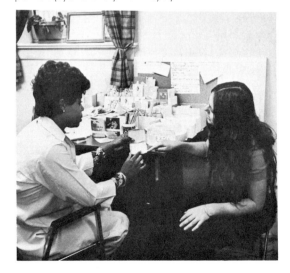

types of factors emphasized in the two models," namely, one's own personal attitudes about sexuality as well as one's actual experience with a partner.

Other research by MacCorquodale (1984) has shown that attitudes toward gender roles are associated with attitudes toward premarital contraception. She found that both women and men who held egalitarian gender-role attitudes were more likely than were other persons to believe that contraception should be shared by both partners. More frequent and effective usage of contraception as well as a greater likelihood that discussions about birth control had taken place prior to sexual activity were also found among persons holding egalitarian gender-role attitudes.

The "Nice-Girl" Dilemma

It's certainly possible to affirm our sexuality and yet, for religious or moral reasons, refrain from premarital sexual activity. It's quite a different matter, however, to be unwilling to admit even to oneself one's own sexual feelings and the fact that one is engaging in premarital sexual intercourse when such is actually the case (G. Fox, 1974). Yet, such ambivalence and denial are not unusual, especially among young women, because of the different "sexual scripts" males and females tend to follow as a result of divergent socialization (Laws and Schwartz, 1977).

Sociologist Greer Litton Fox (1977a), for example, points out how society's idealization of the "nice girl" can influence a sexually active young woman not to use contraceptives. She explains:

> Regular use of contraception requires preparedness and preplanning, acknowledgement prior to coitus of the probability of coitus, and a willingness to take responsibility for sexual behavior. But the only excuses a young woman may give for sexual intercourse prior to marriage and still claim some vestige of niceness to herself are coercion (rape) and, more importantly here, to be so uncontrollably in love as to be virtually swept away by the spontaneous and unrestrainable passions of the particular moment. Obviously, to be prepared for coitus with contraceptives would give lie to the rationale that each act of intercourse was unanticipated and unplanned, merely a temporary and transitory lapse of virtue. In short, in order to be responsible to her "virtue" or "niceness," the nice girl construct requires that a woman be irresponsible sexually with regard to contraceptive use. (p. 816)

Such a young woman faces a dilemma. Because a "nice girl" doesn't engage in sex before marriage, to use contraceptives is to declare to herself, her partner, and the physician, clinic, or drugstore where she obtains the contraceptives that she *is* engaging in sexual intercourse and is therefore *not* a "nice girl." Yet, if she neglects to use contraceptives, she may find herself announcing to the world in another way that she is not a "nice girl"—by becoming premaritally pregnant. (See also Shah and Zelnik, 1981.)

Risking Pregnancy: Costs and Rewards

In her book, *Taking Chances,* sociologist Kristin Luker (1975) describes contraceptive risk taking as "a weighing process between a series of fairly well-defined costs and benefits" (p. 36). The process she calls *decision-making theory* is in many respects similar to what we describe as *exchange* (or *cost-reward*) *theory* in Chapter 1 of this book. The basic presupposition is that humans are goal-seeking creatures who wish to gain benefits while keeping costs low. Luker's focus is on the internal processes taking place as a person sorts out factors that appear costly and those that appear rewarding.

"In making decisions about contraception [women] try to attain many goals, only one of which is not getting pregnant," asserts Luker in discussing her study of women who had visited an abortion clinic to have their pregnancies terminated. She points out that although bearing a child might seem a cost to be avoided, there are also costs in ending a pregnancy through abortion or preventing it through contraception. At the time of her study, costs associated with abortion included financial costs, social disapproval, being required to go through psychiatric testing, and being labeled "disturbed" or "having personality disorders."

When it comes to using contraception to prevent pregnancy in the first place, costs are again perceived by many women. Some costs listed by Luker are (1) the costs of acknowledging one is engaging in sexual intercourse, even being known as "sexually available"; (2) the costs to romantic spontaneity; (3) the difficulties often encountered in trying to obtain and then maintain effective contraception; (4) the costs of facing male attitudes that may include indifference, lack of cooperation, trickery (telling a woman she doesn't need contraception because the man has had a vasectomy), opposition to the use of contraception, and male insistence on dominance in the relationship; and (5) biological and medical costs, such as experiencing the side effects of some contraceptive methods.

On the other hand, Luker (1975, chap. 4) found that at the time of taking a contraceptive risk, some women saw not costs but rather potential benefits in becoming pregnant—even though later they changed their minds and sought abortions. Since it is gen-

erally believed that a premarital pregnancy can be nothing but costly, the fact that some women anticipated such an event as possibly rewarding may seem surprising. What benefits could they expect? Some women were convinced that "being pregnant proves that you are a woman." As Luker explains, "To be pregnant is to be at the core of the traditional definition of the female role, and it is one way of dealing with the new and sometimes frightening roles that society is demanding of women" (p. 66). Similarly, some women felt that becoming a mother would signify their worth as persons and saw pregnancy as a path to enhanced self-esteem, as well as providing someone (a baby) to need them and love them. Some took risks in an attempt to find out if they were fertile, especially if they had some reason to believe they might not be. "Fertility is like money in the bank," writes Luker, "it is nice to know it is there, even if there are no immediate plans to use it" (p. 69).

Some of the women in Luker's study anticipated rewards in their relationships with other people as a result of pregnancy. Some believed a pregnancy might force the male partner to define his commitment to the relationship and possibly marry the woman. Others thought of pregnancy as a way to punish their parents or to force them to pay attention to their daughter or recognize her as an independent adult. For some, becoming pregnant was a way of crying out for help from social agencies—a cry that was not likely to be ignored. Lastly, Luker found a few women who viewed taking chances as rewarding in itself, believing that "the risk of pregnancy brings an excitement of its own to the sexual act or enlivens an otherwise dull existence" (p. 76).

Luker concludes that in contraceptive risk taking, women are "tacitly bargaining with themselves . . . to determine the costs and benefits of contraception, the costs and benefits of pregnancy, and the likelihood that pregnancy will occur" (p. 85).

Males and Contraception

"Who should be responsible for contraception?" When sociologist Greer Litton Fox (1974) asked this question in a pilot study of 275 college students, nearly three-fourths replied that responsibility should be shared by both the male and female partners. However, when Fox looked closely at answers *female* students gave in a second pilot study that asked some related questions, she found that although the *ideal* of shared responsibility was so widely held, the reality was quite different. A high proportion of women felt that contraceptive responsibility falls primarily to the female. Some explained in pragmatic terms: "She's the one who could become pregnant—not *him.*" Some felt males didn't take contraception seriously. Some felt that male methods were less effective anyway but believed that males could at least share the responsibility by helping their female partners obtain and pay for contraceptives.

At the same time that these college women recognized the reality of the situation, they indicated both ambivalence about their own part in contraception (the "nice-girl" construct once again) and considerable resentment over having the burden of contraception placed disproportionately on their shoulders while men could go comparatively free. Fox tapped into this when she asked the women why many college men don't use contraceptives. "The respondents suggested first of all that men consider contraceptives a female responsibility," she writes, "second, that men won't use contraceptives because they get in the way of their own pleasure, and

third, that men don't care enough about what happens to the girl to bother with contraceptives" (p. 19).

Fox concludes that the use of contraceptives is perceived as having different meanings for the sexes. Young women tend to view their own part in contraception negatively, feeling that the need for them to take the responsibility means their male partners don't really care about them and that furthermore, there is some "vague moral taint" involved in obtaining contraceptives. However, in contrast, the women in Fox's study tended to attach positive meanings to male contraceptive use. She explains:

> The male's use of contraceptives or his sharing in their use is taken as a sign of extra caring, a proof of his commitment and love for his partner. Because the male partner himself loses little by not using contraception ("*he* is not stuck with a pregnancy") and indeed may actually stand to gain from not using them (thereby increasing his "pleasurable sensations"), when the male *does* use them he does so *gratis*, almost as a sacrifice. (p. 20)

In another study, Fox (1977b) found that among sexually experienced unmarried young women, those most likely to be effective users of contraception were those who held nontraditional gender-role attitudes along with a belief that they could control their own lives rather than remain at the mercy of external forces or "luck." However, she found that neither variable (nontraditional gender-role attitudes and sense of control) separately or jointly explained the contraceptive behavior of males. Fox emphasizes that "clearly, the male contraceptor needs more attention from researchers." (See also Edwards, 1987.)

One study of over four hundred white, black, and Hispanic male high school students in a large Northeastern city indicated that the majority had either not used contraception at last intercourse or had practiced withdrawal or relied on their partner's douching (Finkel and Finkel, 1975). Although two-thirds of the young men in this sample realized that douching was not a good method of contraception, less than one-third realized that pregnancy was possible even though withdrawal was practiced. (See Table 5-F.)

Of the 72 percent of sexually active respondents who said they had not used a condom during their most recent sexual experience, about one-fourth said they didn't feel contraception was important, another quarter said they believed their partner was using some method of contraception, 32 percent reported they hadn't had a condom with them at the time, and a final 16 percent said they believed their partner could not get pregnant at that particular time (Finkel and Finkel, 1975:259).

Contraceptive Negotiation

"Contraceptive practice, it must be emphasized, is an ongoing, two-party affair," writes psychiatry professor Warren B. Miller (1973), "and in the beginning of every sexual relationship (every stable relationship in particular), there are important negotiations that take place" (p. 200).

However, whether such negotiations actually take place seems to be problematic, judging from some of the materials just examined. At the same time, a study by sociologists Linda Thompson and Graham Spanier (1978) indicates that a partner's influence is a "strong contributor to contraceptive use in young adult men and women" (p. 490). According to Thompson and Spanier, "discussion with the sexual partner

TABLE 5-F Number and percent of correct responses to true-false statements on reproduction and contraception: high school study

STATEMENT	NO.	%
A douche (female washing herself after sexual intercourse) is a good method to prevent pregnancies. (F)	272	66.3
A male's sperm lives less than one day inside a woman. (F)	278	67.8
Rubbers (scumbags, condoms, bags) help prevent unwanted pregnancies. (T)	376	90.2
A female can most easily get pregnant just before her period begins. (F)	192	46.4
Rubbers (scumbags, condoms, bags) help prevent VD. (T)	313	75.4
During sexual intercourse, if a male takes out his penis before coming, his partner may get pregnant anyway. (T)	133	31.9

SOURCE: Adapted from Madelon Lubin Finkel and David J. Finkel, "Sexual and Contraceptive Knowledge, Attitudes, and Behavior of Male Adolescents," *Family Planning Perspectives* 7 (November/December 1975):257.

about contraception and sharing knowledge about contraception with the partner foster effective use of birth control."

If communication never begins or breaks down later, problems in the area of contraception are likely. After several years of observing women who sought prenatal care or abortions at the Stanford University Medical Center, Miller (1973) concluded that at a number of stages in a woman's sexual career she is most vulnerable to an unintended pregnancy. One such time for unmarried women is during the early stages of a relationship when a couple become sexually involved before a "contraceptive pattern" has been worked out through negotiation. Another vulnerable time is during a crisis in the relationship. "Even though two partners may

GUESS WHO'S BUYING CONDOMS?

In the 1970s, the women's health movement taught [women] to take responsibility for [their] own bodies and protect [themselves] from unwanted pregnancy and disease. In line with that lesson, more and more women are buying condoms—and at least one company is taking note and cashing in.

The Mentor Corporation, a Minneapolis-based company, is marketing a new line of condoms packaged in pastel colors and sold on women's-hygiene shelves in pharmacies.

About 40 percent of prophylactic buyers are women, says Al Mannino, Mentor's vice president of health-care products; ten years ago, according to research by Pharmacist Planning Services, the figure was less than 10 percent.

Concern about acquired immune deficiency syndrome (AIDS), along with fear of other sexually transmitted diseases, has created a new awareness of sexual risk. A recent update in the "Harvard Medical School Health Letter" suggests that anyone married or "securely monogamous" for fewer than several years could be susceptible to the disease when body fluids are exchanged during sex. For those at risk, condoms provide a measure of protection.

Condoms are also increasingly popular because of concern over the side effects associated with other forms of contraception. (Prophylactics are the third most common form of birth control in America—exceeded only by sterilization and the Pill.)

Mentor Corporation intends to capitalize on the trend by making its product available nationally; the company has even added a thin adhesive layer to the inside of each condom so that it won't slip off.

SOURCE: Cynthia Werthamer, *Ms.* XV (July 1986), p. 35.

have developed a working pattern of communication and cooperation regarding contraception," Miller points out, "either one may forget or simply abandon this previously established routine under the stress of a serious argument." Some women may at such times entertain a conscious or unconscious desire to become pregnant as a means of preventing the relationship from ending.

Another period of vulnerability is after a breakup between the partners. At such a time, for example, a woman might stop using oral contraceptives. "A surprise weekend or late effort to repair the broken relationship may find the woman contraceptively unprepared," writes Miller (p. 201).

Access to Information and Contraceptives

In spite of increased sexual activity and the large numbers of out-of-wedlock pregnancies occurring each year, many persons oppose sex education programs that provide contraceptive information. The advertising of condoms—even for the purpose of reducing the risks of sexually transmitted diseases—has long been banned in the United States (Redford et al., 1974). By 1987, however, in view of the health threat posed by AIDS, the Surgeon General and other concerned health officials were calling for an end to such advertising restrictions so that the public could be made more aware of the condom's function in disease prevention.

Uneasiness about premarital contraception remains. "If a daughter confides to her mother that she is shoplifting to support a drug habit, would you then advise the mother to instruct her daughter on how to shoplift without getting caught?" This question was addressed to the syndicated advice columnist "Dear Abby" (Van Buren, 1978) and expresses the reasoning of many adults who wish to limit the availability of contraception in the hopes that young persons will then be less likely to engage in sexual relations out of fear of the consequences. However, as sociologist Phillips Cutright (1972a) has pointed out, denial of access to contraception has *not* discouraged sexual activity among unmarried adolescents, and there is no reason to believe that "access to effective medically supervised contraception and abortion" will increase such activity. But such access could make a great difference in the numbers of premarital pregnancies occurring among adolescent young women.

PREMARITAL SEX, GENDER ROLES, AND SOCIALIST EXPERIMENTS

Sociologist Richard F. Tomasson (1970) suggests that "where females have greater equality and are subject to less occupational and social differentiation, the premarital sex codes will be more permissive than where the female's status is completely or primarily dependent on the status of her husband" (p. 180). If his proposition is correct, we would expect the socialist countries to have the most permissive sex codes because the equality of the sexes is an important part of socialist ideology. Such an ideology leaves no room for the double standard, which gives

premarital sexual privileges to males but not to females.

However, an egalitarian ideology could mean either that *both* males and females should be free to engage in premarital coitus or else that *neither* males nor females should be free to engage in premarital coitus. Several socialist experiments give evidence of a struggle between these two positions.

Soviet Union

Freedom in sexual matters, or discipline in sexual matters? This was the question Russia wrestled with repeatedly. In the early years after the 1917 Revolution, the Communist party followed the thinking of Marx and Engels in stressing that sex belongs to the *private* sphere of individual freedom rather than to the *public* sphere subject to regulation by the State. At the same time, the institution of the family was devalued and expected to wither away, along with other social institutions considered no longer necessary. As a result of all this, Russia had its own version of the "roaring twenties." A 1920 party journal carried an article asserting that "an unimaginable bacchanalia is going on . . . the best people are interpreting free love as free debauchery" (Geiger, 1968, p. 64).

Sociologist H. Kent Geiger (1968:66–71) points out that the peasants in particular simply accepted the new sexual freedom as "a gift of the Revolution," a "pleasure to be enjoyed to the full." Others believed the Revolution encouraged a more sophisticated view, in which the significance of sex was akin to swallowing a drink of water to quench physical thirst. And some suggested that "sexual property" should be held in common and shared along with all other kinds of property. Closely linked to the drink-of-water theory was what Geiger calls the "elemental-nature" view, which treated sex as merely an instinct to be satisfied. This view was rationalized on the basis of writings of Marx and Engels which emphasized "natural man."

Many persons viewed sexual permissiveness as a symbolic defiance of the entire old order, a patriotic means of opposing bourgeois morality. Others found still different ways to link sexual freedom with the communist cause. Some said they needed alternative outlets for sex drives because their devotion to the Revolution left no time for settling down with a family. Others said a permanent union involved too much risk because the spouse might later turn out to be uncommitted to the cause. Still others suggested that poverty justifies promiscuity because the poor can't maintain a family.

The notion of "free love" in the writings of Marx and Engels actually emphasized "freeing" love from *economic* concerns so that a man and woman could form a union based on deep feeling for one another rather than on other considerations. But the term *free* was widely misinterpreted, as was the idea of "love." Among the students, there arose the opinion that the way to enter into love was through sex. If good Marxists were to love, then they must realize that sexual attraction formed the base on which love could be built. If the sexual foundation didn't work out, the whole superstructure would topple.

Such rationalizations and the accompanying behavior troubled the older generation of Marxists. For one thing, it soon became clear that even in a social order that promised equality of the sexes, women were the least likely to benefit from the sexual anarchism being advocated by some. Through mockery and ridicule, young Communists used a new "male line," telling women they were not true comrades if they still followed bourgeois prejudices about sex outside of marriage. Lunacharski indignantly remarked, "The fright-

ened girl thinks she is acting like a marxist, like a leninist, if she denies no one" (quoted in Geiger, 1968:63).

However, the old values were still strong among the majority of the population, and many persons were genuinely concerned about the sexual excesses that seemed to follow in the wake of the overturned social order. Yet it was hard to come up with convincing reasons for sexual restraint in view of the way many young theorists had begun to interpret Marxist thought. Men, even party leaders, were engaging in sexual adventures that left helpless women pregnant and abandoned while the men went on their merry way, enjoying still more of the new freedoms. As Geiger points out, this problem caused deep distress among those who took seriously those teachings of Marxist philosophy that decried the exploitation of the weak by the strong.

One female writer suggested that a possible solution might lie in freeing women from enslavement to certain ideas, such as the quest for love and identity through attachment to men. The aim of Alexandra Kollontai was to "teach women not to put all their hearts and souls into the love for a man, but into the essential thing, creative work. . . . Love must not crush the woman's individuality, not bind her wings" (Rowbotham, 1972, chap. 6). She didn't deny that sex and love could or even should go hand in hand, but she wanted people to view them as separate feelings. In Kollontai's thought, a sexual union could be either prolonged or transient and still express love, totally apart from institutional forms. She argued that women had the right to enjoy sexual gratifications with a number of men, just as men felt they had such rights with regard to women (Geiger, 1968:62ff.; Rowbotham, 1972, chap. 6).

The new sexual freedom brought other

problems besides the exploitation of women. In Kollontai's words, "Contemporary love always sins in that, absorbing the thoughts and feelings of 'the two loving hearts' it at the same time isolates, separates off the loving pair from the collective" (quoted in Geiger 1968:63).

Energies diverted from the task of building the new society presented another problem. An ascetic wing of the party had emphasized this all along. Lenin, among others, argued that the Revolution "cannot tolerate orgiastic conditions . . . no weakening, no waste, no destruction of forces. Self-control, self-discipline, is not slavery, not even in love." He argued against the glass-of-water theory of sex as being contrary to the true meaning of *free love* in communist thought, which emphasized a union based on deep feeling and comradeship. His own opinion was that a normal man wouldn't drink out of a gutter nor out of a glass "with the rim greasy from many lips" (quoted in Geiger, 1968:84).

Others selectively used Freudian ideas to emphasize sublimation, arguing that a common pool of energy could express itself either in sexual activity or in socially constructive activity. Young people must redirect their sexual drives into the service of the Revolution. They were now told that preoccupation with sex was characteristic of capitalism and bourgeois society and not in keeping with the rigorous discipline needed to build communism. If, under capitalism, religion served as an opiate to deaden the sensitivities of the masses, sex served in a similar capacity and also had a narcotic effect (a statement of Zalkind, quoted in Geiger, 1968:85).

Thus, the pendulum began to swing the other way. During the 1920s, the cry was for human liberation and noninterference in sex as a private matter. But by the end of the twenties, the emphasis was on "social usefulness," with interference and regulation justified on the basis of Lenin's contention that sexual promiscuity was not a private and personal matter at all but rather a matter of social concern, one reason being the possibility of pregnancy (Geiger, 1968:84).

People's Republic of China

In China, the cultural revolution seems to have skipped the early stage of total sexual freedom that characterized the Soviet experience. Instead, the People's Republic, from the outset, upheld a stringent standard of premarital sexual abstinence for both sexes, along with faithfulness after marriage. Prostitution was abolished, and new jobs were provided for the prostitutes (Sidel, 1972,

The recent opening of China to Western trade and technology may be having some impact on attitudes toward sexuality; but, for the most part, the cultural revolution's standard of premarital abstinence remains intact. (Mimi Forsyth/Monkmeyer)

SEXUAL ATTITUDES IN CHINA TODAY

Female sexuality is still not a subject of public discussion. Among the intellectuals, "sexual revolution" is more a sign of decadence than a progressive and liberating force. Among the younger generations, especially college students, there is a growing interest in understanding female sexuality and sexual fulfillment in marriage.

In the People's Republic of China, one's personal and public lives are intertwined to such an extent that an undesirable personal style (usually referring to sexual behavior) is often detrimental to one's career and lifelong development. The loss of virginity before marriage or an extramarital affair is cause enough for social ostracism, job dismissal, or denial of promotion. Although it applies to both men and women, the effect is usually much more serious for the women.

SOURCE: Xiao Lu, "China: Feudal Attitudes, Party Control, and Half the Sky," in *Sisterhood Is Global*, ed. by Robin Morgan (Garden City, NY: Anchor Press/Doubleday, 1984), p. 153.

chap. 3). Women concerned with emancipation and equal rights were not interested in freedom to engage in premarital coitus. Quite the contrary. Chinese women wanted to escape the sexual slavery to men that had bound them for centuries. They wanted to assert themselves as persons and workers, not as sex objects (Rowbotham, 1972, chap. 7).

The Maoists encouraged late marriage for both sexes because love affairs and family concerns were thought to divert energy from educational and career pursuits and from service to the revolution. As part of the propaganda campaign of the early 1960s, young women were warned that early marriage and childbearing would severely damage their health and that of their offspring. Young men under 25 were told that "unrestrained indulgence of the sexual impulse" would hinder their sleep and exercise after work, that it would dissipate their bodily fluids, bring about nervous disorders, and cause such ailments as headache, dizziness, tension, memory decline, mental and physical pain, impotence, and premature old age (Aird, 1972). Such warnings are similar to those that were spread in the nineteenth-century United States through advice books addressed to young men. It was thought that energy would be conserved by refraining from masturbation and sexual intercourse and then could be redirected into occupational success. One historian called this view of sexuality "the spermatic economy" (Barker-Benfield, 1972). It is interesting to observe its revival in China as late as the 1960s.

What, if any, impact the modernization movements of the late 1970s and the opening of China to Western trade and technology may have on sexual attitudes and behavior remains to be seen. There are already signs that a limited amount of prostitution has recurred in recent years (Shearer, 1986); but, as the boxed insert shows, the sexual values of the cultural revolution for the most part appear to have remained intact.

Israeli Kibbutzim

In the early revolutionary phase, the young pioneers of the kibbutz, like their counterparts in the Soviet Union and China, attempted to build a society free of gender-role differentiation. At the same time, this new society would discourage the bonding of women and men into small, isolated family units. Part of this was in reaction to anything "bourgeois," as traditional marriage was considered (Spiro, 1970, chap. 5). For one thing, conventional marriage kept women in a lower status socially, economically, and legally. But another strain that was just as strong in the antifamilistic tendencies of these collectives was the realization that the internal ties of small family units would bind the individuals within them to one another more strongly than to the community as a whole. "Families may easily become competing foci of emotional involvement that can infringe on loyalty to the collective," explains sociologist Yonina Talmon (1972:4). We saw earlier that similar concerns were voiced at one time in the Soviet Union.

Quite naturally, questions began to arise about handling sexuality in the kibbutz. If conventional marriage were abolished, would it mean total sexual freedom? Could anyone have sex relations with anyone he or she desired? The kibbutz had no clear-cut ideology, so things had to work themselves out by trial and error. There were experiments with polygamy, for example, and a rejection of "bourgeois" standards such as premarital chastity and lifelong fidelity (Spiro, 1970). At the same time, there were efforts toward deeroticizing the sexes, with emphasis on how alike men and women were. Women adopted male dress and discontinued their concern with cosmetics and beauty care. Dormitory rooms were shared by men and women in casual, nonsexual roommate arrangements. A mixed shower was instituted but was soon abandoned because the persons involved felt their previous training was too strong and inhibiting.

Sexual relations were themselves considered a personal matter, and premarital intercourse met with no disapproval on the part of the community. Promiscuity (in the sense of casual sex with a variety of partners) was discouraged, but if a man and woman *both* desired coitus out of love for each other and deep emotional attachment, they felt free to engage in intercourse. At the same time, the exclusiveness of romantic love presented problems for the collective in the way it set couples apart. Thus, it became customary for couples to try to keep secret the special ties between them.

This secrecy and restraint in the public demonstration of "coupleness" was one of several counterbalances that Talmon (1972:8–10) suggests were operative in keeping in check the liberal "emphasis on personal autonomy and erotic gratification." Other counterbalances were the sexual modesty and reticence the young people brought from their Jewish upbringing and the rigorous way of life in the kibbutz, with its emphasis on deferred gratification, commitment to the task at hand, and strict self-discipline.

As a result of the strong counterbalances to the earlier free-love notions, there has arisen a comparatively conservative attitude toward sex in the kibbutz. Group activities rather than couple activities are encouraged, and children and adolescents are encouraged to view one another in nonsexual ways, that is, to see one another simply as persons (Spiro, 1965:327). Kibbutz child-rearing practices emphasize "absolute coeducation" in that dormitories and shower facilities are shared up until age 18, but the atmosphere is familylike, and privacy and modesty are practiced—much as it is by brothers and sisters in conventional family arrangements. In addition, a kind of "incest taboo" prevails, which prohibits sexual contact with members of the immediate peer group with whom living quarters are shared (Rabin and Beit-Hallahmi, 1982:33–34).

Sexual relations during high school days

have been discouraged primarily because they are considered distracting and would hinder young people in their work and studies. After high school graduation, however, young men and women are considered full-fledged members of the kibbutz, and sexual relations are viewed as a private matter of concern only to the man and woman involved until they wish to marry. Traditionally, at the time of marriage the couple would apply for a common room, and this gesture would be the only ceremony required (Spiro, 1970:113). However, in recent years, there has been a move toward having a wedding as a meaningful and memorable event (Talmon, 1972:21).

There have been other changes over the years. Talmon has pointed out trends away from asceticism and austerity and a working out of new compromise patterns. She sees evidence that the sense of social mission that once imbued the kibbutz community is declining. Other sociologists have shown that this "laxist tendency" has had an effect in the sexual sphere (Rabkin and Spiro in Spiro, 1970, chap. 9). The traditional sexual code, with its stress on restraint, is still the official standard; but there is more pairing off among high school students. Sexual relations sometimes occur among these couples, and abortions have been arranged for some of the teenage pregnancies that have resulted. Some girls begin dating as early as the eighth grade, and they usually date upperclassmen. High school girls are more apt to be sexually experienced than are boys because many girls of high school age have older boyfriends from among soldiers or young men of the kibbutz (Rabkin and Spiro, 1970). At the same time, sexual promiscuity continues to be frowned upon, and premarital sexual intercourse is acceptable only in a relationship likely to lead to marriage.

As we saw in Chapter 3, the kibbutz in re-

cent years has been characterized by a growing differentiation of gender roles, with women being allotted more traditionally feminine tasks in the work of the collective. Women have also begun showing more concern about dress, even using jewelry and makeup. Even a hairdresser may now be found in the kibbutz. Attractiveness to males and an emphasis on marriage and children seem to be taking on an importance to kibbutz women that was unknown in the early days of the movement. In this context, the permissiveness-with-affection standard appears to be widely accepted.

Socialist Democracy of Sweden

When Tomasson (1970) formulated his proposition regarding the association between female equality and greater permissiveness in premarital sex, he had in mind primarily the Scandinavian countries—particularly Sweden, which was the focus of his sociological study. He refers to research which indicates that "the majority of young Swedes have premarital intercourse and that they begin at an early age." For example, a 1968 study showed that over 95 percent of the married persons in the sample had experienced premarital coitus.

Birgitta Linner, a Swedish authority in family counseling, has pointed out that sex surveys were woefully few in Sweden until rather recently because Swedish sociologists tended to rely on studies done in the United States. Because of this, we have no record of a jump in nonvirginity in the 1920s that might be compared with what was happening elsewhere in the world—such as in the United States, England, France, and Germany—during that time of rapid social change.

However, an event did take place in Sweden in 1920 that laid the groundwork for vast changes in the years to follow. In that year, Sweden passed the first democratic family laws anywhere in the world (Linner, 1967, chap. 1). Husband and wife, according to the new Marriage Code, were to have equal roles and rights and mutual responsibilities within the family—including the assumption of financial obligations for one another and their children—with housework being considered as a financial contribution to the household. Other laws followed in the decades ahead—laws affecting divorce, women's rights, the care of children, benefits for unwed mothers, financial allowances, and so on. Both official government policy and the general social climate were moving in the direction of full equality for both sexes and away from the old double standard in any of its forms.

Sex education has been required in all school grades for many years. This has included efforts to socialize children to look upon their roles in the family and society as being equal and interchangeable rather than linked to gender. Contraceptive information is also considered important and is disseminated through sex education in the schools and through public service advertisements. Although there are moral debates over the issue, the feeling is rather strong in Sweden and other Scandinavian countries that young people should be able to act upon their sexual urges responsibly—using birth control—rather than being told they must refrain from sex until marriage, an attitude which some feel results in unwise early marriages.

Even so, a considerable number of Swedish brides are pregnant on their wedding day (Linner, 1967, chap. 3; Tomasson, 1970:184). This does not reflect a high proportion of "forced marriages" so much as it indicates the norm of sexual intercourse during engagement. It also tells us something about the social acceptance of premaritally conceived children and their parents in Swedish society. Unmarried pregnant women are not encouraged to marry just to "give the child a name" or to protect themselves and their children from the cruel taunts of society. In Sweden, large numbers of unmarried women elect to keep their children born out of wedlock, and the laws and social policy provide generous and humane support (Linner, 1967, chap. 3; Linner, 1966; Morgan, 1984:658). Overall, the emphasis in Sweden is more on permissiveness with affection than on casual sex with a variety of partners. At the same time, there is enough casual sex to cause concern over what Linner refers to as the one "pessimistic aspect of sex in Swedish society," the spread of sexually transmitted diseases.

It should be kept in mind that premarital sexual experience is not a new phenomenon in the Scandinavian countries. As sociologist Harold T. Christensen (1969) points out, "In Denmark . . . sexual intercourse during engagement is a tradition at least three or four centuries old," and it was not at all unusual for couples to wait until pregnancy occurred before going ahead with the wedding. Linner (1966 and 1967) likewise refers to the agricultural roots and peasant culture that are part of Sweden's history; and in this setting, sex relations before marriage and premaritally conceived children were not at all unusual. In fact, the number of children born out of wedlock is lower now than it was in the nineteenth century. Nevertheless, the older generation has had some difficulty in accepting the newer attitudes toward sex in Sweden, no doubt because of greater openness in discussing the subject and the replacement of double-standard thinking with a norm of sexual equality for both sexes.

Tomasson (1970, chap. 6) has written that "a permissive sex ethic, which is essentially a premarital sex ethic that gives females the same rights and privileges that men tacitly

Different sexual expectations in dating situations are not so much rooted in male and female biology as in social learning. (© Beryl Goldberg)

The premarital-sex ethic in Sweden is permissive. However, these four characteristics are also descriptive of Communist China, and there the premarital-sex ethic is restrictive. Both countries have in common the renunciation of the double standard. But while Sweden has moved toward equality in *permissiveness,* the People's Republic of China has moved toward equality in *abstinence.* Even socialist experiments have no "one-and-only" answer to the question of premarital sex.

EXPLAINING THE DYNAMICS OF PREMARITAL SEX

We have seen that throughout history and in various cultures, males have been more sexually permissive before marriage than have females. Traditionally, not only have a higher percentage of males than females engaged in premarital sexual intercourse, but the percentage of males engaging in all other categories of sexual behavior—including masturbation and petting—has also been higher than that of females (Luckey and Nass, 1969; Carns, 1969).

Males and females have generally differed in attitudes as well as in behavior, with males accepting higher levels of sexual permissiveness as right for themselves than females have been willing to accept as right for *themselves.* However, the research of sociologist Ira Reiss (1960a, 1967b) showed that females were more likely to have permissive attitudes toward premarital sexual behavior if love was involved. Research by other sociologists indicates that women have been far more likely than men to report having had emotional ties with or actual plans to marry their first sexual partners (Simon, Berger, and Gagnon, 1972:216–217).

enjoy in other more sexually restrictive societies, is only an aspect of the general status of women in a society." He describes the requisite "general status of women" in terms of four characteristics: a high level of equality with males, minimization of sexual differentiation in roles, relative economic independence from males, and status determined by individualistic achievements rather than by the status of husbands.

These four characteristics are descriptive of Sweden, and Tomasson's proposition fits.

Sexual Learning and Gender-Role Socialization

The different sexual attitudes and behavior of women and men are not so much rooted in biology as they are in social learning. It's true that people used to believe that men had stronger sex drives and greater needs than did women and that women were not interested in sex, but modern scientific research has shown how much men and women have in common in their sexual response. The studies of sex researchers William Masters and Virginia Johnson, for example, provide evidence that females and males experience much the same physiological responses during sexual orgasm, going through four basic stages of arousal and sexual climax. Women experience sexual excitement and enjoy the pleasurable sensations of sexual activity just as men do (Masters and Johnson, 1966).

Responses to Sexually Explicit Materials West German sociologists Gunter Schmidt and Volkmar Sigusch (1970, 1973; Schmidt, Sigusch, and Schafer, 1973) also found that women can be aroused by and react just as strongly as men do to erotic films and slides and to sexually explicit stories. Through carefully conducted, controlled, and measured laboratory experiments in which persons reported on their sexual behavior and sexual reactions in the twenty-four hours before and twenty-four hours after exposure to sexually explicit materials, Schmidt and Sigusch (1970, 1973) found that 87 percent of the men and 72 percent of the women reported some sort of physiosexual reaction (usually a full or partial erection in the men and genital sensations and vaginal lubrication in the women), and that furthermore, "psychosexual stimulation leads to an increase of masturbation to the same extent in both men and women." How-

ever, although there were similarities in physical reaction, the emotional reaction of the women to the films was somewhat more pronounced than was true of men, particularly in the degree to which they reported shock, irritation, or disgust.

These findings differed greatly from the Kinsey studies two decades earlier, which had seemed to indicate that women are not generally aroused by observing portrayals of sexual action in pictures and films or by reading erotic novels and stories. Kinsey (1953, chap. 16, p. 662, paperback edition) suggested the likelihood that "most females are indifferent or antagonistic to the existence of such material because it means nothing to them erotically." A body of literature and drawings produced by females, although sometimes called erotic, was found by the Kinsey researchers to deal mostly "with more general situations, affectional relationships, and love" (p. 672).

Schmidt, Sigusch, and Schafer (1973) attempted to discover if sexually explicit stories in the context of affectionate expression would be more erotically stimulating to females than to males and also whether the introduction of the affection element would cause a greater response in women than would a sexual situation separated from affection. On the basis of their research, these social scientists concluded that "the stories with and without affection do not have a significantly differing effect on men or women." They went on to say:

> Affection is not a necessary precondition for women to react sexually to sexual stimuli in the same manner as men. Even for stories which describe sexual relations in detail excluding and avoiding any expressions of tenderness and affection . . . sexual arousal and sexual activation among females are as great as among males. This finding tends to refute the claim that fe-

male sexuality is basically more dependent on affection than male sexuality. (p. 198)

Commenting on these findings, Paul Gebhard (1973), who became director of the Institute for Sex Research upon Kinsey's death, suggested that the discrepancies with the earlier Kinsey findings may be explained by the wording of the Kinsey question (which depended upon respondents' recall of earlier feelings) and which did not take into account the different cultural conditioning males and females have received. Gebhard points out that women in our culture are trained to be cautious about sex, whereas males "do not receive this defensive conditioning." Thus, when women are suddenly presented with a picture of sexual activity, they may react negatively whereas, when presented with such materials gradually, as in a motion picture, they are likely to experience sexual arousal. The Kinsey research uncovered indications of this tendency, but it was not taken into account when male and female responsiveness were compared. Gebhard reaches the same conclusion as did the West German researchers. He points out that both Masters and Johnson and the Institute for Sex Research have shown "the essential equality of males and females in response to tactile stimuli," that is, the capabilities of both sexes to react when the sense of touch is involved (as in petting, masturbation, or coitus). And he suspects that if culturally produced variables are taken into account, research will show males and females to be "very similar, if not identical, in their inherent capacity to respond sexually to visual stimuli," as well.

Gender-Typed Approaches to Sexuality Gebhard's reference to *cultural conditioning,* on top of studies that show that males and females are not *biologically* differ-

ent with respect to sexual arousal and response, brings us once again to the matter of *socialization,* the training that persons receive to fit them for their roles in society, as we saw in Chapters 2 and 3.

Mary Walshok, a sociologist who has conducted research on the relationship between gender-role typing and sexuality, states that males are typically more "instrumental" in their sexual attitudes and behavior, while females tend to be more "expressive." "On the whole," writes Walshok (1973), "male patterns are characterized by a capacity to treat sexuality as an end in itself, whereas female patterns are less directly sexual and more typically an outgrowth or expression of some more encompassing emotional or social commitment" (p. 2). We've already seen that the degree to which persons are either instrumental (task-centered and goal-oriented) or expressive (person-oriented) is a matter of social learning.

At the very beginning of sexual awareness, gender-typed differences show up. Almost twice as many males as females experience sexual orgasm through masturbation during adolescence; and among females who have experienced orgasm through masturbation, about half do so only after having first experienced orgasm through a sexual experience with a male (Gagnon and Simon, 1973:181). The male peer group encourages boys to experiment with sex, talk about it, joke about it, and so on. Adolescent boys, more than adolescent girls, come in contact with pornographic materials and are likely to report sexual arousal through sexual fantasies and daydreams. When adolescent girls daydream, they are more likely to be thinking about a situation of romantic love than about sex as an end in itself. Sociologists John Gagnon and William Simon (1973:181–82) report that for females, "opportunities for learning and performing sexual activity are not provided" so that "an interest in sexuality for its own sake or for the sake of pleasure" is not developed to the extent it is in males during this period of life.

Gagnon and Simon (1973:12, 73) point out that in the unwritten script usually followed during adolescent petting, "the description is one of male as subject (active, controlling) and female as object (passive, controlled). Males . . . do, females react or gate keep." Less awakened to her sexual self, the female is concentrating on preventing too much access to her body at the same time that the more erotically aware and experienced male is attempting sexual activity which is clearly goal-directed.

Sexual Language: Male-Female Differences Even the graffiti found on the walls of public rest rooms give evidence of gender-typed approaches to sexuality. The Kinsey researchers found that 86 percent of male toilet-wall inscriptions were sexual in nature, both in words and pictures. Females were much less likely to make any sorts of inscriptions; but when they did, they tended to draw pictures of hearts or to write in lipstick phrases such as "Bill and Sue" or "Kathy loves Jeff." Kinsey and his associates (1953, chap. 16) viewed this comparison of the female and male inscriptions as indicative of "some of the most basic sexual differences between females and males." For males, sexual interest appeared to be genital-centered, while for females, it was relationship-centered.

More than twenty years after this finding by Kinsey, sociologists Nancy Kutner and Donna Brogan (1974) studied the sex-slang knowledge of three groups of students at a Southern university (male and female undergraduate students and female graduate students in nursing). These researchers found that "male undergraduates listed a signifi-

cantly larger number of sex-related slang expressions on the average than did the two female groups studied." When asked to list slang expressions for the words *woman* and *man*, males listed considerably more slang expressions for *woman* than they did for *man*. Females, on the other hand, listed similar numbers of slang expressions for *woman* and *man*. Furthermore, "males much more frequently than females listed slang expressions for 'woman' which denoted woman as a sexual object," Kutner and Brogan report. And on the topic of sexual intercourse, males listed sixty-three distinct slang terms, a large number of which indicated male dominance over the female. Females, for their part, listed twenty-nine slang expressions for sexual intercourse. And although they included some of the dominating-male terms, they tended more than males to list such euphemisms as "making love," "going to bed," "having relations," and "sleeping together" (pp. 482–83).

Kutner and Brogan had hypothesized that as women became less traditional in their gender-role attitudes, their awareness of sex slang would increase. The researchers found that indeed, among females, "the extensiveness of sex-related slang vocabulary does tend to increase as nontraditional sex-role orientation increases." But another part of their hypothesis was not borne out: males with traditional gender-role attitudes did not list more sex slang expressions than did males who were nontraditional and thus more egalitarian in gender roles. According to Kutner and Brogan, "it appears that participation in the male subculture with its shared terminology generally overrides the influence of differing sex-role ideologies" (p. 483).

Male Peer Pressure Sociologist Lester Kirkendall (1968) has written of the problems of

In the adolescent male world, peer pressure is strong. Sexual experience with females is viewed as a means of enhancing status among other males. (© Jaeger Weinstein, 1985/Woodfin Camp & Associates)

male virgins, calling attention to the pressures peer groups have traditionally placed upon males who are relatively inexperienced sexually. If a male has not yet had sexual intercourse, he has been made to feel that something must be wrong with him and that he is not demonstrating masculinity. Such pressures toward sexual performance may be felt in high school, college, the military, or in work situations with older males who tease about sexual intercourse.

Gagnon and Simon (1973:68–81) make the observation that the adolescent male world is a *homosocial* (not to be confused with *homosexual*) world, with a great concern for the approval of those of the same gender. Sexual contacts with females, then, become ways of establishing and confirming social status among males. Males talk together about "scoring," "how far one can get," "making bases or hitting a home run," and so on. The emphasis is on the "degree of sexual access achieved," write Gagnon and Simon, contrasting these male conversations

with female conversations where young women describe relationships in terms of the "level of affection offered." Females have traditionally spoken less about sex and more about perceived or hoped-for feelings of fondness or love on the part of the male.

The First Time Sociologist Donald Carns (1973), using data from a national sample of college students, found gender differences even in the management of the first coital experience. Males tended to talk about the experience to more people and more often met with approval than was true of females.

A difference also showed up in *when* persons told their friends, with 30 percent of the males in contrast to 14 percent of the females, reporting that they told someone immediately after the event. Carns concluded that the evidence points to "a pattern of male 'ego-sex' [which] emerges within the context of the so-called 'male bond' (male peers as audiences for sexual prowess)." This is in sharp contrast to the female's management of the first experience of sexual intercourse. Fifty-six percent of the women in Carns's sample told only one or two friends or no one at all. This was true of less than a third of the men.

Carns focused on the first event of sexual intercourse because of its meaning as "irreversible" and "pivotal behavior" in our society: "One possesses one sexual status before the act—'virgin'—and another afterwards." In this light, the way a person handles the event and its public presentation would seem to tell us something about how that person views his or her identity as a sexual being.

Different Perceptions of One's Sexual Being Traditionally, females and males have had different perceptions of themselves as sexual beings. Sociologists John Gagnon and William Simon (1973; Simon and Gagnon, 1969), taking issue with the legacy of Freud that has fostered a tendency to look for sexual ingredients in nonsexual behavior and symbolism, say that we need to reverse the approach and see how other aspects of life affect our outlook on sexuality. Gender-role socialization especially needs to be taken into account.

Training for society's assigned roles, masculine and feminine, produces two different approaches to sexuality. Whereas males learn sexuality "prior to profound linkages with the rest of life," females act out their sexuality "later and in response to the demands of males and within the framework of societal expectations." Gagnon and Simon (1973) write: "For the female, sexual activity does not occur for its own sake, but for the sake of children, family, and love. Thus sexuality for the female has less autonomy than it has for the male, and the body (either of the self or of others) is not seen by women as an instrument of self-pleasure. This vision of sexuality as a form of service to others is continuous with the rest of female socialization" (pp. 181–82).

How Certain Sociological Theories Apply

In accounting for the learned differences in male and female sexuality, sociologists have taken different approaches. Some, arguing from the structural-functional vantage point, say that gender-role learning that emphasizes female sexuality in the context of love and commitment is necessary for a woman's fulfillment of her traditional family-centered role (wifehood, motherhood, and serving the interests of others as the expressive hub of the home).

Others question this approach, raising the objections that males, too, could be socialized to view sex in a context of love, commitment, marriage, and family or that females could be socialized to have more autonomy in sex and learn to appreciate it for its own sake in the way males are trained to. One sociologist has spelled out a detailed analysis of what he calls "sexual stratification" in terms of conflict theory and social exchange. Randall Collins (1971) asserts that historically and cross-culturally, men have usually been the "sexual aggressors" and women the "sexual prizes for men." The model is one of coercion, with a dominant group (males) having control over a subordinate group (females). In some societies, females are clearly viewed as sexual property, taken as booty in war, used by fathers in economic bargaining, considered to be owned by husbands, and so on. Collins argues that the root of male dominance has lain in the physical strength, size, and aggressiveness of the male sex, while female vulnerability stemmed not only from their generally smaller size but also from their role in bearing and caring for children.

Sexuality, Dominance, and Material Resources Referring to the conflict model of stratification of the social theorist Max Weber, Collins shows how it applies to the male-female sexual situation in various types of societies. The first point is that "persons struggle for as much dominance as their resources permit." Thus males, by virtue of their physical strength, freedom from the biological limitations of menstruation and childbirth, and greater economic advantages gained domination over women. The main resource of a female was considered to be her sexuality, to which a man acquired exclusive rights because of his greater resources. In some societies, this exchange resulted from economic bargaining with the woman's father; and in such societies, women "are closely guarded so as not to lose their market value." This has given rise to customs such as wearing a veil, strict chaperonage, and so on. In ancient Hebrew society, for example, if a man seduced and had sexual intercourse with an unbetrothed virgin, he was required to take her as his wife and pay her father the bride price. If the father refused to give his daughter to him, the man still had to pay the father the bride price because the loss of virginity made the woman of less worth on the marriage market (Exodus 22:16–17).

Collins's second point refers to Weber's belief that ideals are used as weapons in struggles for domination. In this case, the double standard, with its emphasis on female chastity, is illustrative.

The third factor is that changes in the structure of domination take place when there are shifts in resources. As certain political and economic changes occur, women gain a better bargaining position. No longer under the control of their fathers, they "become at least potentially free to negotiate their own sexual relationships," writes Collins, "but since their main resource is their sexuality, the emerging free marriage market is organized around male trades of economic and status resources for possession of a woman" (p. 13). Along with sexuality, female capabilities in homemaking and in providing emotional support for males also came to be valued resources as the ideology of romantic love grew.

The Long Survival of the Double Standard The situation described by Collins is a possible explanation for the survival of the double standard because it helps explain the traditionally greater reticence of females to accept for themselves the sexual permissiveness that has characterized males. Collins suggests that "the most favorable female strategy, in a situation where men control

the economic world, is to maximize her bargaining power by appearing both as attractive and as inaccessible as possible." Overt sexuality may not be used to attract the male but only hinted at indirectly as a sort of "grand prize" or ultimate reward because "sexuality must be reserved as a bargaining resource for the male wealth and income that can only be stably acquired through a marriage contract." Because men and women are bargaining with "unequal goods," femininity and female chastity are idealized, and woman is placed on a pedestal so that "an element of sexual repression is thus built into the situation."

The greatest bargaining power of all for women comes with increasing employment opportunities. Freed from economic dependence upon males, the sexual bargains struck by women can be less concerned with marriage and more concerned about other kinds of exchanges. Collins suggests that in a situation where women have their own economic resources, "dating can go on as a form of short-run bargaining, in which both men and women trade on their own attractiveness or capacity to entertain in return for sexual favors and/or being entertained."

Collins began with a picture of coercion in which one socially dominant group oppresses or exploits the other (conflict theory), but he moved on to a situation described in terms of a "free market," "bargaining," trading sexual resources for status and security (in other words, exchange theory). Persons give and receive in a sexual relationship, and the exchange may be a fair one or it may be one in which one person has a greater advantage and receives the higher profits (Libby and Carlson, 1973).

Referring to traditional male-female dating relationships in a society where males dominate, Gagnon and Simon (1973) point out that "the physical exchanges are surrounded by other exchanges of words and gifts that affirm the increasing accessibility of the female's body" (p. 76). Put another way, males have been socialized to use two kinds of bargaining resources in pursuing their sexual goals: *verbal expressions* (assuring females of affection so that intimacy is legitimated from the female perspective) and *material benefits* (paying for dinners and movies, providing the transportation, and so on, indicating an investment that is expected to result in varying degrees of sexual payoffs).

On the other hand, in societies where gender-role differentiation is not emphasized and females and males are in a more equal position by virtue of equal opportunities in the economic system, there is not the same kind of game playing in dating relationships. In Sweden, for example, dating has been more casual, with little emphasis on playing the roles of feminine charmer, using sexual attractiveness as bait, or masculine pursuer on a mission of conquest. Friendship and equality have been emphasized, with females feeling free to take the initiative in establishing relationships and to pay their own way on dates. It is conventional for dating partners to meet at the place of their date rather than an arrangement whereby the man calls for the woman. In the early stages of a relationship in Sweden, there is actually less emphasis on sex than there is in the United States, where kissing and petting are often introduced very early in a dating relationship. Swedish young people tend to take time to let intimacy develop slowly; but when intimacy in other aspects of the relationship has been developed, they tend to move on to the full sexual intimacy of coitus rather than leveling off at heavy petting and "technical virginity" (Tomasson, 1970:180–81). Females in Sweden, less concerned about guarding their sexuality as their chief bargaining resource, do not feel compelled to engage in intercourse because of the insistence of their boyfriends but rather do so only because they themselves want to (Linner, 1967).

Social Meaning of Virginity

The term *technical virginity* has sometimes been used to describe the widespread practice of engaging in various sexual intimacies while still maintaining, technically, a state of virginity. Petting to orgasm through what is sometimes called "mutual masturbation," oral-genital stimulation, and placing the genitals together without proceeding to penetration are examples of such intimacies (Reiss, 1960a; Bell, 1966). It is widely believed that engaging in them will not make persons "nonvirginal."

Sociologists David Berger and Morton Wenger (1973) have challenged the commonly held idea that "everybody knows what virginity is." They point out that the concept that people have in mind when they think of the term *virginity* varies and holds "different meanings in different social contexts." Furthermore, according to these researchers, the lack of agreement on the meaning and norms surrounding virginity "is due to the long-term changes in the economic role of women in modern industrial society."

To find out if their ideas were on the right track, Berger and Wenger asked sociology students at two state-related Eastern colleges to complete a questionnaire designed to find out if the students felt it made sense to think in terms of virginity and nonvirginity and also to find out how students defined these terms.

In answer to the question, "Does it make sense to say a woman (man) has lost her (his) virginity," 43 percent of their sample rejected the concept of virginity for both sexes, while 57 percent retained a belief that the notion of virginity as a *concept* has value.

ZULU CHIEF ORDERS TESTS FOR VIRGINITY

Pietermaritzburg, South Africa (Agence France-Presse)—A Zulu chief at the tribal location of Mafunze near here is having every girl in his area subjected to compulsory virginity examinations in a bid to curb immorality, illegitimacy and prostitution.

Chief Valindaba Ngcobo this week rallied the elder women in various villages to present him with a list of virgins, and in July he will present a bull to the village which records the highest number of maidens.

Seven elderly women have been appointed in each region to examine the young girls in special huts provided for the purpose.

Young women found to be 'deflowered," as he put it, will have to pay the chief a fine of $11. Those who refuse to undergo the test at all, will find their parents facing a $45 fine. Any young man who accepts responsibility for seducing a girl will have to pay the chief an $11 fine and present the girl's parents with two animals—either sheep, goats or cows.

"One of the best ways to stamp out immorality, illegitimacy and prostitution among our young people is by having virginity tests," explained Chief Valindaba. "I started the tests because it is important for a girl to remain a virgin until she is married."

SOURCE: *Greensboro (NC) Daily News,* January 8, 1979.

Flexibility in Definitions   However, what is of particular interest is that even among those who think it makes sense to think in terms of virginity and nonvirginity, there is considerable disagreement about exactly what constitutes virginity or its loss. The researchers asked a series of questions describing various types of sexual behavior and experiences for both males and females, and the respondents were asked to state whether or not each event constituted "loss of virginity." (See Table 5-G.)

Only about one-third of the respondents viewed the rupture of the hymen as meaning a female has lost her virginity, indicating that to most respondents the concept has another meaning than a physical state of being. But 81 percent considered the full penetration of a vagina by a penis to mean the loss of virginity for a female, which the researchers point out "is somewhat consistent with conventional notions of virginity." But they raise additional questions: "How, though, is the bringing of a male to climax consistent with this notion? Or the bringing of self to climax?" With regard to male virginity, slightly over half of the respondents considered the penetration of a woman's vagina, even without ejaculation, to constitute the loss of male virginity. A majority (around two-thirds or more in most cases) did not consider a male to have "lost his virginity" if he had intimate contact but did not ejaculate, ejaculated by a woman's manipulations, or brought a woman to climax or reached orgasm through masturbation.

Virginity and the Sexual Marketplace
From this data, Berger and Wenger conclude that a *variable* concept of virginity exists and that such a variable concept "is in the interests of both males and females in a society wherein there is considerable social stratification (economic and otherwise) by

TABLE 5-G Attitudes toward sexual events and/or behaviors constituting "loss of virginity" ("No responses" account for missing percentages.)

	YES, MEANS LOSS		NO, DOESN'T MEAN LOSS	
	%	NUMBER	%	NUMBER
Has a female lost her virginity if:				
She brings a male to climax?	16.3	33	67.8	137
Her vagina is penetrated other than by a penis?	16.8	34	66.5	135
Her vagina is fully penetrated by a penis?	81.3	165	4.9	10
Her hymen is ruptured?	32.7	66	51.5	104
She brings herself to climax?	40.9	83	40.4	82
Her vagina is partially penetrated by other than a penis?	6.4	13	74.9	152
A male brings her to climax?	21.7	44	61.1	124
Has a male lost his virginity if:				
He has a wet dream?	0.0	0	76.7	128
Penetrates a woman's vagina, but doesn't ejaculate?	53.3	89	22.8	38
He has intimate sexual contact, but doesn't ejaculate?	6.6	11	69.3	115
He ejaculates by a woman's manipulations?	5.4	9	68.7	114
Only if he brings a woman to climax?	12.7	21	62.7	104
He ejaculates by self-manipulation?	1.8	3	73.0	119

SOURCE: David Berger and Morton Wenger, "The Ideology of Virginity," *Journal of Marriage and the Family* 35 (1973):666–676.

sex." According to these sociologists, the variable concept which allows a woman a certain amount of leeway in terms of the point where she crosses the line from virgin to nonvirgin permits her to have a degree of sexual gratification while still maintaining "her sexual value as an exclusive mate." Furthermore, it puts her in a position of advertising her product so that a man is enticed to become a captive "consumer market" at the same time that the woman has a socially sanctioned reason (the ideology of virginity) for not giving away the ultimate reward, thus keeping her market value high.

For males, the variable concept of female virginity also serves a purpose, claim Berger and Wenger. "It allows the buyer with low resources (poor, unattractive, powerless, etc.) to buy 'used goods' while providing the ego-maintaining illusion that he has bought a new product." They are of course using the term "*used goods*" from the standpoint of the traditional ideology of virginity, with its emphasis on being "untouched" and reserved for the exclusive possession of one man. It was also found that persons who had already engaged in sexual intercourse were less likely to feel that it makes sense to think in terms of virginity and its loss. The researchers explain this, too, in terms of a market analogy by saying that the coitally experienced have "lost their market value along a certain commodity dimension, and therefore may wish to maximize their status along it by denying its existence." Those who had engaged only in petting were less apt to deny that virginity is a valid concept.

One point that Berger and Wenger emphasize is that an effective ideology cannot be too specific about what constitutes its violation. Therefore, certain female conduct is viewed as acceptable because it does not deprive women of their one scarce resource (total sexual access) although, as Table 5-G makes clear, there is considerable disagreement about just what conduct does cause a female to pass over the invisible line between virginity and nonvirginity.

Males and Virginity The only response showing considerable agreement about what constitutes loss of male virginity was the item about vaginal penetration. In fact, there is some indication that male loss of virginity is not viewed as a loss at all but rather as a *gain.* Acts indicating physical maturity (for example, ejaculation through "wet dreams" or masturbation) are not thought to change one's sexual status. Rather, according to Berger and Wenger, "it is possession (use) of a woman's unique resource (to be blunt, her vagina) that for males constitutes movement to the status of 'sexually experienced,' i.e., 'powerful' or 'wealthy.' " Having borrowed from exchange theory and conflict theory, these sociologists reach this conclusion: "Virginity, rather than seen as a 'state of being' in society, is viewed as a social-relational concept having to do with the state of conflict between two parties contending for scarce rewards in society, and in which conflict the contenders bring to bear those resources most available to them" (p. 675).

As we have seen repeatedly, the ideology of female virginity is particularly strong in cultures with high male dominance. When varieties of sexual activity short of actual intercourse are practiced in such settings, the unwritten rules may be stricter than they are in the bargaining context of cultures where women have more autonomy. Political scientist Evelyn Stevens (1973:97) writes of the double-standard situation in Latin America, where a young woman usually engages in intimate forms of noncoital sexual activity only with her fiancé and then only as a means of holding his interest in her until they are married. If he is quite certain that she has not engaged in such behavior with any other man, and if she provides him with the assurance that she is not enjoying the behavior, the Latin American male "may encourage or even insist on her 'obliging' him in this way." However, the permissiveness-with-affection standard appears to be gaining acceptance in Latin America to some degree, which may mean a gradual decline in the rigid double standard. One professor at a Colombian university found that among female students in a human-sexuality class, not only was there a high incidence of such noncoital sexual activities as oral-genital contact reported, but one-third reported having engaged in actual sexual intercourse. Of these, two-thirds said their first coital experience had been with their *novio* (sweetheart or fiancé). These findings were contrasted with the less than 2 percent nonvirginity rate among young Colombian women in a 1969 study (Alzate, 1978).

PREMARITAL SEX IN SOCIAL CONTEXT

Sociologist Ira Reiss (1967a; 1967b) has demonstrated that many different sociocultural factors enter into a person's attitudes and behavior with respect to premarital sex. Just as no other behavior develops in a social vacuum, so it is with sex. A basic theory of

Reiss is that "the degree of premarital sexual permissiveness which is acceptable among courting individuals varies directly with the degree of autonomy in the courtship roles and with the degree of premarital sexual permissiveness accepted in the social and cultural setting of those individuals." Increased autonomy for women usually is a factor in increasing courtship autonomy (for example, by eliminating the chaperonage system, lessening or doing away with parental control of mate selection, and making possible greater individualistic bargaining power). However, the second part of Reiss's proposition also comes into play. We saw this demonstrated in our examination of premarital sex in communist countries such as the Soviet Union and the People's Republic of China. The prevailing social norms discourage premarital sexual permissiveness in spite of the emphasis on female autonomy.

Some of the social factors in the United States which are most associated with different outlooks on premarital sex are religion, socioeconomic status, and race.

Religion

Traditionally, the teachings of Catholicism, Protestantism, Judaism, and other faiths have emphasized that sexual intercourse should be reserved for marriage. And research has shown that religion *does* make a difference in sexual attitudes and behavior. The particular religious faith doesn't seem to matter as much as does the person's commitment to that faith. A religiously devout person is less likely to engage in premarital sexual intercourse than is a person who is less devout. (Singh, 1980; Kantner and Zelnik, 1972; Spanier, 1976).

One sociologist who found evidence that religiosity acts as a brake on premarital sexual involvement is Donald Carns (1969), who analyzed data from a national survey of college students. Carns measured religiosity two ways: in terms of *attendance* (including not only worship services but all types of religious functions, such as religious-study classes, choir rehearsals, youth groups, and so on) and in terms of *religious self-image.* That is, respondents were asked how religious they personally perceived themselves to be, regardless of their degree of involvement in institutional religion.

Carns found that the more religious stu-

Research has shown that religion does make a difference in sexual attitudes and behavior. (Hugh Rogers/ Monkmeyer)

dents were (whether rated by their own self-perception or by frequency of attendance at religious functions), the less likely they were to engage in premarital sexual activities. This was true for both males and females. It was also found that the higher persons rated in terms of religiosity, the more likely they were to cite "the wrongness or immorality of premarital coitus" as the reason they abstained. In addition to moral reasons for not engaging in premarital sexual intercourse, highly religious persons also tended to cite social reasons—namely, that their reputations would likely be damaged if they were to have sex relations before marriage. They were particularly concerned about their reputations among other religious persons—what sociologists would call their "reference group," the group of "significant others" by whose standards they measure themselves and whose approval they highly desire.

Researchers Koray Tanfer and Marjorie C. Horn (1985a:11), in their analysis of data from the 1983 National Survey of Unmarried Women, found the same pattern that social scientists found during the 1960s and 1970s. "In general," Tanfer and Horn reported, "the more religious women are less likely to have ever had sex, regardless of how religiosity is measured."

Data from another broad survey, the *Connecticut Mutual Life Report on American Values in the '80s* (1981:6), showed that the level of a person's religious commitment "consistently and dramatically" affects values and behavior. The researchers found that the degree of religious commitment "is rapidly becoming a more powerful factor in American life than whether someone is liberal or conservative, male or female, young or old, or a blue-collar or white-collar worker."

Religious commitment in this study was measured through an eight-item scale that in-

cluded matters such as praying, reading the Bible, having a religious experience, urging others to turn to religion, listening to religious broadcasts, the respondent's personal perception of God's love, and two items on involvement in organized religion. It was found that the higher the religious commitment, as measured by this scale, the more likely were the respondents to believe that sex between two single persons is morally wrong. Higher religious commitment was also associated with the belief that it is wrong to live with a person of the opposite sex before marriage.

The 1985 Gallup poll on attitudes toward premarital sexual experience cited earlier also found a strong link between religious commitment and the belief that premarital sex is unacceptable. Of those who claimed that religion had an important place in their lives, only 40 percent felt that premarital sex was not wrong. In contrast, 86 percent of those who claimed that religion was *not* an important part of their lives did not consider it wrong for unmarried persons to engage in sexual intercourse (*The Gallup Report*, June, 1985).

Socioeconomic Status

When Kantner and Zelnik (1972) examined data from their first national probability sample of 15- to 19-year-old females, they concluded (as did other social scientists on the basis of research conducted both before and after their study) that "the higher the socioeconomic status—whether measured by poverty status, family income or parental or guardian education—the lower, generally, are the proportions with coital experience."

Other sociologists, however, have begun calling for more research on the topic, pointing out that the inverse relationship between social class and premarital sexual permissiveness may be less pronounced than was once the case (Singh, 1980; DeLamater and MacCorquodale, 1979:72–74).

Ira Reiss (1972:176–177) has suggested that the key to understanding what has been happening is to look at the *degree to which persons at all class levels are either liberal or conservative* in their views on politics, education, and religion. Reiss found that of a group of conservatives, those holding lower status were the most permissive sexually. But in a group of *liberals,* the most permissive sexually turn out to be those of the higher classes (college-educated people). Reiss says it is not really surprising that this new permissiveness shows up among persons with college backgrounds, pointing out that this new sexual outlook "emphasizes control of pregnancy and venereal disease and stresses person-centered sexual encounters." "In short," writes Reiss, "it differs from the older, lower-class permissiveness which had an economic base and a fatalistic philosophy."

Both the double standard and a sense of economic powerlessness with limited opportunities have shaped attitudes toward sexuality among persons at lower socioeconomic levels. Traditionally, lower-class males have taken pride in their sexual conquests, boasted of their ability to have sexual intercourse with a large number of females, and categorized girls and women according to their accessibility for sexual intercourse, with virgins rating highest and "easy lays" lowest (Rainwater, 1966a).

Similarly, Bernard Rosenberg and Joseph Bensman (1968) have pointed out that middle-class values of personalized sex have had little relevance among impoverished groups in urban ghettos. Sex and love have not been viewed in terms of emotional or material responsibility, nor on the other hand has there been much evidence of "pure joy in unrestrained sexuality," which is sometimes thought to characterize lower-class persons. Rather, premarital sex has often been considered sheer physical release, "the 'friction of two membranes'—in which the female is the necessary but unequal partner." Sex is also considered a way of winning prestige in peer-group competition and thereby proving one's masculinity. Rosenberg and Bensman write, "Since [sex] is a competitive game, the boy who plays cannot expect to earn points for scoring over an easy mark, a 'pig.' Victory consists in overcoming the largest possible number of inaccessible girls. The conversion of females into trophies reduces them to nonpersons."

It isn't hard to see the connection between gender-role socialization and sexual attitudes and behavior later on. In Chapter 3, we talked about the greater rigidity in gender roles that characterizes persons of lower social status. Boys are taught to be "masculine"—strong, dominant over women, emotionally cool and tough. Girls are taught to be "feminine"—dependent on men and submissive to them, emotionally warm and tender. Adults and peers encourage boys in their sexual pursuits, but at the same time daughters are usually shielded from even the basic facts about sex in the hope that such guarding will keep them innocent, pure, "good girls" in contrast to those who are promiscuous (Rainwater, 1966a). Being sexually restrained, in turn, is believed to win the greater respect and admiration of boys.

Race

An inverse relationship between socioeconomic status and prevalence of premarital sexual intercourse has been especially evident among black young women. With socioeconomic status (SES) measured in terms of the mean years of education completed by a young woman's parents (or the substitute caregivers who raised her), Zelnik, Kantner, and Ford (1981) found that, compared to whites, blacks showed a much *steeper* decline in premarital sexual experience as socioeconomic status rose. (See Table 5-H.)

These researchers found that among blacks, young women from the most educated homes were the most conservative in their attitudes, with one-third of those whose parents had attended college—and one-half of those whose parents had graduated from college—disapproving of premarital sex. In contrast, white women were more likely to approve of premarital sex as level of parental education rose (Zelnik, Kantner, and Ford, 1981:46,69). Sociologist Robert Staples (1981a:93–94) points out that historically, middle-class blacks have attempted to counteract society's stigmatization of blacks as "sexually loose" by adopting "an even more rigid moral code than the majority rule" (p. 93)—a code that forcefully and dramatically shows up in strict regulation of male-female relationships in traditionally black colleges. "Among members of the upwardly mobile lower class, prudence in sexual activity was often a pragmatic adaptation to the requirements of higher education," writes Staples.

In comparing the attitudes of black young women with those of white young women, however, research shows that blacks are more likely than whites to believe that it is all right to engage in premarital sex (Zelnik, Kantner, and Ford, 1981:46). This reflects the more approving attitude toward premarital sex that has been found to characterize black persons in general (*Gallup Report*, June, 1985). And as may be seen in both Tables 5-A (see page 113) and 5-H, higher percentages of black women than white women have actually experienced sexual intercourse and begun sexual activity at a younger age. (See also Bachrach and Horn, 1985; Tanfer and Horn, 1985a.)

At the same time, Zelnik and Kantner (1980:232–233) note that the "racial differential . . . has narrowed considerably over time." The prevalence of premarital sexual intercourse among black women did *not* increase between the 1976 and 1979 national studies of these researchers, whereas the percentage of white young women engaging in premarital sexual intercourse rose from 38

TABLE 5-H Percentage of women 15–19 years of age who had premarital intercourse, by race and socioeconomic status*

	1971			1976		
SES (YEARS)	TOTAL, % (N = 4247)	WHITE, % (N = 2900)	BLACK, % (N = 1347)	TOTAL, % (N = 2116)	WHITE, % (N = 1466)	BLACK, % (N = 650)
<9	34.4	27.0	61.0	45.6	38.2	70.3
9–11	33.4	29.0	55.8	45.5	41.9	64.0
12	26.9	25.0	47.7	39.4	35.9	67.2
13–15	26.2	24.8	42.8	33.7	32.6	50.6
≥16	23.5	22.8	33.7	30.2	29.9	33.8

*Socioeconomic status (SES) was measured by "the mean number of years of completed education of the persons identified by the respondent as the female who raised her and the male who helped to raise her"—usually the natural parents.
SOURCE: Excerpted from Table 3.2 in Melvin Zelnik, John F. Kantner, and Kathleen Ford, *Sex and Pregnancy in Adolescence* (Beverly Hills: Sage Publications, 1981), p. 70.

percent to 47 percent. Even so, among these adolescents, "blacks in 1979 were still about 40 percent more likely than whites to be sexually active." In the 1983 National Survey of Unmarried Women (aged 20 to 29), 9 out of 10 blacks reported having had sexual intercourse as compared to 8 out of 10 whites—again indicating the convergence that has been occurring. The percentage of single black women in their twenties who were *currently sexually active* (defined as having "had intercourse at least once in the four weeks preceding the interview") was 62 percent. Among their white counterparts, 51 percent reported being currently sexually active (Tanfer and Horn, 1985a).

One way to account for the long-recognized pattern of racial differences in premarital sexual experience is to think in terms of social exchange and the resources that are brought into the bargaining in such an exchange. Almost inevitably, additional elements beyond sex itself enter into the sexual bargaining process. If blacks are shown to be more sexually active than whites, it has nothing to do with the old myth that blacks are more "sexy" and have higher sex drives than whites. Rather, the explanation may lie in the fact that white racism has caused blacks to have been relatively blocked in their achievement aspirations at every class level.

Because among blacks there is likely to be less optimism about future educational and job opportunities, many young black women may feel that sexual favors are the only bargaining elements they have in their relationships with men. Thus physical gratification and the approval and attention they bring may seem to be the only kinds of rewards they can reasonably expect. Hammond and Ladner (1969), for example, tell of girls who engage in sexual intercourse in exchange for a movie date or even a ride in a car. One 15-year-old from a background of deprivation told the interviewers that sex relations provided an escape from her feelings of poverty. "[Sexual intercourse] makes you forget that you don't have the kinds of things you need for school," she said, "the money to buy your lunch and clothes to wear and stuff like that. I play hooky sometimes because I don't have those things but then I 'do it' and have a good time and I don't have to worry about those things" (p. 50).

The lack of privacy and crowded conditions of the ghetto also mean that children of the black underclass (below the poverty line) are exposed to sex at a very early age. In the words of one black mother, "I can't hide the facts of life from them because they can see them every day on any stairway, hall, or elevator in the project" (Hammond and Ladner, 1969:43–44). Parents may attempt to protect girls more than boys because of fears of such consequences as pregnancy, but at the same time, parents know that a great deal of sexual experimentation is likely to go on.

Although lower-class black girls are not stigmatized in quite the same way as are lower-class white girls who engage in premarital sex, there are still some elements of an unequal power distribution between males and females in the sexual realm. A sexually experienced 8-year-old girl told researchers, "I don't like any of the boys around here cause they 'do it' with you and then they 'do it' with somebody else and they act like yourself ain't yourself." Already, this young female yearned to be "special" to a male rather than serving as one of his many sexual conquests. "In the later adolescent years, however, sex for girls takes on the important function of being a form of exchange," write sociologists Boone Hammond and Joyce Ladner (1969), "primarily for material goods and services (gifts, money, etc.). Some economically and emotionally deprived girls are able to gain access to certain necessities from boy friends through their participation in sexual activities'' (p. 49).

It is the absence of viable alternatives, then, that makes young black women (particularly in the underclass) more likely to seek sexual gratification. Along with this comes increased vulnerability to exploitation. This is true even though blacks tend to hold more egalitarian gender roles than do whites. The aspiration to be autonomous rather than merely dependent must be coupled with education and economic resources that make such autonomy possible. Many young black women from economically deprived backgrounds lack the resources that would enable them to fulfill their individualistic aspirations. There is evidence that young blacks are keenly aware of the systematic deprivation of economic rewards that their parents experience and that they will later face as adults (Lott and Lott, 1963; Scanzoni, 1977). Because of this deprivation, they may be more likely than whites to turn elsewhere for meaningful rewards and gratifications. The sexual arena is one such source of rewards that are attainable. In addition, lower-status black adolescents (both female and male) are far less likely to use contraception than are sexually active black adolescents at higher socioeconomic levels (Hogan, Astone, and Kitagawa, 1985).

In examining the differences between the sexual experience of white and black young women, it is useful to think in terms of *absolute* and *relative* comparisons. *Absolutely,* higher-educated blacks have more economic rewards than do less-educated blacks; therefore, girls in these families have less reason to pursue alternative rewards (such as physical, social, and material rewards associated with sexual activities). The rate of premarital intercourse thus goes down among blacks as the socioeconomic status rises. *Relatively,* however, when blacks are compared to whites with the same education, there is deprivation. Blacks, even with college and professional training, get fewer economic rewards than do their white counterparts. This relative deprivation may help explain why young persons in higher-status black families nonetheless have higher rates of premarital sex than do whites at the same income level. Dollarwise, they are actually not at the same level as whites with similar training; they are blocked from the full achievement and its accompanying benefits that their education would seem to promise. Thus, alternative gratifications such as sex are apt to be sought after to a greater degree than would otherwise be the case.

However, another explanation is possible. While greater premarital sexual activity among black females *below* the poverty line may indicate a quest for pleasures that are open to them when they are blocked from other gratifications, the sexual permissiveness among black females at *higher* status levels may have something to do with the greater autonomy that has characterized black women because of the historical and occupational circumstances discussed earlier. If so, this would lend added force to the association between less rigid gender roles and less rigid premarital sex codes (as in the case of Sweden). To reiterate: Where females are dependent upon males, the principal good-in-exchange of females (sexual access) must be closely guarded and carefully conserved to retain its value. But when female status is not so dependent upon relationship to a male, sexual activity may be engaged in for the female's own personal reasons rather than as a bargaining resource to obtain status through a marriage contact (Tomasson, 1970; Coleman, 1966:27).

Other studies also show that different explanations for premarital sexual behavior fit different groups of women. For example, *among teenagers*, young women holding traditional gender-role preferences are the most likely to engage in premarital sex—and at an early age. Sex is viewed as a means of overcoming low self-esteem and gaining status through involvement with a male. Furthermore, young women who hold traditional gender-role norms have learned to be subordinate to males and to yield to male wishes—even when it means their exploitation.

On the other hand, *among college-educated women*, the more sexually active are likely to be those espousing egalitarian gender-role preferences. Such women tend to view their sexual activity not as giving in to male demands but as an aspect of their own personal freedom—a statement of individual choice and autonomy. (See summary of studies in Scanzoni and Fox, 1980:27–28).

TRENDS

A question often raised throughout the 1970s and 1980s centered around the changes in women's roles: Does the greater autonomy women have gained through increasing economic opportunities inevitably mean increased sexual permissiveness? The answer is not clear-cut. On the basis of her research, sociologist Mary Walshok (1973) concluded that highly achievement-oriented women tended to take a more traditionally "masculine" view of roles as segmented and distinct so that "work is work, play is play, and sex is sex." As a result, such women could take a "less contextual and romantic view of sexuality."

On the other hand, psychologist Judith Bardwick (1973) took a different perspective the same year that Walshok published her research. Bardwick saw women *in transition* and pointed out the pain and tension felt by many women who had internalized older values that were difficult to discard—even if they had come to view such values as not always in their best interests. Women in transition have not been sure what sexual lifestyle they would like to put in place of the older view, which incorporated sex into love, commitment, marriage, and motherhood, and which provided "justification" for sexual pleasure. Sex in itself has not been able to fill an empty void of self-esteem and identity among many women who expected to find a new sense of meaning through sexual liberation, says Bardwick.

Various spokeswomen for feminism have made a similar point, showing also how many men have taken advantage of the so-called sexual revolution (Mitchell, 1971; Firestone, 1970). One writer for the women's movement, Shulamith Firestone (1970, chap. 6), has written: "By convincing women that the usual female games and demands were despicable, unfair, prudish, old-fashioned, puritanical, and self-destructive, a new reservoir of available females was created to expand the tight supply of goods available for traditional sexual exploitation, disarming women of even the little protection they had so painfully acquired."

In his study of black singles, Staples (1981a:111) found similar sentiments, leading him to conclude that "the real issue is not one of sexual pleasure or abstinence, but the universal need for belonging and security." He states that "to a large extent, sexual freedom gave women neither of these things. The biggest change that occurred was that many men reduced all women to sexual objects." Even the nonrandom sample of 106,000 female readers of *Cosmopolitan* magazine revealed an uneasiness about the increasingly sexually free atmosphere. Half the women felt that the sexual revolution had gone too far and reported they now felt a new tyranny that *required* them to be sexually active—

FEMINISM AND THE "SEX CRISIS"

Certainly we have seen the stereotypes come and go in our own time—from the "virtuous" nonsexual woman to the lusty genitally centered woman of the Masters and Johnson era, to the spiritualized, sisterly lover of the late seventies. If we enter the eighties with no clear, sharp-edged notion of what our sexuality is or "should" be—and with no consensus on the role of sex in our lives and in our revolution—this should not be dismaying. In fact, the biggest mistake we could make would be to cut off the discussion too soon—to close ranks around a doctrine of what is feminist and what is not, what is right and what is unmentionable, or just plain wrong.

Our own recent history should remind us that there is an inevitable tension, an inevitable ambivalence, in any feminist approach to sex. If we seek to affirm our sexuality in all its energy and diversity, we run headlong into the fact of male sexual violence and exploitation. If we try to narrow the diversity and sublimate the energy, we curtail our own options and imagination. There *is* no answer in a sexist society, much less a society which ranks so many of us as "too old" or "too fat" for sex, and leaves most of us, most of the time, literally too *tired* for it. There is only the long struggle to define ourselves *against* our situation—the reappraisals, the footholds gained or lost, the growing sense of who we are and what we might, given half a chance, become.

SOURCE: Excerpted from Barbara Ehrenreich, Elizabeth Hess, and Gloria Jacobs, "A Report on the Sex Crisis," *Ms.,* 10 (March 1982), p. 88.

not out of choice but out of pressure (Wolfe, 1981).

Perhaps the problem has been in the divergent outlooks males and females have brought to considerations of female autonomy. Women have come to appreciate sexuality as something to be enjoyed as part of their own human "personhood" rather than as a bargaining resource to obtain other kinds of benefits. Many men, on the other hand, have found it hard to understand these new female desires and capacities to enjoy sex as males have traditionally done. Such males may simply consider the "scarce resource" (access to a woman's body) to have become more plentiful. Furthermore, its "market value" may be seen as lower due to an increased supply, with the result that men may bargain with fewer rewards in the ex-

change, thus increasing the exploitation of women.

However, at the same time, there are indications of change among males. In the early seventies, Donald Carns (1973) saw two trends occurring simultaneously. Males began moving away from concerns about performance, conquest, the adolescent male bond, and preoccupation with sex isolated from other factors. Women, on their part, began awakening to a new awareness of their sexuality and moving toward a pleasure-centered approach. "One would hope," wrote Carns, "that if indeed these trends are occurring, the genders do not pass each other in the night."

Actually, it is not likely that the two sexes will "pass as ships in the night." Rather, they may very well find themselves in the same harbor. (See also DeLamater and Mac-Corquodale, 1979:67.) Yankelovich (1981) reports that more and more men and women alike are expressing a longing for deep, sustained relationships that can be open, honest, free of game playing, and less centered on a quest for sexual excitement.

Sexual exchange isolated from other rewards is exceedingly difficult to maintain. The parties involved (male *or* female) are likely to find they want something more—love, attention, a sense of "being special" to one another as total persons. This may account for the popularity of the permissiveness-with-affection standard, not only in the United States but in other nations such as West Germany and Sweden as well (Tomasson, 1970; Linner, 1967; Reiss, 1960a, 1967b, 1973; Schmidt and Sigusch, 1972).

CHAPTER HIGHLIGHTS

Some sociologists suggest that the abrupt changes that occurred around World War I might justifiably be called a "sexual revolution," but that gradual changes in the direction of sexual permissiveness since then may be better termed an "evolution." Reiss has pointed out four primary sexual standards related to premarital sex: abstinence, the double standard, permissiveness with affection, and permissiveness without affection. Most of the changes associated with the so-called sex revolution and later evolution have centered around female autonomy and a movement away from the double standard. Beginning sometime in the mid-1960s, two significant changes occurred: an increase in the incidence of premarital sexual intercourse among young women and a lowering of the age at which persons of both sexes first experienced sexual intercourse. The changes evident in the 1960s continued through the 1970s and early 1980s. Factors involved in a decision to use contraception before marriage include (1) a woman's attitudes toward her sexuality, sexual activity, and gender roles; (2) a sense of control over her own life; (3) involvement in a relationship with a male; (4) communication with her sex partner; and (5) the sorting out of costs and rewards related to both contraception and pregnancy. And even though both males and females speak of contraception as a shared responsibility, females indicate that in reality the major burden falls to them.

Some sociologists see an association between less rigid gender roles and less rigid premarital sex codes. An egalitarian ideology of premarital sex can mean either of two polar extremes. Either *both* males and females should be free to engage in premarital sexual intercourse or *neither* males nor females should be free to do so. Several socialist experiments give evidence of a struggle between these two poles, in some cases settling on a standard somewhere in between (especially "permissiveness with affection"). Traditionally, males have been socialized to think of sex in instrumental terms, while females have been socialized to think of sex in expressive terms. Collins utilizes conflict and exchange theories to explain *"sexual stratification,"* a historical pattern in which men have been the dominant group and sexual aggressors and females have been the subordinate group and "sexual prizes for men." Increasing employment opportunities for women can mean increased bargaining power in their relationships with men because women are thereby freed from economic dependence upon men and also from the idea that a woman's bargaining resource is her sexuality. Overall, a person's attitudes and behavior with respect to premarital sex are affected by many different sociocultural factors, including religion, social class, and race. Carns pointed out two trends occurring simultaneously, with some men showing evidence of wanting sex to mean more than performance and conquest while women were indicating a new concern for pleasure and an appreciation of their sexuality for its own sake. The popularity of the permissiveness-with-affection standard may indicate some convergence in the perspectives of considerable numbers of women and men who want something more than casual sex.

P·A·R·T F·O·U·R

ALTERNATIVES TO TRADITIONAL MARRIAGE AND FAMILY

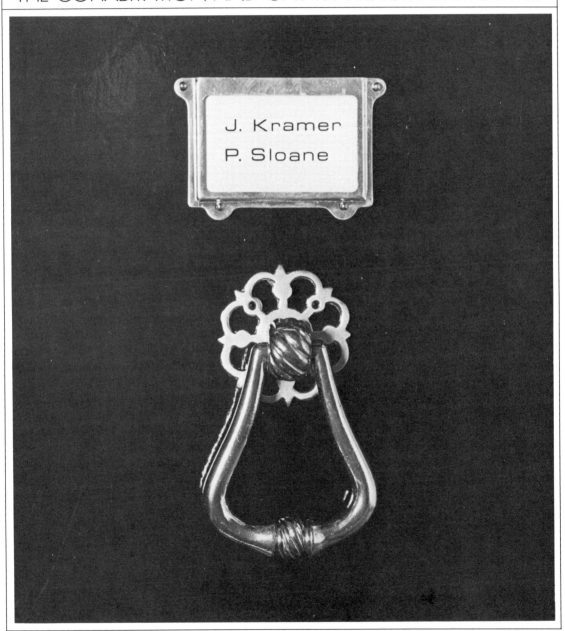

At a conference on religion and social issues, a handsome bearded man in his thirties passes around a photograph of his family as he talks about his love for his spouse and children. The picture shows two men and two children, all smiling happily. The man is a partner in a gay marriage. His partner is the father of the children and has legal joint custody with his former wife, who is grateful for the loving devotion the two men give to the children. She tells her former husband's male spouse that he is part of the family. Often the three parents and the children get together for picnics, birthdays, and holiday celebrations.

In another section of the country, a leading feminist is being interviewed on a talk show. She is asked why she never married and how she feels about marriage as an institution. She replies that marriage as it presently exists is stifling to wives and prevents a woman from fulfilling her total potential. She announces that she has no interest in marrying unless present arrangements of marriage and the family are drastically changed. Until such a time, singleness is preferable.

On another TV talk show, a young unmarried couple tell why they have chosen to live together. The man speaks of the unhappiness of his own childhood, the heartbreak of his parents' divorce, and how this soured him on the institution of marriage. As he speaks, he cuddles the squirming infant on his lap. The woman tells of her concern for their child's well-being. She maintains that she and the baby's father are together because they want to be, not because they *have* to be, adding that their relationship is not dependent upon a contract signed in accordance with society's decrees. Like many other unmarried couples who have chosen to live together, this man and woman feel that marriage can be a trap, forcing people into roles and de-

stroying the freedom and spontaneity they enjoy in their present arrangement.

Because such examples are given wide coverage in the mass media, there is much talk about the "death of the family" in modern society. However, many social scientists, including demographers, view the matter differently. Demographers, specialists in the study of population characteristics, are able to point out trends in births, deaths, marriages, divorces, and other areas of vital concern. "The family (in modified form) will go on," predicts demographer Paul C. Glick (1979:5), emphasizing that "the overwhelming majority of American people still live in nuclear families that include a married couple and/or a parent and one or more children."

At the same time, some persons are interested in different lifestyles and new definitions of *family*. Even Glick's description of the nuclear family is stretched to include solo-parent situations. In this unit, we'll be examining some of these alternatives to conventional marriage and family, giving special attention to unmarried-couple households, homosexual marriage, singleness and single parenthood, and various combined-household arrangements. This chapter will explore the first two of these because both cohabitation and homosexual partnerships are examples of pair bonding that force us to re-examine definitions, customs, and laws pertaining to marriage.

COHABITATION—LIVING TOGETHER WITHOUT MARRIAGE

One of the most talked-about emerging lifestyles in recent years has been the phenomenon usually called *cohabitation*—an arrangement in which unmarried opposite-sex partners set up a household together.

How Widespread Is Cohabitation?

Although we don't know exactly how many unmarried persons choose to live together in a marriagelike situation, a close but cautious look at statistics from the United States Bureau of the Census can provide some clue. Out of all *couple* households in the United States in 1986 (latest available statistics), 1 out of every 25 of the couples was unmarried (U.S. Bureau of the Census, *Current Population Reports*, P-20, no. 412, 1986:2). This means that in over two million households, an adult man or woman was living with an unrelated adult of the opposite sex. As Table 6-A shows, 61 percent of these households consisted of a male householder who had an unrelated woman living with him and 39 percent of them consisted of a female householder who shared her living quarters with an unrelated man.

The Census Bureau doesn't ask questions about the nature of the relationship in such households and, for many years, has reminded users of such data that many different situations are reflected in the findings. For example, an elderly woman may rent a room to a male student. Such situations could also include a live-in employee, such as a companion to an opposite-sex disabled person or a person who does housekeeping or other work in exchange for board and room and/or wages. However, demographers point out that most individuals in unmarried-couple households are in the same age group or an adjacent age group and are thought to be in some kind of personal relationship (Glick and Norton, 1977:32–33). Thirty percent of these households include children under age 15.

In over 2 million households in the United States, an adult man or woman lives with an unrelated adult of the opposite sex. (Michael Kagan/Monkmeyer)

Table 6-A also shows that the number of unmarried-couple households quadrupled between 1970 and 1986. However, even though they have been increasing faster than other types of households, the rate of growth slowed down somewhat by the early 1980s. Glick (1984a:22) projects that unmarried-couple households "are likely to account for only 3 percent of all households and 5 percent of all couple households by 1990." In 1986, 4 percent of all couple households in the United States were comprised of unmarried couples.

The situation is quite different in the Scandinavian countries where, according to soci-

TABLE 6-A   Selected characteristics of unmarried-couple households: 1986, 1980, and 1970 (Numbers in thousands)

CHARACTERISTIC	1986		1980		1970	
	NUMBER	PERCENT	NUMBER	PERCENT	NUMBER	PERCENT
Unmarried-couple households	2,220	100.0	1,589	100.0	523	100.0
Presence of children:						
No children under 15 years[1]	1,558	70.2	1,159	72.9	327	62.5
Some children under 15 years[1]	662	29.8	431	27.1	196	37.5
Sex of householder:						
Male	1,361	61.3	981	61.7	266	50.9
Female	860	38.7	608	38.3	257	49.1
Age of householder:						
Under 25 years	489	22	411	25.9	55	10.5
25 to 44 years	1,344	60.6	837	52.7	103	19.7
45 to 64 years	277	12.5	221	13.9	187	35.8
65 years and over	110	5.0	119	7.5	178	34.0
Marital status of householder:						
Never married	1,143	51.5	778	49.0	(NA)	(NA)
Married, spouse absent	185	8.3	144	9.1	(NA)	(NA)
Separated	161	7.3	121	7.6	(NA)	(NA)
Widowed	146	6.6	142	8.9	(NA)	(NA)
Divorced	746	33.6	525	33.0	(NA)	)NA)

[1]For 1970, children in unmarried-couple households are under 14 years old.
SOURCE: U.S. Bureau of the Census, *Current Population Reports*, Series P-20, no. 391, *Population Characteristics: Households, Families, Marital Status, and Living Arrangements: March, 1984* (Advance Report) (U.S. Government Printing Office, August 1984), p. 5; U.S. Bureau of the Census, *Current Population Reports*, Series P-20, no. 412, *Households, Families, Marital Status, and Living Arrangements: March, 1986* (Advance Report) (U.S. Government Printing Office, November, 1986), p.5.

ologist Jan Trost (1981:401), "nonmarital cohabitation has moved from being a deviant phenomenon to an institutionalized pattern of entering family life." In Sweden, for example, Trost estimates that nearly 1 in 5 couple households now consists of unmarried persons cohabiting under marriagelike conditions (in contrast to about 1 percent in the 1950s).

In his research on newly married couples, Trost found that 99 percent reported having cohabited before marrying. "Since 1972 or 1973 or so, cohabitation without marriage has been considered 'normal' behavior in Denmark and Sweden, and is in no respects at all a deviant phenomenon," he reports.

One indication that nonmarital cohabitation has become a social institution is that laws, authorities, organizations, and the general public increasingly recognize this living arrangement as equivalent to marriage in these countries. Trost points out that "Finland and Norway seem to be where Sweden and Denmark were some years ago" in this respect and contrasts their stage of development toward institutionalizing cohabitation with the situation in the United States, where cohabitation is still, by and large, viewed as a "deviant phenomenon" (pp. 419–421).

This may be changing, however, as premarital cohabitation shows signs of becoming increasingly accepted—at least for couples who eventually marry. Sociologist Patricia Gwartney-Gibbs (1986:423) goes so far as to suggest that it may be becoming "a new normative step leading to marriage." Using data from marriage-license applications in Lane County, Oregon, she found that more than half the couples (53 percent) had the same address before marriage in 1980. Of couples applying for marriage licenses ten years earlier, only 13 percent shared the same home address. Again, this data from one county reflect a fourfold increase and may point to what Gwartney-Gibbs calls "the institutionalization of premarital cohabitation."

Varied Intentions and Arrangements

When a man and woman decide to move in together, even though they have not met licensing and ceremonial requirements, their intentions may vary. In some cases, they may be thinking in terms of a "test run" to see if they're suited to be marriage partners later on. Their living together before that time would be considered a *trial marriage.* In other cases, the couple might be interested in a "do-it-yourself" marriage without the bother of state requirements such as blood tests, obtaining a license, and so on. They think of themselves as married and present themselves to the world as such, even though they have never had a wedding ceremony performed. Their union would be considered a *common-law marriage* in states where such marriages are recognized. A third category of living-together arrangements is entered by couples who are not necessarily interested in either testing out future marriage possibilities or considering themselves married in the common-law sense. They simply set up housekeeping together for companionship and convenience in an *ad hoc arrangement.*

Common-Law Marriage Trial lawyer Barbara Hirsch (1976:3) defines *common-law marriage* as "the lawful union of man and woman by declaration, intention, and conduct, which in certain domiciliary states joins the parties in a relationship that may be severed only by death or divorce." Where common-law marriage is recognized, the legal rights and duties are the same as in any other marriage; and the children of such a union are considered legitimate. But "both parties must actually intend their relationship to be a marriage," Hirsch emphasizes. And of course the couple must be living in a state that recognizes common-law marriage at the time they establish their relationship. Only in such a case could a couple expect the courts to consider their marriage authentic.

Hirsch explains further what common-law marriage means:

> They are Mr. and Mrs. They may file joint tax returns and in all other respects conduct themselves as married people. Having established that relationship, they are married. If they live in a common-law state and that state is their home, then they are married wherever they travel and wherever they later reside. The only way to end a marriage, ceremonial or common-law, is by death or divorce. Annulment doesn't count because that is a legal procedure which declares null and void only a purported marriage which was, in fact, no marriage at all. (p. 4)

The legal recognition of common-law marriage may be traced to the colonial period of American history, when distance made it impractical if not impossible for some couples to travel to a marriage-license office or to find an authorized officiant to perform a marriage ceremony. Currently, only thirteen states and the District of Columbia permit couples to form common-law marriages (Sonenblick, 1981).

There seems to be a growing trend toward

abolishing the institution of common-law marriage, mainly because of the many legal complications associated with it. Questions may arise over the legitimacy of offspring or the settlement of estates. Sociologist William Kephart (1964) refers to the costly court battles that are often necessary for a common-law wife after her husband dies. "Unless she can prove that a common-law marriage existed—seldom an easy task—neither she nor her children are entitled to the property rights or inheritance that normally are theirs" (p. 950). Sometimes upon the death of a wealthy bachelor, women who claim to have been common-law wives step forth hoping to gain an inheritance. And sometimes such claims are made even with regard to a married man. For example, after a 1974 air crash in which a honeymooning couple was killed, a woman filed suit with the airlines claiming she had lived as the groom's common-law wife and had several children by him. Second spouses of persons who have been in common-law marriages often run into particular difficulties with regard to estate settlements because a common-law husband or wife may have had the mistaken notion that getting out of such a marriage is just as simple as getting into it, not knowing that certain state laws may require a formal divorce decree. The subsequent spouse in such cases may have entered in good faith what he or she thought was a legal marriage only to find that the courts consider it to have been an illicit cohabitation because of a former common-law marriage which was never formally ended (Sussman, Cates, and Smith, 1970:270).

For reasons such as these, some legal experts and social scientists believe that the institution of common-law marriage should be abolished and that the only unions considered valid should be those in which the man and woman have secured a license from the state, had a wedding ceremony of some sort,

and obtained a properly signed marriage certificate. Other authorities disagree, pointing out that this would condemn many children "to bastardy" and increase injustice and suffering in the world rather than alleviate it. "This is particularly true among those social and economic classes who have not accepted middle-class standards of marriage," says one professor of law. "Certainly American marriage law should tolerate this much cultural diversity" (Clark, 1968, as quoted in Krause, 1971:18).

Common-law marriage is not easy to define because various states and even various courts tend to interpret it differently. For one thing, whether or not a union has been a valid marriage according to common law is something that is determined *after* the union has been entered. Harry Krause (1971:17–18), a professor of law, refers to a threefold test for such a marriage. The union is regarded as a valid marriage "if the intending spouses have presently consented to be husband and wife, if the marriage has been consummated, and if the spouses have publicly held out each other as such." He explains that "the requirement of 'present consent' to marriage distinguishes the resulting relationship from an engagement to be married at a future time." It also distinguishes it from a trial marriage.

Trial Marriage Before purchasing a new car, it's only rational to take it out for a test drive first. Some people have suggested that marriage should follow a similar pattern, allowing a test period of living together before making the final commitment. Such an arrangement usually goes by the name *trial marriage*. Some proponents suggest a structured form, others an unstructured.

Structured Trial Marriage Structured trial marriages would be institutionalized in some way, with regulations by society to legitimate

THE EFFECTS OF COMMON-LAW MARRIAGE

Under the common-law marriage doctrine, it *is* possible to become married retroactively. Is it, then, possible that a cohabiting couple can be married without knowing it, or even against their wishes? The answer is a qualified yes. The states do not go around slapping unwanted marriages like parking tickets on domestic operations; the status of common-law spouse is generally available to anyone who fills the local bill, but is *imposed* only when one or both parties go to court and successfully claim that status. For example:

Zeke Twombly, a blues guitarist, and his lady, Pinkie, who used to work the graveyard shift at the Top Note Cafe, live together on the outskirts of Mobile, Alabama, for two years. It's love in a cottage surrounded by prim neighbors, and while Zeke and Pinkie haven't really discussed the exact nature of their commitment, they find that the course of true love runs more smoothly when they use his last name and let everyone think that they're married.

Out of the blue, Zeke learns that an elderly fan has left him $4 million, with the stipulation that he enroll in classical music courses and stay off drugs. Zeke, who has always been a closet square, leaps at the terms, taking to his new life like a fish to water; Pinkie is bored stiff and wants out, but she wants to take a piece of the $4 million with her. She files a divorce action.

The court does not know whether Pinkie is telling the truth when she declares that she and Zeke privately agreed to be married. Zeke's denial is taken into consideration, but so are the testimony of their landlord, who swears he would not have rented them the cottage if Pinkie had not been introduced as Zeke's wife, and the records of a New Mexico motel where Zeke and Pinkie spent several blissful days, registered in Zeke's handwriting as Mr. and Mrs. Twombly. Finding no independent evidence to support Zeke's story, the court finds a common-law marriage, entitling Pinkie to some settlement upon the "divorce."

In this unedifying tale, Zeke does indeed find himself married unwillingly and unawares. What this best illustrates is why a majority of states has decided against recognizing common-law marriage; while it certainly offers protection to honest but unsophisticated partners, it also invites abuse, since it is not always easy to tell the fraudulent claims from genuine ones.

However, the courts are extending more recognition to serious relationships that endure without a matrimonial license. As the principles of the *Marvin* case gradually seep throughout the land, the fundamental commitments between homemates may receive much the same protection and acceptance as a common-law marriage.

SOURCE: Jerry Sonenblick, Atty., with Martha Sowerwine, *The Legality of Love* (New York: Jove Publications, 1981), pp. 77–78.

the union. The idea in itself is not new, although new variations continue to be suggested from time to time. Maurice of Saxony was already suggesting trial marriage in the eighteenth century because he considered marriage for life "a betrayal of the self, an unnatural compulsion." His proposed solution was the formation of temporary marriages, with contracts acknowledged as being for a limited period of time (Berger, 1971).

A related idea was proposed by one Judge Ben B. Lindsey. He called his concept "companionate marriage" and first wrote up his ideas for *Redbook* magazine in 1926, only to meet with ostracism and severe criticism after the article's appearance. Shortly afterward, Bertrand Russell proposed a similar idea, suggesting it would be especially applicable to university students as a better way of channeling sexual desires than was the case with the "excitement of parties and drunken orgies" during the Prohibition Era. Russell was rewarded for his efforts by scandal, slander, and the loss of his teaching position at the City College of New York. Americans made it clear that they were not ready for a revision of marriage customs (Lindsey, 1926, 1927; Lindsey and Evans, 1927; Russell, 1929; Skolnick, 1973:248).

Forty years after its publication of Judge Lindsey's article, *Redbook* published another much-discussed article on trial marriage—this time by anthropologist Margaret Mead (1966). Mead proposed a two-step marriage arrangement, each step differing in commitments and responsibilities. The first (or *trial*) part would be called *individual marriage*. It would be entered by a simple ceremony, carry limited economic responsibilities, would not allow children, and would be easy to end. The second (or *permanent*) step would be called *parental marriage*. It would be entered only by those couples who, after the first step of individual marriage, desired to form a lifetime relationship and undertake the obligations of parenthood.

Responses to Dr. Mead's proposal varied from praise for its emphasis on responsible parenthood to criticism for suggesting the temporary arrangement of the individual-marriage form (Mead, 1968). One woman wrote: "I still prefer God's one-step plan, which is *only* for mature couples, united for life, who are prepared for responsible parenthood." Other persons suggested that many couples already followed a similar plan

through existing channels: they enter legal marriage, responsibly use contraceptives for a few years of getting to know one another sexually and socially, then embark on parenthood when they feel the time is right. If the marriage doesn't seem to be working, there is divorce. In view of this, they wondered, what would be the need for such a two-step plan?

Students especially seemed to reject the idea. They couldn't see any reason to go through a marriage ceremony in order to live together and have sex relations if no children were desired. Why have new laws for what many were already doing anyway? One student flatly accused Dr. Mead of wanting "to bottle up freedom, to hedge it with ceremony and publicly acknowledged responsibility." In the end, Margaret Mead (1968) concluded, "It now seems clear to me that neither elders nor young people want to make a change to two forms of marriage. They want to reserve the word 'marriage' for a commitment that they can feel is permanent and final, no matter how often the actual marriages may fail."

There have been other attempts to add a new dimension of rationality to marriage through structured trial unions, all of which would of course require changes in present marriage laws (Berger, 1971). One example was Virginia Satir's proposal at the 1967 convention of the American Psychological Association, which suggested that marriage be made a statutory, five-year, renewable contract. This would provide a built-in mechanism for periodic review of the marriage so that a decision could be made either to go on with the relationship or to let it be terminated (Satir, 1967).

Unstructured Trial Marriage The proposals for structured trial marriages just examined would involve licensing and regulation by society. Many couples see no need for such involvement by the state, preferring to view the man-woman relationship as a private matter (Greenwald, 1970). They see the rationality in the trial-marriage idea but prefer an unstructured form. They simply live together. If they get along well and want the relationship to continue on a permanent basis, they can become legally married. On the other hand, if their living together convinces them they're unsuited for each other, they can go their separate ways.

Again, it must be stressed that the basic idea behind trial marriages is the notion that the selection of a marriage partner should involve rationality. Persons in such arrangements do not hold to the idealism of folklore (such as, "They fell in love, got married, and lived happily ever after—because love conquers all"). A trial marriage is entered in the expectation that rewards and especially the costs of a particular male-female exchange will become apparent *before* a permanent decision about the relationship is made.

Earlier, we saw that mate selection is essentially a process of seeking to strike the best bargain possible. Sociologist George Homans (1961) uses the term *profit* to describe the ratio of rewards to costs experienced by persons in social exchange. In a trial marriage, if the ratio is perceived as unfavorable (too many costs, not enough rewards), the partners are not encumbered by legal requirements to stay together. A "low-profit" situation can easily be terminated. This does not mean that decisions to break up will be painless. Just as in actual divorce, if one partner perceives the reward/cost ratio to be favorable and wishes to continue the arrangement, he or she is the one likely to feel the more hurt and deprived when the relationship ends.

In sum, trial marriage serves as a prelude to marriage and not as a substitute for it. For those who engage in it, it's a kind of experiment—a way of determining whether or not to seek legal marriage with this particular partner or with some other partner (perhaps after another trial marriage) or never with anyone.

Ad Hoc Arrangements The Latin expression *ad hoc* means "for this [special purpose]." Some couples who choose to live together unmarried view their arrangement as simply an ad hoc situation, existing for its own sake. For them, living together is not viewed as an experiment, and the persons concerned do not think of it as a trial marriage (structured or unstructured) or any other kind of marital arrangement. They are not interested in entering legal marriage through licensing and ceremonies, nor are they interested in having their relationship declared a common-law marriage—even if they happen to be in a state where common-law marriages are recognized. They simply want to live together totally apart from the institution of marriage, and they don't want others to consider them "married" in any sense (White and Wells, 1973; Macklin, 1972). Some ad hoc arrangements are short-term; others are ongoing, lasting years.

However, two small-scale studies indicate that females more than males may think of their living together as a possible prelude to marriage and not simply as a substitute or end in itself (Arafat and Yorburg, 1973; Lyness, Lipetz, and Davis, 1972). In other words, while some males may be viewing their cohabitation arrangement as only ad hoc, their female partners may be considering it a trial marriage. This would reflect traditional socialization which encourages females to seek their identity and self-esteem in marriage and motherhood. In addition, any guilt feelings and fear of censure for engaging in sex outside of marriage are easier to deal with if a woman believes her sexual partner is her future spouse.

In sociologist Kristin Luker's study of women seeking abortions (discussed earlier in Chapter 5), she too found that the women in her study tended to think of cohabitation as a trial marriage. This in turn often led to taking chances in birth-control practices. Luker (1975:101) reports that particularly where couples were economically interdependent, "women in the study began to feel after some period of time spent in consensual unions that they were not only being taken advantage of, but that they would be wasting the best years of their lives should the relationship not end in marriage. The pressure to test commitment and to force a declaration of intentions is an ideal precondition for contraceptive risk-taking."

Concealed Arrangements and Open Arrangements

It would be helpful at this point to try to sort out the relationship between *cohabitation* (living together outside of marriage) and *legally recognized marriage* (entered by fulfilling licensing and ceremonial requirements). This brings us back to the definition of marriage presented in Chapter 4.

Marriage, sociologically defined, consists of a relationship in which two or more persons maintain ongoing expressive (including sexual) and instrumental (including economic) exchanges. This definition is broad enough to encompass marriage in many forms—trial, legal, group, gay, traditional, modern, and so on. An important adjunct to this way of viewing marriage has to do with the *public nature* of the arrangement.

It is not likely that anyone would call an affair a marriage. *Affairs* are romantic attachments and regularized sexual liaisons usually carried out secretly and often considered to be of brief duration. While there are

certain expressive interchanges and quite possibly a giving and receiving of material gifts, there is no expectation of the ongoing sexual and economic interdependency that characterizes marital arrangements. What is more, persons involved in affairs try to keep their relationship hidden. Public revelation is the last thing such lovers want!

However, suppose two persons move in together and carry on both expressive and economic exchanges in much the same way as married persons. Yet, they carry on their relationship covertly, even though it is often difficult. Parents, peers, the postal service, the telephone company, insurance companies, the Internal Revenue Service, employers, and others who have an interest in them have no idea that this man and woman are sharing the same apartment. Even though their arrangement is a step closer to marriage than an affair would be, it still cannot be called a marriage—even in the sociological sense. Why? Because their relationship is clandestine and there is a deliberate avoidance of any public disclosure and social recognition.

If persons are secretive about their living together—covert instead of overt—it probably means that they fear punishments that could be imposed upon them by people they consider important in their lives, those whom sociologists call "significant others." Such people might apply negative sanctions so severe that they could disrupt the relationship entirely. If the relationship is that uncertain, tentative, and fragile, it cannot be called a marriage, because a marriage, by definition, is an ongoing exchange.

Two hypothetical couples serve as illustrations of the difference between covert and overt arrangements. Natalie and Kurt decide during college days to share a small apartment together. They don't hide the fact that they are living together, and their friends continue to accept them, visit them, and include them in invitations to various events and activities. Jean and Ed, on the other hand, don't want people to know about their similar living arrangement. They make it a point not to tell their friends out of fear that their friends would shun them if they knew. They are not prepared to accept such a cost because they know it might undermine their attraction for each other. How? Because the cost of rejection by friends might prove to be more significant than the rewards Jean and Ed currently furnish each other. Their arrangement might not seem worth the suffering of social ostracism.

Natalie and Kurt seem to have much more going for them than is true of Jean and Ed. For one thing, the parents of both Natalie and Kurt know about their relationship and do not punish through the withholding of benefits. The parents continue to help with college expenses and also help pay for travel when the couple visits them. Both the financial aid and the willingness to visit with the couple, desiring to be with them rather than shunning them, are important rewards that the parents are not withholding. Their approval of the relationship helps sustain it.

Conversely, Jean and Ed perceive that their parents would cut off all financial assistance if they knew how they were living. Furthermore, the parents would probably be icy cold to them and perhaps even refuse to see

them. This lack of approval plus the loss of economic benefits could also prove of greater significance than their own mutual benefits and thus threaten the ongoingness of their relationship.

Let's assume that several years pass. Natalie and Kurt have completed college, and each enters a livelihood where their living-together arrangement is not likely to incur punishments from people who provide them money (and thus exercise a certain degree of control over them). All this time, Kurt and Natalie have simply continued to live together without legal sanctions, and they plan to continue their arrangement into the future. Can we say they are married? Yes and no. Sociologically speaking, they would appear to be clearly married; they are in an ongoing relationship, publicly declared, in which there is both full expressive and instrumental interdependency. If we look at Figure 6-1, we can see that their situation is neither a trial marriage nor a temporary ad hoc situation. Yet it is not quite the same as a legal union. Their relationship may be called an *ongoing consensual union* (a long-standing situation of living together simply by mutual consent).

Figure 6-1 shows on one side a state of nonmarriage (point 1). This gradually fades into a sociological definition of marriage

FIGURE 6-1 Continuum of relationships between the single state and the married state.

1. NONMARRIAGE		2. MARRIAGE			
		a. SOCIOLOGICAL DEFINITION		b. LEGAL DEFINITION	
The affair	Living together covertly	Living together overtly		Common–law marriage	Legitimized union
(Regularized sexual liaisons)		Trial marriage or Temporary ad hoc arrangement	Ongoing consensual union (not legally recognized)	(In states where legally recognized)	(Fulfilling state requirements for licensing and solemnization)

(point 2*a*), which occurs when there is an overt ongoing exchange of instrumental and expressive benefits. The key word here is *overt*; the relationship is publicly known. However, to be legitimate in terms of a *legal* definition of marriage, (point 2*b*), the relationship must be socially sanctioned by fulfilling state requirements for licensing and solemnization in the presence of witnesses. In between the stage in which a couple may be considered to be married in a sociological sense and the stage in which marriage exists in the legal sense, there is an intermediate stage considered legal in some states only, namely common-law marriage.

In other words, it's not enough to think simply in terms of two statuses, singleness and marriage. To understand the phenomenon of cohabitation, we need to envision marriage as a matter of degrees, with various cohabitation patterns fitting at different points along a continuum. Such an approach can help us integrate the various approaches social scientists have utilized in their conceptualizations of cohabitation.

We need to keep in mind that the majority of cohabitants look forward to being legally married someday—although not, in all cases, to their present live-in partners. Studies have shown this to be true both in the United States and in the Scandinavian countries (Trost, 1981; Newcomb and Bentler, 1980; Blumstein and Schwartz, 1983). Understandably, then, some sociologists see cohabitation primarily as an optional new stage in the sequence of dating, courtship, and marriage (Newcomb and Bentler, 1980; Macklin, 1978; Risman, Hill, Rubin, and Peplau, 1981; Gwartney-Gibbs, 1986). Others see cohabitation as a *variety* of marriage, not an alternative to it, and point out that cohabitants who later marry may view the marriage ceremony as a "rite of confirmation," substantiating their being a family unit, committed

to one another and intending a stable ongoing relationship, rather than viewing it as a "rite of passage," marking a transition to another way of living (Trost, 1981; Lewin, 1982). Still other social scientists look upon cohabitation as an alternative standing on its own merits—a new structure for intimacy apart from traditional marriage laws and customs. In a study of unmarried couples in the Netherlands, Cees Straver (1981) found evidence of two distinct types of relationship—one following the sharing and togetherness model of traditional marriage and the other carving out a path of its own, stressing individual personality development and economic independence. "Each form must be allowed to make its own demands and have its own legal status," writes Straver, with the "sharers" being permitted to obtain the benefits of the legal marriage model they follow and the "independents" being respected in their wish *not* to be considered in some kind of marriage and their desire to "preserve their economic independence from one another" (p. 72).

Cohabitation and the Law

Marriage carries with it certain rights and duties. But since cohabitation (whether a trial marriage or a temporary or ongoing ad hoc arrangement) is not defined as legal marriage, questions have arisen about whether cohabitation similarly entails privileges and duties.

As the decade of the eighties began, scholars and legal authorities from around the world were conferring with one another on how family law should deal with cohabitation—including questions of inheritance rights, insurance, social security benefits, worker's compensation, responsibilities for children born of unwed couples, and so on (Eekelaar and Katz, eds., 1980).

In the United States during the early 1970s, unmarried couples who separated occasionally went to court to determine which partner could keep the water bed or other items from among the goods they had accumulated while sharing an apartment together. Both the number of such cases and the size of the requested property settlements have grown considerably over the years since then.

Widespread attention was especially focused on the $1.8 million suit filed against the actor Lee Marvin by his former live-in companion Michelle Triola Marvin (who had legally changed her surname although she had not married Marvin). Ms. Marvin had taken quite literally the actor's alleged remark early in their six-year cohabitation that "what I have is yours and what you have is mine," and the California Supreme Court ruled she had the right to sue for what she felt was her share of the amount the actor had earned during their time together. However, although the state supreme court had upheld Ms. Marvin's *right* to seek a property settlement just as though she had been a legal wife, the superior court judge who heard her case refused to grant her request for half of Lee Marvin's $3.6 million earned during their years of cohabitation. But the judge did rule that she was entitled to $104,000 for "rehabilitation purposes" so that she could learn or improve skills to aid in her employment, which prompted Ms. Marvin to remark triumphantly, "I am proud to have paved the way for other unmarried women" (*Greensboro (NC) Daily News*, April 19, 1979).

Some cohabiting couples have looked for ways to avoid possible legal problems in the future by drawing up a formal contract at the outset. In his book, *Oh Promise Me But Put It in Writing*, lawyer Paul Ashley (1978:69–77) suggests a number of legal approaches that can be used in developing suitable contracts: trust relationships, partnership agreements, cooperative enterprises, and joint-ownership plans. Such arrangements have to do only with property rights, property management, sharing in tangible profits and losses, and the like. They have nothing to do with the personal and sexual aspects of the relationship.

Indeed, a contract that sought to regulate the *totality* of a cohabiting couple's life together would probably not stand up in courts as a recognized legal contract. Why? Because such a contract "is intended to perpetuate consortium," explains lawyer Barbara Hirsch (1976:96). "It is therefore in derogation of the public policy favoring lawful marriage and legitimate offspring—and therefore unenforceable."

Hirsch points out other ways in which cohabitation practices may not only violate public policy but also may violate actual laws, including certain state laws against fornication (sexual intercourse between a man and a woman who are not married to each other) and certain sexual techniques—especially oral-genital sex. She writes:

> Whether, however, the statutes against fornication, sodomy, fellatio, cunnilingus, transportation across state lines, false registration into hotels, and so forth are actually going to ruin your plans for a skiing trip to Aspen is up to you. The actual risk of criminal prosecution is small, but the laws are there. (p. 39)

Another attorney, Jerry Sonenblick (1981) has put together a book on the "laws of live-in love." One-half of the book is devoted to a state-by-state guide to legal aspects of marriage, cohabitation, common-law marriage, and termination of relationships. Sonenblick uses the term *homemates* in speaking of unwed persons in a committed live-in relationship to distinguish them from what he calls *casual mates* who keep finances and other aspects of their lives separately and give little hint of a shared future together. He feels such a distinction is important because "the courts are starting to recognize that some mates make substantial commitments to each other, while others view living together as a light exchange of companionship and intimacy with few strings attached" (p. 14). Again, our continuum in Figure 6-1 on page 165 should be kept in mind.

Sociologist D. Kelly Weisberg (1975:557) says the central problem in laws affecting cohabitation is "one of cultural lag." As more and more persons engage in behavior that is not legally sanctioned, the legal process may lag behind the social change that has already taken place. "The law thus penalizes participants of alternative families which fulfill the same needs and perform the same functions [as legally defined families]," says Weisberg. Traditional legal definitions have reserved the word *family* for persons who are descended from a common ancestor or who have entered a recognized relationship through formal adoption or marriage ceremonies; and the legal rights and duties associated with this family status have been spelled out by the courts. Laws are designed to discourage the establishment of nontraditional family forms, Weisberg emphasizes, and therefore the judicial system grants to conventional families rights denied those persons who elect to live in other kinds of relationships. (See also Blumstein and Schwartz, 1983:320–322.)

At the same time, sociologist Lenore Weitzman and her colleagues (1978) point out that many of the "rights" attached to husband-wife status are actually disadvantageous for the individuals concerned. The traditional definitions of marriage and family that family laws are designed to promote and protect assume four essential obligations: (1)

the husband is considered to be head of the household, (2) the husband is assigned responsibility for supporting the family, (3) the wife is assigned responsibility for domestic services, (4) the wife is assigned responsibility for child care (Weitzman et al., 1978:306–311). These authors suggest that carefully worded private contracts drawn up by cohabiting, premarried, and married couples can allow for greater flexibility and more egalitarian relationships than can the state-imposed legal marriage contract, which assigns rights and responsibilities on the basis of gender. Although the question of the enforceability of these private contracts is not indisputably settled, Weitzman (1981:335–415) provides examples of numerous court rulings that indicate gradually changing attitudes toward unmarried cohabitation, including a growing recognition of the intentions and expectations of the couples involved and a growing respect for the contracts the two persons have agreed upon together. (See also Myricks, 1980.)

Who Cohabits, and Why?

Most studies of cohabitation have focused on college students. The living-together phenomenon has been especially popular among this segment of the population; and besides, students are a readily available group for researchers to study! A careful review of the research conducted by numerous sociologists on various campuses indicates that approximately 1 out of 4 undergraduates in the United States has lived in a cohabitation arrangement at least once (Macklin, 1978; 1980). Thus, some social scientists suggest that census figures such as those cited earlier may be on the conservative side because they don't include a systematic representation of the college student population (Cole, 1977:76).

At the same time, as sociologists Richard Clayton and Harwin Voss (1977) point out, the extent of current cohabitation in the population in general ("Are you *now* cohabiting?") will be "substantially lower than the lifetime prevalence of cohabitation" ("Have you *ever* cohabited?"). In their nationwide random sample of more than twenty-five hundred men in the age range of 20 to 30 years, they found 18 percent had lived with a woman outside marriage for at least six months at some time in their lives. But only 5 percent were cohabiting at the time of the study, leading Clayton and Voss to emphasize that cohabitation relationships "either terminate or the partners marry" rather than existing as a permanent form of union in most cases (p. 277).

In a national study of never-married 20- to 29-year-old women living in households and college dormitories, researchers Koray Tanfer and Marjorie C. Horn (1985b) found that 12 percent of the women were *currently* living in a nonmarital cohabitation arrangement, whereas 30 percent reported having lived in such an arrangement in the past.

Why has cohabitation come to be accepted to the degree that it has? Most suggested reasons have concentrated on the college student population, where the acceptance of live-in relationships is thought to have something to do with greater sexual permissiveness in general and the popularity of the "permissiveness-with-affection" standard in particular; or perhaps it's related to changes in university regulations, such as the elimination of curfews and different hours for females and males and the availability of off-campus housing and twenty-four-hour visiting privileges in dormitories. Other suggested explanations for cohabitation among college students focus on changes in the traditional status of women, the availability of contraceptives and abortion to cut down

pregnancy risks in such arrangements, a disenchantment with conventional marriage, and a willingness to tolerate a variety of lifestyles (Peterman, Ridley, and Anderson, 1974:344; Macklin, 1972:98).

In her studies of cohabiting couples at Ohio State, sociologist Nancy Moore Clatworthy (1975:77) found that most persons reported living together "for convenience or economic reasons or simply because they liked or loved the person that they lived with." Other reasons cited were "companionship" and "security." No doubt similar reasons would be given by cohabiting couples beyond the college population—along with the belief that cohabitation can serve as a test for marital compatibility. On the other hand, as Newcomb and Bentler (1980:83) suggest, cohabitation "may reflect a broad change in what some people seek from personal relationships." These researchers go on to report their finding that "cohabitors seem to see themselves as more competent, independent, and self-reliant than noncohabitors, and as such may not be as dependent on their relationships for support, contact and intimacy."

Age and Cohabitation Among cohabitants who have never been married, 8 out of 10 men and nearly 9 out of 10 women are under the age of 35 (Spanier, 1983). Thus, not surprisingly, most persons think of cohabitation as a phenomenon among young adults.

If we look only at formerly married persons in cohabitation relationships, however, a very different picture emerges. In this population, the highest proportion of cohabitants are over 35 years of age (64 percent of formerly married male cohabitants and 54 percent of formerly married female cohabitants). In fact, nearly one-fourth of the men and slightly over one-fifth of the women are 65 years old or older (Spanier, 1983). Prior

For some elderly widowed people, pension restrictions on survivor's benefits have prevented remarriage, making cohabitation their only option for living together in a couple relationship. (Ginger Chich/Peter Arnold, Inc.)

to a change in the Social Security Act in 1979, many older widowed persons who wanted to marry felt they were forced into cohabitation arrangements because of a government policy that cut off survivor's benefits upon remarriage. Also, as Weitzman (1981:164) points out, "many private pension plans still terminate a widow's benefits if she remarries, and they therefore provide a strong economic disincentive to remarriage for widows."

Divorce and Cohabitation Cohabitation rates are higher for divorced persons than for never-married individuals (Glick and Norton, 1977:33–34; Clayton and Voss, 1977:283; Yllo, 1978:47). Various researchers have therefore speculated that an unsatisfactory marriage experience may lead some persons to avoid the risk of repeating such an experience by choosing unmarried cohabitation instead—at least for a time. In their study of separation and divorce, sociologists Graham

Spanier and Linda Thompson (1984:203) asked the 205 women and men in their sample how they would feel about living with a potential spouse before remarriage. Half the respondents said they would prefer to do so, and another third said they would consider it. Only 1 out of 6 reported they would be opposed to such cohabitation. In one study of remarried family situations, the prior living together of the couple and any children either had was shown to have positive benefits, helping the adjustment process of the stepfamily being formed and contributing to a supportive environment on the part of the extended kin, whose relationship with the stepfamily in the making appeared to be strengthened (Hanna and Knaub, 1981).

Race and Cohabitation In the large national study of 20- to 30-year-old men, Clayton and Voss (1977) found that blacks were more likely than whites to have lived in a cohabitation relationship at some point. Census data also indicate that in 1980, a time when only 2 percent of all households included a man and woman unrelated to each other and no other adults, 3.5 percent of all black households were of this type (Glick, 1981:113). Demographer Paul Glick, commenting on this data, points out that although nearly 1 out of 5 *unmarried-couple* households was maintained by a black couple in 1980 (when blacks maintained slightly over 1 out of 10 of *all* households), the actual number of black unmarried couples was rather small and the gap between blacks and others was showing signs of narrowing.

Staples (1981a:191) found that those of his sample of black, middle-class singles who chose to cohabit "only adopted the practice of living together after it was firmly established in the white community." At the same time, he points out that historically "the practice of living together without a marriage contract was very common to black people"—especially in the rural South. Many poor black couples were unable to afford marriage licenses and weddings and therefore entered what were often long-standing, devoted, common-law relationships. The difference in cohabitation practices among today's blacks is that such arrangements are found among the middle class as well.

In his sample of black singles, Staples found little difference between the sexes in the actual incidence of living together, but many women showed strong negative or at least ambivalent feelings about the practice. In contrast, the men were quite receptive to the idea. In another study conducted at two Florida universities, the researchers found that only slightly over one-fifth of black women in their study reported having cohabited, in comparison to just under one-half of white women and men and just over one-half of black men (Jacques and Chason, 1978).

In analyzing data from the 1982 National Survey of Family Growth, Christine A. Bachrach (1985) found cohabitation to be nearly three times more common among single Hispanic women (15.7 percent) than among other single women (5.6 percent). In comparing black single women with white single women, Bachrach found that 4 percent of the blacks were cohabiting, while the figure was 7.2 percent for whites.

Staples (1981a:193–194) concludes from the comments of the black women he interviewed that in a cohabitation arrangement "many women find they are denied the legitimacy that marriage confers while being subjected to all its constraints." He also found that among formerly married women especially, there was a tendency to view a cohabitation experience as "time contained"—a temporary living arrangement in which they must take care to avoid "merging into a collective identity with their live-in mate" by maintaining separateness in finances and other areas. These women guard their autonomy carefully, no doubt at least partially because of experiences in their prior marriages.

Religion and Cohabitation In Kersti Alice Yllo's examination of data from a national area-probability sample, she found an overrepresentation of Roman Catholic women in the cohabitation grouping (Yllo, 1978). Other sociologists, in their more limited samples of college students, have noticed a similar pattern (Henze and Hudson, 1974; Peterman et al., 1974). The usual explanation has been based on the assumption that cohabitation is one way for a young Roman Catholic woman to break loose from parental and church restrictions. Such a woman "is perhaps reacting to the greater freedom in the campus setting by experimenting with new ideas and patterns of behavior," suggest Henze and Hudson (1974:726).

Yllo, however, offers a different explanation, which may be more applicable to the broader population that her sample represents. She suggests that cohabitation may be a way of dealing with the Roman Catholic church's position on divorce and remarriage. "Young Catholic women may want to be more sure of their possible marriage partner since divorce is not viewed as an option for them later," writes Yllo. "Also, older Catholic women whose marriages have failed are denied the opportunity to divorce and remarry. Consequently, they may have to settle for a separation from their husband and a cohabiting relationship with their new partner" (p. 45). She sees this as further indication of ways "social structural constraints may affect cohabitation rates."

In their study of 159 married couples, comparing those who had cohabited before marriage with those who had not, Michael Newcomb and Peter Bentler (1980) found that contrary to the studies just mentioned, a greater percentage of Catholics were found among those persons who had *not* cohabited. "Typically, religious affiliation or commitment has an inhibiting influence on nonmarital intimate and sexual behavior, which cohabitation partially represents," say these researchers, pointing out that they found this to be true among both the Catholic and Protestant women in their sample but not among the Jewish women. They suggest that this finding "may represent an aspect of greater liberalism associated with the Jewish religion" (p. 79).

Various Protestant groups have devoted study to the question of cohabitation from a moral and theological viewpoint. A conference of Quakers, who decided upon the term *unregistered marriages* in speaking of cohabitation, remembered that Quaker marriages had at one time not been recognized legally. One outcome of the Quaker questioning was a questionnaire sent out by the National Council of Churches that indicated various attitudes and responses on church policy in cases where cohabiting couples wished to register together for overnight church conferences. (See Mace and Mace, 1981.) Facing such questions is, for many religious groups, much like the situation in many families where a son or daughter wishes to bring a live-in partner home for the holidays and expects to share the bedroom with the partner.

Parents and Cohabitation

In their sample of college students, Henze and Hudson (1974:724) found that while more than 8 out of 10 students would feel comfortable discussing their cohabitation relationship with their friends, only about one-third felt they could be comfortable discussing such a relationship with their parents. It is not difficult to guess the reason. Various

studies have shown that students in cohabitation relationships know or expect their parents to be disapproving of such relationships (Macklin, 1972; Bower and Christopherson, 1977). Staples (1981a) reported this to be true among the cohabitants in his sample of 25- to 45-year-old college-educated, urban black singles. Most indicated to Staples that they did not remain in locations where they had grown up or where their families still lived, thus keeping their cohabitation arrangement hidden.

Other studies show that roughly between about one-fourth (Peterman, Ridley, and Anderson, 1974:348) and one-half (Macklin, 1972:100; Bower and Christopherson, 1977:449) of the parents of cohabitants are thought to be aware of the arrangement; the rest are thought not to know—although they may suspect. Macklin (1972:100) reports that problems with parents mentioned by respondents in her study of female cohabitants included not only real or anticipated disapproval of the male partner but also "fear of discovery, guilt because they were deceiving or hurting their parents, rejection by or ultimatums from parents, and most frequently, sadness at not being able to share this important part of their lives with their parents."

Forming and Maintaining a Cohabitation Relationship

The formation of cohabitation relationships usually comes about gradually. Couples tend neither to jump into them nor to deliberate over them; rather, they just drift into such arrangements. One person stays at the other's place one night, and that makes it easier to stay overnight the next time, until one or the other partners eventually moves in full time (Macklin, 1972; Cole, 1977:70). In some cases, living together does not mean sexual involvement (Macklin, 1972).

According to Cole (1977), a shift in a couple's perception of their relationship occurs when they begin living together. He writes:

> At the point in the process when the partners move in together, the social reality of their relationship undergoes a significant change that calls for a new subjective assessment of that relationship. They must now redefine their social situation to account for the fact that they are cohabiting. This redefinition frequently is accompanied by a reassessment of their feelings toward their partner as well as their own self-concept. If the partners perceive that cohabiting provides them with a favorable reward-cost ratio, they will likely continue to live together. (p. 70)

(Note how Cole is here combining features of social-exchange and symbolic-interaction theory.)

Expectations and Commitment Cole's ongoing research on cohabiting couples has shown only a small minority to be committed to marrying the partner or working hard toward making the relationship a lasting one. Rather, the majority report that they intend to stay in the relationship as long as the association is "mutually satisfying" or "personally enjoyable." "These data suggest that most cohabitants will invest time and energy in a relationship as long as the rewards (satisfactions and enjoyments) outweigh the costs (sacrifices)," Cole (1977:71) emphasizes. A cohabitation relationship is constantly being evaluated and reevaluated, as the participants weigh advantages against disadvantages (Macklin, 1972; Cole, 1977; Libby, 1977a).

Different Types of Cohabitation Relationships Three specialists in family life have suggested that cohabiting relationships tend to fall into one of several categories: the "Linus-blanket" type, the "emancipation" type, the "convenience" type, and the "test-ing" type (Ridley, Peterman, and Avery, 1978).

In the first type (named for the security blanket used by a character in the Peanuts cartoon strip), the relationship is built on "an overwhelming need for one member of the pair to have a relationship with *someone,* with little apparent regard for whom, or under what conditions. To have someone to be with, even though he or she may treat you badly, is better than not having anyone at all" (Ridley, Peterman, and Avery, 1978:130). According to these authors, such a relationship has emotional security as its aim and does not provide opportunities for developing communication and problem-solving skills. Ridley, Peterman, and Avery explain:

> Negative statements made to the insecure person (frequently in the form of criticisms) are often interpreted as a severe questioning of his or her self-worth. The result is that the more secure person perceives and/or acts as if the partner is fragile ("can't take criticism") and that they cannot "rock the boat" without hurting their partner and the relationship. (pp. 130–131)

What these authors term the "emancipation" type of cohabitation relationship is characterized by feelings of guilt, uneasiness, and "unfinished business" on the part of one of the individuals. A desire to break free of internalized past restrictions may push one toward cohabitation; but upon entering such a relationship, internal pressures and feelings of wrongdoing now cause the person to want out of the relationship, with the result that the cycle begins again. Such persons tend to remain in cohabitation arrangements only briefly.

The third type of cohabitation relationship described by Ridley and his colleagues is the "convenience" type, which they say "is perhaps best exemplified in the short duration cohabiting relationship of freshmen or sophomore males." Such a situation "allows the male to have regularized sexual contact and the luxuries of domestic living without the responsibilities of a committed relationship." These authors state that "his major task is to keep the female interested in the relationship when it appears that she is putting more into the relationship than he is" (p. 131). They point out that females may also enter such relationships for "convenience" reasons; although the more common pattern is for males to seek such arrangements, knowing they can count on female socialization to have prepared the female partner to assume domestic tasks.

Last, Ridley, Peterman, and Avery list the "testing" type of cohabitation. The emphasis is on trying out interpersonal skills in a more complex male-female involvement; and at the same time, the partners are learning something else. Ridley and his associates explain:

> In a sense, the partners seem to use the relationship to get to know more about themselves—their likes and dislikes, and to learn more about how intimate relationships of this type apparently lead to a deeper level of self-understanding for both individuals. However, when the relationship solidifies too quickly—prior to the development of individual interests and preferences—the partners feel overinvolved and dependent on the relationship with the accompanying sense of loss of identity. (p. 132)

Prior Cohabitation and the Quality and Stability of Marriage

Do couples who have lived together before marriage have better marriages? The evidence thus far is inconclusive.

Some studies have indicated that the divorce rate of persons who enter marriage after cohabiting is no higher than that among persons who have not cohabited (Risman et al., 1981; Bentler and Newcomb, 1978). In fact, few significant differences have emerged when researchers have compared married couples with cohabiting couples or when they have compared married couples who did not live together before marriage with those who did (see summary of studies in Macklin, 1978, 1980).

In one study, the researcher conducted forty in-depth interviews with persons who were currently either married or divorced and who had either cohabited or simply dated prior to marriage (Rank, 1981). In his small, nonrandom sample, he found that *attitudes toward the transition to marriage*—and not whether or not the couple had cohabited—was the important factor associated with eventual marital breakup. Couples in intact marriages, regardless of whether or not they had cohabited before marriage, tended to see the marriage as simply an extension or continuation of their prior relationship. In contrast, among the divorced respondents, regardless of whether they had lived together or only dated before marriage, there was a tendency to have viewed the transition to marriage as a decided break with their past way of relating and a tendency for the two spouses to have had differing expectations and perceptions of all that married life entails.

In a much larger study of persons who had cohabited with their future spouses, sociologists Alfred DeMaris and Gerald Leslie (1984) found that wives reported perceiving a lower quality of communication after marriage and that both spouses reported lower marital satisfaction than did married couples who had not cohabited. These researchers, aware that their data ran "counter to 'common sense' expectations regarding the advantages of living together before marriage," are persuaded that the findings can be accounted for by the differences between persons who choose to cohabit and those who do not rather than by the cohabitation experience itself. "Rather than acting as a filter that effectively screens out the less-compatible couples," write DeMaris and Leslie, "cohabitation appears to select couples from the outset who are somewhat less likely to report high satisfaction once they are married." They explain that such couples may either have higher expectations for marriage from the beginning or may find it harder than do more traditional couples to adapt to the role expectations associated with conventional marriage. In any case, these sociologists reach the conclusion that "the evidence accumulated to date would indicate that, while living together before marriage is increasingly becoming a common phase of courtship, cohabitation has no particular advantage over more traditional practices in assuring couple compatibility in marriage" (p. 83).

Gender Roles and Cohabitation

Many people believe that choosing to live together apart from traditional marriage will also mean living apart from traditional marriage *roles*. But is cohabitation more egalitarian? Or do couples find themselves slipping into conventional husband-wife patterns?

In Clatworthy's sample of cohabitants in a college setting, 77 percent of the respondents reported that they shared food costs and rent and 59 percent reported that they shared household chores such as laundry, cleaning, cooking, and shopping equally (1975:74–75). On the other hand, Cole (1977:72–73) summarizes seven studies that suggest that "cohabitation is not as equalitarian in the assignment of sex roles and/or household tasks as one might expect" and that furthermore, males and females have dif-

ferent perceptions of their contributions within the household, with females believing that they have the greater work load and males believing that gender-role equality exists.

With regard to household decision-making, Cole reports that his own ongoing longitudinal research on cohabiting couples indicates that three-fourths of them practice "segmentalized decision making," that is, one partner more than the other is responsible for certain decisions according to that partner's expertise and interests. For instance, whoever owned the car before the cohabitation began tends to remain responsible for the car's upkeep. At the same time, many decisions are made jointly. Overall, according to Cole, it appears that females are expected to make more household-related decisions than are males. "It is unclear," he writes, "whether or not this greater female responsibility is indicative of traditional sex-role inequality where the woman is frequently relegated a disproportionate share of the responsibility for household tasks and decisions" (p. 72).

In her large random sample of married and unmarried couples from the general population, Yllo (1978:48–49) found no significant difference between cohabitants and marrieds with regard to decision-making; cohabiting relationships were not found to be more egalitarian on this dimension. Similarly, when the two groups were compared on household division of labor, the data showed that "cohabiting couples are fairly traditional in terms of dividing household tasks along sex lines." Men, whether they were in cohabitation relationships or marriage relationships, "differed in no significant ways as to the type and amount of work they do." And for their part, women in the two groups showed no differences from one another with regard to managing money and responsibility for social activities. But one difference did show up between the two categories of women. Whereas 70 percent of married women under age 30 reported having primary or total responsibility for cooking, cleaning, and repairing the house; only half of the *cohabiting* women in this age group reported such responsibility. On the other hand, approximately two-thirds of women over age 30 bore much or all responsibility for these chores—*regardless* of whether they were cohabiting or married. Since no significant differences showed up among the men, however, Yllo hesitates to conclude that even the younger cohabitants have an overall more egalitarian division of labor than do their married counterparts.

Three other sociologists studied matched samples of married and cohabiting college men and women in research designed specifically to test whether cohabiting couples share chores more equally (Stafford, Backman, and diBona, 1977). Their conclusion? "Women of both groups are still taking most of the responsibility for, and performing most of, the household tasks" (p. 43). They attribute this finding to traditional gender-role ideology and the socialization and parental role models to which persons of both sexes have been exposed during their growing-up years. "Simply removing the institution of marriage and the traditional authority of the male that has accompanied it in Western society will not usher out traditional sex roles," write these researchers. "The nonconscious ideology that . . . keeps women and men in their places will gradually have to be eroded" (p. 55).

In an exploratory study that provides some indication of the impact of an egalitarian ideology, sociologist Lenore Weitzman (1978) and her associates at the Center for the Study of Law and Society at the University of California at Berkeley asked students to prepare their own marriage or living-together contracts. These contracts would be written as alternatives to the traditional legal marriage contract, which assigns rights and responsibilities on the basis of sex.

Some of the students were already married, so they prepared their contracts as "contracts within marriage." Other students were planning to be married but wanted to live together first in a trial union, so they prepared contracts accordingly. The third and largest group were the cohabitants, most of whom "explicitly rejected legal marriage and wrote these contracts to establish a different structure for their relationships," says Weitzman and her colleagues (p. 323).

These researchers found that in general, the personalized contracts written by the couples—whether married, premarried, or cohabiting—"*were more likely to structure intimate relationships as partnerships* and to provide for a more equal sharing of both rights and responsibilities" (p. 374) than is true of the traditional legal marriage contract. The *most* egalitarian contracts were written by the cohabiting couples, and the *least* egalitarian were written by the married couples. Couples planning on marriage were somewhere in between the two.

The major difference between the cohabitants' contracts and those of the married couples related to individualism and the allocation of decision-making and responsibilities. Cohabitants tended to stress each partner's individuality (including self-support and separate finances), while the married persons emphasized togetherness (viewing property and support as "joint endeavors"). As to decision-making and division of labor, the cohabitants were "much more likely to contribute equally to decisions and to share equally responsibilities," in contrast to the married couples, who were "more likely to assign decisions and responsibilities to a single person on a sex-related basis" (Weitzman et al., 1978:371).

It is easier to philosophize about gender-role equality than to live it consistently because the impact of traditional socialization runs so deep. (© 1979 by Susan Berkowitz)

Apparently, in ideology at least, some co-habitants are looking for something different from conventional marriage—a way in which a man and woman can structure their shared life by rewriting the rules of the traditional marriage contract with its gender-specific rights and duties. *Carrying out* the ideology may be another matter, however, as several of the studies have shown. "Repeatedly, people see themselves slipping into stereotyped sex roles in running households," observes sociologist Robert Whitehurst (1974a, as quoted in Stafford et al., 1977:46), pointing out that it's easier to philosophize about gender-role equality than to live it consistently because the impact of traditional socialization runs so deep. (See also Mainardi, 1970.)

In short, cohabitation as it is developing today shows both similarities to conventional marriage and profound differences. (See Blumstein and Schwartz, 1983.) A woman and man are sharing a life together—materially, emotionally, and sexually. Some social commentators therefore speak of cohabitation as a "quasi-marriage" relationship. (The term *quasi* derives from the Latin *quam*, "as," and *si*, "if." Thus, cohabitation is something resembling marriage if not marriage "for real." It's to live *as if* married.) Yet, cohabitation doesn't have the legal recognition and social support so necessary for actual marriage to exist in the fullest sense of that word (as defined in this book).

That brings us to another type of quasi-marriage relationship in which some persons are living in the face of even less social support and in the complete absence of legal recognition: same-sex marriage.

GAY MARRIAGE

Nearly two thousand years ago, the Roman poet Ovid wrote of a man who informed his pregnant wife that family financial conditions were such that they could only afford a boy. Tearfully, he said that if a female were born, the baby must immediately be put to death. When the mother gave birth to a girl, she followed the counsel of a goddess and did not tell the father, who thought he had a son. Only the mother and a faithful nurse knew the truth. The baby was dressed in male attire and given the name Iphis, a name used for both boys and girls.

When Iphis was 13, the father arranged a marriage between his handsome offspring and a beautiful girl named Ianthe. The two were the same age and had been educated together so that a deep bond of love had grown between them. Ianthe's passion for Iphis grew, and she longed for the wedding day, whereas Iphis, though equally in love, kept postponing it. Her desperate mother invented excuses of illnesses or visions interpreted as bad omens. Ovid describes the sense of hopelessness:

> Iphis loved a girl whom she despaired of ever being able to enjoy, and this very frustration increased her ardour. A girl herself, she was in love with one of her own kind, and could scarcely keep back her tears, as she said: "What is to be the end of this for me, caught as I am in the snare of a strange and unnatural kind of love, which none has known before? Cows do not burn with love for cows, nor mares for mares. It is the ram which excites the ewe, the hind follows the stag, birds too mate in the same way, and never among all the animals does one female fall in love with another. How I wish I had never been born! (Ovid's *Metamorphoses*, p. 223, Penguin edition.)

Iphis tried to talk herself out of her feelings. "Pull yourself together, Iphis, be firm, and shake off this foolish, useless emotion. . . . It is hope that conceives and nourishes desire: and your case denies you hope." Rebelliously, she reasoned that none of the usual obstacles kept her from her beloved's embrace; there was no guardian forbidding the marriage, no husband to whom she was bound, no stern father standing in the way of her happiness. It was all the fault of nature. She moaned: "My wedding day is at hand, and now Ianthe will be mine: yet she will not be. I shall thirst in the midst of waters." Crying out to the god and goddess of marriage, Iphis asked why they should even bother to "come to this ceremony, at which there is no bridegroom, where two brides are being wed."

The problem was solved through the intervention of the same goddess who had advised the girl's mother while awaiting Iphis's birth. A miracle was performed within the temple, and Iphis was changed into a young man—a suitable bridegroom for the happy Ianthe.

In mythology, such a gods-to-the-rescue ending might seem a reasonable device for solving the problems of the characters involved. But the solution is not so simple in real life. Persons interested in a same-sex marriage today would be quite unlikely to welcome the intervention of Iphis's goddess. It's true, of course, that some persons undergo sex-reassignment surgery and hormonal treatment because they consider themselves women who are trapped in men's bodies or men who are trapped in women's bodies. But strictly speaking, such persons are transsexual, not homosexual. Their personal image of themselves as female or male doesn't match what their bodies tell them they are. Thus, they want their bodies changed to conform to what they feel is their true sex (Green, 1974, chap. 6).

In contrast, a homosexual male thinks of

MARRIAGE AS A RESTRICTED CLUB

Several years ago, I stopped going to weddings. In fact, I no longer celebrate the wedding anniversaries or engagements of friends, relatives, or anyone else, although I might wish them lifelong joy in their relationships. My explanation is that the next wedding I attend will be my own—to the woman I've loved and lived with for nearly six years.

Although I've been legally married to a man myself (and come close to marrying two others), I've come, in these last six years with Pamela, to see heterosexual marriage as very much a restricted club. . . .

Regardless of the *reason* people marry—whether to save on real estate taxes or qualify for married students housing or simply to express love—lesbians and gay men can't obtain the same results should they desire to do so. It seems apparent to me that few friends of Pamela's and mine would even join a club that excluded blacks, Jews, or women, much less assume that they could expect their black, Jewish, or female friends to toast their new status with champagne. But probably no other stand of principle we've ever made in our lives has been so misunderstood or caused so much bad feeling on both sides.

Several people have reacted with surprise to our views, it never having occurred to them that gay people *can't* legally marry. (Why on earth did they think that none of us had bothered?) The most common reaction, however, is acute embarrassment, followed by a denial of our main point—that the about-to-be-wed person is embarking on a privileged status . . .

Another question we've fielded more than once (usually from our most radical friends, both gay and straight) is why we'd want to get married in the first place. In fact, I have mixed feelings about registering my personal life with the state, but—and this seems to me to be the essence of radical politics—I'd prefer to be the one making the choice . . .

[M]arriage does confer some very real dollars-and-cents benefits. One example of inequity is our inability to file joint tax returns, although many couples, both gay and straight, go through periods when one partner in the relationship is unemployed or makes considerably less money than the other. At one time in our relationship, Pamela—who is a musician—was between bands and earning next to nothing. I was making a little over $37,000 a year as a newspaper reporter, a salary that put me in the 42 percent tax bracket—about $300 a week taken out of my paycheck. If we had been married, we could have filed a joint tax return and each paid taxes on half my salary, in the 25 or 30 percent bracket. The difference would have been nearly $100-a-week in our pockets.

Around the same time, Pamela suffered a months'-long illness which would have been covered by my health insurance if she were my spouse. We were luckier than many; we could afford it. But on top of the worry and expense involved (and despite the fact that intellectually we believe in the ideal of free medical care for everyone), we found it almost impossible to avoid internalizing a sense of personal failure—the knowledge that *because of who we are, we can't take care of each other.* I've heard of other gay people whose lovers were deported because they couldn't marry them and enable them to become citizens; still others who were barred from intensive-care units where their lovers lay stricken because they weren't "immediate family.". . . .

But the single most painful and infuriating rationale for marriage, as far as I'm concerned, is the one that goes: "We wanted to stand up and show the world that we've made a *genuine* commitment." When one is gay, such sentiments are labeled "flaunting."

SOURCE: Excerpted from Lindsy Van Gelder, "Marriage as a Restricted Club," *Ms.*, 12 (February 1984):59–60.

himself as a male—but as a male who is sexually attracted to persons who are also male. And a homosexual female thinks of herself as a female—but as a female who is sexually attracted to persons who, like her, are female. Therefore, most persons interested in "gay marriage" haven't the remotest interest in undergoing a sex change. They want to be what they are and yet be able to be united in

FIGURE 6-2 The "Kinsey continuum" or heterosexual-homosexual rating scale. Definitions of the ratings are as follows: 0 = entirely heterosexual. 1 = largely heterosexual, but with incidental homosexual history. 2 = largely heterosexual, but with distinct homosexual history. 3 = equally heterosexual and homosexual. 4 = largely homosexual, but with distinct heterosexual history. 5 = largely homosexual, but with incidental heterosexual history. 6 = entirely homosexual. (SOURCE: *Alfred C. Kinsey, Wardell B. Pomeroy, Clyde E. Martin, and Paul H. Gebhard*, Sexual Behavior in the Human Female [*Philadelphia: W.B. Saunders Co., 1953; New York: Pocket Books edition, p. 470.*]

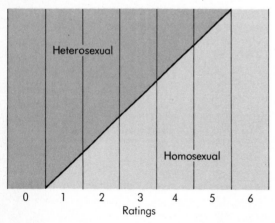

a socially recognized relationship with persons they love—even though the persons they love are not of the opposite sex. (See boxed insert.)

What Is Homosexuality?

Paul Gebhard (1972), former director of what is now called the Kinsey Institute for Research in Sex, Gender, and Reproduction at Indiana University, has defined *homosexual behavior* as "physical contact between two individuals of the same gender which both recognize as being sexual in nature and which ordinarily results in sexual arousal." He defines *psychological homosexual response* as "the desire for such physical contact and/or conscious sexual arousal from thinking of or seeing persons of the same gender." The term *homosexual* is derived from the Greek *homos*, meaning "one and the same," and it may be applied to either males or females who are sexually attracted to members of their own sex. Usually, however, homosexual women prefer to be called *lesbians*, a word derived from Lesbos, a Greek island where, in ancient times, a woman named Sappho directed a girls' school and addressed sensuous poems to her students.

It is beyond the scope of this book to discuss theories of why some persons are *homosexual* (sexually attracted to the same sex) and other persons are *heterosexual* (sexually attracted to the opposite sex), while still others are *bisexual* (sexually at-

DOONESBURY   by Garry Trudeau

tracted to and able to relate to both sexes equally. (See Bell, Weinberg, and Hammersmith, 1981; Paul et al., 1982.) Actually, sex researchers have found that being heterosexual or homosexual isn't so much a simple matter of either/or as it is a matter of degrees along a continuum related to both feelings and behavior. (See Figure 6-2.) Some persons fall more on the heterosexual side of the scale, whereas others fall more on the homosexual side.

Gebhard estimates that between 4 and 5 percent of males and between 1 and 2 percent of females in the United States today could be classified as "predominantly homosexual," defined as a rating of 4–6 on the Kinsey scale (Gebhard, 1972; and in personal interview, February 10, 1978). Gebhard is speaking here of persons whose homosexuality is overt in terms of behavior, not persons who are psychologically predominately homosexual but who have seldom or never acted upon their feelings.

Being Gay In recent years, the word *gay* has come into wide usage by homosexual persons of both sexes. Once serving as a sort of secret code word among homosexuals who wanted to avoid discovery, it has now become a term of pride: "Gay is good," "gay is power," "gay is angry," "gay is proud." Psychotherapist George Weinberg (1972:70–71) distinguishes between being *homosexual* (having "erotic preferences for members of one's own sex") and being *gay,* which he defines as being free of the need for ongoing self-inquisition and ridding oneself of guilt, shame, and regret over being a homosexual. "To be gay," writes Weinberg, "is to view one's sexuality as the healthy heterosexual views his." The emphasis is on self-acceptance.

Persons who regard themselves as gay in the sense described by Weinberg are not apt to be terrified in the way Iphis was by their attraction to members of the same sex. They do not view such attraction as loathsome or unnatural. Indeed, they would even call into question Iphis's observation about the animal world by pointing out that research has indicated that animals *do* sometimes engage in homosexual behavior—including the ram, which Iphis especially cited in her lament (Money and Ehrhardt, 1972:228). Unlike Iphis, the gay person does not wish to be changed but proposes, instead, that society

"Homosexual men and women are best understood when they are seen as whole human beings, not just in terms of what they do sexually" (Bell and Weinberg, 1978:218). (© Jerry Howard 1985/Stock, Boston)

do the changing. The gay person would like to be accepted just as he or she is.

Gay Lifestyles "Too often homosexuals have been viewed simply with reference to their sexual interests and activity," write researchers Alan Bell and Martin Weinberg (1978:25) of the Kinsey Institute. "Usually the social context and psychological correlates of homosexual experience are largely ignored, making for a highly constricted image of the persons involved. . . . Both homosexuality and heterosexuality generate numerous life-styles, and future research may indicate that these are far more impor-

tant indications of people's whereabouts than is sexual orientation per se."

Bell, a psychologist, and Weinberg, a sociologist, conducted in 1970 a comprehensive study of nearly one thousand homosexual persons of both sexes and a comparison group of nearly five hundred heterosexual persons of both sexes. But their study differed from other studies in that they were not trying to find out how homosexuals as a group differed from heterosexuals as a group. They were persuaded that a simplistic lumping together of all persons into one or the other of two groups based solely on sexual orientation would give a faulty picture. After all, we don't think in terms of only one *heterosexual* lifestyle. Why should we assume that only one *homosexual* lifestyle exists? We know that some heterosexuals are in long-term marriages; some opt for "open marriages"; some persons are sexually inactive; some are "swinging singles," and so on. Bell and Weinberg focused on the similar diversity that exists among homosexual persons. Their study makes it clear that there are vast differences among homosexual persons, and there is no *one* gay lifestyle. "An important lesson to be learned from our data," say these researchers, "is that homosexual men and women are best understood when they are seen as whole human beings, not just in terms of what they do sexually, despite the connection between sex and other aspects of their lives" (p. 218).

Bell and Weinberg found that five different types of homosexuals could be categorized from their investigation: (1) *close-coupleds*, persons living in monogamous homosexual relationships similar to heterosexual marriage; (2) *open-coupleds*, persons living with a special same-sex partner but also seeking some sexual and emotional satisfactions outside the relationship; (3) *functionals*, a group Bell and Weinberg compare to "swinging singles" in the heterosexual world; (4) *dysfunctionals,* "troubled people whose lives offer them little gratification"; and (5) a group the researchers term *asexuals,* defined here as isolated, withdrawn persons whose "most prominent characteristic . . . is their lack of involvement with others" (Bell and Weinberg, 1978:217–228).

What Is a "Gay Marriage"?

We have pointed out that marriage exists when two (or more) persons maintain ongoing instrumental and expressive exchanges—that is, when they are both economically and sexually interdependent—and when the relationship is publicly known (at least to a circle of friends) so that it is more than an understanding between the parties concerned. Thus, from a sociological point of view, an overt ongoing relationship of two economically and sexually interdependent women, or of two economically and sexually interdependent men, could be called a marriage. In such cases, the persons involved share bed and board and regard themselves as spouses, mates, or lovers rather than as friends or roommates. Their situation may be compared to the heterosexual cohabitors discussed in the first part of this chapter: they are in an ongoing consensual union but without legal recognition.

Indeed, sociologist Donna Tanner (1978), in her study of lesbian couples, compares the development of such relationships to our continuum in Figure 6-1. First, there is the *trial phase* (much like the affair or regularized sexual liaison on the left side of the continuum), the beginning of the romantic attachment. Next, says Tanner, comes an *insulation* period of living together covertly, one function of which is to enable the lesbian couple "to focus their attention on developing a permanent commitment to each other."

The third stage, *stabilization,* Tanner compares to the ongoing consensual union in our Figure 6-1, where a couple lives in an overt continuing relationship that is not legally recognized. "Similarly," she writes, "the lesbian dyad becomes accepted as a couple by their friends and is invited out socially as a social unit. The partners have by now begun to establish an economic, emotional, and sexual interdependency" (p. 91). It is at this stage that the relationship fits the sociological definition of marriage. Public acknowledgement of their bonding together as a pair is highly important. In Tanner's study, "one couple reflected that they didn't start thinking of themselves as a social unit until they were defined as such by their peers" (p. 78).

Two other researchers used the analogy of heterosexual marital status to describe the situation of gay males (Harry and DeVall, 1978). They studied gay "singles" (those not in a relationship), a classification called "engaged" (men with a special lover but not in a live-in relationship), "married" gay men who were living with their love partner, and "divorced" or "formerly engaged" gay males whose relationship with a lover had ended.

Same-Sex Marriage and the Law

Although a gay marriage might be considered an actual marital union according to a *sociological* definition of marriage, it is not considered a valid marriage from a *legal* standpoint. A test case, *Baker v. Nelson,* occurred when two men appealed to the Minnesota Supreme Court in 1971 after a lower court ruled in favor of a county clerk who had refused to grant the men a marriage license. The homosexual couple contended that since there was no state law specifically prohibiting same-sex marriages, there was no reason to assume such marriages would be illegal.

Mike McConnell and Jack Baker, shown here addressing a university audience, appealed all the way to the Minnesota Supreme Court after they were denied a license to marry each other. (UPI/Bettmann Newsphotos)

Their case further relied on arguments based upon the United States Constitution, in particular the Fourteenth Amendment's guarantee that no state shall "deprive any person of life, liberty, or property, without due process of law; nor deny to any person within its jurisdiction the equal protection of the laws." The petitioners argued that the "due process" clause lay at the root of the United States Supreme Court's ruling on the unconstitutionality of a Connecticut law prohibiting the use of contraceptives by married couples, because such a law was in violation of the *privacy* inherent in the marital relationship.

Furthermore, according to the homosexual couple, the state was violating the "equal protection" clause by discriminating against them as a same-sex couple. Such patent discrimination could be compared to the racial discrimination in marriage laws which the United States Supreme Court had ruled unconstitutional. The case of *Loving v. Virginia* showed that it is in violation of the Fourteenth Amendment for states to make laws against interracial marriage. In that ruling, Chief Justice Warren had written:

> Marriage is one of the "basic civil rights of man," fundamental to our very existence and survival. To deny this fundamental freedom on so unsupportable a basis as the racial classifications embodied in these [antimiscegenation] statutes, classifications so directly subversive of the principle of equality at the heart of the Fourteenth Amendment, is surely to deprive all the State's citizens of liberty without due process of law. The Fourteenth Amendment requires that the freedom of choice to marry not be restricted by invidious racial discriminations. (Kanowitz, 1973:645–648)

The Supreme Court of Minnesota ruled against the homosexual couple, however, stating that these arguments did not apply to their case. While it was true that the state's statute with regard to marriage did not expressly forbid same-sex marriages, the wording was such, said the court, that heterosexual marriage was clearly the intent. Terms such as *husband and wife* and *bride and groom* were used, and the word *marriage* was employed "as one of common usage, meaning the state of union between persons of the opposite sex."

The court referred to definitions found in *Webster's Dictionary* and *Black's Law Dictionary,* both of which refer to distinctions of sex, and declared that it is unlikely that the original draftsmen of the marriage statutes had anything other than this in mind. The court went on to say that "the institution of marriage as a union of man and woman, uniquely involving the procreation and rearing of children within a family, is as old as the book of Genesis." Disregarded as not applicable was the argument of the homosexual couple that "the state does not impose upon heterosexual married couples a condition that they have a proved capacity or declared willingness to procreate."

The court further declared that the ruling that struck down the Connecticut law regarding contraceptive usage by married couples could not be relied on as a basis for arguing against *all* state interference in marriage. "The basic premise of that decision . . . was that the state, having authorized marriage, was without power to intrude upon the right of privacy inherent in the marital relationship," said the Minnesota Supreme Court justices, pointing out that the state's classification of persons authorized to marry does not violate the Fourteenth Amendment.

However, the court admitted that state restrictions on the right to marry are not entirely beyond the reach of that amendment, as was shown in the United States Supreme Court's decision which struck down state laws forbidding interracial marriages. "But in commonsense and in a constitutional sense, there is a clear distinction between a marital restriction based merely upon race and one based upon the fundamental difference in sex" (Kanowitz, 1973:647–648). It was decided by the court that the two men did not have the right to marry one another.

"The *Baker* case presents many of the legal problems that arise whenever the government seeks to regulate fundamental societal institutions," writes legal scholar Arthur Silverstein (1972–73:607) in a discussion of the constitutional aspects of the right of homosexual persons to obtain a marriage license. "The states have surrounded the institution of marriage with a variety of legal benefits and restrictions. As part of this regulation, they have also sought to control entry into that institution."

A specialist in family law, Michael Einbinder (1973–74) describes another case that took place in 1973, *Jones v. Hallahan*. Two lesbians had been denied a marriage license, and the Kentucky Court of Appeals upheld the denial. The court did not draw upon constitutional arguments but based its decision solely on the traditional notion of marriage as a union between opposite sex persons. "In addition," says Einbinder, "the court said that even if a license had been issued and a ceremony performed, the resulting relationship would not constitute marriage" (pp. 785–786).

Efforts toward legal recognition of homosexual marriage would seem to be hindered further by the 1986 United States Supreme Court ruling that upheld the right of states to outlaw certain sexual acts when engaged in by consenting adult homosexual persons— even in the privacy of their own homes. (Although nineteen of the twenty-four states with antisodomy laws in effect at the time of the court ruling considered *all* oral-genital and anal-genital sexual acts to be criminal offenses, regardless of the sexual orientation of the participants, the court declined to rule on whether *heterosexual* persons—including married couples—were protected by the Constitution from prosecution under the same laws. [See *The New York Times*, July 1, 1986, pp. 1, 9, 11])

Homosexual Marriage as an Alternative Lifestyle

Despite the fact that gay marriages are not recognized as legal, many lesbians and male homosexuals *do* form lasting same-sex unions which they may think of and speak of as marriages. The ideals of permanence, faithfulness, and a shared life (both sexually and economically) are often held up, just as in the case of heterosexual marriages. Speaking from the standpoint of the homosexual, Del Martin and Paul Mariah (1972:126) ask how a limiting value can be placed upon the sexual expression of love, whether heterosexual or homosexual. "Is it polarity, the joining of male-female and penis-vagina that makes a 'marriage' whole and therefore 'holy'?" they ask. "Isn't it rather the mutual respect and the mutual love for one another, each to and for the other as a human being, that makes the difference? And isn't love 'socially desirable'?"

Some persons enter gay unions repeatedly, each time hoping that the ideal lover has been found. Others have relationships that endure for a very long time. Martin and Mariah refer to two men who are now in their seventies and have lived together in a homosexual marriage for more than fifty years, although at the same time they consent to one another's occasional seeking of extra sexual gratification outside their own relationship. (They would fit into Bell and Weinberg's (1978) "open-coupled" category described earlier.) Other long-term homosexual unions are exclusively monogamous—"close-coupled," to use Bell and Weinberg's term. Del Martin and Phyllis Lyon (1972), founders of a lesbian organization, have written a book describing their many years together in a quasi-marriage and providing examples of other long-lasting lesbian unions. "It is not uncommon to find Lesbian couples who have been together for twenty years or more," say these authors (p. 111).

Many homosexual persons argue that there would be more long-lasting "gay marriages" if society would lend its support and approval. They attribute the high number of failures to society's pressures and the disdain they are subjected to rather than to any inherent weakness in the homosexual relationship itself. Recognizing the need for emotional support among gay persons, various gay organizations have sprung up in recent years, including religious ones. The Metropolitan Community Churches, a denomination founded primarily for gay people by the Reverend Troy Perry, has weddinglike ceremonies so that gay male couples and lesbian couples can enter into what the group speaks of as "Holy Union," thereby giving the two persons some sense of a public declaration and formalization of their relationship. There also exist gay synogogues for Jewish homosexuals and supportive—if not always officially recognized—organizations within both the Roman Catholic church and most Protestant groups. In addition, most religious groups have been giving serious study to the topic of homosexuality in recent years, including in some cases a reconsideration of traditional religious teachings (McNeill, 1976; Woods, 1978; Twiss, 1978; Jennings, 1977; Nelson, 1978; Scanzoni and Mollenkott, 1978; Batchelor, 1980; Boswell, 1980; Scroggs, 1983).

But Why Marriage? The question may arise as to why homosexual persons can't simply live together without worrying about legal marriage. Of course, many do live together that way right now; it's the only way they can! But some reply to the question by citing both practical reasons and a need for psychic support. On the practical side, there is the matter of finding housing, because they are likely to encounter discrimination if they wish to let their relationship be known openly. Problems with regard to employment also cause difficulty. "Try telling your boss you can't move to a new job because of your lover," writes Dennis Altman (1971:29). His problem would be understood if a heterosexual person were speaking of his or her spouse. Other practical problems cluster around insurance, tax laws, and inheritance rights (the homosexual "spouse" is not likely to receive a share of the estate of a partner who left no will, no matter how long the couple has lived together nor how estranged the deceased has been from his or her biological family). Even something so simple as a hospital visit can become a problem. Altman

(1971:50) refers to a report in the London *Times* which told of a dying lesbian who was permitted visits only by her immediate family and denied the privilege of seeing her partner of twenty years. Some spokespersons for gay civil rights argue that such problems could be solved by the legalization of gay marriage.

Some gay activists think differently. They refuse to refer to their couple relationships as "marriages"—even though such relationships may perform the functions of *marriage* as it is usually defined (Barnhart, 1975). Such persons are persuaded that the idea that gays should marry in a legal sense implies that heterosexual marriage is the norm for close social relationships. They suggest that gay couples instead invent new ways of relating that do not imitate conventional marriage. For some, such "new ways" center around sexual concerns and mean breaking free of the sexual exclusivity understood in the traditional marriage contract. For others, the concern doesn't center around sexual matters at all but rather around gender roles and the notion that marriage means a strict division of labor and a dominance-subordination relationship. The argument is similar to that of some heterosexual cohabitors who reject legal marriage even though the option is open to them.

Sensitive to such feelings, Bell and Weinberg (1978) chose the term "close-coupleds" in reference to gay persons in partnerships that are both "close" and "closed." "We resisted the temptation to call this group 'happily married,' although some of its members described themselves that way," say these researchers, "because we did not want to imply that heterosexual relationships and marriage in particular are standards by which to judge people's adjustment" (p. 219).

However, many homosexual persons are not particularly concerned about terminology. Rather, they are concerned about the psychic costs of being involved in a same-sex union in a society that doesn't recognize the relationship as valid. Altman (1971:66) points out that all the world loves a lover—as long as it's not a homosexual one. He decries the fact that homosexuals do not have the right to express their love publicly without encountering severe ridicule and disapproval. "It is impossible to know to what extent love is strengthened by being public," he writes, "yet . . . I suspect that after a time lovers have a real psychological need for the support that comes from being recognized as such."

Similar anguish was expressed in a letter to a San Francisco newspaper in which a young college-educated male, working his way up in a large corporation, said he could not really expect his career to progress beyond the lower end of middle management without marriage to a woman. The problem was that he already was "married"—but to another male who had come with him when he transferred from another city. His roommate's accompanying him in itself was difficult to explain; but beyond that, the letter writer was mentally tortured by having to pretend constantly that he was single, an eligible bachelor expected to flirt with the women at the office, take them out, and even to give his male colleagues the impression that he was having an affair with some female friend. He said he felt "trapped in a cage of pretending." "I am married!" he stated repeatedly. "I do not look one bit different from other respectable, aggressive, married young men." Yet society does not recognize his marriage, because it is a gay marriage. (Reported in Feldman and Thielbar, 1972:338–339.)

"Our data indicate that a relatively steady relationship with a love partner is a very meaningful event in the life of a homosexual

A COVENANT OF COMMITMENT

"Of course, there have been mock marriages performed in the gay community, with a friend performing the ceremony, followed by a reception at a gay bar for the newly wedded couple. But there have also been genuine religious services held in a church. These aren't weddings, as heterosexuals know them, but covenant services, a recognition in the sight of God and the church of a bond between the two persons involved.

"We had occasion to witness such a 'Celebration of Commitment' at an Episcopal church when a friend, Joyce, invited us to a service for her and Madeline, which was to be performed by her pastor and with her parents in attendance. Joyce was jubilant when she broke the news to us. This tall, pensive, sensitive young brunette had been through years of struggle with her parents, her church and her psychiatrist. Finally she had received the blessings of all three to be herself.

"Dressed in a simple blue suit, her eyes brimming with joyful tears, she solemnly made her vow to Madeline, 'I give you this ring as a token of our covenant, vowing to live in close friendship, to strive for fuller knowledge of your being, and to care for you above all others. I pledge myself to realize your needs, encourage your full potential, and to love you even as I love myself. May God be between me and thee forever.' "

SOURCE: Del Martin and Phyllis Lyon, *Lesbian/Woman* (San Francisco: Glide Publications, 1972; Bantam Books edition, 1972), pp. 104–105.

man or woman," write Bell and Weinberg (1978:102). Their research indicated that such relationships "involve an emotional exchange and commitment similar to the kinds that heterosexuals experience." Homosexual respondents spoke positively of such special relationships "and clearly were not content to limit their sexual contacts to impersonal sex."

Male-Female Differences in Sexual Behavior We saw in Chapter 5 that different socialization has meant differences in how females and males perceive their sexuality. Males tend to think of sexuality in a more detached and instrumental manner, while females learn to view it in a more expressive sense, especially in the context of a loving relationship. These gender-related differences are also seen in homosexual behavior patterns.

Homosexual males, for example, are far more likely to engage in *cruising* (going out specifically to look for sexual contacts in such places as gay bars and nightclubs, gay baths, and so on) and to engage in impersonal sex with strangers (Bell and Weinberg, 1978:73–102; Weinberg and Williams, 1974, 1975). In Bell and Weinberg's (1978:299) San Francisco study, only 16 percent of the white homosexual males and 14 percent of the black homosexual males reported they had *not* engaged in cruising during the year before the interview was conducted. In contrast, 83 percent of both black and white lesbians had not cruised.

On a similar note, numerous studies have shown that homosexual males tend to have many more sexual partners over a lifetime than do homosexual females. Kinsey and his colleagues (1953:475) reported that among persons who reported having homosexual contact, only 29 percent of the women had engaged in such contact with more than one or two partners, whereas 49 percent of the men reported such a pattern, with many having had "scores or hundreds of sexual partners." In Bell and Weinberg's study, three-fourths of the white homosexual males reported having had one hundred sexual partners or more over the course of their lives. This was also true of 59 percent of the black homosexual males. In contrast, only 2 percent of white lesbians and 4 percent of black lesbians reported this many sexual partners. The majority of the women had had sexual relationships with fewer than ten women over the course of their lives. Some of them (3 percent of white lesbians and 5 percent of black lesbians) had only had one sexual partner ever. This was true of none of the men. (See Table 6-B.)

In a West German study of lesbians and homosexual males aged 18 to 35, Siegrid Schäfer (1977) of Hamburg University's Institute for Sex Research found that the median number of sexual partners since the first homosexual experience was five for women but fifteen times that number (seventy-five) for the men. Schäfer also compared both homosexual persons and heterosexual persons as to the number of sex partners they had had during the last year before participating in one of several research studies. As Table 6-C shows, more females (whether homosexual or heterosexual) than males reported having only one partner. But a distinct difference showed up between homosexual and heterosexual males—both in the percentages reporting no more than one sexual partner and in those who reported having more than six.

Behavioral scientists have suggested that both the divergent socialization patterns of males and females and the structural situation in certain parts of the gay subculture may account for such differences. Schäfer emphasizes that while females have been trained to view sex in a context of love, commitment, and fidelity, both homosexual and heterosexual males have been socialized to regard their sexuality "as something in and

TABLE 6-B Homosexual experience with different partners, San Francisco Study

NUMBER OF HOMOSEXUAL PARTNERS EVER	WHM* (N = 574)	BHM* (N = 111)	WHF* (N = 227)	BHF* (N = 64)
1	0%	0%	3%	5%
2	0	0	9	5
3–4	1	2	15	14
5–9	2	4	31	30
10–14	3	5	16	9
15–24	3	6	10	16
25–49	8	6	8	11
50–99	9	18	5	8
100–249	15	15	1	2
250–499	17	11	1	2
500–999	15	14	0	0
1000 or more	28	19	0	0

*WHM—White homosexual males; BHM—Black homosexual males; WHF—White homosexual females; BHF—Black homosexual females
SOURCE: Adapted from Alan P. Bell and Martin S. Weinberg, *Homosexualities: A Study of Diversity Among Men and Women* (New York: Simon and Schuster, 1978), p. 308.

TABLE 6-C   Partner mobility in homosexual and heterosexual samples (West Germany)

| | | | | HETEROSEXUALS | | | | |
| NUMBER OF SEX PARTNERS IN LAST 12 MONTHS (INTERCOURSE) | HOMOSEXUALS (THIS STUDY) | | STUDENTS (GLESE AND SCHMIDT, 1968) | | WORKERS (SCHMIDT AND SIGUSCH, 1971) | | ADOLESCENTS (SIGUSCH AND SCHMIDT, 1973) | |
	Females (N = 151)	Males (N = 581)	Females (N = 366)	Males (N = 1400)	Females (N = 106)	Males (N = 106)	Females (N = 86)	Males (N = 105)
1	43%	5%	73%	63%	65%	33%	67%	44%
6 or more	8%	78%	4%	15%	2%	18%	5%	13%

SOURCE: Siegrid Schäfer, "Sociosexual Behavior in Male and Female Homosexuals: A Study in Sex Differences," *Archives of Sexual Behavior* 6 (September, 1977), p. 361.

of itself," with sexual needs separate from affectional needs. Yet heterosexual males have sexual partners (females) who were socialized to integrate sexuality and affection. Schäfer suggests the possibility that women, plus the institutions of marriage and family, may act as a brake on any tendency heterosexual men might have toward engaging in impersonal sexual contacts with many different partners such as is true of the majority of their homosexual counterparts. "These inhibiting conditions do not exist among homosexual males," writes Schäfer, adding that "this is of course compounded by the standards and norms of their subculture, in which sexual success is an important status symbol" (p. 362). Related to Schäfer's explanation are these comments by Bell and Weinberg (1978):

> Another important reason for homosexual men's large number of partners could be the fact that society provides them with little or no opportunity to meet on anything more than a sexual basis. Driven underground, segregated in what have been termed "sexual marketplaces," threatened but perhaps also stimulated by the danger of their enterprise, homosexual men would be expected to have an enormous number of fleeting sexual encounters. (p. 101)

In recent years, there has been some evidence of a change in the behavior of many gay males because of the fear of contracting AIDS (acquired immune deficiency syndrome), a sexually transmitted disease for which (at this writing) there is no known cure. (See boxed insert.)

In addition to differences in the way males and females are socialized and the structural conditions of that part of the male gay subculture that encourages impersonal sexual contacts and the measurement of self-worth in terms of sexual expression, Bell and Weinberg also suggest that the different ways females and males first experience their homosexuality may influence many of the differences between lesbians and gay males. Lesbians tend to become involved with their partners in an emotional way after knowing them for some time and, only then, begin expressing their love in a sexual way. Bell and Weinberg point out how different this pattern is from the situation of the gay male, "who is apt to have engaged in numerous sexual activities with other males at a relatively early age and whose model of homosexuality consists chiefly of men 'on the make,' of sex without commitment, of the excitement of sexual pursuit" (p. 102).

REPORTED SYPHILIS CASES SHOW SHARP DECLINE

Washington—The number of reported cases of syphilis has dropped sharply during the past three years, and health officials say the decline has been most significant among homosexual men, indicating a major change in sexual behavior because of fear of AIDS.

"A falling syphilis rate is an extremely sensitive indicator of a change in gay sexual activity," said Ward Cates, director of the division of sexually transmitted diseases at the Centers for Disease Control. "Gay men account for more than half of the syphilis in the country."

CDC statisticians said 12 percent fewer cases of syphilis were reported during the first half of 1985 than during the same period in 1984. Cates said the figure has fallen in almost every major metropolitan area.

Since 1982, the total number of syphilis cases has dropped 30 percent, compared to the previous five years, when the number of reported cases increased by 50 percent.

The falling syphilis rates may reflect a trend that began in 1983, when widespread fears about the transmission of herpes virus and the first national publicity surrounding acquired immune deficiency syndrome (AIDS) appeared to force a general reduction in levels of sexual activity.

Three elements suggested that sexual promiscuity has been reduced vastly in the past three years: the falling rates of syphilis, some figures that suggest a decline in one class of gonorrhea, and several recently conducted surveys of sexual behavior among homosexual men that show a marked decline in promiscuity.

"The evidence is as clear as it can be," said Casey Riley, director of Virginia's program on sexually transmitted disease, which reported a 25 percent drop in syphilis cases. "We went into VD clinics and asked people what was happening to their sex lives, and they told us that they are becoming monogamous because of the fear of AIDS."

One recent study of bisexual and homosexual men, conducted by the San Francisco AIDS Foundation, found that more than 80 percent of all homosexual men in the city have reduced their risk of contracting sexually transmitted diseases by making sweeping changes in their sexual activity.

According to the study, more than half of those surveyed said they are now in a monogamous relationship, and the number of people who said they have more than one sex partner fell from 49 percent last year to 35 percent.

"The word is getting out there that the risks are not worth it," said Mark Behar, director of a national organization dedicated to improving education and resources about sexually transmitted diseases. "Education is the reason for these figures."

Although a connection often has been made between the decline of certain rates of VD and the wide fear of contracting AIDS, the number of cases of other sexually transmitted diseases—those less often associated with homosexual men—has risen dramatically.

AIDS is a fatal disease that disables the body's immune system, but both syphilis and gonorrhea are sexually transmitted bacterial diseases that are easily treated with antibiotics.

SOURCE: *Greensboro (NC) News and Record*, Aug. 11, 1985, p. A-20.

At the same time, it must be remembered that many homosexual males establish ongoing same-sex love relationships and live in quasi-marriage partnerships with the special person in their lives. In his study of gay-male couples, psychologist Charles Silverstein (1981) found that some gay men had a tendency to be "excitement seekers" who expressed a need for sexual variety and independence. Others, in contrast, indicated needs for emotional intimacy and continuity, which they sought in long-term relationships. This placed them in a category Silverstein called "home builders." Still others fell in between these categories. (See also Lewis et al., 1981.)

Everyday Life Among Gay Couples   Bell and Weinberg (1978:346) found that 10 percent of the homosexual males and 28 percent of the homosexual females in their sample were living in homosexual-couple relationships comparable to marriage. Comparing these "close-coupleds" with the other homosexual groups in their study, Bell and Weinberg write:

> They were the least likely to seek partners outside their special relationship, had the smallest amount of sexual problems, and were unlikely to regret being homosexual. They tended to spend more evenings at home and less leisure time by themselves, and the men in this group seldom went to such popular cruising spots as bars or baths. . . . Both the men and the women were more self-accepting and less depressed or lonely than any of the others, and they were the happiest of all. (pp. 219–220)

In addition to the close-coupled, 18 percent of the male respondents and 17 percent of the female respondents were in open-coupled relationships. "They were not happy with their circumstances, however," write Bell and Weinberg, "and tended (despite spending a fair amount of time at home) to seek satisfactions with people outside their partnership" (p. 221).

The majority of homosexual couples reported that they shared housework equally and that they combined their incomes totally or in part, although there were certain household responsibilities that fell more to one partner than the other (Bell and Weinberg, 1978:91–101, 323–324).

"Coupled" homosexual persons, like "single" homosexual persons, tended to belong to friendship cliques or networks that served as the functional equivalent of the extended family (Bell and Weinberg, 1978:247–249). Research psychologist Evelyn Hooker (1965) has pointed out that this less visible part of the overall gay community must be recognized if we are to understand the whole. Such friendship groups may get together for spur-of-the-moment dinners or may plan elaborate cocktail parties. Often they will celebrate someone's birthday or the anniversary of one of the homosexual couples.

In Tanner's (1978) study of lesbian couples, she found that anniversaries are often private affairs, "ranging from a bottle of wine at home to dinner at a favorite restaurant." One couple reported celebrating their anniversary every month during the first year, but yearly thereafter. Favorite leisure activities for the lesbian couples in Tanner's study included watching television together or attending movies, getting together with friends, and eating out. Some couples mentioned enjoying concerts and museums together; others told of shared hobbies ranging from camping to chess, from skiing to taking adult evening courses together. "Almost all the couples interviewed said they had dinner parties for friends, usually gay friends, at least once a month," writes Tanner. "This could include anything from ordering Kentucky Fried Chicken to a sit-down dinner with candles with two other couples" (pp. 83–84).

Of course, like their heterosexual counterparts, most homosexual couples spend the greater portion of their time in occupational pursuits. For all these reasons, a comment by Bell and Weinberg (1978) is fitting:

> It is little wonder that so many homosexual men and women reject the label "homosexual," in that it exaggerates the sexual component of their lives, and prefer such terms as "gay," "lesbian," or "homophile." These terms connote much more an entire life-style, a way of being in the world which only incidentally involves sexual activity with persons of the same sex. (p. 115)

The point these researchers make is underscored in the massive study of American couples conducted by sociologists Philip Blumstein and Pepper Schwartz (1983). Focusing on the areas of money, work, and sex, they found that same-sex couples and heterosexual couples (both married and cohabiting) have much in common in their everyday lives as they seek emotional intimacy in their relationships, go about earning a living, make decisions about household finances, divide household tasks, and so on. Differences among categories of couples stemmed not so much from sexual orientation as from gender-role issues and the lack of institutionalized guidelines for cohabiting couples and gay-male and lesbian couples. Such couples had to work out their own ways of relating apart from the established patterns of marriage. (See also Mendola, 1980.)

Of course, some homosexual persons are or have been in marriages with persons of the opposite sex—a point we want to examine next.

Homosexual Persons in Heterosexual Marriages

In Bell and Weinberg's study, 20 percent of the white homosexual men and 13 percent of the black homosexual men reported that they had been married to women in the past. And among the lesbians in the sample, over one-third of the white women and nearly half of the black women had been married to men. Bell and Weinberg suggest that the greater incidence of cross-sex marriage among homosexual women may be related to physiological factors (women are physically able to participate in sexual intercourse without being sexually aroused) and to social factors (the expectation that females will grow up to marry and have children). These researchers also found that it is not unusual for some lesbians to be unaware of their homosexuality until after marriage to a male. These women's marriages tended not to last long, and the cause of the marital dissolution often related to their having formed a lesbian relationship with another woman or to their lack of interest in sexual intercourse with their husbands (Bell and Weinberg, 1978:160–170).

The homosexual males in this study tended to report that their marriages had been more satisfactory than was true of the lesbians, yet less happy than the comparison group of heterosexual males. Homosexual husbands "tended not to have told their wives about their homosexuality before marriage nor to have promised to do anything about it." A considerable number (more than half) of homosexual husbands reported that while engaging in sexual intercourse with their wives, they had sometimes or often fantasized that they were with a male partner instead. Most of these marriages broke up for reasons similar to those of the lesbians in the study: involvement in a homosexual relationship or lack of interest in sex with their spouses. Some reported that wives simply refused to tolerate the husband's homosexuality (p. 165).

In another study, sociologist Brian Miller (1978) classified thirty homosexual husbands into four basic categories. First, there are those who absolutely refuse to think of themselves as homosexual and who dismiss their secretive extramarital sex with other males as nothing more than physical release. They stay apart from the social aspects of the overt gay subculture, and their behavior "is characterized by clandestine, impersonal encounters in parks, tearooms [men's rooms], highway rest stops, and with hitchhikers or male hustlers" (p. 214). A second category consists of men who acknowledge themselves to be homosexual and don't try to fool themselves about their extramarital same-sex behavior. But they are less likely to look for impersonal sexual contacts in the same kinds of places as is true of the first category. They *are* like the first category, however, in that their conventional family lifestyle provides them with a cover, that is, a *public* identity that is heterosexual.

The third category of homosexual men observed by Miller were those who were separated or divorced from their wives and who were somewhat involved in the overt gay subculture's social networks and activities while at the same time "passing" as heterosexual in certain other contexts—especially employment. The final category of homosexual men interviewed by Miller also were no longer living with their wives. But unlike the category just described, these men become *thoroughly* immersed in the gay world and are often self-employed (in many cases with a gay clientele) or work for an employer who does not see their overt homosexuality and gay activism as a problem.

Miller points out that some men may over a period of time move from one category to another to still another in an increasing acceptance of their homosexuality. This gradual process entails reformulating both personal and social identity and is often initiated by "falling in love with another man" (p.

228). Miller points out that the entire process of change in these men's self-images and their reconception of the outer world provides an example of adult resocialization. What had once been viewed as a stigmatized identity (homosexual), and thus not accepted as applicable to oneself, gradually comes to be viewed in positive terms. At some point, such a man begins to identify with gay subculture life and looks to persons in the gay community as his new reference group.

Gay Parenthood

The men in Miller's first category were especially likely to rank their fatherhood role as central to their lives. One reported that his marriage was horrible but that the children were "the consolation prize." Another told the researcher, "My children are the only humans I have ever loved. . . . I need my kids; they're what keep me going" (p. 216). A homosexual husband in the second category reported that his children were the reason he had remained in an unsatisfactory marriage. Each year, he would consider divorce but decide to wait until the children were older. "Now that they are in college, I can't leave because they are my judges," he said. "They'd never forgive me for doing this all these years to their mother" (p. 217).

In Bell and Weinberg's much larger sample, of the white homosexual males and white homosexual females who had been married heterosexually, 50 percent reported having children. An even higher proportion of the black homosexual formerly-marrieds were parents—71 percent of the men and 73 percent of the women (p. 391). The small number of homosexual parents who said they had children age 12 or older who knew about their homosexuality tended to report that the parent-child relationship had not suffered as

DO GAY PARENTS WANT THEIR CHILDREN TO BE GAY?

"Most thoughtful gay parents want their children to be who they are. Most of us realize that early in our own background our feelings were established, and most of us can recall being attracted to members of the same sex at a very early time—certainly before our 10th birthdays. At the same time, most gay parents would prefer that their children not be subjected to hostility and, therefore I suspect, would in one sense be more pleased if their children were heterosexual—not because of any aversion to homosexuality—but merely because of the ugly treatment they would not like to have their children endure. But that's a dangerous line of thinking, for it's as if blacks were to prefer that their children had been white or that parents had preferred that their daughters were sons. It's an ugly part of society which has to be changed."—Bruce Voeller, a gay father and co-executive director of the National Gay Task Force, in reply to a question about whether gay parents worry that their children may be homosexual.

SOURCE: Bruce Voeller and James Walters (interviewer), "Gay Fathers," *The Family Coordinator* 27 (April 1978), p. 151.

a result of the children's awareness (see also Miller, 1979). Sociologist Mildred Pagelow (1976) reports that her research on lesbian mothers indicates it may be easier for these women to let children know than it is to acknowledge their homosexual lifestyle to other relatives, especially parental family members. She writes:

It appears that the majority of Lesbian mothers prefers to be open with their children, especially when they share a home with their lovers; yet they often feel compelled to "pass" with their own parents. Techniques involve suppression of affectionate behavior, little or no physical contact while in the presence of parents, and frequently a rearrangement of clothing and bedroom furniture. (p. 7)

Studies of lesbian mothers have shown them to take motherhood seriously as a central organizing factor of their lives and to face much the same concerns and challenges as heterosexual women in single-parent and blended family arrangements (Lewin and Lyons, 1982; Hotvedt and Mandel, 1982). "Because being a mother is so big," said one woman, "I have much more in common with all mothers than I have in common with all lesbians" (quoted in Lewin and Lyons, 1982).

Many homosexual fathers also have full or joint custody of their children or share a home with a male partner and his children, thus creating a stepfamily situation (Weiss, 1984). Those who don't choose to reveal their homosexuality to their children report that this decision causes them stress and hinders intimacy in the parent-child relationship. Yet, they fear disclosure would result in painful rejection or possibly vindictiveness on the part of the former wife (Bozett, 1980).

In his in-depth interviews with eighteen gay fathers, Frederick Bozett (1980) found that the major catalysts for disclosing their homosexuality to their children were either a need to explain why the parents had decided to divorce or else the development of a committed relationship between the father and another man. "In this way," explains Bozett, "disclosure of the gay identity becomes part of a larger topic, rather than being the topic itself" (p. 176). Bozett emphasizes that "most gay fathers do not disclose their gay identity primarily in order to explain their sexual orientation. The gay father discloses to his children (and to others) primarily in order to explain to them his social and personal world." Having done this, he is able to share his innermost feelings more fully and "need no longer edit his communications with the people who are closest to him" (p. 175). (See also Bozett, 1981.)

Roles in Gay-Couple Relationships

Many people have the idea that homosexual couples pattern their lives after traditional heterosexual marriage, with one partner playing a "husband" role and the other partner playing a "wife" role in all aspects of life, ranging from how the courtship was conducted, through household division of labor, to sexual techniques employed by each person.

Some basis for such a stereotype existed in the past and has continued to a lesser extent into the present. In one unusual case, a San Diego superior court judge ordered a lesbian to pay $100 monthly support to her ex-partner, who had given up her job in another city to be with the woman. The two had participated in a Holy Union ceremony at a Metropolitan Community Church and had signed an agreement in which the one who had given up her job agreed to perform the duties of a housewife, while the other agreed to be the breadwinner for both. When the relationship ended, the woman who had agreed to the "wife" role brought suit against the other woman for breach of contract. The judge saw

the case as analogous to cohabitation situations, where rulings on property and support agreements among unmarried heterosexual couples have been issued (*Advocate*, July 12, 1978; Lewis, 1979:136).

Bell and Weinberg (1978) found only limited evidence of such stereotyped role playing in their San Francisco study. When homosexual males and homosexual females in same-sex coupled relationships were asked whether they or their partner did all the "feminine" or "masculine" tasks around the house, only a few of either sex reported such a domestic arrangement (pp. 93, 101, 325).

Blumstein and Schwartz (1983:148) found that both gay-male and lesbian couples emphasize dividing up household chores in fair and equitable ways. But at the same time, as with heterosexual couples, the person putting in fewer hours in an outside job is expected to do a greater proportion of housework. This was found to be especially true among gay-male couples. Lesbians took particularly great pains to make sure household duties were performed equitably and, in fact, were found to do less housework in general than gay men. According to Blumstein and Schwartz, "This may be because some of them are rejecting a role that has been symbolic of women's low status" (p. 149). (See also Peplau and Amaro, 1982.)

Folk beliefs about a simplistic dichotomy of "active" and "passive" partners in *sexual* aspects of such relationships also are not supported by the evidence. Bell and Weinberg's data showed that both homosexual men and lesbians "are apt to engage in many different forms of sexual contact with their partners and that a very strict adherence to a particular sexual role is quite uncommon" (1978:111). Sex researchers William Masters and Virginia Johnson (1979:213–215) speak of the "my-turn-your-turn" sexual interaction characteristic of homosexual relation-

A WELL-KNOWN LESBIAN COUPLE

One of the most famous lesbian relationships of all time was that of the writer Gertrude Stein and her companion of forty years, Alice B. Toklas. Their stereotypical role playing is much less common in lesbian partnerships today. (Culver Pictures, Inc.)

" 'I am a person acted upon, not a person who acts,' Alice told one of Gertrude's biographers; but she was certainly active when it came to managing their lives. She cooked, gardened, kept house, made travel arrangements, typed Gertrude's manuscripts—and even published them for a time under the imprint of Plain Edition. When guests showed up, Alice was called upon to entertain their wives. The ladies were, of course, 'second-class citizens,' [Allen] Tate recalled. It was a far cry from the lesbian salon of Natalie Barney a few streets away, where women danced in one another's arms and disappeared into bedrooms; but, then, Alice and Gertrude were a bourgeois couple, monogamous and proper. And Alice was—to use the contemporary word—'oppressed'; even 'The Autobiography of Alice B. Toklas' was written by Gertrude. Not until after Gertrude's death in 1946, when she continued to receive their old friends and wrote her famous cookbook, did she really come into her own."

SOURCE: James Atlas, "Alice Entertained the Wives," *The New York Times Book Review* (July 10, 1979), p. 15.

ships, with each partner having a turn as initiator and as responder, as both giver and receiver.

One reason role playing occurred to a greater degree in the past was explained by one woman who remembered the 1950s when many lesbians, particularly in small towns and rural areas, "didn't have any other models to follow so when they found themselves attracted to women, they really thought they must be like men." She concluded that "it's really meeting other lesbians and being in the community that teaches you that you don't have to be masculine to love another woman" (quoted in Ponse, 1978:120). Sociologist Barbara Ponse points to the feminist movement and the widespread questioning of stereotypical gender roles, along with gay political activism and the greater visibility of the gay community, as forces contributing toward the diminishing of role-playing expectations. Another study indicates that androgyny in gay-couple relationships contributes to greater satisfaction because both partners are displaying both instrumental and expressive qualities within the relationship (Ickes et al., 1979).

Types of Gay Marriages

Tanner (1978) divides the lesbian quasi-marriages in her study into three types. She then compares each one to a corresponding pattern in our own typology of heterosexual marriages (described in Chapter 8 of this book).

Tanner's *traditional-complementary* category of lesbian couples corresponds to our "head-complement" category—a marriage arrangement in which one partner is the dominant, unique breadwinner and the other is the dependent homemaker. Traditional gender roles are followed in the division of labor.

A second type of lesbian relationship observed by Tanner is the *flexible nurturing-caretaking* model. Such a relationship allows for more flexibility so that the division of labor is *not* along conventional gender-role lines. However, in this type of relationship, one of the partners tends to be the caretaker, earning more money and also meeting the greater emotional needs of the partner (who in some cases may be a student). "The caretaking partner usually admits to enjoying the feeling of having someone dependent on her and likes the 'mother streak' it brings out in her," writes Tanner (p. 103). Where both partners are employed but the incomes are unequal, the bargaining power differential that results is comparable to the situation in our senior partner-junior partner model of marriage.

The final category described by Tanner is the *negotiated-egalitarian* type of lesbian union, which she compares to our equal-partnership model. Role interchangeability, equal authority in decision-making, and mutual interdependency and reciprocity characterize such relationships. Roles are negotiated and renegotiated as personal and situational changes arise; they are not arbitrarily assigned on the basis of stereotypical gender-role patterns or anything else.

When Gay Relationships End

Tanner's study was based on a sample of twelve lesbian couples. Although at the time of the interviews one of these marriagelike relationships had been in existence for twelve years, Tanner found the average length to be about two years. She collected her data between 1972 and 1975; and by the time her findings were published in 1978, only two of the lesbian partnerships were still intact. "A long-lasting dyadic relationship is rare," concludes Tanner (p. 107).

On the other hand, convinced that far more committed gay-male and lesbian couples exist than is generally supposed, writer Mary Mendola (1980) set out to find such couples through a nationwide distribution of 1,500 questionnaires to be returned by mail. She received more than 400 responses (a 27 percent return) and found that more than two-thirds of the respondents considered themselves to be in a permanently committed same-sex "marriage relationship." Nearly half of the respondents reported they had been in such a marriage only once. About 2 out of every 3 persons who answered the survey reported relationships of at least two or more years' duration, with 17 percent reporting same-sex marriages of ten or more years. Many respondents wrote notes such as the following, which came from an older man:

> My present relationship is now in its ninth year. Previously, I had an eighteen year relationship which ended with the death of my partner. I strongly feel you have a "side" to tell—a side that is not readily known nor very visible. (Mendola, 1980:11)

(Incidentally, Mendola chose to use the word *marriage* to describe the same-sex ongoing relationships she studied, pointing out a dictionary definition of the verb *to marry* as "entering into a close relationship, uniting or forming a union" [p. 6].)

Breaking Up   There's no denying, however, that large numbers of same-sex relationships *do* break up. But why? No doubt the lack of social support is a major contributing factor. Whereas heterosexual couples are given every encouragement to stay together and establish a strong home life, homosexual couples are given no societal support at all. With rare exceptions, any support they get must come from other homosexual persons.

Those couples who have enduring relationships are often envied by those who long to experience such a relationship, and there is much sadness in watching such a relationship come to an end. Jensen (1974) reports that after one gay marriage in her sample broke up, all of the other lesbians in the community endeavored to comfort the partner who was considered to have been mistreated. But at the same time, they voiced fears "that dreams of a lasting homosexual union may only be illusory."

In the larger society, not only are homosexual couples *not* encouraged to remain together; they are positively encouraged to break off their relationships because many persons—including their families, friends, employers, and religious leaders—consider such relationships to be immoral. Sociologist Norval Glenn (1979) found that data from seven different national samples during the mid-1970s indicated that attitudes toward homosexuality continue to be "highly restrictive" in contrast to the greater permissiveness in attitudes toward premarital sexual relations. Close to three-fourths of the respondents, in these samples of 1,500 each, answered that homosexual relations are "always wrong."

Tanner (1978:3) points out that not only must homosexual couples face the lack of social support and the absence of "scripts" or models to follow in establishing and sustaining a gay quasi-marriage relationship; they also face certain unique strains. For example, the two persons must often separate for holidays because relatives expect them to come to their respective parental homes, not knowing they are "coupled" and not likely to approve even if they did know. Then there are the usual problems and conflicts that any couple, whether homosexual or heterosexual, must work out in living together. Jealousy was often mentioned as a conflict area in Tanner's small sample, as was money. "In all of the dyads where money was a point of contention one partner was earning considerably more than the other," Tanner explains, "and the quarrels concerned feelings of dependence or frustration about the inequitable ability of one person to make her financial contribution to the household" (p. 81). In Bell and Weinberg's much larger sample, on the other hand, income disparity for the most part had no particular effect on the relationships of either male or female homosexual couples.

Bell and Weinberg (1978:315) found that the two major reasons lesbian couples tended to break up related to one partner's romantic involvement with another woman or else dissatisfaction with their own relationship. Homosexual male couples tended to report their breakups occurred for reasons beyond their control (for example, a partner's moving away because of employment, military service, or educational opportunities). Others reported that the relationship was unsatisfying to one or both partners. The percentage that broke up because one of the partners became romantically involved with someone else was considerably smaller than was the percentage among their female counterparts.

Blumstein and Schwartz (1983:307–317) found in their research that dissatisfaction with jobs and the intrusion of jobs into relationships, arguments over housework, conflicts over finances, problems with control and dependency, fighting over issues such as frequency of sex relations or the importance of monogamy, and disagreements over the amount of time spent together were all contributing factors in the breaking up of homosexual relationships.

The late Howard J. Brown (1976:141) wrote: "A homosexual trying to make his way in a long-term relationship is like a member of any minority group making an incursion on territory hitherto forbidden: He must be stronger, braver, and wiser than everyone else to avoid foundering." A highly respected physician, medical school professor, hospital administrator, and chief health officer of New York City under Mayor John Lindsay's administration, Brown had begun working to change societal attitudes toward homosexual persons and had announced his own homosexual orientation shortly before being stricken with a fatal heart attack in 1975 at the age of 51.

Not only does the stigma attached to homosexual relationships and the absence of societal support mean that gay persons must work especially hard on their couple commitments; they may also find that these same factors mean that their interdependency is even greater than is that of heterosexual couples. Thus, their breakups are especially painful, with the result that one or the other partner may even contemplate suicide at such a time. In pointing this out, Bell and Weinberg (1978:216) refer to data that indicate that failure to establish an ongoing relationship "may be even more consequential and problematic for most homosexual adults than whatever difficulties they might have in accepting their homosexuality." These behavioral scientists suggest that counselors work with *couples* as well as individuals in order to help homosexual persons in quasi-marital unions to strengthen their relationships and work out difficulties or else "to make their eventual parting an occasion for personal growth instead of alienation."

Gay couples who have sought consecration of their commitment through a "Holy Union" ceremony in the Metropolitan Community Churches are expected to seek a special "divorce" or "annulment" through that

LOSS OF A HOMOSEXUAL PARTNER THROUGH DEATH

I know of a homosexual couple who had lived together for twenty-one years. One of the men died suddenly of pneumonia. A week after the funeral, his brothers appeared at the apartment; they had come to pack up and move out his furniture, paintings, tableware—everything. The two lovers had bought many of these things together over the years, but the apartment belonged to the deceased. The surviving partner told me that he believed that his lover's brothers had long suspected that theirs was a homosexual relationship and that now the brothers were, in effect, challenging him to defend his right to any of the belongings. He said nothing, and was left with nothing.

Forewarned, of course, homosexual couples can prevent this sort of thing (though I have known of cases where the family of the deceased contested his will, where, once again, the homosexual is caught in a vicious circle, for the law does not allow him to marry his partner, but at the same time it cannot assure him that his partner will inherit his estate because the two men were not married). What is almost impossible to avoid, until and unless society recognizes homosexual relationships, is the shock, the horror, and the utter loneliness of facing a bereavement without any of the traditional consolations. Relegated to the status of mere friend, the surviving partner must watch helplessly as members of his lover's family move in and establish their claim as next of kin, as they make funeral arrangements their own way, possibly shipping the body out of town. The fanfare surrounding death in our society is a tried and true way of protecting mourners from the first few weeks of grief, distracting them and at the same time acknowledging the importance of what they are going through. Not only must a homosexual face his grief without such support; he is also obliged, unless he is in an unusual situation, to completely hide what he is feeling. This sets up an unbearable emotional cul-de-sac. I have known men to be shattered by it.

SOURCE: Howard Brown, *Familiar Faces, Hidden Lives: The Story of Homosexual Men in America Today* (New York: Harcourt Brace Jovanovich, 1976), pp. 140–141.

denomination if the marriage ends. Only then are they considered free to enter a same-sex remarriage.

Separation by Death As is true of their heterosexual counterparts, not all homosexual marriages fall apart. Many endure to the very end, and the partners are separated only by one or the other's death.

One of television's *All in the Family* pro-grams captured some of the pathos surrounding such circumstances. Edith Bunker's "spinster" cousin had died, and not until the time of the funeral did the Bunkers learn of her long-term quasi-marriage to her female apartment mate. While Archie pronounced God's wrath upon the relationship and fumed over the bereaved partner's request to keep a sentimentally valued silver tea set, his wife put aside her shock and quickly grasped the human element. She realized that the two women, both schoolteachers, most assuredly would have lost their jobs had their lesbian relationship been made known. With genuine warmth and caring, Edith recognized the depth of her cousin's partner's grief and spoke of how hard it must have been to love somebody so much and not be able to tell anyone about it.

The partners in some gay marriages prepare for the eventuality of death by naming one another as beneficiaries to life insurance policies or provide for each other in wills. In such relationships, however, even where there are wills, relatives sometimes contest them. The boxed insert on this page shows some of the psychic pain experienced by the partner who is left alone. In any case, the desire to provide for the loved one after one's own death illustrates the expectation of permanence that characterizes many homosexual unions. For some, the intent is clearly "until death do us part"—even though society provides no legal recognition of gay marriages at this point in time. (See also Mendola, 1980, Chapter 9.)

CHAPTER HIGHLIGHTS

This chapter has focused on *cohabitation* (an arrangement in which unmarried opposite-sex partners set up a household together) and *gay marriage* (a similar arrangement between homosexual partners).

Heterosexual couples who live together outside marriage may have in mind a *trial marriage* (to test whether or not they want to be married and to prepare for later marriage), a *common-law marriage* (considered a legal marriage in a small number of states), or an *ad hoc arrangement,* in which the relationship exists for its own sake and as a substitute (not preparation) for marriage. Furthermore, the phenomenon of cohabitation forces us to see that it isn't enough to think in terms of two statuses: singleness and marriage. Rather, marriage is a matter of degrees along a continuum. Between nonmarriage and formal legal marriage exists a sociological definition of marriage as an ongoing, publicly declared relationship of sexual, emotional, and financial interdependency. Evidence thus far suggests that most cohabitation relationships either dissolve or the partners get married. To simply continue in an *ongoing consensual union* is not common. Couples usually drift into cohabitation arrangements gradually and maintain them so long as rewards exceed costs. In general, cohabitation rates for divorced persons are higher than for never-married persons. Cohabitation may be called a *quasi-* (or "as if") marriage in that a woman and man are sharing a life together materially, emotionally, and sexually; yet it lacks the legal recognition and social support necessary for marriage to exist in the fullest sense of the word.

Persons interested in another kind of quasi-marriage, *gay marriage,* want to be united in a socially recognized relationship to persons they love, even though the persons they love are of the same sex. A gay union can be considered a valid marriage in the sociological sense, but as yet it is not recognized in the legal sense. A sustained homosexual relationship is thus an *ongoing consensual union,* as in the case of heterosexual cohabitors, but without the option of legal marriage. Those homosexual persons who would like to see gay marriage recognized in law are concerned both about the psychic costs of not having their coupled relationships validated publicly and about the costs in terms of legal privileges and financial benefits denied them.

Many homosexual couples consider themselves married, even if society does not, and work to establish permanent relationships. Homosexual males usually have a far greater number of sexual partners over a lifetime than do lesbians, reflecting divergent socialization, which stresses a more instrumental attitude toward sex for males in general and a more expressive attitude toward sex among females in general. Role playing similar to traditional stereotypical gender roles was at one time somewhat more common among homosexual persons than it is at present. The trend is away from role playing and toward egalitarian relationships.

SINGLENESS, SINGLE PARENTHOOD, AND COMBINED HOUSEHOLD ARRANGEMENTS

In the preceding chapter, we examined two alternatives to traditional marriage which were nevertheless based upon *couple* relationships. However, whether by choice or by circumstance, not everyone lives as part of a pair. Some people live alone. Others live with their children. And still others live in some sort of roommate or group arrangement.

SINGLENESS

In 1970, Roberta Hornig wrote an article for the *Washington Evening Star* entitled "See Aunt Debbie . . . First-Grade Symbol of Swinging Single," which presented the suggestion that grade school children not only needed to see women in roles other than that of homemaker; they needed also to gain a strong image of the unmarried career woman. To aid in this, first-grade reading books could introduce attractive, active, happy, fulfilled "Aunt Debbie," who could show Dick and Jane through her example that alternative lifestyles exist for women. Not all women are wives and mothers. Children could learn that single women can lead interesting, exciting lives and work in occupations that bring great enjoyment (in Bernard, 1972, chap. 10).

Singleness in Historical Perspective

Children in early America heard an altogether different message than that suggested by Hornig's proposal for a positive presentation of singleness. A North Carolina physician wrote in 1731: "[Girls] marry generally very young, some at thirteen or fourteen, and she that continues unmarried until twenty, is reckoned a stale maid, which is a very indifferent character in that country." In Puritan society, women were called "ancient maids"

if they had not married by the time they reached their twenty-fifth birthday (Calhoun, vol. 1, 1919:67, 245). There were no sparkling, vivacious, ambitious, industrious Aunt Debbies around then. The single state received no encouragement whatsoever. In fact, it was positively discouraged.

Both social and economic sanctions were used to push people into marriage. Older single women were ridiculed, often despised, treated as life's failures, and assigned to unpaid drudge-work in the homes of married brothers and sisters. To make matters worse, there arose in literature the stereotype of the neurotic spinster, the meddling busybody, the sour, prim, and proper "old maid" of the children's card game (Watt, 1957, chap. 5).

Bachelors were mocked and treated with harsh disapproval, too. Early American society found it difficult to tolerate unattached persons of either sex. Arthur Calhoun (1919), a social historian, points out that bachelors virtually found themselves "in the class of suspected criminals." Rarely were single men permitted to live alone or even to decide *where* they should live; the courts decided that for them. Many of the colonies had a "bachelor tax" as a further incentive to enter the married state. In Connecticut, Hartford taxed unmarried men twenty shillings a week, and New Haven enacted a law requiring unmarried persons of either sex to live with "licensed" families. Single men and women not living with relatives or in service as apprentices "are forbidden to diet or lodge alone," said the law. The city officials declared that such a law fulfilled the intent of the biblical commandment to obey parents by providing substitute parents for bachelors and spinsters (who were evidently suspected of acting in a wayward manner if they lacked the supervision and restraints of a family). The heads of the specially selected licensed families that took single persons under their

SPINSTERHOOD: ITS CULTURAL SIGNIFICANCE

Spinsters are women who never marry. They are daughters but not wives, often sisters or aunts but rarely mothers, their history the contrapuntal echo of family history. Marriage creates a web of obligations and expectations that binds bride, groom, and their families; through children, it carves channels for the transmission of worldly goods and cultural values from one generation to another. From this perspective, the questions of when marriage occurs, of who arranges it, and of who marries whom are irrelevant; what matters is whether marriage occurs at all. . . . [Studying spinsterhood historically] poses questions pertinent to the history of marriage, the family, and women. Where there are few spinsters, we can ask why there are so few acceptable roles other than those offered by marriage; where there are many spinsters, we must question the centrality of marriage.

SOURCE: Susan Cotts Watkins, "Spinsters," *Journal of Family History* (Winter 1984), pp. 310–311.

care were ordered "to observe the course, carriage, and behavior of every such single person, whether he or she walk diligently in a constant lawful employment, attending both family duties and the public worship of God, and keeping good order day and night or otherwise" (vol. 1, 1919:67–68).

Bachelors were especially under continual surveillance in the New England colonies, being watched by the constable, the watchman, and the tithingman. Whereas today a person might choose singleness in order to be free, it was marriage that freed a man in Puritan society. Only upon taking a wife could he escape the restrictions just mentioned. Furthermore, many New England towns provided building lots when a man exchanged his bachelor existence for the role of husband. In a society that placed a high value on family life and which needed to grow in population, pressures and incentives toward marriage were in abundance.

The main incentives to encourage persons to marry were economic. The bachelor tax drained off part of the single man's income, and in addition he was without the benefits of a wife and children to care for household needs and help him with farm chores or in the shop. Benjamin Franklin's (1745) advice about marriage was that "a single man has not nearly the value he would have in that state of union. He is an incomplete animal. He resembles the odd half of a pair of scissors."

Women, too, were constantly reminded that marriage was expected of them. Almost no other way of securing financial support was open to them. Even so, an early Maryland law was designed to make sure they got the message. A woman who had inherited land was required to marry within seven years. Otherwise, the land would be forfeited to the next of kin or else she would have to dispose of it. The reason for the law was clearly spelled out: "That it may be prevented that noe woman here vow chastity in the world." She was to realize that her land "is gonne unless she git a husband" (quoted in Calhoun, vol. 1, 1919:247). Despite certain laws and informal pressures, some women did choose to remain single. The Plymouth church records of 1667 list the death of Governor Bradford's 91-year-old sister-in-law, describing her as "a godly old

ORIGIN OF THE TERM "SPINSTER"

The denotation and connotation of the word "spinster" has changed greatly over time, paralleling the changing status of single women in their society and their own political consciousness. In the seventeenth century, the term was used generally to refer to the female sex. The task of spinning was part of every woman's daily routine. Late in the century, the word became a legal term for the unmarried woman. Spinning was the prime contribution made by these women to the domestic economy. In the eighteenth century, spinning schools were established by New England's communities to occupy and make socially productive its dependents—orphans, widows, and single women. With the industrial revolution, this socially and economically productive role was lost. The word "spinster" took on the negative connotations of extra, left-over, dried up, and grasping. By late in the nineteenth century, the single woman, particularly of a professional, reform, or intellectual cast, was branded in major medical texts as a "mannish maiden," an Hermaphrodite, no longer strictly female in sex. Yet among themselves, unmarried women used the term "productive spinster," harkening back to a time when the word was used with pride and designated a woman of valued and significant occupation.

SOURCE: Lee Chambers-Schiller, "The Single Woman: Family and Vocation among Nineteenth-Century Reformers," in Mary Kelley (ed.), *Woman's Being, Woman's Place: Female Identity and Vocation in American History* (Boston: G.K. Hall, 1979), p. 348.

maid never married." Other records indicate that Taunton, Massachusetts, was founded by "an ancient maid of forty-eight" (Calhoun, vol. 1, 1919:69).

The old song about the married man who wished he were single so that his pockets would jingle gets to the root of an attitude held by many bachelors—especially in the eighteenth-century South. This was true despite the costs involved (Maryland's part in the French and Indian War was financed by taxes on light wines, billiard tables, and bachelors, for example) because many men felt the responsibility of providing for a wife and children would be an even higher price to pay. In addition, there were men who felt that a free-swinging sex life with a variety of women was preferable to the restraints of settled domesticity with one spouse and attention-demanding children (Calhoun, vol. 1, 1919:246; vol. 2, 1919:208).

Some men remained single not by choice but by circumstance. With the movement westward, there arose a situation in which the supply of women did not match the supply of men. Miners, traders, trappers, loggers, and cowboys often remained single even though many of them might have preferred marriage. Yet both the nature of their work and the scarcity of available women placed obstacles in the way. Newspapers in the 1830s suggested that "the excess of spinsters in our large cities" could be alleviated by transporting them to the new settlements. Such women came to be spoken of in terms of some commodity to be shipped. An 1837 newspaper, for example, reported that "a wagon load of girls for the western market lately past through Northhampton, Mass" (Calhoun, vol. 2, 1919:104).

Sociologist Jessie Bernard (1979:xiii) illustrates the intensity of the pressures urging young women to marry by citing an old parochial school rhyme:

St. Catherine, St. Catherine, oh lend me thine aid,
And grant that I never may die an old maid!
A husband, St. Catherine!
A good one, St. Catherine!
But anyone better than no one, St. Catherine!
A husband, St. Catherine!
Handsome, St. Catherine!
Rich, St. Catherine!
Young, St. Catherine!
Soon, St. Catherine!

Singleness as a Lifestyle Today

In 1973 a new magazine was launched. Its title? Simply one word—*Single.* That a special-interest magazine would come on the scene devoted solely to the concerns of unattached persons would have seemed strange in earlier periods of United States history. But by the 1970s, the single lifestyle was being chosen by growing numbers of persons—in some cases temporarily (but for a longer period, as we saw in Chapter 4 in our discussion of rises in age at marriage) and in other cases permanently. The trend has continued, as can be seen in Table 7-A.

Persons have become more cautious about when (and even *if*) they eventually will enter a legal union—another indication of trends toward rationality in choices about marriage. In terms of exchange theory, we may say that as more persons begin to calculate the costs and benefits of marriage, the greater the likelihood that some of them will assess a pattern of ongoing singleness to be basically more rewarding than legal marriage.

How Many Stay Single?   Most persons eventually marry. In the United States in 1980, according to figures from the U.S. Bureau of the Census, only about 5 percent of

men and women over age 45 had never married (Glick, 1984a:9–13). That picture may be changing, however. "The longer the pattern of increasing postponement of marriage persists, the more likely the prospect becomes that the extent of lifetime singlehood among young adults of today will increase," reports Paul Glick (1979:2). Basing his projections on current patterns, this former senior demographer at the Census Bureau estimates that 10 percent of men who were between the ages of 25 and 29 in 1980 may never marry. Among women in that same age range in 1980, 12 percent are expected to remain single throughout their lives (Glick, 1984a:12–13).

Education and Singleness   According to Glick's estimates, "men who have been educated above the college education level are expected to have the highest proportion who marry within their lifetimes, whereas women college graduates are expected to have the lowest proportion among women." (See Table 7-B.)

Marriage has been viewed traditionally as a major life goal for women—not only for expressive reasons, but as a way of securing economic provision and status. Highly educated women, however, have access to socioeconomically rewarding alternatives to marriage. They have most to gain from greater female autonomy and individualism since they are prepared to enter occupations offering high benefits both in prestige and income. Such women are in no hurry to marry (Allen and Kalish, 1984), and in some cases may choose not to marry at all.

Sociological studies have shown that higher levels of intelligence, education, and occupation are associated with singleness among women (Spreitzer and Riley, 1974:536). In the past, this association was sometimes explained by the suggestion that

TABLE 7-A Persons age 15 years and over and percent never married, by age and sex: 1986, 1980, and 1970 (Numbers in thousands)

AGE AND SEX	1986		1980		1970[1]	
	NUMBER OF PERSONS	PERCENT NEVER MARRIED	NUMBER OF PERSONS	PERCENT NEVER MARRIED	NUMBER OF PERSONS	PERCENT NEVER MARRIED
Male, 15 years and over	88,474	30.0	81,947	29.6	70,559	28.1
15 to 19 years	9,183	98.3	10,425	97.3	11,497	97.4
20 to 24 years	9,788	75.5	10,134	68.8	7,198	54.7
25 to 29 years	10,751	41.4	9,513	33.1	6,592	19.1
30 to 34 years	10,205	22.2	8,538	15.9	5,599	9.4
35 to 39 years	9,034	11.3	6,792	7.8	5,439	7.2
40 to 44 years	6,921	8.5	5,642	7.1	5,838	6.3
45 to 54 years	10,970	5.9	10,938	6.1	11,224	7.5
55 to 64 years	10,350	5.9	10,014	5.3	8,835	7.8
65 years and over	11,272	5.1	9,953	4.9	8,336	7.5
Female, 15 years and over	96,354	22.8	89,914	22.5	77,766	22.1
15 to 19 years	9,090	94.2	10,337	91.2	11,432	90.3
20 to 24 years	10,160	57.9	10,557	50.2	8,409	35.8
25 to 29 years	10,868	28.1	9,741	20.9	6,841	10.5
30 to 34 years	10,229	14.2	8,824	9.5	5,829	6.2
35 to 39 years	9,308	8.4	7,052	6.2	5,708	5.4
40 to 44 years	7,245	5.5	5,939	4.8	6,171	4.9
45 to 54 years	11,692	4.7	11,760	4.7	12,029	4.9
55 to 64 years	11,712	3.9	11,462	4.5	9,807	6.8
65 years and over	16,049	5.2	14,242	5.9	11,539	7.7

[1]Figures for 1970 include persons aged 14.

SOURCE: U.S. Bureau of the Census, *Current Population Reports*, ser. P-20, no. 412, *Households, Families, Marital Status, and Living Arrangements: March 1986*, (Advance Report) (Washington, D.C.: U.S. Government Printing Office, November 1986), p.4.

Because highly educated women have access to socioeconomically rewarding alternatives, they may choose to postpone marriage or not marry at all. (Peter Southwick/Stock, Boston)

women of high education and achievement are "marital rejects" or "pathetic misfits," persons who are "unfeminine" and "undesirable" to males and who therefore remain unchosen. However, the explanation may very well lie in the opposite direction. The active choosing may be on the part of the *women*. One sociologist, after a study of census data that showed a direct relation between female economic attainment and unmarried status, concluded that high-achieving women may consider marriage confining and therefore reject the institution—which is an altogether different matter than saying such women are

unwanted by potential husbands (Havens, 1973:980). Such a tradition has not been uncommon in the academic world, for example. The pioneers of higher education for women often themselves provided positive role models of richly fulfilled and successful single women (Bernard, 1964, chap. 14).

Highly educated men have not faced the dilemma faced by highly educated women. For well-educated women, the situation has generally been one of *either/or*—either major attention to occupation and a life of singleness on the one hand, or marriage on the other (with occupational interests secondary or put aside). But for highly educated men, it has been a matter of *both/and*. No one would think of telling a man upon marriage that he should now seriously consider giving up his career. If anything, marriage may be considered an aid to his career aspirations because having a wife in the traditional sense is expected to relieve him of concerns about everyday household matters (laundry, meals, good order), increase his opportunities for entertaining important guests and clients, and, in general, provide him with the emotional support and encouragement that can be so helpful in advancing his career. This is partly what sociologist Jessie Bernard (1972) has in mind in contrasting the "his" marriage (marriage from the male's perspective) and the "her" marriage (marriage as traditionally defined for females). Even in cases where a woman has elected to follow the path of a high-powered career combined with marriage, she is traditionally expected to be the spouse who makes the greater sacrifices and carries the heavier load of household tasks.

Aware of such costs, more women today give evidence of viewing singleness as a way of life allowing greater freedom and flexibility in pursuing career goals and travel and educational opportunities—benefits they

TABLE 7-B   Selected marriage statistics: United States, 1980

AGE AT SURVEY DATE, RACE, AND EDUCATIONAL LEVEL	PERCENT WHO HAD MARRIED BY 1980		PERCENT WHO MAY EVENTUALLY MARRY	
	MEN	WOMEN	MEN	WOMEN
25–29 years old:				
All races	69	79	90	88
0–11 years of school	75	82	92	90
12 years	75	83	90	90
13–15 years	65	76	74	86
16 years	61	70	84	83
17+ years	57	62	93	83
White	71	81	89	90
Black	58	62	89	75
50–54 years old:				
All races	95	95	97	96
70–74 years old:				
All races	95	94	95	94

SOURCE: Paul C. Glick, ''Marriage, Divorce, and Living Arrangements,'' *Journal of Family Issues* 5, No. 1, March, 1984, p. 13. Statistics were from the U.S. Bureau of the Census, derived from unpublished Current Population Survey data for June, 1980.

might miss by rushing into marriage. As *Ms.* magazine editor and feminist leader Gloria Steinem has said of achievement-oriented women today, "We are becoming the men we wanted to marry" (as quoted in Edwards, 1985:56).

Singleness over the Life Course   Thus far, we have been speaking of singleness only in the sense of never having been married. As we saw in Chapter 6, some persons live in paired relationships even though they are technically considered single (persons who cohabit and homosexual couples). Persons who are homosexual—whether in couple relationships or living as homosexual singles—make up a certain proportion of the never-married percentage cited earlier; but it's wrong to assume a simple equation between singleness and homosexuality per se because, as we saw, many homosexual persons are or have been married to heterosexual partners. (We cannot say, in other words,

that the estimate that 5 percent of the male population is homosexual corresponds to the fact that 5 percent of middle-aged men have never been married.)

Sociologist Peter Stein (1976), in studying the lifestyles of single persons, broadened his definition to include those who may have been in either an actual marriage *or* a marriagelike situation at one point in life but live as singles at some other point. For the purpose of his study, Stein's working definition of *single persons* was "those men and women who are not currently married or involved in an exclusive heterosexual or homosexual relationship" (p. 11).

Another author, Margaret Adams (1976) suggests that the "least ambiguous" definition of single persons is a *legal* definition that includes the never-married, the divorced, and the widowed. "These three groups share the common fate of not having a legal spouse and many similar practical issues of living," writes Adams (p. 18). For her own interviews, Adams concentrated on those within these groups that she felt had most in common in terms of a single lifestyle: the *authentically single* (never-married) and persons who were either widowed or divorced for five years and who had no children.

Out of all the types of households in the United States, the household in which a person lives alone is the second most common. In 1983 (latest available statistics), 23 percent of all households fell into the lone householder category while 59 percent were headed by a married couple (Glick, 1984b:205–206). Figure 7-1 provides a rough picture of how various household arrangements are distributed.

Glick (1984b:206) points out that the number of adults living alone increased by 173 percent between 1960 and 1983. The number of one-parent households increased at about the same rate. During that same time interval, married-couple households increased by only 26 percent, the lowest rate of increase for any category of households. (Unmarried-couple households increased 331 percent, and other nonfamily households increased by 83 percent during that same period.)

This doesn't mean that husband-wife households are showing signs of disappearing. It just means that other types of households have been growing at a greatly accelerated pace. If we shift our thinking from numbers of *households* and think, instead, about numbers of *persons,* we find that census data show that "most Americans still live in married-couple households"—73 percent of the population in 1983, Glick emphasizes. "Yet," he goes on, "the corresponding proportions were even higher a generation earlier; in 1960, fully 86 percent of all household members were living in the homes of married couples" (p. 207).

The question that concerns us here is: Why

are households with persons living alone showing such an increase? (We will also be looking at single-parent and nonfamily households later in the chapter. We have, of course, already examined the phenomenon of unmarried-couple households in Chapter 6.)

Persons who live alone are at various stages of life and differ both in age and marital status. They may be young or old or somewhere in between. They may be persons who have never been married. Or they may be persons who are separated, divorced, or widowed.

As Table 7-C shows, the highest proportion of *women* who lived alone in 1983 were over the age of 45. Less than one-quarter of the 11.8 million women who lived alone in 1983 were younger than 45. In contrast, out of the nearly 7.5 million *men* living alone that year, more than half were under 45 years of age. This is a considerable change from 1970, when only slightly more than a third of men living alone were under age 45.

Among both women and men living alone, the biggest rate of increase has been among younger adults. The increase has, in fact, been so great that Glick (1984b:208–209) speaks of it as "spectacular." "Living by oneself has become more feasible—and even inevitable—for many reasons," writes Glick, pointing out that "greater numbers of never-married and previously married adults are now in the pool of people eligible to live alone." For example, as more persons delay marriage longer, the likelihood of more persons living alone increases. Sociologist Frances Kobrin (1976) speaks of this as the "premarital independence stage" and observes that it has become most pronounced among young males.

The other stage of life represented in a high percentage of one-person households is what Kobrin calls the "post family indepen-

In a block of ten households where the distribution of household types corresponded to the total distribution of household types in the United States in 1983, we would find that approximately:

Six of the households were maintained by married couples.

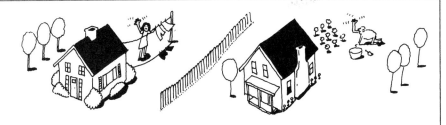

Two of the households were maintained by persons living alone.

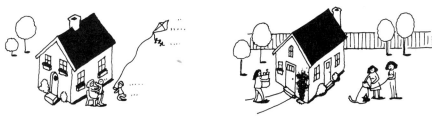

One of the households was maintained by a single parent with children.

One was made up of some other household combination of persons.*

*This category includes household arrangements such as an unmarried couple living together, two elderly sisters or widowed friends living together, three young men sharing an apartment, a grandmother and granddaughter making a home together, same-sex couples, divorced persons who find it economically beneficial to set up a shared household arrangement with a friend in a similar situation, and so on.

FIGURE 7-1 Households by type in the United States in 1983.

TABLE 7-C Numbers of lone male and female householders, and percentage distribution by age and marital status, 1960, 1970 and 1983

YEAR	TOTAL NO. (IN 000s)	TOTAL	AGE <45	AGE ≥45	NEVER-MARRIED	DIVORCED	SEPARATED	WIDOWED
1960	7,063	100	20	80	29	13	11	47
1970	10,851	100	20	80	26	14	9	52
1983	19,250	100	36	64	31	21	8	40
1960	4,435	100	14	86	22	11	7	60
1970	7,319	100	13	87	19	11	6	64
1983	11,799	100	23	77	23	17	5	55
1960	2,628	100	31	69	42	16	16	26
1970	3,532	100	35	65	40	20	14	26
1983	7,451	100	55	45	45	27	12	16

The column grouping header reads: **%, BY AGE AND MARITAL STATUS**; sub-section dividers read "No. Total (Men and Women)", "Women", and "Men".

SOURCE: Paul C. Glick, "American Household Structure in Transition," *Family Planning Perspectives,* 16, No. 5, September/October 1984, p. 209.

dence stage" (most pronounced among older females who have been widowed and for whom the experience of living alone in their own households may be a first). More older persons, in general, are living alone as a result of better health, longer lives, and financial planning that has made maintaining their own households an option. But more widowed women than widowed men are likely to be living alone because older men are more likely to remarry. And when they do remarry, they are likely to marry women a few years younger than themselves (Glick, 1984b:209).

Persons who marry and consider themselves outside the "marital status: single" category may nevertheless find themselves single at some point in life, either through the death of a spouse or through separation or divorce. Such persons also often live alone. The percentage of divorced persons living alone has experienced an especially rapid growth. As may be seen in Table 7-C, about 1 out of 6 women living alone in 1983 was divorced. Among men, the figure was slightly over 1 out of 4. In divorces involving children, mothers are more likely than fathers to have custody of the children and thus to be living with the children while the father lives alone. But close to half of all divorces do not involve decisions about children, and many divorced women also set up lone households (Glick, 1984b:208–209). The increasing level of divorces over recent decades has added more persons to the pool of candidates for a living-alone lifestyle option.

Choosing Singleness Living alone is only one of a number of options open to single

RITES OF INDEPENDENCE

*Alice and Carl Hesse
of Washington, D.C.
are pleased to announce
that their daughter
Susan A. Hesse
of Piedmont, California
is settling into
Joyous Old Maidhood
at bedtime on
Saturday, June 23, 1984,
after which she will cease
looking for Mr. Right
and begin giving
scintillating dinner
parties and soirées.
To help celebrate this
wonderful occasion,
gift place–settings
of Newport Scroll Sterling
by Gorham
are available at
Macy's Department Store.
Thanking you in advance,
Carl and Alice.*

*Dinner Dates to be announced
when Susan acquires a dining table.*

©1984 Susan A. Hesse

NEW CEREMONIES FOR NEW PEOPLE

When Susan Hesse, a 38-year-old creative director, moved into a new apartment, she sent out this announcement to 200 friends and business associates. She phrased it as a good-humored spoof of a wedding announcement, but she also intended it as a serious statement. "I was celebrating my singleness," she explained. She had been married briefly when she was younger, and people had been asking her mother when Susan was going to remarry. "I wanted to say 'I'm single and it's fine,' she said. "I spent a lot of time waiting for Mr. Right, but I'm not waiting any more. This is my life, and it's not on hold."

SOURCE: Beverly Stephen, "Rites of Independence," *Ms., XIII,* no. 5 (November 1984), p. 55.

persons, but the whole idea of options—of choice—is important to keep in mind in discussing singleness in general. One author who has written extensively on singleness and has focused especially on the single woman sees three basic characteristics in an authentic single lifestyle: (1) the capacity to be economically self-supporting, (2) the cultivation of social and psychological independence, and (3) "a clearly thought through intent to remain single by preference" (Adams, 1971). In other words, one doesn't feel forced into singleness because an opportunity for marriage hasn't presented itself. One is single because one *wants* to be. One is single because of *choices* one has made—whether at the outset or later, or as a decision made after the ending of an earlier marriage. Adams (1976:15) thus treats singleness from a different perspective, regarding it not "as a temporary antecedent to the more common condition of marriage," but "as a social status or situation that is complete in its own right." (See also Peterson, 1981.)

"The possibility that some people might actually choose to be single because they want to be, because they feel it would contribute to their growth and well-being to remain so, is simply not believed possible," asserts Peter Stein (1976:4), pointing to the intense societal pressures to marry and the tendency for social psychologists to refer to singles negatively as "those who fail to marry" or those who cannot "make positive choices." To choose singleness means that a person perceives the rewards of that lifestyle to be greater than the rewards of marriage and that any costs perceived are less than the costs that would be required of one in marriage.

From his in-depth interviews with persons who had chosen to be single for the forseeable future, Stein worked out a chart of what

he termed "pushes" and "pulls" that might move a person away from one situation (pushes) and toward another (pulls). This is, of course, another way of looking at relative rewards and costs. Loneliness and pressure from parents to marry, for example, are costs of singleness *pushing* toward marriage. And the desire for emotional attachment and for a family are perceived rewards of marriage *pulling* toward that status. Conversely, a feeling of being trapped and suffocated in a marriage relationship is perceived as a cost to be avoided or eliminated and thus pushes a person toward singleness. Or one might be pulled toward singleness by such expected rewards as opportunities for more varied experiences and psychological and social autonomy. (See Table 7-D.)

For some persons, of course, singleness is not the way of life they would have preferred. Sociologist Robert Staples (1981b:174–175), for example, calls attention to the forced single state in which many black women find themselves because of structural constraints. "Among lower-income Blacks," he writes, "the structural constraints consist of the unavailability and undesirability of Black males in the eligible pool of potential mates." What accounts for this problem? "Due to the operational effects of institutional racism," Staples explains, "large numbers of Black males are incarcerated, unemployed, narcotized, or fall prey to early death." As a result, several million black women may lack an opportunity for marriage. (See also Darity and Myers, 1984:777.)

Middle-class black women also face limitations on their prospects for marriage because of structural constraints. More black women than black men graduate from college. Thus, writes Staples (1981b:174), "assuming a desire for homogeneity in mate selection, it is not possible for every Black female college graduate to find a mate among

TABLE 7-D Pushes and pulls toward being married and being single

Toward Being Married	
PUSHES (NEGATIVES IN PRESENT SITUATION)	PULLS (ATTRACTIONS IN POTENTIAL SITUATIONS)
Pressure from parents	Approval of parents
Need to leave home	Desire for family
Fear of independence	Example of peers
Loneliness	Romanticization of marriage
Cultural expectations, socialization	Physical attraction
	Emotional attachment and love
Guilt over singlehood	Security, social status, prestige
No sense of alternatives	Sexual availability

Toward Being Single	
PUSHES	PULLS
Restrictions within relationship:	Career opportunities
Suffocating one-to-one relationship, feeling trapped	Variety of experiences and plurality of roles
Obstacles to self-development	Self-sufficiency
Boredom, unhappiness, and anger	Sexual availability
	Exciting lifestyle
Role playing and conformity to expectations	Freedom to change and mobility
Poor communication with mate	Sustaining friendships
Sexual frustration	Psychological and social autonomy
Lack of friends, isolation, loneliness	
Limited mobility and availability of new experiences	

SOURCE: Peter J. Stein, *Single* (Englewood Cliffs, NJ: Prentice-Hall, 1976), p. 65.

her peers." At the time Staples was writing, the ratio of unmarried college-educated black women to unmarried college-educated black men was 2 to 1, and the gap was showing signs of further widening. In some categories, there were as many as thirty-eight black women to every black male.

Staples (1981a:227) points out that at one time this imbalance was dealt with by a college-educated woman's willingness to marry a man of less education and lower socioeconomic status, but this is much less likely today. Such women know they do not need marriage for financial support and are not willing to settle for a life with someone who cannot provide the emotional support, intimacy, and companionship built around common interests and outlooks that they desire in a mate.

"One finds a curious pattern in the characteristics of never-married blacks," Staples goes on to say. "There are actually a larger number of men between the ages of 25 and 35 who have never married than women. But the largest proportion of these men are at the lowest socioeconomic level while the greatest proportion of never-married women are at the higher socioeconomic level." He calls

SINGLEHOOD AMONG BLACKS

Singlehood or marriage is more likely to be a dilemma for Afro-Americans. As a group they are proportionately more likely to be unmarried, divorced, separated or widowed. Approximately 52 percent of the black population over age 18 is single. Moreover, singlehood poses special problems for them because of the excess number of women, the different cultural traditions under which they were raised, fewer institutional supports for coping with unmarried life, and the inevitable complications stemming from their status as a racial minority. . . . A white colleague of mine has conducted a study of white singlehood as a viable alternative to marriage. That is not my perspective. Most blacks do not see their singleness as a viable choice but as a condition forced upon them by certain vicissitudes of life in America. This does not mean that black singlehood is a pathological form or that black marriages are that happy or functional. What it does signify is that being single and black is problematic. It requires coping with certain problems that either do not occur in the conjugal state, or happen with less frequency, and for which solutions are more readily available to married people.

SOURCE: Excerpted from the Introduction and Conclusion of Robert Staples, *The World of Black Singles* (Westport, CN: Greenwood Press, 1981), pp. xiii, 221.

attention to the increase in divorce rates among higher-status blacks and points out that "the women in the group are the least likely to remarry."

Many single persons are grateful for lives that permit independence, privacy, and time for solitude. (© Gale Zucker/Stock, Boston)

It is among highly educated black women, then, that singleness is most likely to be a preference. (Better to be *un*married than to be married just for the sake of being married and thus find oneself in a situation that is unrewarding and costly.) But it is a preference that springs not entirely from free choice but also from the structural situation into which the black community has been thrust. (See also Staples, 1985; Rivers, 1986.)

Living as a Single Person Stein (1976) points out that persons tend to think of singles in terms of two basic stereotypes: on the one hand, "*swingers*—the beautiful people who are constantly going to parties, who have uncommitted lives and a lot of uncommitted sex"; and on the other hand, "*lonely losers*," people who are depressed much of the time and sometimes even suicidal (pp. 2–3). Actually, says Stein, the idea that "single men and women are either 'with it' or 'out of it'" is highly inaccurate. (See also Cargan and Melko, 1982.) Single people, like married people, have a variety of experiences and moods. They have good days, bad days, and in-between days. They have happy times, lonely times, exciting times, and dull times. "Yet, overall," reports Stein, "single men and women report many more positive experiences than negative ones" (p. 3).

While independence is the most valued part of being single, a fear of loneliness appears to be the biggest drawback; and singles soon become aware of the need for supportive friendship networks (Stein, p. 99). At the same time, many single persons are grateful for lives that permit solitude and privacy and don't consider loneliness a special problem. Some reported to Adams (1976, chap. 5) that after a busy day in their occupations, they were glad to be able to go home to a quiet house or apartment to unwind without the distractions and demands of a family. This was true of both men and women. One woman told Adams that "in her opinion the type of loneliness with which single people have to reckon produces far less wear-and-tear on the psyche than the more pernicious emotional alienation that can develop between two people when the physical environment is shared but psychological and social exchange are at a minimum, or totally lacking" (p. 91).

Capitalizing on both the "swinging single" stereotype and the image of singles as lonely persons eager to find a mate, various businesses, services, and advertising practices have sprung up in recent years specifically aimed toward the singles market. At the same time, various religious and social service groups are becoming more sensitive to the needs and concerns of single persons and are developing special programs on their behalf.

SINGLE PARENTHOOD

"I still wonder how I could have been so naive as to think that nobody, at least nobody I knew well, would be terribly upset by my decision to have a child on my own." The words are those of a single university professor who, in her late thirties, decided to become pregnant. She goes on to contrast her own motivation with the meaning other people assigned to her decision:

> To *my* mind, I was attempting to fulfill a purely personal need, not to encroach on somebody else's political philosophy. I now know from experience that whatever the motivation of a voluntary single parent, the interpretation others will place on her behavior is that she is making a statement about the value of the nuclear family, about the importance of men as fathers, and about her personal need for companionship. (Mack, 1984:58)

This mother is speaking of one of several ways to become a single parent—intentional out-of-wedlock pregnancy. An *unintentional* nonmarital pregnancy is another way, as is adoption, divorce, or losing a spouse through death.

Births out of Wedlock

Historically, there have always been unmarried women who bore children. When these born-out-of-wedlock children were adopted by married couples, they did not have to grow up bearing the stigma "illegitimate." But if their mothers kept them, they were labeled "illegitimate" or "bastards." The baby was, of course, the same person in either case. It was the situation into which he or she was placed that determined "legitimacy." This labeling would in turn have a profound effect on the child's entire life. But why has such categorization of children taken place? What does it mean?

Principle of Legitimacy The anthropologist Bronislaw Malinowski (1930) wrote that there is a universal rule that "no child should be brought into the world without a man— and one man at that—assuming the role of sociological father, that is, guardian and protector, the male link between the child and the rest of the community." Malinowski called this rule "the principle of legitimacy." He claimed that throughout cultural variations, "there runs the rule that the father is indispensable for the full sociological status of the child as well as of its mother, that the group consisting of a woman and her offspring is sociologically incomplete and illegitimate. The father, in other words, is necessary for the full legal status of the family" (pp. 13–14 in Coser, 1964 reprint).

The principle of legitimacy stems from a functionalist view of marriage and parenthood. You'll recall that in the structural-functional framework, the family is seen as an organism with interdependent parts, each having a particular function to perform, as in the human body. Under the principle of legitimacy, the focus is on the function of the economic provider, a role assigned to the father. Thus a child is said to require a social father in order that the child can receive the status and material benefits that are rightfully his or hers.

Trends Relating to the Legitimacy Issue
Perhaps in some times and places it may have made sense to talk about the necessity of a social father to serve as a pipeline to the status and economic rewards of a particular society. But in modern times, such a requirement is not essential and inevitable for at least two reasons. One has to do with legal redefinitions of legitimacy, and the other relates to the changing roles and status of women.

Legal redefinitions of legitimacy It is possible for societies simply to abolish the legal distinction between legitimate and nonlegitimate. Sweden, for instance, has done precisely that (Linner, 1967:36). A child born out of wedlock has full inheritance rights from its father as well as its mother. Thus, if a man sires two children in marriage and one outside the marriage, all three share equally in their claims on his support, his status, and his estate. This assumes, of course, that paternity can be proven and that the father has any status and assets to transmit to the child. If either or both of these conditions cannot be met, the Swedish state is committed to provide for the child. According to government policy in Sweden, every child without a father is granted the same kinds of social and economic benefits enjoyed by other children.

Similarly, legislation that went into effect in the Union of Soviet Socialist Republics between 1968 and 1970 "has substantially changed the position of children born out of wedlock, and has given them the same status as legitimate children," reports one Soviet author who specializes in family law (Sedugin, 1973:73). In the USSR, an unmarried mother and her child are considered a family—a family just as valid as a nuclear family composed of two wedded parents and their children. If the child's father has not voluntarily acknowledged paternity and if the courts have not given a ruling establishing paternity in a particular case, an unmarried mother may receive state funds to aid in her child's upbringing; or she may send the child to a children's establishment run by the state where he or she is cared for entirely at the state's expense. On the other hand, if a male Soviet citizen "voluntarily acknowledges paternity by making a declaration to a registrar's office, his child enjoys the same rights and has the same obligations with regard to his parents and relatives as children born in wedlock" (Sedugin, p. 74). One of the rights the child enjoys is the right to be supported by both parents.

Supreme Court cases in recent years indicate that the United States may be moving in precisely the same direction as Sweden and the Soviet Union toward eventual abolishment of the legal distinctions between legitimate and nonlegitimate, especially in matters of support and inheritance (Krause, 1971; Ihara and Warner, 1979). However, there is no indication as yet that the United States is prepared to undertake the kinds of programs necessary to equalize opportunities for children who have no male pipeline to the status system.

Legitimacy and changing female roles

The question arises: Why not a female pipeline to the status system? Why couldn't a woman provide for a child the resources that have traditionally come from a man? Increasingly, women are taking advantage of educational opportunities and are gaining access to jobs with levels of income and prestige formerly restricted to white men. Many such women are highly individualistic and extremely achievement-oriented. Among those who have never married, there may be some who choose to legally adopt a child. There may be others who conceive and bear a child out of wedlock and who choose to rear the child alone. Given their high level of resources, there is no reason to suspect that they could not be as adequate a pipeline for conveying society's benefits to a child as any man could be. They can provide adequate objective benefits, and they can socialize the child into achievement-type behaviors through their own example and guidance.

Thus, we see a second reason why a social father may not be requisite in modern society. From the studies of Blau and Duncan (1967), we already know that children who have lost their fathers through death or divorce achieve as much in later life as do children from husband-wife households *from the same social class.* Apparently it is not the presence or absence of the father per se that affects the child's later attainments; rather, it is the benefits that the father provided while he was alive and in his estate, or else that he presently provides through child support. It therefore seems reasonable that a well-trained woman who opts for a lifestyle in which she raises a child alone can do at least as well as women who have been thrust into a status they did not choose nor necessarily want, namely that of provider and solo parent.

Principle of Status Adequacy For the kinds of reasons just discussed, Malinowski's functionalist principle of legitimacy becomes dubious indeed. It needs to be changed and restated to fit the complexities of modern society. Perhaps instead of a "principle of legitimacy," we could think in terms of a *principle of status adequacy.* Very simply, a principle of status adequacy means that every child requires some sociological parent (father and/or mother) or the equivalent in a communal, kin, or political arrangement that can provide the child with adequate socialization and access to the opportunity system. What matters is that a child be cared for, provided for, and guided toward becoming a contributing member of society. A family group made up of only a woman and her offspring need *not*—contrary to the principle stated by Malinowski—be regarded as "sociologically incomplete and illegitimate." But many such mothers and their children need assistance so that the principle of status adequacy can be put into effect.

The latest available statistics show that in 1982, close to 20 percent of live births occurred to women who were not married. Out of every 1,000 black babies born, 567 had unwed mothers. And out of every 1,000 white babies born, 121 were born out of wedlock (*Monthly Vital Statistics Report,* vol. 33, no. 6, Supplement, 1984:6–7). Even more significant is the fact that the vast majority of both black and white births that occur outside of marriage occur to women around or below the poverty line (Cutright, 1972b:382).

The economic discrimination that has especially limited educational and occupational opportunities for black persons helps explain their higher percentages of births out of wedlock. (It might be useful to refer back to the discussion on pages 145–149.) In addition, unmarried black women are less likely to have abortions than are white women faced with out-of-wedlock pregnancies (refer back to Table 5-E on page 117; see also Tanfer and Horn, 1985a:10). And pregnant unmarried black women are also less likely than are their white counterparts to marry before the resolution of the pregnancy (Zelnik and Kantner, 1980:234; Tanfer and Horn, 1985a:11). At the same time, in comparing black and white births out of wedlock, it should be noted that *nonmarital birth rates* (numbers of nonmarital live births per 1,000 unmarried women) have been going down for blacks at the same time they are rising for whites. In 1970, there were 95.5 live births outside of wedlock for every thousand unmarried black women; but by 1982, that figure had dropped to 79.6. In contrast, the 1970 birth rate of 13.8 among unmarried white women jumped to 18.8 by 1982 (*Monthly Vital Statistics Report,* vol. 33, no. 6, Supplement, 1984:31–32).

Not only are both white and black unwed mothers highly likely to come from lower socioeconomic backgrounds (backgrounds associated with more sexual activity and inadequate contraceptive information and behavior); they also tend to be quite young. In only about 1 out of 4 nonmarital births is the mother 25 years old or older. Thirty-eight percent of such births occur to young women in their teens, with women in their early twenties accounting for another 36 percent. (Percentages are calculated from numerical totals in *Monthly Vital Statistics,* vol. 33, no. 6, Supplement, 1984, Table 17, p. 30.)

To disadvantaged young women with few alternative rewards, it may appear as if children—even children society labels "illegitimate"—provide one of their few sources of major life gratifications. Hence there may be little motivation to resist unmarried motherhood, perhaps even to the extent of experiencing several out-of-wedlock births. And that is precisely where the *principle of status adequacy* has relevance. Households headed by poor women tend to be large. Consequently, the children are exceedingly disadvantaged and simply do not receive the kinds of benefits they need to adequately compete in modern society.

The unmarried woman who lacks educational and economic resources may find that single motherhood is something thrust on her rather than freely chosen. She becomes an unwed mother because few other viable options appear open to her. For her, the rewards of being a solo parent are few and costs high. If she is young, her schooling has probably been disrupted. She lacks material resources for her child and is quite likely to have more than one offspring outside of marriage. In terms of the principle of status adequacy, her child requires an *outside* source to serve as the pipeline to the economic and opportunity system. Some support may

10-YEAR-OLD IS MOTHER OF TWINS

Indianapolis (AP)—Twins born to a 10-year-old girl are healthy and gaining weight without use of an incubator, a doctor at Indiana University Hospital said Friday.

Dr. Robert Munsick, who is a professor of obstetrics and gynecology at the university's medical school, said the twin girls, born May 24, were "doing just fine," but will be kept in the hospital "a couple more weeks."

Each of the girls weighed 3 pounds, 6 ounces at birth, and were delivered six weeks premature. The names of the twins and their mother, who was released from the hospital Wednesday, have not been made public.

The twins were delivered normally after labor was induced on their mother.

Munsick said the youngest girl ever to give birth was a 6-year-old Peruvian, whose child was delivered by Caesarian section in the 1930s.

Ten-year-olds have given birth here in recent years, and "11-year-old mothers are almost common," Munsick said.

But a multiple birth for a 10-year-old mother is "extremely unusual," he added.

SOURCE: *Greensboro (NC) Daily News,* June 2, 1979.

come from both her family and from public assistance programs (Furstenberg and Crawford, 1978; Moore, 1978).

In terms of costs and rewards, parenthood that is forced upon a young unmarried woman poorly equipped to handle the situation may be paradoxically entrapping (cutting her and her child off from educational and economic opportunities, for example) at the same time that it may seem somewhat rewarding (providing a certain sense of gratification in the midst of an impoverished life). The basic issue in such a case is not so much a matter of "illegitimacy" as it is of "status *inadequacy.*"

It is a lifestyle very different from one in which an unmarried, well-educated woman *chooses* to have a child. Women with high levels of resources choose such a lifestyle from a variety of alternatives, are well equipped to provide the child with substantial benefits, and are likely to limit the number of children they rear to one or two. The

experience of the university professor discussed on page 219 is one example, as is the case of a physician who chose to give birth to two children out of wedlock and to work in a clinic that allowed her schedule to be flexible enough to combine her career and single motherhood effectively (Rivlin, 1979:92–94).

Unwed Fathers and Legitimacy/Custody Issues State laws have varied on the specifics but, traditionally, men who fathered children out of wedlock have not been able to count on legal rights to custody or visitation. In that respect, laws regarding unmarried parents and their offspring have seemed to favor the mother. On the other hand, it has been the father who has had the power to "legitimate" the child—either by marrying the child's mother or else by taking the child into his own family, acknowledging the child publicly as his, and treating the child as legitimate. The mother, however, could block

Mike Johnson, an unmarried teenage father, won custody of his daughter Jodi, whose 15-year-old mother wanted to give her up for adoption. (© Dale Wittner 1979)

such efforts toward legitimation by the child's father because she was considered to have primary custody of the child and could secure the child's legitimation by giving the child up for adoption. (See discussion in Davidson, Ginsburg, and Kay, 1974:280–329.)

In recent years, unwed fathers have increasingly asserted their rights simply by virtue of being the child's biological father. "Courts, asked to decide between the mother's desire to have the child adopted by strangers and the father's competing claim to

custody, have gone both ways," report three law professors in summarizing trends in this area of family law (Davidson, Ginsburg, and Kay, 1974:315). As more such cases are coming before the courts, the adoption process is being delayed in many cases. If the identity of the father and his permission for the adoption must be sought before permanent placement of the child can be arranged, and if there is the likelihood that a particular unwed father may take legal action to gain custody of the child himself, agencies may exercise great caution. In the meantime, the baby may be growing up in foster homes (Wolins, 1983:118).

In 1979, the United States Supreme Court ruled unconstitutional a New York law that gave to unmarried mothers, but not to unmarried fathers, the right to make decisions on the adoption of their offspring. In the case before the Supreme Court, the unmarried-father's attorney argued that his client, Abdiel Caban, was being denied due process and equal protection of the laws. The children's mother and her new husband wanted to legally adopt the girl and boy who had been born to Caban and her during a long-term cohabitation relationship. Had the adoption request not been stopped, Caban would have been denied even visitation rights and would have had no claim to his son and daughter even in the event of their mother's death.

In another situation, the strains of an unplanned pregnancy resulted in a broken engagement, and the young woman decided to give the baby up for adoption. However, the baby's father objected and sought legal custody of the boy. Upon being granted custody, he subsequently formed a New Orleans-based organization to aid other unwed fathers in similar circumstances.

A number of such stories have been in the news in recent years, and they serve to un-

THE CHANGING RIGHTS OF FATHERS

Counseling of both unmarried mothers and divorcing parents has been affected and will continue to be affected by the increased legal rights of fathers.

In counseling unmarried mothers, the mother contemplating abortion needs to be informed that, although she has a constitutional right to an abortion with which the father cannot interfere, the father may have certain rights if she decides to continue the pregnancy and give birth.

The mother considering adoption needs to know that many states have accorded all biological fathers the right to object to the adoption of a child they have fathered. Furthermore, a father may seek custody of a child when the mother feels the child would be better off adopted. . . .

The mother considering keeping the child and raising it herself needs to know that some states allow a man to seek custody and visitation with a child he has fathered even though he has never lived with the child, was never married to the mother, and, in fact, may be married to another woman.

SOURCE: Marygold S. Melli, "The Changing Legal Status of the Single Parent," *Family Relations* 35 (January 1986), p. 34.

derscore a basic theme of this book—change. Such examples indicate changing definitions of what constitutes a family, just as the phenomenon of cohabitation has been forcing a new look at definitions of marriage. But even more, such examples illustrate changing ideas about gender roles.

As we've seen, the principle of legitimacy rested on the notion that it was the *father* who brought income and status to a family and, on that account, was essential to a child's legitimacy. The emphasis was on the "instrumental" function of fatherhood. We have challenged that assumption in view of the opportunities now open to women, making it possible for many mothers to bring the economic system's rewards to their children just as fathers have traditionally been expected to do. The principle of status adequacy therefore seems more appropriate to the situation in the United States today.

Another traditional idea has held that if a baby is born out of wedlock and not given up for adoption, the *mother* is the parent best qualified to be the "expressive" caretaker of the child. Now that idea, too, is being challenged by a number of unmarried fathers who see their role as encompassing much more than having sired a child. They love their children and want to be actively involved in their children's lives, either through visitation privileges or through actual custody. In other words, unmarried fathers are demanding *expressive* rights and duties at the same time that unmarried mothers are demanding recognition of their *instrumental* capabilities and contributions that allow them to rear their children without the traditional stigma of illegitimacy.

Because of such changing attitudes and circumstances, some authorities in family law call into question the Proposed Uniform Legitimacy Act, which would base legitimacy on the identification of paternity through a court order. Children of fathers who were not known or not available would continue to be

ILLEGITIMACY: HISTORICAL ROOTS IN ENGLISH COMMON LAW

In contrast to the position of the legitimate child whose custody was entrusted exclusively to his father, at common law the illegitimate child was denied even the protection of his mother. He had neither family nor kin; he was *filius nullius,* the child of nobody, or *filius populi,* the child of everybody. Despite these phrases, the common law did not ignore the biological relationship between the child and his natural parents; rather, the relationship itself did not confer status. Thus when the phrase *filius nullius* was used, after the Norman Conquest, it signified merely that the illegitimate child was a stranger in blood to his kin in the sense that he could not inherit property from them. Rather than being nobody's child, he was nobody's heir. At common law, however, the right to inherit carried with it more than the chance of sharing the family property. Because he could not inherit, the illegitimate was excluded from entry to the trade guilds and corporations that were open only to the sons of freemen. By the same token, disabilities were not inherited: the illegitimate child of a bondsman was free.

One consequence of the logic of the concept of *filius nullius* was that the natural parents of an illegitimate child had no right to his custody and no duty to support him. Their consent to his marriage was neither required nor permitted; a court-appointed guardian performed this parental function. Commentators agree that when the law saw fit to give nobody's child a family, its primary motivation was fiscal, not humanitarian: it desired merely to relieve the public of its duty to support the poor. Thus, the Poor Law Act of 1576 authorized the parish where the child was born to impose a weekly charge for his support upon the mother or reputed father, and the poor law authorities commonly placed the child with the mother for nurture until the age of seven. The Poor Law Amendment Act, 1834, placed upon the mother the duty of supporting her illegitimate children until the age of sixteen, and this was taken to imply a correlative right to custody. The Bastardy Act, 1872, allowed the mother to proceed against the putative father for an allowance, not exceeding 5 shillings a week, for the maintenance and support of their illegitimate child, but the proceeding was not thought to entitle the father to custody.

SOURCE: Kenneth M. Davidson, Ruth B. Ginsburg, and Herma H. Kay, *Sex-Based Discrimination* (St. Paul, MN: West Publishing, 1974), pp. 309–310.

---

regarded as illegitimate. Legal authority Kenneth Davidson and his colleagues (1974) summarize the arguments of two outspoken opponents of this act:

The underlying premise of the Proposed Uniform Legitimacy Act has . . . been sharply attacked by Tenoso and Wallach [Book Review, U.C.L.A. *Law Review* 19:845 (1972)]. In their

view, the law's primary goal should not be a search for the father whose identification by a court would then serve to legitimate the child. Rather, the law should recognize that a woman and her children constitute a legitimate family unit and should support this "woman-centered and defined family" as a viable alternative to the existing nuclear family dominated by males. Toward that end, the authors propose a broad legislative program that would recognize all children as legitimate at birth regardless of whether the father can be identified; allow the mother to choose whether the father should be identified at all; require the payment of state support as a substitute for the father's duty rather than as welfare; and provide social welfare resources for all children regardless of the support received from either parent. (p. 324)

Such critics see the Proposed Uniform Legitimacy Act as nothing more than improving a faulty system; instead, they wish to see the whole system radically changed.

Until such changes come about, many unmarried mothers and their children will face the stigma attached to out-of-wedlock births. And, because of the widespread acceptance of the principle of legitimacy, they will also face laws originally built around that principle—laws in some states, for example, that do not give nonlegitimized children full inheritance rights (such as the right to inherit from the parents' relatives). For reasons such as these, some attorneys urge mothers who want to keep and raise their children born out of wedlock to *legally adopt* the children and thus secure their legitimization (Pomroy, 1980, chap. 2).

Single Parenthood Through Adoption, Divorce, or Death of a Spouse

Some single persons become legally recognized parents because they adopt not their own children but somebody else's children. In recent years, changes in laws and attitudes throughout the United States have made it possible for unmarried persons to adopt and rear children.

This practice is upsetting to some unwed mothers who, years ago, were persuaded to give up their children for adoption because social workers advised them that children need to grow up in *two*-parent homes. However, data from available studies do not seem

to provide support for the old fears about a child's being emotionally harmed by growing up in a one-parent situation (Kadushin, 1970). Unmarried persons of both sexes have proven to be excellent parents of adopted children. A Roman Catholic priest, for example, has adopted four over the years, bringing home each child during early infancy. A physician adopted two boys after she was well established in her practice and enough years had gone by to make her feel that marriage was unlikely. A bachelor in his thirties adopted a tiny boy who had been abandoned. A writer, whose engagement was broken when her fiancé found she couldn't have children, later adopted children as a single woman. A schoolteacher adopted a 6-year-old boy with cerebral palsy and was so happy with her son that she decided to adopt two other children—a malnourished young girl from India and a blind toddler from Brazil—through an agency specializing in over-

Unmarried persons of both sexes have proved to be excellent parents of adopted children. (UPI Bettmann Newsphotos)

seas adoptions. Another teacher embarked on single fatherhood by adopting a handicapped child and, later, several other hard-to-place children. A support-and-information group called the Committee for Single Adoptive Parents is based in Chevy Chase, Maryland.

At the same time, although adoption may be an increasingly recognized option for single persons who want to be parents, the number of children available for adoption has been decreasing as more pregnant unmarried women are choosing either to keep their infants or to have abortions. Many agencies prefer to place infants, especially, in married-couple homes, but they may be open to placing with single persons older children, children with physical or mental disabilities, children of mixed racial parentage, children

with emotional problems, or brothers and sisters they don't want to separate (Marindin, 1985). One scholar calls this "an interesting paradox that points to the divergence of goals as determinants of social policy." He points out that "for lack of adequate placements, the most demanding children are placed in the most vulnerable adult units" (Wolins, 1983:116).

In addition to adoption and births out of wedlock, divorce or the death of a spouse are the other routes to becoming a single parent. Table 7-E shows what percentage of lone fathers and mothers are unmarried and what percentage are either divorced, separated, or widowed. The table also shows that less than one-fourth of lone custodial parents do not head their own households but live with others. These consist mainly of very young un-

TABLE 7-E Numbers of lone mothers and fathers, and percentage distribution by householder and marital status, 1960, 1970 and 1983

YEAR	TOTAL NO. (IN 000s)	%, BY HOUSEHOLDER AND MARITAL STATUS						
		TOTAL	HOUSE-HOLDER	OTHER	NEVER-MARRIED	DIVORCED	SEPA-RATED	WID-OWED
			No. Total (Mothers and Fathers)					
1960	2,786	100	79	21	5	29	38	28
1970	3,946	100	83	17	11	33	36	20
1983	8,290	100	78	22	26	43	23	8
			Mothers					
1960	2,406	100	79	21	4	27	42	27
1970	3,545	100	83	17	12	31	38	19
1983	7,395	100	77	23	27	41	24	8
			Fathers					
1960	380	100	79	21	12	54	22	12
1970	401	100	84	16	10	43	18	29
1983	895	100	82	18	14	54	23	9

SOURCE: Paul C. Glick, "American Household Structure in Transition," *Family Planning Perspectives,* September/October 1984, p. 208.

married women who may have few options other than living with their parents (Glick, 1984b:208). Seventy-eight percent of single parents, however, do maintain their own households.

In his demographic assessment of lone custodial parent situations, Paul Glick (1984b:208) points out that although never-marrieds account for the *fastest rate of increase* among lone parents, "by far the largest *number* of lone parents have come, during recent years, from the ranks of the divorced and separated." This is accounted for not only by the increases in marital breakups but also by the fact that more and more divorced persons are waiting longer to remarry or are deciding not to remarry at all. Hence, they remain alone with their children. Over two-thirds of all lone parents living with their children are either divorced or separated. (More discussion of such parents will be found in Chapter 17.) The proportion of single parents living with their children after the death of a spouse is only about 1 out of 12. Death rates among parents of children under age 18 are not high, and remarriage after the death of a spouse means that many such widowed parents do not remain alone.

Living as a Single Parent: Benefits and Costs

Whether they become single parents through an out-of-wedlock birth, adoption, divorce, or the death of a spouse, single parents have much in common when it comes to the responsibilities and challenges of everyday living.

In terms of benefits and costs, single parenting may be considered a rewarding situation when the alternative is shared parenting in a marriage marked by bitter hostilities and destructive conflicts. Persons who have had such negative marital experiences report a sense of relief and satisfaction in rearing their children apart from the former mate.

Another benefit some single parents report, according to sociologist Robert S. Weiss (1979a:259–265), is a heightened sense of self-esteem through having been forced to grow and develop in new ways by the new responsibilities thrust upon them. "Men comment on having become more nurturant, women on having become more self-reliant," writes Weiss. Closely related to the benefit of enhanced self-esteem is the benefit of *autonomy*—the freedom to decide things for oneself about housekeeping standards, mealtimes, leisure activities, money matters, child discipline, and so on, without the necessity of consulting or acquiescing to a spouse who is considered to have made such matters difficult in the past. Weiss found that women from marriages in which they had felt subservient to domineering and unappreciative husbands especially valued their independence as single parents. On the other hand, happily married women who had lost their husbands through death found less satisfaction in their new autonomy. "They recognize the gain, but it does not seem to them very important," writes Weiss of these widows.

A fourth rewarding aspect of single parenthood reported in Weiss's research concerned the nature of the parent-child relationship. Numerous single parents commented on the closeness they experienced with their children. Fathers who had been relatively uninvolved with their children before becoming divorced or widowed found joy in getting to know them in a new way. "I found that they were small people," said one father, "that they had all the same emotions and values and physical needs as big people. And that was very rewarding" (quoted in Weiss,

1979a:264). Mothers, too, reported new feelings of being appreciated, needed by, and important to their children and cultivated a deeper sense of friendship with them, a sense of working together in partnership.

But there is no denying the costs experienced in single parenthood. According to Weiss, "The fundamental problem in the single parent's situation is the insufficiency of immediately available support." There is no longer another adult in the same household to share the responsibility and concern for the child and home and to help in decisions, discipline, emergencies, and all the details of everyday living. Relatives, friends, professionals, and the children themselves can provide some help; but the solo parent still carries the ultimate load of responsibility in a way that isn't true in a two-parent household.

"Responsibility overload" is one of three major kinds of overload Weiss found in his research. The other two were "task overload" and "emotional overload" (Weiss, 1979a:267–276). By *task overload*, Weiss means the sense of frustration and failure that many single parents feel simply because it's impossible to get everything done that needs to be done. The sense of fatigue and, at times, almost frantic desperation is enormous. The basic problem stems from the lack of *spare capability*—a reserve that can be called upon in two-parent families. Weiss explains that the single parent "who is working full time as well as managing a family, and doing well enough at each" may not recognize "that he or she has very little unused capability." He goes on:

> But what has happened is that the single parent, by skimping on a chore here and dropping an activity there, has brought his or her total workload down to the point where it can be coped with—but only just. No room will have been left for meeting new demands. (p. 272)

Then, when a child becomes ill just as a parent is leaving for work or the toilet overflows or the washing machine breaks down, filled with a wet load of clothes needed by the family that day, or a family member is injured and has to be hospitalized for several weeks or the car's battery goes dead or whatever else the unanticipated demand might be, the single parent may feel suddenly overwhelmed and powerless. The proverbial "camel's back" caves in. "That's the last straw," the single parent cries. "I can't take any more!" Such a person is experiencing task overload. "There's simply not enough of me to go around," is how one single parent puts it.

The final category of overload Weiss lists is *emotional overload*. Needing to be constantly available to their children, feeling on duty every moment they are at home, sensing that the full responsibility for parenting is on their shoulders, single parents may feel there is no time or opportunity for relaxation and replenishment. The problem is most acute when no one is available to lend support to help meet the parent's own needs. "It is then as though the parent's emotional economy were running at a constant deficit: everything being disbursed, nothing being received," writes Weiss (p. 276). The single parent thus becomes "emotionally depleted" and feels she or he has nothing left to give. "The avoidance of emotional overload may require a healthy capacity for self-assertion, for the parent's being willing to claim time and energy for self," Weiss suggests. Pointing out that those single parents most determined to be fully devoted to their children are the most vulnerable to emotional overload, he states that "they may discover only by witnessing their own explosions or depressions that they, too, have needs, including needs for relief from the demands of children and for caring attention to themselves."

A number of researchers have studied the psychological well-being of lone parents and their need for social support networks—some system of interconnections with friends, relatives, and other groups that can provide the single-parent family with emotional support, counsel and information, practical help when needed, and integration into the larger community. Michael Smith (1980) draws attention to the relative isolation and lowered level of community participation characterizing single parents. No doubt the overload problem discussed earlier has much to do with this. But one result of lowered participation in life outside the family is, for many single mothers and fathers, loneliness. Smith also found single parents—especially mothers—to have a sense of powerlessness over their lives. Some such women, feeling a need for both emotional support and assistance in rearing their children, return to their own parental homes. There, however, they may encounter unresolved conflicts remaining from their own childhoods and may find themselves in the bind of trying to be parents to their children while being expected at some level to be children to their parents at the same time—a problem that has been called "trigenerational enmeshment" (Dell and Applebaum, 1977; Smith, 1980).

Three other family scholars point out that a return to the family of origin is only one of three major ways a single mother seeks a support network, and the return is not necessarily a physical move to the parents' home but may simply consist of "a psychological reunion with one's relatives . . . a support network that is composed almost entirely of kinship ties within her original family," with the possible inclusion of a "best friend" as well (McLanahan, Wedemeyer, and Adelberg, 1981). The other two types of networks providing support for single mothers were

Constantly "on duty," carrying the full responsibility for parenting on their shoulders, single parents often feel physically and emotionally overloaded. (© 1981 Ed Lettau/Photo Researchers, Inc.)

(1) what these authors call "the extended network" (made up primarily of new friendship ties, women's support groups, and especially other single mothers) and (2) the "conjugal network" (a support arrangement that seeks to approximate or reestablish a conjugal family form centering around a "key male or spouse equivalent" whom the mother considers her major source of support—whether it's someone who lives with her, her former husband, or a man she has dated for some time).

These researchers also found that the divorced mothers in their study tended to fall into one of two categories in terms of their own role orientation. They were either "stabilizers" whose sense of themselves was bound up in their predivorce roles of wife and mother and who wanted to continue this identity. These women found close-knit support networks most helpful. Or they were "changers," who wanted to establish a new identity after their divorces—especially an identity built around a career. These women found loose-knit networks met their support needs best. Women who stressed change at one stage of their postdivorce adjustments might become more stability-oriented at a later stage (and vice versa), with their support-network needs changing accordingly (McLanahan, Wedemeyer, and Adelberg, 1981).

McLanahan and her colleagues concluded from their study that "researchers must avoid making blanket assumptions about the lack of social support among single women living in non-nuclear families." They found that the quality or quantity of social support cannot be measured simply by looking at marital or household status or how close relatives live and how frequently the single parent is in contact with them. Other considerations must be taken into account. These social scientists also caution other researchers not to make assumptions about the quality of friendship ties in the lives of women after their divorces. "The present data indicate," they write, "that for certain women during certain phases of their adjustment, friendship ties may be just as supportive (and intimate) as relationships with significant males" (p. 610). This observation brings us to our next section.

COMBINED-HOUSEHOLD ARRANGEMENTS AND SUBSTITUTE KIN

A wall plaque carries this message:

> We need to have people
> who mean something to us;
>   People to whom
> we can turn,
>   Knowing that being with them
> is coming home.
>
> —R. Cooke

Traditionally, the people "who mean something," to whom one "can turn" in time of need, and who provide a sense of "coming home" have been *kin*, persons to whom one is or has become related through blood or through marriage. But there may be persons who serve as a kind of "substitute kin" even though they are unrelated to one another. In recent decades, there has been much talk about building community. There have been experiments with communal living as well as efforts to create a kind of chosen family of friends with whom joys, sorrows, problems, anxieties, and dreams can be shared even though the friends don't share a common household—an arrangement one sociologist calls an "intimate family network."

In this section, we want to look at some of these functional equivalents of the extended family.

Intimate Network as a Kin Substitute

An anonymous writer in *Ms.* magazine told of how sentimentality over "family solidarity" repeatedly drove her to plan elaborate holiday get-togethers with relatives only to be disappointed again and again. "Generally, the family for which I have sweated so generously ruins my evening," she wrote, adding that this didn't happen when she invited her friends. "My friends, I choose myself. They were not a gift from God." This woman eventually solved her problem by a formula of inviting "eight friends per biological family member" ("The Gift of Honesty," *Ms.*, December, 1973:46).

Some persons find kin relationships more costly than rewarding and seek other relationships to serve as substitutes. There are also persons who look for substitutes because they have no kin they feel emotionally close to with whom significant contacts can be maintained on a regular basis. Relatives may live at great geographical distances, or they may no longer be living at all.

One behavioral scientist, Frederick Stoller (1970), has introduced in family workshops an idea he calls the "intimate family network." Such a plan can serve to alleviate any impoverishment some modern families may feel because they are denied the richly varied experiences and emotional support traditionally associated with kin relationships. According to Stoller, "an intimate network of families could be described as a circle of three or four families who meet together regularly and frequently, share in reciprocal fashion any of their intimate secrets, offer one another a variety of services, and do not hesitate to influence one another in terms of values and attitudes."

Stoller suggests that the number of families should be more than two (to provide richness, varied role models for children, and more problem-solving resources) but usually not more than four, since too large a group would be hard to manage and might also cut down intimacy. Regular and frequent get-togethers would be important in order for the families to come to know one another deeply and develop the capacity to be honest and open with each other even in painful situations.

Reciprocal sharing would mean opening up to one another about how each family lives, its concerns, problems, and so on. Stoller is aware of the value the American family system places on privacy but points out that human life is enriched if *both* privacy and connectedness are experienced. The intimate-network idea would not force a surrender of the right to privacy but rather would provide an opportunity for a "voluntary movement back and forth between open sharing and self-contained areas of living."

The intimate network of families can also provide an exchange of services in the manner that the extended-kin network has traditionally done—not only through aid in times of crisis but also in exchanges of advice, help in special projects (such as painting a house), or child care so that a husband and wife will be free to take a trip together. Stoller also emphasizes the influence intimate-network families can have on one another's values and attitudes, helping one another to grow and develop in new directions.

Although the intimate-family-network concept emphasizes relationships between and among *families*, networks can also be formed among any combination of *unrelated* individuals—single persons, widowed persons, divorced persons, couples with or without children, and so on. The Family Cluster Program, which works through religious and other groups, is one *formal* effort to build such relationships among families and persons living alone or in other household arrangements (Sawin, 1982). But many *informal* networks also exist, particularly in urban areas, where many persons live at great distances from their kinfolk. A close network of friends (some of whom may be work colleagues) forms and meets together for dinners, picnics, trips, holiday celebrations, and so on. Thanksgiving, for example, may become not so much a matter of going "over the river and through the woods to Grandmother's house" as a situation of going across the city and through the halls to someone's apartment opened up to friends.

Shared Living Arrangements

Kate & Allie, a television situation comedy launched in 1984, took as its theme the experiences of two divorced mothers who combined their households into one. By sharing living expenses, furniture and appliances, household chores, mealtimes, and personal and childrearing concerns, these women were able to develop a sense of family that was beneficial both to themselves and the

In television's *Kate & Allie* series, two divorced mothers, who live in a combined household arrangement, developed a sense of family for themselves and the children they brought with them. (CBS Photography)

total of three children they brought from their marriages. Two writers who themselves lived in a shared-household arrangement called attention to an important point being made by the program, namely, that "adults (and children) are capable of living together in all kinds of combinations and permutations other than those that are held together by marriage, sexual passion, or the financial dependency of one sex on the other." "And," they added, "they are capable of having a dynamite good time doing it" (Ehrenreich and O'Reilly, 1984:10).

"We need to know under what conditions shared living arrangements are functional for lone parents," writes social scientist Michael Smith (1980:79). He points out that the presence of another adult in the household "provides at least the possibility for internal support and practical assistance that is not present in the average single-parent household" (pp. 75–76). Smith feels that this type of arrangement for single parents has often been given little attention by researchers because single parenthood is all too often dismissed as simply a transitional stage that will end with a marriage. He suggests several areas for future inquiry, including studies to determine how such arrangements work for the persons involved. If someone leaves a shared household, is it because of a desire for "independent living" or because role conflicts in the shared household became too difficult to handle? In other words, what can be learned from those who leave in order to pursue perceived rewards and those who leave in order to escape what are considered costs?

Divorced persons with or without children are not the only persons who may choose to live in a combined-household arrangement (Brenton, 1974:196–197; Stein, 1976:96–97; Lindsey, 1981; Rosenthal, 1983:203–316). Single and widowed persons may find house or apartment sharing a solution to problems of high living expenses, loneliness, and dividing the task load. Numerous elderly persons have in recent years formed a "chosen family" in this way. The Census Bureau would list such households under the category "nonfamily," but such persons may nevertheless regard themselves "like family" to one another because of emotional ties rather than ties of blood, marriage, or adoption. Such households may show considerable variation in composition. Some may have only two persons; others may have five or six. In some cases, two persons of the opposite sex may set up a household together for reasons of economic sharing and companionship and yet not form an unmarried cohabitation arrangement. Rather, in the words of a woman who lived in such an arrangement for several years, they choose to be "roommates, but not lovers" (Prager, 1979).

According to the U.S. Bureau of the Census (*Current Population Reports*, ser. P-20, no. 410, 1986), 24.1 million households in 1985 were classified as "nonfamily." Over 20.6 million of these households consisted of persons living alone, and nearly 2 million were households made up of unmarried cou-

ples. In the remaining nonfamily households—about 1.5 million—persons were living with one or more other persons not related to them. According to the Census Bureau, in most such nonfamily households containing nonrelatives, only *one* nonrelative is likely to be present.

Residences containing more than eight persons not related to the householder are not counted by the Census Bureau as households but are rather listed as "group quarters." During the 1960s and 1970s, various forms of rural and urban communal living were popular with some persons who sought in a group of biologically unrelated persons a sense of "chosen family" that could fulfill many of the functions traditionally fulfilled by extended kin. Group living in a common dwelling and the pooling of economic resources was the common pattern. Some such "intentional communities" continue today.

More common, however, especially in urban areas, are joint households that do not consider themselves "communes" in any strict sense. These are modified communal-living arrangements. If zoning laws permit, a group of persons may decide to live together simply as a matter of convenience and to share rent costs. In this way, persons may be able to afford living in parts of a city not possible otherwise and can enjoy valued aspects of city life as well as being close to their employment. Some groups get together through word of mouth or advertisements and rent old mansions in deteriorating neighborhoods. Such groups have been described as being either hotel-like or familylike (Mooney, 1979). *Hotel-like situations* are those where housemates hardly know each other and go their separate ways, except for living under the same roof. *Familylike households* value and encourage togetherness.

One single woman who moved into such a household in Washington, DC, says, "Family houses are typified in an ad I saw in a vegetarian restaurant: 'We give each other a lot of support, so don't answer this ad if you hate to be hugged.'" She describes what living with several other persons has meant to her:

> Sharing a house means you can come down to the living room Sunday morning in your bathrobe, have someone to read something funny to, have someone to go with you afterward to the art gallery.
>
> I came from the suburbs. This is warmer, wider, more real, better. (Quoted in Mooney, 1979)

For many single persons, shared living arrangements may be a practical way of solving feelings of isolation and loneliness (Stein, 1976:96–97).

CHAPTER HIGHLIGHTS

Statistics indicate that most persons eventually marry. However, as more and more young persons postpone marriage, the likelihood of lifetime singleness for many will increase. Over the course of a lifetime, a person may experience singleness (in the sense of not being in a paired relationship) at one or more points—as a never-married person or as a divorced or widowed person. Persons are likely to *choose* singleness if they perceive the rewards of singleness to outweigh the costs of singleness and the costs of marriage to outweigh the rewards of marriage. Men with education beyond college are the least likely to remain single over the course of a lifetime. The highest percentage of women who never marry is comprised of those women with a college education or above. Staples points out that singleness is especially pronounced among highly educated black women because of the shortage of suitable black men with comparable education.

The second most common type of household in the United States (second only to married-couple households) is the household in which a person lives alone. The majority of women who live alone are over age 45; the majority of men who live alone are under age 45. But among both women and men who live alone, the biggest rate of increase is among younger adults.

Many single persons are parents—because they have adopted children, because they are keeping and rearing their own children born out of wedlock, because they are the custodial parents of their own children after a divorce, or because their spouses have died.

About 1 out of 5 live births occurs to an unmarried woman. In 1982, out of every 1,000 black babies born, 567 had unwed mothers. Out of every 1,000 white babies born, 121 had unwed mothers. At the same time, it must be noted that the *nonmarital birth rate* (number of live births per 1,000 unmarried women) has been rising for whites at the same time that it has been decreasing for blacks. The high percentage of out-of-wedlock births among black women relates to the economic discrimination black persons have experienced and their blocked educational and occupational opportunities. Black women are also less likely than their white counterparts to marry before the resolution of a pregnancy and less likely to have an abortion. The majority of births outside of wedlock occur to young women and poor women. In addressing this issue, the "principle of status adequacy" seems more appropriate than Malinowski's "principle of legitimacy." In modern times, the universality of Malinowski's notion that a social father is necessary as a pipeline to a society's status and economic rewards may be challenged on two grounds: (1) changing legal definitions of legitimacy and (2) changing gender roles, which make it possible for the child's mother to be the pipeline to the opportunity system. A growing interest in visitation and custody rights for unwed fathers is also related to changing attitudes about gender roles. Single parents, whether they are alone because of divorce, the death of a spouse, single adoption, or out-of-wedlock birth have much in common in facing the challenges of daily life. Rewards of the single-parent status sometimes cited are (1) relief from a painful marriage situation, (2) heightened self-esteem from personal growth experiences, (3) a greater sense of autonomy, and (4) a closer parent-child relationship. Weiss listed the costs of single parenthood as "responsibility overload," "task overload," and "emotional overload." Various researchers have shown the need single parents have for social support networks as a source of emotional support, counsel and information, practical help, and integration into the larger community.

Persons who are single, with or without children, may find a sense of family through shared living arrangements. Combined households of divorced persons and their children, roommate situations, homelike group arrangements for several elderly persons, and modified urban communal arrangements are some of the living options open to single persons who don't wish (or can't afford) to live alone.

·8·

THE STRUCTURE OF MARRIAGE: FOUR BASIC PATTERNS

Entering the state of marriage could be compared to entering a building. However, not all buildings are structured alike, and neither are all marriages. The following cases illustrate four basic blueprints, or models. This doesn't mean that every marriage must fall neatly and totally into one or another of the patterns described (there are frameworks in between the categories, blurring into one another), but the case descriptions help us see some basic structural distinctions.

CASE ONE

During the first half of the nineteenth century, when physical punishment was sometimes used to enforce husband supremacy, a writer recalled a man in her neighborhood. This respected church and community leader regularly beat his wife with a horsewhip, claiming that such behavior was necessary "in order to keep her in subjection" and to stop her from scolding. Emily Collins commented on her neighbors: "Now this wife, surrounded by six or seven little children . . . was obliged to spin and weave cloth for all the garments of the family . . . to milk . . . to make butter and cheese, and do all the cooking, washing, making, and mending . . . and, with the pains of maternity forced upon her every eighteen months, was whipped by her pious husband, 'because she scolded' " (Calhoun, vol. 2, 1919:92–93).

CASE TWO

Cindy and Tom have been married for seven years. They have a 5-year-old son and a daughter, age 2. They consider their marriage and family life ideal and say they can't understand the feminist movement (which they still refer to as "women's lib"). "What is there to be liberated from?" asks Tom. "Women never had it better. Look how nice Cindy has it—just being able to stay at home, be her own boss, have her own hours, while I go out and earn the living! She wouldn't have it any other way, and neither would I. We both like knowing that she's here when the kids need her, and I enjoy coming home to a neat, orderly house and a delicious dinner. Oh don't get me wrong! She isn't my slave or anything. We work together on a lot of household projects on weekends, and I'm always glad to pitch in and help her when she needs me—like helping out with the dishes some evenings when I don't have meetings to attend, or helping put the children to bed."

Cindy agrees that she enjoys her role as full-time homemaker. "I like to sew, and I like to have time to chat with friends on the phone or down at the park while the kids play in the playground. I don't feel at all trapped. Tom gives me an allowance every week in addition to the household money, so I always have spending money that I don't have to account to him for. Really, I like my life and feel I'm fulfilling woman's true role—to love, encourage, and serve my family. And I feel I can help Tom advance in his career best by being just what I am, a loving, devoted wife who supports and backs him up, believes in him, and tries to make life smooth at home. They say that behind every great man is a woman; I want to be that woman in Tom's life."

CASE THREE

Marilyn is an elementary school teacher. Her husband, Al, is the manager of a local department store that is part of a large national chain. Married eighteen years, they have three children, ranging in age from 9 to 15. When her youngest child reached school age, Marilyn returned to teaching after not having taught for several years, except for serving occasionally as a substitute teacher.

Now back at full-time teaching, Marilyn still does not consider it her primary career. "If Al and I feel the children are being harmed in any way and that they need me at home, I'll not hesitate a moment to give up teaching," she says. "I enjoy my work, and it's nice having my income for extra things, but it's not absolutely essential. Al and I believe that the husband should be the main breadwinner. He's the captain, and I'm second mate. That means his work takes precedence over mine. For example, if the company asks him to move (and that's happened many times already during our marriage), my teaching position is no reason to insist we stay here. I'm sure I could always find a similar position at our new location; and if not, I'll just stay home and be a good wife and mother. Or I can always put my name on a list for substitute teaching."

CASE FOUR

Janet and Roger both have demanding careers to which they are highly committed. Arriving at a suitable lifestyle for them and their 4-year-old daughter has not been easy, but they have determined to work out an *egalitarian marriage* in the fullest sense of that term. This means that each takes seriously the responsibility of being a parent and giving time and loving attention to Gretchen. They have not assumed that the task of arranging for child care is Janet's task, nor have the necessary funds come from Janet's salary—as though she were the parent holding major responsibility for their child. Rather, both Roger and Janet feel they must *share* the responsibility for Gretchen's needs as well as share the responsibility for household chores.

Janet and Roger also feel that they should have equal power in family decision-making and that neither one's career is more important than the other's. Thus, if Janet (a psychology professor) decides to accept an offer from a university in another state, her lawyer husband is willing to leave his lucrative law practice and set up a new practice in the new location (following his wife, in contrast to the traditional custom of a wife following her husband). At the same time, if Roger wanted to pursue some new opportunity (in politics, for example), Janet is willing to seek employment at some school in the area where Roger's new plans would take him. They might even consider the possibility of a "commuter marriage" if it became necessary at some point.

UNDERSTANDING THE STRUCTURE OF MARRIAGE

The story of the nineteenth-century authoritarian husband and the modern hypothetical case studies serve to illustrate clearly that people may structure their marriages quite differently.

In defining *marriage* earlier, we saw that there are two sides to marriage, two main parts of the structure—the practical, or *instrumental, side* (earning family income, performing household tasks) and the personal, or *expressive side* (love, sex, empathy, companionship). What goes on in these two areas of marriage is affected by the positions and roles of men and women. The opening four stories showed that marriage may be structured as a relationship between an owner and his property (the nineteenth-century husband who beat his wife to keep her in subjection), between a head and its complement (Tom and Cindy), between a senior partner and a junior partner (Al and Marilyn), or between two equal partners (Janet and Roger). We'll be looking at each of these patterns and variations on some of them.

OWNER-PROPERTY MARRIAGE PATTERN

The story cited in case 1 was not unusual in the nineteenth century. The husband who used a horsewhip on his wife to keep her in subjection was held by the New York courts to be within his rights. If what was termed "a reasonable instrument" was used, wife beating was legal in almost all states as late as 1850. As social historian Alice Felt Tyler (1944:426) points out, "Women were legally considered perpetual minors; if unmarried, the wards of male relatives; if married, a part of their husband's chattels. . . . In legal status servile and incompetent, by social canon revered and closely guarded, in cold fact a vitally necessary part of a dynamic economic and social system." A married woman and all she possessed (including any earnings she might make) were legally considered to belong to her husband. Her very being was considered to be merged into his; the two were one, and the one was the husband.

Writer Eva Figes (1970) speaks of such a concept of marriage as "basically the purchase of sexual favour in return for board and lodging." The limited alternatives for women meant that the bargain was harshly one-sided. From a Marxist perspective, men historically could be compared to the ruling or dominant group, the bourgeoisie; women to the ruled or subordinate group, the proletariat. Helen Campbell, the writer of an 1893 publication on women wage earners, began with "a look backward" to show how "physical facts worked with man's will . . . and early rendered women subordinate physically and dependent economically." She quotes other writers of the period to the effect that "woman at once became property. . . . Marriage . . . became the symbol of transfer of ownership," just as a formal deed signified a purchaser's right to possess his land. It is *economic dependence on the oppressor*, argues Campbell, that is the basis of all oppression (Campbell, 1893:26–27).

Positions and Roles

In the picture of marriage just described, the position of the man is that of owner, and the position of the woman is that of property. This position, or status, indicates how the two persons stand in relationship to one another. But within this status, each has a distinct part to play—a *role*.

Under the owner-property arrangement, the woman's major role was that of wife-mother. It was a hyphenated role in more than word only. A woman who was a wife was expected to be a mother as well; there was no notion that wife and mother could be two separate roles. For a married man, the role of husband-father was likewise not separated. If a man were a husband, he was supposed to be a father as well. That his wife should provide him with children was considered, furthermore, to be one of his basic marital *rights*.

The marriage contract implies both rights and duties for both partners. The rights of one partner may involve having certain duties performed on the part of the other partner. And the duties a spouse carries out may be done in order to assure that the rights of the other spouse are met. For example, in a traditional marriage, a husband might arrive home from work (his *duty* to provide for his family) and expect to find dinner ready (his *right* to have household needs cared for by his wife). His wife has prepared the meal (her *duty* to cook and do other household tasks for her family) because her husband has put in a hard day's work (fulfilling her *right* to be financially supported).

Wife's Duties and Husband's Rights

Under the owner-property arrangement of marriage, the role of wife-mother carried with it certain duties in both the practical and personal sides of marriage. Looking first at her duties within the *instrumental,* or task-oriented, dimension (the practical side), we find the following *norms,* or expectations, of how she was to behave:

1 Her chief task in life was to please her husband and care for his needs and those of the household.
2 She was to obey her husband in all things.
3 She was to bear children that could carry on her husband's name.
4 She was to train the children so that they would reflect credit on her husband.

From the husband's standpoint, the fulfillment of these norms by his wife was a matter of rights—*his* rights. He considered himself to possess the right to have his wife please him, obey him, care for his household needs,

bear him children, and so on. Such rights were inherent in the position of owner.

Two points stand out and summarize the role duties of the wife-mother within the position of property. One, the woman has no existence independent from that of her husband; legally, she is considered a nonperson. By definition, she is merely an extension of him—of his interests, desires, needs, wants, ambitions, goals, and so on. Two, the power question is settled and beyond dispute. The husband is boss and the wife must be subject to him. Whenever there is a disagreement or clash of wills, the wife as his property merely submits to her husband's will. By this means, order and stability are maintained. Embedding the authority question in a fixed way within the normative structure of the wife's role duties is considerably different from what we shall observe in other marriage arrangements.

Did Women Feel Oppressed? Campbell's classic economic history of women details the scope of household tasks performed by the woman of the preindustrial era. Not only did she have all the childrearing and household-maintenance tasks that women have usually been expected to perform, she also "had to spin, weave, and bleach; to make all the linen and clothes, to boil soap, to make candles and brew beer. . . . She frequently had to work in the field or garden and to attend to the poultry or cattle" (Campbell, 1893:50).

The question naturally arises: Did women feel oppressed? Most Marxists would probably admit that they did not but would label this as "false consciousness"; that is, women *believed* they were as content as they could reasonably expect to be, but this was a false or inaccurate picture. Further, the Marxist might say that had wives realized just how bad their condition actually was, they simply would have revolted en masse and sought liberation from husband oppression long ago.

It is difficult to know how most wives felt about their position as property. A few put their feelings into writing so that we know there was discontent on the part of some. However, not many alternative roles were open to women besides that of wife-mother. Likewise, it is hard to think of alternative images other than the wife-mother role that little girls could observe as they grew up, given the rigid gender-role socialization that occurred during that era. It seems likely that most men and women believed in the appropriateness of the marital arrangement as they knew it—the owner-property model, with its respective rights and duties for husbands and wives.

Campbell's study goes to the heart of the matter as she describes the situation in which even wage-earning women found themselves at first. "For ages, [the woman's] identity had been merged in that of the man by whose side she worked with no thought of recompense," wrote Campbell. All the traits that were considered "feminine" were expected to be cultivated (submissiveness, clinging affection, humility), while stronger traits, such as assertiveness, were suppressed. These combined factors stood in the way of any resistance to injustice and mistreatment. Campbell (1893:51–52) makes her point forcefully: "The mass of women had neither power nor wish to protest; and thus the few traces we find of their earliest connection with labor show us that they accepted bare subsistence as all to which they were entitled, and were grateful if they escaped the beating which the lower order of Englishman still regards as his right to give."

Some concerned feminists not only saw the inequities but called attention to the need for consciousness-raising if women were ever going to experience the removal of unjust laws and customs. At the 1848 Seneca Falls (New York) Convention, the first women's rights conference held in the United States, one of the resolutions adopted was "that the women of this country ought to be enlightened in regard to the laws under which they live, that they may no longer publish their degradation by declaring themselves satisfied with their present position, nor their ignorance, by asserting that they have all the rights they want" (reprinted in Rossi (ed.), 1973b, p. 419 in 1974 Bantam edition). Injustices in owner-property marriage laws and customs were singled out for special attention.

Husband's Duties and Wife's Rights

Having seen the wife's duties (which are also the husband's rights), we might wonder about the husband's duties (and, correspondingly, the wife's rights). It is at this point that we discover the most important reason that the owner-property arrangement could be maintained. The husband's chief duty was to provide economic resources for the family's survival and well-being. Because the wife depended on her husband for these essential resources, he had considerable power over her. In other words, her deference was exchanged for his benefits. His power was therefore *doubly* reinforced because it rested both on the norms which prescribed wifely obedience and on the needed benefits with which he supplied his wife.

In exchange for performing her duties, the wife was rewarded by financial support, fulfilling her marital *right* to material provision. She also shared in whatever prestige her husband was able to attain. She received acclaim from kin and peers based on her husband's achievements and social status. In addition, she received esteem, support, and approval from others (including her husband) because she performed her own apportioned duties so well. ("What an excellent wife and mother she is!" "She certainly keeps a neat house, and she can bake the tastiest pies in the world!" "She makes sure her children are well-behaved and mannerly, too.")

These exchanges of husband-wife rights and duties constituted an ongoing cycle. The husband's duty to provide fulfilled the wife's right to be provided for. This provision in turn motivated her to continue performing her wife-mother duties, which meant that the husband's rights were thereby fulfilled. Because of this, he continued to feel motivated to keep on providing for her, with the result that there was an uninterrupted fulfillment of role duties in the prescribed fashion. The basis for these role exchanges lay with the husband as owner and the wife as property, with the man's having exclusive access to economic resources and possessing power that men and women believed to be legitimate and right.

Expressive Dimension

All that has been said thus far has concerned the instrumental dimension of marriage, with its emphasis on economic provision and task performance. What about the person-oriented side of marriage? Again, thinking in terms of rights and duties, the wife's chief duty in the expressive dimension apparently was to provide sexual gratification for her husband. And it was his right to receive that benefit or resource from her. In exchange, it was likewise his duty to provide sexual benefits to his wife. However, although provision of sex was incumbent on both partners, the quality of sexual performance was probably far less crucial. The husband was not obligated to sexually gratify his wife at a very high level. And the wife was not expected to

In the owner-property arrangement, societal norms sanctioned wife-beating, and there was little that women could do about it. (*Feminist Art Journal*)

be particularly sensuous toward her husband; all that mattered was that she be available and "not refuse him his pleasure." Moreover, it is not clear that the spouses were expected to provide one another with a very high degree of other expressive rewards, such as companionship and empathy.

Finally, the husband's ultimate power meant that if there were any disagreements over sexual or other expressive matters, the wife simply had to give in to his will and judgment. If she wanted to visit relatives or neighbors and he wanted her to spend the evening at home with him, she did as he said. If he wanted to have sexual intercourse when she was not so inclined, she submitted to his will. Her own expressive satisfaction wasn't considered important. The double standard was widely practiced by men; they could get whatever kinds and degrees of sexual satisfactions they desired through prostitutes. Mary Wollstonecraft complained about this as early as 1792, when she published her *Vindication of the Rights of Woman*. She wrote: "Their husbands acknowledge that they are good managers, and chaste wives; but leave home to seek for more agreeable . . . society; and the patient drudge, who fulfills her task, like a blind horse in a mill, is defrauded of her just reward; for the wages due to her are the caresses of her husband'' (p. 113). Undoubtedly many wives under the owner-property arrangement felt such deprivation, but there was little they could do except suffer in silence.

Between husbands and wives, "emotional isolation was accomplished through the strict demarcation of work assignments and sex roles," writes historian Edward Shorter (1977:55). Why? Because societal norms dictated that the traditional family be based upon considerations of lineage and property rather than on affection. What mattered were certain definitions of social order. Contrasting past and present attitudes, Shorter writes:

> Whereas the modern couple would brim over with expressive behavior, hand-holding, and eye-gazing as they embarked upon the interior search, the traditional husband and wife were severely limited: "I'll fulfill my roles, you fulfill yours, we'll both live up to the expectations the community sets, and *voilà*, our lives will unfold without disorder." It would never have occurred to them to ask if they were happy. (p. 55)

HEAD-COMPLEMENT MARRIAGE PATTERN

The positions of husband-as-owner and wife-as-property gradually evolved into those of husband-as-head and wife-as-complement. The kind of marriage Tom and Cindy have in case 2 is a head-complement arrangement. Here both the wife's rights and the husband's duties increase. No longer is it a one-sided system in which the wife has little more than

survival rights (food, shelter, clothing) while the husband reaps benefits from her services. In marriages where wives are viewed as complements, or counterparts, to husbands, the husband is expected to meet his wife's love-and-affection needs, her desires for sexual pleasure, her yearnings for warm emotional support, companionship, understanding, and open communication. Take Cindy and Tom, for example. Cindy's responsibilities may at first seem similar to those of wives in the "property" arrangement, but an altogether different marital compact is in effect. Tom is *not* considered Cindy's owner, or master. In the head-complement bargain. two persons who have chosen to join their lives together decide to organize their living arrangements in a particular, convenient way. The husband fulfills his end of the bargain by going out into the world to earn the family income; the wife fulfills her end by remaining home to care for the house and children.

Freed from the necessity of earning a living, Cindy can give her time and attention to her role as family coordinator, keeper of the hearth, and emotional hub. At the same time, she is often able to arrange time for voluntary activities, thus representing the family in the community through participation in charitable work, religious services, political activities, scouting, and parent-teacher organizations.

Tom, on the other hand, is freed from many responsibilities and encumbrances related to the ordinary demands of daily life (such as meal planning, shopping, cooking, cleaning, washing clothes, sewing on buttons, answering social invitations, writing letters and birthday cards to relatives, and the myriad of other tasks that usually fall to wives). Thus, Tom is able to devote more time, attention, and energy to his occupation. He has a helpful, supportive, encouraging wife behind him, making it possible for him to achieve much more than if he had to be on his own. He has someone who fills up something that would be missing from his life otherwise, someone who completes him, rounds out his life—in other words, a *complement*. He may fondly speak of Cindy as his "other half."

This marital arrangement fits with the structural-functional approach to marriage described in Chapter 1. It suggests a biological analogy, with an emphasis on the specialized function of each body part. The husband in this pattern is expected to function as the family's "head," while the wife is expected to function as the family's "heart."

Instrumental Side of the Head-Complement Arrangement

As in the owner-property marriage arrangement, couples who follow the head-complement pattern are expected to fulfill both rights and duties with respect to one another. These rights and duties are associated with the husband-father role and the wife-mother role, and again the *duties* of each spouse serve the *rights* of the other spouse. The norms associated with the spouse roles spell out what the respective duties of the husband and wife are.

Looking first at the practical or instrumental side of the head-complement marriage, we find that most of the norms associated with the wife-mother role under the earlier owner-property marriage arrangement have not changed much. The woman's chief task is still to please her husband and care for the needs of the household. She is still expected to bear and rear children who will carry on the husband's name and be a source of pride and gratification. And she is still expected to find her meaning by living through her husband and children rather than seeking a life of her own. Likewise, she is to make sure that she orders her life so that credit is reflected on her husband. Good complements are expected to bring good compliments!

Yet change has occurred in one of the expected areas of behavior—the issue of obedience. No longer is power rigidly fixed within the established norms as it was under the owner-property arrangement ("Wives must obey their husbands"). Now it becomes somewhat more problematic. The marital power issue is less settled. Gone are the days when the wife was expected to submit to the husband without question.

Instead, as her husband's counterpart, the wife is expected to give final deference. That is, she yields to her husband's will in the end and gives in to his wishes, but before that time she is free to discuss her own opinions on the particular issue. Under the owner-property arrangement, the husband could say, "Do this!" and the wife did it. Now he says, "Let's do this." The wife may reply "Why?" or "No, I don't think so." The husband in turn asks why his wife feels as she does, and then he decides, "We'll do this anyway!" or "You're right; maybe we shouldn't."

(Drawing by Weber, © 1977 The New Yorker Magazine, Inc.)

"They have this arrangement. He earns the money and she takes care of the house."

The final decision is still the husband's. But it differs from his rulership as exercised under the owner-property arrangement because, as head, the husband now takes into consideration the wishes of the wife as complement. To borrow from computer language, we may say that the husband permits the wife to make "inputs" into the husband's decision-making. Of course, she may or may not counsel in a particular matter, and he may or may not consult on certain issues. In some cases, the husband may "allow" his wife to make the decisions. In certain other cases, the two may decide on a course of action jointly. But always the final options are in the husband's hands, he is like a supreme court beyond which no further appeals are possible.

These shifts are subtle but meaningful in that they represent some increase in the wife's participation in power. At the same time, there are corresponding shifts in the husband's *rights.* He has now lost the right to be the absolute ruler. In terms of exchange theory, with its emphasis on costs, rewards, profit, and loss, we may say that the loss of absolute rulership rights has been a cost to the husband. Although he still retains final authority and control, his role is now that of a president in a democracy rather than that of a totalitarian dictator. This loss by no means deprives him of all profit in the marital exchange. He still receives ample rewards from his wife within the instrumental dimension of marriage and retains the rights to receive from her the fulfillment of her duties associated with the wife-mother role as described earlier.

But what about the husband's duties in the instrumental realm? Here again nothing much has changed insofar as his unique obligation to provide for his wife and children is concerned. This access to economic resources continues to be the basis for his still possessing considerable marital power. The wife's rights and rewards associated with her husband's provision for her also remain much the same as before—except for one important shift. In the head-complement pattern, the wife has the right to work—whether or not she exercises that option. With her husband's consent, she may become a wage earner under certain conditions (usually serious economic needs within the family). The existence of the option elevates her power potential, as we shall see.

Expressive Side of the Head-Complement Arrangement

Moving to the expressive or person-oriented dimension of marriage, we see once more the effects of the wife's improved negotiating position. Under the owner-property arrangement, sex was exchanged between the spouses on a duties-rights basis; but the degree of satisfaction was not terribly significant, nor were other aspects of expressiveness, such as companionship and empathy. However, throughout the nineteenth and into the twentieth century, there gradually arose the notion of companionship marriage, with emphasis on the centrality of the "affectionate function." Little by little, it was becoming normative for husbands and wives to be friends and lovers. They were expected to be much more to one another than merely sources of income, status, housekeeping, sexual exchanges, and children. They were expected to enjoy one another as persons, to find pleasure in one another's company, to take one another into confidence and share problems and triumphs, to go places together and to do things together.

Couples also came to expect something beyond the old just-go-through-the-motions kind of sex. They wanted sexual intercourse to be gratifying in a new way—an experience more special and delightful than it once was. Husbands and wives were expected to provide for each other's sexual rights in a reciprocal-duty fashion. If the wife did her best to make sure that the sexual expression of love was pleasurable to her husband (thereby performing her duty and fulfilling his right), she expected in turn that her husband would do his best to provide her with sexual pleasure as well (thereby performing his duty and fulfilling her right).

The same was true in serving as sounding boards for one another's problems, or in being open to each other's needs for self-disclosure regarding inmost thoughts and feelings, or in being companions to one another during leisure time. Each had rights and duties in all these areas. All of this was quite different from the former arrangement of owner-property where the emphasis was more on the wife's duties and the husband's rights with regard to sex, with little importance at all attached to companionship, empathy, and being a "best friend" to one's spouse.

One reason that these alterations occurred stemmed from women's sense of expressive inequities. (Recall Mary Wollstonecraft's complaint about wives who felt cheated when deprived of their husbands' caresses. And this was as early as the eighteenth century.) With improved negotiating power derived from economic opportunities and the option to become wage earners, women began pressing for greater rights within the expressive or personal side of marriage, desiring to make the rights-duties exchange more fair and reciprocal. Warm expressive exchanges surely must have been much more difficult to carry out between an "owner" and his "property" under the old system. The status and power differences were just too wide for the spouses to be deep friends very often or very long. But as power differences began to decline with wives in a better bargaining position, changes were gradually brought about in the personal side of marriage, making it more rewarding for both wives and husbands. In exchange terms, the cost (husband's loss of some power) was offset by gains in the expressive dimension.

SENIOR PARTNER/JUNIOR PARTNER MARRIAGE PATTERN

When a wife takes an income-producing job at the same time that the couple continues to define the husband as the primary breadwinner, there is a shift away from the head-complement pattern. The wife's position as "complement" to the "head" is changed to that of *junior partner*. Correspondingly, her husband's position as head is changed to that of *senior partner* in the relationship. This shift results from the economic inputs the wife now brings to the marriage. Her income means that she is no longer totally dependent on her husband for survival; and furthermore, at least part of the family's living standard is attributable to her resources.

She also is likely to have more power in marital decision-making because, as various studies have shown, working wives tend to use their resources as a way of obtaining more bargaining leverage (Scanzoni, 1970; Blood and Wolfe, 1960). For some employed wives, this leverage may not be used often or at all; but the potential is always there. The wife is bringing money into the home just as the husband is, and she can always use that fact to gain what she feels is right in a particular decision.

Since she has helped earn the money, she wants a voice in how it is used. She may point out the unfairness of her husband's insistence on making huge expenditures without consulting her, particularly when she knows such expenditures would be impossible without her contributions to the family income. Or on the other hand, she might object to her husband's nagging about the price of something she purchased—even though it was purchased out of her own earnings rather than out of some "allowance" from him as in the days when she was a "complement." She might suggest ways they can negotiate about financial arrangements, perhaps coming to the conclusion that they should have separate bank accounts. Or they may decide on a plan in which each puts so much into family support and household needs and keeps another amount set aside for personal use, and so on.

The point to be stressed is that the actual or potential power stemming from a wife's employment removes her from the position of being an adjunct to a benevolent head whose ultimate jurisdiction is undisputed. As a junior partner, the wife has a greater share in the power and the husband a lesser share than in the other marital arrangements discussed. In the terminology of economics that lies behind exchange theory, we might say that the wife's *gain* in power (stepping up into partnership) becomes the husband's *loss* in power (stepping down from headship). This does not mean of course that there are not gains for him also—such as in the greater monetary resources now available to the family.

It must be kept in mind that power, in economics terminology, is a "scarce good." It is something that is limited in supply. How this commodity is divided up depends upon the respective resources of the bargainers. With the wife's greater access to the opportunity system, her resources for bargaining are increased, and so is her power. However, the husband still commands more power than his wife; because, although he is a partner rather than a head, he is the *senior* partner in the relationship. He continues to be viewed as the family's chief provider and is the one through whom the family derives its social status. But now the distance between the positions held by him and his wife is narrowed, and his power is not quite so final and definitive as in the head-complement arrangement.

Al and Marilyn, the department-store manager and schoolteacher in case 3 at the beginning of this chapter, illustrate the senior partner-junior partner arrangement. Their marriage displays several characteristics that are common in this structural form. First, there is Marilyn's moving in and out of the labor force. She worked in the early years of marriage, then dropped out until the youngest entered school, then returned to work again. Second, there is a lack of commitment to her career. If she feels she is needed at home, Marilyn says she won't hesitate to give up teaching. If her husband's company wants to transfer him, she is ready to move and take her chances at finding another teaching position in the new location. If she can't find a suitable job, she is willing simply to be a homemaker.

Third, the priority of the husband's career is emphasized. "Al and I believe that the husband should be the main breadwinner," Marilyn says. "That means his work takes precedence over mine." Al earns considerably more than Marilyn does, and with this higher income comes a higher degree of power in family decision-making. "He's the captain and I'm second mate," reports Marilyn. Furthermore, the family's social status derives primarily from Al and his position in the company rather than from Marilyn's schoolteaching.

Rights and Duties: Instrumental and Expressive

The rights-duties exchange in a marriage where the spouses follow the senior partner-junior partner pattern is quite similar to that of the head-complement pattern. The main difference is in the wife's increased power and the husband's lessened power in marital decision-making. Her working and bringing in income means greater influence in both instrumental and expressive matters. However, it is still considered her duty to fulfill her wife-mother role in caring for the children and looking after household matters—although the husband might (when it is convenient) be more willing to help with such tasks than is the case under the head-complement arrangement where the wife is considered a full-time homemaker. But it is still considered the husband's right to have these domestic duties performed by his wife.

Likewise, the *primary* responsibility for providing for the family is still assigned to the husband. It is still the wife's right to have the husband support her (even though she might contribute to that support), and it is the husband's duty to be the main breadwinner (thereby freeing his junior partner to go in and out of the job market in a way that he cannot). In the expressive or person-oriented side of marriage, the rights-duties exchange is identical to that of the head-complement arrangement (except again for increased power on the part of the wife). Each partner has the right to receive and the duty to give marital rewards in the form of sex, empathy, and companionship.

Movement between Positions

The example of Al and Marilyn shows clearly that there is not some kind of chronological progression between the positions of head-complement and those of senior partner-junior partner. Rather, many wives (such as Marilyn) move back and forth between the junior partner and complement statuses, with their husbands correspondingly moving from senior partner to head and vice-versa.

Young wives are often employed at the beginning of marriage and are thus classified as junior partners. Many of them subsequently drop out of the labor force (usually to have their first child) and are thus reclassified as complements. After a period of time, they may return to work in order to help meet expenses, particularly the increased expense of rearing a child, and once again these women are junior partners. But they may go back to the complement status a year or two later—often because they wish to give personal care to the child or else because of the birth of a second child.

Shifting in and out of the labor force continues to occur among many women past childbearing age as well, in marked contrast to the work experience of men. Except under unusual circumstances (injuries, illnesses, work layoffs, and so forth), men do not start and stop employment repeatedly. In the female socialization process, however, gender-role stereotypes and social pressures discourage strong commitment to jobs and careers. And since societal norms still assign to husbands major responsibility to be family breadwinners, wives have not felt the same compulsion to be part of the paid labor force.

Furthermore, since the major responsibility for child care and domestic chores has traditionally fallen on wives, some women may begin to wonder if the physical and psychological drain of two jobs (homemaking and employment) is worth it. Thus, they quit for a while until restlessness, loneliness, or a desire or need for extra money drives them temporarily back into the labor force once again. Discrimination in hiring practices and advancement opportunities, plus unequal pay scales, have also undoubtedly lessened incentives toward career commitment on the part of many women—especially before rather recent legislation made possible legal redress for such grievances.

Moving in and out of the labor force means

marital statuses shift back and forth as well. It is quite likely that the negotiating advantages of junior partnership increase the longer and more consistently the wife works. The wife who has worked steadily for five years may be expected to have greater marital power than the wife who has been in and out of several jobs during that same period. Why? Because between jobs the latter wife repeatedly shifted into the complement position and thereby moved her husband into the position of head, while the wife with a steady employment pattern remained in the junior-partner position.

Work Motivation

Why do some wives choose to be employed instead of devoting themselves to full-time

Now that the option to employment is open to them, women are increasingly exercising it; and many are expecting much more from their jobs than income alone. (© Hella Hammid/Photo Researchers, Inc.)

homemaking? The question itself is significant. People don't ask why *husbands* are in the labor force. Why? Because everyone knows that up until quite recently men haven't had the option *not* to work. Women, on the other hand, haven't had the option to work—except to a limited degree. Now that the employment option is open to them, women are increasingly exercising it; and many of them are expecting much more from their jobs than the income provided.

A wife's *reason* for working is an important consideration in examining the status of junior partner. For example, a woman who doesn't enjoy working outside the home and who never feels that her family *needs* her earnings is not likely to join the labor force and become a junior partner. But another woman may enjoy working regardless of family financial need, thereby becoming a junior partner by choice. A third woman may not want to work, yet becomes a junior partner out of necessity.

When a woman works for enjoyment, she is going after personal benefits. Her taking a job indicates a move toward autonomy. The woman who works to supplement family income, on the other hand, bases her employment behavior on group needs and interests—those of her husband and children. *Reaching for rewards* motivates the woman who works for enjoyment. In contrast, *avoiding costs* motivates the woman who works from necessity—the costs of having insufficient resources. Such a wife works out of coercion—because she has to, not because she wants to.

However, the evidence indicates that increasingly women are interested in working out of choice. Thus, their employment behaviors are becoming more and more like those of men. Although it is true that the option not to work has been closed to men, studies show that few men would care to exercise such an option even if it were available. This is true of both white-collar and blue-collar workers. From his studies in the sociology of occupations, Walter Slocum (1966:14) concluded that "no substantial group of able-bodied males between the ages of 25 and 65 in America is willingly without work." As we shall see later, one of the most traumatic consequences of retirement for many older males is being forced to give up their jobs and the sense of meaning those jobs provided for them. The same holds true for younger and middle-aged men who have unexpectedly been dismissed from their jobs because of company mergers, reorganizations, budget cuts, new technology, or other reasons beyond their control.

There are numerous reasons why work is so central, not only in America but in every industrialized society. Besides the obvious function of work in providing subsistence (and evidence continues to show that wages *do* matter), work is the means to individualistic achievement, the way of attaining highly valued rewards—a sense of self-worth, prestige, social status, fulfillment, enriching life experiences, satisfaction in service to others, power and influence, and so on. Women and men alike value these prizes offered by an industrial society, and thus we may expect work to have an attraction for both sexes.

Wives who move into the position of junior partner in the marriage relationship are often seeking occupational rewards similar to those of their husbands. However, since in the senior partner-junior partner arrangement the husband continues to be defined as the *chief* family provider, his occupation is regarded as more important than his wife's. Although this marriage pattern means more power for the wife than is true of the owner-property and head-complement arrangements, there is not total equality. Senior-partner husbands are expected to be more committed to their occupations than are junior-partner wives. The norms attached to

the provider role do not permit husbands to move in and out of the labor force.

Related to the significance attached to the husband's occupation are certain norms which help structure the roles of husband-father and wife-mother. In all three marital arrangements looked at so far, there is a basic assumption of parenthood. To enter marriage automatically assumes that an attempt will be made at some point to form a family. However, when the family is formed, the norms prescribe that the mother is ultimately responsible for child care, just as the father is ultimately responsible for economic provision.

The fact that the wife as junior partner is expected to have children and to be responsible for them tends to reinforce the subordinate nature of any occupation she might pursue. Household cares and family needs are expected to predominate over her work goals, and therefore she is prevented from pursuing the direct-line, orderly sequence of occupational and achievement endeavors which characterizes the life of her husband as senior partner.

EQUAL-PARTNER MARRIAGE PATTERN

The vast majority of marriages in America and in other industrial societies are represented by the head-complement and senior partner-junior partner models. Probably few of us can think of many contemporary examples comparable to the nineteenth-century illustration of the husband who insisted on his wife's subordination and whipped her to ensure the owner-property arrangement. Yet, most of us could name many couples who remind us of Tom and Cindy (head-complement) or Al and Marilyn (senior partner-junior partner) as described in the hypothetical case studies at the beginning of this chapter.

However, there is a fourth way that marriage may be structured, and an increasing minority of marriages may fit this pattern. We are speaking of an equal-partner arrangement. The option to work which removes a wife from the status of property not only opens up the possibility that she may become a complement or a junior partner; there is also a step beyond the junior-partner status—a wife may be an equal partner.

In an equal-partner marriage, both spouses are equally committed to their respective careers, and each one's occupation is considered as important as that of the other. Furthermore, there is role interchangeability with respect to the breadwinner and domestic roles. Either spouse may fill either role; both may share in both roles. Another characteristic of an equal-partner marriage is the equal power shared by husband and wife in decision-making. Lastly, this marriage form differs from the other forms in that there is no longer the automatic assumption of the hyphenated wife-mother and husband-father roles. The basic marital roles are simply wife and husband, and marriage is not considered automatically to require parenthood. In our opening case studies, the equal-partner marriage is represented by Janet, the psychology professor, and her lawyer husband, Roger.

Equal Career Commitment

Based on research in England, a team of social scientists state that the "crucial element in distinguishing the dual-career family from other forms of family structure is the high commitment of both husband and wife to work on an egalitarian basis and a life-plan which involves a relatively full participation and advancement in work." Importantly, the term *dual-job family* is not used; these researchers use the word *career* deliberately. A career involves continuity and commitment. And in the dual-career setting, both the husband and the wife have high aspirations to achieve in the world of work, desiring to exercise to the full their individual competencies in their respective occupations, with both spouses performing tasks that are highly productive or that carry great responsibility (Fogarty, Rapoport, and Rapoport, 1971:334–335; see also Scanzoni, 1980).

A major feature, therefore, that marks off the equal-partner position from such positions as head, complement, senior partner, or junior partner are the *norms* endorsing the dual-achiever pattern. Speaking in terms of the rights of marriage, both partners have the *right* to careers (not merely jobs), and one career is not necessarily more significant than the other. That, of course, represents a radical departure from the other three ways in which marriages have been structured. In fact, some sociologists (arguing from the functionalist viewpoint) have suggested that such a marriage arrangement can't work.

Talcott Parsons (1955), for example, argues that gender-role segregation and specialization are necessary to the equilibrium or stability of a marriage. If the husband is chief breadwinner and the wife centers her life in home and family, a sense of competition is not likely to develop between the spouses as might be the case if both were achievers in the occupational realm. The development of such rivalries, according to Parsons, tends to disrupt the marriage. At the same time, even he has admitted that "it is, of course, possible for the adult woman to follow the masculine pattern and seek a career in fields of occupational achievement in direct competition with men of her own class." However, such departure from the traditional domestic pattern was rather rare at the time he was writing, leading him to conclude that "its generalization would only be possible with profound alterations in the structure of the family" (Parsons, 1942).

The equal-partner marriage *is* an attempt to alter the structure of the family. The goal of such an arrangement is not to destroy marriage but rather to *change* marriage so that the partners can fulfill individual aspirations unhindered by gender-role stereotypes and traditional ideas about the division of labor. It is an emerging form that may very well represent the wave of the future.

Travel and Living Arrangements Occupations are major factors in determining where persons live and where they travel. Traditionally, a married couple has lived together in one household in a location determined by the husband's place of employment. If the husband's job meant settling in Michigan, the couple moved to Michigan— even if the wife's preferences might be to remain in Oregon.

Furthermore, if extensive travel was required in the husband's work, few questions were raised about his right to make such business trips or about the wife's duty to stay home and attend to the household while he was gone. In some cases, the husband's occupation might even mean long periods of actually living apart from his wife—such as in the case of a merchant seaman or fisherman, or if a man was in politics, the military, or fields of science which require extensive fieldwork. Such travel and living arrangements have been optional for men but rarely for women.

In the equal-partner arrangement, however, the wife gains these options as well. Her career may require her to travel a great deal, especially if she is in the professions, or in sports, journalism, the performing arts, business, and so on. In a very small sample of dual-career marriages in which the wives held positions in universities, research labo-

ratories, hospitals, and business, sociologist Lynda Lytle Holmstrom (1972) explored attitudes and behaviors related to the issue of the wife's travel. She found in her sample that "most husbands in the professional couples were very supportive of their wives traveling without them and felt they should have this opportunity." Some couples "accepted very easily both the idea of being apart from each other and the fact that during the wife's absence additional domestic responsibilities would fall on the husband." Other couples emphasized the difficulties, particularly in cases where the wife was gone for a long time (such as a month) and there were children left under the husband's care; but even so, the wife's travel was viewed as a necessary part of her career. In one interview, after the husband had mentioned the hardships of having the full responsibility of the household fall to him while his wife was away, he was asked if he would prefer that his wife would not take such trips. His reply was, "No, no. It's just hard." He laughed and added, "I mean, if I feel that she shouldn't go away, then I feel that I shouldn't go away. . . . It's just part of the game."

"Commuter Marriages" Not only do dual-career couples face the issue of the wife's traveling in connection with her career just as the husband travels in his work; there is also the possibility that the spouses' separate occupations may require them to work in different geographical locations. The wife's career may require her working in Buffalo, New York, while the husband's career may require him to work in Chicago. Then what happens? Some couples may decide to spend their weekdays at their place of work and their weekends together in alternate locations or at some spot in between.

"People in two-location marriages are attempting to construct an alternative lifestyle which has few structural or cultural supports," write sociologists Betty Frankle Kirschner and Laurel Richardson Walum (1978:525). Most people's definition of marriage includes the idea that a husband and wife live under the same roof, and it isn't easy for relatives and friends to understand a couple's decision to live apart because of career demands. Acquaintances often wonder if the marriage is in trouble. One woman told Kirschner and Walum that only after months of patient explanation to her colleagues in her new location did they stop referring to her "ex" husband.

These researchers report that wives find it easier than husbands to find support systems, largely because of the women's movement and its encouragement of women's career as-

pirations. In traditional *male*-centered moves, such as leaving wives because of military service or immigrating into a new country before arranging for families to come, males had strong support systems. However, say Kirschner and Walum, "the woman-determined two-location family . . . leaves the male either as a new or renewed single. In either case, friendship and support systems may be difficult to establish or maintain because of lack of understanding and discomfort on the part of others" (p. 522). Friends of the couple may stop socializing with a spouse who stays behind. In addition, both the husband's male friends and the extended family may "denigrate his manliness" and wonder what kind of man he is to "allow" his wife to go off on her own or stay behind in her own career when he moves elsewhere. And some male friends may even feel envy, assuming he is now free to live as a swinging single.

To counteract such lack of support and the other stresses of living apart, couples develop various strategies for cultivating intimacy even though the geographical distance between them may be great. In spite of their high commitment to their respective careers, two-location couples who are making commuter marriage work make sure that they set aside time for interaction with each other in various ways. Kirschner and Walum explain:

> For example, the telephone for many couples becomes a daily or near-daily way of reaffirming coupledness. Some establish a regular time for their "phone date." One couple with limited financial resources would phone and after one ring hang up; the single ring was a symbolic hello, "I'm thinking of you." One woman reported that the knowledge that her husband would phone her at 11:00 P.M. each night sustained her through the day. Others write daily. The members of one couple agreed to write each other at the same time each day so they could sense a shared activity. One couple ex-

(Drawing by Martins, © 1977 The New Yorker Magazine, Inc.)

"I was shot out here to the New York office, my wife's company whisked her off to Denver, and Lord only knows what happened to the children."

changed diaries. And couples plan occasions such as weekends, vacations, and holidays in which they will be together face-to-face. (p. 519)

For commuter couples, say these sociologists, time becomes extremely focused. "Time together is not 'wasted' on dutiful social obligations or meaningless socializing with uninterested others." It is spent with the realization that the hours together are short, and soon the wife and husband will have to return to their separate houses or apartments and their separate careers. Or they will have to put down the phone or end the letter.

At the same time, Kirschner and Walum report that the time apart also takes on an intensity of its own and shows up in heightened efforts to *achieve* in the spouses' respective careers. Career success may help them "justify to themselves their unorthodox living arrangements." But in addition, such couples "also report that it is easier to get work done since they have greater freedom to follow their own work rhythms without having to accommodate the needs of their spouse" (Kirschner and Walum, 1978:520). Nevertheless, such couples tend to think of their living arrangement as temporary and look forward to living together again when new career opportunities make such a move possible.

Kirschner and Walum (1978:523–524) report that those couples who are likely to have the least stressful two-location lifestyle are those who have high career commitment on the part of both parties; recognition by the husband of the importance of the wife's career; financial resources to meet the added expenses of maintaining two dwelling units, phone calls, travel to see one another, and so on; shorter rather than greater geographical distances between the spouses' respective locations to allow for getting together more

often; and long-established patterns of interaction. Couples who have been married for some time are better able than newlyweds to adjust to a commuter-marriage lifestyle. (See also Gross, 1980; Gerstel and Gross, 1984.)

Commuting Isn't Always the Solution
Some couples reject the idea of long-distance commuting, although they say they might be open to the possibility if no other solution were available. In some marriages, career-related moves may be decided on a husband's turn—wife's turn basis. If a husband has an occupational opportunity open to him that would require moving to another location, the wife may follow and seek to pursue her career in the new location also—even though it might mean sacrifices on her part. But then the next move will be determined by the wife's career, If better opportunities open to her elsewhere, it will be her husband's turn to follow.

Other couples might negotiate in other ways. In some cases, *neither* will accept a position elsewhere unless something really worthwhile is open to *both;* and no moves will be undertaken until such an arrangement is found. The point to be stressed here is that the traditional norm of a married couple's moving and living in conjunction with the husband's career interests is for dual-career couples no longer automatically assumed. In equal-partner marriages, the issues of residence and travel are likely to become increasingly problematic. Some employers and organizations are trying various innovative approaches to help ease some of the job-related dilemmas faced by dual-career couples (Hall and Hall, 1979:210–212).

Role Interchangeability

The role of the wife in an equal-partner marriage is a radical departure from her role in the other positions discussed. The norms now prescribe that she has the duty to provide for her husband. At the same time, norms attached to the husband role also maintain that it is a husband's duty to provide for his wife—just as has always been the case. Since both the husband role and the wife role involve breadwinning, we have a case of *role interchangeability*. This is in contrast to the rigid *role specialization* that occurs under other marital positions. In situations of owner-property, head-complement, and senior partner-junior partner, each partner has a particular sphere according to his or her sex—for the male the occupational, for the female primarily the domestic.

Since there is role interchangeability in the equal-partner marital pattern and both sexes can fulfill breadwinner behaviors, there not only exists the norm that the wife as well as the husband has the right to a career; there also exists the norm that the husband as well as the wife has the right to be provided for. In other patterns of structuring marriage, it has been the husband's duty to provide and the wife's right to be provided for. But in the equal-partner situation, each spouse has both the duty to provide and the right to be provided for. The traditional work ethic, which assumed that a man proved his self-worth and masculinity through occupational achievements, centered around his obligations to provide economic benefits, status, and prestige to his wife and family. But with the roles of both partners defined as interchangeable achievers, the husband can expect to share in the wife's status and bask in the prestige resulting from her accomplishments just as she has always done and will continue to do in his.

Option Not to Work Although the provider-achiever role is interchangeable in an equal-partner marriage, such an arrangement does not necessarily require that both partners work full-time all the time. Either partner has the option not to work as well as the right to a career and the duty to provide. It may seem contradictory simultaneously to hold norms in which the husband or wife has the option not to work and yet at the same time has the duty to provide. However, while all the marriage structures we have examined are in constant process, the equal-partner pattern is especially in motion. It is continually being negotiated and renegotiated so that at one point a partner may be exercising his or her achievement rights, while at another time for various reasons the option *not* to work (the right to be provided for) is being exercised.

Will Men Become Househusbands? The question raised earlier now becomes very real: will males, who have traditionally been work-oriented, be likely to exercise their option not to work? Occasionally, one hears reports of couples who trade off "house-spouse" and provider roles; that is, one year the husband stays home to look after the household and children while the wife works and supports the family, and the next year the pattern is reversed. However, at the present time few occupations allow for such flexibility. Even more than that, because of the way society's reward system is related to occupational achievement, it is not likely that many men for very long would find it rewarding not to work.

There might, however, be exceptions in certain types of work. A writer who works full-time for a newspaper, for example, might find it very rewarding to absent himself from his employment for several months to write a novel to which only evenings and weekends could be devoted were it not for his wife's financial support. A similar situation could arise in other creative arts as well—music, painting, sculpturing, and the like.

Note that in exercising the option not to work at a regular income-producing occupation, such men are not actually giving up work. They are changing the kind of work they do and are finding freedom for some pursuit that requires much time but is not always immediately income-producing. However, because of the reward system in an industrial society, they are seldom likely to be full-time "househusbands" in the tradition of the housewife role, although there are occasional exceptions. One man in Sweden, for example, wrote a regular feature for a magazine in which he described his life as a *hemmaman* or househusband. His wife worked as an art director, while he stayed home to cook, clean, make beds, do the laundry, and care for their 6-year-old child. He had previously worked in advertising but found his job boring, whereas he said he enjoyed child care, didn't mind housework, and thought a reversal of the traditional roles made sense in order to make it easier for his wife to pursue her career, since she made more money than he anyway ("The Happy 'Hemmaman,' " *Life* 67, August 15, 1969:46). Such a situation, it could be argued, is more like the *head-complement* form than the equal-partner pattern for marriage—only this time the wife is the unique provider and is likely to hold the greater power because of the resources she brings to the household, while the husband is the complement.

Division of Labor In traditional marriage arrangements, the husband has had the duty to provide for his wife and the right to have his wife take care of household tasks. In the equal-partner pattern, role interchangeability means that both the husband and wife

The happy "hemmaman" (househusband). (Enrico Sarsini/ © 1969 Time, Inc.)

have the reciprocal duty to be breadwinners and the reciprocal right to be supported. But what about household tasks? Does the wife as co-provider have the *right* to have these tasks performed by the husband? And does the husband, having the right to be provided for, have the *duty* to perform such household tasks? The answer is yes, if the exchange is to be fair. How this will be carried out will likely vary with the individual couple, but the mutual responsibility is there. Sharing household duties is a part of the equal-partner marriage pattern just as is the sharing of occupational duties.

That this is not simply "theory" with no relation to everyday life may be seen in some of our own research findings (Scanzoni, 1980; also 1978). Among a regional household probability sample of married white women aged 22 to 33 years, we found that nearly a quarter of the women (23 percent) reported that they shared the provider duty equally with their husbands. These equal partners also indicated that their husbands shared with them the tasks of child care, cooking, dishwashing, clothes washing, and food shopping to a greater degree than was true in the senior partner-junior partner and head-complement marriages in the sample. For their part, *wives* in equal-partner marriages were more likely to share with their husbands household repair tasks than was true of junior partner and complement wives.

Equal Power in Decision-Making

As Figure 8-1 shows, the increasing power of the wife is perhaps the most prominent feature to be observed in moving through the four basic ways marriages may be structured. In the equal-partner position, it becomes standard or normative for both husband and wife to acknowledge that the balance of power is equal; neither spouse has more power than the other. The husband relinquishes any vestige of traditional ideas of masculine superiority, dominance, and the right to have the wife defer to her husband.

The basis for this normative egalitarianism lies in the equal career commitments of the husband and wife. A century ago, philosopher-economist John Stuart Mill (1869) argued that if two persons invest equally in a business, both partners will want equal power in order to protect their own and their mutual interests. Likewise, two spouses with equal investments in their marriage (because of the tangible and intangible resources contributed through their respective career commitments) will want equal marital power. Without this equal power, the career interests of one or the other could be threatened.

Option of Parenthood

In marriages structured around the positions of owner-property, head-complement, and senior partner-junior partner, major rewards were defined as coming from children—especially for wives. There were also certain costs involved—again especially for wives since they were mainly responsible for child care. Because of this responsibility, women tended to forgo serious career commitment and its rewards. In fact, women who did choose to pursue a career over children were generally considered selfish or neurotic.

In recent years increasing numbers of young women have rejected the notion that it is selfish to want a life of their own. They refuse to subordinate individualistic interests and rewards to the interests of husbands and children. Indeed, the argument can be turned around to say that husbands may be selfish to insist that wives have a certain number of children (or any at all) and then be responsible for them. Some persons are raising the question: If individualistic occupational rewards are so valuable, why should only white men have access to them? And if children are so important, why shouldn't husbands be responsible for taking care of them as much as wives are?

Therefore, in equal-partner marriages, the roles of husband and wife are not attached to father and mother roles as they are in the other marriage patterns. The norms for both the husband role and the wife role make having or not having children a matter of choice. And if the choice is made to have children,

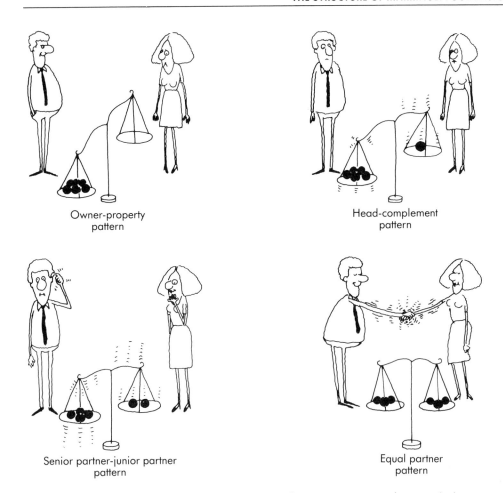

Owner-property
pattern

Head-complement
pattern

Senior partner-junior partner
pattern

Equal partner
pattern

The wife's power has more weight as her position moves from property to complement to junior partner, until in the equal partner pattern the balance of power between husband and wife is equal.

FIGURE 8-1 How the balance of power changes according to the four marriage patterns.

both parents are equally responsible for their care.

Interestingly, our research has shown that equal partners (more than junior partners and much more than complements) control the spacing and the number of children they will have in such a way as to maximize the wife's career interests (Scanzoni, 1980).

MARITAL PATTERNS IN MOVEMENT

It should be clear by now that the positions of owner-property, head-complement, senior partner-junior partner, and equal partner—equal partner are not rigid, distinct categories in the sense that each marriage fits *exactly* into one of these "boxes." In the first place there may be movement between the categories. A wife may be a complement, take a job and become a junior partner, quit six months later and become a complement once again, and so on.

Second, few marriages would fit exactly and indisputably on *all* dimensions into any one of the categories. There is room for indefiniteness, a blurring and blending rather than clear-cut lines separating the statuses. It might be helpful to think of a continuum, a thermometerlike arrangement in which marriages attain degrees of equal-partner

In equal-partner marriages, if a decision is made to have children, both spouses are equally responsible for their care. (© Erika Stone, 1979)

status, degrees of senior partner–junior partner status, degrees of head-complement status, perhaps even (though much less likely today) degrees of the owner-property status. In other words, couples may be more or less in or near one of the statuses.

It should also be kept in mind that while certain marriages may be found at particular points on the continuum today, they may be at a different point than they were two years ago; and they may be at another point two years from now. For example, a couple might be described as having a head-complement arrangement in their marriage. When the wife decides to take on a part-time job selling cosmetics door to door, pursuing it very casually as somewhat of a hobby in her spare time, she may move up to being slightly more than complement. As she begins devoting more time to her occupational interest, earning more money although still only on a part-time basis, she might become almost but not quite a full junior partner. A year later, she might move to a full-time job and take on wholly the junior-partner position in her marriage. If she were to save up money for special training and then were to embark on some career with equal commitment to that of her husband, she might take on an equal-partner status at some point.

AN ALTERNATIVE MARITAL PATTERN: WIVES AS SENIOR PARTNERS

There are some situations where wives are thrust into the position of senior partner in the marriage—not necessarily because they seek it, but because they have no choice. It falls to them by default. They assume primary responsibility for the family because their husbands are unable or unwilling to take such responsibility.

There are other situations where wives are senior partners in the marriage because of a conscious choice by the wife and husband that the wife's occupation will be considered the more important and that she has the primary provider role.

Matrifocal Situations in Lower-Income Families

Anthropologist Helen Safa (1971:36–38) has written of a common pattern in cultures of poverty: the family becomes *matrifocal* or "mother-centered." The strong mother-child bond takes precedence over the husband-wife bond; the role of the husband (if he is present) is peripheral.

Safa points out that this form of family life has arisen among lower-income families as a way of coping under conditions of poverty. The primary function of the family is viewed as childrearing, and "marriage is not expected to provide the intense emotional intimacy sought in the middle-class nuclear family." Both husband and wife have strong ties outside the family, either with kin or same-sex friends, and they tend to rely on these relationships rather than on each other for emotional support and assistance. "Lower-class women cannot invest the conjugal [marital or husband-wife] relationship with the heavy responsibilities it carries in the middle class," writes Safa. Why? Because such wives "cannot be sure that men will be adequate providers, or will not have to leave to find work elsewhere, or may not abandon them for another woman."

Another researcher who has studied lower-class family lifestyles is sociologist Lee Rainwater (1966b:190–191). He points out that the matrifocal family is common among lower-class families in general and not only among black lower-class families, as is some-times thought. According to Rainwater, lower-class families tend to be "matrifocal in the sense that the wife makes most of the decisions that keep the family going and has the greatest sense of responsibility to the family." Women in these families get advice from female relatives and tend to consider their husbands to be unconcerned about day-to-day problems of family life. Structural factors have caused this situation to be especially pronounced among lower-class black families.

Safa (1971:39, 46) makes the point that socioeconomic forces "have systematically robbed the man of any basis of authority in the black ghetto family; they have curtailed his role as economic provider, as leader in his own community, and as spokesman for his family in dealing with the outside world. As a result, the woman has been forced to take over many traditionally male roles." Safa argues that wife dominance is further reinforced by welfare programs: "Because men are temporarily or permanently absent from many black homes, or cannot be reached during working hours, social workers and other government officials dealing with these families often direct most of their attention to the women. In effect, they treat her as head of the household, whether she has a husband or not." (See also Staples, 1985.)

Households Headed by Females Alone

Safa (1971:36) and others who have studied the culture of poverty refer not only to matrifocal families but also to *female-based* families, a more restrictive term applied to those families who are headed by females alone. In 1983, 11 percent of all households were families maintained by a female householder with no spouse present. But if we break down the statistics by race, we find that among black households, nearly a third (31 percent) were families maintained by a woman alone, compared to 9 percent of white households. Among Spanish-origin households, nearly 1 in 5 was a woman-maintained family. (U.S. Bureau of the Census, *Current Population Reports,* p-20, no. 388, 1984:1–3).

In Chapter 7, we talked about the principle of status adequacy as it applied to women who chose to have children outside of marriage and who had the means to provide for them. We contrasted this with cases of status inadequacy among unwed mothers who were young, poor, and often had more than one child out of wedlock. Here we want to concentrate on women from this "status inadequacy" category—women who live in poverty, may have large numbers of children, and hold no particular commitment to the idea of single parenthood. Yet, they find themselves forced into this role by circumstances—not only pregnancy outside of marriage but perhaps through desertion or divorce or because of the death of a husband.

Female-headed households account for a large proportion of the poor—persons who live below the poverty line. The poverty threshold set by the government for a nonfarm family of four in 1982 was $9,862. For two persons it was $6,281 (U.S. Bureau of the Census, *Statistical Abstract of the United States: 1985,* issued Dec., 1984, p. 429). There were 7.5 million poor families in the United States in 1982, and 46 percent of those families were maintained by a female householder with no spouse present. Among black families below the poverty line, 71 percent were families maintained by women alone. Among whites, the corresponding figure was 35 percent. (U.S. Bureau of the Census, *Current Population Reports,* P-60, no. 144, 1984:1–2, 72).

Economically Deprived Black Families Maintained by Females Alone

Throughout this book, while we have contrasted information on blacks and whites, the underlying premise has been that their family patterns are basically similar. Any differences do *not* spring from something innate or consciously planned but rather stem from the way society has been structured. Those blacks who have been most vocal about family lifestyles have not made an effort to set up a unique and distinct family form (for example, a black matriarchy) but rather have moved toward the dominant form of the larger society in which the male has traditionally held the unique or chief provider role. During the 1960s, for example, the Black Muslims and other groups seeking to enhance black identity placed great emphasis on male authority and female subordination and stressed the head-complement pattern for marriage (Malcolm X, 1964, chap. 13.).

This emphasis was apparently in reaction to decades of economic discrimination practiced against black males by the white society. Black women who were forced to work in order to survive came to possess economic resources that resulted in their gaining power in the family. Black males, deprived of access to economic rewards, were also deprived of power within the household. This situation has given rise to considerable folklore about the so-called black matriarchy, including the unfounded assertion that there is something within black cultural values, traceable to plantation days or even to Africa, that predisposes blacks to favor female-dominant households.

All available evidence is to the contrary. Even among blacks who have not espoused the Muslim emphasis on a pattern of male headship and female subordination, it is clear that the overwhelming majority do not prefer households headed by females alone but rather want the married couple form of family lifestyle (Rainwater, 1966b; Liebow, 1967; Schulz, 1969; Scanzoni, 1977; Staples, 1985). At the same time, although it's not preferred, the female-headed household is often accepted as an unavoidable means of economic survival. And the percentage of such households has been growing in recent years, as Figure 8-2 shows.

But don't forget that nearly two-thirds of black society live above the poverty line (U.S. Bureau of the Census, *Current Population Reports*, P-60, no. 144, 1984:1). And over half of black *family* households are families headed by a married couple (U.S. Bureau of the Census, *Current Population Reports*, P-20, no. 388, 1984:2, Table B). In such families, gender-role equality is a pertinent issue. Here we are concerned *only with that slightly more than one-third of black society which is a genuine American lower class or underclass*. (See Figure 8-3.) These persons are different from poor whites and poor Spanish-speaking people in that they encounter much more severe economic discrimination due to their race. Paths to mobility out of the lower class are exceedingly limited; poverty is cyclical, generation after generation. Black males in this situation have been held back from fulfilling the provider role and have been forced into other kinds of behaviors in relation to women and to economic survival.

From his studies of black ghetto life, sociologist David Schulz (1969:82–85) describes several categories of such male behaviors. Some lower-class black men play the role of *pimp*, not only in the usual sense of living off the labors of several prostitutes but also in situations where they live off women who

FIGURE 8-2 Composition of black family households in the United States, 1970 and 1985. (*Source:* U.S. Bureau of the Census, Special Publication PIO/POP-83-1, *America's Black Population: 1970–1982: A Statistical View* (Washington, D.C.: U.S. Government Printing Office, 1983), p. 19; and U.S. Bureau of the Census, *Current Population Reports*, Series p-20, no. 411, *Household and Family Characteristics: March, 1985* (U.S. Government Printing Office, Sept., 1986), p. 8.)

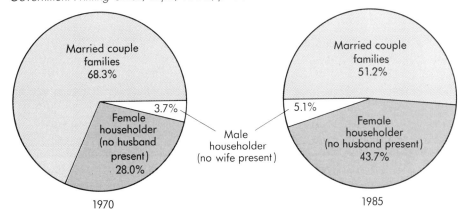

Married couple families 68.3%

3.7%

Female householder (no husband present) 28.0%

Male householder (no wife present)

Married couple families 51.2%

5.1%

Female householder (no husband present) 43.7%

1970

1985

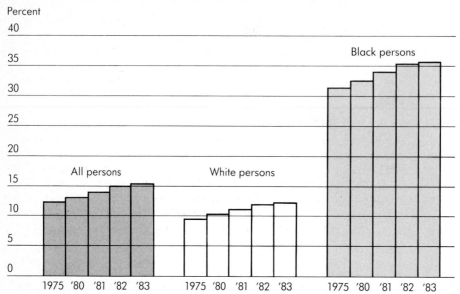

FIGURE 8-3 Percent of persons below the poverty level in the United States: 1975 to 1983. (*Source:* U.S. Bureau of the Census, *Statistical Abstract of the United States: 1985* (105th edition) (Washington, DC: U.S. Government Printing Office, December, 1984), p. 430.)

earn their income legitimately in domestic service or as clerks or welfare recipients. Often these are younger men who demand that their women provide them with a high standard of living (by ghetto standards), including the means to "dress like a dandy," while they reward the woman with their capacity as lovers.

Another category listed by Schulz is the *supportive companion* who meets a woman regularly on weekends and gives her spending money and a good time but wishes to avoid the responsibilities of marriage and parenthood. Then there is the category of the *supportive biological father* who senses some responsibility for children he has fathered, even though he may be married to someone else. To the children's mother, he plays only the role of boyfriend but at the

same time does not run away from certain economic duties.

One step beyond this category is that of the *indiscreet free man* who has a legitimate family plus one or more illegitimate families and who spends much of his time, income, and energies on the "other woman" and any children he has fathered by her. He does not hide his behavior from his legal wife and often compares her to his girl friend, causing much family conflict. The legal wife often feels trapped in the situation because she has numerous children and needs his support. With no alternative sources of rewards, she is forced to "make do" with the limited rewards her husband offers. In contrast, a fifth category, the *discreet free man,* keeps his extramarital activities covert or else has an understanding with his wife. He too showers large outlays of money and attention on his "illegitimate" family but doesn't flaunt these outside interests in such a way as to antagonize his legal family.

Schulz (1969:128) points out that the sixth category, *the traditional monogamous type of father,* is (although rare) considered the most desirable among underclass blacks. Such men are faithful to their wives and children and consider their homes and families to be their major concerns. "Typically such a father will have good relationships with his children and high status in the family regardless of his ability to earn a living."

The first five of these six patterns cast some light on why there are so many female-headed households in lower-class black society. Black women have had to interact with men who have largely been excluded from economic opportunity. These men have simply not been able to provide the kinds of socioeconomic rewards that members of modern societies (both black and white) have expected males to supply. Consequently, alternative strategies have evolved in which lower-class black men and women attempt to exchange economic and expressive benefits in ways that differ from the dominant societal pattern.

At the same time, black women are aware of exploitation by men who act out roles ranging from pimp to discreet free man. If actually married to such men, the sense of exploitation may lead some women to deep resentment. Thus, the high rates of black lower-class separation and divorce are more readily understood. The sense of exploitation may also explain why many black women are willing to remain *unmarried* female heads as well. Schulz (1969:136) explains that some of the black women in his study expressed a fear of marriage "because no matter how good a man might seem before marriage,

after he 'has papers' on you he might well change."

In short, many lower-class black women find themselves thrust into roles they did not seek, nor do they necessarily prefer, but which have been forced upon them as a result of economic discrimination against black men. When these women remain married, they often find themselves having considerably more power than their husbands who have difficulty functioning as providers. On the other hand, lower-class black women who live apart from their husbands may find themselves in situations made punishing through a combination of meager resources and numerous children.

Female Dominance Not the Goal

Female leadership by default, as in the situations just discussed, is something quite different from female *dominance* intentionally sought as a step beyond equality. Most feminists have not expressed a desire to be dominant over men, which would just be the old system in reverse. Rather they are interested in principles of egalitarianism.

Given the way occupational achievement and its rewards are valued in industrial societies, it is unlikely that many males will be interested in a complete reversal of traditional gender roles so that the wife becomes the sole breadwinner and head, while the husband can be supported and led. There are exceptions to this, of course. A common example is the situation in which a married male college student is financially supported by his wife for a temporary period.

There are other instances where personality factors play a part; in a particular husband-wife unit the wife may be stronger, more forceful, and seem to exercise greater decision-making power than her husband.

The husband's psychological makeup may be such that he prefers his wife to be the dominant partner and finds security in her strength. However, such cases are the exception. Because of the occupational-opportunity system, most marriages at present are structured with husbands as heads and wives as complements, or husbands as senior partners and wives as junior partners, although there is movement in the direction of increasing numbers of equal-partner marriages. In the equal-partner arrangement, both spouses take leader-achiever-provider roles, thereby allowing greater role flexibility for both. This pattern seems far more likely to be the wave of the future than a pattern that would totally reverse roles, placing women at the top and men at the bottom.

At the same time, an emerging alternative indicates that some couples are working out for themselves other possibilities—a negotiated pattern that is not, strictly speaking, role reversal, although it may appear so at first glance.

Occupationally Superior Wives

As opportunities for women expand in the marketplace, the probability increases that some couples may find themselves in situations where the wife's occupation is more prestigious and financially rewarding than the husband's. She may become, in essence, the senior partner—not because her husband isn't able to fulfill breadwinning responsibilities and not because she wishes to exercise greater power and dominance over her husband (as critics of the couple's lifestyle may charge). Rather, she is simply committed to her career and has high achievement aspirations, and her career is considered to have higher priority than that of her husband. Both the husband and wife may feel comfortable with such a wife-as-senior-part-

ner arrangement and find it personally satisfying (Atkinson and Boles, 1984).

According to the latest available statistics, in 1981, about 1 out of 6 married couples in which both spouses were employed had wives with higher earnings than their husbands. The Census Bureau's findings further indicated that wives who earn more than their husbands are more likely than other employed wives to have had four or more years of college, to work in a professional occupation, and to have no minor children at home (U.S. Bureau of the Census, *Current Population Reports*, P-23, no. 133, 1984:28; also *Special Demographic Analyses*, CDS-80-9, 1983).

Reviewing the literature on marriages in which wives are occupationally superior to husbands, sociologists Maxine Atkinson and Jacqueline Boles (1984) found that although various theoretical perspectives predicted negative consequences for such marital situations and some empirical findings confirmed the predictions, other research did not consistently show negative consequences. Atkinson and Boles decided to undertake their own exploratory study, examining thirty-one different marriages in which wives were senior partners. They based their research on a combination of two theoretical perspectives: symbolic interactionism and exchange theory. In so doing, they looked at *definitions of the situation* (how and why couples themselves may define their marriages as fitting a wife-as-senior-partner pattern) and the perceived *costs and rewards* a husband and wife may find in this pattern.

To be included in their sample, a marriage had to fit these criteria: (1) the wife's occupation was considered the more important, (2) the husband would be willing to relocate for the sake of the wife's career advancement, (3) a decision to relocate was more likely to be based on the wife's career than the husband's, and (4) the couple's marriage and family life revolved around the wife's career rather than around the husband's.

Atkinson and Boles found that most of the senior-partner wives in their sample were in professional and business occupations traditionally defined as male and which are thus associated with higher status and income. In the majority of cases, these women had either already embarked on their careers or were in training for them at the time of their marriages, and both spouses knew at the outset that the wife's career would take precedence.

In other wife-as-senior-partner marriages (42 percent), the pattern evolved later as an accommodation to changing needs of the spouses. In one example cited by Atkinson and Boles, after a husband retired from his career as an officer in the military, his wife returned to college, earned a Ph.D., and became a university professor. "A husband's retirement or disenchantment can provide opportunities or the necessity for the wife to pursue her own career," write these researchers (p. 864). Another example they cite from their sample is that of a husband who resigned from a high-income position with a major company in order to raise chickens as a small farmer. The couple moved to a location that best served the wife's career interests as she set up her own business. (It could be argued that such "your turn/my turn" approaches illustrate the role flexibility in the *egalitarian* marriage pattern as discussed earlier.)

Most husbands in the Atkinson and Boles study worked in occupations that allowed them great flexibility in terms of both work schedules and locality, and 42 percent were self-employed. Only slightly more than a third of couples in which the wife's career was emphasized over the husband's had children living with them.

In assessing costs and rewards in this marital pattern, couples reported that being negatively evaluated by friends, relatives, work colleagues, and others was the major *cost* associated with their lifestyle. Wives were perceived as domineering and unladylike; husbands were viewed as losers, irresponsible, and less than real men in the eyes of many critics. Besides the social costs of being considered deviant, other costs mentioned by wives were having to bear the major responsibility for the family's financial support, fatigue, guilt over not being "a good wife" (particularly in household-chore performance), and insufficient time to be with the husband and children. The researchers found husbands consistently cited fewer costs or disadvantages than wives did, but the three costs cited most by the husbands were the time spent by the wives away from home, doing without household services traditionally provided by wives, and making sacrifices in their own careers.

In terms of *rewards* in marriages where the wife's career has higher status, both wives and husbands stressed three categories of benefits: achievement rewards, rewards within the marriage relationship, and (in cases where the respondents were parents) rewards for children.

Under *achievement rewards*, wives mentioned having the opportunity to pursue their chosen careers, financial gain, and feelings of independence and enhanced self-esteem. Husbands valued having freedom and resources to pursue their own interests. A majority of husbands also reported that their wives helped them in their own careers through business contacts wives made possible and through exchanging ideas and advice.

Under *rewards associated with their marriages,* over half the wives in the Atkinson and Boles sample mentioned greater freedom from household tasks and receiving emotional support from husbands. Husbands emphasized benefits to the marriage even more than wives. Not having to be the unique family providers, not having emotionally dependent wives, having wives who kept themselves attractive, and experiencing the pleasure of their wives' joy and pride in achievement were rewards cited by more than half the husbands.

Both husbands and wives reported that *major benefits children gained* from the wife-as-senior-partner marital pattern were increased time spent with fathers and an awareness of the possibilities of gender-role flexibility.

Atkinson and Boles don't view the wife-as-senior-partner marital pattern as simply the opposite of the husband-as-senior-partner, however. Societal norms and pressures influence ideas about the marital exchange. Thus, even though the wives are considered to have the primary responsibility for providing the family income, the husbands are not considered to have primary responsibility for household chores. "There is a cultural variable to take into account," write these sociologists (p. 867). In other words, traditional gender-role socialization and norms have left their mark, and senior-partner wives tend to take on the major responsibility for tasks around the home that have been traditionally assigned to wives. At the same time, the husbands in such marriages were found by these researchers to contribute more time to such chores than husbands in any of the other four marriage patterns.

Senior-partner wives also were found to follow certain traditional gender-role prescriptions which helped serve the purpose of compensatory mechanisms to make up for the couple's societally defined "deviant" lifestyle. In this sense, the wife in the senior-partner role could not be considered to exemplify full equality or beyond. As Atkinson and Boles write, commenting on some common patterns of behavior reported by senior-partner wives in their sample, "Catering to husbands' whims, salving males' egos, and striving to be sexually alluring are not indications of equality but rather of adaptations to patriarchal norms of appropriate female gender behavior" (p. 867).

On the other hand, husbands looked for special things they could do for their wives as well. The researchers suggest that such building up of "idiosyncratic credit" (doing something in one role to compensate for not fulfilling certain expectations in another role) is one of the most often employed mechanisms for coping with the strain of being considered socially deviant. It is a way of " 'excusing' or justifying deviant behavior by emphasizing other values" (p. 865). Other ways of minimizing the social costs of negative evaluations by others utilized by couples in which the wife had the superior occupation were *concealing information* about the difference in job status between husband and wife and *covering it over* through humor, boasting about talents and accomplishments of the husband, and other mechanisms designed to reduce stress and tension by denying the importance of being perceived as deviant.

It's possible that, as greater gender-role flexibility is accepted in society, couples who opt for a marital pattern in which the wife's occupation is given primary importance may experience less strain and find their chosen arrangement less costly. In the meantime, it can be viewed as a specially defined exchange relationship in which "wives exchange income for the opportunity to achieve and for household and emotional support from husbands; [and] husbands exchange household and emotional support for freedom from income provision responsibilities and for opportunities to engage in risky and less remunerative occupational pursuits" (Atkinson and Boles, 1984:867). Such exchanges on a *temporary* basis were touched upon in our discussion of the equal-partner marital pattern. But in the wife-as-senior-partner pattern, this system of exchanges describes the couple's habitual way of relating indefinitely.

CHAPTER HIGHLIGHTS

Under the owner-property model of marriage, a wife had no existence independent of her husband. She was dependent upon him for financial support, was required to obey and submit to him, and was expected to fulfill her wife-mother duties according to his wishes. The husband, for his part, was expected to be a *responsible* "owner" and take care of the material needs of his wife and children. His power was doubly reinforced because it rested on (1) wifely obedience as a societal norm and (2) his role as the sole income earner. As women gained independent access to economic resources, they improved their bargaining position within the marriage relationship. The owner-property model of marriage began to give way to the head-complement model in which a husband and wife were expected to be more to each other than sources of income, status, housekeeping, sexual exchanges, and children; they were now expected to be friends and lovers as well.

However, when the husband is defined as the main provider but the wife takes a job that contributes to the overall family income, her position as "complement" to the "head" changes. She becomes the *junior partner,* and her husband is the *senior partner.* His occupation still has primacy, because the wife in this pattern of marriage is less committed to continuous labor-force participation than is her husband. Wives in the junior-partner position are expected to put family and household needs before work goals, preventing such wives from pursuing the direct, orderly sequence of occupational and achievement endeavors that has traditionally characterized men's lives.

In an *equal-partner* marriage, both spouses are equally committed to their respective careers, and each one's occupation is considered as important as the other's. Both partners share equally the duty to provide and the right to be provided for, and both are equally responsible for household tasks. Both wife and husband have equal power in decision-making, including decisions about whether and when to have children. Parenthood is not automatically assumed in this pattern for marriage but is considered optional. The goal of the equal-partner arrangement is not to "destroy" marriage but to *change* it so that both partners can fulfill individual aspirations unhindered by gender-role stereotypes and traditional ideas about the division of labor.

In a minority of marriages, the wife is committed to an occupation with higher status and earnings than that of the husband. Such couples have found ways to minimize the costs of being regarded deviant and report numerous rewards associated with their personal choice of a wife-as-senior-partner alternative marital pattern and the system of exchanges they have worked out.

Throughout the world, women have always worked—a fact acknowledged in the old folk saying: "Man works from sun to sun, but women's work is never done." But women's work, whether in the hot fields of an agricultural economy or over hot stoves as family caretakers, has been undervalued and usually unpaid. As such, it has often gone unrecognized. Without access to *earned income* and the freedom and power such earnings convey, wives traditionally have been considered economically dependent upon their husbands and under their husbands' control. That's why the owner-property pattern of marriage was taken for granted in custom and law. But as opportunities for *paid* work began opening up to women, the owner-property marriage model showed signs of weakening and being replaced by the newer models of marriage discussed in the preceding chapter. Let's now turn our attention to how these changes came about.

HISTORICAL PERSPECTIVE ON WOMEN IN THE LABOR FORCE

As women gained independent access to economic resources, they inevitably improved their bargaining within marriage. Though changes were slight and gradual, women began to realize the inherent contradiction in being able to gain resources on their own while still being considered the property of their husbands. In 1848, the first Woman's Rights Convention called attention to numerous grievances, pointing out wrongs perpetrated by men and reinforced by laws men had drawn up. Among the complaints were these: "[Man] has made [the woman], if married, in the eye of the law, civilly dead. He has taken from her all right in property, even to the wages she earns" (quoted in Rossi, 1973b). There were many injustices under

such a system. Some husbands even hired out their wives and then appropriated their wages. Such unfair practices gave rise to agitation for new legislation on property rights for married women, and various states began to enact laws that were more equitable.

Even prior to the modern era, some women did have certain limited occupational opportunities. Often such women were single or widowed, and they were involved in the guild system. During the Middle Ages, women worked as cobblers, belt and sweater makers, leather dressers, purse makers, furriers, bakers, saddlers, tanners, goldsmiths, lace makers, and embroiderers of such items as church vestments, hangings for religious display, and coats of arms. In some areas of Europe, guild records indicate that over 200 occupations were open to women (Campbell, 1893:46–49; Lasch, 1973; Oakley, 1974a, chaps. 2–3). But when the guild system ended, women lost the few opportunities they had begun to possess.

During the colonial period in America (from 1620 to 1776), there were almost no female wage earners, except for those employed in domestic service. A few women did engage in home-based spinning and weaving and other types of work associated with textiles and clothing production. A woman named Betsy Metcalf discovered that meadow grass could be bleached and braided into straw goods, and this process led to a large and lucrative industry. And the American Revolution, like all wars, saw wives step into positions of heading family businesses and farms temporarily vacated by their husbands.

It should be kept in mind that this historical description refers chiefly to white women. The great majority of black women were laboring as slaves on Southern plantations. And just as it was cotton that kept black women in slavery past the 1790s, so it was cotton that at that time altered economic opportunities for white women. According to Campbell (1893:68–72), "It is with the birth of the cotton industry that the work and wages of women begin to take coherent shape." For the first time in history, large and ever increasing numbers of women began to get out from under their own domestic roofs to work under commercial roofs (spinning mills), earning sums of money hitherto unknown. In this version of the factory system, women from the beginning took a larger part than men. For example, in the first federal count of spinning-industry employees in 1816, there were 66,000 women and female children. There were 24,000 boys under 17 years of age, and 10,000 males 17 years and older.

The women who worked in those New England factories throughout the first half of the nineteenth century were mostly young, single, and poorly educated. Their wages were about half or a third of those paid to men. Nevertheless, the numbers of women engaged in a variety of occupations continued to increase throughout the nineteenth century. The mechanization necessary to carry on the Civil War created a whole new series of trade-type occupations, and the reduced numbers of available men made it possible for many women to enter these newly emerging trades.

Exactly how many women were working is hard to answer accurately because the Census Bureau had difficulty getting families to admit that they contained employed females. This hesitancy was due to fear of disapproval, since many persons considered female employment undesirable and frowned on women who dared to deviate from tradition. The 1870 census recorded the number of women workers as 1,836,288. But it seems evident that there were additional women workers who were not enumerated. By 1880,

Various economic and legal changes meant a gradual recognition of women as persons in their own right, causing profound changes in the marital balance of power. This nineteenth-century cartoon lampooned women's quest for equality. (Library of Congress)

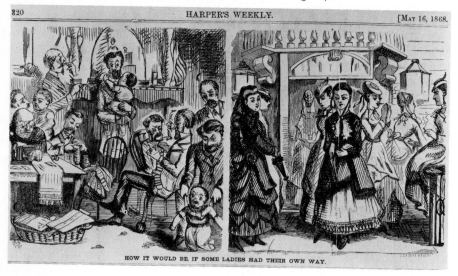

HOW IT WOULD BE, IF SOME LADIES HAD THEIR OWN WAY.

the figure had risen to 2,647,157; but again there was concern about underreporting. The 1890 census showed a 10 percent increase in women wage earners over the 1880 figure. By 1900, 21 percent of all women over 14 years of age were employed, although only 6 percent of all *married* women were in the labor force (Cain, 1966:2).

That 6-percent figure for married working women is probably higher than anything that occurred in the prior century, and the record in this century has been one of dramatic change upward in the actual numbers and proportion of employed wives. By 1940, the proportion had doubled to 14 percent and has continued to increase over each decade since, as Figure 9-1 shows. By 1980, *half* of all married women with husband present were in the labor force; and by 1984, the figure was 53 percent (U.S. Bureau of the Census, *Statistical Abstract of the United States: 1985*, 1984:398).

Employment Opportunities and the Marital Power Balance

This steady increase in access to and control of economic resources by *married* women is perhaps the most significant point about the 200-year upward trend in female employment. The availability of work opportunities and the chance to gain resources on their own caused wives to question the existing marital-role structure. They began demanding more rights, more of a voice in decision-making, more control over their own property, and so on. During the nineteenth and twentieth centuries, numerous legal changes gradually took place which played a large part in removing the wife from the position of property and recognizing her more as a person in her own right (Calhoun, vol. 2, 1919:126–129; Brownlee and Brownlee, 1976:265–266). When women were permit-

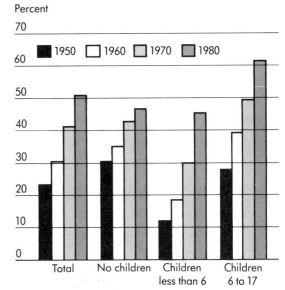

FIGURE 9-1 Participation rates of wives in the labor force, by presence and age of children: 1950 to 1980. (*Source:* U.S. Bureau of the Census, Special Demographic Analyses, CDS-80-8, *American Women: Three Decades of Change* (Washington, DC: U.S. Government Printing Office, 1983), p. 17.)

ted to inherit, earn, control, and dispose of their own property to a greater measure than before, the traditional marriage arrangement was profoundly affected. The changes brought about in marital-role structures (increased rights and power for women) in turn would affect still further labor-force participation by women (with more women feeling they had the right to work outside the home); and again in feedback fashion, this would affect marriages still further (with increased power for wives because of their increased economic resources).

What we see at work here is the principle of alternative rewards described in Chapter 4. A person's power over another person depends on the resources he or she holds out to that person, how dependent that second person is on these resources, and whether or not that second person can find alternative sources for such benefits elsewhere. At the beginning of the nineteenth century, a woman had few options open to her besides marriage. If she wanted to be provided for, she needed a husband. This gave men a tremendous amount of power over women. Utterly dependent upon a man for economic resources, a woman became his property through marriage. However, as employment opportunities increased for women, a woman could provide for her own needs. Why sit idly by waiting to get married when one could engage in the numerous occupational pursuits opening up to women? As the nineteenth century ended, almost half (46 percent) of all single women were employed.

Although it was true that only 6 percent of married women worked outside the home and their rates of employment increased more slowly than those of single women, the *availability* of employment had a considerable impact on even those wives who didn't choose to enter the labor force. As the nineteenth century progressed, there opened up the possibility of choosing another set of rewards than those held out by husbands, and the existence of that option weakened the power of husbands—whether or not their wives actually worked. The *possibility* of a wife's becoming a wage earner gradually became part of the role rights of the wife-mother, thereby putting married women in a position where they had the capability of bargaining instead of merely yielding to their husbands' wishes. Women were no longer bound to unquestioning obedience out of a sense of helpless dependence on male economic support. Instead, wives could offer suggestions, disagree, counsel and advise, even try to insist on a particular course of action.

In moving from her status as property, the married woman could go in one of two directions. The existence of the option to earn income meant either that she could stay at home to look after the household but would now be her husband's counterpart or *complement,* or she could work outside the home and thereby take on the *junior-partner* status in marriage. In either case, the fact that the employment option was always there meant that her negotiating power in marriage was increasing.

Debate over Industrialization and the Valuation of Women's Work

Some scholars disagree over whether the status of women in Western culture has been raised or lowered through industrialization. Similar questions arose in Chapter 3 where we looked at "developing" societies—those currently experiencing movement from agriculture-based economies toward urbanization and industrialization. There we saw that modern technology and the factory system may eliminate many occupations in which women traditionally engaged, thereby hurting many women; but at the same time, industrialization has opened new opportunities for many women and has given them access to economic, status, and educational benefits previously denied them.

Sociologist Ann Oakley (1974a) sees industrialization as devaluing women's work and status. Contrasting preindustrial Great Britain with the situation afterward, she writes of the esteem that had been given to women's productive labors in agriculture, trade, and home-based industries and speaks of ways industrialization stripped women of their former status. The culmination was a removal of productive work *from* the home at the same time that women were expected to remain centered *in* the home. According to Oakley, the result was "the modern differentiation of gender roles and the modern division between domestic and productive work."

On the other hand, historian Edward Shorter (1977) is convinced that an examination of the "real lives of women in eighteenth-century farm-and-craft families" of the Western world reveals a status of considerable inferiority. He takes issue with those who argue that industrialization was "bad for women." "Over the long haul," writes Shorter, "the participation of women in the *paid* labor force was enormously increased rather than diminished—a fact that initiated the dismantling of the staggering patriarchy of the peasantry" (p. xviii).

In the early days of the New England settlement, it is true that women's productive work was recognized and valued, but at the same time "women were considered adjunct and secondary to men in economic life," writes social historian Nancy F. Cott (1977:20), pointing out that "divorce records of the eighteenth century clearly differentiated the two spouses' economic roles." The husband was expected "to supply or provide"; the wife was expected "to use goods frugally and to obey." Cott suggests that the meaning of women's economic status was "diluted" and less obvious during the period when all family members worked together as a "self-contained productive unit," but that the law made clear that the earnings and property of women belonged to their husbands. And when women did work outside the home, "wage rates reflected the expectation that they would rely on men as providers." Furthermore, women lacked opportunities to train for professions, since higher education was closed off to them (Cott, 1977:21–22).

While undeniably the transition to an industrialized society involves many complex factors, including the impact on women's sta-

Scholars disagree over whether the status of women in Western culture has been raised or lowered as a result of industrialization. (© Eric Kroll/Taurus Photos)

tus, it would seem inaccurate to say that women in the United States gradually came to be less valued as productive workers and more dependent upon men as providers. Ideologically at least, husbands were regarded as heads of households and primary breadwinners even in *pre*industrial early settlements where husbands and wives labored side by side in cottage industries and on farms.

The picture may have been different in England, and it is that country on which Oakley (1974a:32) focuses when she writes that "for men [industrialization] enlarged the world outside the home, chiefly by expanding the range of occupations available to them." For women, on the other hand, it came to mean a contraction of the world into the cramped space of the home, doing away with family labor and the family wage and creating the role of the dependent housewife who looks out on the world through the window above the dish-filled kitchen sink (Oakley, 1974a, chap. 3). Industrialization took place earlier in Great Britain than in the United States; and further, the rigidly structured British class system separating the nobility and the commoners may have entered into the greater equality of female and male co-workers in crafts and farm work during preindustrial days. Oakley writes that although the common law embodied the notion "that women ought to be subject to men," ordinary people ignored it in their everyday lives. She explains:

"Common law" was the law of the nobles. Farming people and artisans depended in their dealings with one another on customs that decreed the independence of women and their equality with men. These customs dated back to the beginnings of English society, to the Anglo-Saxon era, when not only was there equality between the sexes in practice, but also, effectively, in law. (chap. 2; p. 28)

What we need to keep in mind is that, as Shorter reminds us, *over the long haul*—regardless of all that has been problematic along the way—women seem to have benefited by industrialization because of the increased options open to them. Oakley's comment about industrialization's role in enlarging the world outside the home for *men,* "chiefly by expanding the range of occupations available to them," could gradually over the years seem just as applicable to women. And it is this opening up of options beyond the four walls of the home that has, as we have seen, made its impact felt on how husbands and wives perceive the structure of marriage.

EXAMINING WIVES' EMPLOYMENT DEMOGRAPHICALLY

At this point, we may find it useful to examine national census data to discover some of the factors associated with the labor-force participation of married women. Viewing a subject from the standpoint of *demography* (the study of vital and social statistics characterizing a certain population) can help us get an overall picture. Race, for example, is one such demographic factor we need to examine.

Race

Although the gap between the percentage of black and white married women in the labor force has been narrowing in recent years, *black wives continue to be more likely to be employed than are white wives* (Wallace, 1980; Glick, 1981; U.S. Bureau of the Census, *Current Population Reports,* p-60, no. 142, 1984:33–34 [table 13]). This reflects the combined effects of historical and current patterns discussed earlier—the long-standing economic discrimination against black males which forced black females into the labor force and the resultant norms which grew up among blacks so that female employment came to be accepted and respected (See E. Smith, 1985; Moses, 1985). At the same time, the economic discrimination that black women themselves feel—both as blacks and as women—stands out in Table 9-A.

Many black wives work because they have to rather than because they necessarily want to. Sociologist Ivan Nye (1974a:28) has pointed out that "for minority families, those without an employed wife are moderately deprived with respect to other minority families and extremely deprived compared to whites." In 1982, black married-couple fam-

TABLE 9-A Median* and mean personal incomes by sex and race, 1982

	MEDIAN INCOME	MEAN (AVERAGE) INCOME
Males		
White	$14,748	$18,071
Black	8,838	11,050
Females		
White	5,967	8,295
Black	5,263	7,349

*The median is the midpoint in a group of numbers arranged from lowest to highest (or vice versa). In the matter of income, it means that half of the persons in each category have incomes above the median listed for that category, and half have incomes below that amount.
SOURCE: Figures are from the U.S. Bureau of the Census, *Statistical Abstract of the United States: 1985*, 105th ed., December 1984, p. 452.

ilies in which the wife was not employed had a median income of $12,469. But that figure jumped to $25,359 if the wife was employed. (See Table 9-B). Clearly, a wife's income can make a significant difference—especially among groups which have otherwise been granted fewer rewards from the economic-opportunity system.

On the other hand many black wives are in the labor force not only because they *have* to be but because they *want* to be. Since among blacks it is normative for women to work, black females grow up expecting to work (Scanzoni, 1977:228–232). A study undertaken by the U.S. Department of Labor (1970) indicated that black women more than white women were committed to the idea of paid employment even if their financial situation made it unnecessary. In an attempt to measure attitudes toward work, women in the age range of 30 to 44 years were asked: "If by some chance you (and your husband) were to get enough money to live comfortably without working, do you think you would work anyway?" In such a hypothetical situation, black women at all socioeconomic levels were interested in continuing to work to a greater extent than was true of white women, with the exception of those white women in higher-level occupations, who also indicated high work commitment.

Paid Work, Women, and Children

In analyzing census data on the participation of women in the labor force, demographer Malcolm S. Cohen (1969) concluded that of

TABLE 9-B Median family income by type of family, race, and labor-force status of wife, 1982

TYPE OF FAMILY	MEDIAN INCOME	
	BLACK	WHITE
All families	$13,599	$24,603
All married-couple families	20,586	26,443
Wife in paid labor force	25,359	30,801
Wife not in paid labor force	12,469	21,849
Male householder, no wife present	14,661	21,416
Female householder, no husband present	7,458	13,496

SOURCE: U.S. Bureau of the Census, *Current Population Reports*, ser. P-60, no. 142, *Money Income of Households, Families, and Persons in the United States, 1982*, 1984. Adapted from Table 13, pp. 33–34.

all demographic factors associated with a married woman's working, it is the number of children she has and how young they are that most influence her employment behavior. His observation still holds true today—even though the percentage of employed mothers is much higher than it was at the time he wrote.

One fact that emerges from census data is that employed women tend to have fewer children than do women who are not employed. This finding could be explained by either assuming that women who want to work choose to limit their family size so that employment is possible or easier, or one could argue that women who have larger numbers of children are not in the labor force (even if they would like to be) because child-care responsibilities at home act as barriers to employment. In other words, does having children keep women from employment, or does employment keep women from having as many children? These questions will be discussed more fully in a later chapter on reproduction.

Of course, many women with children *do* work—even women whose children are quite young. In 1950, some 12 percent of mothers with children under 6 years of age were working. By 1960, the figure had jumped to

19 percent; and by the end of that decade, it had increased another third to 30 percent and continued upward through the 1970s and 1980s. Table 9-C shows the growth in labor-force participation rates of married mothers of preschoolers between 1970 and 1984 (latest available statistics).

Another interesting picture emerging from the demographic data may be seen by referring back to Figure 9-1 on page 277. Married women with children between the ages of 6 and 17 have a higher labor-force participation rate than do even those with no children under age 18, where home responsibilities would be less. One explanation might be that women who have no children or whose children are grown may find their husbands' incomes adequate for the standard of living they wish to maintain. But for others, the presence of children brings economic burdens. To attain a desired standard of living, the family may find that two incomes will be necessary; so the wife goes to work full- or part-time to buy that new freezer or color television or to help with house or car payments. There are also the direct costs of childrearing—providing for food, clothing, medical and dental needs, savings for college, and so on. Families with preschoolers face childrearing expenses too, of course; but in these cases the woman considering employment is hindered by the problem of finding someone to care for the children while she is gone. Mothers of *school-age* children simply find it much easier to enter the labor force.

Those mothers who always planned on employment but who took time out for childbearing and childrearing also help swell the ranks of employed mothers of school-age children. These are women who were employed earlier (in many cases) but whose work pattern was interrupted by choice. They considered themselves out of the labor

TABLE 9-C *Labor-force participation rates for married mothers of preschoolers, by age of child, March 1970 and March 1984*

AGE OF YOUNGEST CHILD	MARCH 1970	MARCH 1984
1 year and under	24.0%	46.8%
2 years	30.5	53.5
3 years	34.5	57.6
4 years	39.4	59.2
5 years	36.9	57.0

SOURCE: Howard Hayghe, "Working Mothers Reach Record Number in 1984," *Monthly Labor Review,* December, 1984, p. 31.

market only *temporarily* for one comparatively small stage of their lives. When the children go to school, the mothers go back to work (U.S. Department of Labor, 1973:22–24).

Traditionally, the presence of preschoolers in the family has not affected the employment status of black women as much as it has the employment status of white women. Again, this finding relates to economic need and the higher proportion of family income provided by these wives. It also relates to the tradition and norms supporting female employment among blacks. At the same time, as in so many areas, the gap in patterns characterizing blacks and whites is narrowing. Mothers of Hispanic origin now have the lowest rates of participation in the labor force, which may be partially explained by their cultural heritage as well as their comparative lack of educational and occupational opportunities (Hayghe, 1984:33). Table 9-D compares the percentages of white, black, and Hispanic mothers in the labor force according to their marital status and at various stages of their children's lives. It also focuses on the number of children living in families (defined by the Census Bureau as discussed earlier) whose mothers are in the labor force.

Maternal Employment and Effects on Children A question often arises at this point: How are children likely to be affected by their mother's employment? Until rather recently, most people believed that children of employed mothers would suffer emotional damage and be hindered in their development because of the long, daily physical separation from their mothers. However, in the 1960s, behavioral-science research began bringing to light findings that went a long way toward dispelling such beliefs. In various studies, as children of working and nonworking mothers were tested and compared, no

important differences showed up. Psychological testing was used in order to compare the anxiety scores and personality-adjustment scores of children whose mothers were in the labor force and of children whose mothers were full-time housewives. In addition, social scientists compared children's school grades, observed their social and emotional development, and so on. Some studies focused on preschoolers and others on school-aged children. But all in all, the findings did not support the old notion that a woman's working will somehow harm her children (see Ferriss, 1971:106 for a brief summary of these studies; also Hoffman, 1974).

In 1963, Ivan Nye and Lois Wladis Hoffman co-authored a book entitled *The Employed Mother in America* that attempted to gather together all available relevant research on the subject of maternal employment conducted between 1957 and 1962. Ten years after the book was published, Hoffman (1973:212) wrote: "The working mother had been considered quite a devil, and a great deal of the research reported in the book had originally been undertaken in the hope of documenting the ill effects of maternal employment. But the data simply would not cooperate." (See also Lamb, 1984:73–75.)

Hoffman points out that it really shouldn't have been surprising that "examined as a general phenomenon, the standard study with adequate controls yielded no significant differences between the children of working and nonworking women," because maternal employment in itself is too wide a variable to study. All kinds of women work at all kinds of different jobs, under various conditions, with children of different ages, and so on. Such things as these would have to be considered. Hoffman points out that we may expect differences in effects of a mother's working according to whether the woman is a member

TABLE 9-D Labor-force participation rates of mothers and number of children in families, selected characteristics, by race and Hispanic origin, March 1984

CHARACTERISTIC	WHITE	BLACK	HISPANIC ORIGIN
Participation Rates of Mothers			
Total with children under age 18	60.2%	63.3%	48.7%
Age 6 to 17, none younger	67.9	70.3	58.3
Under age 6	51.3	56.8	41.0
Under age 3	47.0	52.1	36.0
Married, spouse present	57.9	70.3	49.1
Divorced	80.5	75.2	63.4
Separated	63.8	61.3	42.9
Widowed	59.6	59.3	([1])
Never married	53.5	49.4	35.7
Children In Families (in thousands)			
Total under age 18	48,473	7,743	5,235
Mother in labor force	27,047	4,675	2,343
Mother not in labor force	20,463	2,840	2,802
In married-couple families	40,641	3,775	3,934
Mother in labor force	22,403	2,517	1,826
Mother not in labor force	18,238	1,228	2,108
In families maintained by women[2]	6,869	3,740	1,211
Mother in labor force	4,644	2,127	517
Mother not in labor force	2,225	1,613	694
In families maintained by men[2]	962	228	90
Father in labor force[3]	871	170	69
Father not in labor force	91	58	22

[1]Data not shown where base is less than 75,000.
[2]Families where parent is never-married, widowed, divorced, or separated.
[3]Includes children living with fathers on or off a military post.
NOTE: Children are defined as "own" children of the family. Included are never-married sons, daughters, stepchildren and adopted children. Excluded are other related children such as grandchildren, nieces, nephews, and cousins, and unrelated children.
SOURCE: Howard Hayghe, "Working Mothers Reach Record Number in 1984," *Monthly Labor Review*, December 1984, p. 33.

of the working class or the middle class, whether she works out of necessity or out of choice, whether her children are younger or older, boys or girls. Other important considerations are the hours the woman works, the plans she makes for her household, child-care arrangements, her attitudes about her role, and so on. "But even those studies which introduced such breakdowns found few negative effects and several positive ones," Hoffman reports.

She does, however, refer to one study that "suggested a bit of caution." In a study she conducted of working mothers of elementary school children, she found that children whose mothers feel *guilty* about working may be negatively affected. It is not the mother's employment in itself that seems to cause the problem, but rather the mother's attitude toward it and how she responds.

Hoffman found that some women who enjoyed working felt guilty about this and evidently tried to compensate by overindulging their children. For example, children of these mothers helped less around the house than children of nonworking mothers and were indulged in other ways as well. The results of this showed up in their interactions with other children and in their school performances. The children of mothers who worked and felt guilty about it "played more with younger children than with their age mates; they were less likely to initiate interaction with their classmates; their academic performance was not up to par." It is important to note that "the women who liked their work were more typically—though not exclusively—the middle class, and better educated." Thus, Hoffman's conclusions are significant: "These are almost the only negative effects of maternal employment found in the middle class to date, and they appear to result not from employment *per se* but from guilt about employment" (Hoffman, 1973:212–213; Nye and Hoffman, 1963:95–105).

On the other hand, writes Hoffman, there is considerable support for the idea that maternal employment can have a positive effect, particularly on girls. The daughters of high-achieving women are also likely to be high-achieving and to have less restrictive self-concepts because of the role models their mothers provide. Such girls are less apt to limit their career horizons because of gender-role stereotypes (Hoffman, 1973:213; also see Hoffman and Nye, 1974).

With regard to the effects of a mother's working on sons, there is little data available except for a few very limited studies. Hoffman refers, for example, to a study of a small sample of gifted boys. The low achievers in

the group had more employed mothers, but the high achievers had more mothers who were *professionally* employed—that is, they were women who did not merely hold a job but were committed to a career in a profession (Hoffman, 1973:214n; also see Hoffman, 1974).

Two other researchers who studied children's *attitudes* toward their mothers' employment also found that "when the mother has positive feelings about her job, the effects on the child tend to be positive." If the mother's employment is not a source of conflict for her but a part of life she enjoys, the child also tends to view the mother's working

The daughters of high-achieving women are also likely to be high achieving and to have less restrictive self-concepts because of the role models their mothers provide. (© Elaine Rebman 1985/Photo Researchers, Inc.)

SOME COMMENTS OF CHILDREN FROM TWO-EARNER FAMILIES

Melinda, 13: There was never a time when both my parents didn't work. My parents are away a lot all through the week because besides having regular nine-to-five hours, my father sometimes works through the night and then he'll come home in the morning to change. Both my parents have a lot of meetings.

It seems special when they are home. We take more advantage of it. But it definitely makes me more independent, because they're not around to do everything for me and make all my decisions. If my mother were at home all day, she would do more cleaning and would always have everything ready for me. It's like babying me all my life, so I definitely think it's better that she work, because I am becoming much more independent. I feel free that I make my own decisions, because I've proven that I can by doing it. . . .

Jed, 12: . . . My mother hired a babysitter on a daily basis, so they don't need to be home most of the time. We've had this babysitter for about three years now and she's almost like a part of the family. So even if my parents aren't home, there's always somebody I can talk to.

A friend of mine told me he would like not having his parents home a lot, so that he could learn how to be independent when he grows up, but I think that's silly, because when you're a kid, that's your chance to have someone to depend on. Why not use that time to have somebody to depend on, and then when you grow older you can learn to depend on yourself?

SOURCE: Excerpted from Dorriet Kavanaugh, "Four Bright Children Speak Out on Having *Both* Parents Work," *New Woman,* March-April 1979, pp. 28, 32. As reprinted from original source, Dorriet Kavanaugh, *Listen to Us* (New York: Workman Publishing, 1978).

---

as something constructive and "part of normal family life style" (Trimberger and MacLean, 1982:472). Still other studies indicate that a major benefit of maternal employment is the development in both daughters and sons of more flexible gender-role attitudes (Lamb, 1982, 1984; Mortimer and Sorensen, 1984).

Limited research on day-care centers thus far indicates that attendance at centers of high quality neither benefits nor harms children's intellectual development nor does it weaken their emotional ties with their mothers. In terms of *social* development, "the existing data indicate that day-care-reared children, when compared with age-mates reared at home, interact more with peers in both positive and negative ways" (Belsky and Steinberg, 1978:944).

Arranging for Child Care Most young children whose mothers are employed are not in group-care centers. According to government figures, between one-fifth and one-fourth of employed mothers have arranged for their children to have *parental* care during their working hours (U.S. Bureau of the Census, *Current Population Reports,* ser. P-23, no. 129, 1983). Either the father or the mother may be the caretaker. This may be accomplished by juggling work schedules carefully, by taking advantage of "flexi-time"

4-MONTH-OLD ATTENDS COLLEGE CLASS

Asheville (AP)—There are two points to command the interest of students in an "Introduction to American Government Class" at the University of North Carolina at Asheville.

They are Dr. William Sabo, who recently was chosen Teacher of the Year at the school, and his infant son, who sleeps in a sling across his father's chest as Sabo teaches.

"This way we don't have to leave him with a baby-sitter. That makes it nice," Sabo said. . . .

Sabo and his wife, Theresa, have themselves on a split-second schedule this summer so that they can care for the baby without the help of a sitter.

Mrs. Sabo works as a psychometrist at Highland Hospital. He teaches two classes, the American government class from 9:40 to 11:10 a.m. and a humanities class from 11:20 a.m. to 1:20 p.m.

"I come out of the first class, change notes, meet her at the street, hand her the baby and go back and teach the second class," Sabo said. "She brings Jeff home while I teach the second class. She meets me after class. I drive her back to work and then bring Jeff home. We have it timed to the second." . . . .

SOURCE: Lynne Billings, *Greensboro (NC) News and Record,* Sept. 2, 1984.

arrangements in some businesses which allow employees to choose their own hours rather than insisting that everyone work the same eight-to-five period, and by working at an income-earning profession or job in the home (see Bird, 1979). If neither parent can be home with preschool children, the children are most likely to be cared for by some other relative or a nonrelative either in the children's own home or in someone else's home. Table 9-E shows the principal types of child-care arrangements utilized by employed mothers of different marital statuses.

Seventeen percent of employed mothers find it necessary for various reasons to use a combination of child-care arrangements. For example, nursery-school or day-care center hours may not adequately fit with a mother's working schedule, or the father's work schedule may be such that he can't be with the children for a certain period of time before the mother's arrival home. In such cases, other arrangements have to be made for child care for a certain interval of time. School-aged children, for example, may take care of themselves and a younger sibling for a short period of time in some instances.

Only about 15 percent of employed mothers of preschoolers utilize day care centers and nursery schools as their principal arrangement for child care. The most likely users of group care are women employed full time, women with one or more years of college, and women with high family incomes. Black women are somewhat more likely to use group-care services for small children than are white women and women of Spanish origin. Women in central cities and suburban areas are more likely to use group-care arrangements than are women living in nonmetropolitan areas—a fact that may be associated with the availability of such services (or lack of them) in different places (U.S. Bureau of the Census, *Current Population Re-*

TABLE 9-E Percent distribution of principal type of child care arrangements used by mothers 18 to 44 years old for their youngest child under 5 years, by marital and employment status: June 1982. (Numbers in thousands. Data restricted to employed women having at least one child under 5 years old.)

MARITAL STATUS OF MOTHER AND PRINCIPAL CHILD-CARE ARRANGEMENT	JUNE 1982		
	TOTAL EMPLOYED	EMPLOYED FULL TIME	EMPLOYED PART TIME
All Marital Statuses			
Number	5,086	3,263	1,824
Care in child's home	30.6%	25.7%	39.3%
By father	13.9	10.3	20.3
By other relative	11.2	10.3	12.7
By nonrelative	5.5	5.1	6.3
Care in another home	40.2	43.8	34.0
By relative	18.2	19.7	15.6
By nonrelative	22.0	24.1	18.4
Group care center	14.8	18.8	7.5
Mother cares for child while working	9.1	6.2	14.4
Other arrangements[1]	0.2	0.3	0.1
Don't know/no answer	5.1	5.3	4.7
Married, Husband Present			
Number	4,093	2,524	1,569
Care in child's home	30.4%	25.5%	38.0%
By father	16.8	12.8	23.1
By other relative	8.8	8.5	9.3
By nonrelative	4.8	4.2	5.6
Care in another home	40.7	45.0	34.0
By relative	18.0	19.5	15.7
By nonrelative	22.7	25.5	18.3
Group care center	13.4	17.3	7.2
Mother cares for child while working	10.5	7.1	16.1
Other arrangements[1]	0.1	0.2	0.1
Don't know/no answer	4.9	5.0	4.6
All Other Material Statuses[2]			
Number	993	738	255
Care in child's home	31.6%	26.2%	47.5%
By father	1.9	1.5	3.0
By other relative	21.0	16.6	33.8
By nonrelative	8.7	8.1	10.7
Care in another home	38.2	39.6	33.8
By relative	19.0	20.5	14.6
By nonrelative	19.2	19.1	19.2
Group care center	20.2	23.8	9.7

TABLE 9-E (*continued*)

MARITAL STATUS OF MOTHER AND PRINCIPAL CHILD-CARE ARRANGEMENT	JUNE 1982		
	TOTAL EMPLOYED	EMPLOYED FULL TIME	EMPLOYED PART TIME
All Marital Statuses			
Mother cares for child while working	3.3	3.2	3.9
Other arrangements[1]	0.5	0.6	—
Don't know/no answer	6.1	6.5	5.2

‾Rounds to zero.
[1]Includes child taking care of self.
[2]Includes married, husband absent (Including separated), widowed, divorced, and never-married women.
SOURCE: U.S. Bureau of the Census, *Current Population Reports,* ser. P-23, no. 129, *Child Care Arrangements of Working Mothers: June 1982* (Washington, D.C.: U.S. Government Printing Office, 1983), pp. 4–5.

FIGURE 9-2 Percentage of employed mothers 18 to 44 years old who use group care services as the principal type of child-care arrangement for their youngest child under 5 years old: June 1982. (*Source:* U.S. Bureau of the Census, Current Population Reports, Series P-23, No. 129, *Child Care Arrangements of Working Mothers: June, 1982* (Washington, DC: U.S. Government Printing Office, 1983), p. 12.)

Percent using group care services

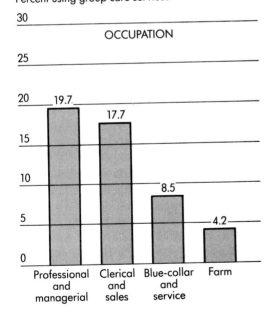

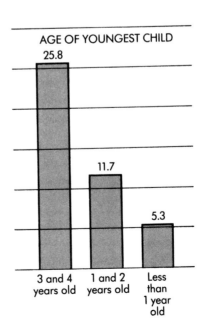

ports, ser. P-23, no. 129, 1983:11–13, 22–23).

Two other demographic factors that have shown up in government-sponsored research may be seen in Figure 9-2. There we see that mothers of infants and toddlers are less likely to use group-care services than are mothers with children past these age groups. And, in terms of the mother's occupation, profes-sional and managerial women are more likely than are women in other occupations to use group-care services as their main arrange-ment for caring for their children during working hours. Because their hours are often long and variable, women in such professions often have unique problems in finding ade-quate child care, as is pointed out in the ac-companying boxed insert.

THE SEARCH FOR LIVE-IN CHILD CARE

Every Sunday night and Monday morning, thousands of illegal aliens—women who are originally from Panama, Jamaica, Haiti, Mexico, and Colombia—join crowds of American commuters on their way to work. Their destination is not a sweatshop or a farm field, but a suburban or city home with children in it.

The reason is obvious. The rise in the number of women holding professional, managerial, and entrepreneurial jobs—women who can afford to get off the child-care-center waiting lists and look for private in-home child-care help—has created a demand that is not being met by the supply of legal American workers. In a real sense, this worker shortage, coupled with the inadequacy of group care, is a threat to the continued ability of American women to penetrate well-paying, high-level jobs. Because such jobs often come with the requirements of overtime, dinner meetings, and travel, women need household help with more flexible hours so that they can manage careers and children too. Without such help a woman's executive position—not to mention her sanity—may be at risk. And without available workers, the working mother is often forced to hire illegal aliens who live a shadowed existence, or students who can commit themselves to work for at least a year. . . .

Why has the problem of household help been so underexposed? For one thing, it is hard to erase the "Upstairs, Downstairs" impression that only the idle rich need help with their children. Furthermore, the stigma that makes household work and child care seem demeaning has endured. Since World War I, it was often the only kind of work available to black women and immigrants. With its low pay, long hours, and lack of status, it has become work to be avoided, and as opportunities for women of all colors have increased in the workplace, many have been quick to leave domestic employment behind. At the same time, more and more women have taken jobs with long and variable hours, business trips, and after-hours conferences, and they urgently need at-home help. But their consciousness of the stigma attached to domestic work prevents them from publicly speaking out about the difficulties of getting the help they need. And guilt about not taking care of their own children—still ingrained in most of us, despite our intellectual understanding that no guilt is warranted—also makes it hard to shift a portion of child-care responsibility to someone else.

The fact is that despite the history of low pay for domestics, today in some areas this work commands wages at least comparable to clerical jobs, and often much more. In an extreme case, one friend had to pay $350 a week to get the kind of person she could trust with her baby. In New York City, employment agencies that specialize in household help laugh at offers of under $150 per week for five days of work (though $200 seems to be average), with vacation and holidays, and room and board, if the workers are to live in. And the women they supply for these jobs are very often illegal aliens. In fact, instructing such an agency that you want to hire only a legal resident may mean getting no candidates at all.

When your newspaper want ad screens out illegals, it usually brings no responses. Calls to state employment services also end in futility. Indeed, state labor officials spend much of their time, and many tax dollars, certifying that no Americans are available for household work. This certification is part of the bureaucratic nightmare involved in a family's "sponsoring" an illegal alien, often one who is already working for the family. Sponsoring means that you as an employer must first convince your state labor department, and then the U.S. Immigration and Naturalization Service, that you have a job available and need this particular alien to perform it. "Sponsorship" is also the goal of the illegal alien. She wants only what waves of immigrants who came before her wanted: to become a legal U.S. resident and to work for a living.

SOURCE: Frances Cerra, "Live-In Child Care," *Ms., 14,* no. 2 (August 1985), pp. 50–52.

Some mothers of young children, desiring the rewards of employment but aware of the costs of less time and energy for involvement with their children, are opting for part-time employment. They feel this arrangement is more compatible with their parental role (Thomson, 1980). In many careers, however, such an option doesn't exist at the present time. Some companies are trying to help employees solve the child-care dilemma, as the boxed insert shows.

COMPANIES GET INVOLVED IN CHILD CARE

Cincinnati—Last year was a nightmare for Carol Berning. Each day after dropping off her two pre-school children at the baby sitter's, the 34-year-old consumer research manager for Procter & Gamble went to work with a knot in her stomach.

Instead of analyzing data for such products as Tide, Cascade and Ivory Liquid, she found herself staring at her youngsters' pictures and worrying. Their sitter had been letting them play in the street, and worse, she was taking them on unscheduled trips across the Ohio River to Kentucky. Then, unexpectedly, the sitter resigned and the chore of finding a replacement was soon absorbing much of Mrs. Berning's workday.

As it turned out, P.&G. provided the baby sitter. Last July, the huge consumer products company announced that it would open two day-care centers for the children of its workers and other Cincinnati residents. It was a $375,000 move that thrust P.&G. into the growing ranks of corporations that are helping parents deal with the dual pressures of work and family.

About 2,000 corporations—triple the number of just three years ago, with most of the increase in the last 12 months—now underwrite some form of child-care assistance, according to the Conference Board. That's still only a fraction of the nation's 6 million total employers, but it includes IBM, AT&T, Polaroid and several other pace-setting corporations that have traditionally set the agenda for American business.

Not since World War II, when companies involved in the war effort routinely provided day care for the children of Rosie the Riveter and other members of the predominantly female work force, have corporations shown such a willingness to become involved in the family. Fueling today's childcare movement is a new corporate conviction that helping employees cope with parental responsibilities improves productivity. . . . Many companies are concluding that unless they help their working parents—especially those in their 30s, who represent the next generation of management—meet family responsibilities, they run the risk of losing them to competitors who do provide child care. . . .

More and more companies are offering benefits that were viewed as superfluous a generation ago but that are now considered the best way to recruit and keep valuable workers and to lessen absenteeism.

The benefits include longer maternity and, increasingly, paternity leaves; cash subsidies to help defray day-care costs that, for parents, can range from $1,500 to $10,000 a year; and, in a few innovative companies, a service that sends nurses into a worker's home to care for a sick child so the parent can go to work. Corporations are also giving in to the demands of women employees for job-sharing, part-time schedules and work-at-home programs.

SOURCE: Excerpted from William Meyers, "Child Care Finds a Champion in the Corporation," *The New York Times*, Aug. 4, 1985, Section 3, pp. 1, 6.

Some parents of *school-aged* children provide them with responsible guidelines for staying alone during hours when a parent or other adult is unable to be present. Family researchers Hyman Rodman, David Pratto, and Rosemary Smith Nelson (1985) found no significant differences on various measures of social and psychological functioning between such "self-care" children and those cared for by adults. These social scientists prefer to speak of *self-care* arrangements rather than using the more common terms *latchkey* or *unsupervised* because of the negative connotation of such terms and the picture of irresponsibility and neglect they suggest. "Most parents prepare their children for the self-care arrangement," say Rodman and his colleagues. They "have rules for their children to follow, maintain daily telephone contact with them, and appear to do a good job of supervising their children in absentia" (p. 414). (See also Cole and Rodman, 1987.)

Employed Wives and Education

Education is another important demographic variable associated with female employment.

The higher a woman's education, the more likely she is to be in the labor force (U.S. Bureau of the Census, Special Demographic Analyses, CDS-80-8, 1983:18–19).

At first, it might seem surprising to note that better-educated wives are employed in higher percentages than are those with lower education, where family financial needs may seem greater. Again, it is a matter of rewards and costs. The more years of schooling a woman has, the more her market value is increased and the greater the earnings available to her. Furthermore, the better educated she is, the more likely she is to find employment in jobs that are professional-technical or managerial—jobs that economists William Bowen and T. Aldrich Finegan (1969:114–132) refer to as "more desirable" in that they "offer more psychic income" than do other kinds of jobs. In other words, highly trained women are attracted to the labor force because of both the tangible and intangible rewards it offers them.

In contrast, the opportunity system doesn't offer lower-educated women the prized rewards it offers the highly educated. In the first place, jobs for those with little schooling are scarce, and even when they can be found, they are low paying. Furthermore, jobs open to women without skills and training do not offer "psychic income" in the form of prestige, power, enhanced self-esteem, opportunities for creative expression, and the enjoyment of interesting work. To such women, the costs of working may seem to outweigh the limited rewards—particularly the costs involved in leaving their children. Among whites especially, gender-role socialization in blue-collar and underclass homes prepares females to think of motherhood and homemaking as being the major sources of gratification in a woman's life. Being a junior partner may seem less reward-ing to these women than being a complement. Hence the kind of statement sometimes made by women with fewer years of education who cannot understand some of the goals of feminism: "I can't for the life of me see why those women want to get out and get a job when they have husbands who can support them! I've *had* to work for many years and believe me, I'd give anything just to be able to stay home with my kids all day." Their jobs often seem dull and dead-end, and they would like to be free of them.

ATTITUDES TOWARD MARRIED WOMEN'S EMPLOYMENT

Whether or not a married woman is employed is strongly related to how her husband feels about the matter. This was one of the findings of a longitudinal study of 30 to 44-year-old women conducted by the U.S. Department of Labor (1973:43). At the time of the first interview during the three-year study, wives who thought their husbands were positive or at least neutral toward the idea of wives' employment were more likely to be in the labor force than were wives who felt their husbands were opposed to working wives. In the third year of the study, there were substantial increases in the percentage of employed wives among those women who at the first interview had indicated their husbands approved of a wife's being in the labor force. Evidently the knowledge that their husbands wouldn't object to their job seeking encouraged these wives to do just that. In contrast, among those wives who at the first interview reported that their husbands disapproved of a married woman's paid employment, there was a drop in the percentage of labor-force participation by the time of the third interview. Studies in the years since

THE MAN BEHIND THE SUCCESSFUL WOMAN

After 20 years of marriage to bestselling author Barbara Taylor Bradford, Bob Bradford, 57, now devotes his time to his wife's career. At present, he is supervising the production of the TV version of her novel *Voice of the Heart*.

"Years ago," he told me, "I was producing movies. Barbara was a journalist, but she had always wanted to write a novel. Yet she never had time for the quiet, disciplined life it takes to write a successful book. My work involved travel—busy, pressured, 18-hour days. Barbara sustained me all those years at the expense of her own career. Now it's her turn. I owe it to her. I devote all my time, energies and skills to her success."

But what about *his* identity, *his* ego?

"I don't have to prove myself anymore. I've had all my victories, my glamours. I don't care if they call me Mr. Taylor Bradford." He laughed. "And that has happened. I don't mind. I know who I am."

Is that position as helpmate sometimes threatening to his masculinity?

"Only men who have serious problems of their own feel threatened by their wives' success. It's a defect in men's character if they feel diminished by their wives. I prefer working with women—strong, brainy women. Men are too self-centered. Barbara has a natural gift for storytelling. I'm happy I can help her. It's her turn," he said again. "Her turn."

SOURCE: Barbara Gordon, "How to Share Life with a Famous Wife," *Parade*, April 21, 1985, p. 6.

---

then have continued to show the impact husbands' attitudes have on wives' employment and wives' *attitudes* about participation in the labor force (Spitze and Waite, 1981; Spitze and Spaeth, 1979).

One study found that among households where wives worked for pay, the greater the husband's education the more likely he was to feel positively about the wife's working, and the more likely the wife was to *think* that her husband felt positively (Scanzoni, 1975b). Less-educated men are more likely to hold negative views about wife employment, probably because they feel that a wife's holding a job could be interpreted as a failure on the husband's part.

Since the income of less-educated men is lower than that of men with more education, their wives' income makes up a higher proportion of total family income. These earnings and the wife's participation in the labor force may be viewed as threatening to the husband's self-esteem. Such men may believe that wife employment casts aspersions on their attainments as men. "After all," they may reason, "what kind of man is it who can't support his own family? A real man should be able to make ends meet without having to send his wife out to work!" If a man has negative feelings toward employment for married women (no matter what his own education level happens to be), he is likely to voice his displeasure and try to influence his wife not to work.

Why Some Husbands Disapprove of Wives' Employment

But why should we expect some husbands to feel threatened and resentful about wife employment? Why can't they be glad for the added income or take pride in a wife's accomplishments or rejoice in the newfound satisfaction she is experiencing in her job? Recall that in terms of conflict theory men may be viewed as a dominant group and women as a subordinate group. A dominant group that feels it is losing power may seek to put a stop to such erosion. Thus, the issue of a married woman's working comes to be viewed as a challenge to male dominance. A negative reaction sets in because many men are reluctant to give up the power and privilege that have been associated with the traditional male role of sole provider.

On the basis of his research and analysis of social trends, Daniel Yankelovich (1974:44–45) observed in the 1970s that "for the approximately one out of five men who say that their work fills their psychological as well as their economic need (primarily in the professional and managerial categories), a working wife is no threat, especially when her economic contribution is not needed." However, for men with less education and less prestigious occupations, a wage-earning wife could appear threatening by making the husband's work seem less valuable. For a man whose "job is just a job," providing few psychological rewards, daily labor has traditionally been made worthwhile by the pride he took in the hard work and personal sacrifices entailed in taking care of his family's material needs. "Accepting these hardships reaffirms his role as the family provider and hence as a true man," Yankelovich pointed out. For such a man, a wife's employment deprives him of the unique breadwinning function that is so bound up in his concept of masculinity.

More recently, Yankelovich (1981, chap. 8) has shown that a cultural shift has been taking place. He writes that a shared societal view "equating manliness with earning power, has persisted in the culture with great force; until the late 1960s it was held almost universally." Up to that point in time, nearly 90 percent of people he surveyed defined a "real man" in terms of being a "good provider." A decade later, only 67 percent equated manliness with breadwinning in this way. "The cultural definition persists," says Yankelovich, "but in attenuated form." Furthermore, as employment has become an option increasingly exercised by middle-class, well-educated women for the sake of both psychological and financial rewards, "the cultural meaning of a woman working outside the home has shifted subtly from an act that diminishes the manliness of the 'head of household' to one that enhances the status of the woman without adversely affecting the man" (p. 100, Bantam edition).

Such changes do not come about without tension and struggle, however, especially among groups with strong traditions of male dominance. In research among low-income Puerto Rican families in New York City, for example, social scientist Oscar Lewis (1968) found that notions of *machismo*, or manliness, characteristic of Latin cultures made it especially difficult for husbands to accept the idea of a wife's employment even though the family sorely needed her income. "The newfound independence of the working wife was probably the greatest source of domestic conflict among the sample families in New York," reports Lewis, adding that the conflict often was so intense that violence erupted and wife beating was quite common. The Puerto Rican husbands in the study were accustomed to being in control of both the family in general and the family finances in particular. Wives who worked no longer found it necessary to rely on their husbands for household and personal expenses. In addition, these wives had a new freedom to do as they wished and go where they pleased. Husbands resented such independence for wives, while wives for their part demanded more equal rights in the household. "The strains on family relationships were often severe," Lewis writes, "and almost every informant commented upon this problem." A psychologist who has given attention to Mexican-American families also refers to strains in family relationships that have occurred in male-dominant Chicano society as more and more women have shown an unwillingness to accept the traditional roles assigned them (Murillo, 1971).

At the same time, social scientist Lea Ybarra (1982) cites a number of studies that call into question the prevailing notion that most Chicano families today are male-dominated. In her own study of low-income, middle-income, and upper-income Chicano couples in California, "results indicated that the Chicano families interviewed exhibited a wide range of conjugal role patterns, ranging from a patriarchal (or role-segregated) structure to an egalitarian (or joint-role) structure, with many combinations of these two polar opposites evident" (p. 172). Furthermore, "the outside employment of the wife . . . proved to have a statistically significant correlation with an egalitarian conjugal role structure" (p. 177). Household tasks and childrearing responsibilities were more likely to be shared by the husband and wife if the wife was in the labor force. As one female respondent told Ybarra:

> Working seems to have gotten me started in the way I think now. If a woman can share the work-

ing world with the man, why can't he share the housework? If we share the home and the children, why can't we share the responsibilities that come with them? (p. 175)

Apparently, many Chicano husbands see the logic in this reasoning and embrace it themselves.

Nevertheless, older ideas about the roles of women and men in marriage, which limited a wife's right to be part of the labor force, have by no means disappeared in the general population. In their study of several thousand married couples throughout the United States, sociologists Philip Blumstein and Pepper Schwartz (1983) found that disagreement over whether wives should be employed persists in many families. Among couples who disagree over the topic, "there are more wives who want to work than husbands who want to let them," these researchers found (p. 118)—although they also found a small number of husbands who put pressure on their wives to get a job when the wives preferred staying home to care for the house and children. Disagreements over the wife's right to work was found to cause strain in marriages, with couples experiencing such disagreements reporting less satisfying relationships than did couples who didn't disagree on the topic.

At the same time, these researchers found that among couples in which the wife was employed, the balance of marital power became more equalized and the husband's respect for the wife tended to increase as well—especially if the wife was committed to year-round, full-time employment (Blumstein and Schwartz, 1983: 139–144).

Gender-Role Norms and Husbands' Attitudes toward Wives' Employment

Our own research indicates that husbands who hold more egalitarian gender-role norms are more favorable to wives' employment than are husbands who hold more traditional ideas about gender roles (Scanzoni, 1975b). On the other hand the more strongly husbands believe a married woman's most important task in life is caring for her husband and children, that her greatest satisfaction should be through her family, and that if a wife does work she should not try to achieve to the degree a man does nor expect to be paid as much as a man who must support his family, the *less* likely they are to favor wives working.

Husbands who are better educated tend to be more egalitarian in gender-role norms, believing that males and females should have equal opportunities to do whatever their abilities and training have suited them to do. Such men are also less likely to feel threatened by wife employment. To sum it all up: Where education is greater and gender-role norms are more egalitarian, husbands are less negative toward wives working and less likely to discourage or prevent their wives' participation in the labor force.

Vestiges of Traditional Notions of Marriage in the Law

Changes in laws often take place much more slowly than do changes in people's lives. In spite of increased economic opportunities for women and the fact that over half of the wives in the United States are in the labor force, the traditional marriage contract and the laws that surround it have assumed husband dominance and wife dependency. This awareness prompts sociologist Lenore Weitzman (1974, 1981; Weitzman et al., 1978) to wonder how many persons would consent to the marriage contract if they knew its terms! "The marriage contract is unlike most contracts," says Weitzman (1974:1170). "Its provisions are unwritten, its penalties are un-

specified, and the terms of contract are typically unknown to the 'contracting' parties."

What are the terms of the traditional contract? Weitzman lists three: the husband is regarded as head of the family; the husband is assigned the duty of support; and the wife is obligated to take care of the house and children. Joan Krauskopf (1977), a professor of family law, adds a fourth item that has characterized marriage in the vast majority of states—the separation of assets. This has been a good-news, bad-news kind of situation. The good news is that married women were granted the right to ownership and control over their own property, including income earned through outside employment—a right women did not have before the second half of the last century. The bad news is that the homemaker, busy with the domestic and childrearing tasks assigned her by the legal marriage contract, could one day find herself in a situation where the courts decided she didn't *own* anything because she hadn't *earned* anything and her husband had listed all assets in his own name only. The wife's contributions as a homemaker have traditionally been considered to have no monetary value.

Forty-two states have followed this separate-property system and have formulated laws and customs rooted in English common law. The other eight states—Arizona, California, New Mexico, Texas, Nevada, Idaho, Washington, and Louisiana—have marriage laws based not upon English common law but rather on law developed in Spain and France. Called a "community property system," the law in these eight states assumes that wives and husbands legally own half of one another's property and are entitled to their share both during the marriage and in the event of termination by divorce (Weitzman et al., 1978:309–310; Krauskopf, 1977:93; Weitzman, 1985:53–54).

Weitzman (1985:54) points out that the "stark contrast" between the separate-property and community-property states has become less pronounced in recent years because of (1) the passage of equal-rights amendments in a number of separate-property states, "which have been interpreted to give housewives access to the property that their husbands acquire during marriage," and (2) legislation in most separate-property states that now provides for court-decided "equitable division" of property upon divorce. At the same time, important differences in the basic principles of the two legal traditions continue to play a part in *how* courts approach the marital property division, including what "equitable" is considered to mean.

However, both community-property and separate-property (or "common-law") states have followed the common-law notion that primary responsibility for family support rests on the husband's shoulders (Weitzman, 1974:1180). "One effect of placing the primary support obligation on men is to further reinforce the husband's position as head of the household," write Weitzman and her colleagues (1978), "and, more specifically, his authority over family finances." They go on:

> The obligation is a mixed blessing for both the husband and wife. The husband is given power at the price of the pressures and responsibility of carrying a potentially crippling burden. The wife is given support at the price of limiting her economic capacity (and self-image), for the law assumes that she will always be economically dependent on a man. (p. 308)

Although the husband is responsible for providing his family with life's necessities, he is free to determine what those necessities are. Courts are reluctant to interfere in private household matters when a marriage is intact. Thus, a wife cannot press for her right to be supported by her husband *as long as she is living with him*. If she leaves him and sets up a separate household, or if he leaves her, she can then go to court and demand the support to which she is entitled. "In other words, the husband may stay at home and starve his wife, but he may not desert her and starve her," quips Krauskopf (1977:100).

In one notorious 1953 case (*McGuire v. McGuire*), a husband with assets valued at over $100,000 insisted that his family live in a house with no bathroom, no kitchen sink, a furnace that was inadequate for the house, and little furniture. He refused to give his wife any money for clothing, household necessities, or church donations; and to make sure he kept control of expenditures, he paid for groceries by check. When she took her complaints to court, the wife found how empty the right to be supported by her husband was. She was told that although the husband's attitude left "little to be said on his behalf," it was not the court's business to determine a family's living standard. In her case, "as long as the home is maintained and the parties are living as husband and wife it may be said that the husband is legally supporting his wife and the purpose of the marriage relation is being carried out" (quoted in Weitzman, 1974:1184; see also Krauskopf, 1977:98).

In the story of Cindy and Tom (illustrating a head-complement marriage) at the beginning of Chapter 8, Cindy delighted in the fact that Tom gave her an allowance in addition to money for household expenditures. However, in terms of legal requirements as set forth by the courts, he could withdraw that allowance and cut down money for household expenditures at any time; and Cindy would have no legal recourse. At the same time, Cindy could not demand payment for her household services because those services are already considered to belong to Tom

HOUSEHOLD WORK: A WIFE'S OBLIGATION?

Because a wife is obligated to provide domestic services for her husband, the courts have refused to enforce contracts under which she was to receive compensation for her labor. The courts have reasoned that if a wife already owes these services to her husband, a contract in which she is to be paid for them is void for lack of consideration. The courts thus have refused to honor contracts in which the husband agreed to pay his wife for housekeeping, entertaining, child care, or other "wifely tasks." Even when the husband and wife have agreed that the services the wife would perform were "extras" like working in the husband's business or doing farm labor, courts have voided the contract which obligated the husband to pay her for them.

SOURCE: Lenore J. Weitzman, "Legal Regulation of Marriage: Tradition and Change," *California Law Review, 62* (July–September 1974), p. 1189.

as part of his marital rights, and one can't be expected to pay for something one already owns. "The law's assumption that a wife 'owes' her domestic services to her husband thereby undermines the economic value of the wife's work in the home," assert Weitzman and her co-authors (1978:308–309). "It also allows the law to disregard the importance of the wife's labor in building the family wealth and property." Cindy spoke of being the support behind Tom, making life smooth for him and doing all she could to help him advance in his career. And Tom appreciates her contribution; he knows he wouldn't be where he is without her. Yet another man might devalue his wife's economic contribution and boast of being a self-made man—even though his wife carefully managed the budget, worked without compensation in the family business, and provided nonmonetary benefits in the form of services such as making the family's clothing, cutting her husband's and children's hair, cultivating a garden to keep food bills down, baking bread, and so on. (See also Weitzman, 1981, chap. 3.)

A writer born in the early part of the nineteenth century—Frances Dana Gage—once put down her thoughts on this topic in a work entitled, "The Housekeeper's Soliloquy." One stanza included these lines: "Wife, mother, nurse, seamstress, cook, housekeeper, chambermaid, laundress, dairywoman, and scrub generally, doing the work of six/ For the sake of being supported." Women not in the paid labor force are not seen as "working women"—no matter how hard they work. Some researchers, social analysts, and legal experts have been calling attention to inequities—in divorce settlements and in many other areas—that result from this viewpoint (Weitzman, 1981, 1985; Oakley, 1974a, 1974b, 1981).

Symbolic Significance in Traditional Name Change at Marriage

The English common-law tradition has left its mark on many marriage laws and customs in the United States. Basic to this tradition was the idea that at marriage, a wife's legal identity became merged into that of her husband. That her labor belonged to him was considered a logical component of such a merger.

WOMEN'S UNPAID ECONOMIC CONTRIBUTIONS

(Charles Gatewood)

Our short-sightedness about women's economics also reflects the way statistics are compiled. Numerical measures universally fail to count women's unpaid contributions to the economic well-being of the nation, in their roles as homemakers and mothers, and as participants and volunteers contributing to the economic growth of civic and community life.

John Kenneth Galbraith gives us some insight into homemakers' unmeasured economic roles. As he states in his *Economics and the Public Purpose:*

> The value of the services of housewives has been calculated at roughly one-fourth of the total Gross National Product. However, the labor of women to facilitate consumption is not valued in the national income or product. This is of some importance for its disguise: *what is not counted is not noticed* [italics added]. For this reason, it becomes possible for women to study economics without becoming aware of their precise role in the economy.

(Along these lines, I find it interesting that the work of a maid or housekeeper is counted in the Gross National Product, but if the maid or housekeeper marries her employer, she is no longer counted.)

SOURCE: Dee Dee Ahern with Betsy Bliss, *The Economics of Being a Woman* (New York: Macmillan, 1976), p. 3.

Blackstone's eighteenth-century *Commentaries on the Laws of England* sum up the notion that the wife ceases to exist as a person in her own right.

> By marriage, the husband and wife are one person in law; that is, the very being or legal existence of the woman is suspended during the marriage, or at least is incorporated and consolidated into that of the husband: under whose wing, protection, and *cover,* she performs everything. (Blackstone, as quoted in Stannard, 1977:9)

One way in which the wife's assumed merger into the husband can be seen symbolically is in the wife's taking of her husband's surname. She is, in name at least, no longer the person she has been up until the time of her marriage and may thus even be referred to as "the *former* Mary Smith." Her identity is especially obliterated in the "Mrs. John Doe" form, which ignores even her first, or given, name. Many couples today are electing to use a hyphenated form so that both the wife's and the husband's name can be retained. Others choose various other ways of symbolizing their egalitarian ideals, including the option of the wife's keeping her birth name just as her husband keeps his. In a fascinating history of names used by wives, Una Stannard (1977) shows that when the custom of taking the husband's name at marriage originated, women (already used to being known as "the wife of") actually viewed permission to use the husband's surname as a privilege—as symbolizing status through identification with a man! Rather than giving up something, it meant gaining something—prestige through the accomplishments of a male. Now that other options are open to women, women in increasing numbers want to be known for their own achievements. For many women, that may also mean a desire to be known by their own name continuously throughout life.

At the same time, women who see their status as tied to that of their husbands are usually reluctant to use "Ms." instead of "Mrs.," and they guard jealously their right to carry their husbands' names even after a husband's death. One woman has refused to pay bills addressed to her in her own first name prefixed by "Ms." Rather than viewing this term as a recognition of her own individuality, she sees this form of address as robbing her of the highly esteemed status she has won through her husband's achievements.

Such examples provide further proof of the way custom and law have combined to emphasize various elements of the owner-property and head-complement models of marriage. Certain assumptions are made about the roles of husbands and wives—assumptions based upon the economic side of marriage.

Gender-Role Ideology: Effects on Women in the Work Force

Assumptions made about appropriate gender roles—assumptions built around the owner-property and head-complement models of marriage—have left their mark not only on marriage laws and customs but on labor-market attitudes and practices. Social scientist. Eileen Appelbaum (1981) has shown how such assumptions placed limitations on women even after employment opportunities opened up to them.

For example, women were seen as a source of cheap labor because of the assumption that women didn't need money as much as men did. Men had families to support, while the single woman (it was assumed) had only herself to take care of and probably only for the short interval between school and marriage. Married women had husbands to support them and thus didn't require wages sufficient to ensure them a decent standard of living; men, on the other hand, did. "The wages of women thus have largely been culturally determined," writes Appelbaum (p. 13), pointing out that the median earnings of women employed full-time, year-round—which have averaged only about 60 percent of men's earnings in recent years—reflect a societal attitude with long historical roots. She provides evidence that "women's wages were set at 60 percent of men's as early as the Industrial Revolution in nineteenth-century England." (See also Norwood, 1982, and Shack–Marquez, 1984).

It was widely held that since woman's role was one of economic dependence, wages paid to women were supplementary. Wages paid to men were *primary*—the earnings on which a family must depend—and thus must be considerably higher. As Appelbaum emphasizes, "This tendency to underpay women on the assumption that a major share of their support was contributed by men has been responsible, in this century and the last, for much of the poverty of single women, widows, and their families who, in fact, must manage without a male wage" (p. 13).

Appelbaum's detailed study of women's past and present labor-force participation also showed additional ways that prevailing gender-role norms affected women in the work force. For one, social acceptance of a married woman's employment required that she keep the demands of her job subordinate to her domestic duties. This, in turn, meant that her occupational pursuits were taken less seriously than her husband's. "The husband, whose job was held to matter, could not be expected to dissipate energy and initiative providing domestic services to his family," writes Appelbaum (p. 12). "On the contrary, his wife was still expected to behave so as to expedite and advance his possibilities for success or advancement at work."

Thus, wives were expected to interrupt their employment activities to stay home and care for children at different periods of married life. They were also expected to leave their jobs and move at any time to wherever their husbands' occupational requirements or aspirations dictated. This intermittent work pattern, tied to women's frequently changing home circumstances, caused many employers to feel justified in denying women special training and opportunities for advancement. Instead, according to Appelbaum (pp. 14–15), "as the economy grew and the employment of married women increased, employers had both an opportunity and an incentive to structure as many of the new jobs as possible so that they could be performed by a low-paid, intermittent work force. . . . Jobs were simultaneously deskilled and feminized." At the same time, the unchallenging, low-paying, dead-end jobs to

IN AND OUT OF DEAD-END JOBS

The unchallenging, low-paying, dead-end jobs to which women were assigned were in themselves a major cause for the high turnover patterns among female workers. (Ellis Herwig/The Picture Cube)

Though turnover rates have been about the same for women as for men in jobs of similar status, the heavy concentration of women in dead-end jobs has tended to reinforce the impression that women are casual workers, lack commitment to their jobs, and have unstable work histories. High turnover, which resulted in part from the character of jobs in the secondary labor market to which women were assigned, was then used by employers as sufficient reason to deny women access to more responsible positions.

SOURCE: Eileen Appelbaum, *Back to Work: Determinants of Women's Successful Re-entry* (Boston: Auburn House, 1981), p. 16.

which women were assigned were, in themselves, a major cause for the high turnover patterns among female workers.

There were still other ways in which women's employment was affected by traditional gender-role ideology. For example, a division of labor arose in which paid jobs labeled "women's work" were viewed as extensions of women's unpaid work in the home—a fact reflected in the wage rates. The jobs most frequently open to women were those based upon the social expectation that women know how to train children, take care of the sick and elderly, serve food, make and launder clothing, and assist men by relieving them of the routine tasks that would detract from their main occupational pursuits. Table 9-F shows which occupations have been considered primarily female over the first eighty years of this century. Note the high percent-

TABLE 9-F Employment of women in selected occupations, 1900–1979

OCCUPATION	NUMBER OF WOMEN (in thousands)							WOMEN AS PERCENT OF ALL WORKERS IN EACH OCCUPATION						
	1900	1930	1940	1950	1960	1970	1979	1900	1930	1940	1950	1960	1970	1979
All professional-technical	434	1,482	1,608	1,946	2,746	4,576	6,519	35.2%	44.8%	41.5%	40.1%	38.0%	40.0%	43.3%
Accountants				56	77	180	344				14.9	16.4	25.3	32.9
Engineers				6	8	20	40				1.2	0.9	1.6	2.9
Lawyers-judges				7	7	13	62				4.1	3.3	4.7	12.4
Physicians-osteopaths				12	16	25	46				6.5	6.8	8.9	10.7
Registered nurses				394	567	814	1,184				97.8	97.6	97.4	96.8
Teachers, except college and university				837	1,196	1,937	2,207				74.5	71.6	70.4	70.8
Teachers, college and university				28	36	139	172				22.8	21.3	28.3	31.6
Technicians, excluding medical-dental				21	44	49	199				20.6	12.8	14.5	16.1
Writers-artists-entertainers				50	82	229	470				40.3	34.2	30.1	37.8
All managerial-administrative, except farm	74	292	414	672	780	1,061	2,586	4.4	8.1	11.0	13.8	14.4	16.6	24.6
Bank officials-financial managers				13	28	55	196				11.7	12.2	17.6	31.6
Buyers-purchasing agents				6	61	75	136				9.4	17.7	20.8	30.2
Food service workers				93	141	109	224				27.1	24.0	33.7	35.4
Sales managers-department heads; retail trade				35	68	51	135				24.6	28.2	24.1	39.8
All sales	228	736	925	1,314	1,646	2,143	2,779	17.4	24.1	26.8	34.5	36.6	39.4	45.1
Sales representatives (including wholesale)				37	70	76	162				5.2	7.3	7.2	12.4
Sales clerks, retail				1,175	1,384	1,465	1,671				48.9	53.7	64.8	70.7
All clerical	212	2,246	2,700	4,273	6,263	10,150	14,152	24.2	51.8	54.2	62.3	67.5	73.6	80.3
Bank tellers				28	88	216	458				45.2	69.3	86.1	92.9
Bookkeepers				556	764	1,274	1,740				77.7	83.4	82.1	91.1
Cashiers				187	367	692	1,298				81.7	78.4	84.0	87.9
Office machine operators				116	225	414	677				81.1	73.8	73.5	74.9
Secretaries-typists				1,494	1,917	3,686	4,681				94.6	96.7	96.6	98.6
Shipping-receiving clerks				19	24	59	103				14.3	8.6	14.3	21.3

Occupation	Number (thousands)							Percent female						
All craft	76	106	135	236	252	518	737	2.5	1.7	2.2	3.1	2.9	4.9	5.7
Carpenters				4	3	11	16				0.4	0.4	1.3	1.3
Mechanics, including automotive				21	25	49	49				1.2	1.1	2.0	1.4
Printing				35	35	58	101				11.8	11.0	14.8	22.2
Bakers				14	17	32	61				12.2	15.9	29.4	43.6
Decorators and window cleaners				14	24	42	94				32.6	46.2	58.3	72.9
Tailors				16	8	22	12				19.8	20.2	31.4	34.3
Upholsterers				5	6	10	12				8.3	10.0	16.4	21.4
All operatives, except transport				2,995	3,252	4,036	4,353				33.5	34.3	38.4	39.9
Assemblers				N.A.	267	459	688				N.A.	43.7	48.7	53.4
Bottling and canning operatives				N.A.	N.A.	16	17				N.A.	N.A.	34.0	37.8
Clothing ironers and pressers				N.A.	N.A.	137	89				N.A.	N.A.	74.9	76.8
Dressmakers				135	116	92	104				97.1	96.7	94.8	95.4
Laundry and dry cleaning operatives				288	273	105	122				67.7	71.3	62.9	65.9
Sewers and stitchers				N.A.	532	816	772				N.A.	94.0	93.8	95.3
All transport equipment operatives				22	41	134	294				1.0	1.7	4.5	8.1
Bus drivers				4	18	68	163				2.6	9.8	28.5	45.5
Operatives (inclusive)	1,264	1,870	2,452					34.0	24.3	25.8				
All service	1,886	2,954	3,699	3,228	4,418	5,944	8,011	71.8	61.9	60.9	54.3	62.8	60.5	62.4
Private household	1,526	1,909	2,277	1,321	1,586	1,132	1,062	96.6	95.5	94.4	94.9	96.6	96.9	97.6
Food service				839	1,379	1,913	2,943				61.6	70.0	68.8	68.4
Health service				249	488	1,047	1,643				74.6	81.5	88.0	90.4
Personal service				221	326	778	1,369				49.7	57.9	66.5	77.3
Protective service				11	28	59	124				2.0	4.1	6.2	8.8

SOURCE: Eileen Appelbaum, *Back to Work* (Boston: Auburn House, 1981), pp. 7–8. Compiled from U.S. Bureau of the Census, *Historical Statistics of the United States: Colonial Times to 1970*, ser. D182-232, for 1900–1940. U.S. Department of Labor, Bureau of Labor Statistics, *Perspectives on Working Women: A Databook*, October 1980, Bulletin 2080, Table 11, for 1950–1979.

age of women in nursing, teaching (under the college level), secretarial and bookkeeping work, and various other occupations associated with providing care and service.

Appelbaum points out that the late nineteenth and early twentieth century societal expectations which confined women to occupations "viewed as consistent with their place in the family and with the existing sexual division of labor in the home" meant that such occupations would be considered the domain of women simply because of the type of work such occupations represented (p. 6). Men were not attracted to them because of the lower pay and prestige associated with occupational categories filled mainly by women. Sociologist Peter Rossi (1961, as quoted in Garrison, 1974:167) made the same point in his observation that "any occupation in which there is a high proportion of women suffers a special disability. . . . Women depress the status of an occupation because theirs is a depressed status in the society as a whole, and those occupations in which women are found in large numbers are not seen as seriously competing with other professions for personnel and resources."

Traditional gender-role beliefs also operated in the widespread practice of assigning supervisory positions to men because it was thought that "the dominant role of men within the family and the submissive role of women would have been threatened if women held positions of authority when they worked" (Appelbaum, 1981:6).

Last, what sociologist Nona Glazer (1984:170) speaks of as the normalization of "the double day" springs directly from traditional gender-role ideology. Women are expected to be responsible for domestic chores, which means employed women must work all day at one job and all evening and much of the weekend on their other (unpaid) job. "Housework and child care, as well as other myriad tasks, are socially assigned to

women—employed or not—who do not have social solutions to the problems of the double day, but must work out personal solutions," writes Glazer. While it is true that husbands are increasingly sharing in household tasks and child care (Maret and Finlay, 1984), research indicates that wives continue to carry a disproportionate load of housework and would like their husbands to participate more fully (Model, 1981; Blumstein and Schwartz, 1983: 144–146; Pleck, 1985; Coverman and Sheley, 1986).

Changes in Attitudes Toward Women's Employment

In 1938, three-fourths of the American public disapproved of a married woman's working for pay if she had a husband capable of supporting her. By 1978, only one-fourth of Americans felt that way (Yankelovich, 1981, chap. 8, Chart D). Appelbaum (1981:3) offers an economic explanation, pointing out that two basic presuppositions on which the traditional view of gender roles rested were challenged by events beginning in the late 1940s. "The first assumption was that the requirements of business and industry for labor could largely be met out of the available pool of male workers," she writes. "The second was that men were able to command a market wage sufficient, in combination with the unpaid labor provided by their wives in processing and preparing food and clothing, in raising children, and in household care and maintenance, to meet their own needs and those of their families." A changing world has meant the undermining of these assumptions.

"The advent of the multiple-earner family in which both husband and wife worked had a major impact on family income and consumption expenditures," stresses Appelbaum (1981:17). Wives' earnings came to be taken seriously and were not treated as "pin

For Better or For Worse®   # by Lynn Johnston

For Better or for Worse, by Lynn Johnston. Copyright 1984, Universal Press Syndicate. Reprinted with permission. All rights reserved.

money" for extras but as *essential income* for the maintaining of a desired way of life. However, "the meaning and importance of this development did not become fully apparent until inflation, recession, and slow productivity growth threatened the standard of living of American families in the 1970s," Appelbaum observes. Her point is well illustrated by the remark of a middle-aged insurance representative who told researcher Daniel Yankelovich (1981:100) that at first he didn't want his wife to work at all so that she would always be home when he got home. "Then," he said, "when she started to work, I insisted that we live within *my* means, on *my* salary. Now, we live on both paychecks and I don't know how in the world we would live any other way."

In 1981, among husbands and wives who worked full time the year round, wives contributed 38 percent of the family's income. The average income of such dual-earner couples was $34,560 (as compared to the average earnings of married couples overall, which was $25,550). If both husband and wife were employed in professional and man-

agerial occupations, their joint income averaged $39,170 (U.S. Bureau of the Census, *Current Population Reports*, ser. P-23, no. 133, 1984:1).

We may expect the research on dual-earner couples that has been taking place in recent years to continue and grow. Why? Because with the increase of married women in the labor force, more and more husbands and wives will be attempting to find ways to make this lifestyle fit comfortably—including, in many cases, the researchers themselves and their peers. Sociologist Joan Aldous (1981) observes that the phenomenon of employed *middle-class* wives has caught social scientists' attention in a way that earlier examples of employed wives did not, possibly because of the "largely working-class character of these earlier families." She points out that prior to the recent period, when so many professional women have chosen to combine marriage and careers, little attention was paid to the contributions many wives made to family finances. "Wives in low-income, immigrant, black, and farm families particularly earned money," she writes. Because the income-producing often took place in the home (taking in laundry, selling eggs and garden produce, renting rooms to boarders, doing seamstress work, and so on), it has frequently been overlooked. Yet, such women are family earners, emphasizes Aldous, and thus are "workers in the restricted economic sense of persons whose activities are exchanged for money" (p. 116). Many low-income families have long faced the issues of obtaining child care during the hours of employment, handling the double load of job responsibilities and household tasks, and so on, just as middle-class families are facing them today.

Clearly, women's employment has had and continues to have a profound impact on marriage. As Appelbaum (1981:25) notes, many traditional ideas and practices are challenged by the changes and increases in paid employment for women. Within the family, older arguments used to justify a division of labor based on sex break down as women demonstrate an employment commitment like that traditionally associated with men. On the job, "employers can no longer use the rationale that women work sporadically when denying them opportunities for training and advancement," and women will be less willing to take dead-end jobs. "Occupational segregation—with women confined mainly to low-skill, low-paying, low-status jobs—becomes increasingly difficult to justify," Appelbaum stresses. "Thus the new pattern of female employment has tended to undermine the traditional, subordinate role of women in the family and in the labor market."

CHAPTER HIGHLIGHTS

As women gained independent access to economic resources, their bargaining power within marriage increased. By the mid-1980s, over half of all married women were in the labor force, continuing a trend that has gone on throughout the present century. A demographic picture of employed women shows that (1) black wives are more likely to be employed than are white wives; (2) the number and age of children greatly influences a married woman's employment behavior—although more and more mothers (even of preschoolers) are entering the labor force, and most studies don't indicate that a mother's employment has negative effects on her children but rather, that it may actually benefit children by teaching them responsibility and flexibility in their gender roles; (3) the higher a woman's education, the more likely she is to be in the labor force; and (4) a married woman's participation in the labor force is strongly related to how her husband feels about it. For some husbands, a wife's employment reflects on his abilities as family breadwinner; for other husbands, a wife's commitment to full-time work enhances the husband's respect for her. Laws and customs have been built around traditional gender roles which assigned women to the home and *unpaid* work while men were assigned to the world beyond the home and *paid* work. Laws, customs, the division of labor in the home, bargaining power in marriage, and attitudes and practices in the labor market based on traditional gender roles are all being challenged as women in increasing numbers become income earners and dedicated career workers.

PROCESS IN MARRIAGE: EXPRESSIVENESS

An incident a few years ago caused a publisher considerable embarrassment. The company had issued some full-color posters to illustrate a series of religious-education materials. But through some oversight, two picture captions were reversed and not noticed before the orders were shipped. A picture designed to illustrate marriage was labeled "John the Baptist in Chains." And the picture of the fettered prophet was entitled "Marriage."

No doubt the mix-up seems fitting to many people. Men have been known to speak of marriage as a kind of bondage, with freedom traded for the "chains of wedlock" (emphasis on the word *lock*). In recent years, large numbers of women have complained—perhaps even more than men—that marriage is a trap, shackling them into confining roles which prevent full development as persons and as achievers.

Such ideas about marriage come from traditional notions of wedded life as something rigidly fixed and static. Small wonder that the question has been raised: "Is there life after marriage?" (Bernard, 1972, chap. 10). The word *life* suggests energy, vitality, process. Actually, to picture marriage as a state of inaction fits neither with the realities of the husband-wife relationship nor with the cost/ reward emphasis of this book. In the preceding two chapters, we examined marriage as a *structure*; now we want to see marriage as a *process*. The word *process* implies something dynamic, on the move; it derives from the Latin *procedere,* "to go forward." A process suggests continuous action taking place in a systematic fashion. Being in process means that ongoing changes and exchanges are occurring all the time (Scanzoni, 1983a, 1983b). Something is happening between the spouses as they interact daily. Neither they nor their relationship is standing still.

WHAT HOLDS MARRIAGE TOGETHER?

If marriage is constantly in process, what keeps the moving parts from spinning off in separate directions? In other words, what is the "glue" that holds a marriage together?

Cohesiveness—sticking together—involves an effort to resolve the problem of *couple solidarity* versus *individual freedom.* As marriage has been understood traditionally, a man and woman are said to become "one flesh." According to the biblical phrase used in many wedding ceremonies, they are "no longer two but one." In the minds of some persons, this merger into a new social unit must erase all traces of the two individuals as separate entities, somewhat in the manner of the juncture of the Allegheny and Monongahela rivers which lose their distinct identities at Pittsburgh, Pennsylvania, when they unite to become the Ohio River.

Yet many persons today reject the idea of a total submersion of individuality for the sake of couple solidarity. They are asking, "Why can't the one be two at the same time that the two are one?" While it is commonly thought that autonomy can have only the effect of dissolving the glue holding marriage together, it's possible to think of it another way. Autonomy can be a basic ingredient helping to cement the relationship—particularly as marriage partners feel fulfilled in their need to be recognized and respected as individuals and not simply as part of a couple.

Marital-Adjustment School of Thought

One of the earliest attempts to explore the glue of marriage was made by proponents of the "adjustment to marriage" school. The marital-adjustment idea fitted nicely with the notions of functionalism and its emphasis on an organism's need for smooth-working parts working together to preserve the structure.

According to the marital-adjustment school of thought, the glue of marriage is manufactured by *submerging individual interests for the greater good of group solidarity*. The major emphasis is on harmony and stability, the sustaining of a commitment to the marriage (Dizard, 1968:4). Sociologist Harvey Locke (1968:45) spoke of marital adjustment as "the process of adaptation of the husband and the wife in such a way as to avoid or resolve conflicts sufficiently so that the mates feel satisfied with the marriage and with each other." Similarly, sociologist Ernest Burgess and his colleagues (1963:294) wrote: "A well-adjusted marriage may be defined as a union in which the husband and wife are in agreement on the chief issues of marriage, such as handling finances and dealing with in-laws; in which they have come to an adjustment on interests, objectives, and values; in which they are in harmony on demonstrations of affection and sharing confidences; and in which they have few or no complaints about their marriage." The emphasis was always on "adjustment," "adapting," "harmonious relations," "agreement," and avoiding or minimizing conflict.

In describing how, in any group, standards may be designed to prevent disruptions based on individualistic interests, social psychologist Philip Brickman (1974:269) makes a comment that fits well with the basic premise of the marital-adjustment school: "In normative relationships [relationships with behavioral expectations clearly spelled out in advance], although conflicts of interest may exist, individuals are not supposed to be engaged in maximizing their own self interests. Instead they are supposed to be doing what is right or moral or normative, even if this is not in their self interest." In other words, persons are supposed to know what a "good" marriage is and requires. And then they try to fit into that mold, whether or not it "feels right" to them and even though it may mean a submerging of their "true selves"—that is, their own personal desires and aspirations. Often a great deal of pretense and game playing occurs to keep up the image of adjustment and harmony.

Criticisms of the Marital-Adjustment Approach

In recent years, there has been a reaction to the marital-adjustment school of thinking. For example, Robert Seidenberg (1970:304–305), a psychiatrist, writes:

> Central to marital problems . . . is the awkward issue of human rights, rights such as self-fulfillment, autonomy, privacy, as well as expectation of compassion, sharing, and mutuality. Marriages frequently land "on the rocks" because there is an assumption by one or both partners that the marital union somehow abrogates these rights. . . . Loving someone then appears to some as giving themselves liberties to overwhelm, to entrap, and to enslave. . . . No marriage should ever be held of more importance than one of its participants. Persons, not marriages, are worth saving. It is a grand hypocrisy of our morality that we have attempted to sanctify and glorify a compact often irrespective of the plight of the human beings involved.

Such critical reactions to the marital-adjustment school are rooted in a basic fact that champions of adjustment largely ignored, namely, that wives were doing more of the submerging of individual interests than were husbands (Bernard, 1972). The model of marriage that marriage-adjustment proponents worked with (and the pattern to which spouses were supposed to adjust) was what we have called the head-complement structure. At the same time, basic male-female inequalities were glossed over by mere *assertions* that modern marriage was now egalitarian. Such assertions may have been based on wishful thinking, but more likely they derived from observations that marriage was no longer an owner-property arrangement. It was assumed that if a wife wasn't "owned" by her husband, she must then automatically be his equal.

In its most sophisticated form, the argument that spouses are equal because they are *declared* to be such goes like this: Husbands and wives are specialists—the husband in his occupation, the wife in her household. Therefore, they complement one another; and because they complement one another,

When two persons choose one another and remain together sharing their lives, they are viewing their situation as one that is rewarding. (© Ellen Pines Sheffield 1981/Woodfin Camp & Associates)

they are equal. They have differences in tasks, but no difference in rank (Miller and Swanson, 1958). One assumption made in this argument is that the rewards for doing household tasks are somehow comparable to rewards obtained for performing tasks in the occupational realm. Another assumption is that husbands are as dependent on wives as wives are on husbands. We have seen that neither assumption is valid. Women have been assigned the tasks that bring fewer rewards, lower rank, and greater dependence. It is difficult to see how this can be called "equality."

Costs and Rewards: Dynamics of Marriage

Another way of thinking about the glue that holds a marriage together is to think of the exchanges the two persons make and the way they evaluate the costs and rewards of the relationship. When two persons choose one another and remain together sharing their lives, they are viewing their situation as one that is rewarding. It's profitable; they gain something from it. The benefits of the relationship outweigh any costs.

If the relationship should cease to be rewarding to one or the other spouse, efforts can be directed toward altering whatever situation seems to be costly and punishing. If no solution can be found, perhaps the relationship will be dissolved—although in some cases, the anticipated costs of dissolution may seem greater than the costs of remaining in an unsatisfactory situation.

In other words, the process of marriage involves getting and giving. Each person wants his or her "money's worth" out of the relationship—not necessarily in some crassly calculating way involving dollars and cents, but in terms of all sorts of rewards, both tangible and intangible. Gaining rewards involves costs and investments, which means there is going on in marriage a constant assessment of the reward/cost ratio to make sure that the individual and the marital unit are experiencing profit.

In thinking of the reward/cost ratio as being the glue of marriage, the emphasis may seem to be on the individual rather than on group unity. However, self-interest and group interest are not necessarily incompatible. What is best for the individual may also be best for the marital unit and vice versa. Most social scientists concur with a point made by Sidney Siegel and Lawrence Fouraker (1960) in their research on economic bargaining, namely that "the two parties, if they behave rationally and in their respective self-interests, will be forced inexorably to [an exchange] which maximizes their joint benefit." In other words, the most solid and cohesive social system is one in which all parties concerned experience what has been labeled *maximum joint profit* or MJP (Kelley and Schenitzki, 1972:307). There is no reason to think that this should hold less for a marriage than for a business partnership.

According to marital-adjustment notions, marital stability is thought to be achieved through long-suffering endurance and making the best of one's fate, with efforts being directed toward adapting to the marriage no matter how unsatisfactory it is. In contrast, the social-exchange or cost/reward model focuses on bargaining, change, and the rewards the spouses offer each other. Rather than being a process of adjustment, marriage becomes a *continual process of negotiation and profit seeking*. To some persons, this way of thinking may at first seem selfish and crass. Wouldn't it be simpler to say that *love* is the glue that holds marriage together?

Love and Reciprocity

A song in the country-music tradition bears the title "The Cost of Real Love is 'No Charge.' " The lyrics tell of a child who compiles a list of all the things he does around the house and then demands payment from his mother. His mother in turn speaks of all she has done for her son, beginning with the nine months she carried him in her womb, the days of child care, the nights of sitting up while he was ill, the money put aside for his college education, and so on. However, in contrast to the child's list with specific monetary value attached to each task, the mother's list carries no price tags. After each item is a statement saying that the cost to the child is "no charge."

There is a prevailing sentiment that love—especially family love—should be freely given with no expectation of return, "no charge." However, the song itself describes reciprocity. The child wants payment, but the mother tells him he has already been paid and will continue to benefit from all that his parents do for him. At the same time, although she claims there is "no charge," the mother expects something from the child—affection, gratitude, respect, and the fulfilling of responsibilities assigned to him as a member of the family.

Interdependencies of Marriage

What is true of the parent-child relationship is also true of the husband-wife relationship. While popular sentiment would have us believe that this, too, is a situation of "no charge," the dynamics of married living suggest otherwise. The rights and duties associated with marriage, as we saw in Chapter 8, mean that exchanges take place between marital partners continually. Some exchanges occur in the instrumental realm of marriage and some in the expressive realm. Many exchanges take place *between* as well as *within* these two realms of marriage.

Marriage, by definition, means both instrumental and expressive interdependencies. Let's take, for example, a traditional marriage in which the husband is the breadwinner and the wife takes care of the home and children. The husband's provider role is built around his duties to supply his wife (and any children) with economic and status rewards. As the husband fulfills these duties, the wife is having her rights to be provided for met. On one level, this motivates her to perform her instrumental role as homemaker, caring for the children and attending to domestic tasks. The husband, having his rights to a smooth-running household met by his wife's performance of her duties, is then further motivated to perform his own instrumental duties in the economic realm.

However, on another level, since the wife's rights to be rewarded by her husband in terms of economic and status benefits are met, she is also motivated to perform her expressive duties. The wife's supportive, nurturant, affectionate behaviors (not only sexually, but including that) fulfill the husband's expressive rights. This in turn motivates him out of rectitude and gratitude to perform his expressive duties, thereby fulfilling his wife's expressive rights. It also motivates him further to perform his instrumental (breadwinning) duties.

A couple may not be consciously aware that such a process is going on between them. They especially may not be aware of the interconnections between the expressive dimension of marriage and the instrumental dimension as it relates to the economic-opportunity system.

THE EXPRESSIVE DIMENSION IN TRADITIONAL MARRIAGE PATTERNS

What sociologists speak of as the "expressive" dimension of marriage is often that which first comes to mind when people think of the husband-wife relationship. Expressiveness includes three basic elements: *companionship* (someone to be with and do things with), *empathy* (someone who listens, understands, and cares), and *physical affection* (someone with whom love can be expressed through touch, caresses, and sexual intercourse).

At first it may seem strange to think of companionship, empathy, and physical affection as being somehow tied in with the instrumental side of marriage; but research has shown there are very real interconnections. These interconnections—particularly with respect to the economic system—are fascinating to explore.

Husband's Occupation and Expressive Satisfactions

Sociologists have found a relationship between social status and the degree to which couples are satisfied with the expressive dimension of their marriages. Couples with higher status (traditionally measured by the husband's occupation, education, and income) are more likely than lower-status couples to feel that their marital companionship, empathy, and physical affection are satisfactory.

In order to understand what are indeed complex relationships, it helps to think of the family and the economic-opportunity structure as two separate systems, each very much involved with the other. Figure 10-1 provides some idea of how the relationship of these two social structures affects what goes

The economic-opportunity system is the means toward achievement and success. Material rewards (in terms of dollars) and nonmaterial rewards (in terms of a sense of self-worth, social status, and prestige) are obtained through this system.

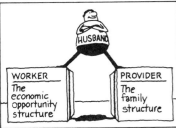

The husband-father, where he is the chief or only family breadwinner, links the family to the economic-opportunity system. His role is that of *worker* in the economic-opportunity system; and in the family system, his role is that of *provider* or *production-agent*.

Goods are produced in order to be consumed. In American society, the nuclear family (husband, wife, and dependent children) is the basic consumption unit. The family uses up goods and services having an exchangeable value (the meaning of "consumption" as economists speak of it). Visible consumption is the way a family demonstrates the extent of its achievement (via the father as provider) through the economic-opportunity structure and is thereby awarded status by other members of the community.

The husband's occupational status, education, and income represent degrees of integration with the economic-opportunity structure. The more rewards he has because of this, the more rewards he is able to provide to his wife and children, and the more positively both spouses are likely to evaluate the expressive dimension of their marriage. As the husband fulfills his chief role obligations as provider, the wife is motivated to fulfill her chief role obligations as the *expressive agent* of the nuclear family.

The key to this ongoing series of mutual (though not generally conscious or rationally planned) processes of exchange is the extent to which the husband carries out his role as provider.

FIGURE 10-1 The family (in the *traditional* pattern for marriage) in relation to the economic-opportunity system. (SOURCE: Partially adapted from John Scanzoni, *The Black Family in Modern Society: Patterns of Stability and Security*, enlarged edition, University of Chicago Press, 1977, pp. 199–200.)

on in a traditional marriage in which the husband is the primary breadwinner.

The economic-opportunity structure may be thought of as a network of ways and means through which success and achievement may be attained in American society. It may also be thought of as a reward system, offering both tangible and intangible benefits. These benefits not only include money, prestige, and status; there are other significant rewards which may not seem so obvious without further reflection. For example, the degree to which a family is incorporated into the economic system is associated with such things as mental and physical health, educational, job, and cultural opportunities, and so on.

Families on the fringes of the economic-opportunity system have more problems with physical health (National Center for Health Statistics, ser. 10, no. 147, 1985). They also have more mental illness, have higher death rates and a lower life expectancy, and face problems of overcrowding, poor nutrition, excessive drinking, violence, lack of privacy, burdensome debts, and low educational and verbal skills—to mention only a few handicaps associated with poverty (Herzog, 1967). The rewards associated with fitting into the economic-opportunity system come to the poor in only meager packages, and the dissatisfaction felt in receiving such scanty benefits carries over into marital dissatisfaction.

We have seen that marriage involves reward seeking. But the level of rewards that may be obtained depends upon the couple's socioeconomic status. In traditional marriages (where the husband is considered the unique or chief provider, whether it is a head-complement arrangement or in the senior partner-junior partner pattern) this socioeconomic status depends upon the husband's standing in relation to the economic-

opportunity structure. This standing may be looked at both in objective terms (the actual *fact* of the husband's income) and in subjective terms (how the spouses *feel* about the level of rewards the husband is able to obtain from the opportunity system).

Research has shown that for both blacks and whites, there are positive relationships between economic factors and satisfactions within the marriage (Blood and Wolfe, 1960). Furthermore, economic satisfactions are strongly related to the family's actual economic position (Scanzoni, 1977). The flow of causes seems to go like this: The husband's education influences his job status, which in turn influences his income. The income in turn influences his wife's economic satisfaction, which in turn influences the expressive satisfaction of both partners (Scanzoni, 1975a).

Actual Income: The Objective Factor A word of caution may be in order at this point. It is an oversimplification to try to formulate a neat, unqualified equation: more money equals more marital satisfaction. We would be telling only half the story if we were to say that the objective fact of income (the actual number of dollars the husband earns) is in itself the determining factor of expressive satisfactions. Such a simple summary of the situation applies mainly to those near or below the poverty line, where the strains of barely making ends meet do take their toll on the marital relationship and there is little doubt that expressive satisfactions would increase if income increased. One respondent from a black ghetto put it this way: "The men don't have jobs. The woman, she starts nagging. He don't have the money so he leaves. She ADC's it. If he had a job the family unit could come back together" (Rainwater, 1970:169).

A wife in such a situation feels an emotional estrangement from her husband because of his poor provision. Because of him, the family is not integrated into the economic-opportunity system with all its promises of success, money, and esteem. Since the objective rewards furnished by the husband are so few, both husband and wife feel a sense of alienation not only from the opportunity structure but also from each other.

This point becomes clear in sociologist Mirra Komarovsky's study of blue-collar marriages (1962). She found that when husbands are inadequate providers wives tend to be overly sensitive to various faults in their husbands and may blame their failure on these factors. In reaction to such faultfinding, a husband may become more anxious about economic inadequacy and may take out his frustrations in drinking, angry outbursts, violence, or emotional withdrawal. The couple tends to avoid topics that matter most (bills, fears about illness, the uncertain future) because they are painful, with the result that a certain remoteness develops between the spouses (Komarovsky, 1962:291–292).

Among couples with an *unemployed* husband, marital communication especially suffers. "Communication between spouses in blue-collar marriages has been described at best as lacking in both quantity and quality . . . compared to white-collar, middle-class marriages," writes researcher Jeffry H. Larson (1984:509), a specialist in family relations. "The combination of a non-communication norm and increased marital role stress during unemployment may lead to increased withdrawal and an almost total breakdown in the quality of communication." Larson concludes that "unemployment seems to splinter an already susceptible marital system in blue-collar families" (p. 510).

Money evidently takes on much greater importance in the lives of those couples who have the least. (© Janice Rogovin 1982/The Picture Cube)

In yet another study, sociologists found that in 9 cases out of 10, wives who ranked the economic aspect as "the most valuable aspect of marriage" were women married to men whose income was less than the median or men who were *downwardly mobile* (defined as having "failed to achieve the occupational level of their fathers"). Money evidently takes on much greater importance to those couples who have the least (Blood and Wolfe, 1960:81).

Feelings about Income: The Subjective Factor A standard of living that is considered satisfying to one person might not, however, be satisfying to someone else. Economic satisfaction is, after all, a subjective matter. For example, suppose that Ann Jones and Barbara Smith both have husbands who earn $20,000. Ann is content with her family's standard of living. She and her husband work together on careful budgeting, own their own home, drive an economy car, and feel they are doing well. Their economic satisfaction extends over into satisfaction with the expressive aspects of marriage as well.

In contrast, Barbara is dissatisfied with the standard of living a $20,000 annual income forces her to maintain. "How can any family get along decently on that paltry amount in these days of rising prices?" she complains.

She nags her husband to look for a better job or even to "moonlight" in order to bring in more money. Barbara would like a better home in a more prestigious neighborhood, more expensive furniture, nicer clothing, more luxury items, travel opportunities, more money to spend on the children, and so on. Her lack of economic satisfaction (despite the objective fact of her husband's income, which is exactly the same as that of Ann's husband) causes Barbara to be less satisfied with the expressive elements in her marriage also. She finds it hard to show empathy and affection to a husband who is not rewarding her as she feels she deserves to be rewarded.

The contrast between the hypothetical Ann and Barbara demonstrates the point of Figure 10-2. Marital satisfactions are related to both objective and subjective economic factors. For couples considerably below the national median income, the line between the objective factor (actual dollars) is likely to be direct. But as husbands' earnings increase toward the median income level and then beyond, the line becomes more and more indirect as subjective factors (*feelings* about economic rewards) increasingly influence expressive satisfactions. The median family income in 1983 was $24,580 (latest available statistics, U.S. Bureau of the Census, *Statistical Abstract of the United States: 1985*, Table 743). Ann's and Barbara's families are living on an income several thousand dollars below that median. But their subjective reactions differ greatly.

The interrelationships between economic satisfaction and the expressive dimension of marriage showed up clearly in our study of more than three thousand married persons (Scanzoni, 1975a). The aspect of expressiveness found to be especially important was *empathy*, because according to the research findings it is empathy that affects the other

FIGURE 10-2 The influence of economic factors on marital satisfaction.

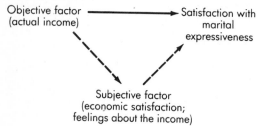

areas of expressiveness—companionship and physical affection.

Empathy in Traditional Marriage Patterns

Empathy means sharing another's thoughts, feelings, and experiences. We are empathizing with other persons when mentally and emotionally we enter into their sufferings, worries, triumphs, or joys. Empathy from others can banish feelings of aloneness and can bring a sense of affirmation, support, and encouragement. People desire to be listened to, taken seriously, given recognition and approval. Psychiatrist Thomas Harris (1967) refers to this need as "the psychological version of the early physical stroking" which is so crucial during infancy (also Berne, 1964).

When people enter marriage, empathy is a sought-after reward. Spouses are expected to be able to confide in each other, talk things over, and find understanding and reinforcement. When such empathy isn't forthcoming from one's spouse, persons may seek alternative sources of rewards. A woman may phone her mother or a friend and pour out her heartaches. Or a man may proposition a female acquaintance with the familiar line, "My wife just doesn't understand me."

Sociological studies have attempted to measure the degree to which persons are satisfied with the empathy they receive in their marriages. Empathy can be looked upon as having two major components—communication and understanding. In three separate large-scale studies, satisfaction with *communication* was measured by asking each respondent how he or she felt about the way he or she could confide in the spouse and discuss anything that comes up. Was such communication perceived to be very good, OK, or not so good? The degree of satisfaction with *understanding* was measured by asking: "How do you feel about the way your wife (husband) understands your problems and feelings? Do you feel her (his) understanding is: Very Good, OK, Not so good?" In general, our findings from all these studies combined may be summed up in the form of five generalizations, each of which will be examined in turn (Scanzoni, 1970, 1975a, 1977; also see Blood and Wolfe, 1960).

For Wives, Economic Satisfaction and Empathy Satisfaction Are Related First, our studies have shown that in general, *among both black and white women, the main positive influence on satisfaction with marital empathy is economic satisfaction.* More than any other variable measured, *economic satisfaction* most influences, explains, or predicts how wives feel about the communication and understanding they receive in their relationships with their husbands.

However, as we have seen, feeling materially rewarded is a subjective matter. How then can a sociologist assume to predict that wives who are economically satisfied will

(Drawing by Frascino, © 1977 The New Yorker Magazine, Inc.)

"You're always telling me you know exactly how I feel. Well, this time I'm calling your bluff. Exactly how <u>do</u> I feel?"

also be satisfied with the expressiveness in their marriages? Might not the degree of satisfaction in either realm simply reflect personality differences?

It is important to keep in mind that explanations and predictions in sociology are based upon research showing what is true of *most* people in a given situation. But this is not to deny that there may be exceptions. In this case, for example, while it is true that most wives' economic satisfaction relates to their husbands' actual income, there are some wives who are satisfied with a lower income and a simpler lifestyle. One illustration might be that of a married couple who choose to carry out humanitarian or religious ideals by identifying with the poor in an urban ghetto or a rural depressed area. Perhaps the husband is a doctor or minister. The wife knows he could be earning a much larger income elsewhere, but she shares his vision and is content with a much lower standard of living than his education and profession would normally imply. However, we must keep in mind that such exceptional cases spring from free choice and are quite different from those cases where persons from birth onward are trapped in a cycle of poverty and forced to endure a lifestyle deprived of the rewards they yearn for. Such people are *not* economically satisfied.

Sociological research looks at random samples which are representative of a total population and draws conclusions based on *probability* or likelihood. It cannot tell us what will be true of each individual case, but it can show us what is likely. We may expect and predict therefore that the empathy a lawyer's wife receives will seem more satisfactory to her than does the empathy a janitor's wife receives. Such conclusions are based on statistics showing what is true of the vast majority, but any one case might not fit the overall picture. The lawyer and his wife

might be on the verge of divorce, for example, while the janitor and his wife might have a warm, loving relationship that has spanned nearly half a century.

It is interesting at this point to notice a slight difference between black wives and white wives with regard to what accounts for economic satisfaction. Among white wives, the biggest indicator is clearly the objective fact of the husband's actual income. Among men, both black and white, feelings of economic satisfaction or dissatisfaction are also linked to the actual amount of money they earn. But among black wives, although their husbands' income and education are important, the research shows these items to be secondary to something else in importance. That "something else" is the wives' own "task-capability ranking." Black wives who rated themselves positively on such matters as intellectual ability, ability to organize things, ability to handle a number of responsibilities, knowledge and experience necessary to hold a job now or later, and abilities in such areas as budgeting, home management, cooking, and child care were also wives who were more apt to be content economically—in spite of the fact that their husbands earned less than the husbands of comparable white women (Scanzoni, 1975a).

Women who view themselves as more capable in skills and tasks may feel that they can therefore stretch limited income further. Economic deprivation has forced them to develop abilities that serve them well in coping with such deprivation. Apparently, the greater this coping ability, the less painful the deprivation is perceived to be; and this in turn means greater economic satisfaction.

The only exception to this pattern is among black wives whose husbands have high education. Then the pattern shifts so that it resembles that of whites; the husband's income becomes the strongest influence on economic satisfaction. It seems that where actual resources are greater (higher income is linked with higher education), there is less need to rely on a coping mechanism in order to feel a sense of economic satisfaction. Instead economic satisfaction is more directly related to one's actual economic situation (Scanzoni, 1975a).

For Husbands, Empathy Satisfaction Relates to Wives' Capabilities A second generalization from our research is this: *among both black and white men, satisfaction with empathy received in marriage is related to satisfaction with wives' capabilities in performing tasks.* There is no denying that economic satisfaction plays an important part in how satisfied a person feels about the communication and understanding received in marriage. This is true for men no less than for women. However, the research findings indicated that white husbands ranked economic satisfaction only in second place as an influence on satisfaction with empathy. And black husbands ranked economic satisfaction third, just after "expressive self-concept" (the degree to which the men considered themselves to be nurturant, supportive, and person-oriented). Placed at the top of the list as the *major positive influence* on satisfaction with marital empathy for both races was satisfaction with their wives' abilities and skills. Husbands who considered their wives to be doing a good job of carrying out mental, social, and practical tasks were likely to be husbands who reported they were satisfied with their wives' communication skills and understanding as well (Scanzoni, 1975a).

One explanation for this finding may be that women who are competent in general are also women who are competent in handling the demanding processes of talking things over and working things through in a marriage relationship. Such wives may have

mastered empathy skills just as they have mastered other kinds of skills.

Another explanation, particularly applicable to *traditional* marriages, relates to exchange theory. Just as wives feel gratitude toward their husbands because of the status and material benefits the husbands provide, husbands may feel gratitude toward their wives because of the wives' competencies and the various benefits that spring from these abilities. Although it is not necessarily conscious, a sense of obligation may be felt by both spouses so that they respond to one another with open communication and warm understanding—in other words, with empathy. The wife responds because of her husband's role as breadwinner, his role outside the home. The husband's response to his wife, according to our research, is based on her competencies both inside the home (cooking, household management, child care, entertaining) and outside the home (knowledge and appreciation of literature, music, and art; intellectual ability, ability to organize things; knowledge and experience necessary to hold a job, and so on).

To try to pinpoint one exact explanation of the relationship between the husband's empathy satisfaction and the wife's task-capability rating is difficult because no doubt more than one explanation is involved. Again we must think in terms of process, perhaps in terms of a computer system with many feedback loops intertwined and affecting one another. If the wife is empathic toward the husband, he is likely to respond with empathy toward her. At the same time, his income enters in, as does her task-performance ability.

However, one finding did emerge which again gets us back to the matter of social status. There is no way of escaping its influence on marital satisfactions. The research data indicated that better-educated wives are the ones likely to be ranked as more competent and skillful. Better-educated wives are also likely to be married to better-educated husbands, and better-educated husbands are those most likely to confer the benefits of higher social status and income. These wives are therefore more likely to be economically satisfied and hence more responsive toward their husbands with empathy for this reason in addition to their possession of skills in communication and understanding. Again it becomes clear that many different interrelated factors feed into the marital-exchange process.

Are Wives or Husbands More Satisfied with Empathy Received?

A third research finding centers on husband-wife differences. *Husbands are more likely than wives to be satisfied with the empathy received in marriage.* An "empathy gap" showed up in all three major studies—in the 1967 sample of over 900 white Indianapolis husbands and wives, again in the 1968 sample of 400 black Indianapolis husbands and wives, and once again in our 1971 five-state probability sample of 3,100 black and white respondents from metropolitan areas of Illinois, Ohio, Indiana, Michigan, and Wisconsin (Scanzoni, 1970, 1975a, 1977).

The finding that husbands are more satisfied than wives with marital empathy could mean either that wives actually receive *less* empathy than husbands do, or else that wives desire *more* empathy than husbands do and therefore cannot be satisfied so easily as husbands.

Perhaps at first glance, the explanation for the empathy gap may appear to lie in the alleged loneliness and isolation of wives in the traditional housewife role. While their husbands are gone all day interacting with colleagues who understand them and discuss subjects of mutual interest, wives have only fragmentary conversations with the postal carrier, supermarket cashier, and children's pediatrician, and must answer endless questions and settle the squabbles of preschoolers. While the husband may feel content with empathy received both on the job and at home, the wife may look to her husband alone for empathy. Yet not only is he not there to give it all day long, but he may also tend to expect *her* to give *him* empathy when he does arrive home and be unwilling to listen to the wife's problems. "I've had a hard day at work, honey. I want to relax and forget troubles for a while." He expects her to reward his economic efforts by soothing and bolstering his spirits.

One problem with the "isolated housewife" explanation for wives' lesser satisfaction with marital empathy shows up in the statistics which indicate that the level of satisfaction is directly associated with level of social status. Higher satisfaction with marital empathy is more likely to be found among wives of higher social status; yet these are the very wives who are more likely to fit the popular picture of the isolated suburban housewife.

Conversely, blue-collar wives are not nearly so isolated. They have relationships that provide intimacy and empathy. Studies have shown that many blue-collar wives have female confidants who serve as the "functional equivalents" of their husbands' workmates. Being less geographically mobile, such wives stay in neighborhoods longer and have time to develop and maintain close friendships. Furthermore, blue-collar wives are more likely to have kin living nearby (Komarovsky, 1962). Yet, they are discontented with the level of empathy found in their marriages. It is not that such wives lack communication and understanding per se; it is rather a case of not receiving empathy from their *husbands*.

Perhaps rather than looking for an explanation in terms of supposed isolation, we might better turn our attention to the matter of socialization. There are two sides to this: Females more than males are socialized to expect a high level of empathic gratifications from marriage. Males, on the other hand, not only may be satisfied with a lower level of empathy, but they are also not socialized to be able to give empathy to the extent that is expected of females (Fasteau, 1974; Balswick and Peek, 1971; Pleck and Sawyer, 1974).

Families, schools, churches, the media, and other influences join in getting across the message that girls are to think of marriage as their absorbing life interest. From the cradle onward, females hear nursery tales about the poor girl or princess who is awakened to life's meaning by the kiss of Prince Charming and whisked off to Blissful Castle to live out her days basking in the warmth of an adoring husband who devotes his life to catering to her every wish. To prepare for that day, little girls learn that females are to develop traits of kindness, tenderness, nurturance, understanding, and emotional expression. They enter marriage expecting to take on (and being granted) the role of "socioemotional hub" or "expressive leader" in the family (Seeley, Sim, and Loosley, 1956:178). And they likewise expect expressive gratifications in return. If they receive less empathy than anticipated, they feel cheated.

Males, on the other hand, are socialized to think of the world of work as their central life interest. Marriage is viewed as an important part of life, but not the be all and end all of life, as many women see it. Thus men tend not to be so totally absorbed in family affairs as are their wives. Being less absorbed, they are satisfied with what they feel are "reasonable" amounts of communication and understanding from their wives.

In the very same marriage, the husband and wife may view the situation quite differently from one another. Sociologists speak of this as the "definition of the situation," referring to how something *appears* to a person or is defined subjectively by him or her. One person may define the situation as favorable while the other may define the same situation as unfavorable. A husband might feel that the communication and understanding that takes place in a marriage is very good, but the wife might feel this area of marriage is very weak. Persons act and react according to their personal definition of the situation.

Another possible explanation for the differences in husbands' and wives' empathy satisfaction also relates to gender-role socialization. Whereas girls are socialized to *give* empathy (and take for granted that they will receive it as well), boys are socialized to *receive* empathy far more than to give it. As children, they watch Mother kissing their bumps and bruises, relieving both physical and psychological hurts, and reassuring them in their fears and discouragements. And they see her do the same for Father. When they grow up, they expect to have wives who will perform the same function, because that's what women are "supposed" to do. Men may be satisfied with marital empathy to a greater degree than wives simply because husbands are *getting from* their wives more empathy than they are *giving to* their wives.

A familiar theme of cartoons and television situation comedies is that of the wife who tries to get her husband to listen and talk with her, only to be met by a series of grunts, "Yes, dears," or requests for a can of beer or a cup of coffee so that he can go on reading the newspaper or watching television in peace. Such scenes are far more likely to occur in lower-status homes than in higher-status families. Boys are taught to be tough, strong, nonintrospective, and to appear "manly" by keeping their feelings to themselves. The only kinds of emotions that may be expressed are those that fit with the masculine image—particularly anger and jealousy. Emotions of tenderness, compassion, and sorrow (especially when tears are involved) are considered to be the domain of the female sex; such behavior in males is looked upon with disdain as being "sissy."

Komarovsky (1962:156) speaks of the extreme difficulty which many lower-status men have when it comes to engaging in reciprocal exchanges of communication and understanding with their wives. The more disadvantaged a husband is (in terms of education, income, and occupational status), the harder he finds it to share feelings with his wife—even if he would like very much to do so.

However, our research showed that wives were less satisfied than husbands with empathy received in marriage *not only* at lower status levels but at higher status levels as well. Could it be that the gender-role socialization that emphasizes less expressiveness in males is also somewhat operative among higher-status husbands? Sociologists Jack Balswick and Charles Peek (1971) suggest that such may be the case. They point out that "American society is ironically short-changing males" in terms of their ability to fulfill marital role expectations. "Society inconsistently teaches the male that to be masculine is to be inexpressive, while at the same time expectations in the marital role are defined in terms of sharing affection and companionship which involves the ability to communicate and express feelings."

Balswick and Peek describe the socialization process in which parents brag about a child's being "all boy." "All boy" is used in

Traditional gender-role expectations have separated women and men into two distinct worlds. (© Christa Armstrong 1979/Photo Researchers, Inc.)

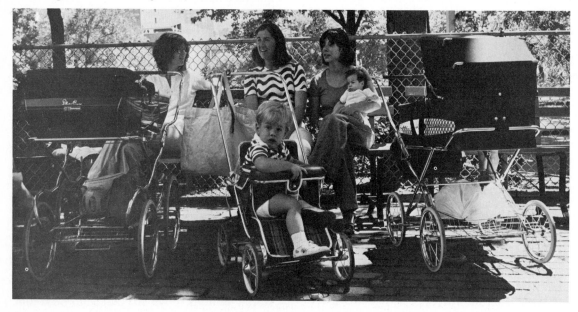

reference to behavior that is aggressive or "getting into mischief, getting dirty, etc., but never . . . to denote behavior which is an expression of affection, tenderness, or emotion." As a result of this socialization process, two basic types may emerge: the emotionally reserved "cowboy," who tries to convey a tough, he-man image and who does not express his feelings toward women even though he has such feelings, and the "playboy," who doesn't even have emotional feelings toward women but views women as expendable commodities to be manipulated and used.

Gender-role stereotypes may cause problems not only with respect to gender-role socialization in childhood but also in the way they separate men and women into virtually two distinct worlds during adulthood. At the middle-class cocktail party, the men gather in assorted groups to talk business, politics, or sports, while the women gather in other assorted groups to talk about children, recipes, schools, and problems of finding household help. In blue-collar settings, the men meet together at the corner bar or enjoy spending evenings "out with the boys" playing poker or bowling, while the women gather with female relatives and friends to share their problems and advice on babies, cooking, sewing, house care, and husbands. Husbands and wives whose interests are so different from one another may find open communication and understanding extremely difficult.

Wives, having been socialized to be nurturant, might be able to give empathy to their husbands in spite of the "different worlds" they live in; but for men it may seem much harder. Not only have they grown up with the idea that inexpressiveness is associated with masculinity, they have also learned to consider women's interests trivial. Yet empathy involves entering into the emo-

When husbands' interests are so different from wives' interests, communication and understanding may be difficult. (Michael Hayman/Black Star)

tions of another and seeing and feeling something as that person sees it. If a husband has difficulty entering into his wife's experiences because he feels a certain disdain for "woman's world" and at the same time is convinced that his wife wouldn't be able to understand and share in the most vital concerns of "man's world," it is not surprising that his wife will not be satisfied with the empathy her marriage offers. (See Rubin, 1983.)

Perhaps empathy would increase if gender roles were less rigid and husbands and wives had more in common. This point was made in a special television drama of recent years. A middle-aged, working-class wife, feeling bored and unfulfilled now that the children were grown and having had her "consciousness raised" through a women's group, tried to describe her deepest feelings to her cab-driver husband. But he refused to empathize

COMMENTS OF A WORKING-CLASS HUSBAND

"They say married people live longer," he said one day, "but I think it just seems longer."

I once asked him why he got married when he views marriage with such lack of enthusiasm.

"What the hell you going to do?" he replied. "You just can't go on shacking up with girls all your life—I did plenty of that when I was single."

He paused to order another beer. "A man, sooner or later, likes to have a home of his own, and some kids, and to have that you have to get married. There's no way out of it—they got you hooked.". . . .

. . . It seems clear that this man is not really complaining about his wife—he is unhappy with *marriage*. He also prefers men as a species to women; except for sexual purposes, he finds women dull and uninteresting. This is not the sort of man who would consider divorce. He is smart enough to know that he would find another wife just as restraining as this one. He also knows that he does not want to go through life as a bachelor.

SOURCE: E. E. LeMasters, *Blue-Collar Aristocrats* (Madison: University of Wisconsin Press, 1975), pp. 37, 41–42.

---

and reacted to her communication efforts by falling asleep, turning away to watch television football broadcasts, or postponing discussion.

He *did* hear her and respond when she asked if she could get a job. The answer was clearly no. The idea threatened his masculine image. However, the wife went looking for a job anyway, and the husband had no idea where she was or if she'd ever come back. That night she phoned and asked him to meet her at a restaurant. Suddenly he didn't care about her job idea. He listened with genuine empathy as she told of waiting in employment offices, and then he said that he knew what that was like, for he too had often pounded the pavement looking for a job and had stood in lines of job applicants. A bond of comradeship and shared experience seemed to grow between the husband and the wife, and suddenly the strong, tough husband began to cry. His wife was moved. Reaching for his hand across the restaurant table, she said she had never felt closer to him. She was receiving the empathy she had longed for.

One reason that empathy satisfaction is greater at higher status levels may be that such couples live in less rigidly distinct male and female spheres and therefore have more in common. Another research finding indicates that husbands at higher levels are more likely to share information and news about their occupations with their wives, thereby giving wives a greater sense of participation in the totality of their husbands' lives than is true at lower levels. Husbands at lower income levels may feel less successful and prefer not to have their employment performances come under their wives' scrutiny any more than necessary (Scanzoni, 1970; Komarovsky, 1962:152ff).

Empathy Satisfaction Differences between Blacks and Whites Another of our research findings is this: *whites are more likely than blacks to be satisfied with the empathy they receive in marriage.* This fourth generalization has nothing to do with inherent racial characteristics of either blacks or whites but rather may be explained by the relationship of each racial grouping to the economic-

COMMENTS OF A WORKING-CLASS WIFE

"When I was a young girl I couldn't wait to get married—I thought it was the most wonderful thing in the world. Now I have my doubts."

The speaker is a woman who has been married for about thirty years. She has two grown children but no grandchildren as yet.

"The men go to work while the wife stays home with the kids—it's a long day with no other adult to talk to. That's what drives mothers to the soap operas—stupid as they are.

"Then the husband stops at some tavern to have a few with his buddies from the job—not having seen them since they left to drive home ten minutes ago. The poor guy is lonely and thirsty and needs to relax before the rigors of another evening before the television set."

She paused to sip her beer.

"Meanwhile," she continued, "the little woman has supper ready and is trying to hold the kids off 'until Daddy gets home so we can all eat together.' After a while she gives up this little dream and eats with the kids while the food is still eatable.

"About seven o'clock Daddy rolls in, feeling no pain, eats a few bites of the overcooked food, sits down in front of the TV set, and falls asleep."

She ordered another beer. Then she said: "This little drama is repeated several thousand times until they have their twenty-fifth wedding anniversary and then everybody tells them how happy they have been.

"And you know what?" she added. "By now they are both so damn punch drunk neither one of them knows whether their marriage has been a success or not."

After a pause to light a cigarette, she said: "I think it's very funny—but I'm not laughing very hard."

I asked her why women seemed so anxious to marry in view of the gloomy state of marriage in our society.

"I don't really know," she said, "but I think it is their desire for children. My children have meant a great deal to me and that is the part of marriage that women like most, in my opinion."

SOURCE: E. E. LeMasters, *Blue-Collar Aristocrats* (Madison: University of Wisconsin Press, 1975), pp. 37, 41–42.

---

opportunity system (Scanzoni, 1977:204–210; 1975a).

Because of the limited opportunities afforded blacks in a white-dominated society, the blacks in our sample as a whole were found to have significantly less education and income and lower job status as compared to whites. Even when education levels are held constant, black men earn less money than white men. According to the U.S. Bureau of the Census, the median income of black men with a high school education was $12,498 in 1982, compared to $17,583 for white men with a high school education. College-educated black men earned a median income of $16,532, while college-educated white men earned $25,368. The figures for men with a graduate school education were $21,902 and $29,068, respectively. (U.S. Bureau of the Census, *Current Population Reports*, ser. P-60, no. 142, 1984, p. 159).

The 1980 census showed an overrepresentation of blacks in certain occupations. The Census Bureau reports, "For example, although blacks comprised about 10 percent of the total civilian labor force, they constituted 14 percent of all operators, fabricators, and laborers and 18 percent of all service workers." The report goes on to state that "in contrast, blacks were underrepresented in managerial and professional specialty occupations (6 percent) and technical, sales, and administrative support occupations (8 percent)." The majority of black men (55 percent) were employed as operators, fabricators, or laborers, or in service occupations. Blacks were also more likely than whites to be unemployed. The unemployment rate for blacks was double that of whites (U.S. Bureau of the Census, Special Publication, PIO/POP-83-1, 1983, pp. 9–11).

These inequities have an effect on black marriages. In discussing the exchanges that go on between a husband and wife, we saw how important economic satisfaction is for exchanges of empathy. However, economic satisfaction among blacks is lower than among whites for the simple reason that the economic situation among blacks is less favorable. It is a matter of *relative deprivation*. Relative to whites, blacks earn less and have lower status. (See Figure 10-3.)

The sociological concept of *reference group* sheds some light on the situation. A

FIGURE 10-3 Median family income by race of householder: 1970 to 1981. (SOURCE: U.S. Bureau of the Census, Special Publication PIO/POP-83-1, "America's Black Population: 1970–1982, A Statistical View" (Washington, D.C.: U.S. Government Printing Office, 1983), p. 7.)

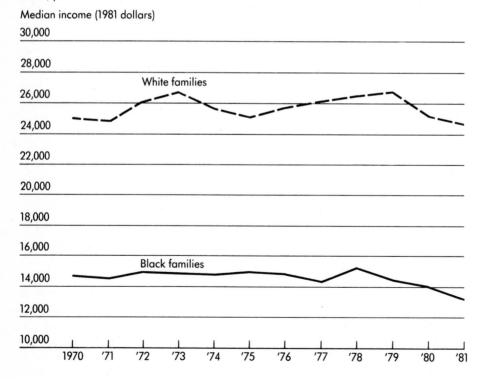

reference group is the group to which individuals or other groups compare themselves; it becomes a kind of measurement standard for assessing how well one is doing. While blacks have made considerable gains in social position as compared to the past, these gains have been accompanied by "psychological losses," according to social psychologist Thomas Pettigrew (1964:187), because many blacks have shifted their frame of reference in recent decades. Whereas formerly blacks tended to judge how well off they were by comparing present conditions with their previous situation, Pettigrew points out, "the rising expectations of the present are increasingly framed in terms of the wider white society."

Pettigrew and others claim that blacks at all status levels feel an intense strain resulting from relative deprivation. In fact, there is some evidence that the higher the status of blacks, the greater are the feelings of relative deprivation (Blau and Duncan, 1967). This may explain our finding that blacks with higher occupational status were no more satisfied with expressiveness in marriage than were blacks of less status—a finding that is not true of whites, where marital expressive satisfaction increases with higher social status.

Although these feelings of relative deprivation influence empathy satisfaction and processes of social exchange within the marriage relationship, they are not deliberate, conscious, and rational. Rather, they result from what sociologists speak of as a *socially structured* situation. Social forces rather than personal preferences and individual characteristics are influencing behavior in such cases. As white society denies equal benefits to blacks who have achieved the same educational and occupational position as whites, a sense of relative deprivation becomes very real to blacks. Since higher-sta-

tus white wives take other white wives as their reference group, they can feel relatively satisfied with the objective rewards of money, prestige, and social status provided by their husbands. But black wives also take white wives as a reference group, and the comparison means relative dissatisfaction or deprivation (Scanzoni, 1977:208).

It is not that black wives respond with less empathy toward their husbands because they "blame" the husbands for not providing the material and nonmaterial rewards that white wives receive. Black wives know that their deprivation stems from the white-controlled economic-opportunity system. Yet, in traditional marriages where the husband is the link between the economic structure and the family, the wives are apt to react toward the husband simply because they can't react directly toward the reward-denying system itself. The process is subtle and usually not conscious. And even at higher status levels, since the husband represents the economic system, he meets with a response on the wife's part that because of *relative* deprivation is no more positive than that of black wives of lesser status who experience fewer *absolute* rewards.

Empathy Satisfaction Influences Other Satisfactions   How couples feel about the empathy in marriage is important not only for its own sake but also for its effect on other aspects of the marital relationship. *Satisfaction with empathy in marriage influences satisfaction with the other expressive elements: companionship and physical affection.* This fifth generalization from our research was found to be true of both blacks and whites. In addition to its own intrinsic benefits to the spouses, empathy evidently serves as a mechanism affecting other aspects of the couple's relationship as well. The more effectively husbands and wives can empathize or communicate and understand one another, the more likely they are to be able to handle satisfactorily decisions and disagreements about time spent together, leisure pursuits, sex relations, contraception, and so on. Thus they are likely to evaluate companionship and physical affection positively (Scanzoni, 1975a).

Companionship in Traditional Marriage Patterns

Marriage, as most Americans idealize it, is virtually synonymous with *companionship.* As one bridesmaid expressed it to a bride on her wedding day, "I envy you. You'll never have to worry about loneliness. You have a permanent 'best friend' now—someone who will always be with you wherever you go. That must be a *wonderful* feeling!"

In other times and places, companionship in marriage has not been emphasized or expected. Ancient Greek men kept their wives secluded to assure the legitimacy of offspring but found companionship with highly cultured mistresses called *hetairai* (Seltman, 1956). And in the early days of the Israeli kibbutz, the husband and wife who were often seen in one another's company were scorned by the community because such spouse companionship was viewed as disloyalty to the larger collective life (Talmon, 1972:12).

Only recently has husband-wife companionship come to be a sought-after reward among some young married couples in Japan. Traditionally, social life has not been couple-centered but sex-segregated, with husbands finding companionship with work colleagues and "bar girls," while wives interact with relatives, children, and female friends. During research on Japanese life between 1958 and 1960, sociologist Ezra Vogel (1963) found that Japanese wives were both curious and envious of American husbands and wives who went out together. Vogel writes: "One wife, upon hearing about a husband and wife going on a trip for a few days responded, 'how nice,' but after a moment's reflection added, 'but what would they talk about for so long?' "

In the United States, however, the companionship ideal of marriage is held up as a major goal toward which every couple is expected to aim. Husbands and wives are expected to accompany each other to most social occasions, to devote their leisure to mutual activities, and to enjoy simply being together as best friends. But how do American couples feel about the companionship they receive in marriage? Our research uncovered some findings that are similar to the findings related to empathy satisfaction.

Social Status and Satisfaction with Marital Companionship First of all, we found that *the higher the level of rewards provided by the husband (especially in terms of education and prestige), the more positively both spouses evaluate companionship* (Scanzoni, 1970:78). Several factors appear to be at work here. First, there is the familiar pattern of the exchange model in which the husband as the chief provider fulfills his instrumental role (financial support) which motivates the wife to fulfill her expressive role (emotional support). The better he fulfills his role, the more she reciprocates with greater expressiveness, calling forth more expressiveness on his part in turn. Companionship, as an important aspect of expressiveness, is thus rated as more satisfactory for higher-status couples.

Also not to be overlooked is that chain of events in which economic satisfaction (subjective), often stemming from economic success (objective), influences satisfaction with marital empathy. If a spouse evaluates positively the *empathy* received in marriage, he or she is likely to consider the marital partner to be a good *companion* as well. Someone with whom one can talk things over and find understanding is probably someone whose company is enjoyable in leisure pursuits, too.

Lifestyle factors may also enter in. Lower-status couples are accustomed to greater gender-role differentiation and sex-segregated leisure activities. Higher-status couples, on the other hand, are more likely to emphasize husband-wife togetherness in leisure pursuits. As a result, they rank the companionship aspect of marriage as more satisfactory than do lower-status couples.

The simple fact of money itself no doubt plays some part, too, in accounting for the relationship between higher social status and a positive evaluation of marital companionship. Leisure activities can require a considerable financial outlay. Camping and sporting equipment, travel, vacation cottages, theater tickets, dining out, entertaining friends—to name but a few of the leisure activities to which many contemporary Americans aspire—all cost money. Higher-status couples possess greater resources and thus have greater access to these means of fostering marital companionship.

Husband-Wife Differences in Satisfaction with Companionship

We also found that *husbands are more satisfied than wives with the companionship received in marriage.* This second research finding is again similar to the finding with regard to empathy satisfaction. Husbands were more likely than wives to evaluate the companionship they received in marriage as "very good." Wives were more likely than husbands to evaluate marital companionship as either "OK" or "not so good." Why the difference? It appears that in both black and white marriages,

husbands may feel they spend enough time in leisure activities with their wives, whereas wives may expect and desire more. Again, the explanation probably lies in the different socialization of males and females so that wives tend to invest the companionship element in marriage with greater meaning and importance than husbands do.

White-Black Differences in Satisfaction with Companionship

A third research finding was this: *whites are more likely than blacks to be satisfied with the companionship received in marriage.* Even though as we have seen there are similarities in evaluations of companionship regardless of race, there are also differences clearly associated with race. When black couples and white couples are compared, the satisfaction with marital companionship is found to be less among blacks than among whites. Again, as we saw in the evaluation of empathy, the principle of relative deprivation appears to be operative.

Physical Affection

Along with empathy and companionship, physical affection completes the trio called "expressiveness in marriage." Physical affection may include a wide range of behaviors—the squeeze of a hand, a kiss, a hug, resting one's head on the spouse's shoulder, stroking the spouse's hair, a tender caress on the back of the neck, a playful pat on the behind, snuggling up together on a couch, sitting on the partner's lap, petting, sexual intercourse.

In popular thinking, sex is considered the most important aspect of marriage; and when a divorce occurs, people often whisper that the couple must have had a sex problem. However, the causes of divorce are much too complex to pin all the blame on sexual dissatisfaction. In fact, marriage counselors can tell of cases where couples were quite happy with the sexual side of their relationship and continued to have intercourse up until the day of the divorce and even afterwards. "Good sex" doesn't necessarily result in overall marital satisfaction. On the other hand, satisfaction with other areas of marriage (economic satisfaction, empathy, companionship) is likely to show up in satisfaction with physical affection as well.

Sex and Sociological Inquiry Aware that sexuality is usually considered a personal and private matter, sociologist James Henslin (1971:1–3) has endeavored to answer the question, "What does sociology have to do with sex?" He writes: "The sociological point of view . . . is that while it is individuals who engage in any given sexual behavior, it is their group membership that shapes, directs, and influences the forms or patterns that their sexual behaviors take. . . . Although sexual behaviors have a biological base, it is membership in groups which shapes or gives direction to the expression of this sexual drive."

Psychotherapist Wardell Pomeroy (1972: 469), formerly an associate of Alfred Kinsey at the Institute for Sex Research at Indiana University, has illustrated how a person's group classification is related to that person's sexual attitudes and behavior. Pomeroy put forth the rather dramatic suggestion that one could tell which of two adolescent boys would be more likely to attend college simply by looking at their respective sex histories. How? By comparing the boys' sex histories with the Kinsey findings on different categories of people (based upon racial-cultural grouping, educational level, occupation, parents' occupation, rural-urban background, religious group, and so on).

The sex history of one boy, for example, might indicate that he has had intercourse with a number of girls, doesn't take his clothes off for sex relations, cares more about the act than about emotional involvement with the girl, disapproves of mouth-genital contact, masturbates less than he did in his earlier teens, and has infrequent "wet dreams." The sex history of the other boy may indicate that he masturbates actively but has little or no sexual intercourse, reacts strongly to erotic stimuli, engages in petting a great deal and may try oral-genital contact, and considers sex more enjoyable in the nude. The first boy, says Pomeroy, is displaying a sexual pattern that stamps him as being from a lower social-status background, and few boys in this category would be likely to go on to college. It is the second boy who is likely to further his education past high school, because his pattern of sexual behavior shows that in all probability he is from a higher social-status background.

Pomeroy's way of drawing attention to the association between sex and status-level differences may seem a bit sensational but it helps make the point. His picture of the two hypothetical unmarried young men is based upon actual findings that emerged in the Kinsey studies of the 1940s and 1950s. Just as clearly, the data showed that social status affects the sexual behavior of married couples. For example, it was found that wives with higher educational backgrounds were more likely to reach orgasm during marital coitus and to achieve orgasm more frequently than wives with lower levels of education. Couples of higher educational background were also found to spend more time in sexual foreplay before intercourse (Kinsey et al., 1953, chap. 9).

Marital Sex at Lower Status Levels Couples with lower levels of education and socioeconomic status differ from higher-level couples in both sexual attitudes and practices.

At the same time, researchers into sex behavior have found evidence that lower-level couples have much in common *with each other* in the same culture, in other cultures, and in other periods of history (Pomeroy, 1972:470).

Rainwater (1964), in comparing his own studies of American lower-status marriages with lower-status marriages in Mexico, Puerto Rico, and England, found several common characteristics. In all four "cultures of poverty," there was a central norm that "sex is a man's pleasure and a woman's duty." Second, a double standard was practiced both with regard to childhood sex education and later sexual behavior. Girls were shielded from sex information and expected to be sexually innocent until marriage; boys were left to their own devices and expected to experiment.

A third characteristic sexual pattern among these poverty groups in all four countries was the tendency for males to separate women into categories of "good women" and "bad or loose women." *Bad women* were defined as those who were sexually active and enjoyed sex—for example, prostitutes. Wives were expected to be "good women" who were uninterested in sex. In studies of a Mexican village, anthropologist Oscar Lewis (1951:326) found that men generally felt that sexual play was for the seduction of other women and deliberately refrained from arousing their own wives sexually because they didn't want their wives to "get to like it too much." The fear is sometimes expressed that female sexual enjoyment may lead to affairs with men other than their husbands.

What do marriages at lower status levels have in common that accounts for these attitudes toward sexuality? As Rainwater (1964) pondered that question, he came up with the hypothesis that *rigidly segregated gender roles* may be the key. Couples whose roles are widely separated are unlikely to have close sexual relations, and wives especially are unlikely to find marital sex gratifying.

Several years before Rainwater suggested his hypothesis, the British social anthropologist Elizabeth Bott (1957) had come to a similar conclusion in research on urban families in England. As representative of couples with segregated gender roles, Bott referred to a semiskilled factory worker and his wife who placed little importance on shared interests and joint activities, preferring instead a "harmonious division of labor." The wife's comments indicated that "she felt physical sexuality was an intrusion on a peaceful domestic relationship rather than an expression of such a relationship." In contrast, couples in Bott's study who stressed joint activities and male-female equality were couples in which the husbands held professional, semiprofessional, and clerical occupations. For these couples, a mutual enjoyment of sex was considered an important part of shared interests in general.

Change and Resistance   According to sociologist Lillian Rubin (1976), some of the Kinsey researchers' findings about working-class sexual attitudes and practices no longer fit. In her nonrandom sample of fifty blue-collar families (with wives under age 40), whom she compared with a smaller sample of twenty-five professional families from the middle class, Rubin saw signs of change, which she summed up as follows:

> Among the people I spoke with, working-class and middle-class couples engage in essentially the same kinds of sexual behaviors in roughly the same proportions. But working-class wives express considerably more discomfort about what they do in the marriage bed than their middle-class sisters. (pp. 137–38)

SEX IN WORKING-CLASS MARRIAGES

. . . it is the men who now more often speak of their wish for sex to be freer and with more mutual enjoyment:

"I think sex should be that you enjoy each other's bodies. Judy doesn't care for touching and feeling each other though."

. . . who push their wives to be sexually experimental, to try new things and different ways:

"She thinks there's just one right position and one right way—in the dark with her eyes closed tight. Anything that varies from that makes her upset."

. . . who sometimes are more concerned than their wives for her orgasm: "It's just not enjoyable if she doesn't have a climax, too. She says she doesn't mind, but I do."

For the women, these attitudes of their men—their newly expressed wish for sexual innovation, their concern for their wives' gratification—are not an unmixed blessing. In any situation, there is a gap between the ideal statements of a culture and the reality in which people live out their lives—a time lag between the emergence of new cultural forms and their internalization by the individuals who must act upon them. In sexual matters, that gap is felt most keenly by women. Socialized from infancy to experience their sexuality as a negative force to be inhibited and repressed, women can't just switch "on" as the changing culture or their husbands dictate. Nice girls don't! Men *use* bad girls but marry good girls! Submit, but don't enjoy—at least not obviously so! These are the injunctions that are laid aside with difficulty, if at all.

SOURCE: Lillian Breslow Rubin, *Worlds of Pain: Life in the Working-Class Family* (New York: Basic Books, 1976), p. 136.

Rubin illustrates by speaking of the conflicts that arise in working-class marriages as husbands become interested in spending more time in foreplay and experimentation with different sexual techniques, yet meet with resistance on the part of their wives. Some wives, for example, reluctantly go along with their husbands' desires for oral-genital sex because they feel it is their duty to please their husbands, or because they fear they will cause their husbands to fulfill sexual desires elsewhere if they refuse. Sometimes they give in to their husbands' wishes out of genuine caring, even though they personally feel uncomfortable. And sometimes their willingness "is offered as a bribe or payment for good behavior—not surprising in a culture that teaches a woman that her body is a negotiable instrument" (p. 140).

Whereas the middle-class women in Rubin's sample tended to be relaxed about the topic, recognizing that oral sex "is a widely practiced and acceptable behavior," working-class wives tended to be filled with guilt. One woman summed up the feelings of most of the others in the sample when she said:

> I always feel like it's not quite right, no matter what Pete says. I guess it's not the way I was brought up, and it's hard to get over that. He keeps telling me it's okay if it's between us, that anything we do is okay. But I'm not sure about that. How do I know in the end he won't think I'm cheap? (p. 141)

Rubin shows that the guilts and anxieties spring not only from past socialization but also from the mixed messages given by many blue-collar husbands who continue to think in terms of "cheap tramps," "those kind" of women, and so on. The men themselves, in spite of certain liberalized sexual attitudes, don't seem to shake off "good girl/bad girl" distinctions easily. Some wives are confused, knowing that on the one hand their husbands boast of wives' "innocence" and limited knowledge in sexual matters; but on the other hand, the husbands are suddenly expecting wives to engage in what might strike the women as strange and exotic behaviors that don't fit their image of themselves as good wives and mothers. Ambivalence on the part of husbands is also seen in their complaints about wives' not being more assertive and initiating sexual relations, while at the same time accusing wives of being too "aggressive" and "unfeminine" when they *do* try to take the initiative.

Even their husbands' new concern about wives' orgasms is not always welcomed by blue-collar wives. "For some," writes Rubin, "it has indeed opened the possibility for pleasures long denied. For others, however, it is experienced as another demand in a life already too full of demands." To illustrate, she quotes a mother of six children, who not only is employed part-time but also cares for an elderly, sick father in addition to all the housekeeping responsibilities:

> It feels like somebody's always wanting something from me. Either one of the kids is hanging on to me or pulling at me, or my father needs something. And if it's not them, then Tom's always coming after me with that gleam in his eye. Then, it's not enough if I just let him have it, because if I don't have a climax, he's not happy. I get so tired of everybody wanting something from me all the time. I sometimes think I hate sex. (p. 151)

Sexual Satisfaction and Social Status
Rainwater's (1965:63) studies of American marriages at different class levels are applicable here. In researching degrees of sexual interest, enjoyment, and commitment, he found "a continuum from strong positive involvement with marital sexuality to strong rejection" (see also Bell, 1974). Social status plays an important part in one's position on the continuum. Among middle-class wives, 86 percent indicated very positive or positive feelings about marital sex, as did 69 percent of working-class wives. But 31 percent of working-class wives reported negative and rejecting attitudes—more than double that of middle-class wives who reported such feelings. Among lower-class or *under-class* wives (those below poverty level), less than half reported positive or very positive evaluations of sex in marriage, and 54 percent expressed negative and rejecting feelings. Both the more rigid gender-role segregation and the fewer economic rewards at this level are no doubt operating in the wife's lower satisfaction.

Blood and Wolfe's (1960:224–229) study of Detroit marriages also indicated that wives' satisfaction with marital expressiveness decreased as social status decreased. Our own findings concur with those of Blood and Wolfe and Rainwater. While it can't be

Sexual satisfaction in marriage is often related to social factors, such as a couple's economic situation and husband-wife empathy, as well as personality factors. (© Joel Gordon 1979)

denied that personality factors enter into physical expressiveness in marriage, social factors also play a significant part. In an achievement-oriented society, a sense of self-worth comes to be linked with success in the economic-opportunity system. It hurts to realize that one is only on the fringes of that system. This feeling of disappointment and dissatisfaction affects husband-wife empathy and carries over into feelings about physical affection as well (Scanzoni, 1970:79–107; 1975a).

Komarovsky (1962:93) observed this phenomenon in her study of blue-collar marriages. One 29-year-old woman said that sex was "wearing off" after ten years of marriage and five children. The wife indicated dissatisfaction with her economic situation and remarked that she might have more interest in sex if her husband were "getting along better." In Rainwater's (1965) interviews, a blue-collar wife complained of her husband's irresponsibility in money matters and his failure to be mobile into the middle class and in-

dicated that these negative feelings about her husband negatively affected her feelings about their sexual relationship. And in another case, the couple was lower class, and the husband was unemployed. Because he had no interest in finding work and the rent was past due, the wife commented that she had lost all desire for sexual intercourse, saying that now she just tolerated it (Rainwater, 1965:90–97).

Seeking Sexual Satisfaction outside Marriage If persons feel their spouses aren't meeting their sexual needs, are they justified in seeking sexual satisfaction with other persons outside the marriage? Among the working-class men in a five-year participant-observation study by sociologist E. E. LeMasters (1975), there persisted a belief that men had greater sexual needs than women and thus had the right to engage in extramarital sex when their needs weren't being adequately met within marriage. Except in highly unusual situations, however, no such rights were granted women; women were assumed to have less need for regular sex. "In other words," says LeMasters, summing up the attitude of the blue-collar men in his sample, "a woman who seeks extramarital sexual partners is a 'slut,' whereas a man who engages in the same behavior is 'starved' for sexual relief by his wife" (p. 96).

Some observers suggest that, as such double-standard thinking disappears (as has been happening within the middle class especially), and as new and more open concepts of marriage are introduced, some couples may establish new ground rules for marriage that *allow* for sex with other persons besides one's spouse (Libby, 1977b). One idea is that a disappearance of the double standard would mean that women would have options for sexual permissiveness previously taken for granted by men only—an idea similar to the reasoning applied to pre-marital sex. Indeed some researchers have suggested a connection between greater per-missiveness in *pre*marital sex and the expec-tation that *extra*marital sex will take place later on (Reiss et al., 1980). In one study of unmarried college students, those students who were already engaging in sexual inter-course were more likely than other students to report that they expected to have outside sexual involvements after they were married (Bukstel et al., 1978). In another study of 321 undergraduate male and female college students, researchers David Weis and Mi-chael Slosnerick (1981:356) found that "the group most likely to report that the various extramarital situations [both sexual and nonsexual] would be acceptable were males who disassociate sex, love, and marriage and who are highly permissive with respect to premarital coitus."

However, sexual exclusivity and sexual possessiveness have been ideals bound up in the notion of marriage as we know it in our society; the two spouses are considered to belong to one another and to have unique rights of sexual access to one another. *Adul-tery* is the legal term for having sexual inter-course with someone other than one's own spouse, and it is negatively sanctioned by public opinion, the law (where it is consid-ered grounds for divorce), and Jewish and Christian religious teachings ("Thou shalt not commit adultery" is one of the Ten Commandments).

Surveys conducted by the National Opin-ion Research Center have shown that about three-fourths of adults believe that extramar-ital sex is always wrong (Reiss et al., 1980). Research also indicates that the general pub-lic is far more willing to tolerate *pre*marital sexual permissiveness than it is to tolerate *extra*marital sex (Glenn, 1979). Sociologist Robert Bell (1971:63) suggests two reasons

for the stronger societal disapproval of extra-marital sex than of premarital sex. First, since a married person already has a socially approved partner to meet his or her sexual needs, it is assumed that there is no good rea-son to pursue outside sexual experience. Second, it is believed that sexual involve-ment outside of marriage will threaten the in-dividual's marriage relationship. Thus, the condemnation of adultery is part of societal concern for the institution of the family.

Commuting Couples and Extramarital Sex Sociologist Naomi Gerstel (1979) has questioned two assertions commonly made about extramarital sex: (1) that whether or not spouses engage in sex outside of mar-riage depends in large measure on their op-portunities to do so and (2) that changes in the *structure* of marriage (for example, movement to the egalitarian form) are linked almost inevitably with changes in basic *norms* that have governed marriage as an in-stitution (for example, sexual exclusivity).

Gerstel shows that neither assertion can be indisputably supported. Using commuter marriage as a test case, Gerstel pointed out that here was certainly an example of struc-tural change (equal-partner marriage in which the spouses' careers kept them in sep-arate residences most of the week) and an example of "increased opportunity" for ex-tramarital sex because the spouses were out of one another's sight so much of the time. Yet, among her seventy-four respondents, only 8 percent who hadn't had affairs prior to commuting became involved in extramarital sex after the commuting began. Sixty per-cent of the commuters had never had an ex-tramarital sex involvement either before or during commuting, and 11 percent who had engaged in extramarital sex *before* commut-ing did *not* do so after the commuting pattern had begun. Another 21 percent had had af-

THE FAITHFUL DESPERADO

I just completed seven years of marriage without having to scratch the famous Itch. It's not something I dwell on, but when I speculate—usually idly—on having an affair, I'm surprised to have been faithful since my wedding. . . .

I know this is a normal, healthy, happy life that I'm intellectually committed to not betraying. But emotionally, it's not easy. In a busy home, the relentless demands of keeping things organized bring a hankering for an uncomplicated liaison. This isn't just a male trip, either; my wife feels the same pressures. Will neither of us again know the helpless thrill of a new love? It's an unsettling thought only halfway through life.

Fortunately for fidelity, it's not a simple contest of intellectual constancy versus renegade emotion. There's no such thing as an uncomplicated affair. Besides the excitement, I remember the lies, the sneaking and remorse that accompanied extra-relationship affairs when I was single. Even when I wasn't serious about a steady girlfriend, I could barely face her after seeing someone else.

If I felt so bad when I was uncommitted, I can't see myself now being faithless, then coming home, without dying of shame. My wife and I share the bundle of big and little intimacies that make up our life together—making love when we get the chance, understanding unspoken signals, saying "I love you" and meaning it, teaching our 2-year-old "Star Light, Star Bright," sharing the successes and frustrations of our work, trading our standing jokes and our standing arguments. If I violated any of this I'd feel as if "Cheater" were etched across my teeth every time I tried to force a smile. Avoiding that distress is a powerful emotional check on infidelity.

And yet, I'm still drawn to someone who seems special. Sometimes speculation moves beyond the idle and banter beyond flirting. There it is on the horizon and moving closer: involvement. But you can tell when the person and the setting and the moment for an affair are nearing coincidence. Maneuvering is fun, like walking along the edge of a cliff. The contemplation is thrilling, the prospect is daunting, the leap might be liberating, the consequences disastrous. Better to step back in the end. Better to step back early on.

On the other hand, maybe my reasons are more practical. For one thing, who has the time? We go flat out all week with kids, work, meetings and chores from 6:30 in the morning until 11 at night, when we crash for a half-hour of reading and talking. I couldn't squeeze in any extracurricular activity even if I wanted to. Then, too, being born 10 years too soon to be caught in the herpes scare is a relief. Why risk the security that comes with being married and monogamous?. . . .

. . . From appearances, most of my men friends are unperturbably faithful. Am I the only one who gives it a thought? Hell, maybe their wives are doing it. Maybe my wife is. She has all the temptations I do, and being beautiful, smart, sexy and funny, she's more eagerly sought. Kidding each other about conquests is one of our inside jokes; who knows for sure when there might be something to it? Maybe many older men who felt in their late 30's as I do now are smiling and saying "Sonny, just you wait." For my part, I can't see why the next seven years should be any different, either for happiness in marriage or opportunities outside of marriage, than the last seven, and I made it through them.

In the end, the surprise at being faithful is topped by another surprise: it's the very ambivalence that makes fidelity and marriage work. That tension means we're not taking each other for granted; we're sticking together, itch notwithstanding. It boils down to feeling special, not just that my wife loves only me, but that this vulnerability of mine belongs only to her. The surprise is on the Desperado: he came down from his fences and let himself love somebody. I may wistfully rue the opportunities missed, but I'll have a deeper satisfaction, and at bottom, I think, a supreme excitement, in the love we share. Will it stay like this? I hope so.

SOURCE: Lance Compa, "The Faithful Desperado," *The New York Times Magazine,* August 4, 1985, p. 60.

fairs before commuting and continued to have them afterward.

Gerstel is making the point that over 80 percent of the persons in her sample behaved after commuting just as they had behaved before. Those who had previously incorporated extramarital sex into their lifestyle continued to do so. And those who were sexually exclusive both before and after commuting showed that *internal* constraints (norms and ideals held about marriage and/or a personal commitment to the spouse) were more influential in their behavior than the "reduction in *external* social constraints" (that is, "lowered observability and responsibility toward the spouse").

Among her respondents who had changed in some way after commuting, the 11 percent who stopped having extramarital involvements may have felt "that they must compensate for their separation with greater sexual fidelity," says Gerstel. "Alternative relationships might be more threatening, as there is a chance for them to develop into real substitutes" in the commuting situation. She continues by summing up the underlying reasoning that may lie behind many commuting spouses' decisions:

> Commuters have already tampered with the marital bond by living in separate residences. To tamper to an even greater extent by having affairs would reduce the marital ties to a near minimum. (p. 168)

But what about those who began having extramarital sexual affairs only after the commuting pattern began? From her in-depth interviews, Gerstel concludes that "in most cases, attitudes (that exist before separation) rather than opportunity seem to be the primary determinant of actual extramarital liaisons" (p. 157).

Extent of Extramarital Sex   Leaving commuter couples, it's common knowledge that among married persons in general, a certain proportion do have sexual intercourse with persons other than their spouses. The exact incidence of extramarital sex today is not known, although in the Kinsey studies of the 1940s it was found that by age 40, half of the married men and slightly over a quarter of the married women in their sample had experienced extramarital sex. In studies since that time, certain sampling problems have made the results questionable—although some sociologists believe that the percentage of persons engaging in extramarital sex may have increased since the time of Kinsey's work (Libby, 1977b).

In their massive study of American couples, Blumstein and Schwartz (1983) found that 30 percent of husbands married ten years or more reported at least one instance of sex with someone other than their wives. Among women married ten or more years, the figure was 22 percent. Their evidence also suggests that the *meaning* of sex outside marriage may be different for women than for men. "A woman's non-monogamy is more likely to be an affair than is a man's," write Blumstein and Schwartz (p. 279). Their interviews indicated that "men more often search for variety, while women prefer a special relationship." Once again, we see the influence of divergent gender-role socialization. (See also Spanier and Margolis, 1983; and Thompson, 1983, 1984.)

According to Blumstein and Schwartz (1983:298), persons who are less committed to permanence in their relationship and who aren't certain their marriages will last are more likely to have extramarital involvements than are persons who believe otherwise. This was found to be true even when such persons reported they were happy in their marriages and pleased with their sex lives with their marriage partners. They simply were not sure of a future together; hence, they were open to extramarital sex.

Ira Reiss and his associates (1980) have proposed a "multivariate model of the determinants of extramarital sexual permissiveness" to help explain why some persons develop permissive attitudes toward nonmonogamy and others do not. They suggest that social scientists engaged in research and theory-building not only take into account eight *basic* variables associated with attitudes toward extramarital sex (education, gender, age, religiosity, gender equality, political liberality, marital happiness, and premarital sexual permissiveness), but also examine at least six additional variables that may be relevant to a better understanding of extramarital permissiveness. These are *marital sexual satisfaction, marital sexual experimentation, marital power,* the degree of *diffuse intimacy conception,* the degree of *emphasis on the pleasurable aspects of sexuality,* and the degree of *autonomy of the in-*

dividual's interaction with members of the opposite sex. Two other sociologists have expanded this multivariate model further by adding a number of new variables (Saunders and Edwards, 1984). In a preliminary test, one of their major findings was that, "for both sexes, the higher the diffuse intimacy conception, the more permissive the attitude toward extramarital sex" (p. 832). In other words, the degree to which an individual seeks emotional satisfaction of deep intimacy needs by turning to a number of different persons rather than seeking the fulfillment of such needs in the spouse alone relates to the degree to which permissive attitudes about extramarital sexual involvement are held.

In some cases of extramarital sex, the spouses do not conceal their activities from one another and may even make an agreement that each is free to have sexual relationships outside the marriage. Some even participate in extramarital sexual experiences together in arrangements that go by such names as "swinging," "consensual adultery," "spouse swapping," or "co-marital sex" (Smith and Smith, 1970, 1973, 1974; Libby, 1977b; Walshok, 1971; Denfeld and Gordon, 1970; Bartell, 1971; Bell, 1975; Symonds, 1971; O'Neill and O'Neill, 1970; Henshel, 1973; Denfeld, 1974; Varni, 1973; Gilmartin, 1974). A number of studies of consensual extramarital sex drive home a point made by Blumstein and Schwartz (1983:289): "A successful open relationship has built-in rules, whether or not the couple realizes it." (See insert.)

Different Views of Sexuality In the seventeenth century, an English clergyman, Jeremy Taylor (1650, chap. 2, sec. 3–2), suggested these reasons for marital sex relations: "a desire for children, or to avoid fornication, or to lighten and ease the cares

THE RULES IN SEXUALLY OPEN MARRIAGES

An open relationship does not mean that anything goes. Even though some couples claim their understanding has no restrictions, we never interviewed a couple who did not describe some definite boundaries. Some couples devise rules that keep their daily life from being disrupted—for example, never being late for dinner, not spending money on someone else, or not bringing home a sexually transmitted disease. Others establish rules of discretion—for example, not letting the children, relatives, or neighbors know. The most important rules provide emotional safeguards—for example, never seeing the same person twice, never giving out a phone number, never having sex in the couple's bed, or never with a mutual friend. Sex outside the relationship is potentially very disruptive. It triggers people's insecurities and fears. Traditional marriages have dealt with this by ruling out nonmonogamy. Couples who engage in open relationships formulate rules to guide their behavior, to make outside sex very predictable and orderly. These rules remind the partners that their relationship comes first and anything else must take second place.

SOURCE: Philip Blumstein and Pepper Schwartz, *American Couples* (New York: Morrow, 1983), p. 289.

and sadnesses of household affairs, or to endear each other." Taylor's list suggests that persons may think of sexual intercourse in terms of various functions. Some persons may consider the main purpose of sex to be procreation, while others may emphasize recreation or mention the function of sex as communication. Or perhaps they think of it in terms of sheer physical release.

Lower-educated couples have tended to have more children and to find birth control more problematic than have couples at higher status levels. Hence, sex-as-procreation no doubt looms high in the thinking of couples at lower levels, along with views of sex-as-release. Lower-status wives in Rainwater's studies made remarks like these: "It's just getting the sexual urge out of him," and "he needs it like a starving man needs food." A husband reported that "a guy gets heated up and after he has it he feels good," adding that his wife felt better and slept bet-

ter after intercourse, too (1965:113; 1960:135).

As education increases, couples may emphasize other kinds of gratifications associated with sexual intercourse (see Rainwater 1965:111, Table 3–15). Sex-as-communication ("endearing each other," to use Taylor's quaint seventeenth-century expression) is considered an important part of the overall communication and empathy in general that characterizes higher-status marriages. In addition, such husbands and wives appear to give more attention to sex-as-recreation. Sexual intercourse may be considered part of the companionship side of marriage, a pleasant leisure activity or fun time in which the spouses can delight together. Kinsey et al. (1953, chap. 9) reported that couples who spent a half hour or an hour in sexual foreplay were likely to be couples from the better-educated groups in his sample. And Gebhard's (1966) data correlating marital satisfaction and wives' orgasmic experience showed that a couple's *spending time* in sexual activity was the key factor in enabling the wife to experience orgasm. As we have seen, the Kinsey studies showed that higher female orgasm rates occurred among higher-educated couples; and such couples were also found to be more willing to experiment with different sexual techniques (Gebhard, 1971:209). It may be that with higher education comes a greater acceptance and appreciation of the human body and all that sexuality has to offer in human experience. Also, higher-status couples have a greater sense of mastery with regard to birth control, and they may tend to have less fear that recreational sex will accidentally turn into procreational sex!

Frequency of Sexual Intercourse One area of marital sexuality where there seems to be little difference by social status is the matter of how often a husband and wife have sexual intercourse. Studies have shown weekly frequency to depend more on age and on the number of years married than upon social status (Blumstein and Schwartz, 1983). In Kinsey's sample, women who married in their late teens reported an average of nearly three times a week during the early years of marriage. By age 30, the average was slightly more than twice a week. By age 40, the average had dropped to 1½ times weekly; and by age 50, it was once a week. For 60-year-old women, coitus was reported to take place about once every twelve days (Kinsey et al., 1953, chap. 9).

More recent research has also shown that social status has little to do with coital frequency. Similarly, race has been found to make almost no difference. The length of marriage seems to be what matters most. Couples married less than a year tend to have sexual relations twice as often or more, on the average, than couples married twenty-five years (Ryder and Westoff, 1971:174; Westoff and Westoff, 1971:23–24). The vast majority of couples, however, whether married only a short time or ten years or more, were found by Blumstein and Schwartz (1983) to have sexual intercourse at least once a week.

THE EXPRESSIVE DIMENSION IN DUAL-EARNER MARRIAGES

Although some of what we have discussed so far in this chapter applies to marriages in general, and some even to emerging marriage patterns (such as the study of commuter marriages), the main thrust of the chapter has centered upon *traditional* marriage patterns. We have been focusing on the importance of the husband's position in the economic-opportunity structure, specifically in the case of head-complement marriages in which the husband is the unique family breadwinner. Now we want to examine what happens to the expressive dimension of marriage when the wife is also in the labor force—particularly in those cases where women have not merely jobs, but *careers*.

Wife's Occupation and Personal and Family Social Status

Until recently, few questions were raised about the measurement of a woman's social status in terms of her relationship to a male. A 1966 book on college students, for example, asserted that "a woman's socially defined success is typically dependent not on her own occupational and job mobility but on her husband's" and that a female has but "one departure and arrival in her life cycle: her exchange of a father-determined social status for a husband-determined one" (quoted in Haug, 1973). Sociologist Joan Acker (1973:938) calls into question such assumptions. If women have such status-determining resources as education, occupation, and income, why don't these resources count as they do for men? Furthermore, asks Acker, why do we assume that such resources "are inoperative if the woman is married?"

Another sociologist, Marie R. Haug (1973: 88) says that the practice of measuring a family's social status in terms of the husband-father alone might have seemed justified half a century ago when social scientists were beginning to introduce social-stratification measures. The proportion of employed married women was low at that time. "But there is no rational basis for persisting in outmoded practices in the face of changed realities in the work world," writes Haug.

Haug's criticisms of traditional measurement practices spring from an awareness that increasing numbers of women have occupational roles, that a woman's income, added to her husband's, can make a significant impact on a family's lifestyle (making possible a move to the suburbs or the sending of the children to college, for example) and that, furthermore, there are cases in which the wife's education and occupational status may be higher than her husband's (for example, where the husband has only a high school education and works as a door-to-door salesperson, while his wife has a college degree and teaches school). Why should the family's social status be assigned according to his job rather than hers? Could their occupational rankings somehow both be taken into account? Or should social status be based upon the occupation or income of the one who would be given the higher ranking on the usual scales? These are questions to which some sociologists are giving attention.

Interestingly, a sensitivity to issues related to this matter was evident in the decision of the Census Bureau to move away from the traditional designation of the husband as "head of household" in the 1980 census. Instead, a *householder* ("the first adult household member listed on the census questionnaire") is considered to be the central "reference person." The reason? "Recent social changes have resulted in a trend toward more nearly equal status for adult members of a household and, therefore, have made the term 'head' increasingly inappropriate." (U.S. Bureau of the Census, *Current Population Reports*, ser. P-60, no. 118, 1979:9).

However, most studies in existence have used one or all of the occupation-income-education factors in relation to the *husband* as the basis of determining a family's social position in the class structure. The explanation lies in the fact that most families up till recently have followed the traditional pattern in which the husband was considered the chief provider. If his wife worked (as in the senior partner-junior partner arrangement), his work was still considered the more important. His commitment to his work was greater than hers, and his job, rather than hers, would determine where the family moved. For all these reasons, the husband has been considered more closely interwoven into the economic-opportunity system than the wife.

But as we've seen throughout this book, that particular outlook has been changing. As social scientists Carlton Hornung and B. Claire McCullough (1981:125–126) emphasize, "the married woman's status identity and social position is no longer a *relational property* derived exclusively from the status achievements of her father and/or her husband. Instead, a woman's status identity is increasingly an *absolute property* determined by her own accomplishments in education, occupation, income, and other areas." They go on to suggest that the achievements of both spouses in a dual-earner marriage *co-determine* a family's social status (See also Oppenheimer, 1977). Sociologists Dana Hiller and William Philliber (1978, 1980; Philliber and Hiller, 1978), however, make the point that less certainty has shown up in various studies about the degree to which the entire family's social status is affected by a wife's attainments—although it *is* clear at this point in time that *her own status* is based on her personal educational and occupational achievements.

Expressive Interaction and Wives with Careers

If we think in terms of equal commitment to careers by both marriage partners (an equal-partner rather than a senior partner-junior partner arrangement), we may envision a theoretical exchange model that is quite different from the depiction of the interdependencies in a traditional marriage described on pages 313–315. There we saw that the husband's performance of his instrumental duties (breadwinning) called forth his wife's response in the expressive realm, thus fulfilling her duties of nurturance and affection. In the dual-career exchange model, we have *two* persons doing each of these things. Thus there is a reinforcement or doubling of the processes involved in the expressive side of marriage.

What we see is *husband-wife role reciprocity* based upon equal-partner status and provider-role interchangeability. The process of fulfilling rights and duties changes from the process we examined in the traditional marriage model. No longer do the wife's instrumental duties include chief responsibility for household tasks; they are shared equally with the husband, for they are now included as part of his instrumental du-

ties. But the wife's duties now also include equal responsibility with the husband for supplying the couple with economic and status rewards from the opportunity system. The rights of both husband and wife are met by these exchanges which in turn motivate them further to perform these instrumental duties as well as expressive duties. Their respective expressive rights are thereby fulfilled, further motivating each spouse in both expressive duties and instrumental duties.

What is new here is that now, as the husband perceives that his economic and status rights are being met through his wife's provision, he has an *added* incentive for performing his expressive duties toward her (enhanced empathy, companionship, and physical affection). Another new feature is the way the husband's performance of expressive duties meets the wife's *rights* in the expressive realm in such a way that she is motivated to maintain ongoing occupational achievement. The husband-wife reciprocities that take place in equal-partner marriages are exactly the same for each spouse—which contrasts with our earlier description of the instrumental and expressive interdependencies and exchanges taking place in traditional (head-complement) marriages.

What the theoretical model shows is that we may expect to see a process in which the dual-career couple's relationship with the economic-opportunity structure will have an impact on the spouses' relationship with each other as well; and that furthermore, their expressive interactions will provide added motivation for achievement in the opportunity system so that they are able to provide one another with that system's rewards.

But what does research tell us about the actual lives of couples where both are involved directly in the economic-opportunity system? What do we know about the expressive dimension—the areas of empathy, com-

PARENT AT WORK

People in process.

I visit a friend. We sit in the living room chatting; her husband is working in his study. Their (I almost wrote "her") two-year-old awakens from his nap, crying. I move to the edge of my chair, expecting that she'll answer the call of the child. But she sits calmly. "The baby is crying," I say tentatively. "I know; Fred'll get him." Inwardly, I think, "But he's working!" Outwardly, I ask quietly, "Isn't he working?" "Sure, but it's his day for child care. I get interrupted when I work, too."

SOURCE: Lillian B. Rubin, *Intimate Strangers* (New York: Harper & Row, 1983), p. 210.

panionship, and physical affection in such marriages?

Empathy

In the past, the large-scale studies which have given attention to the effects of a wife's employment on marital satisfaction have concentrated, for the most part, on marriages of the senior partner–junior partner variety. Equal-partner marriages have constituted such a small percentage of marriages until now that they have largely been ignored.

Even limiting our focus to junior-partner wives, we still do not come up with easy, clear-cut answers by examining the sociological literature on the subject. Occasionally, researchers even reach opposite conclusions. For example, after the Blood and Wolfe (1960:101–102) study of Detroit households, Blood (1963:304) concluded that a wife's employment was likely to lead to a more positive evaluation of the marriage if the couple were lower status than if they were higher status, presumably because of the tangible rewards provided by the wife in a situation where money is most needed. The findings of other sociologists suggest just the opposite. Marital dissatisfaction appears to be associated with the wife's employment at lower status levels much more than is likely

in marriages where education, income, and job prestige are higher (Nye, 1963; 1974b).

Two researchers who studied a sample of 1,325 poverty-level families found employed wives indicating less general marital satisfaction than nonemployed wives. Employed wives also felt their husbands were less satisfied as well. The working wives perceived their husbands to be less satisfied with the time the couple spent together, the meals served, and just the fact of the wife's working. Actually, the wife's work was one of the two main areas in which conflict among lower-status couples with employed wives was greater than among comparable couples where the wives were not working. The other conflict area was sex (Feldman and Feldman, 1973).

These findings fit with Goode's observation that lower-status husbands tend to view their wives' working as a usurping of the husband's provider role. From his study of divorced women, Goode (1956) concluded that if a husband feels threatened in his traditional male role, it can negatively affect expressiveness in the marriage. Harold Sheppard and Neal Herrick (1972:27–28), who specialize in employment research, also found that blue-collar worker dissatisfaction was higher among those men whose wives worked. The researchers reported that these findings were "completely unexpected," because they had assumed that the higher family income would mean *less* discontentment. They surmised that perhaps at the blue-collar level "machismo" might be a factor. "It may be that such men don't feel that they've really succeeded if, *all by themselves,* they can't provide their families with the necessary income to pay for the level of living to which they aspire."

In some of our earlier research, we found that although empathy satisfaction was higher in general among higher-status couples than among lower-status couples, a wife's employment did make a difference *within* these respective categories. A higher-status husband whose wife was employed was less likely to be satisfied with marital empathy than a comparable husband whose wife was not employed. In contrast, an employed wife in a higher-status marriage was likely to be more satisfied with marital empathy than was true of a nonemployed wife. It may be that the higher the status of the husband, the more he may have defined his wife's employment activities as a drain on time and energy that could have been better invested in empathy and attention to their life together. On the other hand, the wife in such a marriage may have felt satisfied that her rights were being granted her by being able to carry out her option to work; therefore in exchange she responded to her husband with what she considered to be a satisfactory level of empathy and defined his empathic responses as positive as well. Again, this may be a case of spouses' "reading" an identical situation quite differently (Scanzoni, 1970:129).

Such a husband-wife difference in the definition of the situation also characterized lower-status couples. But what happened was just the reverse of the husband-wife perceptions at higher status levels and illustrates even further that the relationship between a wife's employment and satisfaction with various areas of expressiveness is not clear-cut. We found in the 1967 study (Scanzoni, 1970) that lower-status husbands were more satisfied with marital empathy if their wives worked, while employed wives at lower-status levels were less satisfied with empathy than nonemployed wives. It is possible that husbands placed such positive value on the money supplied by working wives that they were also able to empathize with them as persons who shared the burden of breadwinning. However, lower-status working wives, aware of the societal norms about the husband's primary role of provider, may have projected onto their husbands their fears that the men might feel threatened and "emasculated" by the wives' earnings. These fears and projections in turn might have caused wives to feel that processes of communication and understanding were less satisfactory than would have been the case in marriages where wives were not working.

In a study of employed wives and marital happiness, sociologists Susan Orden and Norman Bradburn (1969) found that *free choice* about working is highly important. They found that "marriages at all levels of the social structure are affected adversely when the woman is in the labor market only out of necessity" while, on the other hand, a woman's working out of free choice has a positive effect on marital happiness. At only one point did these researchers find that the marriage relationship was strained by a wife's working out of free choice and that was when there were preschoolers at home. "At other stages in the life cycle," report Orden and Bradburn, "the choice between the labor market and the home market makes little difference in an individual's assessment of his own marriage happiness" (pp. 405, 392).

Evidence from a later large-scale study of our own also seems to indicate that a wife's working may not be as important in evaluating marital expressive satisfaction as has been assumed in the past. Satisfaction with empathy, companionship, and physical affection was shown to be no different for either husbands or wives regardless of whether or not wives were employed (Scanzoni, 1975b). And after a study of Swedish working wives, Murray Gendell (1963:132–133) reported similarly: "On the basis of these data . . . we must conclude that working wives are neither more or less satisfied with their marriages than housewives." Fogarty and his associates (1971:475) came to a similar conclusion with regard to husbands after studying marriages with employed wives in England. "Taking all families together," they wrote, "it cannot be said that in the social group investigated 'wife working' has any clear-cut effect, whether positive or negative, on husband's estimate of happiness of the marriage." (See also Locksley, 1980; D. Smith, 1985.)

Perhaps all we can say then with regard to marital-empathy satisfaction as it relates to wives' occupational achievement is simply that more research needs to be done—particularly with respect to equal-partner marriages. On the basis of very small samples and limited case studies, we might propose that empathy could conceivably be strengthened and increased in the dual-career marriage. Each spouse is rewarding the other with both economic-status benefits and expressive benefits. Since each is involved in a career, each can understand and empathize with the other's career concerns. There is a very real sense of putting oneself in the other's position and entering into that person's feelings and experiences because they are much like one's own and thus can be understood. Reciprocal advice and counsel can be exchanged between the husband and wife, since there is likely to be a feeling of colleagueship and equality that calls forth empathy. Such couples do not live in the separate worlds labeled "his" and "hers" which traditional gender roles have fostered (Fogarty et al., 1971:477–478).

Colleagueship in Equal-Partner Marriages   In traditional marriages, a husband's colleagues are usually his work associates, not the members of his conjugal family. But in Holmstrom's (1972) study contrasting more traditional marriages with those that follow the dual-career pattern, she found that "when both marital partners have careers, the possibility exists that they will also be colleagues. If so, it adds a new dimension to the marriage" (p. 121). Holstrom found that a sense of professional colleagueship between married partners may take the form of working together jointly on the same projects (where their fields of specialty are similar or complementary) or in exchanging advice, making suggestions, and in general discussing one another's work. Sometimes, their influence on one another's careers takes more subtle forms, often in processes they may be unaware of at the time—such as in the books and magazines they bring into the home, the professional contacts each makes, the people to whom they may introduce one another, and so on.

In contrast, Holmstrom found that women who had given up their careers to devote full time to their marriages responded quite differently when asked about their influence on their husbands' work. They often replied "as a wife" rather than "as a colleague." They tended to see their roles as buffers between the husband and the pressures and demands of his work or as promoting the husband's career by playing various subordinate helping roles "rather than by collaborating or commenting as a colleague might."

Examples from dual-career marriages suggest a sharply contrasting pattern. An academic couple refers to the intellectual stim-

DUAL-CAREER REWARDS: "GILT BY ASSOCIATION"

Circumstances might have changed for physicist Dr. Aaron Yalow, 65, when his wife, Dr. Rosalyn Yalow, won the Nobel Prize in medicine in 1977. But, according to him, they didn't.

"You see," he said, "our mutual careers are a binding force within our marriage. Many people say you have to have mutual respect in a marriage. But what they really mean is that one person is dominant, the other submissive. Rosalyn and I are truly equals. We live parallel lives."

Dr. Rosalyn Yalow continued her career in scientific research throughout the years of their marriage. "In our family," Aaron Yalow explained, "we decided it wasn't that one person had to be mother to our kids [they have two grown children]. We both needed to be parents to them."

How did he feel when his wife became the second woman in history to win the Nobel Prize in medicine?

"Pride, joy," he answered. "I felt all of it. It's always wonderful when a beloved associate does well. In addition to being my wife, Rosalyn, you see, has always been my beloved associate."

Like many of the men I spoke with, Dr. Yalow used humor and irony to describe his feelings about his wife's success. "Being married to a Nobel Prize-winning scientist? Why, I call it 'gilt by association.' "

SOURCE: Barbara Gordon, "How to Share Life with a Famous Wife," *Parade,* April 21, 1985, p. 5.

---

ulation each provides the other with regard to their respective university careers: "Our collaboration now takes the form of long talkathons in which we discuss the subject, develop new points, downgrade old ones, and sharpen our wits on each other's thought" (Bernard, 1964:234). Joanne Simpson (1973), a meteorologist, provides another example as she tells of meeting her husband in a professional association and about their developing, even before marriage, into "a terrific research team with complementary skills." Where one was weak the other was strong, so that the two of them were able to create more than double the sum of their individual efforts. Even when federal civil service nepotism rules prevented their continuing to work together so that their work interests were brought into conflict, the sense of colleagueship continued. Simpson reports, "The conflict is compensated for in part by the common language, the associates, and the intellectual interests which we share."

The empathy that can spring from colleagueship in an equal-partner marriage does not necessarily require that the husband and wife be doing the same work. The mere fact of their both being active in the economic-opportunity system can result in the kind of sharing mentioned above—common intellectual interests, associates, and so on, plus the exchange of counsel, advice, criticism, and suggestions in the empathic spirit that can occur between persons equally involved in career achievement goals.

Companionship

Because of the sheer demands of time and energy required by an occupation, we might expect husband-wife companionship to suffer when the wife takes on outside employment. We did not find this to be true in one major study (Scanzoni, 1975b), although there was some indication that wife employment negatively affected companionship in the 1967 study of Indianapolis marriages (Scanzoni, 1970:38–41). In that particular sample at that particular time, there were indications that companionship satisfaction was greater if the wife was not working. But if the wife *was* working, once again there were variations by social status. In households where the wife held a higher-status job, both husbands and wives were much more satisfied with marital companionship than was the case in households where the wife held a lower-status job. Women with higher-status jobs are usually married to men with higher education and higher-status jobs as well, men who have achieved and who are secure enough in their provider role not to feel threatened by their wives' employment.

Earlier, Blood and Wolfe (1960) had found that wives most satisfied with marital companionship were those who concentrated on entertaining their husbands' business associates and clients and who devoted themselves to understanding their husbands' business problems and helping their husbands get ahead rather than concentrating on careers for themselves. Those next most satisfied were wives who worked as collaborators with their husbands in joint enterprises. Employed wives were the least satisfied with companionship out of these three categories (because "her work partly separates her from her husband"), but such wives were more satisfied than were the traditional stay-at-home housewives. In the words of Blood

and Wolfe, "Lowest of all [in companionship satisfaction] is the wife who 'sticks to her knitting' while the husband is absorbed in his own business. This traditional-type marriage involves relatively little companionship" (p. 167).

One of the findings that surprised Orden and Bradburn (1969) in their study of wife employment and marital happiness was that husbands whose wives worked part-time ranked companionship satisfaction higher than did all other husbands—including those whose wives were employed full-time and those whose wives were not employed at all. It was also found in this same study that the wives who freely chose part-time work were happier than were women who had freely chosen either to work full-time or to be full-time homemakers.

Gendell's (1963:133) study of Swedish working wives likewise led him to conclude that part-time workers were slightly more satisfied in their marriages than were either full-time housewives or full-time employed wives—though the differences were really too small to be considered significant. And Fogarty and his associates (1971:478) also found some indication of greater satisfaction with part-time wife employment in England.

On the other hand, when psychologist Anne Locksley (1980) examined a large representative sample of marriages in the United States, she found no evidence that marital adjustment and companionship were affected either negatively or positively by wives' employment—regardless of whether the wives were working primarily for money or were highly involved in, interested in, and committed to their work for intrinsic gratifications. And sociologists Sharon Houseknecht and Anne Macke (1981:660) concluded from their research that "it is not employment status *per se* that is important in determining marital adjustment but rather the extent to which family experiences accommodate the wife's employment.'' Similarly, in a review of major research on the topic, Drake Smith (1985:489) concluded that "for most husbands and wives participating in studies spanning over 30 years, wife employment status alone appears to have little or no effect on marital adjustment.''

Companionship in career-oriented, equal-partner marriages requires planning and effort. On the one hand, companionship in such marriages could be enhanced by the spirit of colleagueship and the common interests that are discussed and mutually engaged in (such as travel together relating to one or the other's career where possible or reading the same books and journals). On the other hand, *companionship,* by definition, means doing things together in leisure time; and where both husband and wife are fully committed to career interests, leisure time is likely to be at a premium and may at times seem nonexistent.

Part of the problem stems from what Fogarty and his associates (1971) call "overload"—the double job that is usually faced by an employed wife because of the tradi-tional assumption that the management of the home is her responsibility in addition to her outside work. As one researcher has noted, after studying 106 faculty women at a major university, "Today's professional women are going through a process of *role expansion* (adding new responsibilities without relinquishing old ones), rather than a process of *role redefinition* which may be what tomorrow's professional women will experience" (Yogev, 1981:865; italics supplied).

Trying to do two jobs at once taxes a wife's time and energy so greatly that companionship is considerably reduced—something that her husband might resent. Perhaps this is why some of the studies indicated that there was greater satisfaction on the part of both husbands and wives if the wife chose part-time employment. As Table 10-A shows, a surprisingly high proportion of women in the work force have said they would prefer part-time work if they had enough money to live comfortably. More than half the women in executive, professional, and managerial positions in that sample expressed such a preference, no doubt reflecting the intense

TABLE 10-A   Work preferences among working women: by occupation

If you had enough money to live as comfortably as you'd like, would you prefer to work full time, work part time, do volunteer-type work, or work at home caring for the family?

	TOTAL WORKING WOMEN	EXECUTIVE/ PROFESSIONAL/ MANAGER	WHITE COLLAR	HOMEMAKERS
Base	428	156	222	217
Work full time	17%	19%	14%	4%
Work part time	41	51	38	18
Do volunteer work	13	12	15	14
Work at home	28	18	33	61
Other	*	1	1	3

*Less Than 1%

SOURCE: Louis Harris and Associates, *The General Mills American Family Report, 1980–81: Families at Work—Strengths and Strains* (Minneapolis: General Mills, 1981), p. 20. Reprinted by permission.

COOKING COUPLES BRING CHANGES TO THE KITCHEN

Chicago—The rise in the number of households in which both spouses work has led to changes in kitchen design, according to a report by a kitchen remodeling franchiser.

"We have found that an increasing number of couples are cooking together," says Michael Busch, vice president and chief operating officer of Facelifters of Chicago. "The leading reasons for the kitchen redesign are the desire for more efficient counter and cabinet space and for a room that works well for two people.

Interestingly, some kitchens are also being redesigned with desks and computers."

SOURCE: AP report, *Greensboro (NC) News and Record,* August 15, 1985, p. D-14.

---

time pressures they experience in trying to balance heavy occupational demands with responsibilities at home. Yet, this way of dealing with the problem is neither satisfactory nor realistic for many highly educated women. For one thing, suitable part-time employment is not easy to find; and for another, part-time employment does not bring with it the economic and prestige rewards that full-time work commitment does. Furthermore, many women simply prefer a continuous, highly committed work pattern. They are more apt to feel the solution to the time and energy problem lies in persuading husbands to share more of the overload, perhaps even finding companionship through jointly performing household tasks while also making more time available for leisure-time activities.

Sociologist Linda Haas (1980) calls attention to "role-sharing couples" who share *all* traditionally segregated family roles—the breadwinner role, the domestic role (household chores), the handyman role, the kinship role (maintaining ties with kin through letters, gifts, and so on), the childcare role, and the major/minor decision-maker role. The principle is that of *role interchangeability*, as we discussed earlier, and it appears to be a

key factor in reducing overload. Other ways of cutting overload stresses involve spending money for hired help and time- and labor-saving equipment and seeking changes in the work situation where possible, such as flexible scheduling or job sharing (Skinner, 1980).

Dual-career families also need to make adjustments more than do other families in ordering their social life. Fogarty and his colleagues (1971:477) concluded from their studies that dual-career families have special difficulties "in finding time for contacts with relatives and neighbours." And Bernard (1964:240) quotes an academic wife who said, "I must confess that entertaining for me is more of a chore than a pleasure because I keep thinking of all the time that its preparation takes away from my own work." Holmstrom (1972:98) tells of one two-career couple who solved the problem through the husband's suggestion that they entertain friends by using some of their increased income to take them out to restaurants rather than serving a meal at home.

In marriages where husbands and wives can agree on priorities, the quality of their time together can make up for the lack of quantity. An art professor who says "there's a lot to be said for companionship in marriage" has remarked that her career could not have progressed as it has if she had been married to "a nine-to-five man with weekends off who expected attention" during his leisure time. The man she did marry is a highly respected photographer, photojournalist, and teacher who shares his wife's creative interests and who says, "The nice thing is we talk to each other. We always seem to have something to talk about" (Moore, 1974:15). In such marriages, the empathy of colleagueship seems to result in companionship that is considered highly satisfactory despite busy schedules necessitated by the spouses' equal involvement in the economic-opportunity structure (see Garland, 1972:213–214).

Physical Affection

Persons who think in terms of stereotyped gender roles often express worries that a couple's sexual relationship will be harmed if the wife shares the breadwinner role. Fogarty and his associates (1971:356) described these fears: "The assumption here is that women who want to enter the male world of competition would be highly motivated by competitiveness with men and, as a consequence, would tend to emasculate their husbands. The assumption follows that these couples' sex lives would be characterized by impotence and frigidity." However, while acknowledging that such a pattern might occur in certain cases, these researchers did not find evidence from their data that working wives are characterized by desires to lord it over men. Rather, the women in their sample indicated that they worked for reasons of financial security, the need to be creative, and "the desire to be effective as an individual person." As far as the sex lives of the couples in the Fogarty study were concerned, "the

impression is one of a 'normal' range of sexual experience."

In some research, husbands of nonemployed wives reported greater satisfaction with the love and physical affection in their marriages than did husbands of employed wives. But wives saw things differently. Employed wives were more satisfied than were nonemployed wives with the love and physical affection in their marriages. This was found at all status levels (Scanzoni, 1970).

These husband-wife differences might relate to gender-role stereotypes and traditional notions of "masculinity" in both the sexual realm and the provider role (especially at lower status levels) and a sense of resentment that the time and energy wives devote to their jobs may seem to be "stolen" from loving attention and affection that could have been given to husbands instead (particularly at higher status levels, where wives are likely to have more education and higher-level jobs that make greater demands). For the wives' part, the sense of self-worth experienced through direct access to the economic-opportunity system and the sense of contributing financially to the family plus the belief that their working meant their husbands had granted them something wives increasingly define as not only an option but a right—freedom to work—may have meant that the wives experienced a sense of contentment which carried over to their perception of the physical affection in marriage as well.

Much more research needs to be done to determine the impact that wives' employment actually makes on the physical expression of love in marriage. A later study indicated that a woman's working outside the home made no significant difference at all in husbands' and wives' evaluation of satisfaction in this dimension of marriage (Scanzoni, 1975b). Indeed, some social scientists have

TIME AND ENERGY FOR SEX:
A PROBLEM FOR DUAL-CAREER COUPLES

"We have sex about four or five times a week. Very often I'm tired, or sometimes she gets busy for several days. That's when we make appointments so that we get to sleep earlier, so there is time, because otherwise we begin to lose track. So we make sure we get it pulled back together. . . . Maybe once a week she doesn't want to, once a week I don't want to. It's mutual, random, varied. No set pattern, no set time. If she refuses I may be a little frustrated, but rarely. Sometimes I'm relieved because I'm just too tired. Sometimes just neutral. There is always tomorrow.

It's declined. As a friend of mine used to tell me, if you took a piggy bank and put a nickel in for every time you had sex during the first year of your marriage, and then did it for the second year, you would have saved less and less money as the years went on. It's declined considerably, but for reasons of strength, not a lack of interest. We just get tired and preoccupied with things and pressures here and there. We used to make love every night and now we don't. But our relationship hasn't decreased. As I said, the spirit is willing, but the flesh is weak."

SOURCE: From an interview with a 39-year-old meteorologist married to a 36-year-old woman whose business is dealing in antiques, in Philip Blumstein and Pepper Schwartz, *American Couples* (New York: Morrow, 1983), p. 200.

suggested that, rather than hurting a couple's sex life, a wife's employment might enhance it. The husband and wife can relate as two separate individuals who have developed their personal identities in the occupational world; thus each has more to bring to the other in the overall marital relationship, including the sexual aspects of that relationship (Fogarty et al., 1971:356).

Sociologist Alice Rossi (1964:139) has argued this point in countering charges made by defenders of traditional gender roles who claim that equality of the sexes would upset the male-female sexual relationship. While acknowledging that full sex equality would no doubt be the death knell of the traditional arrangement in which "the sex act presupposes a dominant male actor and a passive female subject," Rossi suggests that husbands and wives who participate equally in parental, occupational, and social roles "will complement each other sexually in the same way, as essentially equal partners, and not as an ascendant male and a submissive female." Rather than detract from the sexual experience, equality can enhance it since the "enlarged base of shared experience" in other realms can heighten satisfaction with the sexual experience as well.

Rossi's argument fits with an exchange-theory approach to the equal-partner marriage. If there are equal exchanges of rights and duties occurring in both the instrumental and expressive dimensions of marriage in general, might we not expect equal exchanges to go on in the sexual relationship as well?

Likewise, role interchangeability in the equal-partner marriage might be expected to extend to the realm of physical affection. Psychologist A. H. Maslow (1970) has alluded to such role interchangeability in sexual relations. Maslow devoted his attention to studying characteristics of persons with a strong sense of self-esteem and self-realization, persons "who have developed or are developing to the full stature of which they are capable." He termed such persons "self-actualizing" and found that one of their characteristics was that "they made no really sharp differentiation between the roles and personalities of the two sexes." Maslow explains:

> That is, they did not assume that the female was passive and the male active, whether in sex or love or anything else. These people were all so certain of their maleness or femaleness that they did not mind taking on some of the cultural aspects of the opposite sex role. It was especially noteworthy that they could be both active and passive lovers and this was the clearest in the sexual act and in physical love-making. Kissing and being kissed, being above or below in the sexual act, taking the initiative, being quiet and receiving love, teasing and being teased—these were all found in both sexes. The reports indicated that both were enjoyed at different times. It was considered to be a shortcoming to be limited to just active love-making or passive love-making. Both have their particular pleasures for self-actualizing people. (p. 189)

As opportunities for women to exercise their full potentialities in the economic-opportunity system present themselves, the number of "self-actualizing" wives may be expected to increase. Thus the likelihood of growing numbers of couples in equal-partner marriages fitting the pattern Maslow describes may also increase.

This could have a positive effect on marital sexuality. Blumstein and Schwartz (1983:222–223) found in their study that "couples who initiate and refuse sex on an equal basis are more satisfied with their sex life." They also found that couples who feel they have the right to refuse sex equally actually have sexual relations more frequently and are happier with their *overall* relationship than are other couples. "Such equality means that the partners share control over their sex life," these sociologists explain, "so that neither feels anger at the other's 'excessive' lack of interest and neither feels guilty when he or she is sexually unavailable."

Historical Changes in Sexual Attitudes In studying human sexuality, sociologists look for patterns, trends, and indications of what is happening among groups of people, rather than focusing on individual cases. We have already seen how social status can make a difference in the sexual attitudes and behavior of people. Similarly, a changing social climate over a period of time can also mean alterations in how people view sexual matters (Gardella, 1985). Kinsey and his associates, for example, took into account changes in sexual practices which occurred over a period of forty years. Their sample of women was divided into categories according to decade of birth, beginning with women born before 1900, then those whose birth dates fell during the periods 1900–1909, 1910–1919, and 1920–1929. There were certain areas of sexual behavior where the decade of a woman's birth made much more difference than did her social class in how she had behaved sexually over the years.

Practices such as engaging in sexual intercourse in the nude or utilizing certain petting techniques in marital foreplay (for example, manipulating the husband's genitals or participating in oral-genital sex) were much less common among the older generation in Kinsey's sample than among the younger generation. Kinsey also found that a jump in the percentages of married women who had experienced orgasm had occurred over the four decades. He attributed these changes to a freer climate and more frankness about sexual matters, along with increased scientific understanding. "There were wives and husbands in the older generation who did not even know that orgasm was possible for a female," wrote the Kinsey researchers (1953, chap. 9), adding that even if persons did think female orgasm was possible, they couldn't conceive of it as being either pleasurable or proper.

In recent years, one of the biggest changes in attitudes toward marital sex has centered around the sexual needs, desires, and behavior of women. The laboratory research of Masters and Johnson (1966) has clearly demonstrated the high capacity women have for sexual enjoyment, including the capability of experiencing multiple orgasms within a short space of time. Such findings would no doubt have shocked the sex lecturer who wrote in the early part of this century: "The best mothers [and] wives . . . know little or nothing of the sexual pleasure. Love of home, children, and domestic duties are the only passions they feel. As a rule, the modest woman submits to her husband, but only to please him" (Shannon, 1917:162). Such lecturers and writers failed to realize that the lack of sexual interest in many married women was not a sign of the "natural order of things" or the "innate goodness of the female sex," but rather stemmed from the way females were socialized in a society that emphasized both sexual repression and the double standard. Such books helped perpetuate further the view that women were sexually indifferent and unresponsive.

Marriage Manuals and Changing Attitudes

One way to get some idea of changing sexual attitudes over time is to examine marriage manuals from different historical periods. In an examination of American marital-education literature from the period of 1830 to 1940, sociologist Michael Gordon (1971) found a profound change in conceptions of the role of sex in marriage, a change he sums up in the title of his article on the subject, "From an Unfortunate Necessity to a Cult of Mutual Orgasm."

Many of the nineteenth-century books made it clear that sex should be viewed as a means to an end (procreation) rather than as an end in itself (pleasure). Warnings were sounded on the supposed dangers of excessive sex in marriage, and couples were alerted to the physical exhaustion and damage that might be incurred through overindulgence in sexual intercourse. Some books took pains to spell out exactly what "overindulgence" was, with the advice varying from calls for sexual abstinence except when a child was desired to suggestions that inter-

The typical Victorian wife and mother was expected to channel her passions in the direction of home, children, and domestic duties rather than toward an interest in sexual matters. (The Bettmann Archive, Inc.)

course be limited to certain time periods. "Few should exceed the limit of once a week; while many cannot safely indulge oftener than once a month," instructed one sex manual written in 1866.

The emphasis on rationality, self-control, and moderation in marital sex was nothing new but could be seen in writings from 200 years before. For example, the context of the comments of Jeremy Taylor, the seventeenth-century English divine quoted earlier, make it clear that he was just as concerned about misuses of sex in marriage as about its "proper" exercise. Avoiding fornication, seeking to have children, and desiring to find comfort from cares and to express endearment—these were legitimate ends; but "he is an ill husband that uses his wife as a man treats a harlot, having no other end but pleasure. The pleasure should always be joined to one or another of these ends . . . but never with a purpose, either in act or desire, to separate the sensuality from these ends which hallow it. Married people must never force themselves into high and violent lusts with arts and misbecoming devices, but be restrained and temperate in the use of their lawful pleasures." This statement was still being quoted as advice to couples in a 1917 sex-education manual (Shannon, 1917:162).

Toward the end of the nineteenth century and in the early decades of the twentieth, the winds of change began to blow—first a slight breeze and then a full-force gale. Sex took on a more important role in the marriage relationship, and pleasure for both partners began to be emphasized. Writers talked about "satisfactory sexual adjustment" and by the 1930s were giving instructions on how to achieve such adjustment. Learning and practicing such techniques was seen as an art, the goal of which was perfectly timed, simultaneous organsm for husband and wife.

In almost paradoxical fashion, sex came to be viewed as *work* at the same time it came to be viewed as play. The growing societal approach to marital sexuality moved from the nineteenth-century emphasis on procreation to the twentieth-century emphasis on recreation, but as Gordon (1971:73) points out, it was recreation "at which one must work hard." "Work at sex because it's fun!" became the prevalent idea.

One of the first sociologists to point this out was Nelson Foote (1954), who responded to the 1953 publication of the Kinsey findings on female sexual behavior by writing an article called "Sex as Play." Referring to insights from the social psychology of play, Foote wrote that "play—any kind of play—generates its own morality and values. And the enforcement of the rules of play becomes the concern of every player, because without their observance, the play cannot continue."

An examination of fifteen currently popular marriage manuals illustrates his point. Sociologists Lionel Lewis and Dennis Brissett (1967) found in these manuals an abundance of rules, duties, and do's and don'ts that husbands and wives were instructed to follow rigorously in their sexual relationship. Sex was presented almost as a chore, involving technical competence, skill development, a quest for mastery, a drive for success, and a fear of failure (defined mainly in terms of having or not having an orgasm). Deferred gratifications, self-denial, scheduling the various parts of the sexual act carefully, striving, performance, deliberation, management—these were the matters with which husbands and wives were to be concerned as they enjoyed themselves in recreational sex. Lewis and Brissett offered the thesis that "the American must justify his play . . . he has done this by transforming his play into work . . . work is felt to carry with it a certain inherent dignity." Lewis and Brissett speak of sex counselors and writers as "avocational counselors" in the same sense as teachers of other avocational interests (such as how to play tennis better, how to dance, ski, and so forth).

Sex researchers William Masters and Virginia Johnson (1973) also have written of "the influence of the work ethic on sexual attitudes in contemporary society" which convinces couples that "work is productive and he who works is virtuous, whereas play is wasteful and he who plays is sinful." Such a view, they emphasize, becomes goal-oriented and concerned with instant gratification rather than a mutual expression of affection between the partners in a context of overall communication and enjoyment of one another.

In Gordon's study of marriage manuals from 1830 to 1940, he noticed other patterns besides the swing from sex-as-procreation to sex-as-recreation to sex-as-work. For one thing, there occurred a change in attitudes toward birth control. Early writers were very negative about limiting family size, but some signs of change began to occur in the 1920s. In the 1930s (partially due to some legal changes), contraception came to be seen in a much more favorable light. Earlier, even writers who emphasized sex for pleasure tended to be reluctant to endorse birth-control practices—except periods of sexual abstinence.

The other most noticeable trend observed by Gordon in his study was the growing emphasis on female sexuality. Early books gave the impression that a woman could be expected to show little interest in coital relations with her husband. Later books still emphasized a woman's alleged lesser desire, but it was now suggested that a dormant sensuality lay within her, waiting to be awakened and called forth by her husband's skillful techniques of love. Full participation in *marital* sexual relations came to be viewed as a woman's right, and the husband's responsibility was to make sure she could exercise this right. As part of the trend toward recreational sex, some books began telling wives to seek to make sex pleasurable for their husbands as well.

What does any of this have to do with the subject at hand, namely the effect of a wife's employment on the physical aspects of marital expressiveness? Gordon (1971:77) suggests, in view of trends he observed in his study of marriage manuals, that research is needed to find out "to what extent was the acceptance of female sexuality linked to the increasing number of women in the work force." As we have seen, the common owner-property arrangement of marriage began to change as the option to work opened to women. The wife's rights were increasing, as were her husband's duties toward her in the marital exchange—particularly with regard to fulfilling the wife's expressive rights. It is not surprising then that sexual satisfaction for wives began to receive increasing attention along with the rise in head-complement and senior partner-junior partner marriage patterns.

Yet, later research on female sexuality in more recent marriage manuals has caused Gordon and his coauthor Penelope Shankweiler (1971:465) to wonder if women have come as far as is sometimes thought. "Women in this century have been granted the right to experience sexual desire and have this desire satisfied," they write, "but always with the man calling the tune." They suggest that this is "a manifestation of the minority group status of women," since "if women have been encouraged to take more initiative it is in order that they might give

SEXUALITY AND THE MALE/FEMALE POWER STRUGGLE

The women's movement, with its emphasis on female sexuality, has brought new concern about female orgasm, an aspect of sexuality perhaps more easily discussed by middle-class than by working-class individuals. Female orgasm, conceptualized by feminists as women's sexual "right," heightens the power struggle between men and women. The reciprocal concern with men's alleged increasing impotence provides ammunition for the counterattack. Now that women's capacity for multiple orgasms is well recognized, both men and women, paradoxically, begin to insist that women should experience sexual climax. Some women argue that they have been deprived of orgasms by men whose single-minded concern with their own sexual pleasure prevented them from stimulating their partners in ways that would lead to female orgasm. The male response has been that women who do not actively participate in the sexual encounter (who are inorgasmic) deprive men of the sexual and psychological satisfaction of knowing they have satisfied their mates.

The debate about male impotence sounds a set of parallel concerns. Impotent men complain that women's new sexual aggressiveness, their demand for sexual satisfaction based on male performance, is the root cause of men's sexual problems. Women counter that male impotence is a hostile act designed to punish women. One might label this sexual debate "Whose orgasm is it anyway?"

SOURCE: Jean Lipman-Blumen, *Gender Roles and Power* (Englewood Cliffs, N.J.: Prentice-Hall, 1984), p. 125.

---

more pleasure to their husbands rather than achieve more autonomy in the sexual realm." Gordon and Shankweiler refer to James Coleman's (1966) remark that female enjoyment of sexuality for its own sake can only come about "when a woman's status and ultimate position do not depend greatly on her husband."

Sociologist Jean Lipman-Blumen (1984: 125) writes that "across the social-class spectrum, the marriage bed sets the stage for the power struggle between women and men." (See insert.) Blumstein and Schwartz (1983:222–225,305) make a similar point in reporting the "backlash of dissatisfaction and conflict" that couples in their sample experienced when they went beyond role *shar-*

ing to role *reversal.* "It is here that the images of the husband 'abdicating his maleness' or the wife 'becoming the man of the family' begin to crop up," they write. "It is here that the partners begin to hold traditional roles up to one another as tests that are being failed."

However, equal-partner marriage emphasizes role *interchangeability,* quite the opposite from a pattern in which one person must be "in charge" while the other follows, defers, and submits out of duty. Role reversal that would place the woman in charge over the man would only be a continuation of an old script with new players. In an equal-partner arrangement, the responsibilities of each partner double in both the instrumental and expressive dimensions of marriage. But the rewards double as well. Thus, it is possible to postulate that as more and more marriages are built on the equal-partner pattern, mari-tal expressiveness will be enhanced because of the broader base of joint interests and the increased and strengthened circuits of the marital-exchange process.

CHAPTER HIGHLIGHTS

In the marital-adjustment school of thought, the emphasis is on avoiding conflicts and retaining harmony by adapting—even though such adjustment may mean submerging personal aspirations and interests. A major criticism of the marital-adjustment approach has centered on a realization that wives have been expected to adapt more than husbands. In contrast to the marital-adjustment school is an approach which stresses that marriage is a continual process of negotiation and benefit seeking. If the relationship ceases to be rewarding to one of the spouses, efforts can be directed toward *changing* the costly and punishing aspects of the situation instead of simply adjusting.

The *expressive* dimension of marriage includes three basic elements: *companionship* (someone to be with), *empathy* (someone who listens, understands, and cares), and *physical affection* (someone with whom love can be expressed through touch, caresses, and sexual intercourse). Research indicates that economic factors play an important part in the satisfactions husbands and wives perceive in all aspects of the expressive dimension of marriage.

·11·

PROCESS IN MARRIAGE:
POWER AND DECISION-MAKING

An experienced secretary and book-keeper saw no reason that she shouldn't go back to work now that her children were in school. Her husband said no. Explaining the problem to a newspaper advice columnist, the woman wrote: "My husband said if I want to work outside the home I should work for him. (He owns a small retail business.) I don't want to work for him because he refuses to pay me. He says: 'You don't need any money of your own. If you want something, ask me and I'll give you the money for it.' (In the past when I've asked for money he has had to know where every dime is going.) He enjoys having me ask him for money. It makes him feel important" (Bloomington-Bedford (Ind.) Sunday Herald Times, "Dear Abby," June 9, 1974).

Persons who assert that marriage can stand on love alone are suggesting an imbalanced, precarious posture. Marriage requires two legs—love and justice. Aristotle, in "The Nicomachean Ethics," defined justice as simply "the good of others." And Robert Seidenberg (1970:304), a psychiatrist, points out: "Love without justice is a yoke, which more often than not, not only enslaves but strangulates the human spirit." The wife in the letter quoted feels that she is being treated unfairly by her husband; she defines her situation as one of injustice, no matter what her husband may say about feelings of love for her.

However, if this wife presses for her rights and insists on furthering her own interests even though they are in opposition to her husband's interests, she is aware that a situation of conflict will develop. Negotiation will be necessary so that a satisfactory settlement can be reached and the relationship continued.

The issue of *power* also comes into play. The wife's power is limited by her dependence on her husband for resources. Aware of this, the husband refuses to allow her any discretionary income of her own even if she were to earn it in his place of business ("he refuses to pay me"). Instead he wants her to ask for any small amount as she needs it, thus keeping both himself and his wife alert to her dependence upon him and his power over her ("He enjoys having me ask him for money. It makes him feel important."). Further evidence of his power is the husband's demand for an accounting of how each dime is spent when he does give his wife money; there is a very real tie between his total control of the resources and his power in the marriage in general.

The wife senses that as long as she is utterly dependent upon her husband for material resources, his power over her will be great and she will find it necessary to go along with his wishes while submerging her own interests. Yet she seems to realize that if she can obtain resources of her own (the principle of alternative rewards as discussed in Chapter 4), her power will be increased and her husband's decreased.

POWER IN THE HUSBAND-WIFE RELATIONSHIP

Many persons have the mistaken notion that issues such as justice, negotiation, conflict, and power have no place in discussions of marriage. Such issues are thought to be appropriate when it comes to discussing political affairs or labor-management disputes but not when it comes to discussing the husband-wife relationship. Yet, since marriage is a social system, it involves social processes no less than do relationships between two parties negotiating business interests or two nations trying to work out a trade agreement.

THE SHOCK OF THE MARITAL-POWER ISSUE

Traditional marriage shores up the power of men in subtle ways which I believe few men—even sensitive men of the greatest goodwill towards women—appreciate. When you are playing tennis and the wind is blowing from your back, you may not be aware of the wind at all and think only that you are playing very well. All your shots go in swift and hard. It isn't until you change courts and the wind is blowing against you that you appreciate the force of the wind. Power is like that. You feel it most when it is working against you. Women sometimes marry to find that the wind is suddenly blowing against them. I am speaking now of spirited women, strong women, who are the most likely to resent the sudden change. They feel overwhelmed in marriage by husbands who have been raised to act, if not to be, strong in their dealings with the outside world and to expect devoted care from a woman in the family. Both their outward strength and inner dependency are reinforced by the usual order of things in marriage.

SOURCE: Phyllis Rose, *Parallel Lives: Five Victorian Marriages* (New York: Knopf, 1983). Random House Vintage Books edition, pp. 268–269.

What Is Power?

The word *power* derives from the Latin *potere,* which means "to be able." Power includes the ideas of ability and control. In this sense, "I can" is the essence of power. I can do something rather than being at the mercy of other forces. I can produce an effect on something or someone else. Thus, we speak of how science has increased the ability of humans to control the environment, to have power over nature, and so on.

As psychologist David Winter (1973) points out, the behavioral scientist is concerned specifically with *social* power. Winter's definition sums up the usual meaning of power as it is spoken of by psychologists, sociologists, and political scientists: "Social power is the ability or capacity of [one person or group] to produce (consciously or unconsciously) intended effects on the behavior or emotions of another person [or group]" (p. 5).

To put the whole matter very simply: *power* is the ability to have one's way and achieve one's goals—even though others may resist.

How Sociologists Measure Marital Power

The concept of *marital power* has posed problems for sociologists, both in terms of defining it and measuring it. In fact, a great deal of controversy has raged over this subject in recent years as various sociologists who study the family have disagreed among themselves (Cromwell and Olson, 1975; Scanzoni, 1979b). The problem in defining marital power has occurred because some sociologists use the term synonymously with other terms, such as authority, decision-making, or influence, while other sociologists make distinctions between the various terms.

Sociologist Constantina Safilios-Rothschild (1970) makes the criticism that too many studies have examined only husband-wife *decision-making* in measuring marital power while failing to pay enough attention to what goes on behind the scenes, such as "the patterns of tension and conflict management, or the type of prevailing division of labor." She suggests that the total configuration of these behavioral patterns must be examined, and not one aspect alone, if power is to be understood. In Safilios-Rothschild's thinking, family power structure should be thought of in terms of three components: *authority* (who is considered to have the legitimate right to have the most say, according to prevailing cultural and social norms), *decision-making* (who makes the decisions, how often, and so on), and *influence* (less obvious maneuvering; the degree to which a spouse is able to impose his or her point of view through various subtle or not-so-subtle pressures even though the other spouse initially opposed that point of view.)

Another problem pointed out by some sociologists is that there may be various levels to familial power structure. Which level is being explored? Are we concerned with who makes particular decisions, or who decides that this person may make those decisions? Or even beyond that, who determines who will decide which spouse will make the decision? (Ryder, 1970; Komarovsky, 1962; Safilios-Rothschild, 1969, 1970). The picture begins to look like the proverbial "house that Jack built"!

In other words, suppose a husband and wife reach an impasse on a certain decision. Finally, just to get the matter settled so that the couple can go on with other things, one of them says to the other, "*You* decide. Since we can't make up our minds, I'll turn the matter over to you and I'll abide by your decision." The spouse who gets to make the decision may seem at first glance to be the one with the greater power; after all it is his or her wishes that will be carried out. However, as Safilios-Rothschild (1970:540) points out,

One way of measuring power in marriage is to determine which partner has the final say in major decisions—for example, decisions involving finances. (Conklin/Monkmeyer)

"the one spouse may relegate one or more decisions to the other spouse because he finds these decisions relatively unimportant and very time-consuming." The "relegating" spouse in such cases has considerably more power than the one who might appear to make the decisions, because the relegating spouse "can orchestrate the power structure in the family according to his preferences and wishes."

Survey Method of Studying Power Sociologists study power in marriage by using two basic methods: *asking* or *observing*. The "asking" method is sometimes called the *survey method* or the *reputational method.* A sample of husbands or wives (or both) is drawn, and questions are asked about the balance of power in their marriage. Sometimes a sample of children is drawn to find out which parent the children think has the greater power in the family. Variables such as social status, stage of the life cycle, and other factors are also introduced in an effort to find patterns that may aid in understanding marital power better. Questions used in the survey method may have to do with decision-making or with handling conflicts. Or a key question might be as direct as this: "Who is the real boss in your marriage?" A question used in several studies including our own research is this one: "When you disagree about [particular items the respondent has listed as areas of disagreement in his or her marriage], who usually gets his way, you or your spouse?" The spouse with the higher score of "winning out" in disagreements is considered to have the greater power.

One frequently used method of measuring marital power has been to ask respondents who makes the final decisions in each of a number of areas. The list might include matters like the choice of work for either spouse, vacation decisions, what kind of car to buy, and so on. Blood and Wolfe (1960) utilized this method in their pioneering Detroit study of husband-wife relationships. Yet, their approach to the issue of power has been criticized because each of the eight items they listed was given equal weight. In other words, when they tabulated the final results to find out a person's power score, decisions about the weekly food budget were treated as being just as important as the choice of the husband's job or the purchase of a house.

The problem of measuring power is further complicated by a lack of consistency in the kinds of questions asked even when marital power is thought of only in terms of decision-making. Blood and Wolfe (1960) singled out eight areas of household decision-making; and while some studies have duplicated these, other studies have utilized lists containing other items. Thus, it is difficult to compare studies (Safilios-Rothschild, 1970).

Another problem in connection with the survey approach relates to the respondents who are being queried. Some studies have focused on wives only, whereas other studies have sought to find out husbands' perception of decision-making power. There are also studies in which *both* husbands and wives are asked their perceptions of power within their marriages and studies designed to find out what children perceive about their parents' marriage. Comparison of various studies again becomes a problem, because it has been amply demonstrated that different members of the family may perceive the power structure differently (see Turk and Bell, 1972; Scanzoni, 1965; Safilios-Rothschild, 1969; Brown and Rutter, 1966; Hess and Torney, 1962).

In addition to the problems clustering around the kinds of questions that are asked and the persons who are asked them, there remains the more basic problem of limiting measurements of power to the matter of decision-making alone. Some sociologists suggest that rather than focusing on the *outcome* of decision-making, it might prove more fruitful to concentrate on the *process* by which decisions are arrived at (Olson and Rabunsky, 1972; Scanzoni, 1979b; Hill and Scanzoni, 1982; Scanzoni and Szinovacz, 1980). But how can sociologists study the processes of decision-making that go on within family units? This brings us to the second commonly used method for investigating marital power.

Observational-Experimental Method of Studying Power Whereas the survey method is built around asking, the observational-experimental method is built around watching and listening. Laboratory situations are set up so that couples may be observed while they settle disagreements and make decisions. The sessions are usually tape-recorded or videotaped and later evaluated by a panel of judges who code the observed behavior according to a specified rating scale. (For example, they might keep a record of who made the most interruptions in a family discussion, who made the greater number of suggestions in a husband-wife dialogue about some disagreement, and so on.)

Game techniques may also be utilized so that a couple is faced with decision-making in simulated situations (Greenblat, Stein, and Washburne, 1974). Sometimes a series of short stories are used as stimuli so that the husband and wife must come to an agreement about hypothetical problem situations and find ways to resolve conflicts. Their interactions are observed in an effort to see who exercises the greater power, who is most persuasive, or who gets his or her way (see summaries in Turk and Bell, 1972; Liu, Hutchinson, and Hong, 1973).

There are, of course, problems with the observational-experimental method just as there are with the survey method. Some critics point out that couples or families who know they are being watched may not act naturally and may present a picture somewhat different than they would in actual decision-making situations in their day-to-day living, thus creating an "onstage" effect. But other researchers have answered such criticisms with evidence that much accurate information about family interaction has been gained from observational methods. Two sociologists attempted to compare the two methods by using both on the same random sample of 211 families in metropolitan Toronto. One interesting finding was that "the questionnaire measures showed husband dominance to prevail, while the observational measures showed a balance between the spouses" (Turk and Bell, 1972:220).

Sociologist David Heer (1963) draws attention to a crucial problem common to both methods of researching marital power,

namely, the fact that the person who has the greater power in one area of marital decision-making may have a much smaller degree of power in another area. It is not easy to find ways to ascertain and measure power since "power is not unidimensional." Heer's statement is but one more indication of the difficulties surrounding research on power in marriage. Sociologists speak of these as *methodological* problems, since they relate to methods of conceptualizing, gathering necessary data, and measuring findings. But an awareness of these problems should not mean that we despair of any understanding at all of marital power. While there are many things that sociologists do not know about this concept, there are many other things they do know (McDonald, 1980). And it is on the basis of information we already have that we can proceed to build theory and seek explanations about the part power plays in the marital process.

How Power Is Obtained and Maintained

A basic principle in sociology links power with resources. That is, the more resources a person, group, or nation possesses, the greater is the power held with relation to others who desire such resources. For example, suppose a country we'll call "Plentyland" has resources which another country ("Scarceland") lacks and desperately needs (oil, wheat, certain raw materials necessary for manufacturing, or other goods). Plentyland will have a considerable amount of power over Scarceland and can force Scarceland to act in certain ways, either by threatening to withhold the needed materials or by promising to increase such goods, provide better economic deals, and so on. If Scarceland's resources offered in exchange are not so essential to Plentyland as Plentyland's resources are to Scarceland, it follows that Scarceland is much more dependent upon Plentyland than Plentyland is on Scarceland. Therefore, Plentyland has the greater power and may be expected to exercise considerable influence and control over Scarceland. The point is illustrated somewhat in the price demands and other power exercised by some of the oil-producing nations during the energy crisis of recent years.

Resource Theory and Power in Marriage

But can resource theory be applied to *marital* power? Once again a certain amount of controversy has raged among sociologists (Safilios-Rothschild, 1970; Rodman, 1967, 1972). Safilios-Rothschild questions limiting the concept of resources to assets that will almost without question be found in greater abundance among *husbands* in traditional marriages (for example, education, income,

(Drawing by Frascino, © 1977 by The New Yorker Magazine, Inc.)

"You say you're only a housewife, and I say what do you mean, 'only'?"

occupational status) while ignoring other kinds of resources. "Does not the wife have at her disposal other 'resources' tangible and intangible which she can (and does) contribute or withdraw at will and thus 'control' even the most occupationally successful husband?" asks Safilios-Rothschild (1970:548). As examples of such control of resources, she names food preparation (poorly prepared or the husband's favorite dish), sloppy versus neat housekeeping, sexual enthusiasm or frigidity, the control of the home atmosphere and hospitality (or lack of it) through pleasant or sour moods, and so on.

In spite of her criticisms of resource theory, Safilios-Rothschild is herself speaking in terms of rewards, costs, and punishments. She does not appear to deny the basic sociological principle linking power with the ability to grant or withhold valued resources. Rather, her hesitancy seems to be associated with a reluctance to limit the definition of resources to an *economic* base.

However, in modern industrial societies, it is productive work in the marketplace that counts in terms of social worth. The work of women in the home is not assigned the same value as the work of men, which is converted into dollars. "In a society in which money determines value, women are a group who work outside the money economy," writes Margaret Benston (1969:3–4). She goes on to point out that household work, when performed by a wife, is not considered to be worth money, and since it isn't, society considers it valueless and not even real work at all. This in turn leads to the conclusion that "women themselves, who do this valueless work, can hardly be expected to be worth as much as men, who work for money."

In commenting upon Benston's statement, sociologist Dair Gillespie (1971:457) emphasizes a point we have made throughout this book: Power is linked with one's degree of involvement in the economic-opportunity system. She writes: "Thus it is clear that for a wife to gain even a modicum of power in the marital relationship, she must gain it from external sources, i.e., she must participate in the work force, her education must be superior to that of her husband, and her participation in organizations must excel his."

Blood and Wolfe (1960) utilized the personal-resource theory to explain their findings on marital power in the Detroit study. After seeing that a husband's degree of decision-making power was related to his education, income, and occupational status, these researchers concluded that "the higher the husband's social status, the greater his power." In other words, as the husband brings increasing amounts of resources into the marriage, his wife is increasingly willing to defer to his wishes and consider him to have the right to have his way in decisions. There was also evidence that the wife who brings educational and occupational achievements to the marriage has a greater share in the marital balance of power because of these resources.

A number of sociologists have criticized the interpretations of Blood and Wolfe, pointing out that even the findings of the Detroit study did not consistently fit with resource theory, because low-blue-collar husbands had more power than high-blue-collar husbands—just the opposite of the relationship between resources and power at other status levels. Also, when different areas of decision-making were measured by other sociologists, the findings did not always fit so neatly with the Blood and Wolfe explanation (Safilios-Rothschild, 1969, 1970; Centers, Raven, and Rodrigues, 1971; Rodman, 1967, 1972).

Three sociologists who conducted a large study among husbands and wives in Los Angeles found that some of their findings clearly supported the resource theory of marital power as set forth by Blood and Wolfe, but other of their findings did not. Nevertheless, Centers, Raven, and Rodrigues (1971) do not toss out the notion that control of valued resources plays an important part in husband-wife power relations. They feel it is but one factor among several others. They call attention to personality factors, cultural factors (especially the influence of norms in the couple's culture or subculture about how much power husband or wife should have), and "role patterning" (the way the domain of authority varies by prevailing societal gender roles; in both their study and the Detroit study, wives had more to say about the choice of food, for example, and husbands had more power in choices about the husband's job).

They also agree with Heer's suggestion that the *relative competence* and *relative involvement* of the spouses in specific decision-making areas must also be taken into account in examining family power. Certain decisions might require skills which one spouse possesses to a greater degree than the other. For example, in a particular marriage, one partner might decide on the color to paint the living room and the furnishings to buy because of that person's abilities in interior decorating; the other partner might make the decision about when to purchase new tires for the car based upon greater knowledge of auto maintenance. Also, the spouse who is more involved in or concerned with a specific matter might be expected to be the one to make the final decision on that matter.

Modifications of Resource Theory Several sociologists who see merit in resource theory as an explanation of marital power and yet are aware of certain weaknesses have suggested revisions or modifications. Heer

(1963) suggests a theory of exchange which takes into account *alternatives* to resources provided by one's spouse. In Blood and Wolfe's interpretation, the emphasis had been on a comparison of the respective resources brought by each spouse into the marriage; and the conclusion had been that the more resources either one has in comparison to the other, the greater will be his or her power. Heer adds another comparison: What is the value of the resources provided by the spouse in comparison to resources available to that person outside the marriage? In other words, would the man or woman be better off married to someone else or not married at all? For example, if a wife thought the alternatives were better elsewhere, she might be less willing to defer to a dominating husband, thereby diminishing his power. The wife in such a case may be willing to risk terminating the relationship because she considers the cost of losing the husband less punishing than the cost of submitting to his control.

Heer's modification of resource theory fits with a point we have made repeatedly: a person's power over another diminishes as the second person finds that other sources of rewards are available. Sociologist Willard Waller's (1938) "principle of least interest" is also relevant. According to this principle, the person who is less interested in keeping a relationship going has the greater power. The one to whom a relationship matters more and who feels the greater need is more willing to defer to the other in order to preserve the relationship. When preservation of the relationship ceases to matter so much, the other party loses power. (See pp. 190–192 in 1951 edition; see also Kelley, 1979:44–47.)

Blumstein and Schwartz (1983:283–285) found a clear indication of this principle when they looked at situations of nonmonogamy in their study of American couples.

Their data showed that the less committed partner in a relationship was also more likely to be open to outside sexual relationships. "On the other hand," they write, "the more committed partner is too much in love and prizes the relationship too highly to look at other people." They point out that the greater commitment of this person "hands power to the person who cares less."

But partners who "care less" also stand to *lose* their power as their nonmonogamous behaviors (exercised because of the power they feel they have that allows them to do as they please) begin to make them less desirable to the partner whose commitment they presumed upon. "When a relationship loses its desirability, it loses its ability to command allegiance," Blumstein and Schwartz emphasize, "and the other person is then freer to pursue other relationships or to exert his or her own power, since the emotional cost of such actions is reduced." We saw in Chapter 4 that one way a person's power over another is reduced is if the second person can say, "I don't *want* what you have to offer."

In comparing cross-cultural studies, sociologist Hyman Rodman (1967, 1972) also found difficulties in explaining marital power solely in resource terms and therefore suggested another modification. Rodman found that in France and in the United States, it was true that the higher the husband's education, income, and occupational status, the greater his power in marriage; but just the opposite was found to be true in Greece and Yugoslavia. Husbands with the highest educational levels in these countries had the lowest marital-power scores. How can this be explained?

Rodman proposes a "theory of resources in cultural context," in which he sees the distribution of power in marriage as resulting from the interaction of two factors. One is the comparative resources of the husband and wife, and the other is the prevailing social norm about marital power in a particular culture or subculture. In other words, if a culture expects husbands to have the greater power in marriage, this norm can have a profound effect upon marital power in spite of the comparative resources of the husband and wife. On the other hand, if a culture favors a more egalitarian view of marriage, power is not automatically assumed and taken for granted as an inherent right of the male. Rather, any power one has must be earned, and this is where resources come in.

Rodman views the United States and France as being more flexible with regard to the distribution of power in marriage and more favorable to egalitarian ideology; therefore power is not something that is already "there" for males. Power comes instead from resources; it must be earned. Thus the higher power of higher-status husbands in advanced, industrialized countries is not surprising. On the other hand, in developing nations with strong patriarchal traditions where social norms support the husband's right to dominate, the social classes more likely to embrace modern, egalitarian marriage ideals are those who have had opportunities for advanced education. Thus, in Greece and Yugoslavia, more highly educated, higher-status husbands have been more willing than lower-status husbands to grant wives more power, with a resulting decrease in power for themselves.

In looking at this cross-national data and Rodman's explanations, we are not by any means suggesting that higher-status Yugoslavian and Greek marriages within a strongly patriarchal society are somehow more equalitarian than higher-status marriages in the United States or other advanced, industrialized nations. Rather, the comparisons were concerned with degrees of authority *within*

the respective countries under study in an effort to see how social status and power were linked in a particular cultural setting.

We have already seen how the option to work (expecially when it is exercised) increases a wife's marital power. And we may recall the example of West African tribes in which wives exercised high degrees of power because of their economic holdings. (See Kaberry, 1953, for more detail; also LaFree, 1974.)

All of this brings us back to resource theory once more. Elements of it are there even when we examine Yugoslavian and Greek data. In a 1966 study, two Yugoslavian sociologists found that in their country women who are employed gain in marital power (Buric and Zelevic, 1967). And Safilios-Rothschild (1967) also found this to be true in her study of wives in Athens. In spite of her misgivings about resource theory, she has written that there is some evidence for its holding true for Greek women more than Greek men. When a wife is employed and especially when her occupational accomplishments are higher than those of her husband, her power in the family tends to be increased, "because the possessed resources prove her abilities in such a way that even the traditional-minded males have to accept her competence."

A recognition of the part that beliefs and cultural norms play in marital power, as in Rodman's modification of resource theory, need not be seen as contradicting resource theory but rather as something that interacts with it and aids in an understanding of how power is distributed. Norms lend legitimacy to power; they do not create power.

It cannot be overstressed that power springs from resources. "Haves" possess more power than "have-nots" in a society. Norms are created to lend support to the possession of power and to show that it is "right" for those who hold power to do so. Thus, the norm that husbands should be more dominant in marriage than wives ultimately goes back to the fact that males have traditionally had greater access to the economic-opportunity system and therefore have had greater resources. Husbands *have* had greater power in marriage, and therefore behavioral expectations (or norms) have developed to support their *right* to this greater power. In turn, one's degree of acceptance of these norms can have an effect on marital power, along with one's resources as compared to those of the spouse. As women gain greater resources, and with these resources greater marital power, we may expect norms to develop that will support wives' rights to such power just as they have supported husbands' rights in the past.

The development of such norms will take time, however. As Jean Lipman-Blumen (1984:178) points out, *the norms that have supported the traditional gender-based distribution of power* "are articulated informally in control myths and formally in law." Among the "control myths" she cites are the belief that men are more intelligent than women and thus more capable of running things, the belief that women are naturally more self-sacrificing and nurturant than men and thus may be expected to put their own interests secondary to those of others, the belief that women's most valuable assets are beauty and sexuality, the belief that women talk too much, and the belief that men are looking out for women's best interests and can be trusted to protect women's welfare. These and the other internalized beliefs or "control myths" cited by Lipman-Blumen have taken on the force of "potent social mechanisms, used by males and females to keep themselves and one another in their 'appropriate'—but vastly unequal—places," she writes (p. 75). Today, such "control myths" are being increasingly questioned, scrutinized, challenged, and seen for what they are—a way of controlling behaviors and perpetuating the unequal power relationship that has been built up between men as a group and women as a group.

Power: Legitimate and Nonlegitimate

If the following two hypothetical statements by wives were heard, the observer would immediately be struck by both a similarity and a difference with respect to their comments on their husbands.

Joyce: My husband and I make most decisions together. We talk things over and then decide what to do. But he decides the really important things—particularly if we disagree. For example, he wanted to take a trip to Florida for our vacation and I wanted to visit relatives instead. Needless to say, he won! And I feel he had a right to. After all, he works hard all year to provide our family with a good standard of living. He deserves to decide how to use his time off work and what kind of vacation to take. I feel the same about major expenditures. He earns the money after all! Why shouldn't he be the one to decide how it's spent?

Martha: My husband bought this house trailer we're living in. He didn't even ask what I thought about it—just got it and moved us in. And now he can't even keep up the payments. He's never earned a decent living in all the years we've been married. You can tell that by just looking around our shabby place! But he sure acts like a king around here. "Get me a beer, Martha!" "I need clean socks. You'd better make sure you get to the Laundromat more often. What kind of a wife are you?" Yet he won't buy me a washing machine, and he takes the car every day so that I have to try to find neighbors who'll drive me to the Laundromat. And Pete is always telling me what I can't do, always bossing me around. Like the other night, my friend Judy called and wanted me to go to one of those parties in someone's house where they sell kitchen things, but Pete said, "No, you're not going! I don't want you to." And that was that. But it doesn't seem fair.

In comparing the two statements, we notice first of all that both wives indicate that their husbands hold greater power in marriage than they themselves do. But second, we notice that one wife feels this is right and fair while the other does not. The key factor here is involvement in the economic-opportunity system.

Joyce's husband has rewarded his family with status and material benefits; thus she feels he has the right to the greater power in the marriage. Martha's husband, on the other hand, has not provided such resources and therefore she resents the way he seizes power in the marriage and tries to control her life. Unconsciously, she is acknowledging that he hasn't earned the right to have authority over her. He has failed in what sociologist George Homans (1961:287) has called "the most important single factor in making a man a leader," namely, "the ability to provide rare and valued rewards for his followers."

Joyce feels that her husband's power in their marriage is legitimate. Martha feels that the power her husband exercises is not legitimate. This distinction is an important one which turned up in our Indianapolis study of marriages, and it throws light on many of the problems that have emerged in studies of marital power.

Some sociologist have sought to clarify the two kinds of influence and control over others by distinguishing between the terms *authority* and *power*. Authority is viewed as legitimate, power as nonlegitimate. Sociologist Walter Buckley (1967), for example, defines *authority* as "the direction or control of the behavior of others for the promotion of collective goals, based on some ascertainable form of their knowledgeable consent. Authority thus implies informed, voluntary compliance." *Informed consent* and *collective goals* are key points. In contrast, *power*, according to Buckley, is "control or influence over the actions of others to promote one's goals without their consent, against their 'will,' or without their knowledge or understanding" (p. 186).

But since in normal, everyday usage, the word *authority* includes the notion of power, it may seem awkward to perch "power" and "authority" on two ends of a pole as opposites. The concepts involved, however, are valid. Control or influence over others that is deemed legitimate and involves knowledgeable consent certainly differs from control or influence that is *not* considered legitimate and which is exercised apart from the consent of the governed. But both cases involve *power* as defined at the beginning of this

FIGURE 11-1 A continuum of power.

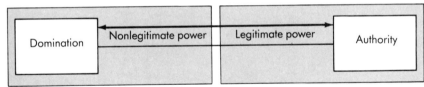

chapter. Thus, we suggest Figure 11-1 as an attempt to clarify the distinction. "Power is power," but it's possible to cross over the line into *nonlegitimate* power.

Nonlegitimate power is neither earned nor consented to. If it moves far enough, it becomes *domination*. Domination includes the idea of lording it over others against their will (the word derives from the Latin *dominus* meaning "master, lord, owner, despot"). In contrast, legitimate power is earned and consented to. As a process involving bargaining and negotiation, legitimate power moves toward *authority*—an institutionalized state. That is, we recognize that a person or group in a position of authority has the *right* to be in charge.

From the standpoint of cost/reward theory, nonlegitimate power is viewed by those under it as being undeserved, taken without having been earned, and not providing sufficient rewards for the leader's followers. It is thus seen in terms of net loss (giving up one's own desires against one's will and giving in to the desires of another). In contrast, legitimate power is viewed by those who submit to it as having been earned and deserved by the one who holds the power. Therefore it is seen in terms of net profit (the rewards provided outweigh the costs of submitting to the will of another).

Nonlegitimate power tends to rely on coercion, threats, and punishment; whereas legitimate power relies on "friendly persuasion" and the provision of benefits. We might compare the distinction to the old problem of motivating the peddler's horse. The peddler might get his wagon moving again by either applying a stick to the animal from behind or by holding a carrot on a string out front to lure the animal onward. Legitimate power tends to emphasize the "carrot approach," while nonlegitimate power puts the emphasis upon the stick.

In the Indianapolis study (Scanzoni, 1970), we found that it is an oversimplification merely to state without qualification that with greater status comes greater husband power—unless we take into account the *kind* of power. Actually, the study showed that lower-status husbands tended to exercise more power in their marriages than did higher-status husbands. Men with less education, income, and occupational prestige tended to resolve conflicts unilaterally, carrying out their own wishes rather than paying attention to their wives' desires. Furthermore, they were less interested in working with their wives in making decisions about matters of spouse disagreement. In the processes of conflict resolution, wives were permitted little participation as compared to the situation in upper-status homes.

We saw earlier that Blood and Wolfe (1960:30–33) had also found that husbands in the lowest status group (low-blue-collar) had more power than husbands in the next category (high-blue-collar), which broke the consistency of the pattern that had otherwise shown that husband power rises with social status. Their only attempt at an explanation was to comment that the group of lowest-status men with high power scores were presumably older men who were carrying on a pre-World War I patriarchal ideology which held that a husband should be the boss.

Komarovsky (1962:225–229), too, found in her sample of fifty-eight blue-collar marriages that the lower-blue-collar husbands had greater marital power than did the higher-blue-collar husbands (skilled workers). She suggests that educational differences might account for this finding. The less-educated couples tended to have more patriarchal attitudes, with masculine dominance viewed as the norm. The better-educated couples (high school graduates) tended to have more egalitarian ideals. Furthermore, the wives in these marriages expected and demanded more of their marriages. Often they were better educated than their husbands, since the relatively high earnings of skilled workers make it possible for such blue-collar men to "marry upward." In some cases, men had even learned their skilled trades as a result of having married high school graduates who had encouraged them to enlarge their achievement aspirations. However, as Komarovsky notes, upper-blue-collar husbands, by marrying better-educated women, "lose the degree of power enjoyed by the semi-skilled over their less-educated wives."

Education is a resource wives may bring into a marriage, and again it is evident that resources bring greater power. The wife's educational resources and the husband's economic resources in skilled-worker marriages bring about more of a balance of power than exists in lower-blue-collar marriages. In upper-blue-collar families, decisions are more likely to be talked over and resolved jointly. This contrasts with the husband's unilateral decision-making and conflict resolution in lower-blue-collar families.

Beliefs and Practices Related to Power   In our own study, we measured both what respondents said they *believed* and what they said they *did* with regard to marital power. We found that beliefs do make a difference and that there was no support for Blood and Wolfe's contention that patriarchal traditions are no longer operative. Respondents were assigned a "male authority ideology" score based upon their responses to two statements read separately at different stages of the interview. The statements were these: (1) "The wife should have equal authority with the husband in making decisions" and (2) "The husband should be the head of the home." Structured responses (which made coding and assigning a score possible) were "strongly agree, agree, disagree, strongly disagree" (Scanzoni, 1970:151).

Among wives, it was found that the higher the social status (based on husband's education, occupation, and income), the more patriarchal were wives' beliefs. With increasing levels of social status, there appeared to be an increasing acceptance of traditional views regarding a husband's right to leadership within the marriage. Conversely, our research showed that the lower the level of social status, the less likely were wives to accept patriarchal beliefs. Lower-status wives rejected traditional notions of masculine authority and leaned toward modern egalitarian ideals. Husbands, for their part, were found at all status levels to believe that the husband should be the dominant person in the marital relationship.

The concepts of legitimate and nonlegitimate power fit nicely here. Husbands evidently feel they have the right to greater power in marriage. Lower-status husbands lean heavily on traditional norms which have given the male the final say as "head of the house." Higher-status husbands have both the traditional norms and economic achievement to support their claim to power. Wives seem to view matters somewhat differently. If husband power appears to be earned (by economic achievement and resources brought to the marriage), wives are willing to grant the right to power *ideologically* as well (by expressing a belief in traditional patriarchal ideals). Thus, with rising status, there comes a willingness on the part of wives to view husband power as *right*, legitimate, earned on the basis of rewards provided. Joyce, in our earlier illustration, is a wife who looks at the matter in this way.

However, lower-status wives are less willing to grant power to husbands ideologically, since the husbands have not earned such power economically, even though the husbands tend to feel that the patriarchal belief system in itself should be enough to assure their greater power in the marriage. The hypothetical Martha in our illustration demonstrated such a marital situation. The husband feels the wife should defer to him simply because he is a man; the wife feels he doesn't deserve such deference since he has been so unsuccessful in the economic-opportunity system. Any power he takes is considered by her to be nonlegitimate and therefore *domination.* The higher-status wife, in contrast, sees her husband's greater power as legitimate and thus *authority.*

The same distinction between domination and authority emerged in our research as we focused on actual practice as well as on beliefs. The method of measurement used was based upon conflict resolution rather than routinized household decision-making (which, as we have seen, poses many problems in drawing conclusions from the data). We reasoned that a more realistic picture of marital power emerges if we examine matters considered important by a couple and over which there is disagreement and then endeavor to find out which spouse has the final say in resolving the conflict.

In a nutshell, our findings were these: The lower the social status of the husband, the more frequent is his settling of issues unilaterally ("We will do what I say! And that's that!") and the less he tends to share decisions with his wife ("Let's talk it over and try to find an answer that suits us both"). Conversely, the higher the status of the husband, the less unilateral is his power and the more he is likely to share decisions with his wife. Rather than saying, "I have the last word by virtue of tradition and economic success," the higher-status husband is more likely to display an attitude that says, "Maybe we can come to a compromise," or "I don't want to make the final decision by myself; let's work on it together."

Thus, although as social status increases both husbands and wives believe the husband should have the greater power in marriage, in actual conflict resolution there is greater participation by both spouses than in lower-status marriages. Less frustrated in the occupational realm and more secure in the power they hold (because it is earned and thus considered legitimate in the eyes of their wives), higher-status husbands are willing to act in a way that is more or less egalitarian, even when contested issues are being discussed. Lower-status husbands, on the other hand, may hang on tightly to every shred of marital power that tradition has granted them since they have no power elsewhere, not having achieved in the economic system and thus lacking the resources that bring power. They therefore *take* power, even though, in their wives' eyes, they have not earned it. In such marriages, in spite of the egalitarian ideals of the wives, husbands tend to make unilateral decisions in areas of disagreement. They are less apt to permit or encourage the participation of their wives in making such decisions, and this lack of shared power is resented by the wives.

In both cases (higher-status and lower-status traditional marriages), husbands hold the power. But *the way wives see that power* is different. Higher-status wives tend to see it as right and proper; lower-status wives do not. Higher-status wives get to share in husbands' power; lower-status wives do not. In a certain sense, we might see here a distinction in types of power that has been made in psychoanalytic theory. Freud, Adler, and Horney all took pains to show a difference in *positive power,* which originates in strength, and *negative power,* which originates in weakness (see summary in Winter, 1973:157). As viewed by lower-status wives, the domination of their husbands is negative power.

Keep in mind that we have been speaking here of marriages in the *traditional* sense, in which the husband is the chief or only provider—the one considered to have the major responsibility for the couple's or family's financial support. (See also Blumstein and Schwartz, 1983:56–59.) Research on equal-partner marriages, with each spouse equally committed to a career and equally a provider of economic resources, might be expected to show a considerable change in the marital-power picture. Hints of this were found in the Indianapolis data. We found, as have other researchers, that a wife's employment is associated with greater power in her marriage—both in terms of her beliefs (more favorable to equality than to patriarchy) and her actual behavior (she tends to make more decisions alone rather than sharing them jointly with her husband) (Scanzoni, 1970:159–162; Heer, 1958; Blood and Wolfe, 1960; see also Scanzoni, 1978, 1979b; Blumstein and Schwartz, 1983).

The research findings from the large-scale study of four types of couples conducted by Blumstein and Schwartz (1983:55) showed clearly that "in marriages, and among heterosexual couples who live together, when women earn more, they win more clout." These sociologists suggest that men have learned to think of money in terms of identity and power (a major reason being "the equation that money equals power" so prevalent in the work place), whereas for women, money represents security, autonomy, self-sufficiency, freedom from dependency. In relationships with men, women have had to learn that "money talks."

These gender differences especially stand out in Blumstein and Schwartz's finding that "money establishes the balance of power in relationships, except among lesbians." The data showed that the lesbian couples in their sample wanted to share all financial responsibilities equally, wanted neither partner to be *dependent* upon the other, and did not use income as a way of establishing dominance in the relationship. Among gay-male couples, in contrast, Blumstein and Schwartz found that "income is an extremely important force in determining which partner will be dominant" (pp. 53–77). On the basis of these findings, these researchers have concluded that male attitudes toward money and power are carried from the public sphere into the private sphere and operate in even the closest relationships. Women in close relationships with men, both as wives or cohabitation partners, are therefore finding that earning their own income is crucial if they want to experience a sense of autonomy and the power that comes with freedom from economic dependency. They are thus more evenly matched for bargaining or decision-making in their particular relationship.

DECISION-MAKING

In marriage, as in any relationship between intimates (friends, lovers, parents and children, siblings), an ongoing process of giving and receiving occurs (Lederer and Jackson, 1968; Davis, 1973). The power structure plays an important part in this exchange, but simply knowing who has the greater influence leaves many questions unanswered. *How* are decisions made? How are problems solved? How are disagreements resolved? What is the process that goes on as compromises are worked out or plans are developed, and so on?

In seeking answers to such questions, we need first to note two kinds of giving and receiving that take place in relationships. One is the giving and receiving of information or

EXAMPLE OF COUPLE NEGOTIATION
IN A LESBIAN PARTNERSHIP

Those couples reporting that their income disparity had a negative effect on their relationship may have had an experience similar to Kathy and Toni's, where the disparity was so great it was bound to cause some problem. Kathy, a stockbroker, earned in excess of $40,000 a year. Toni, a freelance writer, averaged only about $8,000. Recalled Kathy, "When we started our relationship I did not want to make Toni feel like she was dependent on me. So we sat down and made out a budget for household necessities and we each contributed half. This soon became a major problem. Because of the fact that she didn't earn nearly as much as I, I had to lower my standard of living to accommodate a budget that she could afford. This didn't work out at all and continually caused us problems."

Added Toni, "When we started out, I didn't want her to get off on a trip of her feeling like she 'had to support' me. No one has supported me since I was sixteen."

Eventually, the couple negotiated a settlement that seemed to satisfy both. Explained Kathy, "We finally looked at money and its relative importance in our lives. Money didn't actually mean that much. What was important was our time and we felt that our time was equally valuable. What we got paid for our time was something that had very little to do with anything about or within ourselves—what we got paid for our time was all based on decisions we had little input into and seemed fairly irrational anyway.

"So we finally agreed to contribute to household expenses according to our income. If I earned four times as much as she, then I contributed four times as much to the household account. This gave us a lot more freedom and we began to live in a lifestyle that I was more comfortable with. Naturally, if our income relationship changes, then the percent contribution will also change. After all, she could strike it rich one of these days, or the stock market might fold tomorrow."

SOURCE: Sasha Gregory Lewis, *Sunday's Women: A Report on Lesbian Life Today* (Boston: Beacon Press, 1979), p. 142.

---

messages (*communication*) and the other is the giving and receiving of what William Lederer and Don Jackson (1968:177–186) call a *quid pro quo* or "something for something"—an agreement that one person will do or give something in response or reaction to something the other person does or gives. Probably the best word for this latter type of social exchange is *negotiation. Negotiation* may be defined as arranging the terms of a contract, transaction, or agreement by talking matters over and working things out. The word has its roots in the Latin *negotior* which refers to "doing business" or "trading." The husband-wife relationship involves negotiation in that there generally is mutual discussion and an arrangement of terms of agreement concerning areas of married life. How will the spouses divide up household chores? How will they decide whether or not to have children? How will they decide on leisure, friends, visits to relatives, and other aspects of social life? What kind of house or car should they buy? How can they arrange their

WHY WOMEN NEED ECONOMIC INDEPENDENCE

Economic *security* is not enough. Children need economic security but women want economic *independence.* Without her own money, a woman has no mobility, no bargaining power, no true freedom. Even if we never spend a penny on ourselves, just knowing we have our own money to spend as we see fit is a measure of adulthood.

. . . If a woman in a bad situation cannot walk out the door and know she will be able to feed and house herself and her children, chances are she won't walk out. She probably won't even make a demand for fairness for fear it will get her thrown out.

There is no delicate way to frame this reality except to say, in most families, *money is power.* Some men wield the power by withholding the truth about how much they earn or where it is invested. Others use money, material things, or vacations as a system of reward and punishment. Even in households where the husband gives the wife his paycheck and she controls the budget and pays the bills, she is powerless unless she controls the source and access to income. Otherwise, dependent women are like children who must behave in order to get their allowance or students who must obey because they cannot afford to go to college on their own.

SOURCE: Letty Cottin Pogrebin, *Family Politics: Love and Power on an Intimate Frontier* (New York: McGraw-Hill, 1983), pp. 95–96.

sex life so that it will be satisfactory to both of them?

In arriving at terms of agreement, the husband and wife do not necessarily settle a particular issue once and for all. As circumstances change or as desires of one or the other change, various matters may need to be renegotiated. Again, the idea of process enters the picture. Marriage involves an *ongoing* series of exchanges—in other words, continuous negotiation and renegotiation. Even in a relationship that over the years seems to have settled into very routinized ways of doing things, the partners can be caught unawares by new circumstances and face the issue of renegotiation. Time brings changes. The children grow into different stages and require new kinds of guidance or have different needs than earlier. One spouse's health may fail, necessitating a renegotiation on how the household will be run

or how the income will be produced. The retirement period of life may jolt a couple into

Marriage involves ongoing social exchanges and negotiations. (Fred Bodin/Stock, Boston)

seeing areas of their marriage needing re-examination and calling for efforts toward change.

The Latin origin of the term *negotiation* fits well with what goes on in such husband-wife interchanges. In a very real sense, it is a matter of "doing business" through a series of trade-offs. "I did that for him so he should do that for me." "If I gave up a big chunk of my day off to help her out, I don't see why she can't give up some time to bake pies for the guys coming over to play cards tonight—even if she doesn't like my friends!" "Of course, I'm going to hear my wife's speech at the PTA tonight. She always cheers me on when I do things like that; why shouldn't I encourage her, too?" "George got a big raise! Now we can take that trip we've been dreaming about! I'm going to do something special tonight. I asked my mother to take the children overnight, and George and I can have a special evening together making plans—and making love. I'll cook his favorite meal, and maybe we'll even eat by candlelight!" "Well, it seems to me that if a wife works at a job all day, she shouldn't have to come home and do all the housework, too. That's why I try to help Sue with the dishes and cleaning and stuff."

Statements such as these illustrate how rewards and costs shape everyday marital life. The husband who gave up much of his day off to help his wife (costs) expects her to reciprocate by giving up time for him (costs again) in order to reward him as he rewarded her. The husband who has been rewarded with his wife's encouragement and approval is willing to take the time (costs, the extent of which depends on how else he might have used that particular block of time) in order to provide her likewise with encouragement and approval by listening to her speech. The wife who is delighted by the increased rewards of her husband's raise tries to find a way to reward him in turn; she chooses to go the "expressive" route by planning a romantic evening. The husband who is rewarded by his wife's monetary earnings accepts the costs of added participation in household chores to reward his wife with more free time.

Case Study: Bob and Julie

A hypothetical couple named Bob and Julie illustrate how marital negotiation works. Their case seems particularly apt because it combines elements of both traditional marriage (in that Bob is the chief provider) and modern, egalitarian ideals (in that Julie has a job which gives her a greater degree of power than would be likely otherwise). In terms of the four main kinds of marital structures, we would say that Bob and Julie come closest to the senior partner-junior partner arrangement.

Let's assume that Bob and Julie have been married about six months. Without necessarily thinking in terms of bargaining, the two have negotiated with one another as to how their marriage should be structured in terms of rights, duties, and options. Bob was already established as a real estate agent at the time of their marriage, and they have mutually agreed that Julie will teach elementary school for two or three years before they think about having children. Household chores are divided between them. Bob straightens up the apartment and does the laundry. Julie takes care of the meal planning, shopping, and cooking. Additional arrangements have been worked out for other areas of marriage, both in the expressive and instrumental realms. Birth-control methods, use of leisure time, budgeting, visiting relatives, personal habits—these and more have all been subjects of negotiation.

Implicit in such a set of marital negotiations is the question of legitimate power or authority. Bob and Julie have agreed to pattern their marriage so that Bob is the chief provider, which means that he has certain fixed, fully structured rights and duties which are inherent in the breadwinner role. Julie shares in breadwinning, but her commitment to work is less than Bob's. It is understood and agreed upon by both husband and wife that the support of the family will be mainly Bob's responsibility. He is the senior partner.

Bob's position gives him the stronger leverage in decision-making processes and conflict resolution within the marriage. Thus, when Julie suggested Bob's doing the cooking several evenings a week, since her own schedule seemed pressured with commuting and extracurricular school activities, Bob rejected the suggestion. "Sure, my hours are more flexible than yours," he said, "but still my work requires me to be on call constantly. If a prospective customer wants to look at a house, I've got to be free at *their* convenience, not mine. I can't be tied down with cooking! But I'll tell you what I will do. I can help you out by doing the shopping, and that will give you some extra free time. You'll still have to plan the meals and make out the list so I'll know what to buy; but I'm willing to save you the time and energy that you'd have to spend on picking up the stuff. How's that for a compromise?"

As we have seen, the person in an exchange relationship who has the greater resources to offer tends to have more legitimate authority. Therefore, that person tends to shape or influence decision-making in his or her favor. If, for example, Julie were the full-time support of her husband while he completed college, she might have considerably more authority than in her present situation. Or if she were not employed at all, she would have less.

As matters now stand, however, Bob has more legitimate power than Julie does. This is true not only because of his greater financial resources, but also because of the chief-provider role he fills. His job is looked upon by both him and his wife as being more important than hers. He can always argue that whatever might interfere with his career will be punishing or costly to both of them. Sociologist William Goode (1963:21–22) has pointed out that upper-status men obtain many rights and have a high degree of power because they can always claim that family demands must not interfere with their work. Such a man, writes Goode, "takes precedence as *professional, not* as family head or as a male; nevertheless, the precedence is his. By contrast, lower-class men demand deference as *men*, as heads of families" (italics in the original, p. 22).

So long as Julie accepts the senior partner–junior partner structural arrangement and values the rewards Bob supplies her, she will tend to recognize Bob's authority as legitimate. "After all," she says, "*someone* has to have the final say if we can't agree on something. Somebody has to be the last court of appeals. We feel it's only right that it should be Bob. Even though we like to think of each other as equals, and we certainly talk everything over, there's still a sense in which Bob is sort of 'in charge' of the marriage. He has the main responsibility to provide for us. My income comes in handy, but it's his that we always depend on. Mine might stop someday because we'll probably have children, and I'll quit work. But Bob can't do that. He has to shoulder the greater load, so I guess he deserves to have the greater power."

Maximum Joint Profit Bob and Julie are maintaining a relationship in which each considers the exchange to be profitable. They are providing benefits to one another (at cost to each individually), but in return they are receiving certain rewards. They are maintaining an ongoing situation of *maximum joint profit*, to use a term from economics. The situation is comparable to that in which a single buyer of a certain commodity and a single seller of that commodity enter into bargaining. Maximum profit for each is the goal. Psychologist Sidney Siegel and economist Lawrence Fouraker (1960:1,9) have pointed out that such a situation "appeals to the mutual interests of the participants, and would seem to call for harmonious cooperation between them." But at the same time, "the interests of the participants are exactly in opposition, and acrimonious competition would seem to be the behavior norm." If these two opposing factors (cooperation and competition) can be made to work together in the decision-making process, it becomes possible for the two parties in the negotiations to be forced into a contract which is in their *mutual* interest. Each individual and the relationship as a whole benefit. Both buyer and seller are satisfied that profit has been maximum for each. At the same time, the transaction sets up a bond between the bargainers and a climate conducive to doing further business together.

In the ongoing exchanges of Bob and Julie, the greater authority of Bob as senior partner and chief provider has been acceptable to Julie. The "costs" of her deferring to him in certain decisions and stalemates are considered to be fewer than the rewards she receives from him; therefore she is satisfied with her margin of profit in the relationship. Bob, too, feels that his rewards from the marriage are high. The offers and counteroffers of their various negotiations have resulted in a situation of maximum joint profit.

Distributing Rewards and Costs Justly

However, at any point in these exchanges, one or the other partner may come to define the distribution of rewards and costs as being unfair. Homans (1961:74) calls such a perception of inequity "the problem of *distributive justice*." In other words, has the distribution of rewards and costs between the persons been just and equitable? Rewards should be comparable to investments for person A relative to person B if the bargain they have struck is to be considered fair by each.

To illustrate, let's assume that there comes a time when Bob's sales have fallen off and his commissions are down. Julie's salary has remained constant, and her income is now higher than Bob's. Yet she is continuing to do the cooking and finds it a real hardship in view of her tight schedule—especially now that she is helping the fifth graders put out a school newspaper and is staying an extra hour after school. Bob, in contrast, has more free time on his hands than ever and is almost always back at their apartment long before she arrives home. Julie has begun to resent his unwillingness to prepare the evening meal. She feels that she is providing many rewards to him at the same time that she is incurring costs that she considers unacceptable (the necessity of rushing home to cook after an exhausting day of teaching), and, in her opinion, Bob isn't bearing sufficient costs. She feels he "has it a lot easier" than she. Her schedule is fixed while his is flexible, he is home more hours than she is, he is providing less income now than she does. In view of all this, his refusal to cook seems unjust. Julie begins to negotiate, making clear her feelings about the matter. Since there has been a shift in the relative resources of this husband and wife over time, the gap in their relative authority is much less.

In order for the situation to change and the problem to be resolved, Julie and Bob will have to have some honest discussions. Earlier, we saw the important role that empathy plays in marriage. Being able to listen to, understand, share with, and enter into the feelings of the other person is important in any close relationship—and particularly so in the daily interaction of a husband and wife. Numerous studies have underscored the importance of *quality communication* in marital satisfaction and happiness (Montgomery, 1981). Thus, social psychologist Philip Brickman (1974:27, 228) emphasizes that if a situation is going to be changed through bargaining over a particular issue, "a prerequisite . . . is the ability of the parties in the situation to communicate with one another about their various alternatives and intentions." At the same time, he stresses that problems of communication should not be considered the *cause* of the need for renegotiation or the cause of conflict. The prime cause of a bargainer's desire to change situational profits is a sense of *inequity* rather than a lack of communication. But communication is essential if renegotiation is to take place. An inability to communicate could only worsen the difficulties and delay the solution.

Carlfred Broderick (1979:45–54) points out some common barriers to effective communication. Persons may *refuse* to communicate, or else they may communicate "in such an aggressive way that the listener is driven to a defensive position," he writes. A third barrier to effective communication is "masking feelings behind intellectual analyses, projecting them onto the receiving partner and, in general, failing to be up front and straightforward about what is actually felt and thought."

Such barriers have not been erected in the interchanges between Bob and Julie, and as a result they can move forward in their negotiation process. Going back to where we left them, we find that as soon as the sense of unfairness crystallizes in Julie's mind, she brings up the matter again to Bob. She makes a suggestion to alleviate the unfairness (Bob should cook), and in view of their changed circumstances and her better bargaining situation, Bob is more open to her proposal

Numerous studies have underscored the importance of quality communication in marital satisfaction and happiness. (Shirley Zeiberg/Taurus Photos)

than previously. Julie has not let her resentment smolder but has acted immediately. After time spent in negotiation, the couple arrive at a new exchange in which Bob agrees to do the cooking—with certain qualifications. He will cook for a three-month trial period to find out how costly it will be to him and also to find out how things go with his job situation. But for the time being at least, Julie has persuaded him that it is only fair for him to take on this household duty. Bob accepts the legitimacy of Julie's request, and both persons begin to maintain their new, renegotiated sets of costs and rewards. Both have established what has been variously called "balance" or "equilibrium" (Alexander and Simpson, 1971), and there is a sense of "distributive justice." Once again, both parties feel that current exchanges are operating for maximum joint profit and mutual gain.

The process of negotiating and renegotiating exchanges in marriage is illustrated as a series of steps in Figure 11-2. Bob and Julie's story focuses on just one area of renegotiation, but such renegotiations may take place in many other areas as well—often concurrently. For example, in the area of sex relations, one spouse might suggest having intercourse more frequently or trying new positions and techniques, and this matter could be renegotiated. For another couple, leisure time and companionship might be issues requiring renegotiation as one spouse complains of the other's absorption in occupational interests (Blumstein and Schwartz, 1983:174–175).

Written Contracts

All of the ongoing exchanges between a husband and wife are interconnected. And altering one exchange is bound to have certain effects on other exchanges as well. These complex webs need to be kept in mind in cases where couples decide to write their own marriage contracts.

Circumstances change, and people change. To sit down at the beginning of a marriage and spell out in advance *all* the possibilities and contingencies that might emerge, all the negotiations and renegotiations that would have to take place, would require writing something as intricate, detailed, and meticulous as the most complex legal document. Even then, as new situations arose, there would have to be constant amendments (and negotiations about making the amendments!). Some couples might find such an exhaustive contract cumbersome to follow and burdensome to change. Others might find the working out of such a contract challenging and rewarding.

A major theorist in sociology, Emile Durkheim (1893), noted that much of the force even of legal contracts lies with the noncontractual rules that surround them. It simply isn't possible to write everything into a contract. In social exchange, trust is essential—just as "good faith" is highly important

FIGURE 11-2 Marital negotiation and renegotiation.

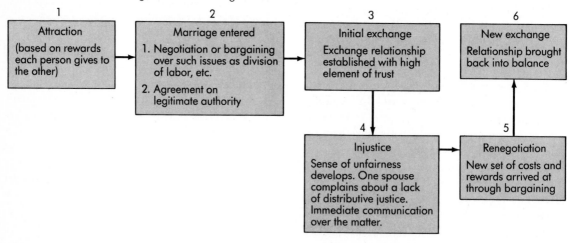

in ongoing exchanges between buyers and sellers in the business world (Blau, 1964; Fox, 1974; Kelley and Schenitzki, 1972; Siegel and Fouraker, 1960).

Persons must *believe* that others will fulfill their obligations—that they will do what is fair and just by them. And in a dyad (two-person relationship) such as marriage, many behaviors must be left relatively unspecified with the understanding—implicit or explicit—that each person is seeking the best interests of both (maximum joint profit).

Without such confidence that others will reciprocate, it is exceedingly difficult for stable, ongoing social relations to exist (Blau, 1964:99). However, trust cannot be written into a contract. It develops because two parties strongly value the rewards that each supplies to the other. Neither person wants to risk losing them, and, therefore, each puts forth an effort to act toward the other in good faith.

At the same time, Lenore Weitzman (1981:241–243) makes the observation from her research that men are more likely than women to speak of written contracts as being *incompatible* with trust within a relationship. "The explanation for this difference may lie in the traditional power difference between the two sexes," she writes, pointing out that women tend to think of written contracts as providing security and protection. "The larger the power differential in any enterprise," Weitzman explains, "the more likely it is that the subordinate party—the serf or the tenant or the consumer—will prefer a clear statement of each party's rights and responsibilities, while the more powerful party will prefer to rely on 'trust.' " She goes on to point out, however, that when two persons are in a relationship *that is not* characterized by a marked power differentiation, "a contractual delineation of responsibilities seems more reasonable (and less threaten-

Jacqueline Kennedy and Aristotle Onassis reportedly drew up a 170-point contract. (AP/Wide World Photos)

ing) to both parties." Her own research showed that both married and cohabiting couples who had worked out a personal contract for their relationship tended to structure the relationship as a partnership with equal rights and responsibilities for both individuals.

Thus, the idea of personally tailored marriage contracts should by no means be dismissed as having little value. Even though trust cannot be written into the contract, and even though changing circumstances cannot be foreseen, a couple's decision to work out a verbal or written agreement of what they expect of one another and the marriage *is nothing more nor less than negotiation.* Couples who work out such a set of ground rules for their relationship at the very outset may not only find the end product—the contract they come up with—useful for their situation. They may also find that the exercise of developing their own set of expectations has served as a training ground for future negotiations as well. (For suggestions on what

LEGAL/FORMAL PRENUPTIAL AGREEMENTS IN MATTERS OF MONEY

Lawyers before the wedding? Yes, indeed. Increasingly, American couples are consulting lawyers *before* they get married in order to draw up prenuptial agreements, otherwise known as marriage contracts. The rich and the famous have always had them. Jackie and Aristotle Onassis reportedly drew up a 170-point contract. Now people with thousands of dollars, not millions, are doing likewise. . . .

Until now, marriage contracts have been used mainly by two types of couple. One is the elderly couple who, when they remarry, may wish to insure that their assets go to their respective children or grandchildren. So each signs an agreement waiving any inheritance rights to the other's assets. The second situation involves one partner who is marrying again after a messy divorce. In this case, the marriage contract in essence negotiates a divorce settlement ahead of time, determining in advance the disposition of property and alimony. . . .

You can put into a marriage contract almost anything you want—even such stipulations as how many children to have and who is responsible for what chores. But family-law experts say that, while living arrangements specified in a contract are morally binding, they are unenforceable in court. For a prenuptial agreement to be upheld in court, it must be shown that it is fair, that it was executed voluntarily and that it was entered into in good faith.

- To meet these criteria, the prospective bride and groom must:

- Each have a lawyer. This is a contract you are negotiating, and each of you must be represented by counsel or the contract may later be ruled invalid.

- Make a full financial disclosure. Each of you will then know what you are getting and what you are giving up.

- Negotiate in good faith. No threats or coercion. Language like "sign it, or the wedding is off" may be grounds for invalidating a contract later.

SOURCE: Nina Totenberg, "How to Write a Marriage Contract," *Parade*, Dec. 16, 1984, p. 14.

might be included in a personal marriage contract, see Weitzman, 1974:1249–1255; 1981:255–290.)

Decision-making processes become more problematic as gender-role preferences change (Scanzoni and Szinovacz, 1980). The traditional way of doing things in marriage kept decision-making simple—even unnecessary in many areas—because each spouse knew exactly what was expected of him or her. Husbands did certain things, and wives did certain things. Under such a system, Julie would have known it was her duty to cook, for example; she and Bob would not have had to spend the time bargaining as they did. Nobody would have thought in terms of negotiation or written contracts spelling out exactly what would be expected of each spouse on the basis of their own personal desires. The traditional gender-based system of dividing up marital rights and responsibilities and distributing power was easily understood, fast, and uncomplicated. But for all its benefits in efficiency, couples paid a price in the lack of freedom and flexibility inherent in such a rigid arrangement.

Yet such freedom and flexibility are what many couples now desire and value. Such couples may therefore expect their joint decision-making to involve a series of negotiations such as our story of Julie and Bob illustrates. Negotiation will be necessary especially if, at any given time, a husband and wife are at different points along the continuum of gender-role preferences. Couples with mixed gender-role preferences—especially when the husband is strongly traditional and the wife holds egalitarian preferences—are those most likely to experience sharp, frequent, and serious conflicts. (See Scanzoni and Szinovacz, 1980, chaps. 2 and 3.)

CHAPTER HIGHLIGHTS

Power may be defined as the ability to have one's own way, achieve one's goals, and have intended effects on others' behaviors and emotions. A basic principle in sociology links power with resources. Because males have traditionally had greater access to the economic-opportunity system and have thus had greater resources, husbands have held greater power in marriage. Therefore, behavioral expectations (or *norms*) have developed to support husbands' rights to this greater power. But as women gain greater resources, we may expect norms to develop supporting *wives'* rights to greater marital power. Power may be exercised in a way that is *legitimate* (earned by the one who exercises it and consented to by those over whom it is exercised) or in a way that is *nonlegitimate* (seized by someone who has not earned it and who doesn't have the consent of those over whom it is exercised). Legitimate power relies on "friendly persuasion" and the provision of benefits to those under it. Nonlegitimate power, in contrast, tends to rely on coercion, threats, and punishment.

Negotiation may be defined as arranging the terms of a contract, transaction, or agreement through talking matters over and working things out. Marriage involves an ongoing series of negotiations and renegotiations as couples work out agreements about the many areas of married life. This continuous openness to negotiation is another example of marriage as *process* rather than as something static. Written contracts must take this into account. Where persons each gain rewards from one another and seek to act in the best interests of both, they are maintaining a situation which aims for *maximum joint profit*, that is, highest possible gains and benefits for *both* persons as individuals and a desire for what is best for the *relationship*. The respective gender-role preferences of a husband and wife also need to be taken into account if we are to understand the decision-making process. A couple's basic disagreement on gender roles is likely to lead to disagreements and conflicts in a wide range of areas within their marriage.

·12·

PROCESS IN MARRIAGE:
CONFLICT AND ITS MANAGEMENT

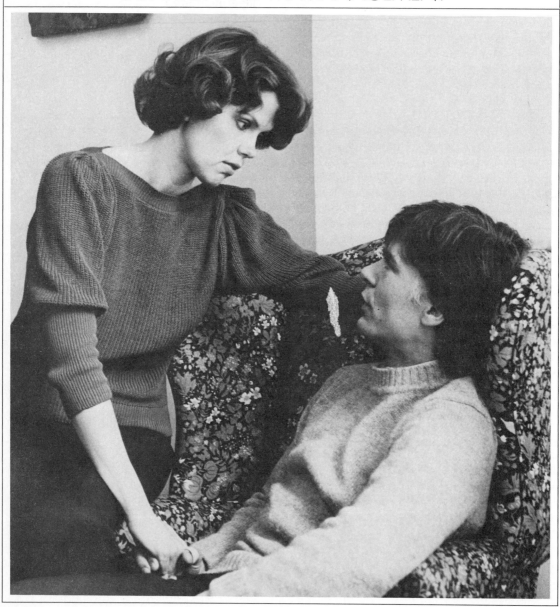

Remember Bob and Julie, the couple we met in the preceding chapter? Let's observe them again as something new happens in their ongoing exchanges. Their situation isn't one of discussion and mutually agreeable negotiation this time, but rather one of out and out *conflict*.

It started when Bob decided they should buy a new car. Julie insisted they couldn't afford it and there was no use even thinking about it. Bob now feels a sense of "distributive injustice." He feels that his investment in the relationship is not producing desired payoffs.

Bob seeks to renegotiate the matter, and communication is established quickly; but in the bargaining that follows, it becomes clear that Bob's authority in this particular matter is less than his wife's. Real estate sales have continued to be low, and Bob's earnings have remained less than Julie's for several months. There is no assurance that matters will change in the near future. If the couple were to buy a new car, Julie's larger income would be the main resource to make the monthly payments. At a certain point in the negotiations between Bob and Julie, *conflict* emerges.

WHAT IS CONFLICT?

Social conflict may be defined as *a struggle over limited resources and/or incompatible goals so that it appears that the more one party gets, the less the other party can have.* This definition is based on a combination of Coser (1956:8) and Kriesberg (1973:17).

The struggle concerns *limited* resources, because if the resources were infinite there would not be the problem of dividing them up so that all parties would feel they had enough. Farmers in an area with abundant rainfall are unlikely to engage in conflict over water supplies. But in an area where water is scarce, two farmers are likely to engage in conflict when one finds the other has dammed the creek to hoard the scanty water supply for his own farm needs. Two children who race for the one remaining swing in the playground are also likely to engage in conflict because the resources are limited ("I got here first!" "No, I did! It's mine!"); but on another day when all the swings are empty, they will each take one and play together amiably.

Similarly, *incompatible goals* may be the basis of conflict. If one person wants to go one way and the other person wants to go in the opposite direction, they cannot walk together and simultaneously reach both goals. One can yield to the other so that they pursue one of the goals, or they might take a third goal as a compromise. Or they might go their separate ways with each pursuing his or her own goal. In a marriage, for example, one spouse might desire a large family while the other desires maximum freedom from anything that would tie them down. One person sees marriage in terms of child-centeredness and wants at least four children; the other person sees marriage in terms of couple-centeredness and wants no children. Their goals are clearly incompatible. Another illustration might be a spouse who is deeply involved in social issues and wants a simple lifestyle with much of their income given to humanitarian causes, while the other spouse wishes to live lavishly. Again, the two goals are incompatible, and conflict is likely to emerge.

Struggle and Resistance

Struggle and *resistance* are key words in defining *conflict* (Kriesberg, 1973:4). Struggle occurs when counteroffers are refused outright or no modifications are suggested. The negotiations have reached a seeming dead end. Yet one or both parties continue to press their claims, and one or both keep *resisting* because they believe that it is *not* in their best interests to accept the claims of the other. Each perceives that it would be too costly to do so. In the case of Bob and Julie, Julie feels the financial cost. Because their material resources are limited at this particular time, she wants to put as much money as possible into regular savings rather than spending it. Bob's goal, on the other hand, is to have a new car. He not only feels that the reward of the car is being denied him but that his status and authority are being undercut as well—a loss that is costly to him.

During the process of conflict, communication may continue in the sense that both parties press their claims and each completely understands and accurately perceives what the other wants. Clear communication in itself, however, is no guarantee that conflict will cease. In other words, it's not enough to talk things over and clear up possible *misunderstandings* (although that's important). Rather, the two parties have to work at *changing the situation* so that grievances and inequities are removed in a way that is satisfactory to both sides.

Communication Problems and Conflict

At the same time, it would be foolish to say that communication plays no part in situations of conflict. Conflict often tends to be associated with garbled communication or with a breakdown of communication. Data from laboratory studies and from investigations of wars show that misperceptions, miscalculations, and misinterpretations can seriously affect conflict (Kelley and Stahelski, 1970; White, 1966). Many Americans became deeply concerned about the seriousness of the cold war between the United States and the Soviet Union some years ago when Premier Khrushchev made the statement: "We will bury you." They interpreted it to mean that the Soviets planned to destroy the United States. However, Khrushchev was simply using a Russian phrase that means, "We will outlive you" (Klineberg, 1964:153 as quoted in Brickman, 1974:153). In other words, the thought was something like, "Our nation will outlast yours. We'll be around long after you."

Misperceptions especially can affect the resolution of conflict. In the case of Bob and Julie, Bob might be saying that he wants *any* new car, whereas Julie may be understanding him to insist on a luxury car—since this is what he has always spoken of in the past. Bob might be understanding Julie to say she wouldn't even consider *any* new car under *any* circumstances, whereas Julie's resistance has mainly been buttressed against the idea of an expensive, luxury car that she is persuaded lies beyond their means. Somehow these two persons have failed to convey their own feelings and to hear what the other is saying. By attributing to one another motives and intentions that are not there at all, they have hindered effective communication.

This common problem of misperceptions has led many family counselors to lay great stress on both *clarity* and *feedback* (or "checking out") in communication. The sender of the message needs to be clear and specific if problems are to be solved and decisions made. And as psychologist Sven Wahlroos (1974:54, Signet edition) emphasizes, the receiver needs to "test assumptions verbally," using such comments as " 'Do you mean that . . . ?' or 'Let me see if I understand you correctly; you want to . . . ?' or 'I want to see if I can state your position fairly; please correct me if I misunderstood you at some point.'" (See also Broderick,

1979, chaps. 2, 3; Miller, Nunnally, and Wackman, 1975, chap. 5; Miller et al., 1982.)

Sometimes communication is simply broken off at some point during the conflict process. The parties concerned may decide they have nothing more to say to one another, and attempts to negotiate are given up. However, silence itself may become a form of communication. Social scientists T. C. Schelling and M. H. Halperin (1961:8) note that "failure to deny rumors, refusal to answer questions, attempts to take emphasis away from certain issues, all tend to communicate something" (as quoted in Brickman, 1974:153). Giving someone the "silent treatment" can be a strategy used to *punish* the other person, a way of showing hostility and anger instead of a desire to work through the problem. Or one of the parties may engage in what counselors call "crazy-making behavior," such as when body language and actions convey a message contradicting the person's verbal message. Wahlroos (1974:13), for example, speaks of the husband who "says that nothing is the matter, but through his nonverbal behavior (long face, pouting, sighing with eyes directed upward, shoulder shrugs, etc.) indicates that he is terribly displeased." By giving two opposing messages about reality, the husband is "implying that his wife cannot trust her senses," writes Wahlroos.

In the case of our hypothetical couple, however, neither is engaging in a strategy of silence. In fact, their talks about the car have been anything but silent at times! And, as is often true in a case of conflict, one or both of the parties may make some move to get the conflict "over with" so that life can get back to normal.

In this particular case, Julie seeks to resolve it by *fiat*—by giving an order or issuing a directive. Her pronouncement is, "No, we're not going to get a new car for you at this particular time." By using her authority based on their relative incomes, she attempts to end the conflict by simply refusing Bob's wishes outright. Her statement has the effect of what family counselors Mendel Lieberman and Marion Hardie (1981) call a "communication stopper." (See insert.)

TEN "COMMUNICATION STOPPERS"

1 *Directing, ordering, commanding* (e.g., "Stop crying," "Try harder," "You must. . . . ") typically produce fright, defensiveness, resistance, and resentment. These forms teach authoritarianism and disqualify feelings. At one extreme they may arouse retaliation, revenge, or rebellion. At the other, they may contribute to the formation of a meek, fearful, placating personality.

2 *Threatening, warning, punishing* (e.g., "If you do, you'll be grounded (fired)"; "You'd better. . . . ") produce resentment, fear, anger, and resistance, invite testing or sabotage, and teach authoritarianism. This approach may arouse rebellion, revenge, or retaliation, or it may result in passivity, despair, or manipulation.

3 *Preaching, moralizing* (e.g., "Nice girls don't do that"; "You should. . . . ") tend to induce guilt, reduce self-esteem, shift the base of moral or ethical authority from a well-developed, internal, adult capacity for judgment to an other-directed reliance on what people "out there" will think, or, at the other extreme, may build resistance to socially accepted values.

4 *Persuading, arguing, lecturing* (e.g., "The fact is . . . ," "When you're older,

you'll realize. . . . '') emphasize the persuader's or lecturer's "rightness," may habituate the other person to his or her "wrongness," invite counterarguments, increase defensiveness, reduce openness, and invalidate feelings.

5 *Advising, recommending* (e.g., "What you should do is . . . ," "Why don't you. . . . '') imply superiority, deprive the Receiver of the esteem-building experience of solving his or her own problem, may encourage dependency, and invite a "yes but" game.

6 *Criticizing, name-calling, characterizing, blaming* (e.g., "You fouled up our plan," "You never . . . ," "You always . . . ," "Liar," "Thief," "You're a typical lawyer") lower self-esteem, induce guilt feelings, reduce openness, arouse resentment and retaliation at one extreme, or may lead to acceptance of and surrender to the negative judgment at the other extreme.

7 *Sarcasm, teasing* (e.g., "So the world is all wrong and you're all right") arouse feelings of rejection, resentment, hostility, and possibly the frustration of being unable to discern the real message hidden by the indirect one. This is a crazy-making device.

8 *Diagnosing, psychoanalyzing, mind reading* (e.g., "You're just saying that because you're overtired"; "It's just a phase you're going through"; "You're just hostile to men") are generally experienced as threatening to privacy and as rejecting one's self-perception, arousing anger and defensiveness at one extreme, or possibly undermining basic self-trust and self-perception at the other. This is another "crazy-making" response.

9 *Withdrawing, Diverting* (e.g., "I won't discuss it any further"; "Not now") communicate a lack of respect for the other and possibly anxiety in the Sender. The "silent treatment" often has, in addition, a punishing effect. Unresolved transactions typically lead to storing up grievances and distorting later transactions.

10 *Cross-examining, interrogating, fact-finding* (e.g., "You must have done something to bring it about"; "Are you sure you're telling the truth?") ignore the other person's feelings, may communicate mistrust, and divert attention to what happened there and then, instead of to the feelings, purposes, attitudes, and intentions present here and now between the interrogator and his or her victim.

SOURCE: Mendel Lieberman and Marion Hardie, *Resolving Family and Other Conflicts: Everybody Wins* (Santa Cruz, Calif.: Unity Press, 1981), pp. 70–72.

NONLEGITIMATE POWER IN CONFLICT SITUATIONS

At any point in the conflict process, legitimate authority can be transformed into nonlegitimate power. When one person or group makes demands that seem excessive, the party on whom the demands are being made tends to feel exploited (Blau, 1964:22). Demands become "excessive" when they are not justified by sufficient levels of rewards. In our illustration, the wife makes a demand ("Forget about the car"), but the husband considers it excessive. Bob doesn't feel that Julie is offering any reward that would justify her demand or that would somehow "make up" for the sacrifice that would be required on his part by giving up his wishes for the new car. Second, Bob still thinks of himself as chief provider, deserving to exercise the greater power in the marriage. He considers his current financial setbacks to be merely temporary, and he doesn't feel that his wife has the right to be as arbitrary as he feels she is.

When demands become excessive in the eyes of persons who are nevertheless forced to comply with them, such persons feel they are being coerced into situations they would not choose for themselves. These situations are regarded as painful, punishing, and costly. The power being exercised over them is no longer viewed as right or legitimate authority; rather it is seen as raw, nonlegitimate power. An example of such a conflict situation occurred in the 1974 feud between members of the National Football League Players Association (NFLPA) and the team owners. Players demanded numerous changes in the way summer training camps and exhibition schedules were being conducted. Life in the training camps was austere and uncomfortable. Rigid restrictions governed virtually every aspect of the men's lives. Curfews kept the players confined to the camp after a certain hour. Lights-out rules and bed checks demanded that they be in bed when they were ordered to be, and guards made regular rounds to make sure everyone was asleep. There were rules against using alcohol, wearing mod clothes, and dating local women (with heavy fines for those who failed to comply). Not surprisingly, the football players began to call such regulations "leash laws" and insisted that they be eliminated. Some men, resentful of being told how to run their lives and of being penned up in what they regarded as a kind of detention camp, were willing to give up football. Others engaged in all-out conflict in the form of a strike. They felt the power of the owners was nonlegitimate because of demands the players considered excessive. "It's the owners' way of showing their power

and maintaining their monopoly of all decision making," the NFLPA executive director was quoted as saying. He went on to say that whereas that kind of control had worked in the past, it would not work any longer. On the other side, the team owners felt that their power was legitimate and that since they paid the bills they had every right to tell the players what they might or might not do (Stump, 1974).

Breakdown of Trust

One consequence of exerting nonlegitimate power is that the trust we spoke of earlier can become corroded. Parties who feel exploited begin to doubt that the other party really cares about their best interests. Instead, the other person appears to be unduly selfish and more concerned with profit for *himself* or *herself* than with maximum joint profit. This became a common gripe among the football players. They felt underpaid and complained that the owners had worked out a system in which the men were working almost for nothing during the preseason months of practice and exhibition games. The owners appeared to care only about lining their own pockets. Similarly, this breakdown of trust was beginning to occur between Bob and Julie. Bob resented her telling him they could not purchase the car, and he began to wonder if she was hoarding her earnings selfishly toward her own goals rather than caring about him.

Regulated Conflict Is Not Resolved Conflict

By trying to settle the conflict through simply giving an order, Julie was seeking to reestablish the kind of exchange relationship that existed prior to the conflict. She wanted the conflict to "be over with." Thus, she took advantage of her present position of power based on control of the resources. But to Bob, that power seemed nonlegitimate. He is unwilling to let the conflict end in such a manner. He wants the conflict to be *resolved*, not merely *regulated*.

Any relationship based on nonlegitimate power is potentially unstable and can easily become unbalanced or even unglued. Persons who feel exploited want to change the status quo and thus are apt to resist and struggle in the face of what they consider unfair demands and insufficient rewards. Therefore, Bob simply refuses to accept his wife's decision and persuades her to reopen communication. "The conflict is *not* settled," Bob declares, convincing Julie that they should engage in renegotiation. This time he is able to strike a bargain with her. While it is true that originally he had set his heart on

a particular luxury model, he had begun thinking matters over and become increasingly willing to settle for a less expensive car—even a subcompact. Julie concedes that with careful budgeting they may be able to afford a car of this kind. They decide to visit various automobile showrooms and choose a car together.

The conflict has been resolved satisfactorily in the sense that the original injustice has been removed along with the sense that nonlegitimate power is being exercised. Feelings of exploitation are also gone, and the sense of trust is restored. The struggle over authority and allocation of material resources is ended in that each party feels not only that his (her) own aims have been achieved but also perceives that the other feels the same way. The renegotiation has led to a new exchange relationship in which the relative au-

FIGURE 12-1 Directions in which marital conflict may move: resolution or regulation.

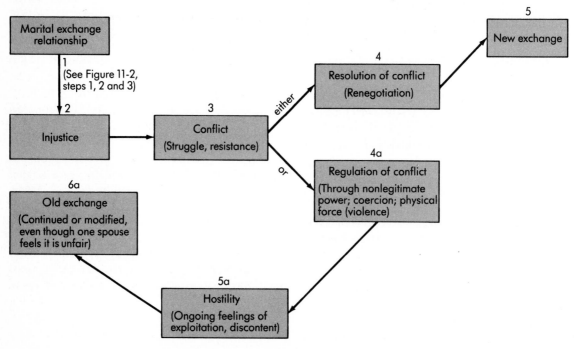

thority of each party is deemed legitimate, and the costs and rewards experienced by each are considered fair. In other words, a new balance of genuine mutual profit has been accomplished. (See Figure 12-1.)

Something else has likely been taking place in the relationship of Bob and Julie—though not necessarily consciously. Persons or groups in any social situation are continually making "comparison levels for alternatives" (Thibaut and Kelley, 1959:21–23). Comparisons are made between the current profit level (rewards minus costs) and what profit levels might exist in other potentially available situations. Persons are more likely to remain in their present situation if they define the rewards offered there as greater than those elsewhere. In the case of Bob and Julie, their renegotiation and conflict resolution have reinforced their sense of overall profit so that the situation in which they find themselves seems more desirable than any alternative one. They have no desire to end the relationship.

TYPES OF CONFLICT

In order to understand conflict more fully, it helps to look at some ways it may be categorized by type.

Zero-Sum and Mixed-Motive Conflict

In a bullfighting contest, either the matador or the bull win—not both. The goal of the game is to conquer the opponent. Social conflict may also be of this type and is sometimes called *zero-sum*; the contesting parties expect to have either all or nothing.

However, another type of conflict has different objectives. Rather than a "winner-take-all" approach, there occurs a "mixed-motive situation." This kind of conflict is far

"First of all, is this new anger or merely some old anger you're just getting around to expressing?"
(Drawing by Frascino, © 1977 by The New Yorker Magazine, Inc.)

more frequent in social interaction than is the zero-sum type. In *mixed-motive* conflict, the contesting parties also want to gain benefits at the other's expense, but they do not wish to totally crush the other. It is in the interests of both, their maximum joint profit, to continue the relationship if at all possible. The term *mixed motive* is used, writes social psychologist Philip Brickman (1974:5), "since each party may be partly motivated by a desire to cooperate around the common interests in the relationship and partly motivated by a desire to compete for the more favorable share of those resources which must be divided up."

In our story of Bob and Julie's negotiations over the new car, the conflict was mixed-motive. Each wanted to gain at the expense of the other, but neither wanted to wipe the other out in zero-sum fashion. Each saw value in maintaining their relationship and wanted to cooperate on the basis of all they held in common, even though their competing interests were pulling in different directions. Bob was not ready to insist on a new car to the point of breaking up the marriage, nor was Julie ready to resist to this point. Thus, they had to deal with mixed motives: competition on the one hand and cooperation on the other.

Personality-Based and Situational Conflict

Another hypothetical couple, the Wilsons, sought a counselor's help because of severe conflicts in their marriage. Ted Wilson complained that his wife neglected household chores to read or watch television. "And she's always nagging me to give her time off from taking care of the kids. What kind of woman is she if she can't stand taking care of her own children and can't keep the house decently clean? Something's wrong with her!" At this point, Betty Wilson broke in: "He's always saying something's wrong with me! Why doesn't he ever look at himself? The first thing he says when he comes in the door each evening is, 'What's for dinner?' or 'Don't you have anything cooked *yet?*' He's only affectionate if he wants sex. He only cares about himself. He won't even baby-sit so that I can take some evening-school courses."

Viewing the Wilsons' problem solely as a *personality-based* conflict, the counselor told Betty she should accept her wife-mother role and "adjust to her womanhood" rather than fight against it. She should stop rebelling against her responsibilities as a homemaker and should leave her husband free to pursue his occupational interests. Her interests should be secondary to those of Ted and the children. Ted, for his part, must learn to be more understanding. "Show Betty more affection and consideration," the counselor advised.

The Wilsons went home, tried out the counselor's advice, and found it didn't work. After a few more months of conflict, they visited a different counselor.

To the second counselor, the Wilsons' case was one of *situational* conflict. Resolution of such conflict lies in changing the situation rather than trying to change the people to fit the situation. The Wilsons were helped first to see what lay at the root of their problem. Betty felt frustrated in her homemaker role not out of malice or laziness but because she felt blocked from finishing college. She watched programs on public television and read books constantly to keep stretching her mind beyond what she felt housekeeping would allow. The counselor helped the couple see that trying to force Betty to "adjust" or "adapt" wasn't the answer. What they needed to do was to negotiate and find ways to make it possible for her to continue her education.

The Wilsons worked out a plan for sharing household chores and child care, and both the negotiation process and the sharing have strengthened their relationship. Watching his wife's accomplishments and happiness, Ted has a new respect for her and finds himself being much more affectionate now that the old hostilities are gone. Betty is so grateful for Ted's willingness to finance her education as well as his sharing of child care and home responsibilities that she feels a new love for him. And even housework isn't the same old drudgery that it was in the days of her sulking and resentment. The Wilsons are finding that the changed situation is removing their old complaints about each other.

While conflicts may have either a situational or a personality base, perhaps far more than is generally realized, marital conflicts stem from factors relating to *situations* that spouses could seek to remedy, instead of simply complaining about one or the other's "unpleasant personality" or how hard it is to get along with him or her. Resolving social conflict over incompatible goals or limited resources is not a matter of "adapting" or "adjustment"; rather it calls for *change*.

Basic and Nonbasic Conflict

It is one thing to engage in conflict within agreed-upon rules of a game; it is quite another to have a conflict about the rules. The first kind of conflict is *nonbasic*. When the rules themselves are called into question and contested, the conflict is clearly *basic*.

To illustrate, let's return once again to our story of Bob and Julie. We saw how they resolved their conflict over a new car by renegotiating within the existing rules or role norms that characterize their kind of marriage arrangement. However, at another point, Bob is offered a job in another locale—a position he considers much more challenging and financially rewarding than his current job. But an exciting opportunity has also come up for Julie in their present location. She has been invited to develop and direct a special computer-based reading program for the local schools, while at the same time pursuing a doctorate in educational curriculum at a nearby university. The stage is set for conflict over their different goals.

Under the rules or norms of a senior partner-junior partner marriage, Bob would expect Julie to forgo her opportunities in special education and move with him, since his role has been defined as chief provider. As such, his occupational demands necessarily take precedence over most other family demands. Another norm characterizing traditional-marriage arrangements has been the expectation that marriage will mean children. It is virtually taken for granted that the union of a husband and wife should produce children at some point in order that the gratifications of the father and mother roles may be experienced.

To complicate Bob and Julie's situation further, Bob has started to talk about having a child soon. He feels that his new position will make it possible to manage the economic costs of a baby and suggests that it's time to have one. Julie need not continue working, Bob says, since he will be able to support a family totally if he takes the new job. Thus, still acting under the "rules of the game" for the kind of marriage Bob and Julie have been maintaining, Bob begins to negotiate a new exchange with his wife. He believes that the rules furnish him with legitimate authority to ask her to move with him and to undertake motherhood soon after.

Julie, however, has other ideas. Having always leaned toward modern, egalitarian sex-role norms, she is now beginning to ask questions about the senior partner-junior partner arrangement. The opportunity of a career in developing and administering computer-based reading programs seems challenging. Bob's requests therefore strike her as unjust. She feels that her costs will rise and her rewards drop substantially if she goes along with her husband. She begins to struggle and resist. Conflict has emerged.

Julie bargains, saying she is willing for Bob to move and for them to commute alternately on weekends. Through her conflict and in her specific negotiating process, she is, in effect, beginning to challenge the norms that govern the senior partner-junior partner arrangement. Open communication was established as negotiations began, but as the conflict progresses certain deep issues begin to move to the fore. Should Julie have children or should she remain voluntarily childless? Should their marriage continue to be based on role specialization, or should they shift patterns to one based on role interchangeability so that Julie would be considered an equal partner in a dual-career arrangement?

These conflicts are clearly basic in that they involve contention over what the rules of the game should be. The game (marriage) will be very different if fundamental rules are changed. Rules governing American football are very different from those governing European football (soccer). In politics, the rules in the United States say that the President shall not use force to resist the courts or Congress. But in many countries today, generals and presidents openly use military force to get their way when parliaments or courts cross them. These are two very different political games.

The earlier conflict of Bob and Julie over the purchase of a new automobile was nonbasic. We saw that even nonbasic conflict is likely to bring about situational changes. This is doubly so for basic conflict. But in addition, for any social system, basic conflict can mean instability or even total collapse. For instance, if an American president could persuade a general to mobilize troops to resist a congressional order to remove him from office, there would occur the most serious and devastating disruption of American democracy in two centuries. Or if two companies were to experience basic conflict over the rules of their buyer-seller relationship, they might simply terminate the association. Such a breaking off of the relationship would not be so likely to occur over nonbasic conflict, which is more easily negotiable.

Issues Involved in Basic Conflict Both in the personal (expressive) and practical (instrumental) realms of marriage, basic conflict may occur. We have defined marriage as a relationship involving sexual and economic interdependence between the partners. The norms surrounding the relationship include the expectation that the husband and wife will have sexual intercourse with one another and that they will share their material wealth. If one partner arbitrarily decides to change those rules, we have a classic illustration of basic conflict.

For example, a distressed middle-aged woman wrote to a newspaper advice columnist with the following story: She and her husband were both in their second marriages, and for six years they had found together what she described as a happiness neither had dreamed possible. Almost nightly, they had sexual relations, which both enjoyed immensely: Then the husband joined a religious cult and changed his attitudes entirely. The wife wrote: "He said he could no longer kiss me, or touch me, or sleep in the same bed with me because if he did he could not enter the kingdom of heaven because he would be committing adultery since we had both been married before!" After eight months of living this way, the wife was seeking help because the conflict was of the most basic sort (Bloomington (Ind.) *Herald-Telephone*, "Dear Abby," March 16, 1973).

How basic conflict may occur over economic sharing is illustrated in the later life of novelist Leo Tolstoy and his wife, the Countess Tolstoy. Tolstoy had become obsessed with a concern for nonmaterialistic values and a desire to share his royalties and other wealth with those who were poor. His wife considered him selfish and neglectful of his own family. Why should he give away *their* money to strangers? Didn't she deserve some reward for all her years of hard work in caring for their home and rearing the children? For Tolstoy to give away his royalties appeared to his wife as a breaking of the fundamental rules of the game as they applied to economic provision and sharing. The *consumption* of resources for survival and for status is a basic issue in marriage, just as is economic *production.*

As we have seen, each of the four ways marriage may be structured also has rules about which partner is the unique or chief provider. The issue of whether or not to have children is also basic—particularly where marriage has been viewed in traditional terms.

At the same time, there may occur *non-basic* conflicts within the same general areas that have been discussed (sex, the provider role, the consumption of resources, and the issue of children). Such secondary conflicts may center around the hours the husband or wife is working, how to discipline the children, how often and with what techniques sex relations should take place, or how to keep expenditures within the budget. But underlying each of these secondary conflicts is an assumption that there is agreement as to the four basic core issues (that is, that there will be sexual intercourse, that the provider role has been acknowledged to be the primary responsibility of one or both partners, that parenthood will be undertaken or avoided voluntarily, and that consumption and lifestyle will be of a certain kind). To the degree that such basic consensus exists, struggles that are less central can more satisfactorily be resolved.

In the case of Bob and Julie, Julie's objective is to resolve their basic conflict in such a way that she will become an equal partner with her husband, with her career and interests considered just as important as his. She is also increasingly open to the possibility of remaining childless and avoiding the mother role entirely. This is a very different "game" or arrangement than the couple had before, when Julie seemed content to be a junior partner and planned to work only a few years before settling down to have a family. Yet it is precisely those former rules and that earlier game that Bob wants. Since each spouse wants to play a different game with a different set of rules, how can they resolve their mutual struggles and resistances? How can they hold their relationship together and avoid separation or divorce?

Some persons might argue that if the husband could somehow retain final authority, as was traditionally the case, then basic conflicts such as these could be resolved. The husband could simply declare, "This is what we will do," and the issue would be settled. However, that argument overlooks the twin questions of justice and accountability. Husbands have generally tended to resolve conflicts in ways they thought best, with "best" meaning ways that seemed favorable to themselves simply because they were considered to have the final authority. Again it seems appropriate to echo John Stuart Mill's argument of a century ago that there is no inherent structural reason for one partner in a voluntary association to be the final authority. It would be unjust in a business partnership, and it is unjust in a marriage.

Moreover, traditionally husbands had authority but *no accountability,* much as did preparliamentary monarchs. But today even a president who says the "buck stops here" is accountable for the exercise of nonlegitimate power. He is accountable to Congress who can impeach him, the courts who can reverse him, or to voters who can turn him out of office. Thus, in marriage, an appeal to some ultimate authority based on gender whose decisions cannot be disputed, modified, or rejected, or who could not be removed from his position of authority is simply not considered fair or wise in modern society. What Lord Acton said about political power applies as well to the notion of the male (or female) as absolute final arbiter in marriage. "Power tends to corrupt, but absolute power corrupts absolutely."

There are several alternative modes of conflict resolution that Bob and Julie can pursue. Assuming reasonable communication and willingness to negotiate, Bob can agree to a bargain in which the rules are indeed changed. Julie would then become an equal partner. As for the matter of starting a family, neither having nor not having children is essential to the equal-partner marriage pattern. The matter is optional. Thus, Bob may try to negotiate with Julie about having a child. If they do decide to have one, issues such as timing and child care become additional matters for negotiation. How extensively should they rely on nursery and day-care facilities? How responsible will Bob be for child care?

Besides bargaining for a child, Bob may also aim negotiation toward persuading Julie to move with him. Let us assume she can find educational and career opportunities in the new locale comparable to those in the old. When Julie agrees to pursue these opportunities rather than her original plans, a new exchange is established in which both spouses experience maximum joint profit. Julie has a new game; she is now an equal partner. At the same time, she has conceded to relocate and also to have a child—both, however, under conditions that she does not consider excessively costly or punishing. Bob, for his part, has gained the benefits he wanted (the move and the child), but he agrees to a new game based on role interchangeability in which he is now merely a co-provider and in which Julie possesses as much authority and autonomy as he does.

However, the story could have a different ending. Upon facing their basic conflict, Bob and Julie may simply decide on another mode of resolution—ending the marriage. The key is whether or not Bob is willing to accept the basic changes in the rules for which Julie is pressing. In other words, is he willing to accept a new game? If he is not, it is difficult to see what meaningful concessions Julie can make, given her objectives. They are resisting each other over very basic issues; and since both perceive that so much is at stake, no significant negotiations or bargaining can take place. The couple may therefore decide that it is in the best interests of both of them simply to separate and file for divorce. (See Figure 12-2.) Each compares the level of alternatives (rewards and costs) within the marriage with alternatives outside it. Each concludes that the latter alternatives are more desirable or "profitable" (fewer costs, greater rewards) than those in their present situation. And so they leave it.

The overwhelming evidence suggests that conflict is an inevitable part of any ongoing social relationship—including marriage. (Ken Karp Photography)

INEVITABILITY OF CONFLICT

Up until recently, sociologists tended to view social conflict as "bad." In terms of the structural-functional approach, conflict was thought to disrupt and tear apart social sys-

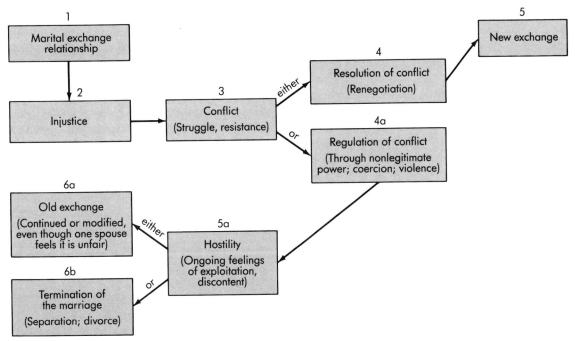

FIGURE 12-2 Three possible outcomes of marital conflict: *resolution, regulation,* or *termination* of the marriage (compare with Figure 12-1).

tems. Conflict within the institution of marriage was thought to have only negative consequences and was to be avoided at all costs.

Currently, the overwhelming weight of evidence suggests that conflict is an inevitable part of any ongoing social relationship—including marriage. Given the processes of social exchange and given the likelihood that all parties involved are seeking to maximize rewards and minimize costs, a certain amount of conflict on occasion is to be expected. There are bound to be occasions of struggling over incompatible goals or resisting the profit seeking of others because of the costs to oneself.

Beneficial Conflict

Given its inevitability, the issue becomes not how to avoid conflict but how to resolve it.

Increasingly, social scientists agree that conflict may often strengthen the bonds of a social relationship and make it more rewarding

(Drawing by Joe Mirachi, © 1977 by The New Yorker Magazine, Inc.)

"Let's face it, Ron. The only time we meet each other's needs is when we fight."

(Blau, 1964; Coser, 1956). Conflict, when satisfactorily resolved, removes injustice and punishments. The end result of conflict can be such that maximum joint profit is greater than it was before. "Opposition," says sociologist Peter Blau (1964:301), "is a regenerative force that introjects new vitality into a social structure." The new bargains that grow out of the conflict mean that numerous aspects of the total relationship can be revised, altered, and made more rewarding than if resistance and struggle had not occurred.

This "regenerative" process can be viewed not only from the micro perspective, such as the husband-wife unit; it can also be viewed on the macro level, where nations contend with one another or groups within society dispute with one another (for example, labor and management). Historically, the feminist movement has meant social conflict between women and men. Females have sought to increase their share of scarce resources (material rewards, education, prestige, power) inevitably at the expense of male dominance and control. The struggle of blacks against whites has been of the same type. When a minority group presses for a greater share of rewards disproportionately enjoyed by a majority group, there is conflict. During the conflict, there is likely to be suffering (costs) on both sides; but when the conflict is resolved satisfactorily, both sides are likely to benefit and experience maximum joint profit.

Looking back over the past two centuries, virtually all social scientists would conclude that the conflicts between blacks and whites and between males and females have indeed been "regenerative" or "healthy" for Western societies. American society is probably stronger and more stable than it would have been had not resistances occurred. And it is not only that these minority groups are becoming better off. It may be assumed that men and whites in general are also better off as a result of gains made by women and blacks. Although it has been costly to males and whites in terms of traditional rewards (privileged position, unchallenged economic advantages, greater power, and so on), new rewards have been emerging as compensation. For example, society benefits through a greater utilization of talents when certain persons aren't blocked from achievement because of race or sex. Freedom from racial or gender-role stereotypes may enable persons to be themselves and relate as human beings who are united by all they have in common rather than separated by artificial differences. Numerous husbands may find themselves emancipated from many pressures as wives share the economic load; and both husbands and wives may come to enjoy their companionship in a new way, free of the constrictions of older gender-role expectations.

Destructive Conflict

However, Coser (1956:73) raises the question: "If conflict unites, what tears apart?" In saying that conflict has the potential of being cohesive (holding social groups together and bringing benefits), we are not denying that conflict also has the potential of being divisive (tearing groups apart, breaking up relationships). Conflicts can bring about the dissolution of business partnerships, entertainment teams, alliances between nations, friendships, and marriages. If a husband and wife, for example, try to resolve conflicts by continually resorting to nonlegitimate power, feelings of exploitation, discontent, and distrust may be generated. The partner who feels exploited might eventually leave the relationship. As we saw earlier, there is some indication that working-class husbands try to resolve conflicts through exercising power that their wives do not recognize as legitimate because the husbands have fewer resources and give their wives fewer economic-status benefits than is true of middle-class husbands. This may be one reason why divorce rates are higher among working-class marriages than among middle-class marriages. Conflicts tend not to be resolved in ways that are regenerative but rather in ways that are disruptive.

We will be discussing an especially destructive way of handling conflict later in this chapter when we examine the topic of marital violence.

AREAS OF CONFLICT IN MARRIAGE

What kinds of issues are involved in conflicts between husbands and wives? Table 12-A compares the results of three major studies. Note that in all three, *money* tops the list. Issues concerning children were also found to constitute a major area of disagreement in a considerable proportion of marriages. The term *tremendous trifles* under the "Miscellaneous" category refers to matters pertaining to one person's habits, preferences, or manner of conducting day-to-day living that the other finds disturbing. Examples are decisions about colors to paint the house, concerns about punctuality, disagreements over the thermostat setting, not hanging up clothes, and so on. Such matters can become highly significant in a husband-wife conflict, particularly when one feels the other is exercising nonlegitimate power and taking unfair advantage.

TABLE 12-A Major conflict areas in marriage (percent of respondents reporting each area)

CHIEF DISAGREEMENT	BLOOD AND WOLFE, 1960	SCANZONI, 1970	SCANZONI, 1975
Money-related matters (producing and spending)	24%	38%	33%
Child-related matters (e.g., discipline and number)	16	19	19
Friend-related matters		10	1
Kin-related matters	6	3	3
Companionship, leisure, recreation (kind, quality, and quantity)	16		8
Activities disapproved by spouse (problem drinking, gambling, extramarital affairs, etc.)	14		3
Rates, household division of labor	4		3
Miscellaneous (all else, including religion, politics, sex, communication in marriage, "tremendous trifles," etc.)	3	21	13
"Nothing" reported, "Nothing specific," not ascertained	17	9	17
Total %	100%	100%	100%
Number of Respondents (n)	(731)	(916)	(3,096)

SOURCE: Adapted from Blood and Wolfe, 1960, p. 241; Scanzoni, 1970, p. 157; Scanzoni, unpublished data from the study described in 1975b.

Economic Matters

Given the interrelationship of the family with the economic-opportunity system, it is not surprising that issues relating to money and jobs are so important to husbands and wives. Self-worth is intricately bound up with achievement and acquisitiveness in a modern industrial society, and husbands and wives are apt to have great concern about whether or not they are living up to personal and societal expectations. Their concern might sometimes take the form of disagreements over occupational matters (the *production* aspect of the economic side of marriage) or over matters of expenditure (the *consumption* aspect). The couple might disagree about the wife's career aspirations or about the husband's working overtime or moonlighting on a second job, or about changing jobs. They might have conflicts about how much they should pay for new furniture, about how far to go into debt, about a spouse's extravagance (or conversely, a spouse's miserliness and hoarding), about having a joint checking account, about savings investments, credit cards, and a myriad of other matters. Blumstein and Schwartz (1983) found that regardless of actual income level, couples in their study who fought over money were more likely to argue about how their money was being managed than about how much income they had.

Disagreements over Children

Since children require a considerable investment on the part of parents, they constitute another area of great importance and potential husband-wife disagreement. Emotionally and financially, as well as in terms of time and energy, parents spend a great deal on children. In spite of the costs, however, parents may also view children as sources of rewards. Husbands and wives may disagree about the best way to ensure that the rewards of children will exceed the costs. To one spouse, the very idea of having children in the first place might appear to be too costly; while to the other spouse, "starting a family" may be a cherished goal. Similarly, there may be conflict about the spacing of children or the number desired. In one situation, a father continued to pressure his wife to "try one more time for a boy" after they had eight daughters. The wife balked at the suggestion.

Child-related marital conflicts are not only centered around having children (if, when, and how many) but also about how to rear them. One spouse might be strict, while the other is lenient; the result is often severe disagreement about matters of nurture and discipline. Clashes about techniques of securing obedience from small children, or about how much allowance to give the elementary schoolchild, or about how much freedom to grant adolescents are not uncommon as husbands and wives share the task of parenting.

Other Conflict Matters

In a follow-up study of *wives only* from the earlier (Scanzoni, 1975b) study of marriages in ten major Northern metropolitan areas, we tapped areas of conflict in a different way by first asking respondents to name the one most important thing they wished their husbands would either do or stop doing and then asking whether or not they felt their husbands' behavior in this matter was fair to the wives (Scanzoni, 1978).

Fourteen percent were unable to name any such area that was a problem at the time of the interview. But among the remaining wives, socioeconomic issues again topped the list. Slightly less than a quarter wished their husbands would either work harder and earn more or else *not* work so hard and spend more time with the family; or they wished their husbands would stop spending so much money, or start spending more on certain items, and so on. Issues related to children concerned 15 percent and comprised the third largest set of conflicts.

However, in contrast to the other studies, a new set of conflicts was in second place—matters related to peer/kin relations. Nearly 23 percent of the wives wanted their husbands to stop spending so much time with the husbands' relatives or the husbands' friends or to "stop wanting other women." Or they wanted their husbands to let them visit their own relatives more or let them entertain more often.

Other areas of conflict involved husbands' failures to perform household tasks (12 percent); socioemotional issues—such as wanting more attention, affection, and empathy from husbands and either more or less sexual interest (8 percent); issues centering around the wives' desire for autonomy and their husbands' resistance or lack of support in that desire for independence (4 percent); and various miscellaneous issues (16 percent).

Conflicts in marriage, whether about money or children or anything else, may be settled amicably through negotiation or may lead to a breakup of the marital relationship. Sometimes, however, they explode into actual violence—a possibility that until recently has been given little attention by researchers, perhaps because of the "touchiness" and unpleasantness of the subject and the common belief that violence occurs only in "abnormal" families (O'Brien, 1971; Gelles, 1980).

VIOLENCE IN MARRIAGE

One June day in 1974, an Indiana minister and his wife went for a drive. The trip ended tragically. When their bodies were found one week apart floating in the Wabash River, law officers theorized that an assailant must have slain the couple and stolen their car. Later, however, the automobile was found submerged at the point where it had been driven 200 feet into a stream. After an extensive investigation, a coroner's jury concluded that the plunge into the water had been deliberate and that the minister planned to kill his wife and possibly himself. The charge of homicide was considered definite, although there was some doubt about the suicide attempt in view of evidence that the minister had tried to escape but had been trapped when his shoe caught on something in the car. In its study, the jury learned that the couple, both in their mid-thirties and married only six months, had been having severe marital difficulties.

This case may seem as bizarre as it is tragic. Yet, according to the National Commission on the Causes and Prevention of Violence, what appear to be automobile "accidents" have not infrequently been found to have been intentional acts of murder and suicide (Mulvihill, Tumin, and Curtis, 1969). Not only is the family car sometimes the murder weapon itself; it also serves as the setting for many murders in which other weapons are used—such as in the case of a woman depressed over her forty-fifth birthday who asked her husband to go for a drive with her and then, as he slid behind the steering wheel, shot him and then herself.

Other common settings for family murders are the kitchen (a central location for interaction between family members and often the site of arguments) and the bedroom (where husband and wife are closed off in privacy with one another at the end of the day, providing an occasion where built-up tensions and hostilities may suddenly erupt) (Steinmetz and Straus, 1974:39, 93). Sometimes both settings are involved, as in a 1979 North Carolina case in which a husband became upset with the cold breakfast his wife had served. They continued their argument in the bedroom, where the husband allegedly reached for a gun and shot his wife in the head, then killed himself. And in a bedroom of a California rest home that same year, an 81-year-old woman was charged in the murder of her 85-year-old husband after she allegedly beat him severely during a quarrel.

"People are more likely to be hit, beat up, physically injured, or even killed in their own homes by another family member than anywhere else, and by anyone else, in our society," writes sociologist Richard Gelles (1979:11). But the problem isn't limited to our society. Gelles goes on: "Nearly one out of every four murder victims in the United States is killed by a member of one's own family, and this is the case in Africa, Great Britain, and Denmark." Family homicide is a gruesome reality in which husbands kill wives, wives kill husbands, parents kill children, children kill parents, brothers and sisters kill one another, people kill in-laws and grandparents, and so on. Viewed this way, the family looks more like a bloodstained battlefield than a peaceful haven of love and tenderness.

Most families, of course, are not broken up by the murder of one family member by another family member. Yet many other kinds of violence may be far more common than is generally realized. Only in recent years has the fact of family violence been acknowledged and research conducted on the topic. During the 1960s, attention, primarily in the medical and mental health fields, began to be paid to "the battered-child syndrome" (Kempe et al., 1962; Kempe, 1971), with some very *limited* attention to battered wives. With few exceptions, it was not until the seventies that notice began to be taken of the extent of violence between spouses, the problem of battered elderly parents, and other forms of violence within families (Steinmetz, 1977; Gelles, 1980).

In this section on conflicts in marriage, we want to focus primarily on violence *between husbands and wives* and introduce the general topic of family violence. Later, in our discussion on childrearing in Chapter 14, we'll be examining the child-abuse aspect of family violence.

Why Not More Research into Family Violence?

Since in the minds of most people, the family is considered to be a place of warmth, love, affection, tenderness, and caring, it seems hard to accept the idea that so much violence can occur within family settings. When it does occur, people tend to want to look the other way—as though not seeing something means it isn't there; or they may dismiss it as a rare exception involving some kind of personal pathology. Members of families where violence occurs don't want to admit that their families are not living up to what families are "supposed" to be and feel ashamed that they are somehow different from other families. Thus they may not seek help until the situation is extremely desperate.

Sociologist Suzanne Steinmetz (1977) speaks of how this "myth of family nonviolence" is perpetuated and reinforced:

> Evidence suggests that lawmakers, historians, and social scientists, as well as the general population, tend to deny the existence of family violence or to assume violence only occurs in sick families, families living in inner-city ghettos, or families characterized by some other pathology such as drugs, alcohol, gambling, or mental aberrations. By this means it is possible to resolve the dissidence between the socially desirable view of the family and the unpleasantness of reality. (p. 5)

For a long time, violence in the family was not viewed as an issue for societal concern because, as sociologist Murray Straus (1974) points out, "no sizable influential group in the population . . . defined it as a problem." He suggests that just as social and cultural forces made it a long neglected topic, social and cultural forces can be credited with its recent emergence as a high priority issue. "First," he writes, "the public and social scientists have been sensitized to violence because of such events as the slaughter in Vietnam, political assassinations, rising homicide and assault rates, and violent social and political protest" (p. 14). A second factor contributing to increased attention to family violence has been the reemergence of the women's movement, which has raised consciousness of how acts of physical coercion associated with male dominance have victimized women. Third, the older *consensus* model of society employed by many social scientists began to be challenged by *conflict* and *social-action* models, which held that conflict is essential to the pursuit of justice by individuals and in order to keep groups from stagnating.

Gelles (1980:144) suggests a fourth factor to be added to Straus's list: efforts had to be made to dispel the belief that it is impossible to conduct family violence research. "Researchers commencing projects in the early seventies were constantly told that reliable and valid research on domestic violence could not be carried out," he notes. "Investigators were reminded that they would literally have to ask, 'Have you stopped beating your wife?' " The issue was a sensitive one; the problem of defining violence as a concept had to be met; and the assumed difficulties in finding research samples had to be overcome. But numerous social scientists came forward to meet the challenge, and research data on domestic violence—rather than hearsay and folk wisdom—began shedding new light on the topic. (See also Gelles, 1982; Gelles and Cornell, 1985.)

How Widespread Is Violence in Marriage?

Some of the earliest pioneering researchers on marital violence endeavored to find out the extent of its occurrence through interviews with applicants for divorce. In one such study, 17 percent of those interviewed spontaneously mentioned physical abuse as a reason for the deterioration of their marriage and a major factor in initiating divorce action (O'Brien, 1971).

In another study, George Levinger (1966) examined records of 600 applicants for divorce in the greater Cleveland area, where, by order of the court, divorce applicants with children under 14 years of age were required to meet with experienced marriage counselors. In analyzing the counselors' interview records, Levinger found that physical abuse was a complaint in more than one-third of the cases, with wives complaining far more than husbands of being physically hurt by the spouse. Nearly 37 percent of the women applying for divorce voiced such a complaint, compared to 3.3 percent of husbands. Social-class differences were also found. Among the middle-class couples in Levinger's sample, 22.8 percent of wives and 2.9 percent of husbands complained of being physically abused by the marital partner. Among working-class and lower-class couples, 40.1 percent of wives reported that their husbands hurt them physically, and 3.5 percent of husbands complained of physical abuse by their wives. While such figures may provide some rough idea of the extent of physical violence in marriages that end in divorce, they do not furnish us with data on marriages in general. Thus, generalizations from these figures should be avoided.

Since violence has often been regarded as almost exclusively a phenomenon of the lower socioeconomic strata of society, the extent to which it occurs in middle-class marriages may strike many as surprising. While it is true that more violence occurs in lower-class marriages than occurs at higher levels, there is nevertheless evidence that a considerable amount of physical abuse does occur among middle-class couples. Slightly more than 1 out of 5 middle-class wives in Levinger's study of divorce applicants reported violence as compared to 2 out of 5 working-class and lower-class wives.

Murray Straus, a sociologist who has devoted a great deal of attention and exploratory study to the issue of violence in marriage, conducted one study in which 385 university students filled out questionnaires indicating whether or not their parents had used or threatened to use physical force during the last year in which the student lived at home. Sixteen percent of the students indicated that one or the other parent had *threatened* to hit or throw something at the spouse; had actually done so; or had pushed, grabbed, or shoved the other during a disagreement. However, as Straus (1974) cautions, "An obvious limitation of this data is that it describes only unbroken families with a child in college, which is far from representative of the population as a whole. . . . Consequently, a description of the amount of violence between family members based on this data is likely to be an underestimate." Also, the information tells us only about a single year of a couple's married life, and it may be incomplete inasmuch as parents might be hesitant to engage in violence in the presence of their children—even though they might resort to it in private.

Another sociologist, Richard Gelles (1973a), in a series of in-depth interviews with eighty couples, found that in more than half of these marriages, at least one instance of husband-wife physical force had occurred at some time.

Several years later, Gelles, Straus, and Steinmetz joined together in a large-scale research effort designed to study family violence in a national sample of over two thousand families. These researchers found that "one out of six couples in the United States engage in at least one incident of violence each year" (Gelles, 1979:92; Straus, Gelles, and Steinmetz, 1980). Furthermore, writes Gelles (1979:92), "over the course of a marriage the chances are greater than one in four (28%) that a couple will come to blows."

However, as Murray Straus and his colleague Suzanne Steinmetz (1973) write, "The fact that almost all family violence, including everyday beating, slapping, kicking and throwing things, is carried out by normal everyday Americans rather than deranged persons should not lead us to think of violence as being desirable or even acceptable." Rather, they suggest asking *why* so many families resort to violence. Gelles (1973b) emphasizes that psychological explanations in which "mental illness" is viewed as the major reason for physical abuse are inadequate in themselves. There needs also to be an examination of social situational factors such as childhood socialization patterns, socioeconomic status, community or subcultural values regarding violence, structural stress (unemployment, excess children, and so on), and immediate precipitating situations that bring on acts of violence in some families.

Why Violence Occurs

To understand violence, we may want to recall our definition of conflict as a struggle over limited resources and/or incompatible goals in which it appears that one person or group will have its way at the expense of the other party or group. Conflict need not and often does not result in violence. However, in some situations persons may resort to violence because it may seem there is no other way out. Sociologist William Goode (1971) points out that when persons begin to feel a continuing imbalance between investments and payoffs in the daily exchanges of family life, they may engage in conflict over this imbalance. For various reasons, they may feel they cannot take one of the other roads usually open in such a situation—escape, submission, or righting the balance. As a result, the conflict "can escalate to the point of violence because no simpler or easier resolution emerges."

In some marriage and family situations, one of the other routes may be chosen. Some persons decide that escape is the answer; thus, the child runs away from home or a spouse deserts the family or files for divorce. In other cases, submission (though given grudgingly and with resentment) might appear to be the only way to "keep the peace." Yielding to the demands of a domineering spouse, for example, may seem easier to the other spouse than bringing injustices out into the open and engaging in conflict. Goode's third alternative, righting the balance, would seem the most desirable way to handle what one or the other spouse feels are imbalances in the husband-wife exchange. This is the renegotiation process we spoke of earlier as exemplified in the way Bob and Julie handled their conflict over the new car.

Articles and books have been written to help couples approach the problem of conflict in this way and to fight "creatively," "fairly," and "properly"—in other words, to fight constructively rather than destructively (for example, Bach and Wyden, 1968; Lieberman and Hardie, 1981). As sociologist Jetse Sprey (1971) has written, "The successful management of conflict requires the ability to negotiate, bargain, and cooperate: a range of behavioral skills." However, some persons fail to develop such behavioral skills

and seek a solution to dissension by either escaping or submitting to the wishes and demands of the other person even if they seem unfair. Or out of desperation, either party in a conflict may resort to the fourth alternative mentioned by Goode—actual violence.

It should not be assumed that the *absence* of conflict means everything is fine in a husband-wife relationship. Seething resentments and hostilities may underlie an outwardly calm marital life. (See Broderick, 1979, chap. 6.) In the example of our hypothetical couple, suppose that neither had expressed feelings of injustice. Julie might have kept to herself (or shared with some relatives or women friends) her feelings that Bob was acting unfairly by not doing the cooking. Resentments could have piled up, but to avoid conflict she would not have voiced her complaints to Bob. Instead, she might have acted increasingly distant and cool toward him. As it was, she was able to bring up the matter and work with Bob toward a constructive solution through negotiation—even before an actual conflict emerged in which each would have struggled for his or her own way. The couple did engage in actual conflict over the car Bob wanted, but again they were able to resolve it since they didn't try to bury the problem but instead were willing to renegotiate after Bob pressed for what he felt was fairness.

Why the Family May Be a Setting for Violence

Suppression of perceived injustice in order "not to rock the boat" or to be "selfless" or "altruistic" can generate strong feelings which could explode at some unexpected time. Several observations of sociologist Lewis Coser (1956:62) are worth noting in this regard. He points out that "there is more occasion for the rise of hostile feelings in primary than in secondary groups." *Primary groups* are groups composed of persons having a close relationship to one another in which, as much as possible, the total range of roles and the complete personality of each is known to the other. The family is probably the most obvious example of such a group. Secondary relationships, on the other hand, involve persons who know and relate to one another segmentally; they share only certain aspects of their lives and see one another only in specific roles. A patient may know a doctor only in the role of physician and know nothing of the physician's role as spouse, parent, church or club member, friend, and so on. The patient and physician are involved in one another's lives only on a secondary level; the physician's relationship with his or her spouse, children, and closest friends, however, is on a primary level. Areas of one's personality and interests which are not disclosed in a secondary relationship are revealed and out in the open in a primary one, such as the family. "If you could see him at home, you'd know what he's really like," is a common bit of folk wisdom.

Coser emphasizes that since primary relations tend to involve the total personality, feelings of intimacy are strengthened. Sharing all aspects of life makes people feel close to each other. Paradoxically, however, such intimacy has the potential of breeding hate as well as love. This happens because persons in close contact are bound to "rub one another the wrong way" on occasion. But since conflict is usually considered "bad" and disruptive for primary relationships, deliberate efforts are made to avoid it (Foss, 1980). The desire to engage in conflict is suppressed out of concern for affectionate sentiments, peace, and group cohesiveness. However, suppression of conflicts often means that an accumulation of hostilities is occurring, and any eruption of these feelings is likely to have great intensity both because

persons in primary relations are so totally involved in one another's lives and also because the hostile feelings have grown to huge proportions by not having been allowed expression earlier (Coser, 1956:62–63, 79).

An outburst in which spouses furiously unleash their gathering storm of hostilities is not likely to solve problems or help their situation. Hostilities and conflict are not one and the same. In the words of Coser (1956:40), "Whereas conflict necessarily changes the previous terms of the relationship of the participants, mere hostility has no such necessary effects and may leave the terms of the relationship unchanged." To renegotiate, bargain, or engage in actual conflict is like the safety valve on a boiler. "Letting off steam" keeps the entire mechanism from exploding (Blau, 1964:304).

When husbands and wives keep hostilities and resentments to themselves, sudden convulsions may occur at any time in the form of devastating, heated verbal exchanges or actual physical violence. Often *both* verbal aggression and physical violence take place. Straus (1974) conducted a study to test the hypothesis that verbal aggression is a substitute for physical aggression. The results showed just the opposite: "The more verbal expression of aggression, the more physical aggression." In using the term *verbal aggression,* Straus is not referring to settling an argument through rational discussion, negotiating, and talking over and working through disagreements. Rather, he is focusing on aggressive tactics such as yelling and insulting the spouse, calling the spouse derogatory names, sulking and refusing to talk (the "silent treatment" can be very aggressive), and angrily stomping out of the room.

Types of Violence

John O'Brien (1971), a social researcher who has given attention to violence in divorce-prone families, defines *violence* as "any behavior which threatens or causes physical damage to an object or person." Examples of family violence in the divorce records he examined included wife beating, child beating, threats with a gun, extreme sadomasochism in sex relations, and the starving of the spouse's pet cats. Straus (1979, 1980a), in gathering data on family conflict and violence, used what he termed "the conflict tactics (CT) scales." Tactics listed under the physical-violence index of the CTS were (1) "throwing things at the spouse"; (2) "pushing, shoving, or grabbing"; (3) "slapping"; (4) "kicking, biting, or hitting with the fist"; (5) "hit or tried to hit with something"; (6) "beat up"; (7) "threatened with a knife or gun"; and (8) "used a knife or gun." Some sociologists suggest that a distinction should be made between two types of violence. Steinmetz and Straus (1974:4), for example, speak of violence in which physical force is used to cause pain or injury as an end in itself in contrast to violence in which "pain or injury or physical restraint" is used "as a punishment to induce the other person to carry out some act."

Perhaps we could think of the distinction in terms of what we might call *explosive violence* and *coercive violence.* The child who throws a temper tantrum, the wife who suddenly begins pounding her husband's chest when he tries to smoothe over a disagreement by making sexual overtures when she wants to talk, and the husband who kicks over a chair in a fit of rage may all be expressing explosive violence. They feel angry and frustrated and feel some need to "get it out of their system" through striking out. *Coercive violence,* in contrast, is goal-oriented and directed toward accomplishing a task, namely to persuade someone to do or not to do something, to punish the person, or, in some other way, to exercise control through physical force. The parent who

shakes the child in order to extract the truth when lying is suspected is demonstrating coercive physical force. "You'd better tell me the truth or I'm just going to shake it out of you!" The husband who reacts to finding his wife in bed with another man by beating them both black and blue is demonstrating coercive violence (though no doubt combining explosive elements as well). "There, that'll show you both! That'll teach you never to do anything like that again, you no-good whore!"

Coercion may, of course, be verbal and involve threats of rewards withheld or certain nonphysical punishments; but as a stressful situation escalates, actual physical aggression may be resorted to as one person tries to control the other. The husband blocks the door and snatches away the car keys, yelling at his wife, "I said I don't want you to go!" Conversely, the person who is attempting to resist the coercion may resort to violence. The wife kicks her husband, scratches his arm with her fingernails in an attempt to get back the car keys, and tries to push him away from the doorway as she shouts, "Let me go, you bully!"

Socioeconomic Status and Violence

We have already seen that husbands who are blocked from success in the economic-opportunity system are likely to attempt to resolve disagreements through exercising power that their wives consider nonlegitimate. There is also some evidence that violence is one of the ways this nonlegitimate power may be exercised in marriage (Allen and Straus, 1980).

A husband might turn to brute force as a means of dominating his wife if it seems the only way he can persuade her to comply with his wishes. As one blue-collar wife told Komarovsky (1962:227), "Women got to figure men out, on account of men are stronger and

HUSBAND RAISES ROOF OVER DIVORCE

Enumclaw, WA—A man bulldozed his three-bedroom, $85,000 home after his wife filed for divorce, and the destruction apparently was legal because he first took the time to pick up a demolition permit, police said Sunday.

Neighbors in the quiet residential area immediately called police when Raymond Kree Kirkman began tearing into the house Saturday.

"When I got the call over the radio, I thought it was the usual domestic case where the husband is tearing up the house—you know, throwing things around," said Officer Fred Eaton. "When I got there, I made him stop for a minute."

But, said a police dispatcher, Kirkman "had a legal permit for a building at the property he did show our officers."

Kirkman showed Eaton the demolition permit he had picked up for an $11.50 fee in this city about 30 miles south of Seattle.

"There were no restraining orders" from the divorce proceedings, said the dispatcher, who declined to give her name. "So the property was communal and there was nothing restraining him from doing it."

Kirkman's estranged wife, Sandy, 26, was out of town Saturday when a neighbor called her and told her that her husband was destroying the house with a piece of heavy machinery. She said she thought the neighbor meant a sledgehammer or other hand tool.

The couple has been separated since last summer and Sandy Kirkman had been living in the house with her three children. She filed for divorce last Monday.

"I told him I wanted to keep the house. I guess he didn't want me to have anything," she said.

Raymond Kirkman was not listed in the telephone book, and could not be reached for comment Sunday.

He was jailed Sunday for investigation of an assault on a television camera crew that went to film the wreckage.

SOURCE: AP report. *Greensboro (NC) News and Record,* Oct. 14, 1985, p. A2.

---

when they sock you, they could hurt you." Another wife told of a time her husband pulled off a banister and ripped up three steps in a fit of anger toward her—which caused her to stop and think of what might happen if that physical strength were applied *directly* toward her. Thus, according to Komarovsky, "the threat of violence is another ground of masculine power," particularly at lower socioeconomic levels. In her sample of blue-collar marriages, Komarovsky found that 27 percent of husbands with less than twelve years of education and 33 percent of wives with less than twelve years of education reported that conflicts were handled through violent quarreling, with occasional beating and breaking things. Among the high school graduates in her sample, 17 percent of the husbands and 4 percent of the wives reported such violence in marital quarreling (p. 363). In another study, Steinmetz (1977:126) found that the higher a husband's and wife's education and the higher their socioeconomic status (measured in her study by husband's education and occupation), the less likely they were to use physical force to settle marital conflicts and the more likely they were to use discussion (see also Gelles, 1979:141).

O'Brien (1971) also reports evidence of a connection between violence and the family's place in the economic-opportunity structure. O'Brien's sample of 150 divorce applicants included 24 percent upper middle class, 29 percent lower middle class, and 47 percent working class. In 1 out of 6 families, violence had occurred to such an extent that it was considered a major reason for initiating divorce.

O'Brien separated the 25 cases of families spontaneously reporting violence from the 125 cases where violence had not been reported as a reason for divorce. He found evidence that physical force on the part of the husband-father was commonly linked with underachievement in the breadwinner role. (See Table 12-B.) Since his sample did not include families with husbands chronically unemployed, the lower class was not represented. Otherwise even more evidence of vi-

olence would likely have shown up. The greater incidence of violence characterizing underclass families in ghetto areas, says O'-Brien, "reflects, not a subcultural disposition toward violence, but rather a greater incidence of men in the father/husband role who fail to have the achievement capacities normally associated with this role" (p. 697).

But why should men become violent with their wives and children because they, as husbands and fathers, haven't been achievers in the economic-opportunity system? Some men may react aggressively out of a sense of frustration at being blocked from the rewards which achievement in that system would have brought them. Unable to attack the system directly or the forces which they feel hold them back from its benefits, such men turn their attacks upon their families. Their reaction is what we have described as explosive violence.

On the other hand, it is quite possible that coercive violence as well as explosive violence takes place in homes where the hus-

TABLE 12-B Comparison of achievement status of husbands in violence and nonviolence subgroups of unstable families

	PREVALENCE IN:	
ACHIEVEMENT STATUS OF HUSBAND	VIOLENCE SUBGROUP (NUMBER = 25)	NONVIOLENCE SUBGROUP (NUMBER = 125)
Husband was seriously dissatisfied with his job	44%	27%
Husband started but failed to complete either high school or college	44	18
Husband's income was the source of serious and constant conflict	84	24
Husband's educational achievement was less than his wife's	56	14
Husband's occupational status was lower than that of his father-in-law (wife's marital mobility downward)	37	28

SOURCE: John O'Brien, "Violence in Divorce-Prone Families," *Journal of Marriage and the Family* 33 (1971), p. 695.

band has not achieved at a high level. Lacking legitimate authority earned by his accomplishments in the realm of work, such a husband may nonetheless feel that he has the right to domineer over his wife. He accepts an ideology of male supremacy, even if his wife views his power as nonlegitimate and does not submit to it unquestioningly or happily. If there is no other means of getting his way, such a husband may try physical force. One behavioral scientist says that the husband's perception of a failure to be in control underlies his violent outbursts (Whitehurst, 1974b:76). In the thinking of such a husband, not to be "in control" of his wife and children is not to be fully a man.

Research by Craig Allen and Murray Straus (1980:203) provides evidence that "the more the wife's resources exceed those of her husband, the more likely the husband is to have used physical force during the referent year" in which these social scientists collected their data. Three other researchers concluded from another study that "certain types of status inconsistency (i.e., underachievement in occupation by the husband) and certain types of status incompatibility (i.e., when the woman is high in occupation relative to her husband) involve very high risks of spouse abuse, particularly life-threatening violence" (Hornung, McCullough, and Sugimoto, 1981:675; see also Walker, 1984:16).

Goode (1971:624) points out that social systems contain four major elements by which persons may move others to carry out their wishes: (1) money or other material resources, (2) prestige or respect (such as commanded by a person in a position to which others look up), (3) winsomeness (likability, attractiveness, friendship, love), and (4) force or the threat of force. In other words, we are back to the "carrot-and-stick" analogy. Persons may get their way through

either rewards or punishments meted out to those whom they wish to control. Husbands who lack positive resources with which to reward their wives are likely to find it more difficult to extract submission or compliance from them. Thus, they turn to the one resource that appears to remain to them—physical force.

O'Brien has taken ideas from conflict theory as it applies to the larger society and has shown how these same ideas may be applied to the family. He points out that those in a superior position in a social system may hold such a position because of an *ascribed status*—a status they have not earned but have been granted by virtue of their membership in some social category (whites in a white-dominant society, males over females, feudal lords over peasants, and so on). In such a social system, those in an inferior position may accept and support the arrangement, believing that the group in the superior position has the right to rule because of its advantaged skills and resources. However, says O'-Brien (1971:695), "One of the most common situations leading to a rejection of the legitimacy of those in high status is when their achieved status fails to measure up to their ascribed status." If the superior group is not able to back up its privileged position with a display of adequate resources, or if it fails to distribute such resources fairly to those over whom it holds power, a conflict situation emerges which may erupt in violence (Grimshaw, 1970). Perceiving a threat to the legitimacy of its superior position, the dominant group may resort to coercive action (violence) against the subordinate group that has dared to challenge its supremacy. Applying these ideas to the family, O'Brien concludes that "one should find that violence is most common in those families where the classically 'dominant' member (male-adult-husband) fails to possess the superior skills, talents or resources on which his preferred superior status is supposed to be legitimately based" (p. 693).

Another researcher emphasizes the importance of the *wife's* resources or lack of them. Wives who are not employed and who have little education are those most likely to remain in situations where their husbands beat them and are least likely to seek outside intervention. Such wives may feel trapped in an undesirable situation but are persuaded they have few, if any, alternatives. In contrast, those with jobs are less dependent upon their husbands and are more likely to seek help from social service agencies or the police and are also more likely to leave the marriage (Gelles, 1979:103–104; see also Kalmuss and Straus, 1982; Strube and Barbour, 1983, 1984).

An additional reason for more violence at lower socioeconomic levels may relate to childhood gender-role socialization, in which boys are encouraged to develop what Jackson Toby (1966) has termed "*compulsive* masculinity," with an exaggerated emphasis on roughness and toughness as a sign of manhood. Toby suggests that boys at such levels, having grown up with little opportunity to understand, appreciate, and wield *symbolic* power (such as the power of a physician or business executive), may look on violence as "the most appropriate way to protect one's honor, to show courage, or to conceal fear, especially fear of revealing weakness" (see also Straus and Hotaling, 1980).

Having looked at some of the reasons for the higher incidence of marital violence at lower socioeconomic levels, we must not conclude that such violence is unknown among middle-class couples. "Believing that abuse of wives and children is confined to the lower class is yet another way people try to see acts of others as deviant and their own behavior as normal," write Gelles and Cornell (1985:16). Roger Langley and Richard Levy (1977, chap. 4) write about a physician who became angry with his wife because she left the door open one hot summer day when the air conditioner was on. The physician knocked his wife down, stomped on her spine, and caused permanent paralysis. In another case, the wife of a scientist told of being hit in the stomach until she vomited blood. Other abused women to which Langley and Levy refer are wives of attorneys, psychiatrists, professors, ministers, and men in other highly respected occupations and professions.

As psychologist Lenore Walker (1979:22) points out, "The recent public focus on battered women has brought many of these middle- and upper-class women out of hiding. The publicity being given the problem is creating a climate in which they think they will finally be believed." Marital violence in middle-class homes has been less visible because it is more apt to go unreported to law enforcement authorities and public agencies than is marital violence at lower socioeconomic levels. Many middle-class wives feel they must protect their husbands' reputations and careers as well as their own standing in the community (Walker, 1979; Langley and Levy, 1977; Giles-Sims, 1983). Thus, such wives have traditionally kept the matter private and hidden for as long as possible, covering their bruises with dark glasses, makeup, special hairstyles, and high-necked, long-sleeved clothing. For battered wives at any class level, the environment of fear and uncertainty about when another incident of violence might be triggered may cause a woman to "live in constant violence by experiencing the expectation of it," write Edleson, Eisikovits, and Guttmann (1985:244). They call for a new agenda of research and theory-building to provide better understanding of men who batter women. (See also

IT CAN HAPPEN IN WHAT APPEAR TO BE THE BEST OF FAMILIES

Terry Davidson's book, *Conjugal Crime,* contains a chapter describing her painful childhood in a church parsonage. Her father was a respected minister, often called by the police to help in domestic-violence situations where a calming counselor was needed. Yet, in his own home, the minister was a cruel tyrant. Davidson recounts what life was like for her and her brother as they were forced to watch their father beat their mother:

> We were to watch calmly, without reacting, without visibly flinching, whenever this self-righteous man punched my mother, pummeled her, kicked her, taunted and mocked her. We were not to intervene. He expected us to approve and learn from it. When he knocked her abjectly to the floor, kicking her body where it wouldn't show, he would proclaim, snarling, ''You asked for it!'' If he noticed her moans of pain, he'd only hurt her more, threatening, ''You're trying to attract the neighbors: now you'll really get it.''

> At these times I was not allowed to leave the room, or hide, or even cover my face. If I cried out, he'd turn his fury on me. So I'd stuff my hand into my mouth and somehow stop time and feelings until he was finished. Then he'd rush out of the house, go off in his car, and not come back until the household was asleep. And I would run sobbing to my mother, ''Please, let's leave him, I hate him, I'm going to *tell.*'' But who could I tell? Who was stronger than he was? I wasn't allowed to speak of it, anyway.

SOURCE: Terry Davidson, *Conjugal Crime* (New York: Hawthorn Books, 1978), p. 139 in Ballantine Books edition.

Bernard and Bernard, 1984; Feazell, Mayers, and Deschner, 1984; Goldstein and Rosenbaum, 1985; Pagelow, 1981.)

Gender Roles and Marital Violence

''The cultural norms and values permitting and sometimes encouraging husband-to-wife violence reflect the hierarchical and male-dominant type of society which characterizes the Western world,'' writes sociologist Murray Straus (1977:68). He points out that the development of ''compulsive masculinity,'' beliefs in male superiority which give men rights over their families, beliefs about wives as being ''childlike'' and ''property'' over which husbands may exercise control, and the sex-based division of labor which gives women primary responsibility for child care and makes them financially dependent on husbands (thus often locking the wives into emotionally and physically injurious marriage situations)—all of these notions have a part to play in the battering that goes on in families. ''Wife-beating is not just a personal abnormality,'' stresses Straus, ''but rather has its roots in the very structure of society and the family; that is, in the cultural norms and in the sexist organization of the society and the family'' (p. 61).

Other social scientists have also examined the issue of gender roles and marital violence (Dobash and Dobash, 1979; Ulbrich and Huber, 1981; Breines and Gordon, 1983; Brown, 1980; LaRossa, 1980; Gelles, 1979). One study of abuse in *dating relationships* showed that "those males who chose to endorse those characteristics our culture has traditionally considered masculine, while rejecting those considered feminine (e.g., tenderness, compassion, gentleness) were more likely to abuse the women with whom they were romantically involved" (Bernard, Bernard, and Bernard, 1985). The researchers found that women who did *not* conform to the traditional feminine role were more likely than traditionally feminine women to be victims of dating violence. This finding fits with Brown's (1980) point that, in marriage, a husband's lack of acceptance of his wife's movement toward egalitarian gender-role preferences can increase the likelihood of marital violence (Figure 12-3). Men who follow a "compulsive-masculinity" script apparently find it threatening to have the male dominant/female subordinate model questioned or challenged. (See also Whitehurst, 1974b.)

In considering the topic of domestic violence, the question of *husbands* as victims of assault may arise. Research indicates that while wives may use violence on husbands just as husbands may be violent toward wives, wives are far more likely to resort to violence only to protect or defend themselves from sexual abuse and physical attacks by their husbands (Gelles, 1979). Thus, although there are battered husbands—and even murdered husbands—"the real issue is the social, political, and legal context of the violence," writes Gelles. "This becomes a question of victimization. When men hit women and women hit men, the real victims are almost certainly going to be the women" (p. 141). Sociologist Susan Steinmetz (1977) explains why:

> When the wife slaps her husband, her lack of physical strength, plus his ability to restrain her, reduces the physical damage to a minimum. When the husband slaps his wife, however, his strength, plus her inability to restrain him, results in considerably more damage. (p. 90)

There is also evidence that husbands are more likely than wives to engage in the most dangerous forms of violence, such as beating up the spouse or using guns, knives, and other means of inflicting serious injury. Husbands who engage in violent acts are likely to do so repeatedly (Straus, 1980a:32). At the same time, Straus and his colleagues found in their national sample that wives who engaged in violent acts were almost twice as likely as husbands to throw things at the spouse, thus supporting "the pot and pan throwing stereotype" (Straus, 1980a:31–32).

Steinmetz (1977) makes the point that women are equally capable of performing violent acts toward their husbands when conditions are equalized—such as through the use of a weapon or where a husband is much weaker physically. Steinmetz reports a case in which an elderly husband was scarred and bruised from assaults by his wife who was thirty-one years younger than he and considerably stronger. She had severely bitten his ear on one occasion, blackened his eyes on another, and another time inflicted such a serious injury that physicians feared he might lose the vision in one eye! If we look at homicide statistics for *spouse murders only,* we find that about half the victims are husbands murdered by wives and half are wives murdered by husbands (Straus, 1977:60; Steinmetz, 1978:3; Gelles, 1979:139).

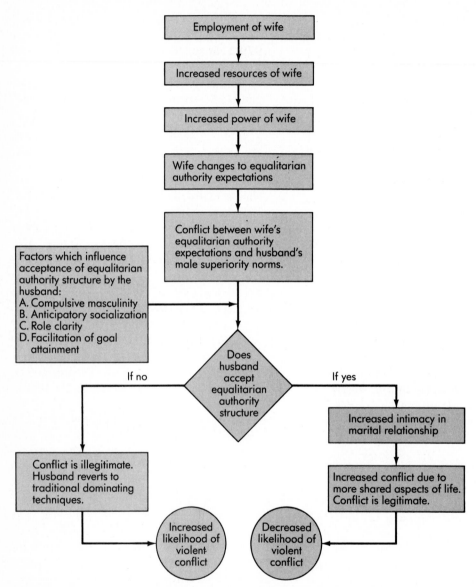

FIGURE 12-3 Flow chart depicting interrelationships of employment of wife, marital equality, and husband-wife violence according to Brown's theoretical formulation. (SOURCE: Bruce W. Brown, "Wife-Employment, Marital Equality, and Husband-Wife Violence," in Murray A. Straus and Gerald T. Hotaling, eds., *The Social Causes of Husband-Wife Violence* (Minneapolis: University of Minneapolis Press, 1980), p. 184.)

Gelles (1979) calls attention to two violence situations where wives are particularly the persons at risk: *marital rape* and *beatings during pregnancy*. Since sexual intercourse is considered a right of marriage, only a handful of states have legislation that recognizes forced intercourse by a husband as being no different than forced sexual acts by someone else—in other words, rape. Some men, particularly those lacking social and psychological resources that could act positively in the power balance in marriage, may consider an act of marital rape as a way to exercise nonlegitimate power. They see it as a way to coerce or humiliate or dominate their wives (Gelles, 1979:127; Russell, 1982). Psychologist Irene Hanson Frieze (1983:552) concluded from her study on marital rape that "it appears that battering and rape are very closely linked and that rape is more closely associated with higher levels of physical violence in a marriage and with problems in the family upbringing of the husband than with a couple's sexual dynamics."

Similarly, when wives are pregnant, they may be victims of beatings by their husbands (Gelles, 1972:145). Gelles (1979:113) suggests several possible reasons. Some couples are poorly informed and may think that sexual intercourse must cease during pregnancy; thus some husbands may take out their sexual frustrations by beating their wives. In other cases, the transition to parenthood and the changes associated with expecting and having a baby may bring stress which, when coupled with economic stress, erupts in violence. Gelles also speaks of some husbands' reactions to wives' mood changes, complaints, and irritability brought about by biochemical changes during pregnancy. In still other cases, husbands may be responding angrily to the prospect of an unwanted child and may show their rage by battering their pregnant wives. The act may be in part a kind of "prenatal child abuse," Gelles (1979:116) suggests, or it may be an effort to prevent a live birth from taking place, since "for many families violence which brings about a miscarriage is a more acceptable way of terminating an unwanted pregnancy than is abortion." Several wives in one of Gelles's own studies reported having experienced miscarriages after beatings by their husbands, and one wife who had been beaten while pregnant told of giving birth to a handicapped child.

While Gelles (1979) underscores a number of factors—including economic problems—that contribute to what he terms a "deadly tradition of domestic violence," one point is particularly pertinent in view of a basic theme of this book. He writes:

> An underlying cause of family violence is the fact that the family is perhaps the only social group where jobs, tasks and responsibilities are assigned on the basis of gender and age, rather than interest or ability. An elimination of the concept of "women's work"; elimination of the taken-for-granted view that the husband is and must be the head of the family; and an elimination of sex-typed family roles are all prerequisites to the reduction of family violence. (pp. 18–19, references omitted)

As was shown in Figure 12-3, a movement toward egalitarianism in marriage can work to either increase or decrease the likelihood of violent conflict. The key is the attitude of the husband (Brown, 1980; Straus, 1980b). Straus (1977, 1980b) stresses that while, in the short run, some men may react violently to the idea of relinquishing the ascribed power and privilege inherent in the traditional male role, in the long run, movement toward equality of the sexes may be expected to help decrease acts of violence between spouses. Research already indicates that the lowest rates of marital violence are found in those families where decision-mak-ing is shared democratically by wives and husbands (Gelles, 1979:141; Straus, Gelles, and Steinmetz, 1980).

CHAPTER HIGHLIGHTS

Social conflict may be defined as a struggle over limited resources and/or incompat-ible goals. *Struggle* and *resistance* are key words in understanding conflict. When one party *resists* the other's wishes or claims, they are engaged in conflict. *Struggle* occurs when counteroffers are refused outright or no modifications are suggested. Communication isn't enough to settle conflict; beyond talking about the conflict sit-uation, the parties must work to change it.

In *zero-sum* conflict, each party seeks to have all or nothing. Only one can win. In *mixed-motive* conflict, the parties are motivated by a desire to compete with each other on the one hand and to cooperate with each other on the other hand. *Person-ality-based* conflict has a psychological base and is rooted in problems within the per-son, whereas *situational* conflict is engendered by structural factors outside the per-son. Resolution of situational conflict lies in changing the situation rather than trying to change the people to fit (or adapt to) the situation. *Basic* conflict is conflict over the rules of the game and wanting to change the rules. *Nonbasic* conflict, on the other hand, is conflict within mutually agreed-upon rules without calling the rules them-selves into question.

The overwhelming weight of evidence suggests that conflict is an inevitable part of any ongoing social relationship—including marriage. Conflict may strengthen a rela-tionship because, when satisfactorily resolved, it removes injustice and can mean greater maximum joint profit. On the other hand, conflict can be divisive (tearing groups apart, breaking up relationships). Disruptive conflicts are likely to be those where nonlegitimate power is exercised, trust is destroyed, and the person who feels exploited and unfairly treated wants out of the relationship. Sometimes conflicts explode into violence. Although family violence occurs at all socioeconomic levels, there is a somewhat greater likelihood for it to occur among husbands and wives of lower education and social status. "Compulsive masculinity" and other ideas associ-ated with traditional gender-role norms appear to play a major part in family violence.

P·A·R·T S·I·X

CONTINUING PROCESSES OF THE FAMILY EXPERIENCE

·13·

CHILDREN: TO HAVE OR NOT TO HAVE?

Ellen and Bill Peck decided not to have children. Soon the pressure was on! People reacted to their childless state with varying degrees of curiosity and hostility. Ellen points out that the question, "Are you going to have any children?" was never asked. Instead it was, "When are you going to have children?" (Katy, 1972; Peck, 1971).

This couple's decision collided with the belief that women are intended by nature to have children and that women's bodies and psyches are programmed toward that objective. Couples who resolve not to have children are viewed as deliberately thwarting nature's goal. Such folk beliefs are reinforced by a network of formal and informal societal pressures urging couples to become parents, and those who don't are stigmatized or pitied. These attitudes and societal pressures, collectively, are sometimes labeled *pronatalism* (from the Latin, "in favor of birth") because they promote and encourage childbearing.

Attempting to counteract subtle and not-so-subtle pronatalist influences, Ellen Peck (1971) wrote a book entitled *The Baby Trap;* in addition, she and her husband helped found an organization called the National Organization for Non-Parents (NON), which didn't hesitate to proclaim that "None is fun!" and emphasized the advantages of remaining childless (or "child-free," to use their preferred term). NON later changed its name to the National Alliance for Optional Parenthood while retaining its original vision. "In order for people truly to have an option," state the organization's promotional materials, "we must continue to work to make nonparenthood a socially accepted and respected lifestyle."

But is it true, as some claim, that couples have babies merely because of societal pressures (since societies cannot continue without replacement of their members)? Or is having babies simply a matter of nature's trickery—a kind of cosmic con game in which persons are carried away in the ecstasy of sexual pleasure only to be rudely awakened by a squirming, squealing, demanding infant who emerges to mock the lovers with an attitude of "Aha! You thought you were just having fun, but look what you got instead—me!" Or might it be that people have children because they want them and *value* them? No doubt all three explanations contain elements of truth.

REWARDS, COSTS, AND THE MOTIVATION TO HAVE CHILDREN

We have seen how the comparison of costs and rewards operates in the husband-wife relationship, beginning even before marriage in the mate-selection process and continuing through the negotiation and renegotiation process after the marriage takes place. Now we want to see how a theory of rewards and costs helps to explain how couples make decisions concerning reproduction. Assuming they are physically able to have children, will a particular husband and wife *want* to have them? If so, how many and when?

In ancient Hebrew society, no one would have thought to ask if married couples should have children. Had not the Creator commanded, "Be fruitful and multiply"? Children were considered God's gifts, "the fruit of the womb . . . his reward." The scriptures declared that a man needed a quiver full of children as an archer needed arrows. A barren woman was to be pitied. "Give me children or I die!" cried Rachel, the wife of the patriarch Jacob. Married couples desired children to help at home and in the fields and to support them in old age. Sons were needed to carry on the family name and inherit the land. Such an attitude toward children has been common throughout history in traditional, patriarchal, agricultural societies.

A sociological study of *why* people have children would have seemed out of place in biblical times. But such studies are of great interest in today's world. All too little research has been carried out in this area, and what has been done has often been faulty on methodological grounds. Increasingly, however, in dealing with questions of population growth (on the *macro* level), or "Why are John and Jane Doe going to have another baby?" (on the *micro* level), social scientists see the need to give attention to the matter of motivation (Campbell et al., 1982). The birthrate at a given time in history cannot be explained simply and solely in terms of effective contraceptive technology or the lack of it. Although some persons are inclined to explain declines in the birthrate since the late 1950s by pointing to "the pill," it should be noted that there was also a low birthrate before and during the Great Depression in the United States several decades before the advent of the pill. And even in the early days of the Roman Empire, the emperor Augustus was concerned about low birthrates and therefore devised various incentives to encourage Roman citizens to have large families. By the time of the late Roman Empire, the problem had grown even more acute because crushing tax burdens and unpaid forced public service made it difficult to support a family of any size (Boak, 1955).

Clearly, the perceived rewards and costs of having children play their part in family planning. In ancient Hebrew society, the *rewards* were uppermost in mind, and large families resulted. In Imperial Rome, the *costs* were of prime concern, and population replenishment was insufficient. But what about today? Why do some couples want children while others do not?

REWARDS OF PARENTHOOD

Psychologists Lois Wladis Hoffman and Martin L. Hoffman (1973) have examined research studies and theoretical literature focusing on reasons why children are valued. Drawing upon their findings, we might group incentives for having children into four main categories according to the rewards children may provide parents (see also Berelson, 1972). Children may be viewed as beneficial to parents for reasons of (1) self-enhancement, (2) family continuity and aid to parents, (3) pleasure, affection and a sense of belonging, and (4) altruistic and religious satisfactions.

Rewards of Self-Enhancement

Embarking on parenthood brings a new social identity and a sense of arriving at adult status. "More than finishing school, going to work, or even getting married," Hoffman and Hoffman (1973:47) claim, "parenthood establishes a person as a truly mature, stable, and acceptable member of the community. . . . This is especially true for women, for whom motherhood is also defined as their major role in life." Since few alternative roles are available for uneducated, lower-status women in particular, having a baby is looked upon as perhaps the most important way of gaining identity at this class level.

Closely related to the new sense of self and adult status may be a sense of achievement through parenthood. It might be thought of as *personal* achievement, either through having physically produced a child (or several children in social or religious circles where large families are highly esteemed) or through meeting creatively the challenges of rearing children and gaining a sense of pride in a job well done.

On the other hand, parents may experience *vicarious* achievement, a sense of sharing in their children's accomplishments as though these accomplishments were happening to the parents themselves. The mother who never had a chance to take music lessons basks in the reflected glory of her child's performance at a piano recital. The football-loving father swells with pride when his son is chosen high school player of the year. Later, as grown children do well in the occupational sphere, parents feel that their own prestige is enhanced as well. "My son, the doctor" is more than an old joke.

Hoffman and Hoffman (1973:56) also call attention to the reward of power and influence that parenthood brings people, along with a sense of making an impact on one's own life and the lives of others through bringing a child into the world. They suggest that particularly for persons who feel powerless in other areas of life, producing and molding a human being can provide a sense of having an effect on the world that is not otherwise possible. Studies have shown that persons who feel powerless are less likely to use contraceptives (Kar, 1971; Groat and Neal, 1967), and the Hoffman and Hoffman explanation may fit. On the other hand, of course, the overall sense of powerlessness might *contribute* to the nonuse of contraceptives because the couples involved may feel that contraceptives would do little good anyway—that getting along in life is a matter of fate and "breaks" rather than self-mastery and rational control.

Power and influence over others' lives can provide persons with feelings of importance. Contacts with social agencies and on the job usually put lower-status persons in positions where others have power over them while they have little, if any, power over others. But at home they can experience a sense of power denied elsewhere. Social customs and laws allow parents to exercise tremendous control over children. Parents can issue commands; they can insist on having their wishes followed and can, within reasonable bounds, force children to comply. Parents can experience that power which stems from being the chief or only source of material and emotional benefits to others who need them (their children). Such "power benefits" in parenthood may play a part in explaining why lower-status couples tend to have larger families.

Socioeconomic Status and Fertility Demographers have long noted the inverse relationship between social class and fertility. That is, *fertility* (the number of children born) goes up as socioeconomic status goes down. In the words of a 1920s song, "The rich get richer, and the poor get children." These statements do not tell the whole story because much more is involved than social status alone in explaining fertility rates, but, in general, we may say that lower-status families have more children, on the average, than do higher-status families (U.S. Bureau of the Census, *Current Population Reports,* ser. P-23, no. 49, 1974, p. 38; U.S. Bureau of the Census, Special Demographic Analyses, CDS-80-8, 1983, pp. 6–8; Wineberg and McCarthy, 1986). The higher a woman's education, the fewer children she is likely to have. The average number of births experienced by ever-married women who had completed thirteen or more years of education was 1.6 per woman in 1982. Women who had completed fewer than twelve years of education had an average of 2.5 births per woman (*Family Planning Perspectives*, 1985a:36). The *overall* average of births per ever-married woman that year was 1.9.

The answer to the question "Why do lower-status couples have more children?" may be that often they want more. They are not so motivated as higher-status couples to prevent births. True, the costs of having children (particularly in the financial realm) are great for lower-status couples, but apparently many feel such costs are more than compensated for by the rewards. As we have seen, for women with few outlets or opportunities for achievement outside the home, the bearing and rearing of children can be extremely gratifying. And for lower-status men, large families can be a source of pride and an opportunity for exercising power not possible elsewhere. Various studies have shown that lower-status men tend to be more authoritarian in their families than are higher-status men (Sears, Maccoby, and Levin, 1957; Hoffman, 1963), underscoring a point made by Blau and Duncan (1967:428): "Whereas successful achievers have their status as adult men supported by their superior occupational roles and authority, the unsuccessful find a substitute in the authority they exercise in their role as fathers over a number of children." In addition, children may be looked upon as a form of wealth. In a report for the Population Council, Bernard Berelson (1972) wrote that childbearing is one of the few ways the poor can compete with the rich. "Life cannot make the poor man prosperous in material goods and services but it can easily make him rich with children" (see also Blake, 1979).

At the same time, we need to realize that women at or below the poverty level are far more likely than others to have one or more *unwanted* births during a lifetime (Alan Guttmacher Institute, 1979:20 *Family Plan-*

Lower-status families tend to have more children than do higher-status families. (Paul Conklin/Monkmeyer)

ning Perspectives, 1985a; Rosoff, 1985; Grady et al., 1986). The poor don't always have more children simply because they want more but because of circumstances over which they feel they have no control. Their socioeconomic condition has restricted educational opportunities; and lower education, in turn, is associated with a higher likelihood of contraceptive failure. Poor persons often don't have access to reliable contraceptive methods nor understand how to use them effectively.

Similarly, access to safe abortions in cases

of unwanted conceptions may be denied them because of governmental policies on funding. (On June 30, 1980, the U.S. Supreme Court upheld the constitutionality of the Hyde Amendment—the controversial congressional-funding ban that stopped Medicaid payments for abortions unless a poor woman's life was in danger or in cases of promptly reported rape or incest.) Upon the implementation of the Hyde Amendment in 1978, the burden of assisting poor women in paying for abortions fell to the states alone (rather than being shared with the federal government under the customary Medicaid arrangement). As of 1983, "federal funds could be used for abortions only when the life of the pregnant woman would be endangered if the pregnancy were carried to term" (Gold and Nestor, 1985:28). In that same year, thirty states adopted their own restrictive policies and refused funding for abortions in any other than "life-only" situations. The result has been that the vast majority of poor women desiring abortions in these states (and a number of others with only slightly less restrictive policies) have access to *neither* federal nor state funding.

According to the Alan Guttmacher Institute (1979), a corporation for research, education, and policy analysis:

> Many Medicaid-eligible women denied governmental help in paying for their abortions, and unwilling to face possible death or injury at the hands of illegal abortionists, are carrying their unwanted pregnancies to term. The consequences of such unwanted births for the young mothers, the young fathers, their children and society are deep and long-lasting. (p. 31)

Rewards of Self-Preservation and Family Continuity

In "Hallowed Ground," the nineteenth-century poet, Thomas Campbell, wrote: "To live in hearts we leave behind/Is not to die." One way to make sure there are hearts left behind in which to "live on" is to have children. Offspring assure the continuation of the family line, the carrying on of the family name, uninterrupted control of a family business, perpetual ownership of family property, and other benefits associated with permanence.

It has long been common folk knowledge that persons desire children as a way of achieving a kind of immortality, and sociological studies provide verification. Men, more than women, tend to mention the survival of the family name as a reason for wanting offspring (Rainwater, 1965:147–148; Hoffman and Hoffman, 1973:48). In India, for example, demographic research showed that when men were asked to state the benefits of having a wife, a common response was "so our descent will continue." Such an evaluation of a wife's benefits was second only to the wife's value in looking after the husband's needs and performing services for him (Poffenberger, 1969).

Self-preservation benefits in having children not only relate to continuing the family line. In traditional societies, children have been valued for their economic utility. Particularly in agricultural societies, children have been considered assets because they provide families with a supply of workers. In the household, children can help with domestic chores; and older children can care for younger children, freeing mothers for other work (in the fields, for example). Children themselves can assist in agricultural tasks from a very early age.

In societies lacking adequate government plans for old age, children are expected to take responsibility for aging parents, often providing them with a home and nursing care as well as with financial support. Especially in underdeveloped and developing nations, a prime motivation for having large numbers of children is to assure that some will be living to provide for the parents in the parents' old age (Hoffman and Hoffman, 1973:57–58).

Rewards of Pleasure, Affection, and Belonging

Children may be desired because of widely held sentiments about the enrichment they bring to a couple's lives. Youngsters can mean fun, excitement, and laughter in the home. They are persons adults can relax with and play with, enjoying jokes, riddles, teasing, and roughhousing. Sparkle and zest are brought into adult lives. The novelty of a new baby ends the old, dull routine. Such an ideal picture is in the minds of many in anticipating children as pleasure sources for parents.

Furthermore, by having a baby, parents feel they have brought into being someone to love and be loved by. Children provide the promise of warm affection, a sense of belonging. A strong primary group is formed. Even if it seems that no one else in the whole world cares, having children is considered to mean that there is always someone who does care, thereby banishing feelings of aloneness. Parents expect that a loving relationship with their children will continue even if the husband-wife relationship itself comes to an end through death or divorce.

There is some evidence that, especially in blue-collar homes, the companionship and affection provided by children compensates for a lack between the spouses in these expressive areas. Rainwater (1960:87) found in his studies of blue-collar homes that wives, especially, tended to form intense relationships with their children because the children seemed to provide a sense of worthwhileness that they did not receive from their husbands. Rainwater reports: "The children (at least when young) seem easier to manage and arouse fewer conflicts than does

the difficult task of relating to grown men whom they do not understand too well and of whom they are often a little afraid."

As far as the men themselves are concerned, they too may find that children provide opportunities for physically demonstrating affection in a way that is discouraged elsewhere. In Chapter 10, we discussed the effects of the socialization of men which may inhibit open expressions of affection toward their wives—particularly in blue-collar homes where greater gender-role differences are emphasized. However, with children, such men may feel more comfortable about giving open demonstrations of feelings. They

Men may find that children provide opportunities for expressing warmth, tenderness, and physical affection in a way that is discouraged elsewhere. (Hays/Monkmeyer)

can feel free to touch, cuddle, hug, kiss, tousle children's hair, hold them on their laps, and so on. "It is possible . . . that children provide for men one of the few relationships where they can express warmth and tenderness," write Hoffman and Hoffman (1973:53).

Altruistic and Religious Satisfactions in Having Children

In a study sponsored by the Planned Parenthood Federation of America, sociologist Lee Rainwater interviewed 409 husbands and wives at various socioeconomic levels in an effort to find out why couples want and have particular numbers of children. In examining his respondents' rationales for large and small families, Rainwater (1965:181–182) found that he could abstract one central norm, namely the belief that "one should not have more children than one can support, but one should have as many children as one can afford."

Altruistic Considerations Rainwater found a widespread belief that parents who didn't have as many children as they could afford were "selfish." Such an opinion was especially prevalent among men who wanted large families. It was less true of women who wanted large families for themselves but, at the same time, could understand that other couples might choose to limit family size in order to provide more benefits for children already born. Yet the notion has persisted that persons who have large families are somehow more virtuous, self-sacrificing, altruistic, less materialistic, and less apt to spoil their children than are persons with small families. However, in recent years, concerns about a worldwide "population explosion" have challenged this way of thinking to a considerable extent, and the opinion is fre-

quently voiced that the truly altruistic couple may be the one willing to forgo the pleasures of an additional child, whereas "selfish" people are those who insist on adding new persons to an already crowded planet.

Hoffman and Hoffman call attention to another aspect of altruism, namely the concerns of various minority groups for an increase in their numbers and power. They refer to a study of black and Chicano college students in which there was support for the idea of having large families, with typical responses being, "We should double the actual number of Chicanos as soon as possible," and "Black people need more power and you can't have power without people; birth control for blacks is legalized genocide" (Buckhout et al., 1971; Hoffman and Hoffman, 1973:50–51). In this way of thinking, having children is viewed as a service performed in the interests of bettering the conditions of an oppressed people.

Some black leaders disagree strongly. After describing the economic hardships large numbers of minority persons face in a society that has discriminated against them and the sense of entrapment an unwanted pregnancy can mean to poor families, U.S. Congresswoman Shirley Chisholm (1970) made this comment:

> Which is more like genocide, I have asked some of my black brothers—this, the way things are, or the conditions I am fighting for in which the full range of family planning services is freely available to women of all classes and colors, starting with effective contraception and extending to safe, legal termination of undesired pregnancies, at a price they can afford? (p. 122)

Religious Considerations Religious satisfactions in having children provide another kind of reward for parents. For some couples, having children is a sacred duty. Parenthood

A BLACK LEADER SPEAKS OUT ON THE ABORTION QUESTION

It had begun to seem to me that the question was not whether the law should allow abortions. Experience shows that pregnant women who feel they have compelling reasons for not having a baby, or another baby, will break the law and, even worse, risk injury and death if they must to get one. Abortions will not be stopped. . . . The question becomes simply that of what kind of abortions society wants women to have—clean, competent ones performed by licensed physicians or septic, dangerous ones done by incompetent practitioners.

So when NARAL [the National Association for the Repeal of Abortion Laws] asked me to lead its campaign, I gave it serious thought. For me to take the lead in abortion repeal would be an even more serious step than for a white politician to do so, because there is a deep and angry suspicion among many blacks that even birth control clinics are a plot by the white power structure to keep down the numbers of blacks, and this opinion is even more strongly held by some in regard to legalizing abortions. But I do not know any black or Puerto Rican *women* who feel that way. To label family planning and legal abortion programs "genocide" is male rhetoric, for male ears. It falls flat to female listeners, and to thoughtful male ones. Women know, and so do many men, that two or three children who are wanted, prepared for, reared amid love and stability, and educated to the limit of their ability will mean more for the future of the black and brown races from which they come than any number of neglected, hungry, ill-housed and ill-clothed youngsters. Pride in one's race, as well as simply humanity, supports this view.

SOURCE: From Shirley Chisholm, *Unbought and Unbossed* (Boston: Houghton Mifflin, 1970), excerpted from pp. 113–122, as reprinted in Lerner, 1972.

provides these husbands and wives with a sense of fulfilling a divine command to "be fruitful and multiply." It brings an assurance that "God has blessed the union" or offers an opportunity for outwardly demonstrating compliance with church teachings against contraceptives.

A major difficulty in studying the relationship between religion and fertility springs from the successful efforts of various pressure groups in the late 1950s to eliminate a question on religious affiliation that was considered for inclusion in the United States census. However, over the years other research has shown religion to be a factor in the number of children couples have been

likely to have. In the 1965 National Fertility Study, for example, married women under 45 years of age who were Protestant had an average of 2.3 children and expected a total of 3.0. Catholic women had an average of 2.8 and expected a total of 3.9 children. Jewish women had 2.1 children and expected to have a total of 2.9 (Westoff and Westoff, 1971:164–161, 227; Ryder and Westoff, 1971:68). Over the next twenty years, differences in fertility by religion narrowed greatly. Catholics continued to have more births than did non-Catholics—but not to the degree that had once been the case. Catholics had only 0.04 more births than did Protestants in 1982, in contrast to 0.14 more births in 1973 (*Family Planning Perspectives*, 1985a).

Roman Catholicism Numerous studies have shown that Roman Catholics, as a result of their religious ideology, both *have* more children and *intend* to have more children than do couples of other religious groups. At the heart of Catholic teachings on marital sexuality has been an emphasis on a special mission assigned to husbands and wives "to collaborate with God in the generation and education of new lives." The point was reiterated in *Humanae Vitae* (1968), the Encyclical on Birth Control issued by Pope Paul VI: marriage is considered to be ordained toward begetting children. This teaching has traditionally influenced the actual number of children in Roman Catholic families and birth intentions for the future among both the general population of Catholics and those who are university students (Scanzoni, 1975b, 1975c; Heckert and Teachman, 1985).

However recent years have shown signs of change, especially in contraceptive practices. Demographers Charles Westoff and Elise Jones (1977) illustrated that change dramatically by pointing out that 8 out of 10 Roman Catholic women married between 1951 and 1955 conformed to their church's teaching on birth control during their first five years of marriage. That is, they either used no method of contraception at all or else used only the rhythm method, which is approved by the church. However, among women married during the 1971–75 period twenty years later, less than 1 out of 10 conformed to church teaching during their first five years of marriage. Using data from the 1975 National Fertility Study, Westoff and Jones noted a "convergence of Catholic and non-Catholic contraceptive practice" in spite of official church teachings, which remain unchanged among the Roman Catholic hierarchy. (See also Westoff and Jones, 1979a; Balakrishnan et al., 1985:211.)

The trend has continued (D'Antonio, 1985). Researchers Jacqueline Darroch Forrest and Stanley Henshaw (1983:163) found that "religion makes little difference in patterns of contraceptive use among women of the same age and marital status." They point out that where the periodic-abstinence (*rhythm*) method is used, Catholic women are those most likely to be using it, but "only a tiny percentage of Catholics report that they rely on that method."

Judaism Studies have consistently shown the fertility of Jewish women to be the lowest of the three major religious groups (Ryder and Westoff, 1971:70). One reason may be that Jewish teachings have not emphasized procreation as a religious duty in the way that Catholicism has. Methods of birth control were known even in biblical times (Genesis 38:9), although large families were strongly encouraged. But with changing conditions over time—exile, movement to cities, dispersion, and so on—the older laws were modified. A man's duty in preserving the human race was considered fulfilled if he had fathered two children (Himes, 1936:69ff. in 1970 edition). The Talmud includes passages permitting contraception and even sterilization for women under certain circumstances (such as health problems or out of concern for her other children). These liberal views of birth control were challenged during the Middle Ages, however, when Jewish leaders began opposing contraception and urging couples to have as many children as possible to enlarge the Jewish population, which had suffered great losses through persecution, massacre, disease, and malnutrition.

While some Jewish rabbis and educators

point out that today Judaism recognizes "that family planning is a necessity of modern life, in view of complex moral, hygienic, and economic factors" (Gordis, 1967:36–41), others express a concern similar to that of Jewish leaders in the Middle Ages. They speak of "the national Jewish need for survival in this post-Holocaust period" and believe "birth control is not a matter of 'individual conscience'" (Lamm, 1980:133–134). There has also been some concern over the downward fertility trends in Israel since the 1950s (Westoff, 1974:111–112). Speaking of the differences in opinion among some Jewish leaders, Rabbi Roland B. Gittelsohn (1980:185–186) writes: "The modern Jew confronts a most painful dilemma between a knowledge that the human population of this earth must be curbed if disaster is to be averted, and an insistence that it is important—for us and for humankind in general—that we Jews survive."

Protestantism Only during this present century have Protestant churches moved away from a position on birth control that in many respects was like that of the Roman Catholic Church (Kennedy, 1970:153). Most major Protestant denominations today, however, would agree with this 1952 statement by a commission of the American Lutheran Church: "Married couples have the freedom so to plan and order their sexual relations that each child born to their union will be wanted both for itself and in relation to the time of its birth. How the couple uses this freedom can properly be judged not by man but only by God. The means which a married pair uses . . . are matters for them to decide with their own consciences" (quoted in Rehwinkel, 1959:41–42).

Some research has indicated that among non-Catholic groups, members of certain fundamentalist sects and Mormons are likely to have more children than do other non-Catholics (Ryder and Westoff, 1971:70–71; Westoff and Potvin, 1967:130ff.; Toney, Golesorkhi, and Stinner, 1985).

Other Reasons Children Are Valued

As part of a large international study of why children are valued and how fertility patterns are affected by the satisfactions children are considered to bring parents, researchers Lois Wladis Hoffman and Jean Denby Manis (1979) examined data for the United States according to whether the respondents were male or female, parents or nonparents, and according to racial or ethnic membership. Table 13-A provides an expanded list of reasons why children are valued. These reasons were given by respondents to the open-ended question: "What would you say are some of the advantages or good things about having children compared with not having children at all?" Both women and men attached great importance to the fun and stimulation children can bring, along with various aspects of love and companionship.

COSTS OF PARENTHOOD

In an effort to alert children to the problems of an overcrowded world, a book for elementary school children contains this exercise in imagination: Youngsters are told to picture the lifestyles of two different families.

One family has two children, and these children have bikes and skates, nice clothes, music lessons, and a chance to go to summer camp. The parents take vacations, enjoy good food (including steaks), and occasionally take the whole family to restaurants. Plans are already being made for the children to go to college.

The other family in this exercise of the

TABLE 13-A The advantages of having children—specific responses[a,b]

	WOMEN					MEN		
	PARENTS			NONPARENTS		PARENTS		NON-PARENTS
SPECIFIC ADVANTAGE	White	Black	Hispanic[c]	White	Black	White	Black	White
Primary group ties and affection:								
Bring love and companionship	33.9	45.7	25.0	21.4	28.6	23.8	26.9	11.8
To have a complete family	16.3	12.0	21.9	19.3	21.4	21.9	19.2	21.5
To benefit the H/W relationship	13.4	7.6	15.6	19.7	7.1	12.2	11.5	12.9
To give love to the child	11.8	13.0	15.6	11.9	28.6	11.0	7.7	10.8
To give to child (not spec. love)	4.0	2.2	6.3	6.7	7.1	4.1	7.7	3.2
Love and companionship in old age	4.6	2.2	0.0	7.4	7.1	3.5	3.9	4.3
Stimulation and fun:								
Stimulation, fun, activity	52.3	45.7	50.0	35.8	21.4	46.7	65.4	23.7
Pleasure from watching them grow	16.6	12.0	12.5	10.5	14.3	16.3	26.9	12.9
Expansion of self:								
Purpose to life	14.0	7.6	18.8	7.4	7.1	10.3	19.3	4.3
Learning experience	11.3	6.5	12.5	7.7	0.0	6.9	3.9	3.2
Self-fulfillment	5.5	2.2	0.0	6.0	7.1	3.1	0.0	2.2
Part of experiencing life fully	4.2	1.1	3.1	3.9	7.1	3.1	0.0	2.2
To recreate myself; a child like me	4.0	1.1	3.1	2.8	0.0	6.6	7.7	4.3
Carry on the family name	1.4	2.2	0.0	6.0	0.0	3.1	15.4	7.5
Carry on the family line	0.6	1.1	3.1	2.1	0.0	1.9	3.9	5.4
Immortality	0.0	1.1	0.0	1.8	0.0	1.3	0.0	4.3
Adult status and social identity:								
Something useful to do	8.9	2.2	12.5	3.5	14.3	3.8	0.0	1.1
You feel adult; more mature, etc.	6.4	5.4	3.1	4.2	0.0	6.3	3.9	1.1
Socially expected and/or natural	6.6	3.3	3.1	4.6	14.3	6.3	3.9	2.2
Gives man an incentive for working	0.3	1.1	0.0	0.0	7.1	5.0	0.0	3.2
Achievement and creativity:								
To create a life, a human being	2.8	3.3	0.0	6.7	7.1	2.5	0.0	7.5
Satisfaction from doing a good job	5.3	5.4	3.1	7.0	7.1	4.4	3.9	11.8
Economic utility:								
Security in old age	1.2	5.4	0.0	4.6	0.0	1.9	3.9	2.2
Help in household chores	2.3	10.9	3.1	1.4	0.0	2.2	3.9	1.1
Morality:								
Makes you a better person	4.1	5.4	9.4	2.8	0.0	2.2	7.7	0.0
Miscellaneous:								
You can teach them	3.0	3.3	3.1	2.8	0.0	4.4	0.0	3.2
Vague positive attitude	2.2	2.2	6.3	4.2	0.0	1.9	0.0	1.1
There are no advantages	0.4	0.0	0.0	5.3	0.0	0.6	0.0	6.5
N	1,125	92	33	288	14	321	27	95

[a]A maximum of four responses per person were coded.
[b]Racial categories with fewer than ten cases have been omitted.
[c]Includes Chicano or Mexican-American, Latin American, and Puerto Rican.
SOURCE: Lois Wladis Hoffman and Jean Denby Manis, "The Value of Children in the United States: A New Approach to the Study of Fertility," *Journal of Marriage and the Family,* August 1979, p. 586.

imagination has ten children. They have to share two bicycles among them. There isn't enough money for these children to take music lessons or go to summer camp. The younger children seldom wear anything but hand-me-downs. This family almost never has steak or goes to restaurants or even has very much meat or other nourishing foods— at least not in the way the two-child family does. The children in the large family therefore have colds more often. They also don't do as well in school and can't study quietly at home because of the lack of privacy. Their parents don't feel the family can afford to send the children to college (Frankel, 1970:48).

Readers of this children's book are being confronted with a traditionally unpopular and underrated fact: There are *costs* as well as rewards involved in having children.

Material Costs in Having Children

From prenatal care through delivery, from childrearing days through college, children are expensive (Espenshade, 1973, 1984; Edwards, 1981; Olson, 1983). Economists point out that the financial costs of children are twofold: *direct* costs (money spent for children's needs) and *indirect* or "opportunity-loss" *costs* (alternatives which have to be passed by or given up for the sake of the children).

Direct costs of having children are quite obvious: food, clothing, shelter, medical and dental care, toys and recreation, vacation trips, education, and much more. Exactly what such costs add up to varies according to social class, the ages of the children, the number of children (the more children in a family, the less spent per child, but the more spent altogether), and the family's lifestyle (for example, are they rural or urban?). Costs rise as the child grows older, and of course costs rise as more children are added to the

family. However, the cost of the first child is approximately twice as much as the cost of a second child in a two-child family.

Indirect costs of having children may not be so obvious. They include such losses as doing without that extra room planned for a den because the new baby needs a bedroom. Or parents may have to forgo savings and investment plans because children make it necessary to spend most of the income immediately. The family's standard of living might be lower because caring for children's essential needs means less money left over for consumption items desired by parents (Mueller, 1972).

One indirect or "opportunity cost" of having children is the loss of potential family income which often results from a mother's being kept from labor-force participation. If a mother is employed, some of the family's income will likely be used to pay for child care during the hours she is at work. Such consequences of having a child (or an additional child) are included when economists compute estimated material costs of parenthood.

At the same time, couples may be well aware of the sacrifices and expenses involved in childrearing and still feel the experience of parenthood is worth it all. "Economic considerations appear to be important in setting an upper limit to the number of children desired," write Hoffman and Manis (1979:595), "but it also appears that, if the needs that children satisfy are important enough and, if there are no acceptable alternative ways of satisfying these needs, considerable costs will be endured in order to achieve the benefits" (see also Blake, 1979).

Costs of Children to the Husband-Wife Relationship

According to popular folklore, having children draws a husband and wife closer together. It doesn't always work that way. Social psychologist Jum C. Nunnally (1972) points out that for years, psychologists have given attention to the effects of parents on children, but only in recent years has some attention been given to the other side of the coin, the effects of children on parents.

Nunnally became impressed with this aspect of parent-child relations while working with a colleague on studies of schizophrenic children. "Although it could not be firmly established from the research results," Nunnally writes, "I developed the definite impression that the disrupted home from which the schizophrenic child frequently came was more a product of the child's disrupting the rest of the family than the cause of the child's schizophrenia." He explains further: "The child was a constant source of strain for the other family members—causing embarrassment before neighbors and continual trouble in school, indifferent to affection, requiring many forms of expensive care, and a source of shame to parents and contention between them." Nunnally found that in a number of case studies, there appeared to be a gradual deterioration of the families as time went on.

Traditionally, marriage has been viewed as a step in which "two become one." Parenthood means that two become three—or four or even more. And this can spell difficulties even in homes that do not face the kinds of problems Nunnally studied.

On the basis of research among a probability sample of more than five thousand adults, sociologist Karen Renne (1970) reported that "people currently raising children were more likely to be dissatisfied with their marriages than people who had never had children, or whose children had left home, regardless of race, age or income level." She offers several explanations for this finding. First, there is the possibility that couples are less apt to file for divorce if their are children at home. Thus, couples with children may continue in unsatisfactory marriages while childless couples would feel more free to separate. Although she did not test this assumption, Renne suggests that "presumably the unhappiest marriages among childless couples and those whose children have grown up have already been dissolved."

A second possible explanation has to do with the demands parenthood makes on a woman and man, since it means an abrupt role transition—one for which many couples are not prepared (Rossi, 1968). It is one thing to be a wife or husband; it is quite another to be a mother or father as well. The relationship between the spouses may be altered drastically by the baby's arrival. Robert Ryder's (1973) research analysis of a study conducted by the National Institute of Mental Health indicates that having a child may result in a wife's feeling dissatisfied with the amount of attention her husband pays to her—either because husbands are less attentive after a baby arrives or else because wives simply desire more attention and assistance at this time.

The finding that marital satisfaction is lowered by the presence of children has shown up in numerous studies (Spanier and Lewis, 1980; Glenn and McLanahan, 1982; Polonko, Scanzoni, and Teachman, 1982; Belsky, Lang, and Rovine, 1985). Sociologist Harold Feldman (1971) found that husbands and wives who had a close relationship with one another during the wife's pregnancy were not brought closer together by the child's birth but rather felt their marital satisfaction dropped. He postulates that to such closely knit couples, a baby may be an "interference factor," producing a decline in husband-wife companionship, with the husband in particular feeling cheated of his wife's attention. Where an *increase* in marital satisfaction occurred after becoming parents, the couples were less likely to have had a closely knit husband-wife relationship beforehand. It may be that such couples expect to be drawn closer together as they find in the baby a common interest, a conversation piece, and a reason to work together in joint tasks.

Some research has shown that the affectional and sexual relationship of a husband and wife may be negatively affected by parenthood (Christensen, 1968; Feldman, 1971). Infants mean interruptions and require parents to be constantly "on duty." The time and energy demands of parenting may mean less time and energy for the kind of sex life a couple had enjoyed previously. As children grow older, privacy increasingly becomes a problem. Spontaneous moments of romance at unusual times become difficult, and plans and strategies for uninterrupted lovemaking may have to be arranged. In a study of four categories of *employed* wives (mothers with infants, mothers with preschoolers, mothers with both infants and preschoolers, and childless wives), Douglas Abbott and Gene Brody (1985:82) found that "all categories of mothers reported having more disagreements regarding affectional expression than did the childless wives." These researchers see these results as reflecting "an ecological reality." They explain that employed wives, when still serving as primary caretakers of their children, may find their responsibilities overwhelming. As a result, "affectional concerns, by necessity, then assume a low priority."

In considering the overall impact of children on a marriage relationship, factors such as family income, race, and wife employment may all have a part to play. Much more research needs to be done, taking these and other variables into account. (See Houseknecht, 1979.) For example, Renne's research cited earlier showed some evidence that for black men, the economic pressures of parenthood, rather than parenthood itself, are major factors in determining dissatisfaction. For black women, another factor may enter in. Black wives with children present did not report less dissatisfaction when family income was higher, in contrast to black husbands with children present. One possible explanation is that black wives are likely to be contributing to the family income, and the presence of children makes employment much more difficult.

Still another factor that needs to be taken into consideration in understanding how children affect marital satisfaction is *choice* or *intentionality.* In a study of two categories of couples—a group of highly educated couples who had delayed both marriage and parenthood and then deliberately chosen to be parents and a group of childless couples who had just as deliberately chosen *not* to be parents—Harold Feldman (1981) found that levels of satisfaction with their marriages were very similar for the two groups. He concluded from this data that "when couples have intentionally chosen their own life-styles, those respective life-styles are equally satisfactory and viable" (p. 599).

One final way that having children may affect the husband-wife relationship is in the area of disagreements. In Chapter 12, we saw that husbands and wives tend to disagree over money and children more than over other concerns of marriage. One cost of having children is the necessity of spreading family income over a wider range of persons and needs. Disagreements over childrearing practices may also be costly to the husband-wife relationship, causing dissension that would have been avoided had the couple not had children.

Costs of Children in Terms of Freedom

Even if husbands and wives agree on childrearing practices, the actual carrying out of all the day-to-day responsibilities involved may seem costly in terms of freedom. Parents are expected to be concerned about their children's mental, emotional, physical, spiritual, and social development. Such a task means an investment of enormous amounts of time and energy which the parents might otherwise have put into individualistic pursuits.

Children complicate life, not only in terms of the sheer physical work they occasion but also in the way they can upset schedules, interfere with plans, and make exceedingly complex what were once simple procedures—things like going on a trip ("We'll have to take the playpen," "Did you get Cindy's diaper bag and baby food, honey?" "Where is Michael's medicine for car sickness?") or planning a night at the movies ("But, Darling, I've tried every baby-sitter I know of! It's not *my* fault Judy called us at the last minute to cancel out") or even a trip to the grocery store ("Peter! Where are your boots? Oh, why must it always rain on shopping day?" "No, the baby gets to ride in the shopping cart; there isn't room for you." "Jennifer! Don't stand on the shelf like that—watch out for those jelly jars! Oh, no!" CRASH).

Other costs of children include being inconvenienced, making adjustments in living conditions (such as growing accustomed to noise, messes, less privacy, and crowding), emotional stress (worrying over a sick child, fearing the worst when a teenager is late getting home with the car), and feeling tied down and unable to carry out travel and recreation plans freely.

Hoffman (1972a) found in one study that some university students felt their own parents had been failures at childrearing and were afraid they might not be any more successful themselves in bringing up children. To these students, the difficulty of rearing a child and the fear of failure meant viewing childrearing as costly. But for those students who expected success in parenthood, childrearing and all its difficulties were thought of in terms of a challenge—a value, not a cost.

Much more research on satisfactions and dissatisfactions in having children remains to be done. Sociologist Ann Goetting (1986) points out the methodological limitations and inadequacies in conceptualizing and measuring parental satisfaction that have flawed much of the existing body of research. She especially calls attention to the lack of longitudinal studies, which could show how the passage of time enters into parents' feelings about the rewards and costs of parenthood.

GENDER ROLES AND FERTILITY CONTROL

Bob and Julie, the hypothetical couple we followed in Chapters 11 and 12, found that attitudes toward gender roles and attitudes toward having children are closely linked. When their outlook on marriage was more traditional, they both considered Bob to occupy the chief provider role even though Julie worked, too. During the early months of marriage, Julie was not committed to a career but fully expected to drift in and out of the labor market, depending on the needs of her family. Both she and Bob planned that she would quit work when they had a baby and would probably remain at home while the children were small.

Then things began to change. As Julie became interested in commitment to a career, her conception of her role moved from *traditional* (being a wife and mother is a woman's most important calling, and a woman must subordinate her interests to those of her family) to *egalitarian* or *modern* (a woman should strive to use all her talents and abilities to achieve in the economic-opportunity sphere, just as a man is expected to do). No longer was Julie so willing to give up her work in order to bear and rear children. She began wondering if she even wanted any children. A large part in the ongoing negotiations of this couple centered on decisions about children.

Increasingly, social scientists have begun giving attention to how fertility control relates to gender roles (Cramer, 1980). Do choices to bear or not to bear children have anything to do with how men and women conceive of the "proper" or "desirable" roles for males and females? How does employment affect a woman's fertility? Employed wives have fewer children than non-employed wives, but does this mean that they deliberately choose to have fewer children because they want or have to work? Or do they work because they have no or few children and therefore fill up their time with a job?

Many studies have shown not only that employed mothers in the United States and other industrialized countries have fewer children but also that unmarried women who plan to be in the work force desire smaller families (see summary in Hoffman and Hoffman, 1973:64; Hoffman and Manis, 1979:595; Fox, 1982; Sweet, 1982).

On the other hand, this pattern of wife employment and lower fertility is not so clearcut in nonindustrialized societies. Sociologist Paula Hass (1972) has examined the proposition that the crucial variable in determining the relationship between wife employment and family size is the extent to which the mother role and the worker role are viewed as incompatible. In developing nations, women have often had a tradition of combining work and motherhood, and working has not meant a lowering of fertility. Women could easily be workers and mothers for at least two reasons. First, the home is the center of economic activity, with women often working in simple cottage industries (such as weaving or pottery making) or in agricultural tasks, with children close by. Second, child care is readily available in the form of the extended family, with a number of relatives usually willing to serve as substitute mothers.

However, the changes involved as societies move toward urbanization and industrialization make the worker and mother roles less compatible. Extended families are not so close by, and child-care arrangements become more difficult. Employment normally takes place away from the home in devel-

As alternative rewards such as educational and employment opportunities become available, women in developing countries may choose to have fewer children. (Barbara Kirk/Peter Arnold, Inc.)

oped societies, geographically separating mothers and children. In such cases, it becomes exceedingly difficult for a woman to be employed and at the same time to be the mother of many children. We may expect her to have fewer children if she wants to continue working. But even more crucial, according to Hass, are the woman's attitudes. If she is highly educated and does not think in terms of traditional gender-role stereotypes, and if she is motivated to achieve occupationally and views the role of worker as an *alternative* to motherhood, she is likely to limit her family size to avoid role incompatibility as much as possible.

Hoffman and Hoffman (1973:65–67) make a distinction between employment as an alternative to fertility and employment as a barrier to fertility. A woman who chooses the gratifications of occupational achievement as an *alternative* to the gratifications of children will have lower fertility not because employment prevents her from having more children but because she wants fewer children in order to devote herself more fully to her occupation. In contrast, the woman who views employment as a *barrier* to higher fertility will have fewer children because working makes motherhood more difficult; she might prefer to have a larger family but knows that as long as she must work or wants to work, it would be hard to have additional children.

Hoffman and Hoffman suggest that if employment operates only as a barrier and not as an alternative to motherhood, child-care facilities could have the effect of increasing rather than decreasing fertility by removing the obstacles that cause much of the mother-worker role incompatibility. Social-policy planners sometimes overlook these distinctions between employment-as-barrier and employment-as-alternative by stating simply that providing job opportunities for women will bring about declines in birthrates. The attitudes, motivations, and gender-role norms held by women are more crucial than is the fact of employment in itself.

Our own large-scale study, which investigated whether and how gender-role norms affect fertility, provided data which clearly show that *the gender-role norms women hold affect both the number of children they intend to have and the number of children they actually do have* (Scanzoni, 1975b). Let's take four hypothetical cases to see how this association between norms and fertility works.

HYPOTHETICAL CASE 1

Dorothy is 28 years old, black, and has a master's degree in social work. Her father is a high school teacher, and her mother is a librarian. Dorothy's husband is a gynecologist. The couple have been married for three years and have no children at this time, although they would like to have children later. Dorothy has been employed as a social worker since before her marriage, and she plans to take off only a couple of months when they have a baby and then return to work.

HYPOTHETICAL CASE 2

Ginny is 22 years old. In answer to the question "Occupation?" she replies, "Housewife—or better yet, homemaker." Ginny is white, Catholic, and married her high school boyfriend at age 18, the same month they graduated. Ginny comes from a family that is religiously devout, participating in the mass regularly; and she and her husband also devoutly practice their religious faith. During Ginny's growing-up years, her father was an auto mechanic and her mother was a full-time housewife. Ginny's husband presently sells appliances in a large department store. The couple have two children and are expecting a third in two months. "This one wasn't planned for," Ginny laughs, "but we'll be glad to welcome him to the family anyway—especially if it's a boy! Our first two are girls." She reports that they had their first daughter in the first year of marriage, and thus she has never held a job.

HYPOTHETICAL CASE 3

Twenty-year-old Debra is black and the mother of three children. The first child was conceived before her marriage, and the last two were born ten months apart. "We tried to keep from having the babies so close together," she says. "But things just didn't work out. It's just too easy to get pregnant. We couldn't keep it from happening, and I expect it'll happen again." Debra's mother works as a cook in a school cafeteria, and her father is a service station attendant. Debra did not complete high school and works part-time as a housekeeper whenever her husband's mother can come over to take care of the children. Debra's husband is employed as a taxicab driver and is seldom home, a point of contention between them.

HYPOTHETICAL CASE 4

Linda—32 years old, white, non-Catholic—is a lawyer with a busy practice. She and her husband (also an attorney) have been married seven years and have two children carefully spaced three years apart. Their son is 4 years old; their daughter is 1. Both are cared for by a live-in housekeeper, who loves them as though they were her own grandchildren.

If a sociologist were to interview these same women twenty years from now, which women would be likely to have the greatest number of children? Which would be likely to have the fewest?

How Gender-Role Norms Affect Decisions about Having Children

Based upon data from our research project as well as from other studies, it is likely that Dorothy (case 1) and Linda (case 4) would have the fewest number of children. Both Ginny (case 2) and Debra (case 3) would be likely to have larger families than either of the other two women. Gender-role norms play a large part in explaining these differences. But remember these are hypothetical case studies, used for purposes of illustration only. Sociologists are not concerned with predicting the behavior of particular *individuals* but, rather, give attention to patterns of behavior and trends among groups of persons who have certain characteristics in common. These hypothetical cases are presented in an effort to illuminate some of our findings from a large probability sample.

Dorothy's Case Demographer Paul Glick (1981) cites government statistics to show that highly educated black women have tended to have very low birthrates. He explains that "Black women with advanced college education may tend to find it necessary to limit their family size especially severely in order to be competitive in the world of work" (p. 112). We saw earlier that the *tradition of labor-force participation for black wives* has encouraged more egalitarian gender roles at all status levels than has been true of comparable whites (Scanzoni, 1977). But at higher status levels, additional factors enter in to reinforce this traditional bent toward greater egalitarianism. Take Dorothy's

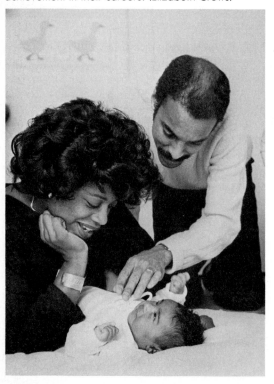

Highly educated black women tend to have very low birthrates because of their strong commitment to achievement in their careers. (Elizabeth Crews)

case, for example. Dorothy comes from a family in which both parents had college educations and both held professional positions. Their higher socioeconomic status indicates that they were likely to socialize their children toward more egalitarian gender roles than were families of lower socioeconomic status. Furthermore, Dorothy herself is highly educated and committed to a career, and at age 25 married a man whose education, occupation, and income indicate high social status. All of these factors fit well with findings about both black and white women in our research project (Scanzoni, 1975b).

The study showed that the higher the family-background social status, the greater would be the egalitarianism that showed up in gender-role norms. Similarly, greater egalitarianism was also associated with higher levels of education. Higher education and greater egalitarian in gender-role norms meant such women were likely to marry later than other women. Also, *married* women who were found to score high on egalitarian gender-role norms were more likely than were other married women to be employed full-time. Finally, the data all fit together in such a way as to make this point: The greater the *egalitarianism* in gender-role norms and the fact of *full-time employment*, and the *greater the education* and the *later the age at marriage*, the lower the total number of births younger married women intended to have.

Ginny's Case Moving on to the second hypothetical case, we find that Ginny illustrates some other patterns that showed up in our research. Unlike Dorothy, Ginny grew up in a blue-collar home where the parents held traditional gender-role norms and socialized their children accordingly. Ginny herself holds traditional gender-role norms reinforced by her religious faith, which she adheres to devoutly. She married young, did not go on for further education after high school, had children early in marriage, and has experienced one timing failure in child spacing. Some findings from our research clearly relate to Ginny's situation.

In research of this sort, certain factors fit with one another much like pieces of a jigsaw puzzle so that gradually the whole picture begins to be seen. For example, the lower the family social-status background was and the lower the level of education a woman had reached, the more traditional were the gender-role norms she held. Similarly, the more traditional a woman's gender-role norms were, combined with lower education, the more likely she was to marry much earlier than other women. Also, the more traditional were the gender-role norms held by a married woman, the less likely she was to be employed full-time. And among Roman Catholic women, the more traditional were the gender-role norms they held, the greater their religious devoutness was found to be.

What does this have to do with how many children Ginny is likely to have? Traditionally, the greater the religious devoutness, the greater has been conformity to church teachings on birth control. Thus, religiously devout Catholics (those who receive communion at least once monthly) have been those least likely to have fertility-control patterns resembling those of white non-Catholics in comparable life situations. Recently, as we have seen however, the gap seems to be narrowing, and Ginny's childbearing career may be less predictable on this count (Westoff and Jones, 1979a).

Remember Ginny's comment about their third child's being unplanned? This could also be an indicator of more children later on. Our research showed that couples who report having children when unintended (timing failures) also tend to report having more children overall. At the same time, something interesting showed up among the Roman Catholic women in the study. Catholics who had experienced timing failures in the past were more likely to hold more egalitarian gender-role norms in the present (Scanzoni, 1975b). It is not clear whether this means that displeasure with contraceptive failures caused women to become more individualistic later on or whether there had been individualistic tendencies that were put aside for the sake of family-centered interests during the earlier years of marriage and then reemerged.

Our study also showed that among nonemployed Catholic wives, there was a positive relationship between the husband's income and the number of children. More income meant more children—both in the present and intended in the future. Catholics have tended to accept, more than non-Catholics, the idea that "good persons would have as many children as they can afford." If the earnings of Ginny's husband increase, the couple is likely to have more children.

Shall We Try One More Time for a Girl? (Boy?) There is another way in which gender may enter into the number of children Ginny will have. Recall her statement that the first two children were girls and they were now hoping for a boy. Several studies have indicated that couples like to have children of both sexes (Williamson, 1976). If a husband and wife have two or more girls and no boys or two or more boys and no girls, they are more likely to "try again" for another child than are couples who have a child of each sex. The Princeton Fertility Study, a longitudinal study in which the same couples were studied over a sixteen-year period, provided data which indicate that the sex composition of the family does affect family size.

Couples who fail to achieve the desired sex composition within the number of children originally intended are likely to change their plans and have additional children in an effort to have the sex composition they want (Westoff, Potter, and Sagi, 1963:205–207). Couples are more likely to have a third, fourth, or even fifth child if all the preceding offspring were of the same sex; and this is especially true if the preceding offspring were girls. The final report of the Princeton Fertility Study showed that "couples whose first two children are boys are 11 percent more likely to have another child than are couples whose first two children included a child of each sex." But "if the first two children were girls the probability of a third birth is 24 percent higher than if there was a child of each sex" (Bumpass and Westoff, 1970:93–94).

Other social scientists have pointed out a continued preference for boys, not only in traditionally patriarchal societies such as Chinese families in Taiwan (Wu, 1972), but also in modern industrial societies. After an exhaustive survey of studies conducted in the United States and Europe between 1931 and 1975, social demographer Nancy Williamson (1976:63) reports "evidence of slight boy preference especially for firstborns, desire for one of each sex, and preference for a predominance of boys over a predominance of girls if a balanced number of each was not chosen." And while men have a *stronger* preference for sons than women do, women also lean toward boy-preference—though to a lesser degree.

One study based upon a large nationwide probability sample showed that just under one-half of 15- to 45-year-old married women in the United States have a preference for male children. Just under one-third prefer female children, while sightly less than one-fifth express a preference for boys and girls equally (Coombs, 1977). Preferences were measured according to how respondents replied to the question: "If you were to have exactly three children, would you most like to have three girls, one boy and two girls, two boys and one girl, or three boys?" Unless the respondents indicated the strongest possible preference for one sex or the other (5 percent said they would like all boys, and 3 percent said they would like all girls), they were asked a series of questions about *alternate* choices and then scored according to the way their preferences leaned.

A 1954 study of men and women of marriageable age was duplicated nearly twenty years later among university students by different researchers. Similar findings emerged both times: when asked which sex these men and women would prefer their first child to be or when asked which sex they would like an only child to be, they overwhelmingly chose a boy ("Sexism on the Stork Market," *Human Behavior*, January 1974, pp. 45–46 [comparison of Dinitz, Dynes, and Clark, 1954, with Peterson and Peterson, 1973]). There was, however, a slight increase in the percentage of persons to whom the sex of their firstborn didn't matter; and when it came to the sex of an only child, the percentage of men who wanted a boy decreased from 92 percent in 1954 to 81 percent in 1973. Among women, there was little change as to preferred sex for an only child; about two-thirds indicated a preference for a boy in both surveys. Since the shift in attitudes occurred only among the men, psychologists Candida Peterson and James Peterson felt that the explanation lay in economics rather than the ideology of the feminist movement. Girls are no longer considered a financial liability as they were in the days when they were considered extra mouths to feed until the day they were married off. Now daughters grow up and support themselves just as sons traditionally did—which may in itself be more indicative of feminism (in the sense of changes toward egalitarian gender roles) than these researchers were ready to admit (Peterson and Peterson, 1973).

Sociologist Gerald E. Markle (1973, 1974) found that among university students, one-third had no preference regarding the sex of their first child; but among those who did indicate a preference, the choice was 12 to 1 in favor of a boy. And in a general sample of persons living in Tallahassee, Florida, Markle found that the preference for a boy was 19 to 1. Markle's studies showed that respondents holding *traditional* gender-role ideologies were much more likely to state that they preferred their first child to be a boy than were respondents holding *egalitarian* gender-role ideologies. This research demonstrated what Markle had hypothesized from a survey of literature showing that, in virtually all cultures around the world, male babies are preferred; namely, that "an ideology of male superiority" affects first-child sex preference.

But what if there were a movement away from notions of male superiority and male privilege? An egalitarian ideology tends to abolish ideas about the unique character of boys, thus lowering their "market value" and reducing desires for them. As a result, the overall number of children desired by couples should be lowered because the pressure to "keep trying for a boy" would be eliminated. But in our hypothetical case study of Ginny, the desire for a boy is strong and is reinforced by the traditional gender-role norms held by her and her husband. Chances are that they will have more children in an effort to make sure they have one or more sons.

Debra's Case Moving on to hypothetical case 3, we find that Debra's lower social status (both in terms of the present and her parental background), lower education, early

age at marriage, premarital pregnancy, and past timing failures are all factors calling for predictions of high fertility over the course of her married life. A return visit by an interviewer twenty years after the first interview would likely turn up information that Debra had become the mother of a large family.

Why? In addition to the factors mentioned, plus some of those that applied to Ginny in case 2, three other findings from our research apply to Debra. First, a shorter interval between the time of marriage and the time of the first child's birth is a good indication that a higher number of children will be born in the marriage than if the interval had been longer. Second, the higher the number of children, the lower the satisfactions that are felt to be experienced in both the economic and expressive dimensions of marriage. And third, the greater the traditionalism in gender-role norms (related to socialization in childhood, socioeconomic status, education, age at marriage, and so on), the less likely are wives to be currently using efficient and effective means of contraception and the lower is their confidence that they will be able to prevent unintended births and "spacing and number failures."

Linda's Case The remaining hypothetical case study focuses on Linda. The propositions that describe Dorothy in the first case study also apply to case 4. Linda's egalitarian gender-role norms, high education, high socioeconomic status, later age of marriage, and full-time employment before her children were born as well as full-time employment at present all combine to indicate the likelihood that her family will remain small. In fact, her family may already be completed in that she has two children, a boy and a girl (although given her egalitarian gender-role views, this one-of-each-sex composition shouldn't matter), and she has confidence that unintended births will be prevented because she has had no timing failures in the past, having effectively used efficient methods of contraception. Two final propositions from our research fit Linda's case: (1) among employed wives, the greater the job status and income, the lower the number of children and (2), among white non-Catholic wives who are employed or who are well-educated, the greater the egalitarianism in gender-role norms, the less likelihood there is of past contraceptive timing failures ("accidental" conceptions). Thus the lower the fertility overall, since among all groupings (black, white, Catholic, and non-Catholic) timing failures and number of children are positively related.

The one reason that Linda might possibly choose to have an additional child relates to her having found satisfactory child-care arrangements, with the result that her mother role and career role are not incompatible at this time. But given all the other information we have on Linda, it is unlikely that she will have more children.

Summary Statement on Gender-Role Norms and Fertility In summarizing these hypothetical cases illustrating our research on how gender-role norms affect fertility, we can state the following: The greater the *individualism* (a woman's desire for personal and occupational achievement and for freedom to pursue her own interests), the less will be the *familism* (a woman's desire to center her life around husband and children). And the lower the familism, the lower will be the number of children intended and the number of children actually born. Similarly, we found that among unmarried university students, the more egalitarian the gender-role norms held, the fewer the number of children intended (Scanzoni, 1975c).

What about men? It appears that men who hold egalitarian views and are open to achievement aspirations in women are also willing to have fewer children. But men have a relatively lower sense of compulsion in the matter. In marital negotiations, we may expect that more egalitarian husbands will simply go along with their wives' limited birth intentions rather than actively taking a part or assuming a leadership role in formulating such plans. On the other hand, husbands who are more traditional might actively attempt to influence their wives' thinking, particularly if the husbands desire more children than do their wives. Or such husbands might simply be less cooperative with respect to contraception. ("Ah, come on, Joanie, don't be a spoilsport! Nothing's going to happen just this one time! And so what if it does? It might be kinda nice to have a new baby.") However, a great deal more research needs to be done on marital decision-making about having or not having more children.

CONTRACEPTION, STERILIZATION, AND ABORTION

A century ago, a federal statute known as the *Comstock Law* (named for a self-appointed vice hunter named Anthony Comstock) made it illegal to distribute birth-control information and materials through the mails. Druggists who sold contraceptive devices were arrested. Various states had their own legislation making it a crime to distribute contraceptive literature, illegal for physicians to prescribe contraceptive devices, or even (as in Connecticut) against the law for couples—single or married—to use contraceptive devices.

Many of these anticontraceptive measures continued into this present century, some until recently. The clergy denounced birth control as sinful, and Theodore Roosevelt warned of "race suicide." Condoms were referred to as "rubber articles for immoral use." In the 1920s, when the birth-control-movement leader Margaret Sanger needed diaphragms to distribute to women who came to her birth-control clinic, she was unable to obtain such contraceptives in the United States and had to purchase them from abroad. American manufacturers were by then permitted to manufacture contraceptive devices but refused to make the reliable Mensinga diaphragm and, instead, made unsatisfactory cervical caps. However, it was illegal to import contraceptives. Margaret Sanger's clinic therefore obtained them through illegal channels, importing them from Germany by way of Canada, from where they were smuggled across the border in oil drums (Kennedy, 1970:42, 183, 218).

Times have changed. Birth control is a fact of life in modern industrial societies, having gained widespread public acceptance and support. How successfully couples practice the limitation of their families depends on a combination of motivation and methods.

Contraceptive Practices

During the 1960s, a large drop in the rate of unwanted births occurred. Contraceptives were becoming more extensively used and used earlier, the more efficient methods were becoming more widely used and used more consistently, and there appeared to be greater motivation to avoid pregnancy among many women (Westoff, 1972). According to the National Survey of Family Growth (NSFG), conducted periodically since 1955 by the National Center for Health Statistics, nearly two-thirds of births to married women occurring within the five years prior to the 1965 survey were *unplanned.* Either these women didn't want the births at all, or else they had become pregnant sooner than they had wanted to.

By the time of the 1973 survey, a dramatic change had taken place. Then only 37 percent of births during the five years before the survey were unplanned births. A decade later, only 29 percent of such births were unplanned (*Family Planning Perspectives,* 1985a:36).

However, even though there has been a drop in unwanted births, nearly 30 percent of children born to married women are still the result of unplanned pregnancies. And about 10 percent of children born to married women, according to NSFG data, are unwanted children (*Family Planning Perspectives,* 1985a).

Norman B. Ryder (1973:141–142), a sociologist who specializes in population research, emphasizes that both *methods* and *motivation* enter into contraceptive success and failure. Ryder defines *contraceptive failure* as "an unplanned pregnancy which occurs in an interval during which use of contraception is reported." He found that we can better understand contraceptive failure if we look at a couple's intentions. Were they attempting to *delay* the next pregnancy or to *prevent* it altogether? He found that regardless of the method used, more failures occurred when couples planned only to delay a pregnancy. Evidently, if there are plans to have another baby sometime anyway, more chances are taken, whereas efforts at contraception are more rigorous if the desire is to prevent an *unwanted* pregnancy. Motivation makes considerable difference. (See also Grady et al., 1986.)

Methods of Contraception Used "Today, at least nine out of 10 women, both married and unmarried, are familiar with all methods of contraception," report researchers Jacqueline Darroch Forrest and Stanley Henshaw (1983:157). They contrast this with the early 1970s, when less than three-fourths of married women were aware of methods such as the intrauterine device (IUD) and spermicides in addition to the more familiar birth control pill and condom.

By 1982, 93 percent of married women at risk of an unintended pregnancy were using some contraceptive method. (Wives *not* at risk of an unintended pregnancy are those who are already pregnant, postpartum, trying to become pregnant, or unable to conceive because of nonsurgical or noncontraceptive sterility.) Tables 13-B and 13-C show what currently married women have been doing to prevent or postpone pregnancy. Table 13-B shows similarities and differences in the contraceptive practices of black wives and white wives in the United States between 1973 and 1982, while Table 13-C examines the contraceptive practices of wives in Canada according to religion, which again shows the movement away from adherence to traditional Roman Catholic teachings on birth control.

Pregnancy Risk and Gender-Role Norms

Some methods of birth control are less effective than others in preventing pregnancy. To use them is to take chances. Examples are male withdrawal before ejaculation, douching immediately after sexual intercourse, and "natural family planning" methods requiring periodic abstinence. (Various forms of natural family planning, including the older calendar rhythm method, are the only methods officially endorsed by the Roman Catholic Church.)

In analyzing our research on how fertility relates to gender-role norms, we found that women who sought *individualistic* rewards more than familistic rewards were unlikely to use such high-risk methods of contraception. They tended to use more effective methods—the pill, intrauterine devices (IUD), or very diligent use of the diaphragm with a spermicidal cream or jelly—or their husbands carefully used condoms. Women who ranked higher on *familism* than individualism, on the other hand, were using methods that placed them at high risk of pregnancy (Scanzoni, 1975b).

It became apparent that the risk-taking level in contraception indicates the degree to which women are indifferent to the *costs* of children or even actually desirous of the *rewards* of children. Women who hold more traditional gender-role norms may think of an unplanned pregnancy as a "surprise," perhaps, but they are not likely to think of such an event as a "disaster," as might women holding egalitarian gender-role norms and individualistic aspirations. Women who strongly believe in pursuing their own interests (such as career achievement) cannot afford to be indifferent to the costs of children. Any children born to them must be carefully planned both as to number and timing. Egalitarian wives are therefore more motivated than are traditional wives to choose the most reliable birth-control methods and then to use those methods with great care to avoid failure.

This finding is one more piece of evidence that motivation plays a highly significant role in fertility control. Improved methods made possible by advances in research and technology are of great importance but are not, in themselves, enough. No matter how *theoretically* effective a particular contraceptive technique is, its *actual* effectiveness will, in large measure, depend upon the user. Women who forget to take their birth-control pills or couples who occasionally neglect to insert diaphragms or to use condoms can expect contraceptive failures, not because the

TABLE 13-B Number of currently married women 15–44 years of age and percent distribution by current contraceptive status and method, according to race: United States, 1973, 1976, and 1982. (Statistics are based on samples of the household population of the conterminous United States. Data for 1982 are preliminary.)

CONTRACEPTIVE STATUS AND METHOD	ALL RACES[1]			WHITE			BLACK		
	1982	1976[2]	1973[2]	1982	1976[2]	1973[2]	1982	1976[2]	1973[2]
	Number in Thousands								
All currently married women	28,231	27,488	26,646	25,195	24,795	24,249	2,130	2,169	2,081
	Percent Distribution								
Total	100.0	100.0	100.0	100.0	100.0	100.0	100.0	100.0	100.0
Sterile	40.9	30.0	23.9	41.1	30.7	24.0	37.8	24.4	22.7
Surgically sterile	38.9	28.2	22.9	38.9	29.0	23.2	36.3	21.6	20.8
Contraceptively sterile	27.9	18.6	16.4	28.2	19.3	16.5	23.2	12.7	14.6
Female	17.4	9.5	8.6	17.0	9.6	8.2	21.0	10.9	13.6
Male	10.4	9.0	7.8	11.2	9.7	8.4	2.2	*1.7	1.0
Noncontraceptively sterile	11.1	9.7	6.5	10.7	9.7	6.6	13.2	9.0	6.2
Female	10.1	8.9	6.3	9.8	8.9	6.3	13.1	8.7	6.1
Male	*1.0	0.7	0.2	*1.0	0.8	0.3	*0.1	-	*0.1
Nonsurgically sterile	*2.0	1.7	0.9	*2.1	1.7	0.8	*1.4	2.7	1.9
Pregnant, post partum	7.2	6.8	7.3	7.2	6.8	7.4	6.1	6.8	6.8
Seeking pregnancy	6.7	6.5	7.0	6.6	5.9	6.8	8.5	9.6	7.1
Other nonusers	5.0	7.6	8.7	4.5	7.1	7.8	9.8	13.3	17.9
Nonsurgical contraceptors	40.1	49.2	53.2	40.6	49.5	54.0	*37.8	45.9	45.4
Pill	13.5	22.5	25.1	13.4	22.6	25.1	15.6	22.2	26.3
IUD	4.8	6.3	6.7	4.8	6.3	6.6	5.9	6.2	7.6
Diaphragm	4.5	2.9	2.4	4.7	3.0	2.5	3.3	1.8	1.2
Condom	9.8	7.3	9.4	10.2	7.5	9.9	4.3	4.6	3.2
Foam	2.0	3.0	3.5	2.0	2.9	3.5	*2.1	3.8	3.0
Periodic abstinence	3.2	3.4	2.8	3.3	3.5	2.9	*2.4	*1.4	*0.8
Withdrawal	*1.2	2.0	1.5	*1.2	2.1	1.6	*0.1	1.8	*0.4
Douche	*0.1	0.7	0.6	0.0	0.6	0.5	*1.0	2.7	1.8
Other	*1.0	1.0	1.3	*0.9	1.0	1.4	*2.1	*1.4	1.0

[1]Includes white, black, and other races

[2]Includes unmarried women living with a partner

*Figure does not meet standards of reliability or precision (30 percent or more relative standard error).

SOURCE: U.S. Department of Health and Human Services, National Center for Health Statistics, Christine Bachrach and William Mosher, "Use of Contraception in the United States, 1982," Advance Data from Vital and Health Statistics, No. 102, December 4, 1984 (Hyattsville, Md.: Public Health Service) p. 3.

TABLE 13-C Percentage distributions of married women 18–49, by current reproductive and contraceptive status, and of currently married users, by method, according to religion, Quebec and the rest of Canada

STATUS AND METHOD	TOTAL (N = 3,283)	CATHOLICS		PROTESTANTS	
		QUEBEC (N = 780)	REST OF CANADA (N = 764)	QUEBEC (N = 37)	REST OF CANADA (N = 1,187)
All Married Women					
Pregnant, postpartum or seeking pregnancy	13.0	12.9	13.2	†	12.4
Noncontraceptively sterile	8.7	9.1	9.4	†	9.2
Not using a method	5.2	2.9	8.4	†	3.9
Using a method	73.1	75.1	69.0	73.0	74.5
Users					
Female sterilization	41.7	43.8	40.5	†	44.2
Male sterilization	17.6	18.9	15.5	†	19.8
Pill	15.0	16.9	15.5	†	13.4
IUD	8.0	6.3	9.5	†	7.1
Diaphragm	1.4	0.0	0.9*	†	2.1
Condom	10.8	8.2	9.5	†	9.9
Foam	0.7	0.0	0.4*	†	1.2
Rhythm	3.0	3.7	4.9	†	1.2
Withdrawal	1.3	1.0*	2.5	†	0.6*
Other	0.6	1.2*	0.8*	†	0.3*
Total	100.0	100.0	100.0	†	100.0

*Relative standard error of 0.30 or more
†Too few cases for analysis
SOURCE: T. R. Balakrishnan, Karol Krotki, and Evelyne Lapierre-Adamcyk, "Contraceptive Use in Canada, 1984," *Family Planning Perspectives*, September/October, 1985, p. 214.

perfect birth-control method is yet to be discovered but, rather, because their motivation in using presently available methods is not strong enough.

One problem pointed out by some feminists is that while some of the more efficient contraceptives may carry low pregnancy risks, they carry other kinds of risks. And for the most part, these risks must be taken by women, not men. For example, certain dangers and serious side effects have been associated with use of the IUD or the pill by some women. Barbara Seaman (1972:219) writes:

"If you doubt that there has been sex discrimination in the development of the pill, try to answer this question: Why *isn't* there a pill for men?" Male biomedical researchers counter with claims that the greater availability of female contraceptive methods is not part of a "male chauvinist plot," nor are scientists "proceeding to research and test contraceptives in order to provide more fun for men, while ignoring the health needs of women." Rather, they point to certain complexities in the male reproductive system that have limited the approaches that can be taken (Segal, 1972). However, research on male contraceptives continues, including investigations into the possible use of sex steroids that would inhibit the production of sperm and possible techniques that could immunize a male against certain components of his own body so that antibodies might stop the production of sperm or cause sperm to be infertile (Bremner and de Kretser, 1975). Of course, side effects are a possibility with a "male pill," too.

But for the present time at least, the possibility of side effects from oral contraceptives for women have kept some individualistic, egalitarian wives from using or continuing to use them—even though the pill is generally considered to be the most reliable means (apart from sterilization) of cutting down the risks of unwanted conception. Data from our research indicate that while women with egalitarian gender-role norms do tend to gravitate toward pill usage, women who are equally committed to individualism and egalitarianism may avoid the pill because of concern about physiological effects, choosing, instead, other reliable, low-risk methods and making them work because of strong motivation (Scanzoni, 1975b).

Apart from sterilization, however, the pill is still the most widely used form of contraception. But its usage has been decreasing. (See Table 13-B.) In the United States in 1973, 1 out of every 4 married women aged 15 to 44 years was taking oral contraceptives. By 1982, only 13.5 percent were on the pill.

Use of the IUD also fell during that same period, no doubt because of adverse publicity. Such serious problems resulted from one IUD design, the Dalkon Shield, that its manufacturer was eventually forced into bankruptcy after paying out vast sums in damage awards and legal costs. IUDs of a different design and without the medical risks of the Dalkon Shield also became virtually unavailable

to women in the United States after the other two major manufacturers of IUDs discontinued marketing them in 1985 and 1986. Their decision stemmed from economic concerns, after publicity surrounding the Dalkon Shield problems increased the likelihood of lawsuits against other manufacturers of IUDs as well and made liability insurance almost impossible to obtain (Forrest, 1986).

While use of oral contraceptives and the IUD has declined, use of the diaphragm and condoms has increased. But by far, the favorite form of contraception among married couples in both the United States and Canada is sterilization, as Tables 13-B and 13-C show. Among *unmarried* women, the pill remains in top place.

Sterilization

In 1983, sterilization surgeries exceeded the 1 million mark in the United States (*Family Planning Perspectives*, 1985b). Fifty-eight percent of these sterilization surgeries were performed on females, and 42 percent were performed on males.

Since sterilization is considered to be *the* lowest-risk method of contraception, the question may arise: do couples with egalitarian gender-role norms choose tubal ligations or vasectomies to a greater degree than do couples holding traditional gender-role norms? Much more research needs to be done to answer this question as well as other questions about why couples choose contraceptive surgery, how they feel about it afterward, and so on. In our own research (Scanzoni, 1975b), we were unable to find any meaningful pattern of variables (not even education) to account for the choice of this "radical" means of birth control by either younger or older couples in our sample.

A number of studies have shown, however, that women with limited education and lower socioeconomic status are more likely to have experienced a tubal ligation than are women with more schooling or who are in higher-income families (Westoff and McCarthy, 1979; Westoff and Jones, 1979b:6; Forrest and Henshaw, 1983; Balakrishnan et al., 1985). Lower-educated women may have turned to contraceptive surgery in a desperate attempt to control fertility after several children and unsuccessful attempts to use other contraceptive techniques. Sometimes pressures for such surgery have come from outside, for example from social agencies. In 1974, the Department of Health, Education, and Welfare issued strict guidelines designed to protect poor and minority persons against *coerced* sterilizations—particularly in the case of minors and adults considered legally incompetent. The guidelines resulted from public protests after federal funds were reported to have been used for the sterilization of two black adolescent girls in Alabama. In another case, physicians were requiring that pregnant women on Medicaid who had two or more children must agree to a tubal ligation or else the physicians would not deliver their babies (Vaughan and Sparer, 1974).

Since lower-educated women have traditionally had more children than higher-educated women, it has been easier for them, if they wanted to be sterilized, to meet contraceptive-surgery eligibility requirements set up by the medical profession. Restrictive policies of physicians, hospitals, and health insurance companies have, in the past, meant that more than free choice was involved if a couple chose sterilization. For example, up until 1969, the official manual of the American College of Obstetricians and Gynecologists (ACOG) recommended that contraceptive operations be performed on women *only* if they were at least 25 years old and had five living children. A 30-year-old woman could not be sterilized unless she had four living children, and a woman 35 years old had to have at least three living children

before she could have a tubal ligation. These suggestions were adopted by most hospitals, some of which had even more restrictive requirements for sterilization. However, many of these restrictions were dropped after 1969 when the ACOG manual discontinued mentioning the old recommendations. Although vasectomies have generally been performed in physicians' offices rather than in hospitals, they too have been subject to restrictions—often the doctors' own ideas about the desired age of a man and number of children he must have before being sterilized (Presser and Bumpass, 1972:20).

In 1970, only 31 percent of married women in the United States approved of tubal sterilization, and only 37 percent approved of vasectomy. But by 1982, 7 out of 10 married women approved of both the female and male methods (Forrest and Henshaw, 1983). With the growing acceptability of sterilization, we may expect more and more couples to consider such surgery when they want either no additional children or no children at all. Already by 1979, sterilization had become "the single most popular method [of preventing conception] for couples married 10 years or more" (Westoff and Jones, 1979b:6). Both the male and female surgical procedures can now be performed on an outpatient basis, which has increased their popularity in recent years.

Among both black and white couples, the person sterilized is more likely to be the wife than the husband, although the gap is narrower among whites. As Table 13-B shows, only 2.2 percent of black married women are protected by their husbands' vasectomies. The corresponding figure for white married women is 11.2 percent. As might be expected, the election of sterilization as a method of contraception increases as women grow older. After age 35, the risks associated with the pill increase considerably (Forrest and Henshaw, 1983:162; Fortney, 1987). As couples reach a point of not desiring more children, they may choose sterilization as the least-risky way to prevent further pregnancies. Between the ages of 25 and 29, 25 percent of women in the United States are protected by either female or male sterilization. But the percentage jumps to 62 among women in the age range of 35–39 years (Forrest and Henshaw, 1983:163).

Sometimes persons who have been sterilized regret that decision later—particularly if they remarry after divorce or the death of a spouse. In the Canadian national study from which Table 13-C is taken, 1 out of 10 women who had had tubal ligations reported that if they were to make the decision again, they would not choose sterilization (Balakrishnan et al., 1985:215). Regret rates in the United States are also about 10 percent (Henshaw and Singh, 1986). Reversing sterilization surgery is possible in many cases, although successful restoration of the ability to sire and conceive children cannot be guaranteed in every instance.

Abortion

Up until the historic Supreme Court decision in 1973 that swept aside antiabortion laws, abortion had been illegal in most states except in certain situations (such as rape, incest, or danger to the mother's life). Although illegal abortions occurred in great numbers, it was difficult to study who had them and why. After July 1970, New York was one state that permitted abortion on request; and early studies of the impact of legalization indicated that from 70 to 80 percent of abortions performed in New York City would have been performed anyway— but illegally—had the law not been changed (Cutright and Cutright, 1973:8; Tietze, 1973, 1975; Sklar and Berkov, 1974).

In the years since 1973, it has been possible to study what the legal right to abortion has meant nationwide. As Table 13-D shows, most abortions in the United States are *performed on young* women. In 1981 (latest statistics available), 28.5 percent of women having abortions were no older than 19 years. Another 35 percent were between the ages of 20 and 24.

Marital status also makes a difference. "Unmarried women experience almost twice as many abortions as births," write Stanley Henshaw and his colleagues (1985:92), "while married women have almost 10 times as many births as abortions." Of the 1.6 million abortions reported in the United States in 1981, 81 percent were obtained by unmarried women (never-married, separated, divorced, or widowed).

Researchers note that one result of the Supreme Court ruling "has been a steady trend toward performance of abortions earlier in gestation, when the procedure is safer" (Forrest et al., 1978:274). Ninety-one percent of abortions in 1981 "were performed at 12 or fewer weeks past the last menstrual period (weeks LMP [on Table 13-D])," Henshaw and his colleagues point out, adding that "half of all abortions were obtained at eight or fewer weeks LMP, and fewer than one percent at more than 20 weeks" (p. 91).

Seventy percent of abortions are obtained by white women. However, if we separate the racial groupings and look at *abortion rates* (number of abortions per 1,000 women aged 15 to 44), a different picture emerges. Among white women, the abortion rate is 24 per 1,000; while among women of black and other races, the rate is 56—more than double that of whites. Economic hardship resulting from racial discrimination is no doubt a major contributing factor.

Another interesting research finding relates to the abortion ratio, which takes as its base not numbers of women but, rather, pregnancy outcomes. The number of abortions per 100 live births *and* abortions is the

TABLE 13-D Number and percentage distribution of legal abortions, by selected characteristics of women and method of abortion, United States, 1980 and 1981

	NO.		% DISTRIBUTION	
CHARACTERISTIC	1980	1981	1980	1981
Total	1,553,890	1,577,340	100.0	100.0
Age-Group				
<15	15,340	15,240	1.0%	1.0%
15–19	444,780	433,330	28.6	27.5
15–17	(183,350)	(175,930)	(11.8)	(11.2)
18–19	(261,430)	(257,400)	(16.8)	(16.3)
20–24	549,410	554,940	35.4	35.2
25–29	303,820	316,260	19.6	20.0
30–34	153,060	167,240	9.8	10.6
35–39	66,580	69,510	4.3	4.4
≥40	20,900	20,820	1.3	1.3
Race				
White	1,093,630	1,107,770	70.4	70.2
Nonwhite	460,260	469,570	29.6	29.8
Marital Status				
Married	319,880	298,510	20.6	18.9
Unmarried*	1,234,010	1,278,830	79.4	81.1
No. of Live Births				
0	900,030	911,880	57.9	57.8
1	304,760	312,200	19.6	19.8
2	215,620	219,880	13.9	13.9
3	82,870	84,480	5.3	5.4
≥4	50,610	48,900	3.3	3.1
Prior Induced Abortions				
0	1,042,960	1,022,890	67.1	64.9
1	372,480	389,780	24.0	24.7
2	97,290	112,670	6.3	7.1
≥3	41,160	52,000	2.6	3.3
Weeks LMP				
≤8	799,950	810,300	51.5	51.4
9–10	416,500	423,910	26.8	26.9
11–12	201,750	203,970	13.0	12.9
13–15	73,210	75,770	4.7	4.8
16–20	49,620	49,600	3.2	3.1
≥21	12,860	13,790	0.8	0.9

TABLE 13-D (continued)

CHARACTERISTIC	NO.		% DISTRIBUTION	
	1980	1981	1980	1981
Total	1,553,890	1,577,340	100.0	100.0
Method				
Instrumental evacuation†	1,486,510	1,518,050	95.6	96.2
Medical induction‡	66,170	58,150	4.3	3.7
Hysterotomy/hysterectomy	1,210	1,140	0.1	0.1

*Never-married, separated, divorced or widowed.
†Suction and sharp curettage; includes dilatation and evacuation at 13 weeks' gestation and later.
‡Includes intrauterine instillation of saline, prostaglandin, urea, and, in some cases, combination procedures.
SOURCE: Stanley K. Henshaw, Nancy J. Binkin, Ellen Blaine, and Jack C. Smith, "A Portrait of American Women Who Obtain Abortions," *Family Planning Perspectives*, March/April 1985, p. 92.

abortion ratio. Abortion ratios for nonwhites and whites in the teenage years are about the same. But, say Henshaw and his colleagues, "among women who are unmarried, the ratio is lower among nonwhites than it is among whites at every age." They explain that "nonwhites are less likely than whites to terminate pregnancies that occur outside of marriage by abortion, but they are more likely than whites to terminate marital pregnancies by abortion." These researchers observed that 61 percent of nonwhite women having abortions in 1980 already had one or more children, while only 35 percent of white women having abortions that year already had children. "Nonwhites more often carry their first pregnancy to term and then obtain abortions if a subsequent mistimed or unwanted pregnancy occurs," say these social scientists (pp. 90, 95).

As Table 13-D indicates, only about 1 out of 5 abortions is obtained by a married woman. Apparently, a statement by Cutright and Cutright (1973) still holds true, and it is safe to say that "the bulk of the decline in marital fertility is coming from contraception—not legal abortion."

However, among married couples who feel

that children would be costly and in conflict with individualistic interests, abortion may seem a viable option in the event of an "accidental" conception. Sociologist J. E. Veevers (1973a:358), for example, found in a sample of fifty-two voluntarily childless couples that although most of the wives had never been pregnant, they reported that if pregnancy should occur, they would seek an abortion. One-fifth of these women had already had at least one induced abortion. Demographers Charles Westoff and Norman Ryder (1977:170) also found a relationship between individualistic interests and a more permissive attitude toward abortion. Married women who were *least likely* to believe abortion was permissible were women who had never been employed. Married women *most likely* to believe that abortion was permissible were women who not only were employed but who worked for reasons other than financial considerations. Education was also found to be an important factor. Women with a college education were found to be more approving of abortion than were women with a high school education or less (pp. 167–170).

Gender-role preferences apparently enter into attitudes toward the permissibility of abortion. Sociologist Kristin Luker (1984:193–194), in studying activists on both sides of the abortion debate, concluded that "this round of the abortion debate is so passionate and hard-fought *because it is a referendum on the place and meaning of motherhood.* . . . While on the surface it is the embryo's fate that seems to be at stake, the abortion debate is actually about the meanings of *women's* lives." She points out that "women who oppose abortion and seek to make it officially unavailable are declaring, both practically and symbolically, that women's reproductive roles should be given social primacy." In contrast, *pro-choice*

women see such an insistence on the primacy of women's reproductive roles as being costly. "Practically, it devalues their social resources," Luker writes (pp. 200–201). "If women are only secondarily in the labor market and must subordinate working to pregnancy, should it occur, then their education, occupation, income, and work become potentially temporary and hence discounted." The ability to plan and control their lives, as males have been able to do, is seen to be tied up with the availability of abortion as a backup measure should contraception fail at some point. (See also Finlay, 1981.)

In recent years, much controversy has surrounded the question of abortion. Yet reput-

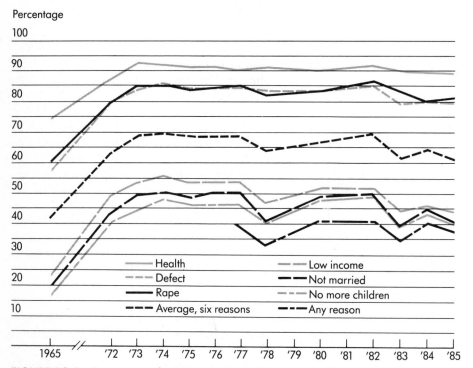

FIGURE 13-1 Percentage of adults in the United States approving of legal abortion under various circumstances, NORC General Social Surveys, 1965–1985. (SOURCE: Reprinted from *Family Planning Perspectives, 17* (July/August, 1985), Digest section report, p. 181.)

able surveys have shown that the percentage of adults approving of abortion under various circumstances has remained much the same since 1972. Figure 13-1 graphically illustrates the percentage of persons who approve of legal abortion (1) for the sake of the mother's health, (2) in cases of rape, (3) if there is a strong likelihood that the fetus has a serious defect, (4) for reasons of low income, (5) because of a woman's unmarried status, or (6) because no further children are desired.

VOLUNTARY CHILDLESSNESS

In the children's story "The Gingerbread Man," we are presented with the sad spectacle of a lonely old couple so desperate for a child that they set out to make one out of cookie dough. In Edward Albee's play *Who's Afraid of Virginia Woolf?* childless George and Martha, constantly at odds with one another, railing with insults and hostilities, nevertheless draw solace from a shared secret—the illusion of the imaginary son they had dreamed up together.

According to popular folk belief, married couples without children are to be pitied. Their lives are considered by outsiders to be incomplete. Surely, the reasoning goes, no couple would remain childless unless it couldn't be helped. Perhaps the husband or wife is infertile, physically unable to reproduce. But even then, adoption is always a possibility. That some couples would deliberately choose not to have offspring strikes many persons as absurd.

There is evidence that most people do want children, but research in both the United States and Canada has shown that 2 to 5 percent of couples prefer to remain childless (Veevers, 1972, 1979, 1980; Silka and Kiesler, 1977; Polonko, 1979; Mosher and Bachrach, 1982; Hoffman and Levant, 1985). An even higher percentage of unmarried college students in several studies have indicated a preference for childlessness over their lifetimes—though, of course, many may be expected to change their minds later (see summary of such studies in Silka and Kiesler, 1977; Polonko, 1979).

If it is true that around 1 out of 20 currently married women deliberately wants to avoid motherhood despite all the pronatalist pressures of relatives, friends, the media, and even the government (through income-tax laws), the question becomes *Why?* The little research that has been done thus far on voluntarily childless couples indicates that the answer lies once again in perceived rewards and costs (Polonko, 1979). Veevers (1974, 1980) points out that some couples who choose not to have children think chiefly in terms of cost avoidance, but other couples look at the reverse side of the coin and emphasize the rewards of an adult-centered lifestyle.

It is possible to think of the rewards of *not* having children in much the same way that we earlier considered the rewards of having children. Couples who desire the child-free lifestyle might think in terms of the following:

Rewards of Self-Enhancement and Self-Preservation

Social identity and a sense of adult status can come through means other than parenthood—most notably through individual achievement in a career or public service. We have already seen that some couples may look upon having children as a way of gaining a sense of self and experiencing vicarious accomplishments (by "living through" their children), but other couples feel that children could hinder self-enhancement and block a husband and wife from being all that they could otherwise be. Such voluntarily childless couples feel that children would drain away time and energy that could otherwise be devoted to pursuing individualistic interests and making names for themselves. They want to be remembered for their own contributions to the world rather than the contributions of their children.

Rewards of Affection, Belonging, and Pleasure

Whereas couples who want children speak of the expressive rewards expected in parenthood, couples who don't want children may view children in a "three's a crowd" fashion and fear that commitment to parenthood would detract from commitment to the marriage itself. Veevers (1974) reports that some of her respondents made comments such as, "A child would come between us. I wouldn't be able to be as close to my husband if I had a child . . . " or "If you have children, then not all of your emotional involvement would be with each other anymore and you would have lost something." Couples who opt for the child-free lifestyle are willing to "put all their emotional eggs into one basket," as one respondent told Veevers. Affection and belonging are important for such women and men, but they want to find such affection and belonging in the husband-wife relationship alone rather than seeking these rewards through children. As Veevers expressed it: "A dominant component [of the child-free lifestyle] is commitment to the ideal that a married couple should be a self-sufficient unit, who look to each other for the satisfaction of most (and perhaps all) of their social and psychological needs. . . . They relate to each other not only as man and wife, but also as lover and mistress and as 'best friends.' The presence of children makes such dyadic withdrawal difficult if not impossible" (p. 397).

In another study, sociologist Karen Polonko (1979, chap. 4) compared voluntarily childless wives with wives who intend to have children and found that the majority of the voluntarily childless "believe that children will decrease their satisfaction with spouse closeness, companionship, romance, and the opportunity to experience new things with their spouse."

This theme of "experiencing new things" and freedom to pursue individualistic and couple interests and adventures also shows up in other studies of child-free couples. Veevers (1974) reports that a recurrent theme among her respondents was the search for novelty; the avoidance of routine; the quest for new experiences, new situations, and new tasks; the desire to travel; and the freedom to just "pick up and go" at a moment's notice. Childless couples also reported that they enjoyed being able to pursue adult activities and adult entertainments without having to be concerned about family recreational activities, child-centered play, and constant consideration of "what is good for the children." They liked, for example, being able to attend movies with adult themes rather than being limited to Disney-type films in the interest of family togetherness.

Altruistic and Religious Satisfactions in Not Having Children

"People who don't want to have children are simply selfish! They think only of themselves and their own convenience." Such has been the familiar accusation hurled at couples who voluntarily choose to remain childless. But with growing concern about population pressures, food and energy shortages, crowding, and all the related problems of too many people on too small a planet, the accusation of selfishness has been aimed at a different target. Couples who want the rewards of children in great abundance are the ones who are now likely to be labeled self-indulgent and unconcerned about the good of humanity. Couples who forgo the experience of parenthood may be considered, by at least some persons, to be altruistic.

And indeed altruistic motives may very well figure into the decisions of some couples to remain childless. In our own university-student sample, although no question was asked about preferred childlessness per se, we did find that a prime motivation for limiting family size was a deep concern about population pressures (Scanzoni, 1975c). Two researchers, Susan Gustavus and James R. Henley, Jr. (1971), who studied seventy-two childless couples applying for sterilization, found that concern over population growth was one of several reasons these men and women gave for not wanting any children.

Veevers (1973a:363–364) reports that concern with population problems "does provide a supportive rationale indicating that one is not necessarily being socially irresponsible and neglectful of one's civic obligations if one does not reproduce" but that among her sample, such concern was not a motivating force for not having children but was "an *ex post facto* consideration." It was something a childless couple could latch onto after making their decision, but primarily "their satisfaction with being childless is related to concerns other than to their contribution to the population crisis."

Hoffman (1972a) makes a similar point. Referring to the report of a psychiatrist working with couples having marital difficulties, she states that a recurring theme that emerged during therapy was that of the husband who didn't want children but *pretended* to want them in order not to appear harsh and unloving. "With the socially negative view so prevalent," writes Hoffman, "it has probably been unacceptable to admit the de-

sire for childlessness even to oneself." Such individuals may be the ones most open to concerns about not adding to the world's population because these concerns provide an altruistic rationale for their personal preferences. At the same time, there is no denying that among some socially conscious couples, consideration of population pressures may be a very real motivation in their initial decision not to have children rather than simply a rationale to justify their decision later.

When it comes to the question of *religious* satisfactions in not having children, the issue may be harder to determine. To some persons, the very notion of religious satisfactions in childlessness would seem absurd because religious beliefs have traditionally been bound up with notions that children are "blessings from heaven" and that parenthood is a sacred duty. Indeed, in both the Veevers and the Gustavus-Henley samples of childless couples, there is an indication that rejection of such notions includes rejection of the religious beliefs and institutions from which they derive. Veevers (1973a:357) writes of her sample of fifty-two voluntarily childless wives: "Most individuals are either atheists or agnostics from Protestant backgrounds, and of the minority who do express some religious preference, almost all are inactive." Respondents in the study by Gustavus and Henley (1971) were also likely to report that they had no religion. And in Polonko's (1979) sample of ninety-five voluntarily child-free wives, participation in religious services averaged less than once a year. Nearly one-third reported no religious preference, "and most of these women further classify themselves as atheists or agnostics," reports Polonko (chap. 4). Although two-thirds stated a religious preference, one-fifth of them attended religious services less than once a year, and close to another fifth reported they never attended. Only one of the wives said she attended church more than once weekly. Only 12.6 percent of the voluntarily childless wives in Polonko's sample were Roman Catholic.

Traditionally, religious supports for voluntary childlessness have been nonexistent. However, at least one Protestant scholar sees in voluntary childlessness the possibility of a church-sanctioned commitment somewhat like that of celibacy for reasons of religious service. Just as a person might renounce marriage in order to devote himself or herself to serving God and others with a maximum of freedom, mobility, and time available for one's mission, so might a married couple choose not to have children in order to give full concentration to their ministry. So writes Mennonite theologian John Howard Yoder (1974) as he suggests that church mission and service agencies could benefit by encouraging voluntarily childless couples who embrace this lifestyle in order to dedicate themselves to religious ministries. Similar thinking is taking place among some Roman Catholics. An article in *U.S. Catholic*, for instance, proposes "a new alternative . . . made possible only in this time—that childless marriage be recognized as a religious ideal when it is undertaken in order that the couple might pursue a higher calling of service to God and humanity" (Everett and Everett, 1975:39).

Choosing the Child-Free Lifestyle

Jean E. Veevers has given much study and consideration to factors related to the decision of couples not to have children. Several of her findings are of special interest because of what they tell us about how and why the decision not to have children is made. (See Veevers, 1972, 1973a, 1973b, 1974, 1979, 1980.)

Many of Veevers' (1973b) respondents reported having come from unhappy homes in which their parents remained together rather than getting a divorce. The children learned not only that having children doesn't necessarily mean either personal or marital happiness but also that children can even be the cause of strife in marriage. Furthermore, parents who endure miserable situations "for the sake of the children" may be teaching children that parenthood is entrapping, preventing the option of divorce. Women in the sample who grew up in such homes had negative impressions of motherhood, impressions that were made all the stronger by the fact that their mothers had been "basically dissatisfied with their housework and child-care roles."

Some voluntarily childless wives in Veevers' sample had been "only" children. Thus it may be that the absence of role models and the lack of opportunities to interact with siblings caused some of these women to feel incompetent for or uninterested in the mother role for themselves.

On the other hand, some of the wives in the sample came from large families in which they were the oldest of the children and had responsibility for all the younger brothers and sisters. Being cast in the "little-mother" role, these women learned early that children limit one's activities. Often during girlhood, these women had to baby-sit when they would rather have pursued their own interests or attended school events. Taking care of real children provided an experience quite different from that known to little girls who play only with dolls. "The dolls never misbehave in unmanageable ways," writes Veevers, "they never preempt or preclude other activities, and when they become burdensome or boring they can be readily but temporarily abandoned." Not so with real babies. And girls who grow up in the oldest-daughter position in the family often learn that early. They may thus have little desire for taking on the mother role in adulthood.

Egalitarian gender roles and wife employment may also enter into the choice not to have children. Earlier we saw that these factors were related to limiting family size; but for some couples, they are also related to avoiding parenthood altogether. Veevers (1974) writes: "Most of the childless wives interviewed report that their marriages are characterized by very egalitarian sex roles, with an orientation in which the husband and wife are considered to be of equal value to the relationship, with equal levels of authority and equal levels of competence." Furthermore, "egalitarian role relationships may be both a consequence and a cause of childlessness." (See also Hoffman and Levant, 1985.)

With one exception, all of the childless wives in Veevers' sample work and plan to work indefinitely. About half of the women reported a deep commitment to their work and derive a sense of identity from it, and many have high professional aspirations. "The remaining half work mainly for extrinsic rewards, such as money and the satisfactions of interacting with others in job situations," Veevers (1974) reports.

Polonko also found the voluntarily childless in her study to be "characterized by intensely egalitarian gender-role and pro-childless norms." Such women "perceive children to be very costly to their satisfaction with their spouse relationship, standard of living and career," writes Polonko (1979, chap. 4), and all three of these areas are quite highly valued. The voluntarily childless women in her study had achieved higher income and occupational prestige than had the wives who had not voluntarily chosen childlessness. Polonko suggests that for voluntarily childless wives, career *success* is a key factor in decisions to remain child-free, along with

Egalitarian gender roles and wife employment are sometimes factors in the decision not to have any children at all. (© Michal Heron 1981/Woodfin Camp & Associates)

perceptions that the wife's career and the care and attention required by children would be incompatible. Other studies have indicated that occupational success in high-status jobs is associated with intentions to remain child-free (see Silka and Kiesler, 1977). As Table 13-E shows, among 18- to 34-year-old women of all marital statuses, women with the greatest amounts of education and women in professional- and managerial-level occupations are those most likely to expect to remain childless throughout their lives. There is also some indication that among lower-status women with aspirations for upward mobility, the likelihood of preferring a child-free lifestyle is greater than it is among other lower-status women. In contrast, lower-status men who prefer childlessness are more likely to be men with lower educational and occupational aspirations (Kenkel, 1985).

How the Choice Is Made Veevers (1973a:359–360) found that nearly a third of childless couples decide before marriage that childlessness will be a part of an informal marriage "contract." From the very begin-

TABLE 13-E Births to date and lifetime births expected per woman and percent expecting to remain childless, by ethnicity and socioeconomic status: June 1981

CHARACTERISTIC	BIRTHS TO DATE	LIFETIME BIRTHS EXPECTED	PERCENT EXPECTING TO REMAIN CHILDLESS
Race/ethnicity:			
White	1.1	2.0	11.2
Black	1.6	2.2	9.0
Spanish origin	1.5	2.3	7.1
Education:			
Less than high school	1.8	2.4	6.9
High school graduate	1.2	2.0	10.0
Some college	0.8	2.0	11.9
College graduate	0.6	1.8	16.5
Graduate training	0.6	1.7	19.5
Labor force status:			
In labor force	0.8	1.9	13.6
Employed	0.8	1.9	14.0
Unemployed	1.0	2.1	9.8
Not in labor force	1.7	2.3	5.5
Occupation:			
Professionals/managers	0.6	1.7	19.0
Sales/clerical workers	0.8	1.9	13.6
Blue-collar workers	1.2	1.9	11.8
Service workers	1.0	2.1	10.6
Farm workers	1.3	2.4	11.9
Family income:			
Under $5,000	1.5	2.3	8.0
$5,000 to $9,999	1.3	2.1	10.5
$10,000 to $14,999	1.1	2.0	12.0
$15,000 to $19,999	1.2	2.0	9.5
$20,000 to $24,999	1.1	2.0	10.3
$25,000 and over	0.9	2.0	12.2

NOTE: Includes women of all marital statuses, 18 to 34 years of age. Women of Spanish origin may be of any race.
SOURCE: U.S. Bureau of the Census, Special Demographic Analyses, CDS-80-8, *American Women: Three Decades of Change*, 1983, p. 7.

ning, there is no intention to have children. In most cases, these women in Veevers' sample had made the decision during adolescence and later sought future mates who agreed, but in some cases, the women had not considered a childless marriage until meeting their future husbands.

Among the other two-thirds, childlessness came about as the result of continually post-poning having children until a future time. But the "right time" never came. For most couples, this postponement seemed to go through four stages—first, a definite period of waiting; second (when the agreed-upon time is up), an indefinite period of postponement when the time to have a baby becomes increasingly vague; third, a critical state in which the possibility of permanent childless-

WHAT ABOUT HAVING ONE CHILD ONLY?

While most couples decide to have two children, a small but growing number remain childfree. About 10% choose the third alternative—to have one child. . . .

Parents of only children are quick to point out the advantages of the one-child family for themselves. "Being the parent of one child is having the best of two worlds" in the view of one parent. "I can experience the joys and frustrations of being a parent without getting so tied down by parenting responsibilities that I haven't time to pursue my own interests". . . .

The image presented by one-child parents of a close, democratic, affluent family-style is considerably different from the long-admired American portrait of the "Walton" family-style with its tangle of relationships and clear lines of authority. One mother in a one-child family observed that the end results are different. "Parents with several children often seem to view parenting as an all-consuming job. For my husband, daughter, and me, life is more like a three-way adventure."

SOURCE: Sharryl Hawke and David Knox, "The One-Child Family: A New Life-Style," *The Family Coordinator, 27* (July 1978), excerpts from pp. 215–217.

ness is openly acknowledged for the first time; and fourth, an explicit decision (or the recognition of the implicit decision that has been gradually made) that they will never have children. Other researchers write of ongoing patterns of negotiation rather than a series of postponements (Cooper et al., 1978).

In another study, focusing on the respective power in the husband-wife relationship when there is *disagreement* about whether or not to have children, it was found that if the husband first suggested childlessness, the wife was likely to come around to agreement with him, often after years of negotiation. But if the wife wanted a child-free marriage and the husband did not, the husband was not likely to be persuaded by her wishes. Divorce in such cases tended to be the outcome (Marciano, 1978).

Interestingly, in Veevers' sample of wives who wished to be child-free, the door was not closed on possible adoption of children some day. Veevers (1973a:362–363) points out that the importance of the option of adoption lies in the twofold symbolic importance: "the

reaffirmation of normalcy" [because of the societal view that "normal, well-adjusted" people will want and like children] and the avoidance of irreversible decisions." (See also Veevers, 1980.)

One sociologist has argued that the inclusion of women open to the possibility of adoption muddies the definition of voluntary childlessness—that openness to the adoption option indicates a lack of firm commitment to a child-free lifestyle (Houseknecht, 1981). At the same time, she, too, recognizes the negative societal attitudes that have to be faced by those who choose never to have children (Houseknecht, 1982; see also Calhoun and Selby, 1980).

INVOLUNTARY CHILDLESSNESS AND ALTERNATIVE ROUTES TO PARENTHOOD

For large numbers of couples, childlessness is not a matter of choice. A fertility problem prevents their having children. According to the latest data from the National Center for

SURROGATE MOTHERHOOD: A SPECIAL CASE

Malden, Mass.—A healthy baby girl was born Thursday to a woman who had agreed to have a child for her sterile sister by impregnating herself with her brother-in-law's sperm.

Kristen Jennifer was born at 3:35 a.m. at Malden Hospital, into the waiting arms of her mother-to-be, Carole Jalbert.

Jalbert, who was present throughout the labor of her sister, Sherry King, exclaimed, "Oh, my baby! My baby!" when the 7-pound, 6½-ounce baby was born, the statement said.

"To this day, I feel like an aunt. I was just babysitting," said King, the surrogate mother. She added that the delivery "hurt, but it was worth it."

Owen King, husband of the biological mother, said the child was "the culmination of a two-year project with a pretty heavy emotional investment."

"When the baby was born, to say we felt ecstasy and just incredible cheerful joy is an understatement," King said.

He was there when his wife gave birth, as was the father, Ernie Jalbert, and the two sisters' parents. "I think every man should see something like that," Jalbert said at the news conference. . . .

The family began working in 1983 for a child for Carole Jalbert, 39, who is unable to bear children because of a hysterectomy 18 years ago.

SOURCE: Excerpted from Associated Press report, *Greensboro (NC) News and Record*, Nov. 8, 1985, p. A-12.

Health Statistics (*Advance Data from Vital and Health Statistics*, no. 104, 1985), in 1982 there were 1.4 million childless married couples unable or unlikely to have offspring. In addition, another 4.6 million couples, though not childless, were also unable or unlikely to experience any future births. These statistics do not include couples who have chosen contraceptive sterilization.

The National Center for Health Statistics classifies a couple as infertile if neither spouse is surgically sterile and "if, during the preceding 12 months or longer, they were continuously married (presumed to be sexually active), had not used contraception, and had not conceived" (p. 4). According to the American College of Obstetricians and Gynecologists, the infertility problem can be traced to the male about 40 percent of the

time and to the female an equal percentage of the time. In about 20 percent of cases, *both* partners contribute to the fertility difficulty (Nelson, 1984; "Information Update: Infertility in Men," *Family Life Educator*, Winter 1982, pp. 10–11; Moghissi, 1978).

The overall percentage of couples classified as infertile has remained between 13 and 14 percent. Among couples in which the wife is in the age category of 20 to 24 years, however, the percentage nearly tripled between 1965 and 1982, climbing from 4 percent to 11 percent (National Center of Health Statistics, *Advance Data from Vital and Health Statistics*, no. 104, 1985). Although reasons for this jump were not included in the government data, one of the coauthors of the report, William D. Mosher, said in an interview that this age group's fertility may have been

HYSTERECTOMY DOESN'T BAR PREGNANCY

Boston—For the first time, doctors say they are enabling a woman without a uterus to have a child by implanting her egg into the body of a surrogate mother.

The woman's egg was fertilized in a test tube with her husband's sperm and then placed into the uterus of a friend, who is now in her fifth month of pregnancy.

So-called surrogate mothers have been used before. But in those cases, the surrogate's own egg was fertilized with sperm provided by the husband of an infertile woman. The surrogate carried the fetus until birth and then turned over the child to the infertile couple.

"What is the first is a situation where a woman who has by all accepted standards been infertile will be able to obtain her own genetic baby," said Dr. Wulf H. Utian.

Utian is director of the Laboratory for In Vitro Fertilization and Embryo Transfer at Mt. Sinai Medical Center in Cleveland, where the procedure was performed. He described the case in a letter published in Thursday's New England Journal of Medicine.

At Infertility Associates International, an agency in Bethesda, Md., that matches couples with surrogates, director Harriett Blankfeld said similar embryo transfers have been attempted before, but she agreed that the Cleveland case is the first apparent success.

"Embryo transfer is a whole new horizon," she said. "It offers the infertile couple the opportunity to have a child that is biologically both theirs. The host mother is truly, in every respect, an incubator."

Utian said the procedure could be used to help many women who produce healthy eggs but cannot conceive. Among them are women who have recurrent miscarriages or women with uterine abnormalities, such as those caused by the drug diethylstilbestrol, or DES.

In this case, a 37-year-old woman had undergone a hysterectomy after her uterus ruptured during pregnancy. Three of her eggs were later removed, and one of them was fertilized with her husband's sperm. Then it was placed into the uterus of a 22-year-old friend who had already had two normal pregnancies.

"The baby appears to be normal, and the pregnancy is completely uncomplicated," Utian said.

When the child is born, it will be turned over to its genetic parents.

SOURCE: Associated Press report, *Greensboro (NC) News and Record*, Nov. 22, 1985, p. A17.

affected by the increase in sexually transmitted diseases and by the popularity of the IUD during the period of this study (Cimons, 1985). Women who use IUDs and who have had multiple sexual partners (and thus more exposure to the risk of sexually transmitted diseases) are more likely to develop pelvic inflammatory disease and tubal infertility than are nonusers of the IUD or IUD users who have had only one sexual partner. Certain *types* of IUD, especially, have been found to increase the risk of problems that may lead to infertility in some women (Cramer et al., 1985; Daling et al., 1985).

However, there are many different kinds and causes of both male and female infertility; and sometimes infertility can be treated and its problems overcome through surgery, hormone therapy, or drugs (Porter and Christopher, 1984). In other cases, involuntarily childless couples who want the experience of parenthood may turn to various alternative ways to have a child (Nelson, 1984; Zimmerman, 1982; Francoeur, 1985). Some of these possibilities are *artificial insemination* (in which semen from a woman's husband or a donor is inserted by syringe into her vagina at the time of her ovulation), *in vitro fertilization* (in which a ripe ovum is removed from a woman's body, fertilized by her husband's sperm in a special container, then reinserted into her body to proceed as a normal pregnancy within her uterus), *surrogate motherhood* (in which a woman consents to be artificially inseminated by the husband of a woman unable to conceive and then bears a child for that couple), and *embryo transfer* (in which an in vitro fertilized ovum from one couple is placed into another woman's uterus to develop until birth, at which time the baby is given to the genetic parents).

These new reproductive technologies, while giving hope to many women and men and providing options for parenthood once undreamed of, are also raising new legal and ethical questions (Donovan, 1986; Cushner, 1986). They have also introduced new complexities. "It is now possible for a child to have up to five parents: an egg donor, a sperm donor, a surrogate who gestates the fetus and the couple who raise the child," writes one legal scholar (Andrews, 1984:56, as quoted in Donovan, 1986:57).

Involuntary childlessness can be an emotionally traumatic experience for many couples, and they tend to develop various strategies for dealing with their situation. (Zimmerman, 1982; Porter and Christopher, 1984) Some couples choose to *adopt* a child rather than pursue the possibilities of infertility treatment or alternatives now made possible through reproductive technology (see Bachrach, 1983, 1986).

MACRO VIEW OF REPRODUCTION

If the nursery-tale introduction to childlessness is "The Gingerbread Man," the equivalent introduction to a macro view of the world population situation could be the story of the old woman who lived in a shoe and had so many children she didn't know what to do.

Ansley J. Coale (1974), for many years director of the Office of Population Research at Princeton University, has vividly described what is taking place as world population increases at a rate more rapid than at any time in history. He points out that the *growth rate* (the number of persons added per year per 1,000 population, taking into account both births and deaths) was, up until 10,000 years ago, about 0.02, and it took at least 35,000 years for the population to double. Between A.D. 1 and 1750 (the year when the modern accelerated growth phenomenon began), the growth rate was 0.56 per 1,000, which meant

Some couples experience parenthood by adopting children. (Arthur Grace/Stock, Boston)

5 BILLIONTH BABY DUE TODAY

Washington—Somewhere on Earth, a child born today will become the 5 billionth person living on the planet, according to estimates of the Population Institute.

"This particular baby . . . is a sobering symbol of the shocking rapidity at which the world's population is multiplying," said institute President Werner Fornos.

Population experts have been anticipating the arrival of the world's population at the 5 billion mark, although not all agree on the exact time of that occurrence, and some have said that the milestone may have already passed.

"Five billion probably puts the world population about at its carrying capacity," said M. Rupert Cutler, executive director of Population-Environment Balance. "It will be difficult to feed, clothe, shelter and employ many more people at more than a subsistence level of life."

SOURCE: *Greensboro (NC) News and Record,* July 7, 1986, p. A-1.

the world population doubled every 1,200 years. However, according to United Nations studies, the growth rate is expected to be about 20 per 1,000 over the next several decades—which would mean a doubling of the world population this time in just under thirty-five years!

Coale illustrates the cumulative effect of even a small number of doublings by referring to an old legend in which a king offered his daughter in marriage to any man who could supply one grain of wheat for the first square on a chessboard, two grains for the second square, double that amount for the third square, and so on. "To comply with this request for all 64 squares," writes Coale, "would require a mountain of grain many times larger than today's worldwide wheat production."

He points out that if the 20 per 1,000 growth rate were to continue so that the population would double every thirty-five years, the earth would be in a similar situation to the legendary king's chessboard. "The consequences of sustained growth at this pace are clearly impossible," says Coale. He explains why. "In less than 700 years there

would be one person for every square foot on the surface of the earth; in less than 1,200 years the human population would outweigh the earth; in less than 6,000 years the mass of humanity would form a sphere expanding at the speed of light."

According to *The Population Institute Annual Report* (1982, p. 37), "it took from the beginning of recorded history to the year 1830 for the world to achieve its first one billion people." Within a hundred years, it had achieved its second billion; and thirty years after that, a third billion. By the mid-1980s, global population was already over 4.8 billion, and United Nations and World Bank projections indicate it will reach 6 billion by the end of the century unless various nations are able to reach their fertility goals, which could bring the population down to 5.7 billion by the year 2000 (Fornos, 1985).

Fertility Rates in the United States

Throughout most of the developed world, there appears to be a trend toward two children as the preferred family size (Westoff, 1974b:113). The United States is no exception. The trend toward smaller families shows up in the lowered fertility rate pictured in Figure 13-2. In 1983, the fertility rate (65.4 live births per 1,000 women aged 15–44 years) was the second lowest ever recorded in the United States (National Center for Health Statistics, *Monthly Vital Statistics Report,* Vol. 32, no. 13, 1984, p. 1).

Another tendency that has grown in recent years is for many women to delay motherhood until their thirties so that they can give their full attention to educational and career pursuits (Ventura, 1982; Wilkie, 1981). Women who have their first births at older ages tend to be better educated, in the work force, and employed in professional occupations. (See Figure 13-3.)

Where Population Growth Is Occurring

It should be kept in mind that not all parts of the world are growing equally. In some nations, there is even governmental concern

FIGURE 13-2 Fertility rates in the United States: 1930–83. (SOURCE: National Center for Health Statistics: Annual Summary of Births, Deaths, Marriages, and Divorces: United States, 1983. *Monthly Vital Statistics Report,* vol. 32., no. 13 (Hyattsville, MD: Public Health Service, Sept. 21, 1984), p. 3.)

Births per 1,000 women aged 15–44

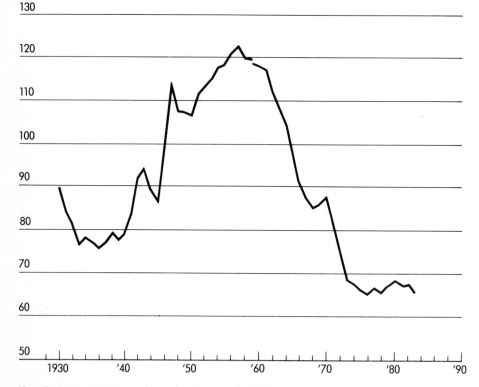

Note: Beginning with 1959, trend line is based on registered live births; trend
line for years prior to 1959 is based on live births adjusted for underregistration.

Percent of first births

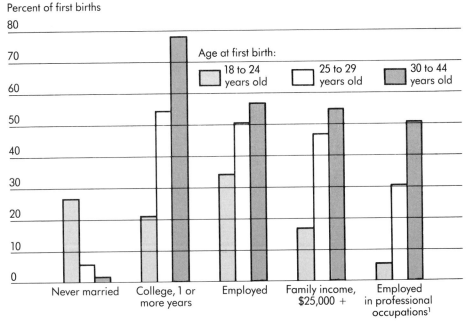

¹Percentage based on employed women.

FIGURE 13-3 Characteristics of women who have had a first birth in the last year, by age: June 1982. (SOURCE: U.S. Bureau of the Census, Current Population Reports, Series P-20, No. 387, *Fertility of American Women: June 1982* [Washington, DC: U.S. Government Printing Office, 1984]).

that not enough people are being born. In other nations, the annual population increase seems staggering and is associated with poverty, inadequate food supplies, extremely crowded living conditions, and other social problems.

In the developing countries, the rapid population growth is due not only to high birthrates but to low death rates. Demographers speak of the bringing into balance of this lag between death rates and birthrates as the "demographic transition." During the transition, as less-developed countries undergo changes through which they move toward urbanization and industrialization, death rates decline because of medical advances, improvements in sanitation, nutrition, and the

like. At the same time, the birthrate in these countries continues as before for a considerable period of time. Population then grows because of this difference in birthrates and death rates. After the transition to urbanization and industrialization is completed, the birthrate also declines, mainly because of changed attitudes toward the value of having children and because of educational and work opportunities for women. The wide gap between numbers of deaths per 1,000 population and numbers of births per 1,000 becomes much smaller.

Rafael M. Salas (1985), executive director of the United Nations Fund for Population Activities, points out that "75 percent of the world's women live in developing countries" and have lower levels of literacy and education, higher birthrates, and less access to occupational opportunities than do women in developed countries. Salas writes: "Women have remained in the periphery of development till now, and their participation can be increased only by providing training and education and enabling them to exercise their reproductive freedom." He urges recognition that "because a woman's status and opportunities are clearly related to demographic variables, improvement of the status of women should also be a component of population policy" (p. 5).

At the same time that developing nations are growing so rapidly, fertility in the twenty countries that have 80 percent of the world's "developed" population is "at, near, or below the replacement level" (Westoff,

1974:109). *Replacement level* means an average of 2.1 births per woman over a lifetime of childbearing. (Demographers speak of the likely average number of births per woman over an entire lifetime of childbearing as a nation's *total fertility rate*. It is based on births per woman at different age levels in a given year.) See Figure 13-4.

Trends and Government Policies

Governments are aware of the consequences of population growth or lack of growth, and they may utilize various measures to either cut down or encourage fertility. Where there is a concern about *too rapid growth* and the problems of crowding, housing, pollution, limited resources, burdens placed on community services, and similar matters related

FIGURE 13-4 Global stabilization imperative. (SOURCE: Adapted from *The Population Institute Annual Report, 1982–1983* (Washington, DC: The Population Institute, December, 1982), p. 36.)

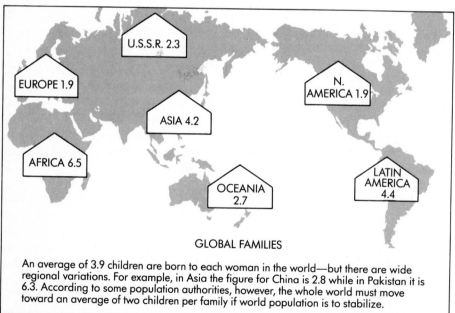

U.S.S.R. 2.3

EUROPE 1.9

N. AMERICA 1.9

ASIA 4.2

AFRICA 6.5

OCEANIA 2.7

LATIN AMERICA 4.4

GLOBAL FAMILIES

An average of 3.9 children are born to each woman in the world—but there are wide regional variations. For example, in Asia the figure for China is 2.8 while in Pakistan it is 6.3. According to some population authorities, however, the whole world must move toward an average of two children per family if world population is to stabilize.

CHINA RELAXING STANDARD OF ONE CHILD PER FAMILY IN RURAL AREAS

Peking—China is gradually retreating from its avowed commitment to a population control policy of one child per family in rural areas in the face of widespread protests and resistance from peasants.

Over the past year, many of China's provincial governments have adopted new rules allowing couples living in the countryside to have a second child under special conditions.

An official of China's State Family Planning Commission said in a recent interview that after five years of experience, authorities in Peking have decided to relax the one-child limit in rural areas in order "to make our policies more rational and acceptable to our people."

"We are only advocating the one-child family in the cities," said Shen Guoxiang, deputy director of the commission. "In the rural areas, where people have been found to have difficulties, they can have a second child."

The definition of "difficulties" will vary from province to province and from locality to locality. But Shen said that in some areas peasant couples will be permitted a second child "if the first child is a girl."

"Until the turn of the century, there must be some people who can have only one child, and those families will be mainly in the cities," Shen said.

He emphasized that China is not in any way abandoning the fundamental goal of its birth-control campaign—to limit the population to 1.2 billion in the year 2000. In its 1982 census, China counted 1 billion people.

Shen said Peking will continue to fix quotas for the number of births allowed in each of China's 29 provinces and regions, which then pass on similar numerical limits to cities and villages.

He did not explain how the government can relax its policy in the countryside, where four-fifths of the people live, and still meet its population target. . . .

The peasants have a number of reasons for objecting to the one-child rule more vehemently than do city people.

In economic terms, peasants profit from having extra hands to help with the work. This has been particularly true in the past five years. Under market reforms fostered by the national leadership of Deng Xiaoping, peasants have been allowed to engage in a form of private enterprise and to increase their income by raising output, so they have a powerful financial incentive to have more children.

Also, the peasants' level of education is below that of urban residents, and traditional attitudes like the preference for male heirs are stronger in the countryside.

SOURCE: Jim Mann, "China Relaxing Standard of One Child Per Family," L.A. Times-Washington Post News Service, *Greensboro (NC) News and Record*, May 12, 1985, p. A13.

to the well-being of a country and its citizens, governments may seek to encourage birth control through various programs. For example, in 1979, China's national leaders began a strict program of costs and rewards intended to keep couples from having more than one child. (Chen, 1985). This population policy has met with much resistance, especially in rural areas. (See insert.) As social scientist Lucy Jen Huang (1982:781) emphasizes, numerous factors are associated with such resistance, most notably "the love for children, the fear of not having descendents to carry on the family name, concern about being poor and lonely during old age, and the emotional shock of being sterilized." Sterilization is urged for any couple with two or more children, and peasants can lose part of their lands or be required to pay heavy fines if they do not comply (L. A. Times-Washington Post News Service, *Greensboro (NC) News and Record,* May 29, 1983).

India, second only to China (which has the world's highest population), is also making a rigorous effort to curb population growth, with the goal of achieving replacement-level fertility by the year 2000. Government officials plan to use monetary incentives, such as $5,000 saving bonds for couples who have no more than two children, to encourage smaller families. As in traditional Chinese culture, strong preferences for male heirs have kept couples from limiting family size—when daughters are born first (*Popline* report, World Population News Service, May, 1985, p. 1). Other countries that may have to follow the lead of countries like China and India are Nigeria, Bangladesh, Mexico, Pakistan, and Ethiopia, which has faced such severe famine problems in the 1980s (*Popline* report, World Population News Service, February 1985, p. 1).

On the other hand, if a government becomes alarmed that a decline in fertility may

mean military, economic, and political disadvantages or may cause a labor shortage in future years, policies and programs and changes in laws may be instituted in an effort to raise the fertility rate. For example, Romania's *total fertility rate* in 1955 was 3.1 births per woman, but by 1966 it had reached a low of 1.9. Disturbed by this decline, the government repealed its permissive abortion law. Since 1983, the government has taken further measures to encourage more births. For example, childless couples are required to pay a heavy monthly tax, equivalent to about 10 percent of the average monthly salary. Officials have indicated that this penalty on childlessness may be raised even higher. On the other hand, large families are being given increased benefits (*Greensboro (NC) News and Record,* December 16, 1985).

Another government that became concerned over a low population-growth rate was that of President Peron of Argentina. Before his death in 1973, he told the women of Argentina that they had maternal responsibilities to fulfill—and promptly made oral contraceptives illegal (Westoff, 1974:118). Although government control of birth control remains tight today, family planning services are limited, and pronatalist policies are in operation, restrictions have become somewhat less rigid than they were under Peron. Physicians are still forbidden by law, however, to prescribe contraceptives for unmarried women (Morgan, 1984).

Costs, Rewards, and Population

It seems clear that on the macro level, no less than on the micro level, reproduction is a matter of costs and rewards. Too many people can be costly, but so can too few. Governments around the world are increasingly aware of population concerns and have set

CHILDBEARING: A PATRIOTIC DUTY?

Declaring it the "patriotic duty" of Romanian women to bear four children, President Nicolae Ceausescu announced last spring "stern measures" against abortion to be enforced by the police.

Married women must now undergo monthly pregnancy tests at their workplaces, and must have a medical explanation for "persistent non-pregnancy."

Written confirmation from a doctor is required if a woman suffers a miscarriage. Should police decide a woman has lied about the termination of a pregnancy, she faces a year in prison.

Women who do not fulfill their child quotas are rarely promoted, and can lose their jobs.

Romania is one of the poorest Eastern European countries and carries a huge foreign debt. President Ceausescu is reportedly eager to accelerate the birthrate in hope of increasing economic output.

SOURCE: *National NOW Times,* January/February 1985, p. 5.

up various commissions to study demographic trends and to suggest policies (Berelson, 1973). Where there is concern about too much population growth, as is occurring in the less-developed nations, attention must be given to the rewards and costs of children on the micro level in order to affect trends at the macro level. Especially is there a need to present alternative rewards, for (in the words of Hoffman and Hoffman, 1973:69) "as long as children satisfy an important value for which there is no alternative, people will climb over a great many barriers and put up with a great many costs before they will diminish fertility. As long as children satisfy important values, even very trivial reasons for another child will seem valid."

CHAPTER HIGHLIGHTS

How couples perceive the costs and rewards of having children plays a major part in family planning. Incentives for having children tend to fall into four main categories: (1) self-enhancement, (2) self-preservation, (3) pleasure, affection, and belonging, and (4) altruistic and religious satisfactions. Persons at lower socioeconomic levels tend to have more children than do those at higher levels. One reason is that children are a source of rewards for poor people when other rewards are denied them; another reason may relate to a sense of helplessness in controlling their lives, including a failure to prevent unwanted births in many cases. The material costs involved in having children are twofold: *direct costs* (money spent for children's needs) and indirect *opportunity costs* (opportunities passed by or given up for the children). Some studies have indicated that couples who are rearing children are less satisfied with their marriages than are childless couples or those whose children are grown.

Research shows that gender-role norms held by women affect both the number of children they intend to have and the number they actually do have. A summary statement of gender-role norms and fertility is this: The greater a woman's *individualism* (desire to pursue her own interests and fulfill her own achievement goals), the lower will be her *familism* (desire to center her life around her husband and children). And the lower the familism, the lower will be the number of children intended and the number actually born.

Over 90 percent of married women at risk of an unintended pregnancy are now using some contraceptive method. By far the favorite form of contraception among married couples in both the United States and Canada is sterilization. Among unmarried women, the pill remains in top place. Most abortions are obtained by young, unmarried women, with fewer than 1 out of 5 abortions performed on a married woman. About 5 percent of married couples choose to have no children at all because they view children as more costly than rewarding and prefer an adult-centered lifestyle. At the same time, around 13 percent of couples are classified as infertile. A number of such couples may choose alternative routes to parenthood.

Governments may take action to decrease or increase population, depending upon how fertility trends appear to be helping or hindering national self-interest. Where the concern is over too much population growth, as in less-developed countries, attention must be given to the rewards and costs of children on the *micro* level (the "small picture" of individuals and couples) in order to affect trends at the *macro* level (the "large picture" of nations and the world as a whole).

·14·

THE YEARS OF CHILDREARING

How would you like to take care of an egg for a week? That seemingly preposterous question was put to a high school class in Philadelphia a few years ago in an effort to show students what it's like to be responsible full-time for an infant.

The egg had to be raw, not hard-boiled, and thus susceptible to breakage. Careless students who broke their Humpty Dumpties over the week were subject to a trial for "egg abuse," and at the end of the experiment a mock trial was held for such offenders. Some of the instructions for the project went something like this: "If you want to go out, the egg goes with you or you have to hire an egg-sitter. WHAT IF YOU HAVE TWINS??!! Look at the bright side—eggs don't wake you up in the middle of the night" (National Alliance for Optional Parenthood, 1978).

BECOMING PARENTS: A CRISIS?

The egg experiment illustrates the lifestyle changes that occur when persons become parents. As a number of sociologists have pointed out, "if the family is conceived of as a small system of interrelated roles and statuses, then it follows that the addition or removal of a family member necessitates changes and reorganization which may produce stress" (Hobbs and Peck [Cole], 1976:723). During the late 1950s and throughout the 1960s, this concern with possible stress gave rise to a number of studies and reports that suggested that parenthood was nothing less than a crisis for many wives and husbands.

Some of the first parenthood-as-crisis studies indicated that the majority of couples in particular samples experienced an "extensive" or "severe" crisis when their first child was born (LeMasters, 1957; Dyer, 1963). Couples were thought to hold an idealized image of parenthood that didn't prepare them for the reality of a demanding, helpless infant.

On the other hand, later studies presented a different picture. While a baby's entrance into a household obviously changed—even disrupted—the usual routine of husbands and wives, the majority of couples reported gratifications in parenthood. Most spoke of their marriages as being no different (and in some cases, even better) after the first child's birth and did not report a severe crisis experience. If a crisis was perceived, it tended to be measured as only "slight" or "moderate" (see Russell, 1974; Hobbs and Peck [Cole], 1976; Hobbs and Wimbish, 1977; Hill, 1978).

An Example of True Crisis

The word *crisis* may, at first, call to mind a psychological definition that includes an "upset in a state of equilibrium caused by a hazardous event which creates a threat, a loss, or a challenge for the individual" (Bloom, 1963, as quoted in Klaus and Kennell, 1978:24). For example, two professors of pediatrics have summarized studies of the emotional crisis parents undergo upon the birth of a child with a birth defect. At the moment of impact, when the news is first received, the parents go through a period of shock, then one of denial, followed by a period of sadness and anger. Gradually, equilibrium is restored as the parents learn to cope and adapt. The process has been compared to the grieving process that takes place when a child dies. In the case of a malformed infant, the parents are, in a sense, mourning the loss of their expected, perfectly formed child. But at the same time, something else is being required of them. They must become attached to the actual, living, malformed infant that *has* been born; and they must handle this concurrently with the "grief work," or mourning, process. However, as such parents get to know their baby and learn to give him or her the required physical care, feelings of closeness to the child develop and the initial feelings of sadness begin to diminish in most cases (Klaus and Kennell, 1978:23–26; Bristor, 1984; Fortier and Wanless, 1984). (For a summary of studies of families with handicapped or seriously ill children, see Rapoport et al., 1977:117–129; Earhart and Sporakowski, eds., 1984; Doherty and McCubbin, eds., 1985; Barbarin, Hughes, and Chesler, 1985.)

Inadequacies of the Family-Crisis Approach to Studying Parenthood

While it isn't difficult to think of parenthood as a "crisis experience" in cases such as that just described, some scholars have suggested that the term is a bit too strong for the *ordinary* experience of parenthood. While some studies, as we've seen, did show that some couples perceived their experience with their first baby to be a "crisis" (according to sociologist Reuben Hill's [1949, 1978] definition of crisis as a sharp change in which old patterns are no longer adequate and new ones have to be developed), others suggested calling such an experience a "normal crisis" (Rapoport, 1963). Parenthood was thus viewed as a normal event in the lives of most couples, a developmental stage that could be looked forward to and prepared for because it was an experience common to most people. Yet at the same time, the change in status from nonparent to parent was such that the term *crisis* still seemed appropriate.

Some sociologists, however, began thinking in terms other than crisis. Daniel Hobbs, Jr. (1965:372), for example, referred to "the process of transition from the marital dyad to the familial triad." (See also Hobbs, 1968.)

Similarly, Alice Rossi (1968) suggested that "the time is now ripe to drop the concept of 'normal crises' and to speak directly, instead, of the transition to and impact of parenthood." She feels that the words *normal* and *crisis* don't really fit together—for two reasons. If a couple successfully makes the transition to parenthood, the word *crisis* seems inappropriate. And second, the word *normal* appears to suggest only successful transitions to parenthood and would seem to rule out the possibility of unsuccessful transitions and negative parenthood experiences. Daniel Hobbs, Jr. and Sue Peck (Cole) (1976:730) likewise emphasize that "it is more accurate to think of beginning parenthood as a transition, accompanied by some difficulty, than a crisis of severe proportions."

BECOMING PARENTS: A TRANSITION

One may leave an unsatisfactory job or marriage, but there is no turning back once parenthood has been undertaken. "We can have ex-spouses and ex-jobs," writes Rossi (1968), "but not ex-children." The word *transition* derives from the Latin for "going across." With parenthood, a new way of life is beginning for the couple.

Several studies have indicated that wives are more likely than husbands to report having found the transition to parenthood difficult (Hobbs and Wimbish, 1977:686; Belsky et al., 1983, 1985; Harriman, 1983; Belsky, 1985)—not a surprising finding in light of the greater disruptions in wives' lives beginning with pregnancy and continuing through their traditionally greater involvement in child care. And in a study of black first-time parents, sociologists Daniel Hobbs and Jane Maynard Wimbish concluded that the transition to parenthood for these couples was slightly more difficult than it was for the

The transition to parenthood is less difficult if the pregnancy was planned and problem-free and if the birth does not take place too soon after marriage. (© Alice Kandell/Photo Researchers, Inc.)

white couples in earlier studies in which Hobbs had been involved (Hobbs, 1965, 1968; Hobbs and Peck [Cole], 1976). However, they offer no explanation as to why this might be but call for further research. At the same time, they point out that the higher difficulty scores in the sample of black couples did not (any more than in the case of white couples) "warrant the label of crisis to describe their experience" (Hobbs and Wimbish, 1977:688).

As we have pointed out repeatedly in this book, black persons face unique problems stemming from discrimination and blocked access to educational and economic opportunities. Dealing with such problems adds yet another challenge to all the usual chal-

lenges and changes involved in the transition to parenthood. In pointing out that "the reality, racism, and response to racism must be included in any interpretation of parental behavior in Black families," Marie Ferguson Peters (1985:160) emphasizes that "Black families make resourceful and creative adaptations as they cope with discrimination and low income . . . , and their supportive child rearing strategies buffer some of the cruel and demeaning messages Black children receive from a hostile world beyond the Black community." First-time black parents must prepare themselves for this buffering task in addition to all the other facets of the new parenthood role.

What do new parents in general find most bothersome about their new roles? Some of the most common complaints relate to the baby's interruption of routine habits of sleep and freedom to go places, fatigue, money problems due to the increased expenses of an infant, interference from in-laws, the loss of the wife's figure and worry over personal appearance, additional work, decreased sexual responsiveness, a decrease in contacts with friends, less time for oneself and one's spouse, feelings of overwhelming and unending responsibility, unpredictability and difficulty in making plans and schedules, and a sense of being tied down (Hobbs and Wimbish, 1977; Russell, 1974; Miller and Sollie, 1980).

Some new mothers experience inner struggles as they try to balance motherhood with career aspirations and interests. "My baby is a new individual in my life whom I love dearly, but at this point I am not personally fulfilled in simply being a mother," one woman told researchers Brent Miller and Donna Sollie (1980:463). "I am finding it difficult to cope with the boredom and lack of intellectual stimulation in my life." She told of having given up her teaching career be-

WHAT BLACK PARENTS WANT

Black parents have all the problems other parents have, and more. They have to bring up their children to be comfortable with their blackness, to be secure, to be proud, to be able to love. . . . They have had to raise their children under the most horrendous of circumstances. In social, economic, and emotional deprivation. Educational deprivation, too. The quality of black life, while it is improving, has been unspeakable. And not because of anything blacks have done. Because of what has been done to blacks . . . no other group has had the experience of being treated as less than human for generation after generation after generation. . . .

What do blacks want for their children?

Nothing more than every parent in every latitude and longitude wants for his [or her] child. And nothing less.

SOURCE: Phyllis Harrison-Ross and Barbara Wyden, *The Black Child: A Parent's Guide to Raising Happy and Healthy Children* (New York: Peter H. Wyden, 1973), pp. 20–21 in the Berkley Medallion paperback edition.

cause she felt placing her child in a day-care center or with a baby-sitter "would be unfair." But now she felt undecided about what she should do.

Perhaps the comment of another woman in Miller and Sollie's sample sums up what many parents feel during the transition to parenthood. "Because an infant is so demanding," she said, "there are days when one wishes the baby did not exist. Knowing these feelings are normal, however, makes coping with the day-to-day routine possible" (p. 463).

Factors Involved in Difficult Transitions to Parenthood

Sociologist Candyce Smith Russell (1974) did not discard the term *crisis* in her study of first-time parents and factors associated with difficult transitions to parenthood. But she used the word in a special sense. "It is important to make clear that crisis as used in this study is defined as change in self, spouse, or relationships with significant others which

the respondent defines as 'bothersome,' " writes Russell (p. 295).

What were some factors associated with a perception of parenthood as a "crisis" (in Russell's sense) or a "bothersome," difficult transition? Premarital conception, a mother's poor health, and (for men) a low ranking of the role of fatherhood in their scale of values. On the other hand, parents indicated less difficulty in undertaking their new roles if the pregnancy was planned and without complications and if the delivery was problem-free. The more months a woman had been married before having her first baby was also linked with a less-stressful transition to parenthood.

In addition, the baby's temperament entered into how distressing the new experience of parenthood was perceived, with quieter babies associated with lower stress for the parents. Russell writes:

It is likely that there is a reinforcing interchange between a parent's ideal image of a baby and the infant's objective behavior. Quiet behavior may reinforce a parent's image of a cuddly baby and elicit a warm response from the parents, which in turn satisfies the infant's desires. Noisy, active behavior, on the other hand, may not fit parental expectations and may elicit non-soothing behavior which will further excite an already active baby. (p. 300)

Do Rewards Outweigh Costs?

Russell not only looked at the problems parents experienced in having their first baby; she also measured *gratifications* associated with parenthood. And overall, her research showed that "respondents perceived their first year of parenthood as only moderately stressful and as well supplied with rewards" (p. 300).

This emphasis on the gratifications of parenthood must not be overlooked. Otherwise, we see only one side—and the negative side at that. As psychologist Lois Wladis Hoffman (1978:340) emphasizes, "This negative portrayal does not seem to jibe with the overall positive evaluation of new motherhood that many women indicated and with the reports of older women looking back." By "negative portrayal," she means the social-science literature in which both theories and research have focused on a variety of problems associated with new parenthood—for example, evidence of greater traditionalism in gender roles as husbands and wives begin functioning as parents, certain anxieties and marital dissatisfactions during early stages of parenthood, theories about the loss of marital intimacy when the twosome becomes a threesome, and all the "bothersome" elements in first parenthood that have given rise to the "crisis" label already examined.

Hoffman is persuaded that we must take into account the *subjective* experience of motherhood in order to get the total picture. "To summarize the effects of the first child on the woman's role without asking the woman how she felt," writes Hoffman,

"might lead to the conclusion that motherhood would soon be on its way out" (p. 366).

Thus, in her research based on a large national representative sample of white married women under age 40, Hoffman used two approaches. One, she asked the women themselves how they felt about motherhood. And two, she compared the women who had already had their first child with those who had not, looking for any differences between the two groups with respect to gender-role attitudes, employment, education, power in marital decision-making, how much husbands participated in household-task performance, and friendship patterns.

She points out that if we paid no attention to women's feelings about their experience of motherhood but looked *only* at objective comparisons between the two groups (mothers and nonmothers), motherhood might be described in "severe" terms. In comparison to the nonmother, the woman who has had her first child

> has more responsibilities and less freedom; she is more likely to leave employment, and sometimes to curtail education. Her husband helps less with household tasks, to some extent her power in decision-making is diminished, and she is more likely to develop a set of friends separate from her husband. (p. 366)

At first glance, we might expect from this that those women who had actually experienced such changes and restrictions in their lives would be the most likely to rate motherhood negatively, whereas nonmothers might hold in mind an idealistic image and rate motherhood more positively. But Hoffman's findings show just the opposite. "In all open-ended questions, mothers viewed motherhood more favorably than nonmothers," writes Hoffman, "and women with no more than a high school education saw it more positively than those with further education" (p. 364).

RETHINKING PARENTHOOD: WHO BENEFITS?

Everyone can benefit from the reinvention of family roles. Mother is being recognized as a person, and as a person who can think. Father must be recognized as a person, and as a person who can feel.

SOURCE: Maureen Green, *Fathering: A New Look at the Creative Art of Being a Father* (New York: McGraw-Hill, 1977), p. 217.

Hoffman found that new mothers often changed their gender-role ideology in the direction of more traditionalism in order to feel more comfortable psychologically with what indeed tended to happen when the first child was born: an "increased separation of husband-wife roles along the traditional, sex-typed lines" (p. 366). In spite of such separation along gender-role lines and more "apartness" between husbands and wives in general (such as an increase in separate friendships), most respondents felt that having a baby brought them closer to their husbands because it involved the husband and wife in a common task and goal—the child's well-being. Hoffman concludes:

> Whether it is the human capacity to learn to live under the conditions that exist, whether it is a bill of goods that has been successfully sold, or whether motherhood is in fact a very gratifying experience, one effect of the first child is a more positive view of the experience, and even to some extent a change of attitudes to fit, and accept, the new situation. (pp. 366–367)

PARENTHOOD: THE INSTITUTION AND THE EXPERIENCE

Increasing numbers of women and men are questioning traditional gender roles, however, as we have seen throughout this book. And we may expect such questioning to show up in less willingness to fit into traditional assumptions about motherhood and father-hood as well and more willingness to seek instead for new patterns. Yet such questioning need not devalue parenthood; for many, it may enhance and enrich the experience.

To question the traditional assumptions about parenthood doesn't mean an undermining of the parent-child *relationship* but has more to do with the conventional way in which parenthood has been conceptualized and in which child-care responsibilities have been assigned. That's why it is important to distinguish between parenthood as a *relationship* or experience (which can indeed be gratifying as the Hoffman data showed) and parenthood as an *institution* (the form or patterned way of parenthood that has been set up with certain roles and behavioral expectations spelled out in advance for women and men to follow) (see Bernard, 1974; Rich, 1976).

Motherhood

Keeping in mind the distinction between motherhood-as-institution and motherhood-as-relationship, we can see the point sociologist Jessie Bernard (1974:10) is driving at when she asserts that young mothers "are beginning to tell us, it's true: they find joy in their children, but they do not like motherhood." Bernard explains why:

> The way we institutionalize motherhood in our society—assigning sole responsibility for child care to the mother, cutting her off from the easy

ON HAVING A SECOND CHILD

My best friend in high school used to theorize that the reason you missed somebody was because you missed the side of yourself that only that particular person was able to bring out. You missed part of yourself.

When I now think about why I chose to have a second child, my friend's theory strikes me as closest to my reason. There was something of me yet to get out that only another offspring could summon. But while I was still pregnant with my second child, I wouldn't have framed that answer so selfishly. I would have focused on our first child, Moriah: Stephen and I wanted Moriah to have a sibling and to be a sister. I worried that I was too observant, too intense, *too much* for one child, and for *her* sake, we needed to shift the trilateral balance of parents and child to one where there were four personalities. . . .

I never expected to limit myself to two children. I loved being the middle child of six kids. Two children seemed dangerously close to a lifelong double date. It was so *ordinary.* A two-child family lacked the inevitable precociousness of an only child as well as the romance of a big, sprawling brood. Even three was an improvement. In my head, when childless, I never for a moment thought I'd stop at two.

I underestimated the immensity and constancy of the responsibility of *one* child. Yes, even after coming from a large family, after running a play group for two-year-olds as a college student, even after student teaching, I had believed that having a baby would make little difference in our lives. I was wrong about that. And two children *are* more than one. More work, more time, more patience, more money. Also, it is more growth, more challenges, more rewards, more stretching of the elastic organ, the heart, and that barely understood mass of tissue, the mind. There is a Zen saying that "Enough is a feast." For us, these two are enough. These two are a feast.

SOURCE: Excerpted from Meg Campbell, "On Having a Second Child," *Ms.,* vol. 13, no. 3 (September 1984), p. 140.

---

help of others in an isolated household, requiring round-the-clock tender, loving care, and making such care her exclusive activity—is not only new and unique, but not even a good way for either women or—if we accept as a criterion the amount of maternal warmth shown—for children. It may, in fact, be the worst. It is as though we had selected the worst features of all the ways motherhood is structured around the world and combined them to produce our current design. (p. 9)

Bernard emphasizes that this view of motherhood is based largely upon a nineteenth-century Victorian idealization—a conception of motherhood that was "male and middle-class" and which ignored the reality of women's lives even of that period of history. The focus was on "mother as symbol."

Feminist author Betty Friedan (1981:86–87) makes a similar point. Emphasizing that even though women can now choose motherhood "without paying the price of physical mutilation and shortening of life that women had to pay generations ago," the choice of motherhood is still a choice "weighted by the price of psychological mutilation, stunting of talents and economic disaster" that too many women have had to pay. Ambivalence over the assumed cost/reward ratio of

WAITING FOR AN IMPORTANT QUESTION

"I'm still waiting in college audiences for young men to stand up and say, 'How can I combine career and family?' in the same way that young women do."

SOURCE: Gloria Steinem, founding editor of *Ms.* magazine, in an address to the National Association for Female Executives, July 18, 1986, quoted in the *Greensboro (NC) News and Record,* July 20, 1986, p. A-10.

motherhood is at the root of the conflict many women are expressing today in discussions of feminism and family ideals—an anxiety that Friedan sees as "a hangover from the generations when too great a price was paid" in assuming the motherhood role. A woman was presented with only an either/or choice. Either she must sacrifice her career aspirations for the sake of motherhood or she must sacrifice her desire for a rich, warm family life in order to pursue her own individualistic interests and career goals. Men have never had to face such a choice.

"The price of motherhood is still too high for most women," Friedan asserts; "the stunting of abilities and earning power is a real fear, because professions and careers are still structured in terms of the lives of men whose wives took care of the parenting and other details of life." She believes that free choice is crucial to woman's "personhood" and stresses that such free choice "has to mean not only the right to choose not to bring a child into the world against one's will, but also the right to have a child, joyously, responsibly, without paying a terrible price of isolation from the world and its rewarded occupations, its decisions and actions."

Fatherhood

Some scholars and researchers have been calling attention to a myth that has grown up which assumes that parenting and mothering are one and the same (Rapoport et al., 1977:3; Young and Hamilton, 1978:137). Until recently, fathers have been given relatively little attention, except for their traditional role as primary breadwinner. Author-poet Adrienne Rich (1976) points out that

Role sharing means both parents take equal responsibility for their children and consider this responsibility when they integrate occupational and family roles. (Gatewood/The Image Works, Inc.)

FATHERHOOD: FOUR MYTHS VERSUS REALITY

Myth #1: Men do not have a natural inclination toward parenting or nurturing behavior. **Reality:** Parenting skills, like most other skills, are basically learned behaviors, not biological endowments. Social customs have taught women and girls to care for the young: social customs could also teach, encourage, and reward men and boys for the same types of skills and behavior.

Myth #2: Infants (both male and female) show no interest in their fathers. **Reality:** Recent research by Lamb (1975) and others casts serious doubts on our earlier assumptions. When the father takes an active role during the first few months of the infant's life, a strong bond seems to develop between them, just as it does between infant and mother. An infant may be more concerned with basic needs of nourishment, comfort, sleep, and a predictable, positive environment than with the sex of the person who meets these needs.

Myth #3: There is a single and universal description of a "successful father." He is financially secure, emotionally tough, and has a natural strength and inclination to control his environment through rational thought and behavior. **Reality:** As women and men honestly raise questions about traditional sex-role definitions and expectations, both are acknowledging much broader characteristics and options for being a successful woman or a successful man. There is no single definition for masculinity or femininity; neither is there a single or universal definition for a good father or a good mother.

Myth #4: Fathers do not want to be bothered with the daily routines of childrearing. **Reality:** Although many fathers have accepted a narrow definition of their role and feel that their time should be spent on non-child-related tasks, many are eager to participate in direct interaction with their children at all levels. Many more fathers would feel this way if they were encouraged to realize their capabilities as parents.

SOURCE: James C. Young and Muriel E. Hamilton, "Paternal Behavior: Implications for Childrearing Practice," in Joseph H. Stevens, Jr., and Marilyn Mathews (eds.), *Mother/Child, Father/Child Relationships* (Washington, D.C.: National Association for the Education of Young Children, 1978), pp. 135–145.

even the expression to *father* is generally taken to mean "to beget, to provide the sperm which fertilizes the ovum." In contrast, the expression to *mother* carries with it the idea of nurturing and caring for someone.

Many men are beginning to see such a narrow definition of fatherhood as having cheated men of the rewards of greater involvement with their children. Thus unwed fathers are, in some cases today, demanding visitation rights and custody rights. Divorced fathers are also indicating a desire for more than a provider role, even for total or joint custody in many instances. And many fathers in intact marriages now question the wisdom of pouring their energies so totally into occupational pursuits that involvement in family life is shoved aside. They are less likely to believe the simplistic equation: "good provider" equals "good father."

The rethinking of women's roles has had an

impact on men's roles as well and is a major factor in the new attention to the responsibilities of fatherhood today. "Young women now entering the scene want more than merely supportive husbands," writes Bernard (1974:175). "They want fatherhood itself expanded. The sharing of the provider role by the mother is felt to call for a sharing of the parental role by the father in the childcare and socializing function." Bernard emphasizes that role sharing is not the same as *role reversal* (in which the mother is the family provider and the father is the caretaker of the children and house)—although, of course, some couples may choose the role-reversal arrangement if it particularly suits them. But *role sharing* means both parents take equal responsibility for the children and take this responsibility into account as they integrate occupational and family roles.

Many men as well as women apparently want to see *fatherhood* expanded and redefined. Commenting on her book for parents, *Growing Up Free*, Letty Cottin Pogrebin (1982:43) writes that the one line in her book "that many men having singled out as the most resonant is this bit of advice: *Don't be the man you think you should be, be the father you wish you'd had.*" (See insert.) The limited fatherhood style that gender-role stereotyping dictated is viewed as unsatisfying by many men today.

And men are doing something about it (Hanson and Bozett, 1985; Lewis and Salt, 1985). Increasingly, fathers are participating with mothers in prenatal classes and in childbirth itself. Male friends may throw a baby shower for a father-to-be (O'Malia, 1982). Fathers enroll in infant-care classes or join with other fathers in "fathers-only" play groups where fathers can bring their children for playtime, swap ideas and advice, and share their fatherhood experiences (Korpivaara, 1982). Fathers and mothers alike have

been found eager for information on infant behavior, health, growth, and developmental landmarks (Kliman and Vukelich, 1985). A survey of the research literature on fathers and infants indicates that both benefit from the fathers' close involvement with their children from the time of birth onward (Ricks, 1985). Fathers have been discovering the importance of nurturance behaviors in their own lives, and researchers have been discovering the important part played by fathers in the various aspects of children's development (Lamb, 1976; Lamb and Sagi, 1983; Lamb, Pleck, and Levine, 1986; McAdoo, 1986).

Stages of Parenthood

Rossi (1968) points out that the development of a social role has various phases and lists four basic stages of adult social roles: the anticipatory stage, the honeymoon stage, the plateau stage, and the disengagement-termination stage. For example, in the case of a person's role as spouse, the period of engagement is the *anticipatory stage* for that role; the *honeymoon stage* is made up of the early days when the role is new and the spouses are enjoying a special closeness to one another and exploration of one another's uniqueness; the *plateau stage* is the "protracted middle period" that makes up the major part of married life; and the *disengagement-termination stage* occurs when the marriage ends in divorce or death.

Early Stages Applying these four broad stages to parenthood, Rossi speaks of pregnancy as the anticipatory stage. (Making the preparations for adopting a child would be the equivalent for adoptive parents.) In an exploratory study of twenty-four expectant parents, M. Colleen Stainton (1985) found that both prospective mothers and prospec-

BIG CHANGES IN PARENTING

I have been thinking a lot about fatherhood.

I'd swear everyone is. Since the publication of *Growing Up Free,* my book on nonsexist child-rearing, I have made the rounds of some 30 cities doing lectures, interviews, and talk shows where listeners call in to register their views. The subject that comes up most often and arouses the most passion is not, as one might expect, sex after sex roles, or tips for an egalitarian marriage, but how men can be better fathers.

- "My father never knew me," said an intense male voice over a Grand Rapids phone-in show. "I don't want to make the same mistakes. I'm trying to learn how to father my own kids while there's still time."

- "I'll never forget what happened when I was ten years old. My mother had just died and my sister and I were standing beside the casket bawling," recalled a San Francisco man of 70. "When my father saw my tears, he grabbed me by the shoulders and said, 'We're *men;* we're not going to cry. We're going to be strong.' I've swallowed my tears for sixty years and all I've got to show for it is a lifelong lump in my throat and mean memories of my father."

- A New York City cabdriver told me forthrightly: "Being a father is more important to me than being black, being a Baptist, or being a man."

- "When our son said he was coming home from college on the day of my husband's office Christmas party, my husband asked him to come straight to the office," said a woman in Washington, D.C. "The boy bounded in, saw his father across the roomful of people, ran and threw his arms around my husband's neck and hugged and kissed him. At first I was embarrassed for my husband, but then I heard one man after another come up to him and say, 'I'd give the world if my son would do that with me.' "

Things seem to be changing. Fathering is becoming a new kind of verb—an active verb—that describes a new kind of role and a new set of behaviors. Men are affirmatively taking off time to be with their children. They are talking to one another about fathering, learning the parenting trade, and exchanging ideas and impressions the way mothers have for centuries. . . . They are looking to women, not as emotional surrogates and stand-ins for the too-busy dad, but as expert counselors in the art of parent-child intimacy.

All over America, people are thinking about the fathers we have or the fathers we are, and fatherhood is being redefined, reinvented, and redeemed.

SOURCE: Excerpted from Letty Cottin Pogrebin, "Big Changes in Parenting," *Ms., 10* (February 1982), pp. 41–43.

---

tive fathers developed, over the course of the pregnancy, a sense of the fetus as a unique individual and "a growing member of the family."

The anticipatory stage is followed by the honeymoon stage of parenthood, which Rossi (1968) describes as "that postchild-birth period during which, through intimacy and prolonged contact, an attachment between parent and child is laid down." She emphasizes that there is a major difference between this honeymoon stage and the honeymoon stage of marriage, however, because in the early stages of parenthood, parents are getting acquainted with the child for the first time while in the early stages of marriage, the persons knew each other in advance to a considerable degree.

Interest in *sharing* the anticipatory and honeymoon stages of parenthood may be seen in the participation of young husbands and wives together in preparation-for-childbirth classes, the desire of many couples to have the husband present during childbirth (either in a hospital that cooperates with such a plan or, in some cases, by arranging an at-home birth, possibly with the assistance of a midwife rather than a physician, where legal), and in the interest of many young fathers in sharing the care of babies and small children, as we saw earlier (see Rapoport et al., 1977:161–175, 352).

The honeymoon stage of parenthood seems especially important with the first baby because the parents are conscious of trying out various aspects of the parental role for the first time. The sociologist Sandra Titus (1976) calls attention to one illustration of this. By studying records of family life as shown in family photo albums, she found that not only do parents tend to take *more* pictures of the first baby than of subsequent children but they also take special *kinds* of pictures. First-time parents seem interested in preserving on film a record of their own learning of various tasks associated with their new roles; thus, there are photos of the parents as they hold, feed, diaper, bathe, and otherwise care for the baby.

Later Stages There is no precise point marking the transition from the honeymoon stage of parenthood to the plateau stage— the bulk of the years in which parents are preparing their children for life. It is during this plateau period that parents confront various child-developmental issues such as gender-role socialization; moral development; and growth toward independence, discipline, and motivation for achievement (Rapoport et al., 1977:353).

The Committee On Public Education of the Group for the Advancement of Psychiatry (1973) has described what is taking place in parents' lives during those years:

> Parenting involves reliving one's own childhood experiences during each stage through which the child passes. Parents and children develop together and interact with each other. To be able to feel what the child feels enlarges the parents' capacity for empathy in other interpersonal relationships. (p. 16, as quoted in Rapoport et al., 1977:16)

At the same time, the committee emphasizes that parents need not feel guilty for recognizing their own needs as individuals and attending to them:

> Parents are not only vehicles for the care of their children. They were persons before the child arrived; are persons while they are parents; and will be after the children leave.... They were once told to listen to their parents. They are now told to listen to their children. Both directives are valuable. They must, in addition, listen to themselves. (pp. 131–132, as quoted in Rapoport et al., 1977:18)

The final stage of parenthood, Rossi's disengagement-termination stage, like the plateau stage, is not marked by some specific event signifying that parental authority, obligations, and responsibilities have ended. "Many parents, however, experience the marriage of the child as a psychological termination of the active parental role," says Rossi (1968). At the same time, as we have seen, Rossi emphasizes in that same article that a parent can never become an ex-parent in a strict sense. Even after their offspring reach legal age or marry or otherwise strike out on their own, parental interest and involvement usually, to some degree, will continue.

CHILDREARING IN AN ACHIEVEMENT-ORIENTED SOCIETY

Childrearing, like marriage, is a complex process involving actions, interactions, and reactions; and all parties concerned—father, mother, and each child—play a part in this process (see Walters and Walters, 1980). In other words, we're back again to exchange theory.

Exchange Theory and Childhood Socialization

Sociologist Stephen Richer (1968) has developed a theoretical model of how social exchange may be expected to work in parent-child relationships. Building upon the premise that power is associated with resources, Richer attributes the high degree of power parents hold over very small children to the fact that in the earliest years, children are totally dependent upon parents for both material rewards (food, clothing, shelter) and social rewards (comfort, love, affirmation, approval, and so on). Children have few, if any, alternative sources of such rewards, nor do they in themselves possess equivalent resources which would permit bargaining from an equal power base.

The relationship is one-sided until somewhere in the toddler stage, when children discover a resource of their own—one highly valued by parents and which, therefore, gives children a measure of power in the bargaining process. That resource, according to Richer, is *compliance*—doing what others want them to do. Children perceive that their

compliance means a great deal to parents and can make parents happy or unhappy. ("Melissa, please eat your peas. Come on now, be a good girl. It makes Mommy sad when you won't obey." "Timmy! You know you're supposed to tell me when you have to go to the potty!" "Kim, say 'thank you' to Grandma. Kim! Come back here this minute! Say thank you for the present. Oh, that child makes me furious!")

Richer points out that the child's growing awareness of the ability to produce effects on others (the parents' pleasure or displeasure) is a crucial occurrence. "For, though still dependent for basic material and social rewards on his parents, the child begins to experience feelings of autonomy, a necessary prerequisite for later involvement in self-interested exchange (p. 463).

When the child starts school, compliance is found to be valued by other adults as well. Now the teacher's praise and approval can be obtained in exchange for the child's conformity to the teacher's wishes. Schoolmates also increasingly become sources of social rewards. No longer is the child quite so dependent upon parents, and with the availability of alternative rewards for the child comes a diminishing of parental power. The child may now place a higher price tag on compliance: hugs, smiles of approval, and expressions of pleasure may not always be enough any more. Thus the parent may suggest material rewards (a dollar for a good report card or a gift for cooperation in something the child doesn't want to do) or may bargain for the child's compliance in a spirit of *quid pro quo:* you do this for me, and I'll do that for you. The early dependence stage has given way to a reciprocity stage.

During adolescence, the child's power increases even more because the resources offered by the peer group take on such importance. One way parents may try to obtain and

A child's growing awareness of the ability to produce effects on others is a crucial occurrence. (© Alice Kandell/Photo Researchers, Inc.)

maintain compliance is through offering new kinds of rewards which will bring greater peer-group approval for the adolescent (the keys to the car, opening the home for parties, and the like). However, if the young person has alternative material rewards (money from a part-time job) as well as alternative social rewards (peer approval), dependency on parents is all the more decreased—as is parental power.

Richer acknowledges that the picture just presented may seem a bit overdrawn, but it is intended simply to provide a basic illustration of how social-exchange theory may be applied in parent-child relationships. Of special importance is the part socioeconomic status plays in the exchange. For example, parents may view a child's increasing realization that compliance can be granted or with-

held as a situation calling for reasoning and reciprocity or as a situation posing a threat to order and therefore calling for coercion (the stick instead of the carrot). Social class has a great deal to do with which of the two approaches parents will take. Studies have shown that parents at lower socioeconomic levels are more likely to use coercion and parents at higher levels are more likely to employ reasoning and bargaining. "The middle-class home is thus more conducive to the development of an exchange system," says Richer, "whereas the cultural patterns at lower status levels inhibit such a system." And when a child reaches adolescence and physical force and coercion are more difficult to utilize, lower-status parents may find themselves relatively powerless because they have few rewards to offer in comparison to alternative sources of benefits now open to their offspring.

Sociologist Robert Winch (1962) has tested exchange theory in a study comparing the influence on college males of two social systems: the family and the fraternity. *Identification* was the term he used to denote the lasting influence of one person or social system on another person. (We have already seen, in Chapter 2, how important parents consider the reward of such identification on the part of a child who models his or her life after the parent's example and values.) Winch found that since upper-status families (fathers in particular) are better able than are lower-status families to reward their sons with such resources as material goods, time, and expertise, sons from families at higher socioeconomic levels are more likely to identify with their fathers than with the fraternity peer group. But when a family lacks resources and expert power, the son looks to another social system for rewards; therefore, the fraternity's influence increases as socioeconomic status decreases (Winch, 1962; Winch and Gordon, 1974, chap. 3).

Class Differences in Socializing for Achievement

"Members of different social classes, by virtue of enjoying (or suffering) different conditions of life, come to see the world differently—to develop different conceptions of social reality, different aspirations and hopes and fears, different 'conceptions of the desirable,'" writes sociologist Melvin Kohn (1969:7). Another way of saying that persons hold differing "conceptions of the desirable" is to say they hold different values.

Kohn (1969:200) has done extensive research which shows that parental values differ by class and, consequently, parents at different status levels socialize their children in different ways. "Parents tend to impart to their children lessons derived from the conditions of life of their own social class—and thus help prepare their children for a similar class position." For example, in a study of men and work, Kohn found that at higher socioeconomic levels more than at lower levels, there was great value placed upon self-direction characteristics—curiosity about how and why things happen as they do, interest in making sound judgments, self-reliance, taking responsibility, facing facts squarely, being able to work under pressure, and so on. At higher status levels, the men tended to evaluate jobs in terms of *intrinsic qualities* (characteristics inherent in the occupation, such as how much freedom it offered, how interesting it was, the opportunities it afforded to use talents or help other people). But at lower status levels, the men tended to judge jobs according to *extrinsic characteristics* (externals such as pay, job security, fringe benefits, work hours, supervisors and coworkers, and so on) (p. 76).

Not only was the conception of the world of work found to differ by socioeconomic status, the conception of the social world was also found to differ. The lower the social status, the more likely were the men to emphasize a rigid conservatism which opposed questioning old, established ways. They were more likely to resist innovation and change and unable to tolerate nonconformity to the dictates of authority. "The most important thing to teach children is absolute obedience to their parents," was the kind of statement which received much greater agreement among lower-status men. The lower the social position, the more likely were the men to view personal morality in terms of conforming to the letter of the law (again emphasizing the external over the internal), and also the less trustful they were of other people.

These outlooks carry over to the socialization of children. Kohn found that the higher the socioeconomic position of fathers, the more highly they valued self-direction in their children and the less likely they were to value conformity to standards imposed from the outside. The contrasting values of higher-status self-direction and lower-status conformity also showed up in a study of mothers. Although Kohn found that mothers at all status levels considered it important that their children be happy, considerate, honest, dependable, obedient, and respectful of others' rights, the higher the social status of mothers, the more likely they were to emphasize curiosity and self-control as desirable qualities for their children. And the lower the status, the more likely were they to select obedience, neatness, and cleanliness as desirable. Of particular interest is Kohn's finding that a mother's own educational and occupational attainments (rather than her ascribed status based on her husband's attainments) are related to the values she holds for her children. Kohn found also that those working-class mothers who held high aspirations and wanted their children to attend college tended to be women who themselves had had some educational advantages but who had married down. "One gets the impression," writes Kohn, "that for many of them, the child's upward mobility represents an opportunity to recoup the status that they, themselves, have lost" (p. 34).

Kohn's findings on different parental values largely held for both blacks and whites. Socioeconomic status, not race, was the key factor in determining whether parents emphasized in their children either self-determination or conformity to external controls. As a further test of his findings, we included in our 1968 Indianapolis study of black families some of Kohn's items for measuring parental values. Our results were similar: The lower the status of black parents, the more

likely they were to respond that *obedience* was the most important thing a child should learn. The higher the status, the more likely they were to indicate that *autonomy* was the most desired value for their children. We also found, as Kohn did, that the greater the wife's own occupational status, the more likely she was to transmit autonomy values to her children (Scanzoni, 1977).

Resources Provided by Parents

When Gertrude Hunter entered high school, she enrolled in the college-preparatory program without so much as a second thought: "What happened next," she says, "is, tragically even today, all too familiar to blacks." A faculty adviser called her in and handed her back the form that had contained her carefully worked-out class schedule. But all the college-prep courses had been crossed out! Home economics courses had been substituted. The dazed young woman took the paper home, whereupon her outraged mother promptly marched to school to confront the adviser. Gertrude Hunter describes the scene in her own words: "The adviser attempted to placate my mother. 'Mrs. Teixeira,' she pleaded, 'what is a colored girl going to do with college? If she learns cooking and sewing, she can always get a good job.' But when we left the office, I was enrolled in the college course."

Years later, as a pediatrician in a high administrative position with the United States Department of Health, Education and Welfare, Dr. Gertrude Hunter looked back with gratitude to her parents' influence on her life. Knowing they expected her to do well in school, she endeavored to fulfill those expectations. Her father and mother helped her see that who and what she was was good. "As a woman," she says, "I was told I would be able to do whatever I wanted. I was taught that my skin had a beautiful color. This constant, implicit reinforcement of positive self-image was my parents' most valuable gift to me" (Hunter, 1973).

Self-Esteem In the ongoing exchange between parents and children, the resources passed on by parents may be tangible (music lessons, summer camps, college or trade school tuition, and the like) or they may be intangible in the form of attitudes conveyed and aptitudes developed. The building of a child's self-esteem, as in the case of Gertrude

Intangible resources, such as a positive self-image, are among the most valuable gifts parents can pass on to their children. (Charles Gatewood)

Hunter, is one example of such an intangible resource.

Sociologist Alan Kerckhoff (1972:56) calls attention to the way children's interactions with their parents profoundly affect their definition of the world around them so that they come to view it as "friendly or threatening, as a source of opportunity or danger, as controllable or chaotic." In that interaction, a child's self-image begins to evolve; and the world and the self will seem quite different to someone who believes, "I can do anything I set out to do," and someone who believes, "People like me don't have much of a chance in life." Kerckhoff writes: "The self-image is thus a view of oneself in relation to one's environment. Part of that environment is the opportunity structure—how much access to rewards different kinds of people have."

Persons at lower socioeconomic levels tend to see the social stratification system in much the same way as higher-status persons; that is, they rank certain occupations as being more prestigious than others. They generally consider *themselves* to be in lower-status positions in addition to being defined by others in this way, which means, says Kerckhoff, that these attitudes will be conveyed to lower-status children, who then follow their parents in developing a "sense of impotence in society." Since such parents have little faith that the American Dream will actualize for them or their children, they emphasize security and avoiding risk rather than looking for opportunities to seize. The child thus develops an attitude of passivity rather than a sense of mastery. In a home where there are low expectations for achievement and great pressures for compliance, a child is likely to develop low self-esteem.

However, where parents endeavor to build a strong self-image in children, encouraging them to be upwardly mobile, they provide

EIGHTH-GRADE DROPOUT SAW CHILDREN EDUCATED

San Diego—Rose McKinney's education ended in the eighth grade, but the 84-year-old daughter of a former slave saw her 12 children through college and postgraduate schools.

"I never did get back, but the Lord blessed me just the same," said Mrs. McKinney.

Her dozen children include five with doctoral degrees—professors, pastors, psychiatrists, authors, business executives and technicians. Of her 29 grandchildren, 20 are college graduates or attend college now, and several hold advanced degrees in disciplines ranging from communications to economics.

"The McKinneys aren't trying to take over the world," she said, looking back. "They're just interested in getting an education. It's just in 'em."

The family got its start in 1914, when Mrs. McKinney married an impoverished sharecropper in Rondo, Ark. George McKinney died in 1972, but by then a family of scholars was well established.

By the light of a kerosene lamp in the '20s and '30s, she taught her children as preschoolers to read.

"I always wanted them to be outstanding. I wanted them to be useful men and women," she said. "I would pray for them, that when they all got old enough, they would all go to school."

As each child got to college, often aided by academic scholarships, older brothers and sisters pitched in to help. Their father pushed too—sending off for courses from a correspondence school in Chicago in the hopes of getting a high school diploma.

"He never finished it, but he sure tried. He would get his books and study by the kerosene lamp after working the cotton compress all day," said a son, Dr. George McKinney Jr.

At one time, a daughter, Ruth, wanted to drop out of school because "we didn't have clothing like everybody else had."

A speech teacher now, she said, "Many times we'd register for school in September but not start until November because we spent those two months picking cotton to buy clothes and groceries. . . . But my mother said, 'No. You will not drop out of school.' "

SOURCE: AP report, *Greensboro (NC) Daily News*, August 23, 1980, p. A3.

them with a valuable resource for achievement. Some comments of respondents from our study of black families illustrate how parental encouragement and confidence serve as resources that benefit children. "He has given me the incentive to get ahead," said one male respondent of his father. And these comments were made about mothers: "She had a value system that was a middle-class standard, not like poor people." "She always taught me to save money—what little I could get hold of—and take advantage of every opportunity that would help me to get ahead" (Scanzoni, 1977:79). (See also Scanzoni, 1985; Harrison, 1985; McAdoo, 1985; Franklin and Boyd-Franklin, 1985.)

Education and Work Attitudes Since occupational achievement is so bound up with education, a family that values education provides children with a particularly valuable resource in that children will be encouraged and aided in obtaining as much schooling as possible. We found that considerable educational and occupational mobility had occurred among our sample of Indianapolis black families, and there is little doubt that parental attitudes aided in such upward mobility in a great many cases.

Numerous respondents made comments such as these: "She saw that I went to school." "Lots of times I didn't plan on going and he saw to it I got there." "He kept telling me I needed an education." "She wanted me to be very smart." "He helped me by financing the things I needed for school." Several spoke of parental sacrifices which made it possible to finish school instead of having to drop out to get a job. "He went without clothes so I could go to school," said one respondent. "She washed and ironed for white folks and helped out so I could go to school," said another. Others spoke of parents making it possible to attend college, art school, or trade school. Respondents reported emotional support, aid with homework, and other forms of help and encouragement parents had given as well.

Attitudes toward work were also conveyed to them by parents. "I used to jump from job to job," said one respondent. "He told me I couldn't get ahead like that—to stay on the job until I could get to know whether I liked it or not." Some told of fathers who had spoken of hardships they themselves had faced so that their children would know what to expect in the job market. Overall, although these parents were aware of the relative deprivation of blacks, they nevertheless endeavored to encourage their offspring to accept the dominant value system of American society with its emphasis on achievement.

However, not all parents had conveyed such positive attitudes. Some respondents spoke of being taught to expect disappointment, and some were actually hindered from movement toward achievement. Some parents were indifferent, offering no advice about getting ahead and doing nothing to encourage educational attainments. One male respondent said of his father: "He hindered us because he wanted us to quit school and go to work; he did not allow us to participate in school activities." A woman said of her mother: "Because I had to do all the housework, she didn't care if I went to school or not" (Scanzoni, 1977, chap. 3).

Among both blacks and whites, a family's position in the economic-opportunity system has a great deal to do with attitudes conveyed to children. Kohn (1969, chap. 11) suggests that the values parents emphasize in their children are generated and maintained by the parents' own occupational experiences. Lower-status jobs are more constricting and seldom provide opportunities for self-direction, emphasizing, instead, conformity to authority; hence, the lower the status, the more likely does the conformity discussed earlier come to be regarded as a value in its own right on or off the job. In contrast, higher-status occupations permit self-direction and encourage flexibility, creativity, and making one's own analyses and decisions rather than simply obeying orders. Persons with opportunities for self-direction on the job place a high value on self-direction in other areas of life as well and seek to convey such attitudes to their children. According to Kohn's studies, children at higher status levels are thus better equipped to get ahead in a society that stresses achievement. They are more likely to have learned to think for themselves, handle responsibility, meet new and problematic situations, and initiate change instead of merely reacting to it. Lower-status children are less prepared for achievement because their parents have placed primary emphasis on externals and consequences.

Other studies have shown that even the way parents talk in the home affects a child's thinking and speaking abilities and that language patterns vary according to socioeconomic class. As a result, children at higher status levels become better able to label, classify, analyze, conceptualize, and communicate than do children at lower socioeconomic levels (see summary in Kerckhoff, 1972:48–52).

Achievement Motivation and Gender Roles

There is some evidence that high achievement motivation is associated with certain childrearing patterns, namely, early independence training, encouragement of self-reliance, fewer restrictions, and holding high aspirations (McClelland, 1961; also see Brown, 1965, chap. 9). Such patterns would seem to be the opposite of the value orientations of lower-status families (passivity and conformity) and suggest, rather, the mastery and autonomy more likely to be found at higher status levels.

However, differences in achievement socialization are related not only to class but also to gender. Female socialization at all class levels seems to reflect value orientations generally associated with lower-status levels; that is, girls, more than boys, are pointed in the direction of passivity and conformity, and boys, more than girls, are encouraged toward mastery and autonomy. The actual *degree* of gender typing varies by class, but elements of it are there at all status levels.

Sociologist Alice Rossi (1965) showed that the qualities thought to be characteristic of great scientists are the very qualities that have traditionally been discouraged in the childhood socialization of females: high intellectual ability, intense channeling of energy in the pursuit of work tasks, extreme independence, and "apartness" from others. On a similar note, psychologist Lois Hoffman (1972b) points out that socialization practices have usually encouraged females from earliest childhood to want to please others and to work for approval and love. Achievement in tasks is motivated by these learned *affiliative* needs, and "if achievement threatens affiliation, performance may be sacrificed or anxiety may result." Boys, on the other hand, learn to value achievement much more for its own sake and to become involved in work for the sheer joy of mastering a challenging task.

In view of studies which show that gifted girls are less likely than are gifted boys to fulfill their intellectual potential in adulthood, Hoffman's (1972b) thesis is that females are not given adequate parental encouragement in their early strivings toward independence. Parents tend to worry over and protect girls more than boys, fostering dependence and discouraging feelings of confidence and competence. If one is female, there is also less pressure to develop one's own self-identity. "Separation of the self is facilitated when the child is the opposite sex of the primary caretaker," writes Hoffman. Since the mother is usually the primary caretaker, both male and female children form their first attachment to her. However, a boy is encouraged to identify with his father, which prompts an earlier and more complete separation from the primary caretaker and fosters the building of a sense of selfhood. "The girl, on the other hand, is encouraged to maintain her identification with the mother," Hoffman explains: "therefore she is not as likely to establish an early and independent sense of self." She also points out that boys, more than girls, engage in conflict with their mothers, another way in which the formation of a separate self is facilitated.

But perhaps more than building a sense of selfhood through *separation from* the mother, it is the male child's *identification with* the achiever role of the father that encourages greater autonomy. Hoffman is not unaware of that possibility and refers to studies which show that high-achieving females have also identified with their fathers. Changing attitudes and more egalitarian gender-role norms might show that a female's identification with her mother doesn't, in itself, hinder self-direction. "The significant factor may be identifying with a mother who is herself passive and dependent," Hoffman states. "If the mother were a mathematician, would the daughter's close identification be dysfunctional to top achievement?" Research is needed to answer that question, but already there is some evidence that the answer is no. Rather, close identification with such a mother might be likely to encourage the daughter to follow the mother's example and become an achiever herself. Other conditions conducive to female achievement are also more likely to be found in those families where the mother is professionally employed, namely, early independence training and a close relationship with a father "who encourages the girl's independence and achievement while accepting her as a female" (Hoffman, 1974:162–163; 1973:213).

Childhood Experiences of Female Executives

For her doctoral dissertation in business administration at Harvard University, Margaret Hennig studied female presidents and vice-presidents of male-oriented, nationally recognized, medium-to-large business firms and compared them with a control group of women "who appeared overtly to match the top women executives in all factual data but who had never succeeded in rising beyond middle management." The difference between the two groups' achievements appears to lie in the family dynamics of their respective childhoods (summarized in Hennig, 1973; Hennig and Jardim, 1977).

Each high-achieving executive was either an only child or the firstborn in an all-girl family with no more than three siblings. Both parents of each high-achieving female highly valued in their daughter *both* femaleness *and* achievement; being a girl and being a success were not viewed as contradictory or mutually exclusive. Although all but one of the mothers represented the traditional feminine role model in homemaking, they actively encouraged their daughters to explore roles that were usually considered masculine. Both parents warmly supported their daughter and delighted in her accomplishments. In addition, they sought to help her internalize achievement values and satisfactions. They seemed to want her to learn early to set her own goals and standards of excellence and to experience the pleasure of rewarding herself through a job well done.

The executives also reported that their parents had had unusually strong relationships with each other and with them, respecting each person as a distinct individual. As one respondent expressed it: "I had the fortune to have two full and complete parents. That is, both my mother and my father were separate real people and I had a separate and real relationship with each. Most girls have such experience of sharing common interests with their mothers; few share common interests with their dads."

Overall, the father and mother in such homes created a supportive climate free from gender-role limitations so that, over the years, their daughter could try out a wide range of roles and behavioral styles. This "security base" prepared these future executives to overcome any obstacles they might encounter from having been born female. When gender-related conflicts came up, "it was the conflict itself, rather than the achievement, that was perceived as needing to be eliminated," writes Hennig. All during childhood, these women had developed high self-esteem—both from their parents who reinforced and encouraged them and from their own experiences of successful accomplishments. Hennig (1973:30) concludes: "During those early experiences, they accepted such a strong concept of themselves as people that even years of later conflict and pressure to split them into two segments— the feminine affective person and the masculine instrumental person—could not cause them to reduce their achievement drive."

SOCIAL STATUS AND CHILD DISCIPLINE

The word *discipline* may be defined as training to act in accordance with certain standards, or it may be defined as chastisement or correction for failure to conform to such standards. Sociologist Leonard Pearlin (1972) refers to the second sense of the word in speaking of discipline as "a systematic reaction to the behavior of children that parents judge to be either a direct threat to parental values and aspirations or an insufficient effort by children to attain these distant ideals" (chap. 6).

Pearlin's use of the word *systematic* is deliberate: he is making the point that although parents differ in disciplinary practices, these differences are *patterned* and cannot be explained simply as the result of personality variations or as momentary reactions to situations in which parents give vent to certain feelings. Pearlin's study of families in Turin, Italy, produced findings that correspond to Kohn's findings in the United States. Accord-

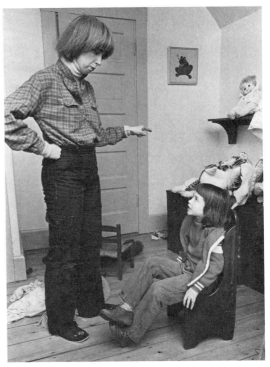

Disciplinary practices in the home are tied to parental values, and parental values are linked with social status. (© 1980 Paul Fortin/Stock, Boston)

ing to their evidence, disciplinary practices in the home are tied to parental values; and parental values, as we have seen, are linked with social status.

Both middle-class and working-class parents emphasize control in the lives of children; but for middle-class parents, the emphasis is on control from within (self-direction), whereas working-class parents stress control from without (obedience to rules and authority). Both social status and the sex of the misbehaving child enter into the reaction of parents with regard to discipline.

Kohn (1969, chap. 6), for example, found that working-class mothers in his sample were more likely than were middle-class mothers to employ physical punishment when children (particularly sons) engaged in wild play (boisterousness, aggressive behavior, belligerent and destructive actions) or when children fought with brothers and sisters. The focus was on "the direct and immediate consequences of the disobedient acts" rather than on perception of the child's motivations. From the mother's point of view, what has occurred in such a case is a violation of good order; such nonconformity to acceptable standards of behavior calls for punishment, according to working-class values.

Middle-class mothers, on the other hand, were able to tolerate wild play even in its extreme forms. But they could *not* tolerate violent outbursts of temper. The overt behavior in the two instances might be exactly the same ("shouting, wrestling, slamming doors, stamping feet, running"), but what these mothers were concerned about was the child's intent rather than the situation itself. Children's rowdiness and excitement in play weren't viewed as alarming as long as their actions were perceived as "letting off steam." However, if the same actions were viewed as violent outbursts—temper tantrums resulting from a child's feeling frustrated at not getting his or her own way— middle-class mothers tended to resort to physical punishment. Why? Again, parental values seem to have been involved—in this case, the middle-class value of self-control. Parents refused to put up with behavior that indicated the loss of such control.

Gender-Based Differences

Misbehavior in children may be thought of either in terms of their doing what they shouldn't do (as in the above illustrations) or in their *not* doing what they *should* do (re-

fusing to carry out parents' requests). Kohn found that working-class mothers tended to punish sons for the first kind of misbehavior but not for the second kind. When boys defiantly refused to comply with their mothers' wishes, the mothers tended to refrain from any form of punishment and instead simply did nothing at all. But when daughters refused to do as they were told, they were swiftly punished. At this social status level, "more is expected of girls than of boys," writes Kohn. "Girls must not only refrain from unacceptable behavior; they must also fulfill positive expectations" (p. 101).

Working-class girls were more likely than were boys at this level to be punished for activities such as smoking, swiping something, or fighting with friends. Once again, we see the part class differences play in gender-role norms. Kohn points out that for working-class parents, "what may be taken as acceptable behavior (perhaps even as an assertion of manliness) in a preadolescent boy may be thought thoroughly unladylike in a young girl." Middle-class parents, in contrast, tend not to make such distinctions based on gender. Their main concern in matters of discipline is that children of either sex will act according to internalized principles (pp. 105–106).

Types of Discipline

In 1958, social psychologist Urie Bronfenbrenner published a comprehensive review of socialization studies from the 1930s onward. Bronfenbrenner was especially interested in class differences in childrearing, and one of his conclusions was this: "In matters of discipline, working-class parents are consistently more likely to employ physical punishment, while middle-class families rely more on reasoning, isolation, appeals to guilt, and other methods involving the threat of loss of love" (as quoted in Kerckhoff, 1972:42).

However, since that time a number of studies have caused sociologists to raise questions about alleged class differences in the usage of physical punishment, and inconsistencies in earlier studies are being reexamined as well (Erlanger, 1974; also Straus, 1971). Pearlin (1972:103) wrote of his Italian study: "By itself, class bears only a modest relationship to physical punishment: Only 8 percent more middle- than working-class parents reported that they had not resorted to any physical punishment in the past six months."

Another sociologist, Murray Straus (1971), found that 52 percent of a sample of university students had experienced actual or threatened physical punishment from their parents during the last year of high school; but there was no relationship between physical punishment and socioeconomic status. Straus was surprised that such class differences didn't show up—especially since the study showed that the highest frequency of physical punishment took place among students who reported their parents emphasized obedience as the most important characteristic of children and the lowest frequency took place where parents considered self-control and thinking for oneself to be the most desired traits in children. Straus suggested that the explanation for the lack of differences according to class may lie in the fact that working-class students in the sample were from homes where upward mobility was emphasized and where parents had identified with higher-status values and socialization practices. Thus the incidence of physical punishment was no greater among them than among middle-class students.

Kohn's (1969) research showed that mothers responded to children's misbehavior in numerous ways—ignoring it, scolding and admonishing, removing the child from the situation or diverting attention, restricting activities, isolating the child temporarily, or punishing the child physically ("everything from a slap to a spanking"). Both working-class and middle-class mothers reported that they generally ignored misbehavior or else admonished their children verbally at this stage (Kohn's sample included only mothers of fifth-graders). Few reported using isolation or restriction, and even fewer punished physically under usual circumstances. Although there was a slight tendency for working-class mothers to be more likely than middle-class mothers to use physical punishment, coercion was not quickly resorted to in either class. Only *persistent* misbehavior was seen to call for punishment. "It would seem, then," says Kohn, "that the difference between middle- and working-class mothers' use of physical punishment is not in the frequency with which they use it, but in the conditions under which they use it" (pp. 93–95)—conditions which we have already examined.

Discipline and Achievement Values

In the socialization process, parents seek to guide their children in the development of characteristics and behaviors which the parents consider to be important for the future—particularly as sons and daughters prepare to fit into the economic-opportunity system in some way. Evidence from the studies of Kohn and Pearlin suggests that the parents' values come from their own place in the economic structure and that these values are then passed on so that children will find a place there that will quite often be similar to that of the parents. When children deviate from behavior consistent with the parents' values, discipline is employed. In this sense, discipline is an important part of socializing for achievement (Pearlin, 1972:99).

CHILD ABUSE

In recent years, increasing attention has been given to the problem of battered children. The subject of child *discipline*, just examined, is different from child *abuse*—although authorities may not always agree on the exact line of demarcation. What starts out as discipline may sometimes become abuse, especially if a parent feels a child's behavior indicates the parent's loss of control over the situation. Sociologist Suzanne Steinmetz (1977:39) explains: "Just as normal discipline is an attempt to restore authority, abuse is a more desperate attempt to do so." In such cases, according to Marian Marion (1982:576), the intensity of physical punishment is escalated because the control achieved by coercive discipline is short-lived and often results in even more deviant behavior on the part of the child. Marion, a specialist in human development and early childhood education, calls this intensification of physical punishment "turning up the volume" and points out that at some point it can become nothing less than child abuse.

The Child Abuse Prevention and Treatment Act passed by Congress in 1974 provided this definition of child abuse:

> Child abuse and neglect means the physical or mental injury, sexual abuse, negligent treatment, or maltreatment of a child under the age of eighteen by a person who is responsible for the child's welfare under circumstances which indicate that the child's health or welfare is harmed or threatened thereby. (quoted in Gelles, 1979:45)

The exact extent of child abuse in the United States is not known, although enough evidence exists to show that it is much more common than has generally been assumed. A study of cases known to professionals in schools, hospitals, social service agencies. and various state agencies (surveyed for the National Center on Child Abuse and Neglect) has indicated that out of every 1,000 children in the United States under the age of 18, 10.5 are abused or neglected annually (Gelles and Cornell, 1985). In 1980, according to the American Humane Association's tabulations, 788,844 cases of abuse and neglect were reported, with sexual abuse "the most rapidly increasing form of reported maltreatment" (p. 48).

In their national survey on family violence, Murray Straus, Richard Gelles, and Suzanne Steinmetz (1980:60), "examined the extent, level, and kinds of violence that took place in the homes of 1,146 American couples who had children between the ages of three and seventeen living at home." Their study was based on a representative sample. Extrapolating their findings to the nearly 46 million children aged 3 to 17 living with both parents in the survey year (1975), these sociologists estimated that between 3.1 and 4 million children have, at some time, been punched, kicked, or bitten by one of their parents. Children who have been beaten up by a parent at some time number between 1.4 and 2.3 million. "Finally," write these researchers, "our data mean that between 900,000 and 1.8 million children between the ages of three and seventeen have had a parent use a gun or a knife on them at some time" (p. 62).

Why Do Parents Abuse Their Children?

While the idea has been prevalent that parents who abuse their children are thereby showing that they are "sick," "pathological," or "abnormal," sociologist Richard Gelles (1979) points to the research he and his colleagues have conducted, as well as other studies, and comes to a different conclusion. "It is now necessary to stop thinking of child abuse as having a single cause: the mental aberrations of the parents," he writes. "It is time to start thinking about the multiple social factors that influence child abuse" (p. 40).

What are some of these social factors? Economic factors, for one. *Unemployment* can be a factor in producing family stress that may show up in violence toward children (Gelles, 1979:35–37). *Social status* also enters in. Numerous studies have indicated that child abusers tend to have lower occupational status and income (see summary in Gelles, 1979:33; Straus et al., 1980).

This is not to say that higher income abusive parents don't exist. They do, but their numbers are fewer. Moreover, the differences in child abuse by social class can't simply be written off as differences in labeling and reporting—even though it's true that physicians and helping agencies are more likely to take a middle-class parent's word for it that a child's injuries resulted from an "accident," whereas a poor or minority person is more apt to be "caught," reported to authorities, and given the label "child abuser." Also, an injured child brought into an emergency room or clinic is far more likely to be diagnosed as abused than is a similarly injured child brought to a private physician's office (Gelles, 1979:63–64). But even keeping these matters of labeling and reporting in mind, enough research evidence exists to indicate a greater incidence of child abuse at lower socioeconomic levels. The pressures of feeling cut off from the economic-opportunity system may build up to the point of explosion, with children bearing the consequences.

Gelles also reports that child abuse is likely to occur *if the parents themselves had been abused as children* or *if the child is the result of an unwanted pregnancy* (pp. 36–37). The Straus, Gelles, and Steinmetz study (1980) showed that *family size* also enters in, with the highest percentage of abuse occurring in families with five children. These sociologists found that in the poorest families, "each additional child increases the likelihood of child abuse." Among families classified as well-to-do in the survey, the rate of child abuse was not related to the number of children. But in families *between* the poor and well-to-do categories, the risk of child abuse increased with each child up to a total of seven. Beyond that, there was no child abuse.

In view of the stress caused by economic hardship as family size grows, Straus and his colleagues (1980:178) have attempted to explain their surprising finding that the very largest families have the least violence toward children. "Perhaps parents with eight or nine children are simply too exhausted to raise a finger toward their children," they write. "But it may well be that the very largest families simply have less stress than five- or six-child homes. . . . The oldest children may be a resource for the parents. They can baby-sit, help with the chores, bring in additional income, and minimize the impact of the last in a parade of children. Another possibility is that those people who desire to have and do raise such large families are so 'child-oriented' that they will be less violent no matter how many children they have."

But among families with four, five, or six children, "the family's economic pie is sliced smaller" with each new child, and the data indicate that "as the strain on the pocketbook builds, parents' tempers tend to fray."

Important patterns also emerged in a study conducted jointly by the Human Resources Department of the state of Georgia and the Atlanta-based National Center for Disease Control, which focused on 2,000 cases of child abuse, including twenty-six in which the children died. Children born out of wedlock were found to be 2½ times more likely to be abused than were children of married parents.

Of natural parents who abused their children, half were mothers. And half of these had given birth to their first child while still in their teens. Fifty-eight percent of all child abusers in the study were male, and many were not the natural fathers of the children they abused. The Georgia study showed that 90 percent of children who were *sexually* abused were girls. Types of abuse suffered by boys included burns, malnutrition, skull fractures, cuts, brain damage, and other multiple injuries (*Greensboro (NC) Daily News,* AP report, January 28, 1979). Of course, girls may suffer such injuries, too.

In view of the stereotypical image of motherhood as synonymous with gentleness, it may come as a surprise to learn that large numbers of mothers abuse their children. Straus and his colleagues (1980:65–67) found that during the year of their survey, 68 percent of mothers had engaged in at least one incidence of violence with their child, as compared to 58 percent of the fathers. "Mothers are more likely than fathers to throw objects at their children, slap or spank them, or hit their children with objects," write these researchers. "There is no difference between mothers and fathers for pushing or grabbing; kicking, biting, or punching; or lastly, beating."

What accounts for the violent behavior of some mothers toward their children? The simplest explanation is that the mother's traditionally greater contact with and responsibility for her children may, at times, cause her to feel so exasperated by a child's demands that she gives way to a violent outburst due to sheer frustration (Gelles 1979:34). Straus, Gelles, and Steinmetz (1980:66) point out that problems with a child are considered to reflect on a mother's competence as a parent more than a father's. Mothers are considered to be responsible for a child's behavior and development, and that responsibility can weigh heavily on them. To illustrate, these social scientists refer to a letter written to advice columnist Ann Landers in which a frightened and guilt-ridden mother told of suddenly slapping her son black and blue because he had given up trying to solve a math problem while the mother was helping him with homework. The mother was terrified to think back on her sudden loss of control in reaction to a stressful situation.

Expectations related to a division of labor based upon traditional gender roles also enter in. As a result, children affect a mother's plans, goals, aspirations, time, and energy more than they do a father's. "When a child is born, if a parent has to quit a job or change personal plans and goals, the parent is usually the mother," write Straus, Gelles, and Steinmetz. "If a child is sick, the parent who stays home from work is usually the mother" (p. 66). The frustration mothers may feel is not merely temporal; rather, "children affect the total range of their mothers' plans, goals, and expectations." Again, we see the importance of rethinking traditional gender roles. The heavy load of responsibility for child care, which can create such stressful conditions for many women, underscores the need for shared parenting in intact families and social support arrangements for aiding single, divorced, and widowed mothers struggling to rear children alone.

These researchers also found that women married to violent men are more likely to use violence in dealing with their children. Mothers who have been hit by their husbands were found to be twice as likely as other mothers to abuse a child. "The same applies to women whose husbands were verbally abusive to them," write Straus, Gelles, and Steinmetz (1980:217). "They, in turn, physically abused their children at more than double the rate of abuse by other mothers (21.2 per cent versus 9.3 per cent)." Some battered-women's shelters are therefore providing special programs designed to help mothers who have followed such a domino pattern of violence to break out of that pattern. In addition to finding relief from the abuse they themselves have endured from their husbands, these mothers are helped to find independent resources that will decrease their feelings of powerlessness, and they are aided in developing new ways of thinking and acting so that they are better able to avoid using abusive tactics on their children (Giles-Sims, 1985).

Children Who Are Most Vulnerable to Parental Abuse

"The most dangerous period for the child is from 3 months of age to 3 years," says Gelles (1979:34). "The abused, battered, or murdered child is most vulnerable during those years when he is most defenseless and least capable of meaningful social interaction."

According to Gelles, three interrelated factors may account for this. First, a very small child is simply less physically durable than an older child and thus can't withstand as much physical punishment or force without severe damage or even death occurring.

Second, parents may become frustrated because infants and toddlers cannot be reasoned with as the parents try to persuade them to do something or stop doing something. Gelles refers to case studies in which parents who had abused their children spoke of doing so in desperation when they couldn't get a baby to stop crying, to cooperate in toilet-training efforts, or to otherwise obey some command.

Third, just by virtue of her or his birth, an infant can be distressing to parents. "The new-born child may create economic hardship for the family, or may interfere with professional, occupational, educational, or other plans of the parents," explains Gelles. "Thus, the new child may create structural stress for parents which is responded to by abuse" (p. 35).

Premature babies, babies with low birth weight, retarded children, and physically and developmentally disabled children—in other words, children who are in any way labeled "different" and require special attention and care, thus placing greater strain on the parents—are also at higher risk of becoming victims of parental violence (Straus, Gelles, and Steinmetz, 1980; Gelles and Cornell, 1985). Teenagers are also at risk. The Straus, Gelles, and Steinmetz research showed that "children under 5 and older teen-age children were the most likely to experience violence that held a high chance of causing physical injury." The researchers refer to the frustration expressed by many parents of teenagers who complain that their adolescent will not listen to reason. "Thus," Straus and his colleagues write, "we find that children too young to reason with and older teen-agers, who refuse to be reasoned with, are both vulnerable to the same resolution of the conflict—violence" (pp. 70–71).

Sexual Abuse of Children

The National Center on Child Abuse and Neglect has defined *child sexual abuse* as "contacts or interactions between a child and an adult when the child is being used as an object of gratification for adult sexual needs or desires" (U.S. Department of Health and Human Services, Children's Bureau, 1980:1). A considerable amount of such sexual abuse, much of it unreported, takes place in a family setting. Sexual relations between close family members occur in spite of the *incest taboo* that was discussed in Chapter 4. As Table 14-A shows, various studies of reported parent-child incest indicate that by far the most common form is father-daughter incest.

Linda Gordon and Paul O'Keefe (1984:27), after examining historical records of father-daughter incest in the light of current research, concluded that "such incest is usually coercive, thus appropriately considered a form of family violence." They argue that "incest more than any other type of family violence is calculated and premeditated, not a result of a sudden loss of control" (p. 32). The incestuous relationship between a father

and daughter may continue for years, with the father insisting on total secrecy and showing no sense of guilt. It is for these reasons that Gordon and O'Keefe link child sexual abuse to *power* rather than to stress. (Both power and stress have been found to play a role in general, nonsexual family violence, according to the research of Straus, Gelles, and Steinmetz [1980, chap. 8].) Gordon and O'Keefe write:

The pattern that we found most consistently associated with incest was extreme male domination of the family. We found this quantitatively in the various indicators of the weakness of the mother—her death, her illness or disability, or her own victimization from wife beating. We found it qualitatively in the victims' and wives' expressions of submission and fear towards the male assailants. This pattern of male domination cannot be considered a stress factor because it is the fundamental structure of the families in question and because it is a pattern defined as within the normal range and often reinforced by prevalent social norms. (p. 33)

TABLE 14-A Parent-child incest

STUDY	DATE	POPULATION	NO. OF INCEST CASES	PARENT-CHILD	FATHER-DAUGHTER	FATHER-SON	MOTHER-SON	MOTHER-DAUGHTER
Weinberg	1955	Court cases (Illinois)	203	166	164	0	2	0
Lukianowicz	1972	Clinic records (Ireland)	55	38	35	0	3	0
Maisch	1972	Court cases (Germany)	78	74	66	4	3	1
Meiselman	1978	Clinic records (California)	58	43	38	2	2	1
Justice & Justice	1979	Clinic records (Texas)	112	103	96	5	2	0
Totals			506	424	399	11	12	2
%				100	94.1	2.6	2.8	0.5

SOURCE: Judith Lewis Herman, *Father-Daughter Incest* (Cambridge: Harvard University Press, 1981), p. 19.

INCEST—ABUSE OF POWER, BETRAYAL OF TRUST

Incest is almost always a devastating experience for the victim. Its emotional and psychological impact is destructive for several reasons—partly because of our cultural reactions to incest, to a greater degree because the child is thrust into an adult role for which he or she is unprepared, and, most tragically, because of the aggressor's betrayal of the child's trust and dependence. The victims are not always innocent in a sexual context, they are not always virginal, but they are generally too young and naïve to understand treachery, and that is the innocence that is so traumatically betrayed in incest. The people they have learned to depend on, trust, and love suddenly turn on them in a bewildering, terrifying, often physically painful fashion. . . . There is no stranger to run from, no home to run to. The child cannot feel safe in his or her own bed. The victim must learn to live with incest; it flavors the child's entire world. The aggressor is always there, incest is often a continuing horror for the victim. . . .

When a father makes incestuous advances toward his daughter, he rarely resorts to force or violence—he has no need. There is a tremendous psychological coercion built into the father-daughter relationship. Not only has the daughter been taught to obey her father, but she looks to him for moral guidance. If daddy says it is all right, it must be. Then, of course, if she considers disobeying her father, the threat of punishment is always hanging in the air. So the victim almost always participates in the incest "voluntarily," not recognizing the subtle coercion that has taken place.

SOURCE: Susan Forward and Craig Buck, *Betrayal of Innocence* (New York: Penguin Books, 1978), p. 19.

Psychiatrist Judith Herman (1981:202) also points out the part a patriarchal family structure may play in fostering the sexual abuse of children. "As long as fathers dominate their families, they will have the power to make sexual use of their children," she writes. Most fathers won't choose to exercise such power, she stresses, but some men will—and do. As in the case of family violence in general, she sees a need for a radical transformation of the gender-based family power structure and traditional gender-role ideology. The need is for "a new and regenerated form of family life established on the basis of equality" if the sexual exploitation of children is to be prevented (p. 206).

What Can Be Done about Child Abuse?

The complexity of child abuse as a societal issue is summarized by Saad Nagi (1977), whose study was designed to aid human service agencies in developing programs and policies. Having commented on advancements in medical technology that have aided physicians, surgeons, and radiologists in diagnosing and treating abused children, Nagi goes on to say:

Unfortunately, the complexity of the problem goes beyond the diagnosis and treatment of physical problems. It entails identifying and treating whatever emotional damage the children might have sustained, motivating parents and others to report cases of suspected abuse, changing the behavior of abusive parents and guardians in order to prevent repetition, deciding when children should and should not be left with their families, and collecting legally admissible evidence for protecting the rights of children. (p. 22)

Nagi points out that the two basic approaches that have been used in dealing with parents who have abused their children are *punitive approaches* (parents are punished for what they have done) or *therapeutic approaches* (parents are directed to counselors for help).

In addition to involving themselves in psychological and family counseling programs, some parents who are concerned about their violent actions toward their children join self-help groups such as Parents Anonymous (modeled after Alcoholics Anonymous) so that they can talk over their problem with other parents in a similar situation. In addition, service agencies and other socially concerned organizations have established shelters for victims of family violence. Various treatment intervention programs have also been set up for abusive parents and for entire families in which child maltreatment occurs (Halperin, 1981; Watkins and Bradbard, 1982).

Yet Gelles (1979) argues that as commendable, useful, and necessary as such programs and efforts are, they are not enough. They are like "an ambulance service at the bottom of the cliff" because they wait until after the child abuse has occurred before they step in to help. The need is to "fix the road on the cliff that causes the accidents," says Gelles (p. 41). And that means research and theory to aid in predicting child abuse and putting forth effort to deal with the various social factors that we have seen lie behind much of the maltreatment of children. (See Straus et al., 1980, chap. 10.) Marion (1982) also suggests that family-life educators can play a part by helping future parents learn "positive alternative discipline strategies."

Sociologist Suzanne Steinmetz (1977:138) refers to examples of some persons who were able to survive brutality in childhood without the disastrous consequences that so often occur or who were able to overcome those that did occur, even though the abuse left its mark (as in the case of Thomas Edison, whose hearing was damaged by the frequent severe beatings he received as a child). Nor is the pattern doomed to be repeated in some fatalistic way. Steinmetz provides a note of hope for former victims of child abuse by referring to a personal communication from an authority in child development who was herself a beaten child. The woman reported that she is frequently asked, "Do all children who are abused grow up to be abusing mothers?" Her reply: "No, some of us grow up to study empathy."

CHAPTER HIGHLIGHTS

A first baby changes a couple's lives so that the "transition to parenthood" is sometimes difficult and has even been called a "crisis" in some sociological studies. The transition has been found to be more difficult for wives than for husbands because of traditional assumptions that mothers will have the greater responsibility for child care and will make the greater sacrifices of individualistic interests. Russell's research has turned up some factors that are associated with a greater or lesser degree of stress in the transition to parenthood.

Russell's research also focused on the gratifications of parenthood. And Hoffman found that mothers view motherhood more positively than do nonmothers. However, mothers often feel compelled to change their gender-role ideology in a more traditional direction to fit with the segregation of husband-wife roles that tends to become more pronounced when the two become parents. On the other hand, many young mothers notice a discrepancy between motherhood set up as an *institution*, with specific patterns of expected behavior (which they view negatively) and motherhood as a *rich experience of relating to their children* (which they view positively). Many fathers today also want a larger part in their children's lives than has been traditionally expected, required, or even allowed (because of work demands and schedules).

Rossi has written of parenthood in terms of four stages: the anticipatory stage, the honeymoon stage, the plateau stage, and the disengagement-termination stage. Each stage has unique features and challenges.

Socioeconomic class differences have been found in how children are socialized for achievement and in ways children are disciplined. And while child *abuse* occurs at all class levels, it occurs with greater frequency where the stresses occasioned by economic deprivation (including actual unemployment) are greater.

·15·

THE EXTENDED KIN

"**Y**ou don't marry a person, you marry a family!" So goes the conventional folk wisdom, neatly summing up a fact of life. Even the most starry-eyed couple looking forward to marriage soon realizes they have to face up to their relationship to their families of origin. After marriage, *her* family and *his* family will likely come to be considered jointly as "our folks." And over the years, this will mean a variety of decisions, ranging from which family to visit for Thanksgiving to how to care for a widowed parent in old age.

THE EXTENDED KIN: WHO ARE THEY?

If we were to plan an old-fashioned family reunion, we would invite two categories of people: persons related to us by blood and persons related to us by marriage. Anthropologists and sociologists use the term *consanguinity* (derived from the Latin word for blood and blood relations) to refer to persons who share a common descent or biological heritage—for example, grandparent, parent, sister, brother, aunt, uncle, and cousin.

The word *affinity*, on the other hand, is used to describe a relationship that exists because of marital ties. *Affines* (from the Latin *adfinis*, meaning "one who is connected by marriage") are persons such as stepparents, stepbrothers and stepsisters, in-laws, and spouses of aunts and uncles. The term *extended kin*, like a family reunion, includes both blood relations and those related by marriage—or what anthropologist David

Extended families include two basic categories of people: those related "in nature" (by blood) and those related "in law" (by marriage or adoption). (Elizabeth Crews)

Schneider (1968) calls relationships "in nature" and relationships "in law."

Relationships "in Nature"

We are born into some relationships. "Two blood relatives are 'related' by the fact that they share in some degree the stuff of a particular heredity," writes Schneider (1968). "Each has a portion of the natural, genetic substance. Their kinship consists in this common possession" (p. 24).

Blood relationships are in one sense permanent. A common biogenetic makeup links together persons in such relationships, regardless of whether they want to recognize their interconnectedness or not. Two brothers may separate early in life and perhaps never speak to one another again. A parent may disown a child. A daughter or son might sever all relations with a parent. But "in nature," the persons are still related; one has not become an ex-brother or ex-parent or ex-son or ex-daughter. To speak about blood relations in this way, explains Schneider, is to speak about the "order of nature," which he then contrasts with the "order of law."

Relationships "in Law"

Schneider points out that whereas heredity or "blood" binds together relatives in nature, "relatives *in law* are bound only by law or custom, by the code for conduct, by the pattern for behavior" (p. 27). A sister gets married, and her husband becomes our relative, our brother-*in-law*. Or a parent remarries, and a child immediately has a new relative—a stepmother or stepfather, possibly stepsisters and stepbrothers. A relationship in law sets up a certain interconnectedness between persons that is not there "naturally."

By the term *law*, then, Schneider (1968:27–29) simply means social customs, rules, and expectations in contrast to biological givens. He thus speaks of three classifications of relatives: (1) those related *only in nature*—for example, the continuing "blood" tie between an unwed parent and her or his baby even after the child's placement with adoptive parents; (2) those related *only in law*, such as a husband and wife, stepsiblings, a spouse and his or her parents-in-law, or parents and an adopted child; and (3) those related *both by blood and by social declaration* (or "law")—offspring and their natural parents (with certain exceptions related to adoption and to issues of legitimacy and illegitimacy), sisters and brothers, grandparents and grandchildren, and so on.

Changing ideas about such classifications show up in changes in family law over a period of time—especially with regard to inheritance laws, support laws, adoption laws, divorce laws, definitions of *legitimacy* and *illegitimacy*, and laws and definitions surrounding what constitutes incestuous marriage (Farber, 1973). For example, states vary not only in whether their statutes permit or prohibit the marriage of certain blood relatives, such as first cousins but also in whether or not the marriage of *affines* (persons related only "in law") is considered incestuous and thus forbidden—for example, marriage between stepbrothers and stepsisters or marriage between in-laws. Under existing statutes in some states, marriages have been declared illegal in cases involving a man who married his uncle's widow, a woman who married her father-in-law, and persons who have married stepchildren or stepgrandchildren (Einbinder, 1973–74: 783–784).

Sociologist Bernard Farber (1973) traces the origin of such laws to certain interpretations of the Bible and to definitions of *affinity* that have placed the person related "in law" in the same position as if she or he were permanently related by blood to relatives acquired through marriage—a view that was linked to concerns about property and which governed estate regulations. According to Farber, a shift in how the family is defined brings about a shift in laws pertaining to affinal marriages. He sees evidence of such a shift occurring.

At the same time, some scholars of family law believe that laws governing who may not marry whom are not keeping pace with many of the rapid changes affecting families today, including multitudinous step relationships arising from divorce, remarriage, redivorce, and so on. Carolyn S. Bratt (1984), a professor of law who has done an extensive study of the religious origins of state incest statutes and the reasoning that has been used to support them, calls for a total reexamination of such laws.

Another authority on family law, Michael Einbinder (1973–74:783–787), argues that affinity statutes have outlived any usefulness they may once have had. He points out that the effect of such statutes has been eliminated in some instances "by holding that the relation of affinity between one spouse and the blood-relatives of the other ceases on the death of either spouse." While numerous states have recognized the inappropriateness of affinity statutes, a minority "continues to include them within the statutory definition of incest," with Georgia applying criminal sanctions against the widest range of affinity relationships (Bratt, 1984; 292, 294).

Marriage: A Special Case

Schneider (1968) speaks of marriage as "the example of a relationship in law within kinship *par excellence*" (p. 96). Furthermore, marriage is "*the* relationship in law which is specifically restricted to mean a sexual relationship." In marriage, a husband and wife are not "natural" relatives by "blood." But in this particular relationship of choice (a choice made either by them or for them), the two are declared by society to have entered an intimate relationship above which none ranks higher. According to the Judeo-Christian tradition, for example, they are declared to be "one flesh."

Sex, marriage, and kinship are intricately bound up together, as the following quotation from sociologist Bernard Farber (1973) makes clear:

> The biological acts of sexual intercourse and birth have everywhere generated norms and values that deal with the relatedness of people . . . the stabilization of sexual relationships provides the basis for defining reciprocities associated with the institution of marriage. These reciprocities involve not only the married couple but also persons related to them. In addition, the act of birth creates the necessity of establishing rules for determining responsibility for children over their life cycle, i.e., as they mature into adulthood, marry, procreate, age, and die; these responsibilities reflect the individual's concern for those related to him by descent. The claims established through marriage and descent thereby create for each individual a reservoir of relatives from whom he can anticipate certain kinds of conduct associated with "family" or "kinship" in the society in which he lives. The extent and nature of these claims vary from one society to another. (p. 4)

Roots and Branches: The Family Tree

Farber's reference to descent reminds us that our kin include those who have come before us and who will come after us. "Within families, all the symbolic input of past generations, all the give and take of present generations, and all the potentials for future generations come into play," writes sociologist Marvin Koller (1974:8).

A great surge of interest in family genealogies accompanied the 1977 television dramatization of Alex Haley's book *Roots*, which

WHAT DO YOU CALL YOUR PARENT-IN-LAW?

Some informants call their spouse's parents by parental terms; that is, spouse's mother is "mother," "ma," "mom," etc., while father is "father," "pa," "pop," "dad," etc. Some use a parental-plus-name form such as Mother Smith (Father Smith), Mother Jane (Father Jim), or Ma Perkins (Pa Perkins). First-naming is also used here, but informants are often quick to state that first-naming is not always the first name used. If they met as strangers there is a tendency toward Mr. and Mrs.-plus-last-name forms, and only later when the spouse's parent permits or invites it is the first-name form used. Informants are also quick to note the prevalence of no-naming here.* One informant in his mid-fifties, married for more than twenty years, claimed that he had never addressed his wife's mother by any form whatever! If it was absolutely necessary to get her attention he made coughing or throat-clearing noises, to which she had learned to respond.

* This is the zero form of address. It may sometimes be articulated as a throat clearing or "uh hum" sort of noise. Erving Goffman first suggested the term "no-naming" to me some years ago.

SOURCE: David Schneider, *American Kinship: A Cultural Account* (Englewood Cliffs, NJ: Prentice-Hall, 1968), pp. 84–85.

traced his own family lineage from its origin in Africa, through slavery, and into recent times. Even earlier, as social historians were showing increasing interest in the everyday lives of ordinary people of the past, ordinary people of the present were being encouraged to record their own family's history. For instance, a 1976 three-day conference at Washington, DC's Smithsonian Institution featured workshops, lectures, and films to help persons "dig at the family tree" by searching through diaries, old letters, wills, scrapbooks, other records, and memories. One of the speakers, anthropologist Margaret Mead, urged the audience to interview their grandparents and also to write something down for grandchildren as a way of anchoring family members in both past and future. Another speaker, psychiatrist Murray Bowen, pointed out that each person is a mix of sixty-four families over a period of five generations. And in ten generations, we're a mix-

ture of just over a thousand families (Shenker, 1976)!

In American society, persons are considered part of both their mother's and their father's family. Anthropologists would say we have a system of *bilateral descent reckoning*. Kin on both sides are recognized, and a person is related to both sides of the family equally. Some societies, however, have a *unilateral system of descent reckoning*. One is considered to belong in a special sense to only one side of the family. This is especially true where societies are organized around *kin groups*; and with certain exceptions, one is assigned membership in only one such group (Lee, 1977, chap. 6). In a society based upon kinship as the "basic organizing principle," writes sociologist Gary Lee, "it is often the case that no other kinds of groups or social structures exist independently of the kinship structure . . . the kin group is the unit within which economic, political, edu-

In a society based on kinship, "the kin group is the unit within which economic, political, educational, and religious interaction occurs." (Alan Carey/The Image Works)

cational, and religious interaction occurs" (p. 152). In such societies, where it is common to have a unilateral descent system, descent may be traced through the father's line (*patrilineal descent*) or through the mother's line (*matrilineal descent*).

Persons in our own society, which is *not* built around kin groups, often give little thought to descent. Schneider (1968:68) points out that most Americans have trouble remembering if their great-grandparents even had brothers and sisters, much less whom they married or how many children they had. And when he conducted an anthropological study of kinship in Chicago and asked informants to "List for me all the people whom you consider to be your relatives," it was quite common for informants to pause somewhere in their listing and ask, "Do you want the dead ones too?" Persons seemed

unsure about whether to consider as relatives persons who were no longer alive. "Further," says Schneider, "there seemed to be a clear tendency for the dead to be omitted entirely in the very early phases of the collection of the genealogy, and only to come to light during later enquiry, often in another connection" (pp. 69–70).

Adult Adoptees' Search for Biological Roots: A Special Situation The desire for a sense of connectedness with biological roots and personal family history is felt especially keenly by many adopted persons. "Adoption agencies today report a groundswell of interest among adult adoptees returning for information about their origins," write psychologists Katherine Kowal and Karen Maitland Schilling (1985:354). Their survey of 110 adult adoptees who had contacted either a social service agency or a search group that provides support and help in obtaining information about birth parents indicated four main reasons the adoptees felt a need to know about their origins. "The most commonly mentioned need was to find some resolution of confusion or a sense of emptiness," write Kowal and Schilling, pointing out that many persons spoke of needing to fill a void in their lives.

Mentioned next most frequently was a need for greater self-understanding. "Subjects frequently said they wanted to know who they looked like or who their children resembled," the researchers report. "Or they felt that certain personality traits were puzzling to them and they wanted to know if there were other biological relatives who shared these traits" (p. 360). A third category of information seekers needed a medical history. "I am now being watched for breast cancer," one woman commented. "Knowing that it is or isn't in my family would help me to deal with it and enlighten me to my possible risk to it myself." Older adoptees were concerned about specific medical problems they had developed and for which they needed a family medical history in order to answer physicians' questions. Younger female adoptees were concerned about hereditary traits that might be passed on to children they might have.

A fourth category of information seekers spoke of a need for belonging. Some in this small group spoke critically about their adopted parents, reporting problems during adolescence especially, and some had lost an adopted parent through death. Kowal and Schilling quote one person who commented on how finding biological relatives was expected to provide a sense of belonging. "It will give me a beginning and some kind of foundation for my life," this adoptee wrote. "I need to justify who I am because I'm very

different from my family and I never felt like I was OK for who I am! I just want to meet someone who is a part of me to help me feel less unconnected to anything." Kowal and Schilling point out, however, that only a small percentage of adult adoptees are motivated by a need to belong and a desire for a surrogate family.

Yet anxiety over the possible psychological or physical loss of adopted children is the biggest fear expressed by adoptive parents in debates over sealed versus open birth records. Adoptive parents who are less fearful of loss and rejection are more likely than fearful parents to have a positive attitude toward open birth records, according to a study by Shirley Geissinger (1984).

As part of another study, social scientists Michael Sobol and Jeanette Cardiff (1983) looked at some reasons adult adoptees who are *not* engaged in searching for biological roots did not choose to search. The main reasons given were that they didn't want to hurt their adopted parents and that since they had a "positive sense of identity with their adopted parents, there was no reason to look beyond the boundaries of the adopted family for a sense of historical and personal perspective" (p. 481). Other reasons for not searching were lack of interest or need, a fear that searching would hurt or disrupt the lives of the birth parents, fear of what the consequences might mean, insufficient time or money, feelings that such a search would be useless, insufficient knowledge and emotional support, and fear of rejection.

Pointing out that most information seekers are mainly concerned about their genealogical history as it relates to their personal identity, Sobol and Cardiff urge professionals to "recognize that for most adoptees, their 'true' parents are those who provided psychological support and nurturance throughout childhood and adolescence. As such, gaining access to one's biological roots does not so much threaten the adopted parent-child relationship as it provides for the opportunity to enhance one's feelings of completeness" (p. 483).

Relatives: Close and Distant

We may think of relatives in terms of *genealogical* closeness—a parent is closer than a second cousin, for example. Or we may think in terms of *social* and *emotional* closeness: we *feel* closer to Uncle Jack and Aunt Sue than to Aunt Ellen and her husband. We may also think in terms of *geographical* closeness or distance: Grandma and Grandpa Smith live across the street, while Grandma and Grandpa Robinson live across the country.

Sociologists make various classifications of kin. Bert Adams (1968:12) is thinking in terms of genealogical closeness when he makes the distinction between the "kin of orientation" (those from the same family of origin—one's parents, brothers, and sisters) and the "secondary kin" (aunts, uncles, cousins, grandparents, and so on). Another sociologist, Ralph Piddington (1965), seems to have in mind degrees of social and emotional closeness when he divides kin into the categories of "noneffective kin" and "effective kin." *Noneffective kin* are persons genealogically related to an individual but with whom social relationships are not maintained.

Piddington further divides the category of *effective kin* (those with whom social interaction is maintained) into two subcategories: *priority kin* (members of one's own nuclear-family and those kinfolk most closely related to it, particularly the parents of each spouse, where there is a certain degree of "recognized moral obligation to enter into appropriate social relationships") and *chosen kin* (more remote kin with whom one is not duty-bound to enter social relationships but with whom such relationships are entered just the same, out of free choice). Most of us can probably think of relatives in our own lives who fit into these various categories.

What Piddington calls the "noneffective kin" would probably fall into a category Schneider (1968) refers to as "that limbo called wakes-and-weddings relatives, shirt-tail relations, or kissin' kin" (p. 74). Persons seen only at funerals and weddings or who are relatives of relatives (thus brought into the extended-kin network on somebody else's shirttails) are persons with whom there is little direct contact. That's what makes it hard, in many cases, to think of them as actual relatives. Schneider points out that most of us tend to think of our relations as "persons to whom we relate"—persons with whom we have social interaction. That is one reason persons have difficulty deciding whether or not a list of relatives should include those who have died. The social relationship—the interaction, the communication—has ceased; yet the dead may continue to occupy an important place on the family tree and in the memories of those who loved them.

Interestingly, Schneider (p. 17) found some regional and religion-based variations in terms used for distant kin. Northerners (especially from the Midwest) tended to speak of "shirt-tail relations." Catholics, more than non-Catholics, referred to "wakes-and weddings relatives." And Southerners were more likely to talk about "kissin' kin" or "kissin' cousins." One common explanation for this last-mentioned term is given by Schneider: "The kiss is the sign that no matter how distant, such persons are nevertheless relatives and therefore are entitled to that sign of being a relative, the kiss" (p. 70).

One exception to the tendency not to count as relatives those with whom social contact is extremely rare or nonexistent is in the case of a famous relative. "During the course of the field work," Schneider writes, "we not infrequently encountered the statement that So-and-So, a famous personage, was a relative. Sometimes the relationship was traceable, sometimes not. When it was traceable, it could clearly be seen that this was the only relative of such distance on the genealogy, whereas closer relatives were unknown or unheard of" (p. 67).

THE EXTENDED KIN: INTERACTION PATTERNS

Earlier we saw the important part played by kin in various times and cultures, particularly in such matters as mate selection, inheritance rights, and economic sanctions. In modern industrial societies of the Western world, however, the kin network does not have power to influence persons to the extent that was once the case (and which remains the case in some cultures). Since the kin no longer control economic resources, they lack the authority that would accompany such control. Industrialization makes it possible for persons to achieve on their own. They are no longer dependent on kinship connections for lands, houses, farms, and businesses; and they are no longer tied to where relatives are—either geographically or occupationally.

Aware of such changes, many persons have concluded that something worthwhile and beneficial has disappeared from modern life. They speak of the isolation of the nuclear family, the depersonalization of urban and suburban living, the evaporation of a sense of belonging, sharing, and community in contemporary society.

But is it really true that the modern nuclear family is isolated from the wider kin network? Has urbanization weakened kinship ties, or do such ties persist despite residential and social mobility? Sociologists have given a great deal of study to these questions and have been forced to do some rethinking over the years.

Isolation of the Kin—Fact or Fiction?

During the 1930s and 1940s, a great deal was written about what came to be known as "classical urban theory," one aspect of which concerned the kin. Certain influential sociologists suggested that people in urban society are characterized more by *secondary* (impersonal) contacts than by *primary* (more intimate) relationships with family and close friends as they are in rural societies. Health needs, help in trouble, education, recreation—these were things no longer provided by kin but, rather, by other institutions and agencies set up for such purposes as part of urbanization. At marriage, it was assumed that couples broke away to form families which served as independent units of social life entirely separated from the extended kin (Wirth, 1938; Parsons, 1943; see also summaries in Adams, 1968; Sussman and Burchinal, 1962; Lee, 1980).

However in the 1950s and 1960s, sociologists began taking another look at the widely held view that urban dwellers lived isolated lives and had few primary relationships. Studies of kinship and friendship patterns among city residents showed that they were *not* cut off from intimate, meaningful social contacts in general, nor were they cut off from kin in particular. What was discovered was simply that urban dwellers have more secondary, impersonal, or segmental contacts than rural persons do. But these secondary relationships are not *replacements* for primary relationships; they exist right alongside them (Adams, 1968:3).

RARE AND EXTREME CASE OF KIN ISOLATION

Duluth, MN—An 80-year-old woman who shunned others, including her children, had been dead in her home for nearly four years when her mummified body was found in February, authorities said Thursday.

Police earlier had estimated that Blanch Hansen had been dead at least one year before her body was discovered Feb. 5.

But St. Louis County Medical Examiner Volker Goldschmidt used city Water & Gas Department records to determine that Hansen probably had been dead since May 1981, according to documents filed with the state Department of Health.

"He estimated she had been dead for a year or more. Beyond that time (one year), there's no way of estimating the exact time of death" using only autopsy results, Dr. Donald Kundel, deputy medical examiner, said Thursday of Goldschmidt's conclusion.

Goldschmidt set the date of death at May 1981 because that's the last time water was used in the house, Kundel said.

No further investigation into her case will be made, since there was no indication of foul play, he added.

Duluth police were aware in February of the drop in water consumption at Hansen's home in 1981, Inspector Fred Sowl, head of the investigative division, said Thursday.

Hansen's two children, who live in the Duluth area, had been feuding for several years and said they had not known her whereabouts.

Her body was discovered after the two children ended their feud by settling the estate of their mother's 82-year-old brother, who died Jan. 29.

"He (Robert Hansen) asked, 'So, where are you keeping Mom?' And we said, 'We thought you were taking care of her'," said Ken Evenson, Blanch Hansen's son-in-law, in February.

Her son found the body. Authorities said she died of natural causes.

SOURCE: AP report, "Death of 80-year-old woman goes unnoticed for four years," *Greensboro (NC) News and Record,* April 12, 1985, p. A-1.

The question of *why* kinship ties persist in modern society is discussed by sociologist Marvin Sussman (1966), who bases his explanation on exchange theory. Persons perceive that they receive valued rewards from kinfolk, and the kinfolk likewise perceive that they, too, receive as well as give valued rewards. Thus reciprocity goes on, with closest ties being maintained with those relatives who are viewed as having the greatest rewards to offer. These rewards may be tangible (for instance, gifts of money or material goods) or intangible (simple enjoyment of one another's company, grandparents' affection and attention to small children, and the like). Sometimes the rewards are in the form of mutual aid and service, such as baby-sitting or looking after the house while the nuclear family is on vacation. Just keeping in touch is in itself perceived as rewarding, whether such communication and contact is maintained through visits, letters, or phone calls. The notion of reciprocity in kin relationships also includes some sense of duty and moral obligation—particularly with regard to one's aging parents. (See also Leigh, 1982.)

Whatever Became of the Multiple-Generation Household?

Most of us have an image of a bygone era in which large families lived happily together under one roof—parents, children, grandparents, maybe even an aunt, uncle, or cousin or two. And then industrialization came along and changed all that. Research by modern social historians, however, indicates that such a picture is more mythical than real. Extended families often lived nearby, but living together in the same house was the exception rather than the rule.

After making detailed studies of household size spanning over three centuries, Peter Laslett and his colleagues from the Cambridge Group for the History of Population and Social Structure have concluded that "mean household size remained fully constant at 4.75 or a little under, from the earliest point for which we have found figures, until as late as 1901." Furthermore, writes Laslett (1972), "there is no sign of the large, extended coresidential family group of the traditional peasant world giving way to the small, nuclear, conjugal household of modern industrial society. In England in fact. . . . the large joint or extended family seems never to have existed as a common form of the domestic group at any point in time covered by known numerical records" (p. 126). According to Laslett, the nuclear or simple family household of parents and children has been and continues to be the basic domestic unit. (See Table 15-A.)

For the most part, variations in household size were not so much related to the presence or absence of kin members as it was to the number of children at home, boarders or

TABLE 15-A Multigenerational households in sixty-one English communities, 1574–1821

TYPE OF HOUSEHOLD	PROPORTION
Households of one generation	23.8%
Households of two generations	70.4
Households of three generations	5.8
Households of four or more generations	0.0
Total	100.0%

SOURCE: Adapted from Peter Laslett, "Mean Household Size in England Since the Sixteenth Century," in Peter Laslett, ed. (with the assistance of Richard Wall), *Household and Family in Past Time* (London and New York: Cambridge University Press, 1972), p. 153.

other live-in persons, and, especially, servants. "Servants were simply children who had changed households, from the parental home to the household of the master," writes Laslett (1972:147). Thus children sent to learn some craft or trade or simply for employment would swell the ranks of the second household while lowering the number in their original home. This practice would seem to account for Laslett's finding a direct relationship between household size and social status: the higher the status, the larger the household, according to statistics from 100 English communities from 1574 to 1821. Persons of higher status were able to hire more live-in workers (servants).

It was also common in the United States to record servants as members of a household. The social historian John Demos (1972:561) found, in his studies of the Plymouth Colony, that the average household size was just under six persons, most commonly consisting of a husband and wife and their children, with perhaps a servant or two and possibly one or (more rarely) two grandparents. Since life expectancy was lower than it is now, the likelihood of having elderly grandparents in the home for very long was not great. Infant mortality was also high. Thus, even parents with large numbers of children frequently did not see all of them reach adulthood. Furthermore, just as was true in Europe, many children in Colonial America left their parental homes early to take up residence as servants in other homes. Such servanthood is described by the historian Edmund Morgan (1966):

> Most of the inhabitants of seventeenth-century New England either were or had been "servants." Today the word "servant" usually means a domestic: the cook, the butler, the chambermaid. In the seventeenth century it meant anyone who worked for another in whatever capacity, in industry, commerce, or agriculture, as well as in what we now call domestic economy . . . slaves were also known as servants, and so were apprentices. Servants, then, might differ considerably in their economic and social status. (p. 109)

The findings of one other study of household structure in North America also deserve mention because they, too, show much less change in multigenerational household living than has generally been supposed. When the sociologist Edward Pryor, Jr. (1972:575, 580) examined Rhode Island census records for two time periods, he found that in 1875, 82 percent of households consisted of nuclear families (parents and children, with no extended kin present). In 1960, the figure was 85 percent. In other words, in 1960, 15 percent of Rhode Island residents had some relative living with them—actually not a great deal less than the 18 percent with extended kin living with them in 1875. As to the presence of grandparents and grandchildren in the home, only 8 percent of Rhode Island households were multigenerational (three or more generations) in 1875. In 1960, 5 percent were multigenerational.

Commenting on a number of studies that showed that parents who survived into old age at the turn of the century did, nevertheless, have a somewhat higher chance of sharing a home with a grown daughter or son than they would today, Lee (1980:195) refers to a point made by Ethel Shanas (1979). Shanas argues that the lesser likelihood of co-residence today does not indicate kin isolation or alienation but, rather, is a statement of the better living situation in which many of the elderly find themselves today. In terms of both health and finances, many elderly persons are well enough off today to be able to maintain the independence they prefer, thus enjoying, with their grown children, "intimacy at a distance" rather than in the same household.

Numerous studies have shown that the parent-child bond continues to be strong throughout life. Victor Cicirelli (1983:33–35), a professor of developmental/aging psychology, points to research indicating that the vast majority (78 to 90 percent) of older people with living children see one or more of their children at least weekly and are in frequent telephone contact with them as well. "Only a very few elderly people have lost contact with their adult children," Cicirelli emphasizes. But at the same time, elderly parents and their children alike generally express reservations about sharing a residence, believing that conflicts would increase if they were to live together under the same roof.

Even so, at some point in time, an aging parent or other relative may find it necessary to move into an already established household. Researchers Scott Beck and Rubye Beck (1984) observe that the incidence of extended household living is much higher than generally assumed—*if we look at longitudinal data* rather than cross-sectional data (which only show the incidence at one given time). Using data from a national probability sample, Beck and Beck found that over a ten-year period, 1 out of 5 white middle-aged couples and 1 out of 2 black middle-aged couples had formed *extended households* (defined as "any living arrangement that includes family members other than the respondent's spouse and children").

Extended Family Ties among Blacks

Among black Americans, the "informal absorption of families and individuals by relatives" has been a tradition from slavery onward (Hill and Shackleford, 1975). This absorption may occur in a number of ways, as is shown by the social scientist Andrew Billingsley (1968:16–21), who has worked out a *typology* of black family structures (a way of classifying black families by type).

Billingsley starts out with three basic types of families: the married couple (the "incipient nuclear family"), the married couple with their children living with them (the "simple nuclear family"), and the solo parent whose children live with him or her (the "attenuated nuclear family"). The terms aren't hard to remember if you keep their meanings in mind. The word *incipient* refers to the initial stage of something, and, of course, the husband-wife union is the necessary foundation stage in order for a simple nuclear family to emerge. The word *attenuated,* on the other hand, comes from a Latin term meaning "to reduce." Billingsley is using it to describe a "reduced" family—one headed by a single (never married), separated, deserted, divorced, or widowed parent, rather than by two parents.

If any of these categories of families takes in other relatives, a distinct type of extended-family household comes into being. The childless married couple (or with children grown and gone) who take in relatives become an example of "the incipient extended family." The married couple with children at home (simple nuclear family) become a "simple extended family" when they take other relatives in. And when other relatives join the solo-parent household, an "attenuated extended family" household comes into being. According to Billingsley, all of these patterns exist in appreciable numbers among black families, and "to know which of the subtypes of extended family is under consideration would help to clarify the generalizations which may be made." In other words, it's as erroneous to speak of *the* black family as it is to speak of *the* white family—as though only one kind existed.

Secondary Members   These various kinds of extended-family households may include relatives who come by themselves or who bring families with them. When a family takes persons who are alone into its household, the family is adding what Billingsley calls *secondary members.* They may be a brother or sister or parent of the wife or husband; or they may be aunts, uncles, cousins, grandparents, nephews, nieces, or grandchildren.

"Most dependent secondary members of black extended families are grandchildren," assert Robert Hill and Lawrence Shackleford (1975) after an extensive examination of the literature and statistics on black extended families. They observe that two-thirds of black children under 18 who are not living with either parent are living with either grandparents or great-grandparents, whereas about one-fifth live with aunts and uncles.

"The historic fortitude and self-reliance of the black elderly is vividly reflected in the fact that they are more likely to take others into their households than to be taken into the households of younger relatives," Hill and Shackleford write, pointing out that, at the time of their writing, only 4 percent of black families (headed by husbands and wives or by women alone) had persons 65 years or older living with them. In contrast, half of black families headed by women aged 65 or older were rearing children under 18 who were not their own.

Subfamilies In addition to welcoming individuals, a family sometimes takes in another family unit. Billingsley (1968:20) refers to such families-within-families as *subfamilies*. They might be an "incipient subfamily" (husband-wife pair), a "simple nuclear subfamily" (parents and children), or an "attenuated subfamily" (a solo parent with her or his children) who have found themselves in circumstances that necessitated moving into a relative's household.

Only a small percentage of all black families are subfamilies. Three out of four such families are made up of a female solo parent (usually separated, divorced, or widowed) and her children. Most commonly, they move in with the woman's parents or parents-in-law—or, in some cases, with her sister (Hill and Shackleford, 1975).

Other Patterns Billingsley (1968) also speaks of· the *augmented family,* a family augmented or enlarged by the addition of one or more persons from outside the family—in other words, nonrelatives. As one illustration, we may think of the 7 percent of black children who live in family arrangements where neither of their own parents is present. Fourteen percent of such children (or just under 1 percent of *all* black children) live with persons not related to them (U. S. Bureau of the Census, *Current Population Reports*, ser. P-20, no. 410, 1986, p. 71).

Some students of black family patterns feel that Billingsley's useful typology should go further and incorporate certain other arrangements: for example, two sisters living together (Williams and Stockton, 1973) or one of the most prevalent patterns of all— "the informal adoption of individuals and subfamilies by relatives who live alone (e.g., widowed grandmothers or aunts)" (Hill and Shackleford, 1975).

Base Households and the Extended-Family Network Extended black family networks tend to have one central place that everyone considers "home"—no matter how far away they live. Social work professor Elmer Martin and educator Joanne Mitchell Martin (1978) call this place the *extended family base household,* pointing out that "family reunions, outings, vacations, celebrations, weddings, and other family activities take place there" (p. 6). This base household, the very center of the extended-family network, is the residence of "the dominant family figure"—the woman or man considered the leader of the extended kin, the person (usually elderly) most revered and respected among all the relatives and recognized as crucial to the family network's continued existence (p. 17).

The dominant family figure keeps the kin network informed of family news, provides counsel and moral support, helps work out family conflicts, passes down family history to younger generations, and instructs the young about their black heritage (including telling stories of what it was like for black people during the dominant family figure's growing-up years, as well as providing instructions on matters ranging from the preparation of soul food to survival techniques for getting along in the world). This person, who serves as the hub of the extended kin, also lays great stress on developing a sense of family. "Fostering a sense of family involves encouraging family members to feel some obligation to their relatives," write Martin and Martin (1978:18). While pointing out the mutual aid system throughout the black kin network, the Martins write that "the first option for anyone in need of a place to stay is the family base. . . . It can consist of three family members one month and ten the next, one generation today and three tomorrow. It can accommodate one family member temporarily until he can find work as well as another for the rest of his life" (p. 39). Housing that allows for such flexibility is much harder to come by in urban areas than it is in rural areas and small towns (p. 85).

Martin and Martin (1978) conducted in-depth interviews with up to twenty persons per family out of each of the thirty extended black families on which they focused—extended families comprised of over a thousand persons in all. Their definition of such families is useful in understanding black extended-family patterns:

> When we speak of a black extended family, we mean a multigenerational, interdependent kinship system which is welded together by a sense of obligation to relatives; is organized around a "family base" household; is generally guided by a "dominant family figure"; extends across geographical boundaries to connect family units to an extended family network; and has a built-in mutual aid system for the welfare of its members and the maintenance of the family as a whole. Our definition grew out of our personal membership in families of this nature and our observations of similar families. (p. 1)

Summarizing a number of studies that indicate stronger kin ties among blacks than among whites (as demonstrated in black patterns of co-residence, mutual aid, and visiting), Lee (1980:195) writes, "The critical question at the moment is not whether this is true, but why." He suggests that both socioeconomic and cultural factors may explain the greater kin involvement characterizing black persons. Economic discrimination related to race has meant that large numbers of black persons found themselves forced to turn to relatives for help in the face of unemployment, inadequate housing, and low income. Bert Adams (1970:587) has noted that "minority status tends to result in residential compounding, and in strong kin ties for the sake of mutual aid and survival in a hostile environment." In addition, a strong cultural tradition that places great value on family relationships may also help account for the close kin ties among blacks. (See also McAdoo, 1982; Taylor, 1986.)

Extended-Family Ties among Mexican-Americans (Chicanos)

Like black families, Chicano families also maintain strong ties among the kin. They know they can count on one another in times of trouble or need and tend to prefer their system of mutual aid over Anglo-controlled agencies (Mirandé, 1977). At the same time, the independent nuclear-family unit is the

Chicano families also maintain strong ties among the kin, but the independent nuclear family unit is the preferred family form. (© Joel Gordon, 1979)

BECOMING RELATIVES BY SPECIAL RITUAL

Compadrazgo or co-godparenthood is the relationship between the parents and godparents of a child christened in church; through their participation in the ceremony, godfathers and godmothers, the parents of the child, and sometimes the priest who baptized the child, become ritually related. Having replaced the "pagan" institution of blood brotherhood, compadrazgo became common all over Europe and still exists in parts of Greece, Spain, Italy, Serbia, and Russia. In England co-godparents were known as god-sibs (that is, "siblings in God"); here, however, the relationship did not endure as an institution and went through the vicissitudes of social change which the etymology of the word—from godsib to gossip—indicates.

. . . In most cases it is the reciprocal relations between the parents of the child and the godparents which explain why this Christian institution flourishes in parts of Europe and South America today. The christening ritual sanctions a relationship between friends and neighbors, the child acting as a symbol—an expression and a guarantee of this friendship. . . .

These ritual relations between friends serve very practical purposes and at the same time offer a means of greater emotional fulfillment and an assurance that an individual does not stand alone. Compadres lend each other money; a woman will work in her friend's house when she is sick; they mourn the death of a relative. Compadres must be kind and friendly and a network of ties . . . helps maintain community order. . . . Throughout Latin America, for example, it is a friendly bond which may be used to forestall sexual aggressiveness; you can avoid trouble with a man who is determined to seduce your wife by making him your compadre! He cannot refuse the offer of friendship and once it is made the wife is henceforth sexually taboo.

SOURCE: Robert Brain, *Friends and Lovers* (New York: Basic Books, 1976), chap. 4.

preferred family form. "One may choose to live near parents and other relatives, or perhaps even with them, out of economic necessity," writes sociologist Alfredo Mirandé, "but the norm is that the nuclear family remains autonomous and in a separate residence" (p. 753). Yet the nuclear family reaches out to relatives on both the father's side and the mother's side, with special emphasis on good relationships with the mother's sisters (Queen and Habenstein, 1974:429). Grandparents are highly loved and respected, and they are viewed less as authority figures than as sources of warmth and nurturance (Mirandé, 1977).

In one study of children in an urban *barrio* in Houston, Texas, Chicano children named only relatives when asked to name persons they loved. In contrast, Anglo children and black children named both family and non-family members, indicating that in their view friends as well as relatives were persons one could love (Goodman and Beman, 1971, reported in Mirandé, 1977).

However, this finding may not only indicate the great importance of kin in the life of the Chicano child; it may also show that the line of demarcation between close friends and relatives is less clear. "Not only are relatives included as friends, but friends are symbolically incorporated into the family," Mirandé (1977:752) points out. Especially noteworthy has been the custom of *compadrazgo,* or ritual kinship, in which persons are linked together as *compadres,* a close friendship tie that is comparable to a kin tie and which originally functioned to provide substitute parents (godparents) for children in the event their own parents died (Mirandé, 1977). "While the *compadrazgo* may take a number of forms, notably coparenthood," write social scientists Stuart Queen and Robert Habenstein (1974), "by providing fictive kinship linkages, its effect is to generate social and interpersonal cohesion and thus to reduce the potential extrafamilial conflict that might arise in a highly family-centered society. Coparenthood, which is considered the most important, links two families through the baptismal ritual" (p. 429).

How Important Are Kin?

Of course, the relative importance attached to friendship and kinship pertains not only to Chicano society but to the larger society as well. For one thing, close relationships require an investment; and we are not likely to enter or maintain relationships in which our investment doesn't pay off. Sociologist Mark Granovetter (1973) suggests that "the strength of a tie is a . . . combination of the amount of time, the emotional intensity, the intimacy (mutual confiding), and the reciprocal services which characterize the tie" (p. 1361). Since everyone has a *limited* supply of time and emotional energy, however, the extent to which we invest these scarce resources in any one relationship can affect the amount of resources left for other relationships (Shulman, 1975). Persons who invest their time and energy heavily in the extended-kin network, for example, and are rewarded in reciprocal fashion, may attach less importance to outside friendship. The re-

verse could be true, also. Or time and effort poured into one's own nuclear family can cut down on time and effort put into extended-kin relations (Robins and Tomanec, 1962).

Life-Span Variations in Kin Interaction

Various researchers have studied the degrees of involvement with kin, friends, neighbors, and voluntary associations at different stages of life (Shulman, 1975; Mattessich, 1978; Leigh, 1982). As sociologist Norman Shulman (1975) emphasizes, "at each stage people tend to establish and sustain networks of relationships geared to the needs and concerns of their particular stage of life" (p. 820).

Data from Shulman's sample of 347 urban respondents indicated that single young adults are least likely to name relatives among those persons closest to them; friends are considered of greater importance. Shulman explains this as resulting from "the non-familial nature of the major concerns of people at this stage of the life cycle," when interest centers on educational and career concerns, enjoying companionship, and seeking a mate—all of which contribute to a preference for interaction with persons of similar age and interests.

When persons enter marriage, however, and especially as they become parents, relatives take on a new importance. "Kin involvement peaks noticeably for individuals with one or more pre-school children," writes sociologist Paul Mattessich (1978:11). "Needs for advice, for help with child care, and for financial assistance act to push people at this stage toward kin, as does the simple desire to 'show off' the children." Kin are probably more interested in seeing the children during infancy and the early years of childhood than at any other stage, according to Mattessich, who points out that this is especially true of grandparents. (See also Belsky and Rovine, 1984.)

The social anthropologist Elizabeth Bott (1957), after intensive interviews with a small number of English families, describes the common life-cycle pattern as consisting of "several phases of expansion and contraction." Informants remembered childhood contact with grandparents, aunts, uncles, and cousins, in addition to involvement with their own parents and siblings. "However," writes Bott, "most people indicated that in late adolescence and early adulthood they had broken away from their parents and siblings to some extent, and contacts with extra-familial kin were dropped or greatly reduced" (pp. 156–157). After this contraction phase, there came another expansion phase after marriage and children.

"Family relationships are never fixed; they change as the self and the significant other family members grow older, and as the changing society influences their respective lives," writes Matilda White Riley (1983:443). "Clearly, the longer the relationship endures (because of longevity) the greater the opportunity for relational changes." Riley, who specializes in the sociology of aging, suggests that the kinship structure has been *transformed* because of the great increases in life expectancy that have occurred during the twentieth century. "Linkages among family members have been prolonged," she writes, "and the surviving generations in a family have increased in number and complexity." She continues:

> Today's kinship structure (which has no parallel in history) can be viewed in a new way: as a latent web of continually shifting linkages that provide the potential of activating and intensifying close family relationships. These relationships are no longer prescribed as strict obligations, but must be earned—created and recreated by family members over their lives. (p. 439)

In other words, persons living today have the potential of being involved in a more complex "kin matrix" than ever before—and for a longer period of time. Riley asserts that we need to look at the interdependencies of the lives of family members as "each person's family life continually interacts with the lives of significant relatives." She believes that the usual "life course" or "life span perspective" often fails to look beyond the individual. "We are indeed concerned with people moving through life," she writes. "Yet we are concerned not with a single life or a statistical aggregate of lives, but with the dynamic family systems of interdependent lives" (p. 448).

To illustrate the complexities of contemporary kinship relationships and interdependencies, let's consider the hypothetical situation of 47-year-old Kate. On a particular Tuesday when Kate has a day off from work, she spends part of the afternoon visiting her 90-year-old grandmother in a nursing home. As the clock nears 2:45, Kate leaves in a rush so that she can be at her daughter's home in time to baby-sit while her daughter goes to her obstetrician for a prenatal checkup. This is her daughter's second marriage, and she is eager to have this baby with her new husband. The 2-year-old grandson whom Kate is caring for this afternoon was the subject of a bitter custody fight. Kate's daughter's former husband, Wayne, appears resigned to having lost his custody battle but would like more visitation time with his son. While Kate is baby-sitting, the phone rings. It is Wayne's mother, asking if she can stop by to bring a gift to the child, who is *her* grandson as well as Kate's.

When an exhausted Kate arrives home, she

finds a letter from a cousin with whom she has had almost no contact in many years. The cousin is asking for advice on a matter about which Kate has some expertise. Kate thinks about it while waiting for her husband. While they are eating dinner, the phone rings. Kate's 72-year-old widowed mother has had a heart attack and is in intensive care. Immediately, Kate must begin making plans to travel 500 miles to be at her mother's side. She must also call the Red Cross to see about notifying her brother, who is a career military officer on an overseas assignment. She thinks about her brother and how they have drifted apart over the years. What will it be like to have renewed contact with him once again?

The hypothetical case of Kate is not far-fetched, or even unusual. It illustrates what Riley (1983:446) calls the "continuing interplay among intertwined lives within the entire changing kinship structure." The impact of divorce on this changing kinship structure (for example, on questions surrounding grandparent visitation rights) also needs to be considered in rethinking extended-kin ties (Bean, 1985–86).

Calling on Kin for Help Regardless of the stage of the life course, interaction among kin is likely to be high during times of disaster, such as floods or tornadoes. For many people at such times, relatives provide a variety of services ranging from baby-sitting to offering temporary shelter, food, clothing, and even small loans (Drabek et al., 1975).

But what about everyday problems and crises not related to major disasters? To whom do people turn? Sociologist Reuben Hill (1970) found differences associated with what stage of the life cycle persons happened to be in. His study focused on three generations of families: (1) a "grandparent" generation, with all children launched; (2) a "par-

ent" generation, contracting in size as children were being launched or were already gone from the home; and (3) a "married-children" generation, just beginning its childbearing stage and thus expanding in size.

When respondents were asked to indicate preferred sources of help in times of crisis, the grandparent generation reported that they turned first to their children (the middle, or "parent," generation). Second, they turned to friends among their own peer group, then to health and welfare agencies, then to private specialists, and, last of all, to their married grandchildren.

The parent generation preferred to turn first to their parents (that is, the grandparent generation) and next to their married children. Turning to friends was the third choice of this middle generation, then to private specialists, and last to their own brothers and sisters.

What about the "married-children" generation? They reported that they turned first to their parents and second to private specialists. Their third choice was friends, followed by sisters and brothers, with help sought from grandparents their fifth choice (Hill, 1970:69).

Why Do Kin Help? The sociologist Alvin Gouldner (1960) has written on the "norm of reciprocity," which helps explain the stability of a social system. Quite simply, *reciprocity* is the process of giving benefits to others (through what we do for them or give to them), which induces them to provide benefits for us in return.

Although Hill (1970:76–80) does not entirely disagree with those sociologists who explain intergenerational kin exchanges in terms of the norm of reciprocity, he attaches importance to two other norms that may be operative as well: *filial obligation,* defined as "the norm of responsibility of children for their parents"; and *noblesse oblige,* the "sense of obligation of the more advantaged family to aid those perceived to be in less fortunate circumstances."

However, both filial obligation and *noblesse oblige* fall under Gouldner's explanation of how the norm of reciprocity works. The parents in their middle years, who are giving to their own parents (the grandparent generation), may indeed feel a "filial obligation," but that sense of obligation stems from knowing that in the past their parents were the ones who gave to them. Gouldner (1960) emphasizes that reciprocity "tends to structure *each* role so as to include both rights and duties" (p. 169). Parents have rights, but they also have duties toward their children.

An example of the lifelong reciprocities between parents and children is the care grown children may give to elderly parents who once took care of them. (Robert Eckert/The Picture Cube)

And children have rights, but they also have duties toward their parents. To some extent, these reciprocities exist throughout life.

Gouldner also refers to a universal norm of *moral obligation* to reward those who have earlier rewarded us. This norm, part of what reciprocity is all about, seems more fitting than *noblesse oblige* in explaining especially the pattern Hill found in which the grandparents may frequently find themselves "dependents," with their grown children (the parent generation) serving as "patrons" (p. 304).

Where relatives receive aid but are unable to give, they may develop a sense of dependency that is humiliating and embarrassing to them and results in less visiting with the kin or participating in kin activities (Hill, 1970:76–77, 304). This lends support to the findings of numerous studies by social psychologists that show that "while reciprocal exchanges breed cooperation and good feelings, gifts that cannot be reciprocated breed discomfort, distress, and dislike" (Hatfield [Walster], Walster. and Berscheid, 1978:107).

Does Mobility Affect Kin Relations?

Three sociologists have described several different kinds of mobility: residential, personal, vertical, and ideational (Burgess, Locke, and Thomes, 1963:363–384). As applied to kin relations, we say that persons reside *geographically* close to or distant from kin. Similarly, persons may be close or distant in terms of the *personal experiences* they have had—trips, social contacts, life-enrichment experiences that set them apart from others in their family, for example. Third, persons may be close to or distant from their kin in terms of *social status* because they or the kin have moved either up or down socioeconomically (vertical mobility). Last, persons may be close or distant from various kin members because of the way they have moved in terms of the *ideas* they hold and the *values* they espouse—for example, their religious beliefs and allegiance to some group may set them apart from the kin or may bring them closer.

Most studies of kinship and mobility have concentrated on either *geographical* (residential) mobility or on *socioeconomic-status* (vertical) mobility. Little attention has been given to the other two areas mentioned above—except where changes in personal ideas, values, social contacts, and life experiences are related to changes in social status.

Geographical Mobility and Kin Interaction

Sociologists Lee Robins and Miroda Tomanec (1962) measured closeness of interaction with relatives in terms of "the number of avenues used for communication, performance of services, and fulfillment of obligations." As might be expected, they found that closeness decreases when relatives are geographically distant. At the same time, they write, "We do not know from our data whether geographic distance also makes relatives *feel* subjectively less close." Maintaining contact with geographically distant kin is costly—whether costs are measured in terms of financial outlay (costs of trips, phone calls, mailing gifts, and so on) or in terms of the time and energy invested in writing letters, planning and making visits, entertaining relatives as houseguests, and the like.

In kin relationships that are considered rewarding, intimacy is maintained regardless of distance. Bott (1957) suggests that the crucial criteria for separating these relationships from other, less intimate ones are "the amount of contact combined with the amount of effort people put into making special visits to the relative" (p. 121). Bott's study showed that persons may be "close" to some relatives even though they live far away. At the same time, they may be less close (in terms of social contacts and feelings of affection) to other relatives who live nearby (pp. 126–128).

Research by sociologist Bert Adams (1968:23–24) showed that unskilled and semiskilled blue-collar persons, persuaded they could find work as well in one industrial area as another, frequently relocated for the precise purpose of getting away from unsatisfactory kin relations. At the same time, good kin relations could keep blue-collar persons living in an area. Relationships matter more than job opportunities in determining where to live—a pattern that contrasts with that of white-collar persons, where "opportunity takes precedence over relationships," says Adams. White-collar respondents told him they would like to be able to see their kin more often, but occupational demands had meant moving away.

Harriette Pipes McAdoo (1981b:157), a professor of social work, refers to the " 'support chains' for geographic mobility" that have operated for many black persons as they have moved to new areas. One person would become settled in an area, then help other relatives and friends to relocate in that same area in quest of better economic opportunities. Such a system "ensured that a person who moved to an area was not totally isolated, but was met with an existing supportive network that would give assistance until a niche had been found." Large numbers of extended kin have migrated in this way.

Status Mobility and Kin Interaction

What happens to kin relations when a working-class person moves into the middle class? Contrary to what we might expect, most available studies indicate that kin interaction isn't greatly affected by status mobility (Klatzky, 1972:40). For example, in a study of 305 black parents representing 178 family units, Harriette McAdoo (1978) looked at four patterns of mobility. The highest percentage of her sample (62 percent) were newly middle class after two generations of working class; another 23 percent had grandparents in the lower class, parents in the working class, and were themselves middle class; still others had parents who had been born into the working class but had moved to the middle class into which the respondents had been born (6 percent); and last, some respondents (9 percent) reported having been middle class for three generations.

What did McAdoo find? "The kin help system had been maintained before, during, and after mobility," she writes. "Parents did not have to cut themselves off from their families to become upwardly mobile. Eighty percent of the families indicated an intensive involvement in the kin exchange system. . . . No differences in kin help were found between those born middle class or working class, nor between the four mobility patterns." She did find, however, that "those newly mobile were more pressured to share with those of lower income than those who were born middle class." (See also McAdoo, 1981b.)

Robins and Tomanec (1962), in interviewing 140 college students, found that although the students came from middle-class homes and expected careers in high-status occupations, "they showed no preference for white collar over blue collar relatives" at this point in life.

Of all relatives, contact with *parents* is especially maintained, regardless of whether persons have moved up or down in status (Bott, 1957:148–149; Klatzky, 1972:38–41). The encouragement and support of parents is important to their upwardly mobile offspring (Adams, 1968:171), and the success of that son or daughter reflects positively on the parents (Bott, 1957:149). On the other hand,

the downwardly mobile person may draw comfort and feel less of a failure through identifying with his or her parents who remain at a higher status level (Klatzky, 1972:40; Litwak, 1960).

Gender Roles and Kin Involvement

Wives, more than husbands, tend to keep up kinship ties regardless of geographical distance. And they tend to keep in closer touch with their own side of the family than with the husband's side (Robins and Tomanec, 1962; Berardo, 1967; Farber, 1966:76–77; Bahr, 1976). The key role played by females in maintaining kin contacts is dramatically illustrated by sociologist Felix Berardo's (1967:553) finding that if a mother died, a family's interaction with the extended kin fell almost as low as if both parents had died. But if a father died, the frequency of kin contact was almost as high as if both parents were alive.

However, sociologist Howard Bahr (1976:77–78) points out that maintaining kin contact through letters, phone calls, and visits does not tell the whole story. "In fact," he writes, "the apparent female domination of the kinship role may stem largely from the husband's default or delegation of kinship tasks. He seems content for the wife to function as chief correspondent, executive secretary, or family clerk. But when the decision is whether to provide economic aid to relatives, or when there is overt disagreement [about the kin], he is likely to make the decision." Bahr's assertion is based on a study of over two hundred couples randomly selected from lists of parents whose children were in the third grade.

Some sociologists, thinking in terms of the traditional family where the wife is not employed, have suggested that a wife's fulfillment of kinship obligations is only to be expected. After all, she has more time available. Since Bahr found that employed mothers, as well as mothers with large families, were less involved in keeping up communication with extended kin, he suggests the "available time" idea may have merit. But although this may be one explanation for the reduced kin contact of mothers with large families, it doesn't necessarily explain why full-time employed mothers were found to be "less likely to affirm obligations to kin and less likely to feel remiss in their interaction with them" (Bahr, 1976:75).

Perhaps we are seeing here what we see in the case of husbands: a concentration on the instrumental tasks of income-producing and achievement in the economic-opportunity system, with less importance attached to performing traditional expressive duties toward extended kin. Interestingly, however, Bahr found that the women "most kin-oriented" in terms of feeling obligation and concern about meeting that obligation were not the full-time homemakers but, rather, the wives who were employed part-time.

That wives, more than husbands, have shown involvement with kin relations is not surprising in view of traditional socialization patterns. As we saw earlier in this book, females are taught to be nurturant and concerned about interpersonal relationships, while males learn early the importance of putting their energies into achievement. Thus, upon marriage, couples may find themselves dividing up tasks and responsibilities on the basis of traditional gender-role norms—which means that caring for kin, like caring for children, is assigned to the person trained for nurturance; namely, the female.

However, just as less rigidity in gender roles is associated with higher levels of education and higher status in general, Bahr (1976) found "an inverse relationship between socioeconomic status, as measured by income, education, or occupation, and the proportion of husbands who defined communicating with kindred as primarily a wife's responsibility" (p. 73). In other words, the more education and the higher the husband's income, the less likely he was to think his wife should be the one to keep in touch with relatives and the more likely he was to feel that he, too, was responsible for such contact.

Women, more than men, have also been found to take on the role of "kinkeeper" for the *extended* family, not only keeping themselves and their immediate families in touch with kin but keeping the various members of the broader extended family in touch with each other as well (Rosenthal, 1985). The "kinkeeper" characteristically passes on news of family members to other family members; telephones, visits, and writes frequently and urges other family members to do the same; and arranges events to bring kin together—family reunions, picnics, and celebrations of anniversaries, birthdays, and holidays. Each side of the family may have such a "kinkeeper."

CHAPTER HIGHLIGHTS

Kin include persons related both by blood ("in nature") and by marriage ("in law"). The persistence of kin ties may be explained in terms of reciprocity; that is, kinfolk perceive their relationships rewarding as they give to and receive tangible and intangible benefits from one another. A tradition of strong ties among kin is especially pronounced among black and Chicano families. Generally speaking, for most persons, interaction with kin tends to vary according to one's stage of life. But regardless of the stage of one's life course, interaction among kin is likely to be high during times of disaster. And if kin relationships are considered rewarding, intimacy is maintained regardless of geographical distance. However, mobility is not only a matter of geography. Persons may move closer to or farther away from their kin in terms of personal experiences, ideas and values, and socioeconomic status, as well. Yet contrary to what we might expect, most studies have indicated that kin interaction 'isn't greatly affected by status mobility, especially when it comes to interaction with parents. Contact with parents is usually maintained regardless of whether persons have moved up or down in status. One indication of traditional gender-role socialization patterns with regard to kinship interaction shows up in findings that wives, more than husbands, keep in touch with relatives, maintaining especially close ties with their own side of the family.

·16·

THE MIDDLE AND LATER YEARS OF MARRIAGE

According to folk wisdom, as the years of marriage go on, the fires of love burn down. The theme is a familiar one in novels, plays, and films. "You just bite the nail and hang on" was the advice given by an elderly father to his middle-aged son in view of the son's marital discontent in Robert Anderson's drama, *Double Solitaire.* A public-television presentation of 1975, the play took its title from the mother-in-law's counsel to the daughter-in-law. While the disenchanted husband was hearing his father's advice to "just remember, bite on the nail," the middle-aged wife was listening to the older woman's recipe for ongoing marital happiness: play double solitaire. Most people, of course, play the card game alone, but, emphasized the mother-in-law, in marriage the spouses can play alone while together. A "double-solitaire" marriage was exactly the kind of marriage the younger woman didn't want.

MARITAL SATISFACTION OVER TIME

Descriptive literature by writers, family counselors, and a certain number of studies by behavioral scientists have reinforced the belief that marriages deteriorate in the middle years. "By and large such observations are based on clinical experiences with persons who have so much difficulty in making the transition that they must seek outside help," writes researcher Irwin Deutscher (1962), whose own findings did not support commonly held notions about, for example, the "empty-nest" period of life, when children are grown and gone and parents allegedly have little to bind them together any longer.

While cautioning that definite conclusions cannot be drawn from the responses of such a small sample (forty-nine urban, middle-class, postparental couples, 40 to 65 years of age), Deutscher (1962) wrote that the majority of wives and husbands viewed this stage of the family life cycle "as a time of new freedoms." In particular, his respondents spoke of the freedom from economic responsibility for the children, freedom to travel or move to another location, freedom from housework and other tasks, "and finally, freedom to be one's self for the first time since the children came along."

At the same time, while many early reports of diminished marital satisfaction over time were based on little more than impressions and clinical findings, some data from more rigorous studies have lent support to such findings (see summary in Rollins and Feldman, 1970:21). For example, Blood and Wolfe's (1960:264) widely cited Detroit study produced the finding that wives became less satisfied as the length of marriage increased. And the Burgess/Wallin longitudinal study, begun in 1937 with 1,000 engaged couples and followed up twenty years after their marriages, showed that among the 153 couples left from the original sample, there was widespread disenchantment, less intimacy, and decreased "marital adjustment" (Pineo, 1961; Troll, 1971).

Our own studies have yielded inconsistent results, again showing the uncertainty and need for further research in this area. A large-scale study of white Indianapolis husbands and wives showed that, in general, satisfaction with *empathy* (communication and understanding) increases—although there are certain variations by socioeconomic status and sex that must be taken into account (Scanzoni, 1970). A later study, however, indicated that the age of a wife or husband (highly correlated with the stage of marriage in most cases) made virtually no difference at all in how satisfactory both black and white persons evaluated their marriages (Scanzoni, 1975a).

Some studies have shown a decline in marital satisfaction during the childbearing and childrearing stages but an increase in satisfaction during the postparental years (Rollins and Feldman, 1970). Such findings have led to the widespread generalization that marital satisfaction follows a U-shaped curve, dropping when the first child is born, leveling out over the childrearing years, then moving back up again when the children have left home. Yet, although there *is* some empirical evidence for such a pattern, the decline in satisfaction is not so dramatic as it may at first appear. The "U" isn't very deep and, in fact, is rather flat "inasmuch as only 4–8% of the variation in marital satisfaction is associated with stages of the family career," emphasize researchers Boyd Rollins and Richard Galligan (1978). These sociologists and others call for caution in view of the way some writers tend to *overstate* the U-shaped effect and thereby give couples entering marriage the impression that they "should prepare for the storm" (p. 82; see also Spanier et al., 1975; Schram, 1979).

In view of the question being asked (namely, How does the passage of time affect marital quality?), it is regrettable that so little research on the topic has been longitudinal (Ade-Ridder and Brubaker, 1983; Spanier and Lewis, 1980). Until such longitudinal studies are undertaken and other methodological problems corrected, our understanding of how marital quality fares over time will remain unclear and inconclusive (Spanier and Lewis, 1980).

Some couples may feel that their marital satisfaction remains high or even increases over the years, while other couples experience a decline and may feel that the descriptive terms sometimes used for mid-marriage disappointment are on target. There may be *disenchantment* (a loss of enthusiasm for the partner and the relationship, a cooling of feelings), and there may be *disengagement* (lessened companionship and interaction between the spouses) (Blood, 1969:325–333). These are the marriages that sociologists John Cuber and Peggy Harroff (1965) have categorized as "devitalized" because of "the clear discrepancy between middle-aged reality and the earlier years." In such cases, the couples report that once they were closely identified with each other, shared many interests, spent a great deal of time together, and thoroughly enjoyed their sex life. Now things have changed, and they do things for and with each other out of duty more than out of the sense of love and delight in one another they once felt. According to Cuber and Harroff, although "the original zest is gone," those couples in their sample who fit into this category tended to "believe that the devitalized mode is the appropriate mode in which a man and a woman should be content to live in the middle years and later" (pp. 49–50).

In attempting to understand the complexities suggested by the various studies on changes in marital satisfaction over the years, perhaps we need to see even *more* complexities rather than trying to boil it all down to a simple truism, such as, "Marital satisfaction does (or doesn't) decline as time goes on." There are structural and situational factors—and not merely personality considerations—to keep in mind. If marital satisfaction is related to socioeconomic status, we need to consider changes in access to the economic-opportunity structure over the family life cycle. How does either spouse's loss of employment on the one hand, or a sizable promotion on the other, affect satisfaction within marriage? How will the marital relationship be affected by a husband's feelings at middle age that he has not reached the goals of which he had dreamed? What if a wife feels unfulfilled in her career goals? How will a wife's decision to seek employment after the children are grown and gone affect her relationship with her husband at this stage of life, especially after a marriage built on traditional gender-role assumptions? Research that takes situations such as these into account is needed. Also, since some studies indicate that marital satisfaction decreases and levels out during the childrearing stages but increases again at the postparental stage, questions need to be raised about whether we are seeing the effect of children on a marriage or simply the effect of the passage of time. Longitudinal research on marital satisfaction among childless couples over the years would be fruitful for comparison.

"Too many other uncontrolled variables such as ages of husband and wife, number of years married, and stage in the occupational career of the husband (and wife) are highly correlated with child-referenced transitions over the family career," say Rollins and Galligan (1978), in commenting on the common assumption that the presence or absence of children or their stage of development is what accounts for a U-shaped curve of marital satisfaction. They go on to say that "the data are, however, congruent with the notion that the presence of dependent children in the home put a 'crunch' on the time, energy, and economic resources of parents and result in a decrease in the marital satisfaction of the parents" (p. 83). These sociologists call for further research and suggest that the lowered marital satisfaction during the childrearing years may be related to the increased accumulation of family roles over the years and the stress or strain experienced in trying to live up to the expectations and obligations of these multiple roles (see also Hoffman and Manis, 1978; Anderson, Russell, and Schumm, 1983).

Another factor to keep in mind is the personal growth that one or both spouses may experience over time. People change, but not always at the same rate or in the same direction. New experiences, new interests, new contacts, new goals, even adopting a whole new philosophy of life may mean that one spouse ceases to be the person the other spouse thought he or she knew and married. Anthropologist Paul Bohannan (1970:36), an authority on divorce, suggests that an inability to tolerate change in the spouse often lies at the root of the growing estrangement associated with a marital breakup. As a person changes over the years, the rewards he or she offers to the spouse (and the costs to the spouse) are likely to change as well. This will require renegotiation if the couple is to reach new agreements of expectations so that each spouse experiences maximum joint profit.

Perhaps we might also speculate that a certain amount of disenchantment occurs because of unrealistic expectations stemming from romantic love. When the helplessness of "falling in love" and being swallowed up in a mystery beyond comprehension gives way to the daily routines of living together, a great deal of magic and passion may seem to disappear. In the words of psychoanalyst Erich Fromm (1956): "After the stranger has become an intimately known person there are no more barriers to be overcome, there is no more sudden closeness to be achieved." Thus the exhilaration of falling in love may be sought with someone else, and once again "the stranger is transformed into an 'intimate' person." The intensity again becomes less and ends in the desire for a new adventure in romantic love—"always with the illusion that the new love will be different from the earlier ones" (pp. 44–45 in paperback edition).

Subjective Evaluation of Marital Satisfaction

Marital satisfaction is really a subjective matter, depending upon how a marriage lives up to the expectations of the individuals concerned. One couple may consider their marriage deeply satisfying, whereas an outsider might see the marriage as dull and undesirable. Whether or not wives and husbands are satisfied with their marriage relationship in the middle years depends upon the rewards they expected to receive and felt they deserved and whether or not these rewards materialize. In exchange-theory terms, we can think of Thibaut and Kelley's (1959:21) *comparison level* or CL, an imaginary point on a scale by which persons evaluate costs and rewards in a relationship (just as a certain point on a thermometer serves as the dividing line between temperatures above and below freezing). If the marital rewards minus costs are at a level that meets the expectations of the particular husband or wife, he or she rates the marital relationship above the comparison point (CL)—though the rating is not necessarily conscious. On the other hand, if the outcomes of a particular relationship (the rewards as compared to costs) fall below an individual's personal CL, the relationship will be rated unsatisfactory.

It's possible that in some marriages, the level of profit diminishes over the years so that the relationship ceases to be as rewarding as it once was. In other words, to one or both spouses, the marital relationship slides below the CL point. This may explain some cases of disenchantment in the middle years. In other cases, one or both spouses may *raise* their CL point and come to expect *more* from the marriage than they did earlier, with the result that the outcomes of the relationship may be evaluated quite differently than was once the case. A person may not be so easily satisfied as was true earlier in the marriage but may feel that he or she deserves a great deal more at this point in life.

Thibaut and Kelley also speak of another standard of comparison—the *comparison level for alternatives* or CL$_{alt}$. The CL$_{alt}$ marks the lowest level of outcomes or profit a member of a relationship will accept in the light of available alternatives. Persons consider the reward/cost ratio of the best other situation available to them and weigh the anticipated profit there against their present situation. For example, a husband or wife might have reason to believe that the rewards minus costs in a relationship with a third party would yield greater profit than does the present relationship with the spouse. In some cases, this might mean divorce and remarriage; in other cases, an extramarital "affair" might result, even though the marriage continues. Or a spouse might come to the conclusion that a *single* lifestyle is a desirable alternative and would offer a more favorable reward/cost ratio than the present marriage. Chapter 17 will focus on the many facets of divorce and remarriage.

THE MIDDLE YEARS: EMPTYING OF THE NEST

Because of increased longevity, couples who remain married may expect to have a longer period of time together after the children have grown than has ever been the case before. Demographer Paul C. Glick (1977:11) suggests that this extended empty-nest period may be "the most dramatic change that has occurred in the pattern of the typical life cycle." (See also Norton, 1983; Rodgers and Witney, 1981). What will this mean for a husband and wife? For the first time in twenty years or so, it will be just the two of them. How will they feel as their children go out on their own and the longer-than-ever postparental period stretches before them?

Wives in the Middle Years

Contrary to the stereotype of the middle-aged woman depressed over the physical

Contrary to the stereotype of the middle-aged woman, depressed over menopause and the emptying of the family nest, many wives at midlife today are energetically attending to their own interests and thankful for the freedom to pursue them at last. (© Bohdan Hrynewych/Stock, Boston)

changes associated with menopause and experiencing a sense of uselessness upon the emptying of the family nest, many wives at midlife today are likely to be energetically attending to their own interests and thankful for the freedom to pursue them at last. The stereotype no doubt arose from observing individual cases that seemed to support it, especially in clinical settings where troubled women sought out help. But it's a mistake to generalize from these instances and to assume that the periods of *launching* (when children are getting ready and beginning to leave home) and *empty nest* (when children have left) must necessarily be difficult and distressing for all mothers. When sociologist Norval Glenn (1975) analyzed data from six national surveys, he found that middle-aged wives whose children had left home reported greater general happiness and greater marital happiness than did middle-aged wives with a child or children still at home. Although he cautions against the assumption that the results would be the same in the case of widows left entirely alone and acknowledges that there *are* cases of individuals who experience negative effects from the postparental stage, he says that in general, he did not find evidence that "the 'empty-nest' or postparental stage of the family life cycle is a traumatic and unhappy period for the typical woman." Other studies have yielded similar findings. Summarizing some of these, Joan Robertson (1978), a *gerontologist* (a specialist in the study of aging), writes:

> The childbearing years are over for most women in early midlife. Longitudinal data indicate that both men and women respond to the *empty nest period* with a sigh of relief and freedom from responsibilities. Most women welcome the freedom to revive or intensify old and new interests. Most seek opportunities for self-definition, new careers, and inner sources of strength. Conversely, some (but fewer than has been traditionally assumed) remain the same by choice and others stagnate—remain the same without making a conscious choice. Some become acutely or chronically depressed and dependent on spouses, families, or others. (p. 378)

Who are the women most likely to experience difficulty as the nest empties? According to family-studies specialist Dena Targ (1979:381), they are "women who define themselves primarily as mothers . . . women who have accepted the traditional feminine role, who have invested themselves in their children, who have not created alternative roles for themselves . . . women who have not

MIDLIFE: A STAGE RATHER THAN AN AGE

Appearances notwithstanding, for women, at least, midlife is not a stage tied to chronological age. Rather, it belongs to that point in the life cycle of the family when the children are grown and gone, or nearly so—when, perhaps for the first time in her adult life, a woman can attend to her own needs, her own desires, her own development as a separate and autonomous being. Thus, the mid-thirties career woman, married two years and about to bear her first child is not concerned with midlife issues. She's worried about diapers and feedings, about hard days and sleepless nights, about how she'll continue her career, about whether she can manage motherhood and wifehood without sacrificing one to the other, or her own life to both. Compare her with a woman of the same age, married eighteen years, whose youngest child is fifteen. For good or ill, she has answered the questions that now face the recently married new mother. For good or ill, that part of life is done. Now, she must find a way to give meaning to the rest of her life—something to do, some way of being, that makes each day worth living.

SOURCE: Lillian B. Rubin, *Women of a Certain Age: The Midlife Search for Self* (New York: Harper & Row, 1979), pp. 7–8.

anticipated and planned for the empty nest period." Wives who have been employed outside the home before the nest empties, or who have developed outside interests other than paid employment (such as voluntary work or further education), tend to adapt to this period most successfully (Schram, 1979:10; Rapoport et al., 1977:274–275; Borland, 1982).

Sociologist Alice Rossi (1980) points out that most of the research on women at midlife that has been done so far has concentrated on the small birth cohorts of the period from 1920 to 1935, women whose childhoods were in some way likely to have been affected by the Great Depression and whose adulthoods were shaped by unique social and economic pressures associated with the movement to suburbia and the larger families desired in the 1950s. Such research may tell us a great deal about what middle age means to many in this particular group of women, but it does not define or describe middle age as a predictable stage of adult development

or tell us what middle age may hold for women in the future. "For women moving into adulthood today," Rossi writes, "an expectation of relatively continuous employment adds a degree of certainty to their sense of the future and may therefore reduce anxiety and stress as they become middle aged" (p. 31).

Rossi emphasizes that we are in "a new period of increased variance in both the timing and sequencing of life events," and this must be taken into account in studying midlife. "Age norms are more fluid," Rossi writes. "More people marry, divorce, remarry, or never marry; increasing numbers of children spend time first in two-parent, then one-parent, then two-parent households; more people have no children at all, and more have late first births" (p. 16). These and other factors (such as making major career changes at various points) need to be taken into account if we are to understand how middle age is likely to be experienced in the years ahead. (See also Neugarten and Neugarten, 1987.)

Husbands in the Middle Years

Various family-development specialists have shown how males at midlife experience the negative effects of earlier, traditional gender-role socialization. "The 'male mystique' requires men to be strong, aggressive, unemotional, and tough, all characteristics which may be called into question during the decades from forty to sixty when the male is confronted with the beginnings of bodily decline, career stagnation, and drastic changes within his family unit," writes Jessica Field Cohen (1979:469).

Cohen refers to a number of studies that indicate that the gender-role paths traveled by males and females may cross at middle age, with males becoming more sensitive and nurturant (*expressive*) at the same time that females are becoming more independent and assertive (*instrumental*). Since for many men, middle age is a time of taking stock of life and recognizing their own mortality, they may feel anxious and uncertain about what lies ahead and feel threatened by their wives' growing autonomy (Cohen, 1979:467; Brim, 1976). They may yearn for attention, support, and nurturance from their wives at the very time their wives are feeling that a new world is opening up to them as women—a time of life in which women at last can attend to their own interests after years of putting husbands and children first. (See also Rossi, 1980; Zube, 1982.)

Social scientist Lillian Rubin (1979), in interviewing 160 women aged 35 to 54, found repeated instances of husbands who missed the old comfortable routines of their marriages when wives' behavior had been predictable and traditional. Some husbands began complaining about their wives' lack of interest in spending money for clothes and other items, whereas earlier they had complained because they considered their wives extravagant! "I don't really want clothes any more," one respondent told Rubin, "I only bought them before because I didn't have anything else important to do with my life" (p. 182). One husband wondered why his wife didn't want to redecorate the house any longer—something she had wanted so much when it wasn't possible earlier (and something "that would have kept her happily in the house a few years ago"). But now she spoke of changed priorities. Commitments to new interests (including paid employment and further education) meant that often their husbands' once-wished-for offers of movies and dinners were now viewed as impositions in wives' busy schedules, with the result that husbands felt hurt, rejected, and confused. Rubin describes what the changes in a wife's life can mean for the marriage:

> That "different kind of commitment" means that, even when she still takes care of the physical needs of family and household, she may not be so readily available to manage their social and emotional needs as well. It means she can't entertain so often because she has work to do. . . . It means that she doesn't want to go to a movie because she's studying for an exam. . . . It means that she may be too preoccupied with a conference tomorrow to want to have sex today. (pp. 179–180)

One woman reported that after she had trimmed down from 300 pounds, her husband's initial delight gave way to brooding and comments about wishing she hadn't lost all that weight. He saw her advancement in her job and her new self-confidence and began worrying that she would no longer be the same person. She told Rubin:

> All I can say to him is, "I love you, but I can't go back to being what I was. I can't do that for anybody." I finally feel that I'm a person with something to offer the world. I'm not going back to what it was like before for anything—no matter what. (pp. 197–198)

Some husbands find such determination on the part of wives hard to accept.

WHAT DOES MIDDLE AGE LOOK LIKE?

Gloria Steinem (AP/Wide World Photos)

More than a decade ago I did a dumb thing by going along with a press mistake and saying I was two years younger. This was prefeminism naturally. At the time I was going with a man who kept telling me that it was insane, suicidal, masochistic and otherwise unhealthy for any woman to tell her age. It's interesting how that one small lie—if it comes out of insecurity, not security—can make you feel completely false and terrible. I started using my actual age about a year later.

Then when I turned 40 I decided to celebrate it publicly. *Ms.* gave me a birthday party, and some reporter kindly said, "You don't look 40." I said, "But this is what 40 looks like. We've been lying so long who would know?" That comment has gotten more response than almost any other I've made, so I know age is still a problem for women—and I keep on telling mine.

SOURCE: Gloria Steinem, "An Unsinkable Feminist Sails into Her 50th Year Jubilant about Her First Best-Seller," *People, 20* (Nov. 21, 1983), pp. 185–186.

MIDLIFE TRANSITION: HIS AND HERS

Because he has spent his life in the work world, he knows its limitations. Even if he enjoys his work, he's beginning to slow down, to look for other interests, to experience the shallowness of his interpersonal relationships. In her life, it's just the other way around. She knows all about those things he misses. She has spent her life developing emotional closeness with others, honing her interpersonal skills to a fine edge. That's where she's most expert. For her, the time has come to test her competence in other ways. She goes to school or gets a job—fearful perhaps, but also filled with excitement, the promise of adventure filling her fantasies. For her, the world often seems shiny and new.

> Every day I go to work is a thrill. I love walking into my office, closing the door, and getting at the things on my desk. I feel like a kid who has a new toy to play with every morning when she gets up. [Slightly abashed at what she's just said] I hope you won't think that's too silly.

In fact, her excitement about her life is anything but silly; it's a refreshing delight to see. But again, it often means new problems in the family. Sometimes they're felt immediately because he's ready to slow down at just the moment she's accelerating her investment in a new career.

SOURCE: Lillian Rubin, *Woman of a Certain Age* (New York: Harper & Row, 1979), p. 207.

Furthermore, for many husbands, the midlife transition brings not only changes to their marriages but also changes in their *job* outlooks. Social scientist Rhona Rapoport and her colleagues (1977) call attention to the rapid technological and organizational changes that often catapult men to the peak of their careers earlier than was once the case. Upon reaching this peak, they may move in any of several directions. They "may feel depressed at a sense of futility in life; they may embark on a second career, or change their life styles completely by opting out of the occupational ladder altogether, or they may recreate their current interests" (p. 274). According to these researchers:

> For men in occupations which require competitive effort to make their way up organizational ladders, this may be a period of choice—between moving upward into more taxing senior positions with greater rewards of pay, power and prestige (though feeling perhaps that one is not as fit or as driven for such things as previously) vs de-emphasizing work aspirations in favour of rewards in family life or other interests. (p. 274)

Rapoport and her colleagues go on to point out that men who become more involved in their families not as a chosen top priority but because of a feeling that they have failed or are likely to fail in occupational advancement may show signs of dissatisfaction, irritability, and depression in response to what is actually second choice. In contrast, those men "who choose [family involvement] as a primary option, emphasizing 'humanistic' values rather than success, may have higher levels of satisfaction than their more 'successful' colleagues" (p. 274).

In addition to changes in their physical bodies, marriages, and occupational aspirations, men at midlife are facing another change—the same one experienced by wives and one that has sometimes been considered unique to wives: the change associated with the emptying of the family nest.

Few studies have focused on how fathers react to their children's leaving home—a neglect that three social scientists label "both difficult to understand and unfortunate." Robert Lewis, Phillip Freneau, and Craig Roberts (1979) speculate that "because males are currently increasing their involvement in the home and some are becoming more nurturing and caring toward their children, it would seem that more fathers will be experiencing unhappiness at the time that their last child leaves home" (p. 515). In their random sample of 118 postparental fathers, these researchers found that 35 percent had neutral feelings about having all their children gone from home, 26 percent felt somewhat happy, 16 percent felt very happy, and the remaining nearly one-fourth reported feelings of unhappiness.

Focusing on the fathers who reported unhappiness over the empty nest, Lewis, Freneau, and Roberts found that men who felt most unhappy "were also apt to be those who felt most neglected by their wives, received the least amount of understanding from them, were most lonely, were least enthusiastic about their wives' companionship, and had the least empathic wives" (p. 517). As we have already seen, many wives at this stage of life are stepping outside the nest themselves—at just the time when their husbands are turning more inward, toward their families, after years of concentrating on occupational achievement. Yet it may seem that now that the men have come home, everyone else has gone!

Another finding of Lewis and his associates

was that the fewer the children fathers had, the greater was the unhappiness felt when the children left home. And the fathers' age seems to be a factor, too. "The fathers who reported most unhappiness were also the oldest fathers," say these researchers, "and those who reported the greatest happiness were the youngest fathers" (p. 517). The data also suggested that fathers who perceived themselves to be most *nurturant* felt most unhappy when all their children had moved away from the family household. Lewis, Freneau, and Roberts say it all adds up to this: when the last child leaves home, the fathers who feel the most unhappiness tend to be those who have the "most to lose." They go on to describe this finding among the men in their sample:

> That is, they had the fewest children and, therefore, had more to lose emotionally with each child's leaving. They tended to be older fathers and, therefore, may have perceived fewer years to share with this child whom they feared would probably never again be so close. They also tended to perceive themselves as more nurturing and caring men, who may have had more to lose with the diminution of the full-time father role and loss of accompanying identities as care-givers and nurturing persons. Finally, these were fathers who probably had the most to lose with their last child's leaving because they tended also to report less satisfactory marriages. (p. 518)

One problem, say these researchers, is that there are "few normative guidelines for fathers at this stage, since males traditionally have been expected to concern themselves primarily with instrumental tasks, such as earning the family's livelihood" (p. 519). Thus, they don't expect the postparental period to be problematic and are likely to reach this point in life without having prepared for what they have been led to believe was something that concerned only mothers.

THE SQUEEZE BETWEEN GENERATIONS

"I feel like a nut in a nutcracker," one middle-aged woman told us. "I'm caught between pressures from my aging parents on one side and my teenagers and their needs on the other."

She was describing a common situation at this stage of life (Rapoport et al., 1977:270). Health, emotional, and possibly financial needs of older parents may make heavy demands upon the middle generation at the very time they are launching their own children and looking forward to time for their own self-realization.

A husband and wife at midlife may even find that once they reach the empty-nest stage, the nest will soon become refilled—either with an elderly parent or a grown son or daughter who has experienced a divorce, loss of job, or other circumstance (Hess and Waring, 1978:250).

In 1984, more than one-third (37 percent) of young adults 18 to 29 years old lived with their parents (Glick and Lin, 1986). Economic factors (such as the high cost of housing and difficulties in finding employment), the postponement of marriage, increases in unmarried motherhood, and high rates of marital dissolution no doubt all have a part to play in the decision of over 18 million young adults to make their home with their parents at a time in life when the parents expected to have the house to themselves. Some adult children have never left home at all, while others have returned after having been out on their own for a time.

"Whether previously living away from home or not, fledgling adults are more welcome when they are under the age of 22 and their stay is relatively brief," write Audra Clemens and Leland Axelson (1985:263), specialists in family studies. On the basis of

their own two small studies and a review of the limited amount of research on the topic, they conclude that "older children and those whose sojourn becomes long-term appear to both cause and experience more stress." For many middle-aged couples, the presence of an adult child places considerable strain on the marriage. Adult children may have ambivalent feelings about the arrangement as well. (See insert.)

"Role allocation in our society is such that those now in middle adulthood easily fall victim to overcommitments," write social scientists Beth Hess and Joan Waring (1978:249). Too many needs, roles, and responsibilities are clamoring for attention at the same time. And there isn't enough time and emotional energy to go around.

Midlife Couples and Their Grown Children

For one thing, parents don't cease being parents just because their children are approaching adulthood or have already reached it. Rapoport and her associates (1977:307–309) therefore prefer not to use the term *postparenthood* but speak of "parenting with adult children" instead. They point out that while it's true in general that "the *active* element of the parenting role recedes" and "the physical energy and time spent on daily parenting activities decreases and may stop altogether," parents continue to be concerned about their children and involved in their lives to some extent. Counsel, mutual aid, and a desire to spend time together often continues into and throughout the empty-nest period. Yet regrettably, say these researchers, "the actual experience of parenting with adult children has received very little systematic study" (p. 308).

During the launching period, as parents head toward the time when their children

BACK TO THE PARENTAL HOME

The return home can stir up past conflicts and resentments. Hostilities that were cooling off begin heating up again. Former habits, attitudes, and modes of communication that may have been phasing out reassert themselves.

"I left home when I was eighteen," says a twenty-six-year-old who recently returned to her parents' home after her divorce, "and I sort of looked forward to moving back with mom and dad. Emotionally, I was a mess after my husband and I split up, and I thought it would be great living with the two people in the world who really know me and care about me. I also thought we'd reached the point where we could deal with each other as responsible adults—I mean, I'd lived on my own for five years before I was married and I've supported myself, not to mention going through a marriage and divorce. . . . But you'd think I was still a little girl who'd never been away. It's the same old routine all over again: 'Did you make your bed?' 'What time will you be getting home?' And the hell of it is, if I left them now, it would be like having another divorce. There's so much feeling mixed up in it—I mean, the way we care for each other and yet the way we grate on each other's nerves."

SOURCE: Elinor Lenz, *Once My Child . . . Now My Friend* (New York: Warner Books, 1981), pp. 188–189.

will reach legal age, marry, or otherwise strike out on their own as adults, the parents themselves may be going through a period of questioning and change—as we've already seen. Parents are likely to be experiencing "middlescence" while their children are experiencing adolescence (Robertson, 1978:377). And while parents may continue to influence their children, their children at this stage of life may influence considerably the values and behaviors of the parents in a kind of "reverse-socialization" pattern (Bengtson and Troll, 1978:225). Witness the impact of young adults of the 1960s and 1970s on the political ideologies, clothing, and hairstyles adopted by the parent generation.

What is occurring is a "complex feedback system of transmission and differentiation involving generations of youth and their parents," report behavioral scientists Vern Bengtson and Lillian Troll (1978:234). Since parents have made such great investments in their children, they may feel they have a stake in assuring generational continuity by transmitting their values to them. But at the same time, their children are asserting their independence and may have a different perspective on the goals their parents consider most important (p. 218). There is give and take from both directions, and it may lead to deepening friendship on the one hand or alienation on the other (Lenz, 1981).

At the time that their young adult children are asking, "What shall I do with my life?" the parents may be asking, "What have I done with my life? Have I made the best choices? What lies ahead in the years that are left?" Once again, a weighing of costs and rewards is taking place. Rapoport and her colleagues (1977) talk about the "critical evaluation" typical of these midlife years. Have life investments been satisfying and worthwhile? "Are they paying off—psychologically, interpersonally, and in terms of how well the children seem to have developed?" (p. 271).

And while looking at the generation following after them intensifies the midlife couple's questions about personal identity, values, and achievements, looking at the generation ahead of them—their aging parents—may jolt them into a vivid realization of their own mortality. Rossi (1980) calls attention to a point made by Bernice Neugarten (1968:97); namely, that persons at midlife gradually change their time perspective so that "life is restructured in terms of time-left-to-live rather than time-since-birth."

Midlife Couples and Their Aging Parents

"In helping the aged parent, the offspring rehearse for their own future," write Hess and Waring (1978:252), "and conversely, the older person, having already lived through middle-age transitions, can serve as a role model and source of advice." But, they go on to say, the way is not always easy, nor is the relationship between the generations necessarily without problems and strains.

Aging parents may require time, emotional energy, and financial aid just when middle-agers are already overcommitted and faced with pressing career demands, community responsibilities, and heavy involvement in the lives of their own growing or grown children (which may include paying for expensive college educations). If a parent is widowed or becomes severely ill, the pressures on the middle generation may be especially acute. "The expenses associated with a parent's protracted illness are a financial as well as an emotional drain," write Hess and Waring (1978). "But demands for companionship can be even more trying" (p. 260). And such demands for attention and companion-

ship may be present where older parents are in good health as well as in cases of sickness and disability.

Hess and Waring (1978) speak of some of the psychological barriers that often block close relationships between middle-aged persons and their parents, including leftover resentments and hostilities from the years when the middle-generation persons were growing up in the family household:

> Although years of separate residence and greater self-knowledge may erase some of the minor difficulties and blunt the edge of some of the major ones, struggles for control, patterns of blaming, and disappointments about achievement, etc., may linger to undermine the possibility of a comfortable relationship between parents and children in the later years. Or they may be transferred onto the in-law relationship, creating a different but no less difficult kind of strain. (p. 251)

The resulting "emotional distance" may mean that the prospect of caring for an aged parent will cause considerable anxiety for many persons. Hess and Waring (1978) emphasize that "the expressed reluctance to take on primary care of an ailing parent may not reflect 'hardheartedness' so much as a strong reality orientation—the situation may be more emotionally stressful than the offspring can cope with" (p. 251). In other words, it isn't only a case of overcommitment in which the offsprings' time and energy resources are so taxed that they are unable to give themselves fully to their parents' needs. It's often a fear that one's own marriage or emotional health will suffer if one (or one's spouse) takes on caretaking responsibilities for an aging parent. Yet even that realization may arouse pangs of guilt. At the same time, the aging parent may feel just as reluctant to become dependent upon a son or daughter—especially if the relationship has been a difficult and strained one in the past.

"I'M TOO OLD TO HAVE A MOTHER"

"I'm too old to have a mother," my friend Adele protested recently as we were discussing the exigencies of having aged parents. I empathized totally. Her mother is 87. Mine is five years older. Both of us are Prime Time citizens, eligible for membership in the Gray Panthers and AARP.

We have raised our children, seen them through college. We have survived their experimenting with drugs, their dropping out, their periods of total rejection. We have supported them and suffered with them, subjecting for the most part, our needs to theirs. Then, just when we arrive at the time when we think we are free, we are thrust again into parenting, this time with our mothers as the wards.

Much has been said about the pitiful plight of the elderly, dumped into nursing homes, shoved into back rooms, ignored by ungrateful offspring, but little consideration has been given to those who, like Adele and me, sustain their parents. . . .

At present longevity, intended as a bonanza, in too many cases, is a nightmare. Doctors and scientists who have addressed themselves to prolonging life have given little consideration to the quality of life. Often when I have queried doctors about efforts to improve my mother's condition, to provide intensive therapy so she might walk again, they smile benignly and shrugging their shoulders ask, "What do you expect at her age?" They have written her off.

We must rethink and restructure the care and consideration of the very old, for their sakes and for the sake of their aging children. The group called the "oldest old" is growing more rapidly than any other segment of the population. Planning and provisions are made when a baby boom is expected. But no planning and provisions have been made for the elderly boom.

SOURCE: Excerpted from "Prime Time," a regular feature in *New Directions for Women, 14* (March/April 1985), p. 10.

Victor Cicirelli (1983:40–41) found that the strains most frequently reported by adult children caring for elderly parents were "feeling physically worn out, emotionally exhausted, and that the parent was not satisfied no matter what the child did." Other reported strains were feelings of being tied down by the elderly parents' needs, the necessity of altering one's own personal schedule, and having to give up many aspects of one's former social life and recreational activities. "Those adult children who perceived their parents as more dependent and as having greater needs for services and who gave their parents more help also experienced more personal strains and negative feelings," writes Cicirelli. What kind of negative feelings? "Feelings of frustration, impatience, and irritation were most frequently reported, followed by helplessness and guilt."

Elder Abuse In some extremely stressful situations, an elderly parent may be physically or emotionally abused or neglected (Douglass, 1983; Cornell and Gelles, 1982; Gelles and Cornell, 1985; Poertner, 1986; Valentine and Cash, 1986; Kinderknecht, 1986; Sengstock and Barrett, 1986). One research scientist specializing in gerontology refers to data from a Michigan study that show that "the most common causes of neglect and abuse appear to include the consequences of adult caretakers becoming over-taxed by the requirements of caring for a frail dependent adult. The burden for caring, without occasional relief, can lead to despair, anger, resentment, or violence among some caretakers" (Douglass, 1983:401). Many persons who abuse elderly parents were themselves abused during their growing-up years by those same parents and thus learned violence in the home (Gelles and Cornell, 1985:105).

Stress appears to be a major contributing factor in elder abuse. As Gelles and Cornell (1985:105) point out, "It is unrealistic to expect all families to be able to assume the responsibility of caring for an aging parent. . . . Families may lack the appropriate levels of personal, social, and economic resources to adequately nurture their dependent, aging relatives." (See also Steinmetz and Amsden, 1983.)

Gender Roles and Caring for Aging Parents In pointing out that "the current trend [in the United States] is toward laws that would legislate familial responsibility—demand that families care for their own," Jo Horne (1985:276–277) highlights a major problem in the assumptions behind such social policies. "Such ideas," she writes, "are based on a false picture of the typical caregiver as a middle-aged woman whose husband is at the peak of his earning power, who is healthy, and who can provide care for an older person in need of support because she is at home." Such a picture is all wrong. The typical caregiver is what Horne terms "young-old"—a woman who is herself at or near retirement age. She is likely to be holding a full-time job necessary for her own (and possibly others') livelihood. She may be single, divorced, or widowed. To take on a care-

giving role at this stage of life and in such circumstances isn't easy, and the risk of "burnout" is real (Horowitz, 1985).

Traditionally, the caregiving role has fallen to daughters (Stoller, 1983). Females have been socialized to take care of others' needs ahead of their own—to be nurturers. Daughters are also expected to remain more closely tied to their families of origin than are sons. Another carryover from traditional gender-role expectations is the assumption that women are less committed to their careers and thus have more free and flexible time available when it is necessary for them to take care of aging parents. This assumption can no longer be made in view of the growing percentage of women in the work force.

Responsibility for a frail elderly parent may include sharing the same house or else maintaining frequent face-to-face or telephone contact to ensure the parent's well-being. The primary caregiver must also devote considerable time and energy to performing various tasks for the aging parent. Such tasks may include providing transportation, taking care of financial matters, filling out Medicare and other forms, making sure the parent takes medication properly, shopping, cooking meals, doing laundry and other household chores, assisting the parent in personal grooming (such as help with bathing and dressing), dealing with service organizations on behalf of the parent, and providing emotional support and companionship.

After a careful review of the research literature on the topic, Amy Horowitz (1985:612) reached this conclusion: "When the needs of an elder parent grow, the sex of the adult child is one of the most important and consistent indicators of caregiving involvement. Daughters predominate as providers of direct services, whereas sons play a more substantial role in decision-making and the provision of financial assistance." Her

CAREGIVING RESPONSIBILITIES FOR THE ELDERLY: BUSINESS RESPONDS

Mixed among the usual concerns with alcohol and drugs, strained marriages and other stress, employee assistance counselors like James R. O'Hair at Westinghouse Defense Electronics have begun to hear about difficulties of a different sort.

"A number of employees have been coming to us with their problems in taking care of their elderly relatives," Mr. O'Hair said. Seeking sources of help, the Westinghouse facility, which is in Baltimore, offered employees a two-week series of lunch-hour seminars with local, state and Federal officials and other experts.

Similar programs have been arranged for employees at Mobil, Ciba-Geigy and Con Edison by Pathfinders/Eldercare, a Scarsdale, N.Y., counseling service. In Illinois, the Metropolitan Chicago Coalition on Aging is also setting up work-place seminars.

The Travelers Corporation recently staged a "care-giving fair" in Hartford. . . . Last month, Travelers established a care-givers support group for employees who wished to share experiences and tips. And today, the company will add care for elderly dependents at home to the flexible benefits programs in which employees can set aside part of pretax income. . . .

Building on the experience at Travelers and eight other companies, the Care-givers Workplace Project of the American Association of Retired Persons is preparing guides and training programs for management and employee-assistance counselors. "The business community is in the early stages of awareness," said John C. Rother, the association's legislative director. "The oldest baby boomers turned 40 this year, which means their parents are likely to be 65 or older," he added. "So management is beginning to hear from the work force, including fellow executives."

Most of the 96 companies that responded to a recent survey by the New York Business Group on Health had not given much thought to this problem. But the survey itself created new awareness, said Dr. Leon J. Warsaw, the group's executive director. He cited a company that examined computer printouts of employees' telephone calls and found two categories of heavy users: "Teen-age lovers, of course, but also people with care-giving responsibilities, who had to call home five or six times to make sure Momma turned off the stove."

Travelers also surveyed its employees, most of them women, and found 20 percent of those 30 years and older were providing some form of care for an older person. Eight percent were devoting 35 or more hours a week to care-giving. Employees were not asked about morale and work performance. But the association of retired persons, the Federal Administration on Aging and the University of Bridgeport, in Connecticut, are looking at the bottom line.

"Unanticipated lost time is the main problem," Dr. Warsaw said. Employees often must leave work to deal with doctors and government agencies that are only open weekdays, from 9 to 5.

As for morale, a study of families by Elaine M. Brody of the Philadelphia Geriatric Center found that 28 percent of women who were staying home to take care of elderly mothers said they had quit work for that purpose. "A similar percentage of those who were at work had reduced their working hours or were considering quitting," she said.

The vast majority of services for older people are provided by their families. . . .

"Most of the bills are paid for by the family or from the person's resources," said Mrs. Brody of the Philadelphia Geriatric Center. She said employers could help by offering flexible working hours, sabbaticals in times of family crisis and day-care benefits. Dr. Friedman of the Conference Board suggests that companies could sponsor their own day-care centers for elderly adults and could also increase corporate giving to community agencies that serve the elderly.

SOURCE: Milt Freudenheim, "Business and Health: Help in Caring for the Elderly," *The New York Times*, July 1, 1986, p. 34-y.

own study indicated that when *sons* are identified as the primary caregivers, they tend to be either the only child in the family, they have only brothers and no sisters, or they live geographically closer than their siblings to the parent (or parents). In other words, in general, "Sons tend to become caregivers only in the absence of an available female sibling."

Horowitz's (1985) study also indicated that not only did sons provide less overall assistance to aging parents (especially "hands-on" services such as the tasks described earlier) but they also found caregiving less stressful than did daughters—even in situations where they *were* providing a level of care similar to that of the daughters in the sample. Horowitz attributes the higher degree of stress experienced by daughters to the multiple role demands and competing claims on time and energy experienced by middle-aged women at the very period in their lives when they are most likely to be enlisted to care for elderly parents.

Another factor may be involved in the difference in stress levels experienced by female and male caregivers: the degree of spousal help and support. "Women often voiced appreciation that their husbands remained neutral toward the caregiving involvement; in contrast, men expected and depended upon both emotional and concrete support from their wives," writes Horowitz

(1985:615). "Thus, caregiving as a primary female role clearly extended to daughters-in-law as well as daughters." A woman may find herself providing primary care for her own parents at one point and for her husband's parents at another point. Horowitz points out that even employment has not been found to keep women from assuming such caregiving responsibilities, although "their employment status may necessitate different patterns of caregiving in the future as well as more shared responsibility among male as well as female siblings" (p. 612). (See also Zimmerman, 1986.)

THE LATER YEARS: GROWING OLDER TOGETHER (OR ALONE)

Esther and Fred Blake are both 64 years old. Although everyone tells Fred that he should be looking forward to his retirement, he rather dreads giving up the work that has meant so much to him for so long. Esther, who has devoted her life to homemaking, has mixed feelings. She looks forward to time for travel and hobbies together, but she also knows from the experience of friends that her own daily routines will be drastically changed with Fred around the house all day. In addition, both are concerned about Fred's 82-year-old mother, who lives alone in an apartment near their home. Her health is failing, and they wonder whether they should consider a nursing home for her or invite her to live with them—which would cut down on their own freedom. They illustrate a point made by Elaine Brody during the 1985 International Congress of Gerontology: "The grandparent generation is providing the care for the great-grandparent generation" (quoted in *Greensboro (NC) News and Record,* July 13, 1985).

Neither Fred nor Esther feels "old." As they recently showed some friends their honeymoon pictures, Fred said he would like to go back to hike over some of those rugged mountain trails again. "At *your* age?" his wife had teased. "What do you mean, 'At my age'?" countered Fred, "you're only as old as you *think* you are!"

The Objective Meaning of Aging

Half-joking remarks like "At *your* age?" or "Act your age!" imply the existence of social norms associated with various stages of life. Since social norms generally guide us throughout life as to how we should or shouldn't act, older people sometimes feel confused and alienated because at their stage, behavioral expectations are less clear.

Some sociologists suggest that decreasing social requirements for behavior could actually be viewed as bringing increased freedom for elderly persons (Bengtson, 1973:23–26). Irving Rosow (1973:36–37) points out that this freedom results from the fact that as persons grow older, limitations are placed on their responsibilities and power; therefore their ability to affect others adversely is sharply reduced. "There is less social stake in their behavior," he writes, "and correspondingly little concern with the options that older people exercise and the choices they make." What they do in their private lives is up to them. "So long as they do not

become a burden to others or indulge in virtually bizarre behavior, within their means they can do very largely as they want and live as they wish."

It is no doubt true that for some persons, freedom from normative constraints is considered a reward—as illustrated in the remark of a woman who said, "You have a perfect alibi for everything when you're eighty" because people readily overlook spilled soup, forgotten appointments, "acting silly," and even insisting on one's own way (letter to "Dear Abby," *Bloomington (IN) Herald Telephone,* May 20, 1975). On the other hand, freedom from social expectations because of decreased power and responsibility to affect the lives of others can be experienced as a punishment or loss. "I'm no longer important to anyone; people don't care what I do anymore" could be the feeling.

Not knowing what is expected of oneself is especially hard in cases of what sociologist Leonard Cain (1964:289) calls "asynchronization": the timing of various events in a person's life in a way that doesn't synchronize with other events (quoted in Bengtson, 1973:17). According to social expectations, people marry, have children, advance in their occupations and enter retirement and widowhood at certain taken-for-granted times. Yet the timing of certain events in one area of life doesn't always correspond with what is taking place in another area. Sociologist Vern Bengtson tells of interviewing a 55-year-old steelworker who, having just retired, was considered to have reached *old age* in the economic-occupational sphere of life. But in his family, he was relatively *young* in that he was the father of a 13-year-old daughter. In a fraternal order, his activities and position caused him to be considered *middle-aged.* This man found it difficult to define himself or know what was expected of him. Friends from work kidded him about being an old man. He didn't know what to do with his time. And his wife was annoyed with his being underfoot all day long (Bengtson, 1973:17–18).

What Is Old Age? There is no simple answer to the question, When does a person become old? Surveys in both Great Britain and the United States have shown that the older a person's chronological age, the later he or she tends to think old age begins (Riley, Foner, and associates, 1968:311). Concepts of old age also vary by social status, with lower-status persons tending to believe old age begins earlier (for example, in the fifties), while persons of higher status tend to think old age begins later (about age 65). Bengtson (1973:21) points out that persons of lower status move through their family careers and their work careers more quickly than do higher-status persons. At lower socioeconomic levels, persons tend to marry earlier, have their children sooner, and become grandparents earlier. In addition, because of limited education, they usually reach as high as they will ever go occupationally at an earlier age than do persons at higher status levels. Not surprisingly then, "old age" seems to arrive sooner.

The Census Bureau defines the elderly population as persons who are 65 years of age and over. This is the age at which individuals become eligible for full social security benefits, Medicare coverage, special considerations under tax laws, and—in the case of many workers—retirement benefits. At the beginning of the century, there were only 3 million persons aged 65 and older; but by 1950, that figure had quadrupled to over 12 million. By the 1980 census, the figure had doubled again, to over 25 million. The Census Bureau predicts that the elderly segment of the United States population will number 35 million by the year 2000 and over 67 million by 2050 (U.S. Bureau of the Census, *Current Population Reports*, ser. P-23, no. 138, 1984:5; U.S. Senate Special Committee on Aging, 1985:11).

Advances in medical science and technology have meant considerable increases in life expectancy. At the beginning of the century, a newborn could be expected to live forty-nine years, but a baby born in 1983 could look forward to living just under seventy-five years. Persons who had already reached their sixty-fifth birthday by 1980 could expect to live 16.4 more years. Table 16-A shows the percentage of persons 65 years and over in various age categories. By the year 2000, it is projected that about 1 out of 2 elderly persons will be 75 years of age or over. The "oldest old"—the age-85-and-over population—is expanding especially rapidly. (See U.S. Bureau of the Census, *Current Population Reports*, ser. P-23, no. 138, 1984:44; U.S. Senate Special Committee on Aging, 1985:1–22.)

The arbitrary setting of age 65 as the beginning of old age provides a *social* definition of old age, just as age 18 or 21 socially and legally defines adulthood. However, there is a big difference. The change in classification from a minor to an adult is usually viewed as a gain; it means that a highly regarded status, with new social and legal privileges and responsibilities, has been conferred upon a person. In contrast, moving from middle age to old age (as it has been defined by social security regulations, for example) may be viewed as a loss. Many privileges and responsibilities are taken away. The status conferred—"elderly person," "golden-ager," "senior citizen"—is *not* a highly regarded one because in an industrial society, being old is not as esteemed as it is in other societies, where prestige is granted on the basis of accumulated wisdom from many years. In

TABLE 16-A Percent distribution of the population 65 years and over, by age: 1950–2020

| AGE | 1950 | 1960 | 1970 | 1980 | PROJECTIONS | | | |
					1990	2000	2010	2020
65 years and over	100.0%	100.0%	100.0%	100.0%	100.0%	100.0%	100.0%	100.0%
65 to 69 years	40.7	37.7	35.0	34.2	31.5	26.0	29.8	32.3
70 to 74 years	27.8	28.6	27.2	26.6	25.3	24.5	21.9	25.6
75 to 79 years	17.4	18.5	19.2	18.7	19.6	20.7	17.1	17.0
80 to 84 years	9.3	9.6	11.5	11.6	12.8	14.2	13.9	10.8
85 years and over	4.8	5.6	7.1	8.8	10.9	14.7	17.4	14.3

SOURCE: U.S. Bureau of the Census, *Current Population Reports,* ser. P-23, no. 138, *Demographic and Socioeconomic Aspects of Aging in the United States,* 1984, p. 17. Adapted from Table 2-6.

industrial societies, education and innovation, rather than past experience, are valued keys to the occupational system's rewards. Change is rapid, and new technological skills are required. Practical knowledge of old ways of doing things is considered of limited worth. Thus older persons are expected to move out to make room for the young.

Social scientist Sarah Matthews (1979) concludes from her research that old age in our society is nothing less than a *stigma*—something that "spoils" one's identity in the eyes of others and makes one seem somehow not fully "normal" as a human being and as an adult (Goffman, 1963). Matthews (1979) explains:

> Old people are assumed by virtue of their age to be physically, and, therefore, mentally incapacitated. The stigma theory that age and poor health are synonymous is used to justify a mandatory retirement age, but it also has an effect on everyday interaction. Old people because of their advanced age are more easily assumed to be incapable of performing adequately as adult members of society. (pp. 61–62)

The Subjective Meaning of Aging

To lump together all persons who have passed a certain number of birthdays under the labels "the elderly" or "senior citizens" gives the impression that "the aged" make up a homogeneous category. The word *homogeneous* comes from the Greek and means "of the same kind." But persons at age 65 and beyond don't suddenly all become alike any more than all persons at 25 are alike. Increasingly, social scientists emphasize that much more than age itself must be taken into account. People vary in their outlooks, goals, self-concepts, and social resources. Social status is particularly important because, as the sociologist George Maddox (1970) stresses, this variable summarizes previous life experience. He goes on to point out that what individuals bring to old age determines, to a large extent, what old age will mean to them. "Social competence, adaptive flexibility, and a sense of well-being displayed by persons in the middle years of life predict the probable display of these same characteristics in the later years," he writes, adding that in a sense, the life cycle is a process in which "success predicts success."

From our earlier discussions of social status, we know that persons with higher education are more likely than are those of lower education to possess the social and personal skills mentioned by Maddox. Sociologist Zena Blau (1973) provides evidence from various studies showing that the lower the social-status level, the more likely persons are to respond to old age with attitudes of *alienation,* "characterized by the feeling that 'there is just no point in living,' by feeling regret over the past, by the idea that 'things just keep getting worse and worse,' and by abandonment of all future plans." Such persons tend to feel they have been failures (having been poor in a society that stresses success) and consider their lives useless. "You know what they ought to do with old men like me?" asked one respondent. "Take us out and shoot us. We're no good for anything" (pp. 156–157).

Old age may also seem difficult for persons at higher status levels, especially when it is accompanied by the loss of significant roles such as that of worker or spouse; but rather than reacting with alienation, the major response is what Blau calls *conformity*—an attitude of adjustment. "Lots of times you don't like the new things," said one respondent, referring to the changes brought by the transition to old age, "but there isn't anything you can do about them. You just have to accept them" (pp. 163–166).

Blau found another small category, however, which she labeled *innovators*: persons who—regardless of social status—are able to take old age in stride, enjoy life in the here and now, and continue to develop new interests and friendships. Persons of both sexes who were both socially active and employed were the most likely to be innovators. The news media frequently call our attention to such persons: the 87-year-old man who began university studies toward his bachelor's degree, the 90-year-old woman who was disappointed to find the authorities would not allow her to obtain a license to drive a motorcycle, the stage and film actors who continue acting into their eighties and nineties.

Research has shown that a person's attitude has a great deal to do with aging. "You're only as old as you think you are" has much truth in it. Blau refers to the writer E. B. White, who said, at age 70, "Old age is a special problem for me because I've never been able to shed the mental image I have of myself—a lad of nineteen." Although the years brought changes, he was able to maintain a sense of inner sameness, continuity, and knowing who he was. Such ongoing self-identity and "agelessness" was due, in large measure, to the fact that he was able to keep up in his craft in spite of the passage of years, a privilege denied most people today. Blau asserts that it is the loss of one's occupational role, "the mainstay of one's identity," that leads people to form a new concept of themselves (pp. 103–104). In an extensive review of research findings on aging, sociologists Matilda Riley, Anne Foner, and associates (1968:302) emphasize that, "in the main, identification of the self as old is most pronounced among the disadvantaged and those who have experienced sharp discontinuity with the past." Widowhood, retirement, and poor health are cited as examples of such sharp discontinuity. We tend to form a sense of who we are through what we do and through relationships with other people. To find it necessary to leave the most significant role associated with *doing* (occupation) because of ill health or compulsory retirement, or to leave what for the majority of persons is the most significant *relationship* role (spouse), is to leave what seems like a part of one's very self.

Role Exiting: Retirement and Widowhood

As we've seen, being old is much more than having reached a certain chronological age or of having undergone certain physical changes; it has a social meaning, and it is this social meaning that is most crucial. Zena Blau (1973:xiii) uses the term *role exiting* to describe the social meaning of aging and to show why persons in our society tend to dread being labeled "old": "For it is the sustained experience of being necessary to others that gives meaning and purpose to the life of all human beings. Opportunities to remain useful members of the society are severely undermined by the exits from adult social roles that are typical of old age." While role exits occur constantly before old age (one leaves the student role to become a wage earner, for example), the role exits most often associated with old age are different because "retirement and widowhood terminate a person's participation in the principal institutional structures of society—the nuclear family and the occupational structure" (pp. 17–18). A person comes to be viewed as a dependent, not a producer—a person with diminished power in society (Dowd, 1975).

Retirement Retirement is a relatively new social institution associated with industrial society and without past precedent (Loether, 1964:518). As sociologist Ethel Shanas (1972:222) emphasizes, giving up work at a set age in order to spend the remainder of one's life in retirement "emerges as a widespread practice only when the level of living within a society is such that persons can be supported by society without themselves being workers." In simpler societies, the pro-

ductivity of the elderly is needed because almost everyone is living near the subsistence level, and enforced idleness would be out of the question. But in modern societies, automation, diminishing opportunities for self-employment, and pressures to make room for job-seeking younger workers all combine to make retirement the rule rather than the exception.

The passage of the Social Security Act in 1935 institutionalized retirement and formally defined *old age* by establishing pension eligibility at age 65. But what this means is that at a certain arbitrarily fixed point in time, a person is suddenly excluded from the occupational structure—the structure that in American society provides such highly valued rewards as prestige, income, and a sense of worth. Blau (1973) describes what this role exit means to a male's self-image in particular. Both the material and social rewards associated with the opportunity system are taken away. After having been socialized to consider occupational achievement as the chief aspect of adult identity, males in retirement find themselves not only without a job but without the identity that went with that job. Adding to the strain is the realization that "retirement is a *social* pattern that implies an invidious judgment about old people's lack of fitness to perform a culturally significant and coveted role." It is a form of social banishment and exclusion and is therefore the hardest kind of role exiting one is called upon to bear (pp. 105, 211–215).

Legislation effective January 1, 1979 raised to age 70 the earliest age at which retirement may be legally required for persons in most occupational groups. And, in 1986, the 99th Congress passed legislation that will protect most workers in the United States from mandatory retirement policies altogether. In predicting that such changes would come about, Matthews (1979) wrote that in reaction to funding problems in the

RETIREMENT: REWARD OR PUNISHMENT?

Dear Dr. Donohue: My husband retired recently, and since has been nothing but a grouch, complaining of this or that ailment. I have heard, but never believed it till now, that these guys just retire to die. Why? It is distressing me terribly. Any comment on this "non-medical" question?—Mrs. R. T.

It may not be as "non-medical" a question as you think. This retirement syndrome is real for many men. Why this downhill slide occurs at a time when life should be most pleasant, without the worries of work, is a puzzle. Some studies have, in fact, shown some sort of a correlation between retirement and heart-related illnesses. Some men need and thrive on the anxieties of daily work. In a discussion of this recently, one physician remarked, "There are some individuals who feel retirement is a just reward for a lifetime of work and others who regard it as a punishment for growing old." We are not sure whether there are direct links between physical ailments and retirement, but we have suspicions that there may be several.

SOURCE: From "Dr. Donohue" syndicated column, *Greensboro (NC) Daily News,* March 20, 1980.

social security system, Congress began to shift away "from an emphasis on what the aged *cannot* do to what the aged *can* do," the goal being to reduce old-age "dependency." Increasingly, more and more people have come to believe that retirement should be based on choice and ability, not age. Matthews believes that even with such changes, "most workers will probably choose to retire 'on schedule,' that is, between the ages of sixty and sixty-five." This has been the pattern in recent years, when nearly two-thirds of older workers have been choosing to retire before they reach age 65 (U.S. Senate Special Committee on Aging, 1985:3).

According to Matthews (1979:170–171),

RETIREMENT: SOMETHING NEW IN HISTORY

Retirement has been recognized as a special problem only since the latter part of the 19th century. Prior to that time, relatively small numbers of individuals survived to become old, and few of the survivors could continue actively in the labor force. Contributory old age pensions (social security) first were introduced in Germany in 1883. Full benefits began in 1891 to workers at age 70 with at least 40 years of work history. By 1916, sufficient funds had accumulated so that the retirement age could be reduced at 65 years. . . . Most industrial nations followed the German pattern; the United States concluded the sequence with the Social Security Act of 1935.

With the institutionalization of retirement, two developments occurred: Job vacancies for younger workers were created by encouraging older workers to leave the labor market, and older workers received partial replacement income for surrendering their jobs.

SOURCE: Excerpted from Anne L. Babic, "Flexible Retirement: An International Survey of Public Policies," *Aging and Work,* 7 (1), 1984, pp. 21–22.

For Better or For Worse®   by Lynn Johnston

(For Better or for Worse, by Lynn Johnston. Copyright 1984, Universal Press Syndicate. Reprinted with permission. All rights reserved.)

"Elimination of chronological age as the legal criterion of the beginning of old age, while it may have minimal economic effects, may have far-reaching effects on the social definitions of the aged." To know they are still regarded as persons capable of contributing to the economy if they so chose could have a positive effect on the self-esteem of older persons themselves. Flexible retirement policies, currently being examined and debated in many parts of the world, can mean both benefits and costs to individuals and society. Another question being raised centers around the traditional irreversibility of retirement and whether or not provisions should be made for reentry into the labor market (Babic, 1984).

"When retired workers seek to reenter the work force, whether because inflation has eroded their income or for other reasons, they often do not find full-time work at desirable wages," reports the National Commission for Employment Policy (1985:8). "Because of pension restrictions, the Tax Equity and Fiscal Responsibility Act (TEFRA), Employees Retirement Income Security Act

(ERISA) provisions and Social Security earnings limitations, most post-retirement workers are limited to part-time work, usually less than 1,000 hours per year." Many older persons find that part-time work has great appeal at this stage of life, however, and are delighted to find a growing trend among many employers not only to hire older persons but to be willing to offer them flexible hours and job-sharing opportunities as well (Fowler, 1986; National Commission for Employment Policy, 1985; U.S. Senate Special Committee on Aging, 1985).

A number of things happen in retirement. No longer can spouses bring home the monetary and status rewards that played such an important part in marital power and in the instrumental and expressive exchanges of rights and duties discussed in Part 4 of this book. Because of the traditional meaning of the breadwinner role, retirement is experienced as much more demoralizing to males than it is to females who retire from the work force (Blau, 1973:29). This might be changing, however, as more women are becoming committed to careers and taking on the equal co-provider role. But for wives who have been full-time homemakers, life goes on much the same as it did before the retirement period, except that their husbands are now around the home all the time.

For men, the changes are many. The daily pattern is disrupted because the once-structured time built around the job is now empty. Social participation is curtailed because male friendships are usually highly dependent upon their occupational involvement. After a man's retirement, his still-employed former work associates continue to talk, joke, and gripe about job-related topics, and both he and they begin to realize that he no longer fits in (Blau, 1973:89).

Although blue-collar workers tend to report lower job satisfaction than do white-collar workers and are more likely to volunteer for retirement, they tend to have greater difficulty in making the transition from worker to retiree. Losing the occupational role means a reduction in feelings of self-worth because blue-collar men are less likely to have other roles to fall back on or tangible evidences of accomplishment that remain (such as college degrees). The occupational role has been their major means of identity. The occupational role has also been highly important to white-collar men, but because of greater resources and role flexibility, they have been found to be better able to make the transition to the retired state (Loether, 1964, 1967).

Widowhood As with retirement, there are differences by socioeconomic status and by sex with regard to the other major role exit associated with old age—widowhood. Of course, a person may lose a spouse before this period of life, but the subject is considered here since it affects such vast numbers at this stage (especially women). In 1981, more than 1 out of 2 women over age 65 had lost a spouse, in contrast to 1 out of 8 men in this age range (U.S. Bureau of the Census, *Current Population Reports*, ser. P-23, no. 138, 1984:85). Figure 16-1 shows the percentage of persons in each of three age categories who are widowed.

There are more widows than widowers for two reasons: women tend to marry men older than themselves, and men tend to die earlier than women. Older women are now outnumbering older men by a ratio of three to two (U.S. Senate Special Committee on Aging, 1985). In 1984, among persons aged 65 to 69 years, there were 81 men for every 100 women. Among persons 80 to 84 years of age, there were only 53 men for every 100 women. Figure 16-2 shows the sex ratio among various age categories of the elderly population.

Since in traditional marriage, a woman's identity and status have stemmed from rewards provided by her husband, the husband's death means not only the loss of a companion with whom one's life was shared but also the loss of the wife role. A new way of looking at life—a reconstruction of reality—takes place during the transition from wife to widow to being one's own person (comparable in a sense to what also happens after divorce). At first, many women continue to think in terms of their former wife role and order their lives after their husband's wishes for a time ("Bill wouldn't want me to . . . ," "I think George would expect me to do it this way," "Carl never wanted me to learn to drive"), but many arrive at a point of reaching out and building a new life (Silverman, 1972).

Sociologist Helena Lopata (1973a) found that widows of lower socioeconomic status (measured by education level) tended to live more isolated lives than did widows at higher status levels. Women with lower education have usually been married to men with low

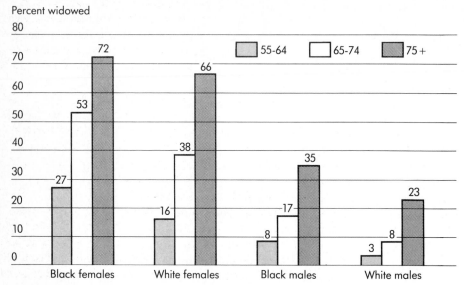

Percent widowed

FIGURE 16-1 Widowhood of persons 55 and over by race and sex: March 1983. (SOURCE: Reprinted from United States Senate Special Committee on Aging, *America in Transition: An Aging Society, 1984-85 Edition* (Washington, DC: U.S. Government Printing Office, June 1985), p. 86.)

incomes, and husband-wife activities were usually highly segregated by sex, which, as we saw in Chapter 10, tends to be associated with lower expressive satisfaction. In one sense, widowhood may be less costly to such women in that they cannot experience the loss of a companionship they never had. For such a woman, writes Lopata, "isolation is made easy by the fact that she was always marginal to the social system and that she was not socialized into any skills for expanded re-engagement into society" (p. 270; Blau, 1973:84). On the other hand, widowhood may be extremely costly in terms of money, as such a woman experiences even greater financial restriction than when her husband was alive.

Lopata's research led her to conclude that losing a husband is less disorganizing to the identities of lower-status women than it is to identities of women with higher education because higher-status women have invested

more time and energy into constructing a world view built around their husbands. In such homes, there is likely to have been more shared interests, greater communication, empathy and involvement in one another's lives, and less stress on gender-segregated activities. Nevertheless, because of the personal and social resources associated with her educational advantages and other benefits, the higher-status woman is equipped to build a new image of herself and the world if she so chooses. Though the change may be painful, as the process goes on she may come to feel "like a fuller human being, more independent and competent than in the past" (Lopata, 1973b:416).

A number of studies indicate that in general, males have greater difficulty adjusting to widowhood than do females. The loss of a spouse in old age takes its toll on men in many ways: low morale, mental disorders, and high death and suicide rates (Bock and

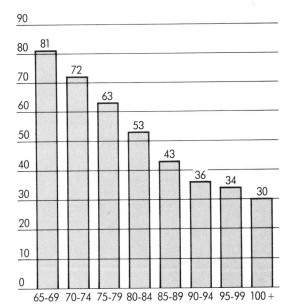

FIGURE 16-2 Number of men per 100 women by elderly age group, 1984. (SOURCE: Reprinted from U.S. Senate Special Committee on Aging, *America in Transition: An Aging Society, 1984-85 Edition* (Washington, D.C.: U.S. Government Printing Office, June 1985), p. 17.)

Webber, 1972). Like retirement, widowhood is (in Blau's terms) a "role exit." But unlike retirement, widowhood isn't a socially imposed exit but results, in most cases, from forces beyond human control. Therefore, widowhood doesn't carry with it the same sense of having been judged and banished by others as retirement sometimes does. But there is still the sense of loss—of being deprived of highly cherished rewards.

In traditional arrangements, the *instrumental* side of marriage is characterized by an exchange in which the husband provides the wife with financial and status benefits and the wife rewards the husband by performing the necessary tasks of daily living, such as maintaining the home. When death ends the marriage, the surviving spouse is left without these instrumental rewards to a great degree: a wife's husband-based status is gone, and often her financial situation is a problem as well, and a husband has lost his means of domestic care. For the first time in his life he may have to cope with laundry, cooking, cleaning, and the like. One result of the traditional gender-linked division of labor in marriage is that an older widow's life goes on much as usual (in terms of housekeeping), while a widower is forced to take on new and often unfamiliar responsibilities. Not only has he lost the role of worker through retirement, but now he must take on a different role (homemaker), and so many changes all at once in the later years of life can be difficult (Berardo, 1970; Vinick, 1978).

In addition to the instrumental, or practical, side of marriage, the *expressive*, or personal, side is deeply affected as well. Again, males appear to fare worse in widowhood. Men are more likely than women to have depended entirely on their spouses to serve in the role of confidant, meeting needs for empathy, understanding, affection, communication, and companionship. But women are more likely to have other sources of personal affirmation outside the marriage, not only because they are more likely than husbands to have kept in touch with kin networks over the years, but also because they are more likely to have deep friendships in which they are accepted and appreciated as total persons (and not viewed primarily in terms of a role, such as worker) and from which they can draw rich emotional support (Zube, 1982). Many older women have friends who are already widows and who can serve as role models, providing older women with an opportunity to mentally rehearse for widowhood in advance. When widowhood strikes, the network of widow friends can provide the new widow with companionship in various activities as well as empathy and aid. Zena Blau (1973:72–75) emphasizes the importance of having at least one intimate friend to

When widowhood strikes, the network of widow friends can provide companionship in various activities as well as empathy and aid. (Shirley Zeiberg/Taurus Photos)

bring continuity to life and emotional support in old age. But at the same time, she shows how much more difficult it seems to be for men than for women to form such close, long-lasting friendships because gender-role socialization has traditionally discouraged the development in males of those qualities that are necessary for building deep interpersonal relationships (see also Lowenthall and Haven, 1968; Powers and Bultena, 1976).

We may speculate that adjustments to widowhood may become less difficult and demoralization less common as emerging forms of marriage replace the traditional head-complement model. As women and men come to share equally in breadwinning and domestic roles, they may be better able to cope with losses in the instrumental side of marriage. It also seems likely that the diminished rewards in the expressive side of marriage brought by widowhood will seem less devastating as both sexes become more alike in terms of nurturance qualities and, through having developed the capacity for intimacy,

can build and maintain other close relationships to bring meaning to life in old age.

The Marriage Relationship in the Later Years

Some couples have many years together before death separates them. Research on the marriage relationship in the later stages of the life cycle is limited at this time, but some findings are coming to light through the efforts of a number of scholars (Riley, Foner, and associates, 1968; Smith, 1965; Palmore, 1968; Stinnett, Carter, and Montgomery, 1972; Parron and Troll, 1978; Streib and Beck, 1980; Brubaker, 1983, 1985; Gilford, 1984, 1986).

As Figure 16-3 shows, about 3 out of 4 men over age 65 live with their spouses as do more than 1 out of 3 women in that age category. The figure shows the percentage of elderly persons living in various other arrangements as well. Note that nearly 40 percent of women over age 65 live alone as do 14 percent of their male counterparts. Only about 5 percent of the elderly live in nursing homes at any given time, although a higher percent will spend at least some time in an institution for the elderly during their remaining years (U.S. Bureau of the Census, *Current Population Reports*, ser. P-23, no. 138, 1984:88; U.S. Senate Special Committee on Aging, 1985:73). Three out of four such persons do not have a spouse.

Just as a growing proportion of widows and widowers are maintaining independent households, a growing proportion of elderly married couples are living in households separate from their children. In cases of illness, the spouses tend to care for each other, preparing meals and so on. Gender-role differentiation tends to become lessened, and shared activities tend to increase because so much time is available for the husband and wife to spend together in the later years of

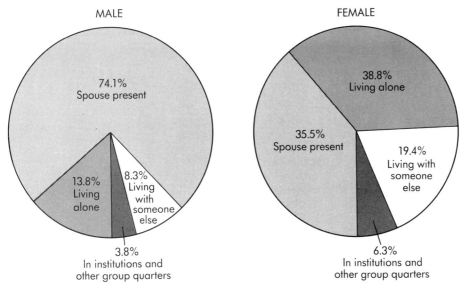

FIGURE 16-3 Distribution of male and female populations 65 years old and over by living arrangements: 1981. (SOURCE: Adapted from U.S. Bureau of the Census, Current Population Reports, Series P-23, No. 138, *Demographic and Socioeconomic Aspects of Aging in the United States* (Washington, DC: U.S. Government Printing Office, 1984), pp. 87, 95.)

marriage. Companionship may be enhanced, both through greater sharing of household tasks after the husband retires and through more joint leisure projects such as vacations or decorating the home (Hill and Dorfman, 1982). High marital satisfaction in the later years is also associated with high morale, but the reverse is true as well (Lee, 1978).

In other words, although many changes occur over the years as a couple go through life together, some sorts of exchanges, in both the instrumental and the expressive realms of marriage, continue so long as the marriage lasts. And those couples who have learned to understand and empathize with one another, to enjoy activities together, and to negotiate in times of conflict have the potential of experiencing high rewards and maximum joint profit to the very end (Parron and Troll, 1978). In cases where chronic illness or other impairments create high amounts of stress in an older marriage, cou-

ple therapy with the aid of an understanding counselor can be highly beneficial (Beckham and Giordano, 1986).

Aging and Sexuality

Contrary to many commonly held beliefs and stereotypes about being sexually "over the hill," sexual interest and activity continue among elderly couples. Advancing age usually means a decline in the frequency of sexual intercourse, but that doesn't mean that sex will necessarily be eliminated from marital interaction. The Duke University Longitudinal Study of Aging showed that the majority of husbands and wives were sexually active until over age 75. And close to 15 percent of the couples indicated a pattern in which both sexual activity and interest were increasing rather than decreasing. Among those couples who reported having stopped

SEX AFTER 70

Of those who mentioned sex in marriage, the important aspect was not the physical act but the warmth of another body, the holding, the intimacy. One 73-year-old man expressed himself fully on the subject of sex:

> I don't know if I'm oversexed, but I'm a lover. I like to pet, kiss, hug. I have more fun out of loving somebody I love than the ultimate end. You know, some people— and this is the failure of sex, too—some people want sex and forget the rest of it—the hugging and the petting and I think that's wrong. People say, "What will happen to me when I get older?" Well, *I'm* still alive! There's no thrill like that today. People try dope, they try smoking, they try drinking. This is the one thing that's good for the body.

SOURCE: Barbara H. Vinick, "Remarriage in Old Age," *The Family Coordinator, 27* (October 1978), p. 362.

having sexual intercourse entirely, however, the median age at which intercourse ceased was age 68 for men and 60 for women. Wives and husbands agreed that husbands were the ones most responsible for stopping sexual intercourse, the main reasons being loss of potency, loss of interest, and illness (Palmore, 1970, chap. 8).

Despite widespread notions about the "sexless older years," many elderly couples continue to enjoy the physical expression of love. (Bruce Davidson/ Magnum Photos)

The Sex Information and Education Council of the United States reports that pervasive stereotypes about the alleged "sexless older years" can be destructive in many ways, negatively affecting the older person's sex life, self-image, and the marriages of older people in general. Such stereotypes also cause problems between aged parents and adult children when widowed or divorced parents consider remarriage, can make diagnosing various medical and psychological problems difficult, and may even lead to false accusations and faulty administration of justice in cases of elderly men accused of certain sex offenses. For example, if elderly women show an interest in small children, they are considered warm and affectionate. But for an elderly man to show such interest brings the risk of being labeled a "dirty old man." It is assumed that his interest in children could only be sexual; and since it's also assumed that old people have no interest in sex, the man's attitudes are thought to indicate a perverted interest which must be watched with fear and suspicion (SIECUS, 1970, chap. 8; Felstein, 1970). Many persons in the helping professions are urging efforts toward greater

NEVER TOO LATE

"I was a widower for five years. Six months ago I remarried and everyone said to me, 'It's good that you married again because you need companionship.' Everyone tells me about companionship. It gets me mad. Sure I want companionship, but I also got married for sex. I always had an active sex life and still do, and I'm 82 years old."

SOURCE: Statement of a man attending a community lecture for persons over 60. In Bernard D. Starr and Marcella Baker Weiner, *Sex and Sexuality in the Mature Years* (New York: Stein and Day, 1981), p. 5.

sensitivity to and understanding of the sexual needs of the elderly—including elderly persons in nursing homes, whose right to privacy and desire for physical affection have not always been recognized or treated wisely (Carroll, 1978). At the same time, Hess and Waring (1978:257) call attention to the concerns of some specialists in aging that "with the discovery of gerosexuality, too much may now be expected of elderly lovers." (The prefix *gero* there comes from the Greek word for "old age" and is the word from which *gerontology*—the scientific study of aging—comes.)

Remarriage in the Later Years

While difficulty in accepting the possibility of aging parents' active sexuality may be one reason that offspring often are less than enthusiastic about a parent's remarrying late in life, other reasons also enter in—for example, fears that a lonely parent is being taken advantage of by the prospective mate or anxieties that the offspring's share of an inheritance will be diminished because of the parent's new spouse (Hess and Waring, 1978:253).

Even so, many thousands of marriages

AT AGE 103, MAN TIES KNOT WITH 84-YEAR-OLD

Beloit, WI—After an 11-year friendship, but only two weeks of being engaged, Harry Stevens, 103, and Thelma Lucas, 84, were married this week at the nursing home where they both live.

"He's a wonderful man and a wonderful lover," Lucas said. "He kisses like heaven."

It was the second marriage for both.

"I love this woman and she loves me," Stevens said before the ceremony Monday. "I'd like to have somebody to live with, somebody that I love."

After the ceremony, the two rode off in wheelchairs festooned with aluminum cans and "Just Married" signs.

SOURCE: Associated Press report, *Greensboro (NC) News and Record*, December 23, 1984, p. F6.

each year involve either a bride or a groom who is over 65 years old. The National Center for Health Statistics reports that within the marriage-registration area (MRA), comprised of the District of Columbia and the forty-two states that provide the center with marriage records, there were, in 1981, over seventeen thousand remarriages in which the brides were 65 years old or older. That same year, in more than thirty thousand remarriages, the grooms were age 65 or over (*Monthly Vital Statistics Report,* Vol. 32, no. 11, 1984:8).

Many sons and daughters of older parents who remarry not only approve but are glad for their parents' newfound happiness. It also relieves adult children of worries about their parents' loneliness and need for companionship, reports sociologist Barbara Vinick (1978) after in-depth interviews with twenty-four remarried elderly couples. Her respondents had received positive affirmation from their children in over half the cases. They found, however, a surprising amount of negative feedback among their own peers upon learning of the remarriage prospects. "People mentioned friends who felt deserted by the remarriage," writes Vinick, "or, not having the courage to remarry themselves, felt apprehensive in regard to a friend's chances for happiness" (p. 361). Over time, friends tended to become more approving of the marriage, but getting together with both friends and relatives tended to decrease as the new spouse became the major "source of intimacy and services" (p. 362).

Most of the remarried elderly persons in Vinick's small sample reported satisfaction. "We're like a couple of kids," one woman told her. "We enjoy life together. When you're with someone, you're happy." Those who reported unhappiness were those who felt that external circumstances had forced them into marriages they later regretted.

Vinick provides an example:

> One such woman, Mrs. R., was approaching the age of compulsory retirement when she met her husband. She did not know how she would get along financially, and had a feeling of desperation about her situation. Mr. R. owned a home, and was financially well off. After a short courtship, they married. Mrs. R. now describes her marriage as like "having stepped into a dark room." Her husband is arbitrary, autocratic and miserly. She is full of apprehension but is pinning her hopes on a move to Florida where she hopes they will be happier. (p. 362)

But, Vinick adds, Mrs. R.'s situation was illustrative of only a minority of persons in the sample. Nineteen of the twenty-four women and twenty-one of the twenty-four men described themselves as "satisfied" or "very satisfied" with their remarriages.

Aging and Alternative Lifestyles

Little empirical data have thus far been gathered concerning aging and alternatives to traditional marriage and family such as those discussed in Chapters 6 and 7—although a certain amount of research has focused on, for example, elderly homosexual persons (Minnigerode and Adelman, 1978; Raphael and Robinson, 1980; Friend, 1980), elderly never-married persons (Scott, 1979), and various group-living arrangements for older persons (Streib, 1978). As we saw earlier, cohabitation has been an alternative chosen by some elderly couples, who have desired love and companionship but haven't wanted to lose widow's pension benefits or (until changes in the law in 1979) social security benefits or who haven't wanted to run counter to their children's wishes that they not marry again (Hess and Waring, 1978; Dressel and Avant, 1978). Some elderly couples, like many of their younger counterparts, may view cohabitation as a trial marriage. (See insert.)

LIVING TOGETHER "EIGHTIES-STYLE"

Fort Lauderdale, FL—Two years ago, Martha Munzer and Isaac Corkland were reunited by coincidence and resumed a courtship interrupted by war—World War I.

They've been living together almost ever since, and today they'll be married in a Pompano Beach synagogue. Then Corkland, 83, and Mrs. Munzer, 80, will take a monthlong honeymoon in Israel. They say part of the reason they're getting married is to make it easier to register in hotels.

The couple met on a blind date in the summer of 1918 and say they fell in love over the next 10 days.

"It was so romantic at 18 to have a young Army lieutenant who was my lieutenant," Mrs. Munzer said.

"I thought she would make a wonderful helpmate." Corkland recalled. "She had such a bright outlook on life."

He was shipped to Europe, and despite their best efforts to keep in touch, they drifted apart after the war. She married after graduation from the Massachusetts Institute of Technology and he became a Tennessee lawyer and married there. But they never forgot each other.

"After Corky became a widower in 1960, he came to New York looking for me, but he didn't find me," she said.

Corkland retired to Florida and took creative-writing classes at Nova University. In one class project, he described his wartime romance.

Soon after, a fellow student showed him portions of a book a friend was writing. The friend was Mrs. Munzer, who was living in Mamaroneck, N.Y., and a widow.

"We thought it was kind of a miracle. Our lives had been apart for 60 years," she said.

The couple says, "our life is only beginning," and Mrs. Munzer's latest book, her eighth, is titled "It Might as Well Be Spring."

"We're just having a ball," she said.

She giggled when asked why the two lived together for the past two years.

"We took a leaf from the younger generation. We decided to see first how we liked living together," she said.

SOURCE: Associated Press report, "Love's Labour's Lost and Found," *Greensboro (NC) Daily News and Record,* March 30, 1980.

Sociologist Gordon Streib (1978) points to a need for more research on various points along a *continuum* of possible living arrangements for elderly persons—possibilities ranging from independent households on one end to a total-care nursing home on the other, with a wide range of collective-living arrangements in between (see also Streib and Hilker, 1980).

The child-free alternative lifestyle elected by many married couples today also needs to be considered with regard to aging—both the couples' own future aging (what will be their support system?) and the fact that their parents may be pressuring them to have children simply so that the older generation may experience grandparenthood! In a humorous essay in *The New York Times Magazine* (July 25, 1976), columnist Russell Baker spoke of a real concern of some persons—the fear of

THE HOMOSEXUAL COMMUNITY CARING FOR ITS OLDER MEMBERS

Since older persons represent a diversity of ethnic groups, religious backgrounds, and socio-economic status, they also include lesbians and gay men. However, the special needs of older gay men and women have often been overlooked.

Senior Action in a Gay Environment, Inc. (SAGE) was created to help meet these needs. SAGE is a part of the gay and lesbian community caring for its elders. . . .

SAGE is a group of trained volunteers—including social workers, doctors, lawyers, psychologists, gerontologists, and other concerned members of the gay community—who joined together in June, 1978, to incorporate the country's first volunteer service organization addressing the needs of older lesbians and gay men. SAGE's services are uniquely designed to enhance the older person's connection with the gay community.

SAGE OFFERS THE FOLLOWING SERVICES BY TRAINED VOLUNTEERS

1 Friendly visiting: at home, in the hospital, or in an institution
2 Escort services: to medical centers, gay religious services, shopping, on errands
3 Telephone contact: daily or as needed
4 Social activities: to provide a congenial setting for meeting, sharing and caring; to reduce loneliness, rebuild relationships, establish supportive connections with the gay and lesbian community
5 Bereavement support: for those facing the serious illness or death of a friend or lover
6 Information and referral in areas of concern to older persons: legal matters (including wills and bequests), home care and long-term facilities. SAGE makes referrals to appropriate social service agencies as well as to gay-oriented professionals including lawyers, therapists, and physicians.

Services are free, and confidentiality is fully respected.

SOURCE: From a brochure distributed by Senior Action in A Gay Environment, Inc., 208 W. 13th St., New York, NY 10011.

being "grandchildless." "What right, one may ask, do these aging Americans have to expect grandchildren?" asks Baker. "The answer is that American society has conditioned them to construct their lives on the assumption that grandparenthood is inevitable, and as a class they have done so." He continues:

The politicians they have chosen to govern them have been the politicians who boasted that they would make the world a better place for their grandchildren. They have borne taxation, taken up arms, supported huge mortgages and spent vast sums on the improvement of their own children, and all in the cause of making America a better place for their grandchildren.

BETTER HOUSING OPTIONS FOR THE ELDERLY

The Australians have developed a housing concept for the elderly which is currently being assessed in some American communities. Hundreds of elderly parents now have the opportunity to live in compact, relocatable cottages in the backyards of their adult children's homes.

The unit is trucked to the site and installed on a timber foundation that has been prepared in advance. The water pipes, electrical wiring and sewage outlet are then hooked up to those in the main house. The average set-up time is one day.

The state housing authority rents the houses for a nominal $15 monthly fee and then moves the houses to new locations when they are no longer needed. Both generations retain a measure of independence, and the combination of privacy and proximity is said to be strengthening family life by reviving the extended family. . . .

Another concept that is proving attractive to the elderly and other singles are housing units called "mingles." These units have multiple master bedroom suites that share a common kitchen and living area. "Mingles" allow unrelated persons the opportunity to maintain privacy yet avoid isolation.

SOURCE: *Family Life Educator, 1* (Summer 1983), p. 14.

THE CHILDLESS ELDERLY

[Research] findings reported here demonstrate that today's childless elderly have levels of well-being that match and sometimes exceed those of parent elderly. That the childless are able to construct a parallel quality of life suggests either that children are not crucial in that quest or that the childless are able to establish effective alternatives to the benefits derived from children. It may be that the knowledge that children are not available as a fail-safe resource produces capable, self-reliant elderly. Of course, this adaptation is a lifelong process. The absence of large numbers in one's friendship network—especially of kin—may not reflect a disadvantage for the older person. We tend to think of younger adults as well-adjusted, interesting, and healthy individuals if they have a few close friends. For these people, relatives (kin) are secondary confidants and friends. Only the person who is unable to develop a close social network of his or her own—the person whom only a relative could love—falls back on the commitment of kin as the sole social support network.

SOURCE: Excerpted from Judith Rempel, "Childless Elderly: What Are They Missing?" *Journal of Marriage and the Family*, 47 (May 1985), pp. 346–347.

What was the point of all this if it turns out that there are to be no grandchildren to enjoy this better world . . . ? (p. 4)

Grandparenthood

In her study of over a thousand Chicago-area widows, the sociologist Helena Znaniecka Lopata (1979) found that while grandchildren were reported to be persons the widows enjoyed being with, they were less likely than were nieces and nephews to be listed as persons to whom the widows could turn in times of crisis or when they felt in need of comfort. "What is quite possible is that the relation provides intense enjoyment for only a brief time while the grandchildren are little, and that the generations drift apart when the grandchildren become strongly involved in their own lives," explains Lopata (p. 246). The average age of the widows in her sample was 65, which would indicate that some of the grandchildren were likely to be heavily involved in the concerns of adolescence and early adulthood, including their own educational, career, and family interests and responsibilities, thereby making them less available as intregal parts of their grandmothers' social-support systems.

Other studies have indicated that when it comes to the morale of elderly persons, friends make a greater contribution than do grandchildren because friends have much more in common with them (Wood and Robertson, 1978; Blau, 1973). In summarizing a number of studies on grandparenthood, two specialists in the study of aging point out that in the United States, the grandparent role is, by and large, an inactive role, hedged about by certain restrictions ("Grandparents are expected not to encroach upon the parental responsibilities of their young adult offspring or to interfere with their authority"), but yet is seen by older persons "as at least one so-cially acceptable avenue for involvement in their children's families" (Wood and Robertson, 1978:369–370). According to Wood and Robertson, who interviewed 257 grandparents:

> While grandparents verbally attributed a great deal of significance to grandparenthood, the behavior of most grandparents in the role was relatively limited. It was true that most grandparents babysat, took their grandchildren to the zoo, movies, and so on, read to and played with them, and gave grandchildren gifts and remembered their birthdays, but the frequency of these activities for most grandparents was only a few times a year. Fewer than half of the grandparents reported ever telling their grandchildren about family history and customs or teaching them a special skill such as sewing, cooking, fishing, or a craft. (p. 369)

At the same time, the grandparent-grandchild relationship should not be sold short. Human development specialist Chrystal Ramirez Barranti (1985:343) emphasizes that changing demographics challenge the belief that the role of grandparents "has moved to the periphery of family life." Rather, increasing longevity, along with other factors, will mean that multigenerational families will be increasing and long-term intergenerational relationships will become commonplace. Pointing out that women and men today are becoming grandparents at younger ages and spending longer periods of their adult lives in that role than was true of previous generations, Barranti goes on to point out that "today's children can expect to spend nearly one-half of their lives as grandparents." She calls for a serious consideration of the grandparent/grandchild relationship as a potential resource for the family as a system. Lillian Troll (1983:63) also argues that "grandparents are not absent from central family dynamics." But she points out that "grandparent interactions and roles are diverse—much more diverse than parental ones, varying in

Grandparents can provide children with love, acceptance, "a sense of security and warmth, an historical sense of self, and the gift of a role model for one's future aging." (© Erika Stone 1984/Peter Arnold, Inc.)

part with social class, ethnicity, and sex, but largely, it seems, with individual feelings and preferences and life circumstances." (See also Bengtson and Robertson, 1985; Cherlin and Furstenberg, 1986.)

While folklore has presented us with the image of elderly white-haired grandparents in rocking chairs or in cozy kitchens with gingham curtains and the spicy aroma of cookies baking for the grandchildren, many grandparents are middle-aged rather then elderly. It is common today for persons to become grandparents in their late forties or early fifties (Rapoport et al., 1977:335). And this can mean a difference in grandparenting style—particularly for grandmothers. Social

scientist Joan Robertson (1977) found that younger grandmothers with more education, high involvement in activities outside the family, outside friendships, and paid employment tended to consider grandmothering "a joyous role" but, at the same time, made it clear "that they are more involved in their own lives and place less emphasis on grandparenting" (p. 173). In contrast, the older grandmothers in her sample had less education, tended to be widowed and unemployed, and had fewer outside friendships and community ties. These grandmothers "speak of grandmotherhood in highly laudable and personal or affective tones," writes Robertson. "Grandchildren are viewed as important to their daily lives because they help fill lonesome hours. This is evidenced in the fact that these women have the highest frequency of interaction behavior with grandchildren—an interesting finding in view of their age" (p. 173). Very old grandmothers—in particular, great-grandmothers—are more likely to see their roles as symbolic and emotional rather than in terms of active involvement, mainly because of declining health and strength and/or geographical distance (Wentowski, 1985).

Little research has thus far been done on the grandfather role. Rapoport and her colleagues (1977:335–337) suggest that much more attention be given to grandfathers. They suggest that while the younger grandmother may be busy with her own interests, glad to be relieved of the duties of active parenting, and uninterested in heavy involvement in a grandmother role (such as caring for grandchildren while her offspring and spouse are at work), the opposite may be true of the grand*father* in many cases. "Having been denied the pleasures of active parenting, he may yearn for a phase of active grandparenting," say these behavioral scientists, calling for research to explore this possibility. If their speculation is found to be true, it will be one more instance of the impact of changing gender roles—just as we saw in our discussion of the launching and empty-nest period of the middle years. One study of older grandfathers (mean age 75 years), however, indicated that for the men in this sample, grandfatherhood was considered a relatively unimportant role in later life (Kivett, 1985).

A number of family specialists are calling for further research on grandparenthood as an integral part of the family system (Troll, 1983; Kivett, 1985; Barranti, 1985). Concluding from an extensive review of existent studies on the topic that "vital and significant relationships exist between grandchildren and grandparents," Barranti writes:

> When a close, intimate grandparent/grandchild relationship has been formed during the child's early years, an attachment quality is developed and nurtured throughout the life of each (Kornhaber and Woodward, 1981). With that attachment comes the experience of being loved, accepted, a sense of security and warmth, an historical sense of self, and the gift of a role model for one's future aging. (p. 348)

CHAPTER HIGHLIGHTS

Some studies have indicated that marital satisfaction over time tends to follow a U-shaped curve, with satisfaction high at the beginning, lower during the childbearing and childrearing years, then higher again during the empty-nest period. Since few such studies have been longitudinal, however, the question of how marital quality is affected by the passage of time remains unsettled. It is known that couples who remain married into the middle and later years are likely, because of increased longevity, to have a longer period together after the children are grown and gone than has ever been the case before.

Contrary to the stereotype of the middle-aged woman, many wives at midlife today are enthusiastically pursuing their own interests and thankful for the time and freedom to do so. Those who have most difficulty when the children leave home are those who have defined themselves chiefly as mothers, accepted traditional gender-role assumptions, and haven't planned ahead by developing outside interests. At the same time that many wives are turning their attention to interests outside the home such as employment and further education, many husbands are questioning their own life-long absorption in occupational endeavors and would like to develop and emphasize the expressive side of life more fully. As a result, some fathers at midlife are finding it difficult to see their children leave home. Some are also finding it hard to accept their wives' new aspirations.

Just at the time when the middle generation is already overcommitted with the many demands of growing or grown children, careers, and community·responsibilities, they may find that their aging parents are requiring increased attention and, possibly, financial aid. In extremely stressful situations, abuse of elderly persons may occur. More often, caregivers report feeling physically and emotionally drained and experiencing various negative feelings, accompanied by a sense of helplessness and guilt. The responsibilities assumed for frail elderly parents are usually assigned along traditional gender-role lines, with daughters and daughters-in-law expected to perform most of the caregiving tasks.

The Census Bureau defines elderly persons as those who have lived for sixty-five years. This definition, based solely on chronological age, arbitrarily classifies persons in a social category that in our society is often devalued and considered nonproductive and powerless. Leaving important social roles ("role exits") at this stage of life may bring a painful sense of loss—especially the leaving of one's role as *spouse* (through the experience of widowhood) and one's role as *worker* (when retirement is negatively experienced, especially if it has not been freely chosen).

For couples whose marriage continues into the later years, high marital satisfaction is associated with high morale. Many widowed older persons remarry. Changing gender-role expectations and the fact that many persons become grandparents while in their forties or fifties have combined to bring changes in grandparenting style, particularly in the case of grandmothers.

·17·

DIVORCE, REMARRIAGE, AND STEPFAMILIES

When Larry and Sue, a couple in their late twenties, announced their plans for divorce, their friends were shocked. They couldn't believe it. Not Larry and Sue! If *they* couldn't stay married, who could?

Psychiatrist Arthur Miller (1970) points out that such reactions are typical of the feelings friends may experience in such situations. An impending divorce may cause friends to seriously examine their own marriages, and they may feel anxious and threatened. Sometimes there has been an idealization of the marriage of the divorcing couple, and the model with which one identified suddenly seems to be crumbling, bringing a sense of disillusionment as well as emotional loss.

The shock is intensified when the news is completely unexpected. In his classic study of divorce and readjustment, sociologist Willard Waller (1930: xiv, 107) wrote of a couple's teamwork in maintaining "the polite fiction" that all is well in their marriage even though they are moving toward divorce. The societal norm that family matters are private matters usually means that husbands and wives are reluctant to air their grievances or quarrel in front of their mutual friends. During the process of alienation leading toward divorce, the couple may make deliberate attempts to "manage their impressions" on others—in a sense giving what sociologist Erving Goffman (1959) speaks of as "a performance," trying to control how others see their situation. They are likely to act as they think they *should* act because others expect married couples to act in certain ways—even though such actions may be contrary to the realities of their particular case.

DIVORCE AS A PROCESS

The reference to a "process of alienation" underscores an important point: just as marriage is a process, so is the dissolution of a marriage. Marriage, with its ongoing exchange of rights and duties, rewards and costs, requires negotiation again and again. But sometimes the bargaining breaks down. The old pact no longer seems satisfactory to one or both parties; yet the couple seem unable to strike a new deal on which they can agree. One may try to coerce the other, seeking to get the conflict regulated rather than resolved. This approach tends only to increase hostility and bitterness, especially when the coercion is viewed by the other spouse as an exercise of nonlegitimate power. The trust element and concern for maximum joint profit is damaged. "If you really wanted what is best for me and for our marriage, you wouldn't be ordering me to do something against my will!" says one spouse. But the other counters: "If you wanted what's best for *me* and cared about what *I* feel is best for our marriage, you wouldn't be resisting me. You'd go along with what I want."

Such was Sue and Larry's situation. Larry loved the outdoors and wanted to get away from the city life that meant so much to Sue. Increasingly concerned about energy conservation and environmental issues, Larry longed to join with some friends of theirs in an organic farming venture in a rural area where the other couple had inherited some land. But Sue cringed at the notion of what she called a "primitive, back-to-nature lifestyle" and couldn't envision herself "chopping wood, tending chickens, and raising goats or something." Furthermore, she had no plans to give up her studies in architecture at the university and the job she had been promised after graduation. She was stunned that Larry would even suggest it.

Larry told his friends he wouldn't be able to join them in their farming experiment, so they found another couple. But Larry blamed

Sue for shattering his dream and making him miss out on what he considered an extraordinary opportunity. Over the months, Larry and Sue grew increasingly distant from each other. Their interests and life-goals seemed to pull them apart, and they found it harder to talk together about things that really mattered. Certain subjects (careers, lifestyles, gender roles) were particularly explosive, didn't lend themselves to discussion and negotiation, and, eventually, came to be avoided entirely. Where each had once felt reinforced by the other, both now felt that the other was almost like an altogether different person, no longer providing the rewards of emotional support that had meant so much to the other's self-esteem. Instead, there were now psychic punishments—nagging, criticism, smoldering resentment, searching for faults to complain about, and a tendency to tear down instead of build each other up as they had once done. These punishments, along with the diminishing rewards, made the relationship seem increasingly costly to maintain. Outside alternatives became more and more attractive (for Larry, the prospect of living and working among like-minded persons; for Sue, the prospect of freedom to pursue her career interests unhindered).

Reassessing the Marital Relationship

Sociologists John N. Edwards and Janice M. Saunders (1981:386) refer to changes in the way one perceives one's spouse and one's marriage relationship during this reassessment that is part of the dissolution process. As a result, a "devaluation of one's reward-cost outcomes" occurs. "If a person has become aware of attractive alternatives and reassessed his or her marital outcomes," they write, "the sense of attachment or identity with that relationship is likely to decrease. One's loyalty to the spouse, involvement in the marriage, and sense of belonging begin to decline." (See also Udry, 1981; Levinger, 1979; Booth and White, 1980.) As Larry and Sue were undergoing this process, the thought of divorce alarmed them at first—they had thought such a thing could never happen to them—but it seemed the only way.

Bohannan's "Six Stations of Divorce"

The process Sue and Larry underwent corresponds to what anthropologist Paul Bohannan (1970, chap. 2) calls the *emotional divorce*. Divorce may seem perplexing because so many things are taking place at once. Bohannan has isolated six aspects or overlapping experiences involved in each divorce. The emotional divorce centers around the deteriorating marriage relationship. The husband and wife "may continue to work together as a social team, but their attraction and trust for one another have disappeared," writes Bohannan. "The emotional divorce is experienced as an unsavory choice between giving in and hating oneself and domineering and hating oneself. . . . Two people in emotional divorce grate on each other because each is disappointed." (See also Weiss, 1975; Spanier and Thompson, 1984.)

While the emotional divorce is taking place, other aspects of divorce may also be occurring. There is the *legal divorce* (the obtaining of an actual decree), the *economic divorce* (the settlement of money matters and the division of property), the *co-parental divorce* (decisions about the custody of any children, visitation rights, each parent's responsibilities, and so on), the *community divorce* (changes in the way friends and others in the community react as the couple's divorce becomes known), and the *psychic divorce* (the sense of becoming uncoupled and regaining a sense of identity as an individual rather than one of a pair).

DIVORCE STATISTICS AND TRENDS

How widespread is divorce? One common way demographers measure marital dissolution is through the *crude divorce rate:* the number of divorces per 1,000 persons in the population. Figure 17-1 shows trends in marriage and divorce rates in the United States over a century.

Crude Divorce Rates

In 1867, when divorce statistics first began to be collected, there were about 0.5 divorces per 1,000 population. For the next sixty years, the divorce rate increased consistently, rising about 75 percent every twenty years. Had this pattern continued, the divorce rate in 1947 would have been 2.8. Instead, a very steep rise occurred in the 1940s. Most observers attribute the sharp increase to the high number of "quickie marriages" that took place amidst the uncertainties and upheavals of that period. As World War II came to an end, so did many of the hastily entered marriages it had spawned. The divorce rate in 1946 was higher than ever before—4.3 divorces per 1,000 population.

Then, just as suddenly, the rate fell again and leveled off during the 1950s, remaining at about 2.1 to 2.3 until 1963. That year the plateau ended, and another climb began. Within ten years the rate had nearly doubled, even exceeding the 1946 figure. For every 1,000 persons in 1973, there were 4.4 di-

Figure 17-1 Crude rates of marriages and divorces per 1,000 population: United States, 1867–1983. (SOURCE: National Center for Health Statistics, 1973, series 21, no. 24, p. 10; *Monthly Vital Statistics Report,* 1979, vol. 27, no. 13, p. 11; *Monthly Vital Statistics Report,* 1984, vol. 32, no. 13, p. 9.)

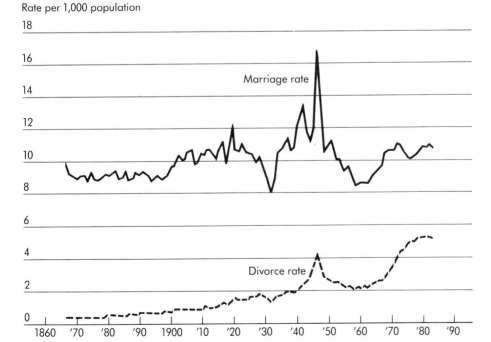

vorces; and by 1975, the divorce rate was 4.9. However, in 1976 and 1977, the divorce rate plateaued at 5.0, the first time in a decade that the rate had not climbed from one year to the next, leading some observers to suggest that this might signal a slowdown from previous spectacular rate increases. Then the rate climbed to 5.2 in 1978 and reached the historic high level of 5.3 in 1979 and again in 1981, only to drop to 5.1 in 1982 and back down to 5.0 in 1983. (National Center for Health Statistics, *100 Years of Marriage and Divorce Statistics, 1867–1967,* ser. 21, no. 24, 1973:9; *Monthly Vital Statistics Report,* Vol. 22, no. 13, 1974; Vol. 23, no. 12, 1975; Vol. 27, no. 13, 1979; Vol. 32, no. 13, 1984).

Refined Divorce Rates

Using *all* persons in the population as a base on which to calculate divorces presents a problem since many persons aren't "at risk" when it comes to divorce (children and unmarried adults). Demographers therefore sometimes use another way of measuring divorces, taking only married women as the base. The results are called *refined rates.* Refined rates are considered more precise because they focus on the logical group out of which a particular category comes. If you're interested in studying first-marriage rates, you take single persons as your base because they're the persons who enter first marriages. If you want to focus on divorce rates, you look at married persons—the category out of which divorces occur. If you want to study fertility rates, you look at women in the childbearing years, and so on.

In 1982, there were 21.7 divorces per 1,000 married women 15 years of age and over, the lowest the refined divorce rate had fallen since 1977 (National Center for Health Statistics, *Monthly Vital Statistics Report,* Vol. 33, no. 11, 1985:1). See Figure 17-2.

The Divorce Ratio

Still another way to look at the extent of divorce within the population is to consider the *divorce ratio,* defined by the Census Bureau as "the number of currently divorced persons per 1,000 married persons who are living with their spouses." In 1970, the ratio for men was 35. By 1985, it had increased to 103 divorced men per 1,000 married men. For women, the ratio increased from 60 in 1970 to 153 in 1985. The lower ratio for men is due largely to the fact that men are more likely than women to remarry after divorce and to do so in a relatively short period of time. Thus, there are fewer divorced men around at any given time to be compared with numbers of married men (U.S. Bureau of the Census, *Current Population Reports,* ser. P-20, no. 410, 1986:5, 69).

Age, Duration of Marriage, and Divorce

"Teenage marriages are twice as likely to end in divorce as marriages that occur in the twenties," write Glick and Norton (1977:15) of the U.S. Bureau of the Census.

Thus, reality is clouded somewhat by speaking of overall divorce rates without taking into account where the bulk of divorces occur—at lower age levels. The instability of teenage marriages, however, doesn't always show up in teenage divorce statistics because the persons involved may have left their teens by the time the marriage breaks up and the divorce decree is final.

Furthermore, the practice of "waiting until the children are grown and gone" may not be as common as is popularly assumed. There are such cases, to be sure; but, statistically, such occurrences are not great. The older couples become, the less likely they are to divorce–especially after the early thirties, when divorce rates drop sharply. In 1982,

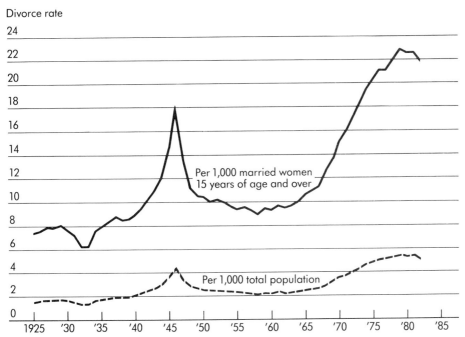

Divorce rate

Figure 17-2 Divorce rates in the United States: 1925–82. (SOURCE: National Center for Health Statistics, "Advance Report of Final Divorce Statistics, 1982," *Monthly Vital Statistics Report,* vol. 33, no. 11, Supplement, Feb. 28, 1985, p. 2.)

"only 10 percent of divorcing men and 7 percent of divorcing women were 50 years of age and over" (National Center for Health Statistics, *Monthly Vital Statistics Report,* Vol. 33, no. 11, 1985:3). However, the average age at which divorce occurs has risen slightly over recent years. Table 17-A shows the percentage of divorces involving persons at various age levels.

Statistics from the thirty-one states comprising the Divorce-Registration Area (DRA) indicate that half of marriages ending in divorce will end within the first seven years of marriage. Only 11 percent of divorcing couples in 1982 had been married twenty years or more. Table 17-B shows the percentage of divorces and annulments involving couples married for various lengths of time. (See also Plateris, 1981.)

Race and Divorce

"Although blacks and whites display generally similar patterns of divorce by social and economic characteristics," Norton and Glick (1979:15) point out, "the incidence of divorce is uniformly higher for blacks than for whites." As Table 17-C shows, the divorce ratio for black persons is more than double that of white persons and persons of Spanish origin. The highest divorce ratio of all is that of black women. In 1985, there were 326 divorced black women per 1,000 married persons with spouse present (in comparison to 142 white women). Black women are also less likely than white women to remarry after divorce (Staples, 1985).

Why should black marriages have higher rates of disruption than those of whites? Be-

TABLE 17-A Percent distribution of divorces and annulments by age of husband and wife at time of decree, and median and mean ages: divorce-registration area, 1972–82 (based on sample data)

AGE OF HUSBAND AND WIFE AT TIME OF DECREE	1982	1981	1980	1979	1978	1977	1976	1975	1974	1973	1972
	PERCENT DISTRIBUTION										
HUSBAND											
All ages	100.0	100.0	100.0	100.0	100.0	100.0	100.0	100.0	100.0	100.0	100.0
Under 20 years	0.6	0.7	0.8	0.8	1.0	0.9	1.0	1.0	1.1	1.1	1.0
20–24 years	11.7	12.5	13.5	13.9	14.8	14.7	15.1	15.2	15.7	15.7	15.9
25–29 years	22.0	22.8	23.4	23.8	24.3	24.0	24.8	25.1	24.2	23.4	23.5
30–34 years	21.3	22.1	21.4	20.8	20.2	19.8	18.6	18.6	18.2	17.9	17.2
35–39 years	16.3	15.1	14.6	14.2	13.8	13.4	12.9	12.5	12.4	12.4	12.3
40–44 years	10.7	10.0	9.8	9.7	9.3	9.4	9.5	9.3	9.6	9.9	10.2
45–49 years	6.9	6.7	6.5	6.7	6.6	6.9	7.2	7.3	7.5	8.0	8.0
50–54 years	4.6	4.6	4.4	4.5	4.5	4.8	4.9	5.1	5.2	5.3	5.5
55–59 years	2.8	2.7	2.7	2.6	2.7	2.9	2.9	2.8	2.8	3.0	3.0
60–64 years	1.5	1.5	1.4	1.5	1.4	1.5	1.5	1.6	1.7	1.7	1.7
65 years and over	1.5	1.4	1.4	1.4	1.4	1.6	1.5	1.5	1.6	1.6	1.6
	AGE IN YEARS[1]										
Median age	33.6	33.1	32.7	32.5	32.0	32.4	32.3	32.2	32.2	32.4	32.6
Mean age	35.7	35.4	35.1	35.0	34.8	35.1	35.1	35.0	35.1	35.3	34.9
	PERCENT DISTRIBUTION										
WIFE											
All ages	100.0	100.0	100.0	100.0	100.0	100.0	100.0	100.0	100.0	100.0	100.0
Under 20 years	2.7	2.9	3.4	3.6	4.0	3.8	4.1	4.4	4.6	4.4	4.3
20–24 years	18.6	19.5	20.8	21.2	22.7	22.3	22.4	22.5	23.0	23.1	23.7
25–29 years	24.1	24.8	24.6	24.8	24.6	24.5	25.1	25.2	24.3	23.7	23.0
30–34 years	19.9	20.2	19.4	18.7	17.9	17.9	16.7	16.3	16.1	15.6	15.0
35–39 years	14.2	13.1	12.8	12.3	11.8	11.3	11.2	10.9	10.7	10.9	11.0
40–44 years	8.8	8.2	7.7	7.9	7.5	7.7	7.9	7.6	7.9	8.4	8.8
45–49 years	5.1	4.9	4.8	5.0	5.0	5.3	5.6	5.7	5.9	6.3	6.6
50–54 years	3.1	3.1	3.1	3.1	3.3	3.4	3.5	3.6	3.6	3.9	3.9
55–59 years	1.8	1.8	1.7	1.8	1.7	2.0	1.9	2.0	2.0	2.0	2.0
60–64 years	1.0	0.9	0.9	0.9	0.9	1.0	0.9	0.9	1.0	1.0	1.0
65 years and over	0.8	0.8	0.8	0.7	0.7	0.8	0.8	0.8	0.8	0.7	0.8
	AGE IN YEARS[1]										
Median age	31.1	30.6	30.3	30.1	29.7	29.9	29.7	29.5	29.5	29.7	29.8
Mean age	33.1	32.7	32.4	32.3	32.1	32.4	32.3	32.3	32.3	32.5	32.1

[1]Medians and means computed on data by single years of age.

SOURCE: National Center for Health Statistics: Advance Report of Final Divorce Statistics, 1982. *Monthly Vital Statistics Report.* vol. 33, no. 11, Supplement (Hyattsville, MD: Public Health Service, Feb. 28, 1985), p. 10.

TABLE 17-B Percent distribution of divorces and annulments by duration of marriage to decree and median and mean duration of marriage to decree: divorce-registration area, 1982 (based on sample data)

	DURATION OF MARRIAGE (PERCENT DISTRIBUTION)						NUMBER OF YEARS MARRIED AT TIME OF DIVORCE	
TOTAL	UNDER 1 YEAR	1–4 YEARS	5–9 YEARS	10–14 YEARS	15–19 YEARS	20 YEARS AND OVER	MEDIAN	MEAN
100.0%	4.2	33.7	26.5	15.6	8.7	11.3	7.0 years	9.4 years

SOURCE: Adapted from Table 10, National Center for Health Statistics: Advance Report of Final Divorce Statistics, 1982, *Monthly Vital Statistics Report,* vol. 33, no. 11, Supplement (Hyattsville, MD: Public Health Service, Feb. 28, 1985), p. 13.

cause educational and economic opportunity have a great deal to do with marital stability. But because of discriminatory practices in a white-dominated society, blacks have not had equal access to such opportunities. As we have seen at various points throughout this book, black males in particular have been relegated to the fringes of the economic-opportunity system. Sociologist Robert Staples (1985:1007–1008) refers to a study by Joe and Yu (1984) which indicates that 46 percent of the 8.8 million working-age black males in 1982 were not in the work force. "Even college-educated black males have an unemployment rate four times greater than their white peers," writes Staples. "Among black males employed in the labor force, one out of three will suffer from unemployment in a given year." Black marriages faced with employment problems have a greater likelihood of disruption than do black marriages without such problems. "In general, unemployed men do not make good husbands and fathers," Staples points out. "Since employment and income are the measure of a man's masculinity in this society, men who have neither do not tend to feel good about themselves or act very positively

TABLE 17-C Divorced persons per 1,000 married persons with spouse present, by sex, race, and Spanish origin: 1985, 1980, 1970, and 1960

YEAR	TOTAL	RACE		SPANISH ORIGIN[1]
		WHITE	BLACK	
		Both sexes		
1985	128	120	251	121
1980	100	92	203	98
1970	47	44	83	61
1960	35	33	62	(NA)
		Male		
1985	103	98	179	97
1980	79	74	149	64
1970	35	32	62	40
1960	28	27	45	(NA)
		Female		
1985	153	142	326	143
1980	120	110	258	132
1970	60	56	104	81
1960	42	38	78	(NA)

(NA) Not available
[1]Persons of Spanish origin may be of any race.
SOURCE: Adapted from Table A-5, U.S. Bureau of the Census, *Current Population Reports,* ser. P-20, no. 410, *Marital Status and Living Arrangements: March, 1985,* (November, 1986), p. 69.

toward their wives and children.'' He emphasizes that ''the pressures that push many black males out of other social institutions within society also work to push them out of marital relationships'' (p. 1009). (See also Ball and Robbins, 1986; Secord and Ghee, 1986.)

Socioeconomic Status and Divorce

Over the years, numerous reports from census data both in the United States and in other developed nations have shown that social status and marital stability are positively related: the greater the social status, the greater the marital stability (Goode, 1962; Cutright, 1971; Norton and Glick, 1979).

Reasons for the association between socioeconomic status and marital stability were already discussed in Chapters 3 through 12. There we saw the part played by an exchange of resources in terms of fulfilling marital rights and duties, and we saw how satisfaction with the instrumental and expressive sides of marriage is closely linked to socioeconomic factors. High marital satisfaction indicates that the partners view the relationship as providing rewards to a greater degree than it exacts costs. Why leave a situation where the profit margin is high? On the other hand, one or both partners may perceive the reward/cost ratio to be so low that the relationship doesn't seem worth maintaining— particularly if alternatives outside the marriage promise greater benefits (Scanzoni, 1979c; Levinger, 1979). Then the question ceases to be ''Why leave?'' and becomes, instead, ''Why stay?''

Exchange theory also helps us see why particular social groups have higher rates of marital dissolution. For example, the heavy concentration of divorce among young persons cannot be adequately understood until

we think in terms of economic factors. Persons with lower education tend to marry earlier. They also tend to hold more traditional gender-role norms and therefore prefer the head-complement form of marriage—or, at most, a senior partner–junior partner arrangement. Such wives are socialized to expect their husbands to provide for them, and so the lower education and resulting lower incomes of their husbands tend to result in less marital satisfaction and a greater likelihood of divorce. If the wife does go to work, the husband may feel threatened by her independent resources to a far greater extent than would a husband with a higher level of education. In addition, the lower education of both partners quite likely means that they possess fewer negotiating skills and are less able to work through conflicts.

Or look again at the higher incidence of divorce among blacks. As we have seen, black men have been able to bring relatively fewer resources to their marriages than white men because of economic discrimination by whites and blocked educational and occupational opportunities. In traditional-type marriages, wives may be disappointed that their husbands are not providing them with a desired level of rewards, and the husbands themselves may feel frustrated by their limited access to the opportunity structure. Furthermore, black wives have often entered the work force out of necessity, providing them not only with alternative resources (money earned on their own rather than money provided by their husbands) but also giving them increased power in their marriages. The strong preferences many black women have developed for individualism and egalitarianism may result in their being more insistent on justice in terms of opportunities for self-determination and the pursuit of both extrinsic and intrinsic occupational rewards.

Thus, the bargaining in black marriages may be "tougher." Black wives may be less willing than white wives to endure certain kinds of costs (or reduced net profit). Also, as Staples (1985:1010) points out, even though a wife may not be dissatisfied with her husband's role in the marriage, "her high income may threaten the husband's authority and status, undermining his self-concept so that *he* becomes unhappy." For many black couples, disparities in occupational opportunities and educational attainments between the spouses (with many black women marrying men of less education than their own because of the restricted field of marriage eligibles) may be factors in marital dissatisfaction and strain (Ball and Robbins, 1986; Secord and Ghee, 1986).

Income-Maintenance Programs: Do They Save Marriages?

The question may arise: if marital well-being is associated with economic well-being, could the marriages of disadvantaged persons be helped by giving such families more money? Studies of the results of various financial-aid plans have thus far provided conflicting answers (Moles, 1979; Galligan and Bahr, 1978; Hannan, Tuma, and Groeneveld, 1978). In some federally funded experimental programs, for example, families that received guaranteed incomes had higher rates of marital dissolution than did families in a control group studied for comparison. It appeared that as wives became less dependent upon their husbands for sustenance, they also became more likely to leave unsatisfactory marriages in which they had previously felt trapped because of a lack of alternatives. On the other hand, sociologists Richard Galligan and Stephen Bahr (1978:289) have examined data that "suggest that direct income supplements may have little effect on marital dissolution" and

point out that other factors related to total family assets and consumership skills must be taken into account in examining the question. (See also Draper, 1981.)

Three other sociologists point out that income-maintenance programs have built into them two possible effects that are sometimes at cross-purposes with each other. The "income effect" could lower divorce rates by decreasing the tensions and conflicts generated by money worries. The "independence effect," on the other hand, works in an opposite direction "by reducing the economic dependence of the more dependent partner (usually the wife) on the marriage" (Hannan, Tuma, and Groeneveld, 1978:611). According to these sociologists, "the effect of an income-maintenance program on marital dissolution depends not only upon the magnitude of the payment a couple receives but also on their level of income before the program, the level of the wife's independence, and the magnitude of the change in the wife's independence." And while pointing out the inconclusiveness of currently available data and calling for further research, two other behavioral scientists observe that "whether or not public assistance payments encourage initial separation, they do seem to retard the remarriage of the already separated" (Levinger and Moles, 1979:136).

What Likelihood Do Marriages Have of Ending in Divorce?

Demographer Alexander Plateris (1979) has examined data from the National Vital Statistics System to see how the risk of divorce varies according to the year in which persons were married. To do this, he studied "marriage cohorts." A *marriage cohort* may be defined as "a group consisting of all couples married during a given calendar year" (p. 1). Plateris emphasizes that "any change in the variety of conditions—social, economic, cultural, demographic—that may influence the overall risk of marital disruption at any given point in time, will affect the various groups of married couples differently, according to the respective stages in their married lives."

One example of change over time that Plateris observed in his cohort study was this: The 1950 marriage cohort reached the level of having one-quarter of the couples divorced by the time of the twenty-fifth wedding anniversary. But one-fourth of the couples married in 1952 were already divorced by the time of their twentieth anniversary. For couples married six years later, in 1958, one-fourth were divorced before they had a chance to celebrate their fifteenth anniversary. And among couples in the 1965 cohort, one-quarter of the marriages had ended in divorce by the time of the tenth anniversary (p. 2).

Another demographer, Paul C. Glick (1984a), has analyzed data from the June 1980 *Current Population Survey* conducted by the U.S. Bureau of the Census. Using this data, and basing his projections on current divorce patterns, Glick predicts that about 1 out of 2 (49 percent) of women and men who were 25- to 34-years-old at the time of the survey will have seen their marriages end in divorce before they reach age 75. This is more than triple the 15 percent level of the generations ahead of them, those persons who were already in the 65- to 74-year-old category at the time of the survey.

As Table 17-D shows, persons who have graduated from college are less likely than other persons to become divorced. Men who have gone on for postgraduate training also have a lower likelihood of becoming divorced. But for *women* with postgraduate education, the likelihood of divorce after first marriage is considerably higher. Such women are usually highly involved in their careers and, possessing independent resources, are less likely to remain in unsatisfactory marriages.

Changing Attitudes toward Divorce

In the mid-1970s, a Chicago-area church introduced, as part of Sunday worship services, the announcement of marital separations. Members of the congregation were encouraged to go up to divorcing couples to express loving concern and acceptance. "We rejoice with Mary and Joe when they get married," the minister is quoted as saying, "but who anguishes with them when their marriage doesn't work?" (*Chicago Daily News*, April 19, 1975:10).

An article in a religious periodical suggested a step further—a ceremony of marital dissolution in which the officiant solemnizes the end of one period in a couple's life and the beginning of another (Shideler, 1971). Some religious leaders caution against assuming that such ceremonies promote or condone divorce; rather, they signify a recognition of the *reality* of divorce and a concern to lend support to the persons affected (Powers, 1976). "A divorce ritual is no more against marriage than a funeral is against life," explains one denominational staff member (quoted in *Newsletter of the National Council on Family Relations Task Force on Divorce and Divorce Reform*, October, 1976:9).

Such support for divorced persons has not always been forthcoming from religious leaders. Around the turn of the century, a writer on Christianity and social issues called divorce the "worst anarchism." Simple anarchy could overthrow the state, Lyman Abbott declared, but the state could be reconstructed. Divorce, however, could de-

TABLE 17-D   Selected divorce statistics: United States, 1980

AGE AT SURVEY DATE, RACE, AND EDUCATIONAL LEVEL	EVER MARRIED			
	PERCENT WHO HAD ENDED THEIR FIRST MARRIAGE IN DIVORCE BY 1980		PERCENT WHO MAY EVENTUALLY END THEIR FIRST MARRIAGE IN DIVORCE	
	MEN	WOMEN	MEN	WOMEN
25–34 years old				
All races	20	24	49	49
0–11 years of school	25	29	51	53
12 years	22	25	51	48
13–15 years	22	24	58	55
16 years	12	13	40	39
17+ years	13	17	41	52
White	20	23	49	48
Black	9	26	52	58
45–54 years old:				
All races	22	22	33	27
55–74 years old:				
All races	15	15	15	15

SOURCE: Paul C. Glick, "Marriage, Divorce, and Living Arrangements," *Journal of Family Issues, 5* (March 1984), p. 16.

stroy the family as an institution and bring about the downfall of civilization. Abbott, like many moral thinkers and writers of his time and since, considered the family (and, more specifically, the traditional form of the family in which the husband-father has been the central figure) to be the very foundation of society. Good social order, according to this viewpoint, could not exist side by side with divorce (quoted in O'Neill, 1967, chap. 2).

Alarmist cries, religious controversies, and legal debates have surrounded the subject of divorce throughout much of history. Changing attitudes today (such as those reflected in the accounts of church-sanctioned divorce ceremonies) and suggestions for reforming divorce laws appear to be rooted in two basic ideals: (1) a concern for the individual's rights and best interests and (2) a demanding view of marriage, with high expectations for companionship, empathy, affection, and self-actualization.

Individualism versus Familism

The worth, dignity, and freedom of the individual are cherished ideals in our society. But, at the same time, there is concern for that which is most beneficial for society as a whole, which sometimes necessitates putting aside individualistic interests. It's an old problem—one that has emerged, for example, in communal-living experiments: *auton-*

omy (self-determination and self-interest) versus *community* (in which group interests are given primary emphasis, even if individualistic interests are submerged or sacrificed).

During the divorce controversies that accompanied the rising divorce rates from after the Civil War onward, much of the debate centered around opposing perspectives on marriage. There was the traditional view that upheld *familistic* ideals on the one hand, and an emerging view that emphasized *individualistic* ideals on the other. From the standpoint of *familism,* marriage meant subordinating personal prerogatives and interests for the sake of the family (and, ultimately, for the sake of one's society because the family was held to be the basic unit on which society rested). O'Neill (1967, chap. 3) writes of moral conservatives who demanded that persons in oppressive marriages remain in them no matter how great the pain. Good would come out of even a bad marriage because of the spiritual growth resulting from the "purging, purifying influence of suffering." Providing a way out of an unsatisfactory relationship couldn't be reconciled with the ideals of familism. The availability of divorce was thought to discourage a couple's working at their relationship. Furthermore, according to an article in a religious periodical in 1903: "When people understand that they must live together they learn to soften, by mutual accommodation, that yoke which they know they cannot shake off. They become good husbands and good wives, for necessity is a powerful master in teaching the duties it imposes" (quoted in O'Neill, 1967, chap. 2).

From the familistic viewpoint, marriage is seen in terms of permanence, duty, and fidelity; but from the *individualistic* viewpoint, marriage is seen in terms of pragmatism, or practical considerations. What is best for the individuals involved? If a marriage doesn't work out, why force persons to remain in it?

Wouldn't it be better for the woman and man, and for society in general, if such marriages simply end? These kinds of questions bring us to the second reason that attitudes toward divorce began to change.

High Expectations for Marriage

O'Neill (1967, chap. 1) provides historical evidence that the form of family life idealized in the last century (the Victorian partriarchal family) was actually quite recent on the historical scene, having gradually emerged since the sixteenth and seventeenth centuries. If we view the modern nuclear family as "an essentially new institution rather than as the last gasp of a dying one," it is easier to understand "why divorce became a necessary part of the family system." O'Neill points out that "when families are large and loose, arouse few expectations, and make few demands, there is no need for divorce. But when families become the center of social organization, their intimacy can become suffocating, their demands unbearable, and their expectations too high to be easily realizable." The system is made workable by the "safety valve" of divorce.

He goes on to emphasize that when divorce is viewed in this way, it can be seen as a necessary feature rather than a flaw in the marriage system. Divorce provides persons who are oppressed in their marriages with a way of escape, "and those who fail at what is regarded as the most important human activity can gain a second chance." (See also Scanzoni, 1983b.)

Religion and Divorce

As divorce rates were rising and attitudinal changes were taking place, churches were taking a new look at the divorce question. There was by no means a consensus of opinion. Those who argued according to tradi-

ANNULMENTS: 15,000% INCREASE IN 15 YEARS

Dubuque, IA—One of the most dramatic changes in the U.S. Catholic church since Vatican II is scarcely ever heard about. Annulments in this nation are up more than 15,000 per cent in 15 years.

In 1968, 338 annulments were granted; by 1983, the number had risen to approximately 52,000.

Yet, even these figures are just the tip of the potential matrimonial iceberg. So far, fewer than 10 per cent of divorced Catholics have sought annulments, which would bring them back to full-church participation. One reason so many are so slow to apply is that they do not know the score—and the church, it appears, has been remarkably reticent about telling them.

An annulment is a declaration by the church that a particular marriage was not a sacramental union in the first place. It does not say the couple were not legally married or that the children are illegitimate.

The church does not consider divorce a sin, so divorced Catholics are still "in good standing" and may participate in the sacramental life. The problem arises when such Catholics decide to remarry—and statistics show that approximately 80 per cent do remarry—because the Catholic church considers sacramental marriage indissoluble. Catholics who remarry without annulment are not excommunicated (as many still think—the excommunication penalty was removed in 1977, but with minimum fanfare). However, they are forbidden the sacraments and treated as adulterers until they get annulments. . . .

SOURCE: Excerpted from Michael J. Farrell, Trends and Reviews Editor, *National Catholic Reporter*, 21 (Nov. 16, 1984), p. 1.

tional interpretations of the Bible called for strict opposition to divorce: Had not Jesus taught that man should not put asunder what God has joined together? But as early as the seventeenth century, writer-poet John Milton (1820:126–128) argued that this teaching itself legitimated divorce because some persons may not have been "joined by God" even though legally married. During the moral debates over divorce in the late nineteenth century, the same point was made by Carroll Wright, Commissioner of Labor and supervisor of the first United States government statistical report on marriage and divorce. Wright claimed that it was "blasphemous" to call the union of two ill-suited persons "a sacrament on the ground that God hath joined them together." Human beings, not God, were responsible for bad marriages, he argued, and persons who had made a mistake and "missed the divine purpose as well as the civil purpose of marriage" should be provided with a way out (quoted in O'Neill, 1967, chap. 7).

A modern Jewish position on divorce reflects a similar viewpoint: "Once it becomes clear that the marriage has failed irremediably, Judaism recognizes that the union has lost its sanction and its sanctity . . . the husband and wife are no longer joined together by God in any meaningful sense, and society stultifies itself by trying to ignore the truth" (Gordis, 1967:43).

Other arguments that have been used in an attempt to reconcile divorce with religious teachings center around the ideals of love, mercy, and compassion, the recognition of human frailties, and the suggestion that "Christ saw marriage as an ideal state rather than an institution to be defended at all costs" (O'Neill, 1967, chap. 3). Even in the Roman Catholic Church, which traditionally has firmly opposed divorce and remarriage, a great deal of rethinking on the subject is taking place today in spite of the official position.

Law and Divorce

Persons in the legal profession and legislators have also been forced to reexamine the divorce question in view of changing social conditions and attitudes. Will tougher laws preserve marriages? Will families break up at higher rates if divorces are easier to obtain? Some answers are provided by both history and cross-national comparisons.

O'Neill (1967, chap. 1) points out that when it was both difficult and expensive to obtain a divorce, divorces were largely restricted to middle- and upper-class persons. "But once the legal restraints on divorce were eased, divorce tended to become a lower-class phenomenon." However, this doesn't mean that less restrictive divorce laws *cause* the breakup of lower-status families. We saw earlier that the "glue" that holds a marriage together is not the law but rather the rewards it provides the partners. Spouses who perceive the costs to exceed the rewards may want to leave the relationship *without* divorce. Desertion and separation (sometimes called the "poor person's divorce") do not grant freedom to remarry as divorce does, but they do provide escape from an unsatisfactory marriage. However, when divorces may be obtained more easily, broken marriages among persons with limited opportunities in the economic system are able to take the divorce route rather than the desertion route.

Max Rheinstein (1972:406), a professor of law, has concluded after thorough research on divorce in the United States and across the world that "a strict statute law of divorce is not an effective means to prevent or even to reduce the incidence of marriage breakdown." Responding to those who blame divorce for "not only broken homes but broken lives," Rheinstein argues that what harms homes and lives isn't divorce but, rather, the breakdown of the marriage that precedes divorce. Divorce is only a legal recognition that the marriage has already broken down; it restores the man and woman to freedom to enter new marital relationships. The freedom of remarriage can be good for society, says Rheinstein (chap. 5), because "it reopens the way for the creation of new homes for the

Divorce is a legal recognition that a marriage has already broken down. (© Bruce Roberts 1976/Photo Researchers, Inc.)

ex-spouses and their children, a home . . . which at least holds the possibility of being more harmonious than that which has broken down."

In his opinion and that of many other concerned persons, society would be better served and marital stability better promoted by helping people to form and maintain satisfactory marriage relationships rather than tightening laws to keep persons locked in unsatisfactory relationships. Even the total banning of divorce wouldn't prevent marital breakups. A number of Latin American countries, for example, do not permit divorce and remarriage, but evasive practices have been devised by which persons (especially those with means) do find ways out of unsatisfactory marriages (Rheinstein, 1972, chap. 16; Galanternick, 1976).

Therefore, a move has been underway to make laws designed to alleviate some of the pain of divorce rather than adding to that pain through strict and severe legal requirements. One evidence of change is the gradual movement away from the *adversary* approach, the approach in which one partner sues the other for divorce (*John Doe v. Mary Doe*), toward divorce by mutual consent. The concept of "grounds for divorce" (adultery, cruelty, desertion, nonsupport, drunkenness, and so on) is giving way to the simple recognition of a *marital breakdown* and the partners' desire to separate.

The National Conference of Commissioners on Uniform State Laws has proposed a model no-fault divorce law that would make marriage a totally voluntary relationship, "lasting legally only so long as it meets the needs of both partners," emphasizes sociologist Jessie Bernard (1970). She believes that divorce "will probably always be an extremely painful experience for most people, as breaking ties always is, even outside of marriage." But at the same time, "the idea of forcing people to remain together is repug-

nant to the present world view" (see also Wright and Stetson, 1978). As this idea has come to be more and more widely accepted throughout the United States, all of the states except South Dakota have made provisions for some form of no-fault divorce (Weitzman, 1985:41).

Alimony and Changing Ideas about Marriage, Divorce, and Gender Roles

One of the biggest differences between no-fault and traditional divorce law may be seen in the redefinition of *alimony* and its purpose. (The word comes from the Latin *alimonia* meaning "nourishment, sustenance.")

Sociologists Lenore Weitzman and Ruth Dixon (1976), in a careful and thorough analysis of changes in ideas about alimony, point out that traditional notions about its role and purpose were tied to traditional notions of gender roles in marriage. Alimony was designed to insure that wives were compensated for fulfilling their marital duties through devotion to homemaking, and it was also designed to reinforce the responsibility of husbands for supporting their wives—even if the marriage ended in divorce. The very existence of alimony reflected the legitimacy of the norms surrounding the exchanges of marital rights and duties as spelled out in the traditional marriage pattern. Furthermore, say these sociologists, in addition to compensating wives for past services and enforcing husbands' support obligations, alimony served as a way of punishing the person considered "at fault" while rewarding the innocent party. If a husband was considered at fault in the divorce, he could be penalized by being required to make high alimony payments. If the wife was considered guilty (for example, in cases of adultery), she could be penalized by *not* being awarded alimony.

SUMMARY OF CHANGES IN DIVORCE LAW

TRADITIONAL DIVORCE	NO-FAULT DIVORCE

Restrictive law
  To protect marriage
	Permissive law
	  To facilitate divorce

Specific grounds
  Adultery, cruelty, etc.
	No grounds
	  Marital breakdown

Moral framework
  Guilt vs. innocence
	Administrative framework
	  Neither responsible

Fault
  One party caused divorce
	No fault
	  Cause of divorce irrelevant

Consent of innocent spouse needed
  Innocent spouse has power to prevent or
    delay the divorce
	No consent needed
	  Unilateral divorce
	  No consent or agreement
	    required

Gender-based responsibilities
  Husband responsible for alimony
  Wife responsible for custody
  Husband responsible for child support
	Gender-neutral responsibilities
	  Both responsible for self-support
	  Both eligible for custody
	  Both responsible for child
	    support

Financial awards linked to fault
  Alimony for "innocent" spouse
  Greater share of property to "innocent"
    spouse
	Financial awards based on equality
	  and need
	  Alimony based on need
	  Property divided equally

Adversarial
  One party guilty, one innocent
  Financial gain in proving fault
	Nonadversarial
	  No guilty or innocent party
	  No financial gain from charges
	  Amicable resolution encouraged

SOURCE: Lenore J. Weitzman, *The Divorce Revolution: The Unexpected Social and Economic Consequences for Women and Children in America* (New York: The Free Press, 1985), p. 40.

Under no-fault legislation, all such notions are challenged and changed. Weitzman and Dixon (1976) show that rather than being used to punish alleged wrongdoing and to reinforce traditional gender roles, the no-fault approach calls for a new concept of alimony based solely on the *needs* of the respective parties. Divorce is not thought of in terms of assigning blame to either person; thus, the idea of alimony-as-punishment is discarded. So is the idea of alimony as compensation for a homemaker's services over the years—which is a major reason many feminists feel this aspect of the newer divorce laws is unjust (see also Eisler, 1977; Weitzman, 1985:360; Bernard, 1985).

According to provisions of the California Family Law Act of 1969 with its pioneering no-fault approach to divorce, judges are asked to set alimony by considering "the circumstances of the respective parties, including the duration of the marriage, and the ability of the supported spouse to engage in gainful employment without interfering with the interests of the children of the parties in the custody of each spouse" (Civil Code Section 4801, as quoted in Weitzman and Dixon, p. 11).

For the supported spouse (which is usually the wife), there exist three types of financial provision, two of which are considered temporary until the formerly supported spouse is capable of self-support. Weitzman and Dixon (1976) use the term *transitional support* for what is sometimes called "retraining support" or "support for displaced homemakers." The idea is that a woman who has devoted her life to homemaking may need to learn or update her occupational skills in order to gain employment outside the home. Once she can support herself, she would no longer need or receive transitional-support payments from her former husband.

Another kind of support is custodial support, which Weitzman and Dixon are careful to distinguish from child support, which is support for the children's needs. *Custodial support* provides income for the parent who is caring for the children, freeing her or him to be a full-time caretaker, especially while the children are very young. A third kind of financial provision sometimes granted under the "new-alimony" system is what Weitzman and Dixon call *support insurance* and compare to a disability pension. It is support awarded to older women who are divorced after a long marriage and are not able to be retrained for gainful employment.

When it comes down to the practical application of the new laws, however, Weitzman and Dixon (1976) found they make little difference. They call attention to the *alimony myth*—the belief that most divorced women receive alimony and that most divorced men pay it. Weitzman (1985:183) points out that under both the traditional and no-fault divorce systems, "alimony is awarded according to judges' (and lawyers') conceptions of what the husband can afford. . . . Even when judges feel that a husband can afford to support his former wife and children, they rarely require him to help them sustain a standard of living half as good as his own."

Weitzman (1985) writes that "most judges appear to view the law's goal of equality as a mandate to place an equal burden of support on men and women without regard to the fact that the parties' capacities to support that burden are clearly unequal by virtue of their differing experiences during marriage." She is convinced that the three categories mentioned above who most need spousal support—mothers of young children, older housewives divorced after marriages of long duration, and women in transition—have not been treated fairly in interpretations and applications of the new divorce laws.

Unexpected Consequences of Divorce-Law Reforms

Weitzman's (1985) ten-year study of the impact of changing divorce laws began on an optimistic note. She reports that she expected no-fault divorce to yield only positive results. Instead, she found the legal reforms were having "unanticipated, unintended, and unfortunate consequences." Weitzman's research showed that under the new laws, women experienced a 73 percent *drop* in their standards of living by one year after the divorce, whereas men experienced a 42 percent *rise* in their standards of living (pp. 337–343).

In answer to the question, "How could a law that aimed at fairness create such disparities between divorced men and their former wives and children?" Weitzman points out that (1) court-awarded child support is inadequate and often not enforced, (2) demands on the wife's resources are greater than demands on the husband's resources after divorce because she usually has custody of the children while he is allowed to keep most of his income and is free to spend it on himself, and (3) in the vast majority of cases, the husband and wife are at different "starting points" and have unequal earning capacities at the time of divorce. "Not only do men in our society command higher salaries to begin with," Weitzman explains, "they also benefit

PROFESSIONAL LICENSES RULED MARITAL PROPERTY IN NEW YORK

The New York Court of Appeals has ruled unanimously that a medical license acquired during a marriage is marital property, a ruling which entitled the ex-wife of a doctor to a share of his future income.

According to evidence submitted in the case, Loretta O'Brien had worked as a teacher while her husband, Michael, completed his undergraduate and medical degrees. Two months after he obtained his license to practice surgery, Michael O'Brien sued for divorce.

The Court of Appeals awarded Loretta O'Brien $188,000, an amount estimated to represent 40 percent of the license's value. In making the award, the court said that professional licenses obtained during marriage are a part of the property of the marriage and thus are subject to equitable distribution in divorce actions.

Recently, a similar case in California was decided the opposite way.

SOURCE: *National NOW Times, 18* (December/January 1986), p. 7.

---

from the common marital pattern that gives priority to their careers." She continues:

> For women, in contrast, marriage is more likely to act as a career liability. Even though family roles are changing, and even though married women are increasingly working for pay during marriage, most of them nevertheless subordinate their careers to their husbands' and to their family responsibilities. This is especially true if they have children. Thus women are often doubly disadvantaged at the point of divorce. Not only do they face the "normal" 60 percent male/female income gap that affects all working women, they also suffer from the toll the marital years have taken on their earning capacity. (p. 342)

Weitzman (1985) also calls attention to inequities in the division of property, especially the rigid application of rules to divide all marital assets equally, rules which "often force the sale of the family home, and compound the financial dislocation and impoverishment of women and children" (p. xi) while failing to take into consideration new forms of property, forms which are the major

assets in most marriages today—namely, *career assets* (professional education and licenses, earning capacities, health insurance, pensions, and other benefits).

"The no-fault law took a major step forward by reducing the acrimony and hostility in the legal process of divorce," Weitzman concludes, "but because it did not provide economic protection for women and children, it failed to achieve its loftier goals of fairness, justice, and economically based equality" (p. 401). She suggests numerous ways in which the law can be improved without returning to the traditional divorce process with all of its own abuses and problems. (See also Bahr, 1983; Wishik, 1986.)

AFTER DIVORCE

Personal adjustment after divorce was a neglected area of study until Waller published his research and theoretical insights on the subject in 1930. A quarter of a century went by before another significant sociological work was published in an effort to understand how persons reorganize their lives after divorce—this time research on divorced women conducted in the Detroit metropolitan area by William Goode (1956). More recently, both behavioral scientists and family counselors have been increasingly focusing attention on postdivorce problems and challenges (Bohannan, 1970; Krantzler, 1973; Bloom et al., 1979; Weiss, 1975; Spanier and Casto, 1979; Spanier and Thompson, 1984).

Goode (1956, chap. 1) saw the process of readjustment in terms of changes in roles. A person leaves the role of husband or wife and must take on a new role. There are also changes and disruptions in existing social relationships when one is no longer part of a married pair. Postdivorce adjustment, according to Goode, involves incorporating such changes and disruptions into the individual's life in such a way that he or she moves beyond thinking of the prior divorce as the "primary point of reference." In other words, the person ceases to think in terms of "I am an ex-wife (or ex-husband)" but, rather, in terms of being an individual in one's own right.

Divorce involves a time of transition and grief, which isn't always easy since societal expectations are unclear (people wonder whether to extend sympathy or congratulations after a divorce), and support is often lacking both with regard to the mourning process itself and in terms of helping persons cope with building a new life. Mel Krantzler (1973), a divorce counselor, speaks of divorce as "the death of a relationship" and suggests that a time of grief is essential for emotional healing just as when an actual person dies. In divorce, the individual is not necessarily mourning the fact that the ex-spouse is gone or wishing that he or she would return—the divorce itself signifies their disinclination to live together satisfactorily. What

(Copyright © 1984 Universal Press Syndicate Reprinted with permission. All rights reserved.)

is happening is grief over the loss of the rewards no longer held out by the relationship, a realization that (in the words of a film title and song, popular in the 1970s) "the way we were" has ended. The enrichment found in the marital partnership has ceased to exist. The net profit is gone.

There is a sense of diminishment of one's very own self in the loss. Waller (1930, chap. 5) recognized this when he wrote:

There is always an element of betrayal when we break with a friend, and our distress is made all the more poignant because we have betrayed not only the friend but the part of us that was in him. . . . The pathos of a marital break attaches . . . to the very essence of the process by which those who have been one flesh are made separate. Personalities that have been fused by participation in common enterprises and that are held together by their common memories can only be hewn apart at the expense of great psychic travail.

A number of researchers and family counselors have observed various patterns, or stages, in the adjustment to separation and divorce—stages much like those Elisabeth Kübler-Ross (1969) observed in her pioneering work with terminally ill patients who had to come to terms with death: denial and isolation, anger, bargaining, depression, and acceptance. The content of the marital-dissolution adjustment stages and their sequence are portrayed differently by various family-life professionals, but an awareness of such common reactions can provide helpful insights to the divorcing person (Fisher, 1981; Salts, 1979; Price-Bonham and Balswick, 1980; Hassall and Madar, 1980).

In the separation and divorce process, persons who once learned to live together must now learn to live apart. The interdependence, the daily routines, the regularized sex life, the companionship, and the built-in habit systems that have developed over time as the two persons shared a life together—are all changed by divorce.

The individual may begin longing for the ex-spouse and the rewards the relationship once held, even though he or she knows this chapter in life is closed and, indeed, may want it to remain closed. "The memory of a person [may be] dear after the person is dear no more," observed Waller (1930:135). He writes of a man who reported looking for the mail to arrive at all times of the day, even though he knew there couldn't possibly be any further deliveries. The man had ambivalent feelings, both longing for and dreading letters from his ex-wife (p. 54). Weiss (1975), too, observed this phenomenon among divorcing persons and, in his book on marital separation, included a chapter entitled "The Erosion of Love and the Persistence of Attachment." (See also Kitson, 1982; Bloom and Kindle, 1985.)

At the time of the breakup, the marriage partners may expect the divorce to bring feelings of relief and happiness and may be surprised at the sadness and moments of nostalgia that come up. Part of the reason may lie in what Bohannan (1970) sees as a *reversal* of the courtship process and the "rewarding sensation" of knowing one has been selected out of the whole world. Divorce means being de-selected, and "it punishes almost as much as the engagement and the wedding are rewarding" (p. 33).

Weiss (1975:64–65) speaks of the different types of distress experienced by the "leaver" and the "left." He found that "those who initiated the separation tend to feel guilty, even anguished, at the damage their departure inflicted on those they were pledged to cherish." On the other hand, "those on whom separation was imposed . . . have been the recipients of traumatic rejection. . . . They may feel aggrieved, misused not only by the one man or woman who ended the marriage to them but by the entire human race. . . . They may accept their spouse's accusations that they are unattractive or cold or doltish or sexually inadequate, and decide that they are utterly without value."

Spanier and Thompson (1984) found in their study that those who had great difficulty accepting the breakup and who reported loneliness after the separation were those who suffered the most severe consequences, including thinking about—and even attempting—suicide. "For men, as well as women," they write, "being in the position of being left, loving the marriage partner until the end, and holding out hope for the marriage foretold a troubled aftermath to separation" (pp. 128–129). In yet another study, sociologist Stan Albrecht (1980:62) found that a feeling of personal failure was identified as the most common factor that made divorce so traumatic and stressful among those in his research sample. He points out that most persons have internalized societal norms about permanence in marriage. "Thus, despite increasingly liberal attitudes toward divorce, its occurrence in one's life is still seen as an admission of failure."

Yet for many couples, an unsatisfactory marriage can be more punishing than divorce. Krantzler (1973, chap. 8) quotes poet-novelist Herman Hesse, himself twice divorced, to show that divorce may open the way for some persons to experience a new exchange of rewards and a creative, fulfilling life that would have been impossible otherwise. "Be ready bravely and without remorse," wrote Hesse, "to find new light that old ties cannot give." Spanier and Thompson (1984:233) found that only about 20 percent of the separated women and men in their study indicated discontent with themselves and life or were troubled with health problems. "The vast majority appear to have gone on with their new life after separation with some degree of pleasure and enthusiasm," they write.

Divorce may open the way for some persons to experience a new exchange of rewards and a creative, fulfilling life that would have been impossible otherwise. (© 1983 Sarah Putnam/The Picture Cube)

CHILDREN AND DIVORCE

Even though life after divorce is a new life, ties with the old life may remain for some time. The after-divorce "continuities" may include such matters as occasionally helping a former spouse with some household chore, picking up mail at the old address, even going out to dinner or shopping together during the "uncoupling" process (Vaughan, 1979). The biggest continuity of all, as might be expected, is the ongoing tie that exists between the former spouses because of their shared interest in the children born or adopted during their marriage. They may no longer be wife and husband, but they are still Mom and Dad.

Children as a Link between Divorced Parents

"Just as the relationship between married spouses is a critical determinant of family interaction," writes social scientist Constance Ahrons (1979:500–501), "so, too, is the relationship between divorced spouses critical to divorced family reorganization and interaction. One of the most stressful tasks facing divorced parents is the redefinition of their coparental relationship."

Prior to the divorce, the two persons each held the position of spouse-parent within the family. Now they must learn to continue their shared parental relationship to their children and also the shared relationship they have *with one another* because of that parenting; at the same time, they are expected to learn to discard the spouse role that was formerly so intricately tied to the parent role. It's often a difficult task, because even the parental role is now different and has to be redefined as part of a new lifestyle in which the parents live separately. Ahrons suggests that a whole new family system comes into being (Figure 17-3). She writes:

> The reorganization of the nuclear family through divorce frequently results in the establishment of two households, maternal and paternal. These two interrelated households, or nuclei of the child's family of orientation, form one family system—*a binuclear family system.* The centrality of each of these households will vary among postdivorce families. Some families make very distinct divisions between the child's primary and secondary homes, whereas in other families these distinctions may be blurred and both homes have primary importance. (p. 500)

One example of such blurring observed among Ahrons' (1979) sample of divorced parents was that of the divorced couple who owned and lived in the same duplex, with the mother occupying one half, the father in the other half, and the children moving freely between the two households. Child psychiatrist Richard Gardner (1977) refers to a similar situation in which former spouses lived in separate wings of a large house, with the children's rooms located in between. Such situations are, however, not usual.

Ahrons' sample consisted of forty-one divorced parents to whom the courts had awarded joint custody of their children, and thus the term *binuclear family system* may be especially appropriate. In joint custody, both parents have "full custodial rights" and are given "an equal voice in the children's upbringing, education, and general welfare" (Cox and Cease, 1978:11–12). Since the parents are expected to consult with one another about important matters involving their children and, in other ways, share in their children's lives, a certain amount of

Figure 17-3   The child's binuclear family system (when both parents remarry). (SOURCE: Constance R. Ahrons, "Divorce: A Crisis of Family Transition and Change," *Family Relations, 29* (October 1980), p. 538.)

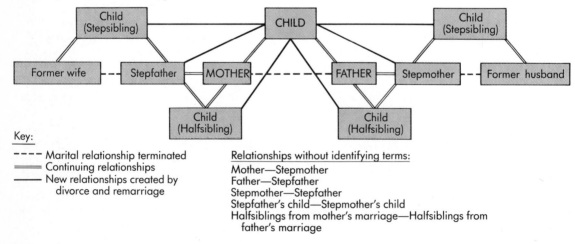

Key:
- - - - Marital relationship terminated
===== Continuing relationships
——— New relationships created by divorce and remarriage

Relationships without identifying terms:
Mother—Stepmother
Father—Stepfather
Stepmother—Stepfather
Stepfather's child—Stepmother's child
Halfsiblings from mother's marriage—Halfsiblings from father's marriage

postdivorce interaction between the two parents is inevitable. The amount of such interaction and how the divorced parties feel about it varies.

Ahrons (1979:505) found a continuum of "relational styles" among the divorced spouses in her sample, ranging from "my former spouse as best friend" to "my former spouse as bitter enemy," with most respondents falling somewhere in between as "neither friend nor foe."

The "best-friend" former spouses were those who showed evidence of respect and caring for one another after the divorce, sometimes sharing news or seeking advice as *friends* as well as co-parents. Some had business partnerships together. Such divorced parents chose to live near enough to have frequent get-togethers so that the children could share experiences with both parents at the same time in child-centered fun times, outings, and family conferences.

Divorced parents in Ahrons' second or "neither friend nor foe" category kept in-person contact to a minimum, discussing by phone most issues that concerned the children. When such parents did get together, the occasion was usually some special event in the child's life—perhaps a birthday or a performance in a school play or sports activity. "There was more unresolved anger in these former spousal relationships than in the first pattern," writes Ahrons, "and the joining together to share the child's experience was marked with some discomfort and formality. The parents had some disagreements about each other's child-rearing practices but most had decided to not interfere with the way the other parent related to the child" (p. 511).

Unlike parents in the "best-friend" and "neither friend nor foe" categories, the third category observed by Ahrons—the "bitter-enemies" category—chose not to get to-

gether at all. Even upon occasions in their children's lives that brought them to the same place, such as graduation ceremonies, these divorced parents did not sit together or otherwise interact, except for polite formalities. Ahrons points out that parents in this category tended to have custody arrangements that were closer to the traditional sole-custody pattern in that one parent had physical custody and a higher degree of control over the child's life than the other. "One illuminating finding of this study is that joint custody rights are not synonymous with equal parental responsibility," reports Ahrons (p. 508)—although, of course, that is the ideal that many strive for. (See also Ahrons, 1980; Furstenberg and Nord, 1985.)

Child-Custody Arrangements

Up until the middle of the nineteenth century, custody of children after a divorce was almost always given to the father. Some English judges reasoned that God had appointed the father to be guardian of the child and that furthermore, fathers could better prepare children for life since they (and not mothers) were involved in society and understood the workings of society. American judges tended to rule according to "best interests of the child" rather than the absolute or divine right of fathers, but the practical outcome of their decisions and the reasoning behind them echoed their English counterparts and English common law. Fathers were generally awarded custody because they were the financial supporters of the children, considered to be the natural protectors of both children and women, and better equipped to educate children for participation in society (Weiss, 1979b:325–326).

Then something happened so that "preference for the mother was the dominant judicial outlook from the time of the Civil War

After divorce, various custody arrangements determine such matters as visitation rights, where a child shall live, and whether the mother or father or both will be assigned legal responsibility for decisions concerning their child or children. (© 1979 Maureen Fennelli/Photo Researchers, Inc.)

through the 1960s," writes sociologist Robert Weiss (1979b:326). What happened was a changed attitude toward the family; it came to be viewed as a haven *from* a cold, impersonal world rather than a school of preparation *for* that world. Under the older way of thinking about childrearing, the "best interests of the child" seemed to assign the custodial role to the father—the one who could train the child for society. Under the newer way of thinking, the child's best interests seemed to decree that the mother have the custodial role because she was the one who could nurture and insulate the child from the hard knocks of life and patiently and soothingly help the child adjust to his or her environment. Ideas about a unique psychological bond between a mother and child and exaggerated claims about the child's needs for the special love only a mother was thought capable of giving led to the *doctrine of tender years*—the term used in law to indicate that the mother, if she is considered fit, should be granted custody of young children. (See also Weitzman, 1985:218–223.)

However, just as attitudes in the 1860s changed from preference for the father in custody decisions to preference for the mother, in the 1960s, attitudes began showing signs of change from a preference for the mother to the notion that the sex of the custodial parent is irrelevant (Weiss, 1979b:325–328). The arrangement that best serves the child's interests in the individual case is increasingly seen as what matters.

Sole custody is the name given to the custody arrangement in which one parent (whether the mother or the father) is given full responsibility for the child, who lives with that parent and is under that parent's control. The other parent (the noncustodial parent) is granted visitation rights but "has no legal right to make decisions regarding the rearing of the child" (Cox and Cease, 1978:10). However, even in this arrangement, the parents may discuss with one another certain major concerns and decisions with regard to their children.

Under *divided-custody* or *alternating-custody* arrangements, one parent has physical custody and legal authority for a designated period of time, and the other parent has such responsibility for the child during another period of time. In other words, the parents take turns being solo parents with legal custody. "The most common divided custody arrangements provide for the children to spend alternating six-month periods with each parent, if the parents live in the same school district, or nine months with one parent and three months with the other if they live in different districts," explain two specialists in family law and counseling (Cox and Cease, 1978:10).

Split custody is another arrangement sometimes granted by courts. In *split custody*, the children are split up. One parent is given custody of some of the children while the rest of the children are in the other parent's custody.

Earlier, we referred to joint custody, in which both parents are granted full custodial rights and are equally responsible for the child—not just during alternating periods but all the time. This arrangement, while apparently increasingly popular with many parents, is often discouraged by the courts, which favor, instead, sole-custody arrangements (Woolley, 1978; Cox and Cease, 1978). The reason for skepticism among some legal authorities usually relates to a belief that two people who can't get along in a marriage relationship aren't likely to agree on how to rear their children and, also, that children's lives will lack stability without one place called "home" and one parent in charge. Yet as Ahrons (1979, 1980) has demonstrated, joint custody need not mean that a child is torn between two separate worlds but is, rather, incorporated into a binuclear *family system* that includes both parents, even though they are in two different households. The whole point of joint custody contrasts with the adversary idea of divorce in which the former spouses are considered bitter antagonists, with the children caught in between. "Joint custody decisions are based on the presumption that both adults are competent, responsible parents who want to continue to relate with their children, although they are choosing to terminate the spousal bond," emphasizes Ahrons (p. 513). Her research, as well as that of others (for example, Woolley, 1978), uncovered a wide variety of innovative ways in which divorced parents worked out the practical aspects of joint cus-

tody. One little girl in such an arrangement, far from feeling divided in her loyalties, explained, "My parents love me enough to let me love both of them" (Woolley, p. 33).

On the other hand, battles over custody can be bitter. Sometimes they require the services of a *divorce mediator*, defined by Lois Vanderkooi and Jessica Pearson (1983:557) as "a neutral intervenor [who] helps disputing parties negotiate a mutually satisfactory settlement of their conflict" (see also Kaslow, 1984; Haynes, 1981). Weitzman (1985:310–312) found that one-third of the women in her study reported that their former husbands used the threat of a custody dispute as a coercive weapon for gaining financial concessions from their wives (see also Chesler, 1985). The problem of child snatching by dissatisfied noncustodial parents has also become an issue of societal concern in recent years and needs more research (Gelles, 1984).

Effects of Divorce on Children

Based on current statistics, demographers Arthur Norton and Paul Glick (1986:16) have projected that nearly 60 percent of all children born in the United States in 1984 may be expected to spend close to a year or more in a one-parent family before their eighteenth birthdays. For 40 percent of children, a one-parent situation will result from divorce. Another 5 percent will experience their parents' long-term separation, 2 percent will lose a parent through death, and 12 percent will live in one-parent families because they were born out of wedlock. Nearly two-thirds of children who will live in one-parent families will spend part of their childhood with a stepparent as well (Glick, 1984a).

To look at it another way: according to the National Center for Health Statistics, in 1982 (latest available statistics), 17.6 children out of every 1,000 experienced parental divorce, as compared to 7.9 per 1,000 twenty years earlier (*Monthly Vital Statistics Report,* Vol. 33, no. 11, 1985:7).

The question quite naturally arises: what does divorce do to these children, numbering over a million annually? How does divorce affect their lives? No one simple answer can be given because the question itself has so many dimensions, and so many factors must be taken into account. Research up to this point has been limited and has yielded conflicting results. "Some studies argue that there is little measurable impact of divorce on the lives of children," write sociologists Larry Bumpass and Ronald Rindfuss (1979:50), "while others have attributed all manner of social ills to this experience."

Bumpass and Rindfuss refer to studies showing that children from disrupted families tend to have lower socioeconomic and educational attainments over the long term and also higher rates of instability in their own marriages. Rather than settling the question of the consequences of divorce in the lives of children, however, such findings may be telling us less about divorce per se than about factors associated with divorce and the postdivorce period—especially the likelihood of economic hardship. Single-parent families—particularly those headed by mothers—are likely to find their living standard lower than before the divorce. The problem is especially acute at lower status levels. Mary Jo Bane (1979), a specialist in urban studies, in calling attention to the fact that lower-income families have higher rates of both divorce and death than higher-income families, concludes that "one would expect both men and women in disrupted marriages to be somewhat worse off than other families" because they are more likely to come from the ranks of the poor to begin with (p. 238). "These economic problems

ought to be the main concern of policy-makers who worry about the children of marital disruption," asserts Bane (p. 286).

A similar point comes through in Bumpass and Rindfuss's (1979) analysis of a large national probability sample of mothers. They found, for example, that among white children whose mothers had not completed high school, 33 percent experienced a disrupted family before they reached age 15, as compared to one-fifth of those children whose mothers had finished high school. "A mother's age at the birth of her child is correlated with education," say these researchers, "but the differences by mother's age are even more pronounced. Children born to mothers under the age of 20 are more than twice as likely to experience a disrupted family than children born to mothers aged 25 or older (39% vs. 15%); furthermore, they are, on the average, six years younger at the time of disruption (4.8 vs. 10.8 years of age)" (p. 60).

Among white children in the sample, about 1 out of 6 had experienced the disruption of the parents' marriage by age 5. Among black children (for reasons we suggested earlier in this chapter), the rates were more than double; more than 2 out of 5 black children had experienced marital disruption by age 5, and 3 out of every 5 were likely to experience the breakup of their parents' marriages before they reached age 16. Bumpass and Rindfuss also point to "another significant aspect of children's experience with marital disruption that is missed by divorce statistics":

> Many children are born after the marital dissolution but before their mother remarries. Among twice-married women in 1970, more than one-fourth had given birth between separation and remarriage. (p. 52)

Such births complicate even further the economic hardship faced by many divorced mothers rearing children alone.

But, of course, not all divorced mothers were married at an early age and lacked educational and economic opportunities; and regardless of a family's socioeconomic status, financial hardship isn't the only consideration to be taken into account in assessing the effects of divorce on children's lives. Children may undergo a great deal of personal pain when their parents' marriage ends (Gardner, 1977, chap. 4). Children sometimes blame themselves, feeling that they themselves somehow "caused" the divorce; or they may feel that the parent who left has rejected them rather than the marital partner. They may feel hurt, confused, angry, and insecure. They may display symptoms of grief that are similar to grief reaction in cases of death. They may entertain fantasies about their parents' reconciliation. After all, divorce is a crisis experience. But it need not be viewed as an absolute disaster with inevitably disastrous effects, damaging the child for life (Luepnitz, 1979).

In interviews with a small sample of twenty-four college students whose parents had divorced before the respondents were 16 years old, psychologist Deborah Luepnitz (1979) found that exactly half the students reported that the initial conflict between their parents was what the students found most difficult and stress-producing. In other words, the predivorce period was harder for them as children than was the divorce itself. Another one-fourth found the postdivorce period the most difficult, and 8 percent found the transition period between the time of the announcement and the time their fathers moved out to be hardest. The remaining 16 percent reported no stress over their parents' divorce. Three of the four students reporting *no* divorce-linked stress attributed this to the lack of bitter antagonism between the parents during the divorce process; the supportiveness of parents, friends, and siblings; and

the fact that they continued to have free access to both parents after the divorce. The other student reporting no stress over the divorce indicated relief that the family was now free of a father who had been violent and in constant trouble with the law.

Luepnitz suggests that perhaps "much of the literature on children of divorce ought to be retitled 'children of marital conflict' " because symptoms often thought to be reactions to divorce were reported by her subjects to be "in response to marital fighting *years* before they became 'children of divorce' " (p. 84). It may be far more distressing for a child to live in a conflict-ridden home than to come from a "broken" one. A number of Luepnitz's subjects reported that before age 9, they experienced severe physical reactions to their parents' fighting—reactions such as vomiting, losing or gaining weight, hair loss, even an ulcer.

Other research likewise indicates the detrimental effects of parental conflict. "It doesn't seem to matter if the conflict leads to separation or divorce," writes educator Cynthia Longfellow (1979) after a review of numerous studies. "The child who experiences his [or her] parents' marital discord is at greater psychiatric risk" (p. 305). Longfellow suggests that little is accomplished by looking for one broad-reaching answer to the question of divorce and its impact on children; rather, we should be endeavoring to sort out those aspects of divorce that are troubling to children: for example, life-event changes (not only one parent's moving out but, possibly, less income available, the necessity of moving to another location, and so on), parental depression, absence of adequate support networks for the single mother in many cases, the parental conflict surrounding the divorce, and how the divorce is understood and processed by the individual child. (See also Glenn and Kramer, 1985.)

Solo Parenting After Divorce

An extensive review of the research literature, as well as a study they themselves conducted, also leads sociologists Helen Raschke and Vernon Raschke (1979) to conclude that it would be beneficial "to give more attention to conflict and its effects on children in all family forms, and less attention to ferreting out the 'ills' of the single-parent family" (p. 373).

Among the family forms examined by the Raschkes were those with both parents present (intact families), single-parent families, reconstituted families (new families brought into being through the remarriage of a di-

vorced or widowed parent), and arrangements in which children lived with relatives or in foster homes. The particular *form* of a child's family was found to make no significant difference in the child's self-concept. (These researchers suggest that a child's self-concept "can be interpreted as a general measure of personal and social adjustment," [p. 369].) What *did* make a difference was whether or not the children perceived an atmosphere of conflict in their families. Where there was greater conflict, the self-concept of the children was significantly lower. On the other hand, perceived parental happiness was positively correlated with the children's self-concept—regardless of whether the family was intact, reconstituted, or a single-parent arrangement. The happier the child's parent or parents, the higher the self-concept of the child. Pointing out that their study of 289 third-, sixth-, and eighth-graders may not provide answers to all the questions surrounding the topic, Raschke and Raschke say one thing is sure: it doesn't provide any support for "the cliché that 'broken homes yield broken young lives'." Thus, the study "should play a role in helping to place the single-parent family in better perspective" (p. 373).

While 3 out of 4 children live with two parents (including families where one parent is a stepparent), the remaining children live, for the most part, in single-parent families. The percentage of children living with only one parent nearly doubled between 1970 and 1985, rising from 11.9 percent to 23.4 percent. The largest proportion of children who live with only one parent live with a divorced parent (U.S. Bureau of the Census, *Current Population Reports,* ser. P-20, no. 410, 1986:71–72; Norton and Glick, 1986). Figure 17-4 shows the living arrangements for children under 18 in 1985 according to race and Spanish origin.

In spite of traditional gender-role assumptions, many fathers can and do successfully rear children alone. (James H. Karales/Peter Arnold, Inc.)

"MY HOME IS NOT BROKEN, IT WORKS"*

One summer day, my son Robert, then five years old, took me by the hand and asked me to go outside with him.

Holding on tightly, he carefully walked around the house with me, looking at doors and windows and shaking his head. There was something he didn't understand.

"Mommy," he finally asked, pressing my hand with his warm, chubby fingers, "is our home broken?"

His words shot through my body, alerting every protective instinct, activating my private defense system, the one I hold in reserve to ward off attacks against women and children.

"Oh, Robbie," I answered, hugging him, "did someone tell you that we have a broken home?"

"Yes," he said sweetly. "But it doesn't *look* broken!"

"It's not," I assured him. "Our house is not broken and neither are we."

I explained that "broken" is some people's way of describing a home with only one parent, usually the mother. Sometimes there was only one parent because of divorce, like us. "There are still lots of homes like ours. And they're still homes."

Robbie looked relieved and went to play with his friends. I stood there, shaking with anger.

What a way to put down a little kid and me, too, I thought. I supported my three children, fed and clothed them. I was there for them emotionally and physically. I managed to keep up payments on the house. Although we struggled financially, we were happy and loving. What was "broken" about us? . . . .

It's true that society does not help single or divorced women raise their children or keep their families intact. The scorn felt for so-called broken homes is expressed in the lack of support systems for heads of those households, in the withholding of federally funded quality child care, job training, and equal pay, and in the meanness with which aid to dependent children is doled out.

The expression "broken home" suggests thay my children never had a chance in life because their father was not present, and what I did doesn't count. I *know* that's not true, and it's not true for millions of other Americans also stigmatized by the term.

*This quotation is used with thanks to Daphne Busby, president of the Sisterhood of Black Single Mothers.

SOURCE: Carol Kleiman, *Ms., 13* (November 1984), p. 154.

Slightly over 1 out of 5 children in the United States lives with a mother in a solo-parent situation. And although only 2.5 percent of children now live with their fathers in such an arrangement, more and more fathers have been interested in seeking custody in recent years—including custody of very young children (Orthner and Lewis, 1979; Greif, 1985a). In spite of traditional gender-role assumptions, many fathers can and do successfully rear children alone (Orthner, Brown, and Ferguson, 1976; Orthner and

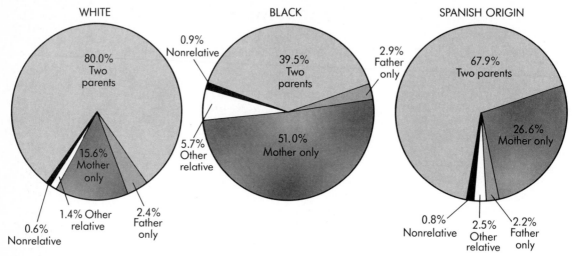

Figure 17-4 Living arrangements of children under 18: 1985. (SOURCE: Adapted from U.S. Bureau of the Census, Current Population Reports, Series P-20, no. 410, *Marital Status and Living Arrangements: March, 1985,* Nov., 1986 p. 71.)

Lewis, 1979; Gersick, 1979; Risman, 1986; Greif, 1985b).

Solo parents—whether mothers or fathers—face the challenges, joys, and problems that all parents face, but they face them without a partner. They have to balance the demands of home and career; find baby-sitters; provide guidance and discipline; actively support their child's school endeavors and other activities and interests; arrange appointments with physicians and dentists; shop for new shoes; bandage scraped knees; and allow plenty of time for fun, listening, telling stories, laughing, and hugging. And they have to do it all alone. (See special issue, "The Single Parent Family," *Family Relations,* January 1986.)

Supportive friendship networks, relatives who care, teachers who take a warm and personal interest, special community and religious activities designed with such families in mind, and groups such as Parents without Partners can make a tremendous difference in the emotional well-being of solo parents

and their children at a time in their lives when encouragement is especially needed. Many of the divorce rituals mentioned earlier were designed to be symbolic of such support. "At precisely the time when individuals are most lonely and need to establish links of communication with others," writes Jeanne Audrey Powers (1976:80), a Methodist minister who has authored divorce ceremonies, "members of the Christian community know least how to respond, and the person is usually met with silence, embarrassment and whispered conversations that end abruptly when the person enters a room."

Her point is poignantly illustrated by an anecdote told to us by a woman who was first widowed and then saw her second marriage end in divorce. When the second marriage ended, one of her children asked, "Where are all the people, Mommy? Why aren't people bringing us casseroles this time and coming to visit like they did when Daddy died?" Apparently, persons in this woman's circle of acquaintances found themselves more willing to provide emotional support and practical assistance for someone whose spouse had died than for someone whose marriage had died.

While some divorced fathers rearing children alone have also reported negative reactions from others, the majority report they receive much support and a great deal of special attention (Orthner and Lewis, 1979:43). One researcher suggests a reason related to traditional gender-role expectations:

> Since, in our society, children of divorced parents usually live with their mothers, there is nothing especially commendable about a single female parent. When, on the other hand, the children live with their fathers, the men are frequently regarded as heroic, or at the very best, commendable for taking on the responsibilities they are not usually expected to do. In a sense, the single male parent may be viewed as a social widower, and as such receives much of the solicitations and direct help which is customarily offered to actual widowers. (Mendes, 1975, as quoted in Orthner and Lewis, 1979:44)

Contrasting societal attitudes toward male solo parents with those toward female solo parents (who are seen to be simply "doing their job," even though the mothers are employed full-time), researchers Kohen, Brown, and Feldberg (1979) point to the example of a divorced mother of a handicapped child who said:

> "No one has felt any commitment to me as a result of my having to take care of Barbara alone—no one has offered any help. When she is with my husband, they get invited out all the time. When people come here, they take it for granted that I'll cook for them. But they'll take food all prepared out there [her husband's house]." (p. 238)

Here, as in so many other areas, we see the impact of gender-role stereotypes.

Impact of Divorce on Gender Roles

At the same time that divorce forces many women to become more autonomous and to develop skills along *instrumental* lines, divorce may be forcing some men to develop skills along *expressive* lines by involving them more fully in parenting—especially where fathers are awarded full or joint child custody.

Kristine Rosenthal and Harry Keshet (1978), social scientists, found that after-divorce parenting, whether part-time or full-time, can be an important resocialization experience for men. The experience makes necessary a rethinking of work commitments as over against commitments of time and energy to their children. Interaction with children may come to have higher priority than ever before. "Parenting which in a marriage was likely to come second to work obligations is now a legitimate function *on par* with the demands of work," say these researchers. "In fact, it acquires many of the characteristics of work, and fathers begin to develop competence, recognize cues for judging themselves as competent, and experience the familiar rewards of a job well done" (p. 471). Aware that this description gives the impression that men tend to make even expressive relations into something instrumental, Rosenthal and Keshet continue:

> The issue of competence and efficiency dominates the self-image of males. The cultural image of competence is cold and impersonal, but it also can be a way to think about feelings and to begin to learn how to function interpersonally. (p. 471)

In their study of 127 divorced and separated fathers, these researchers found that as men gained confidence in their parenting through caring for their children's physical needs—such as giving the children baths, meals, and getting them to school—the fathers experienced good feelings between them and their children and gradually developed greater sensitivity to what was on their children's minds. "Once the feelings of competence begin to be introduced into the area of dealing with children's emotions, reinforced by the child's well being, the whole area of emotions becomes less threatening for men," say Rosenthal and Keshet. And "for men socialized to believe that feelings must be kept hidden and are a barrier to effective functioning, experiencing competency in this area can be a source of positive self-regard" (p. 472). These fathers' movement away from nontraditional gender roles and their greater skills in expressiveness

In nearly half of the marriages taking place today, either the bride or groom or both have been married before. (Michael Kagan/Monkmeyer)

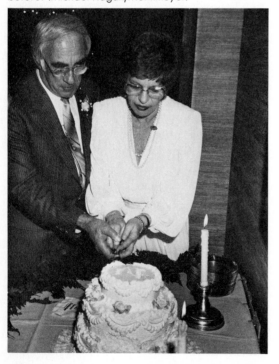

might be expected to carry over into new relationships, including remarriage and what Rosenthal and Keshet call "refamilying."

REMARRIAGE

Remarriage after divorce is popular. "Evidently, divorced men strongly prefer being married, albeit with a different partner," write the demographers Paul Glick and Arthur Norton (1977:6) after examining data showing divorced men to have a greater likelihood of remarrying than never-married men have of marrying for the first time.

For women, the likelihood of remarriage "is largely a function of her age at the time of divorce," writes Lenore Weitzman (1985:204). "If she is under thirty, she has a 75 percent chance of remarrying. But her chances diminish significantly as she grows older: between thirty and forty, the proportion is closer to 50 percent, and if she is forty or older, she has only a 28 percent chance of remarriage."

Women with lower education are more likely than are women with higher levels of education to remarry after divorce. Women with four or more years of college "either enter remarriage more deliberately or decide to remain unmarried," points out Paul Glick (1984a:17). Having other options open to them in the economic-opportunity system, such women may be less willing to run the risk of another unsatisfactory marriage. The costs are too great.

Indeed, for some women at all class levels, divorce may be considered rewarding rather than costly. Some report that after divorce, they experienced autonomy for the first time in their lives, and it's a good feeling. They enjoy the control they exercise over their own lives—how they use their time, how they keep the house, how they rear the children, how they use money, and so on. In citing evidence for this, Kohen, Brown, and Feldberg (1979) explain:

> If a couple divorces, the woman loses most of her right to the man's resources, but she also loses her personal dependence and obligations of service. She now stands in direct relationship to society as the head of her family. . . . Patriarchal authority is now outside the family, not inside, and the woman can choose to some extent the way in which she will relate to those authorities [employers, welfare officials, lawyers and judges, and the like] and the use she will make of whatever formal and informal resources are available. (p. 229)

While not minimizing the very real financial hardships many women face after divorce, Kohen, Brown, and Feldberg report that some divorced women they interviewed tended to feel they had *more* money after divorce, when in actuality they had less! Why?

Because now they had *control* of the money (whether earned income or from AFDC or support payments); and such control made all the difference after having lived in marriages where husbands gambled, spent more than they earned, or withheld needed money from their wives and children. Thus, they felt "better off" in many ways, including financially. For such women, "divorce meant an end to the husband's power to impoverish the family." (p. 239) On the other hand, some women assessed the cost/benefit ratio differently. Women who had been married to high-income husbands, especially, tended to indicate that "problems from loss of income far outweighed the benefits of increased control" (p. 240).

In recent years, remarriage rates have dropped; but even so, approximately 7 out of 10 divorced persons under age 40 may be expected to remarry eventually (Glick,

TABLE 17-E Percent distribution of marriages by marriage order of both bride and groom: marriage-registration area, 1970–81

YEAR	ALL MARRIAGES	MARRIAGE ORDER OF BOTH BRIDE AND GROOM			
		FIRST MARRIAGE OF BRIDE AND GROOM	FIRST MARRIAGE OF BRIDE, REMARRIAGE OF GROOM	REMARRIAGE OF BRIDE, FIRST MARRIAGE OF GROOM	REMARRIAGE OF BRIDE AND GROOM
1981	100.0%	54.7%	11.8%	10.1%	23.4%
1980	100.0	56.2	11.3	9.8	22.7
1979	100.0	56.4	11.2	9.5	22.9
1978	100.0	57.1	11.1	9.3	22.5
1977	100.0	57.5	10.8	9.0	22.6
1976	100.0	58.5	10.7	8.8	22.0
1975	100.0	60.1	9.9	8.6	21.3
1974	100.0	62.9	9.2	8.1	19.8
1973	100.0	64.6	8.7	7.9	18.9
1972	100.0	66.7	8.2	7.4	17.6
1971	100.0	67.7	8.0	7.3	17.0
1970	100.0	68.6	7.6	7.3	16.5

SOURCE: National Center for Health Statistics: "Advance Report of Final Marriage Statistics, 1981," *Monthly Vital Statistics Report,* vol. 32, no. 11, Supplement (Hyattsville, MD: Public Health Service, 1984), p. 9.

Ziggy, Copyright 1986 Universal Press Syndicate.

1984a:18). The median length of time between divorce and remarriage is just under two years (National Center for Health Statistics, *Monthly Vital Statistics Report,* Vol. 32, no. 11, 1984:2). As Table 17-E shows, in only about 55 percent of marriages in 1981 were both the bride and the groom marrying for the first time. Forty-five percent of marriages involved a bride or groom or both who were remarrying.

"Divorce, then, serves not so much as an escape hatch from married life but as a recycling mechanism permitting individuals a second (and sometimes third and fourth) chance to upgrade their marital situation," write sociologists Frank Furstenberg, Jr., and Graham Spanier (1984:53). They suggest that the term *conjugal career* is an apt metaphor and describe remarriage as "conjugal succession"—the substituting of a new relationship for an unsatisfactory one.

Remarriage as a Process

Ann Goetting (1982), another sociologist, describes remarriage as a *process* with six "stations" analogous to Bohannan's six stations of divorce that we mentioned earlier. Goetting thus speaks of the *emotional remarriage* (attraction and bonding, often requiring the overcoming of fears of new hurts and rejection), the *psychic remarriage* ("the process of changing one's conjugal identity from individual to couple"), the *community remarriage* (alterations—often *painful* alterations—in friendships as one moves from the world of the divorced to a friendship network of married and remarried couples), the *parental remarriage* (in which those with children face issues of stepparenthood), the *economic remarriage* (in which a new "marital household as a unit of economic productivity and consumption" is established), and *legal remarriage* (dealing with legal responsibilities and the distribution of resources in view of both the former and new marriages).

Do Remarriages Work Out?

Remarriages after divorce are somewhat more likely to end in divorce than are first marriages. We saw earlier that about 49 percent of first marriages end in divorce. On the basis of current statistics, Glick (1984a:20) predicts that 61 percent of men and 54 percent of women who have remarried will experience *redivorce* as well.

However, these projections should not lead to the conclusion that divorce repeaters are simply "divorce-prone" and have personalities that hinder their remaining in a stable marriage situation. "The term 'divorce-prone' is pejorative and unnecessary," writes

REMARRIAGE AFTER DIVORCE

Because they are not innocent of the possibility of failure, couples who have been married before must hedge their commitment to marriage even more than those married the first time. Persons who remarry are increasingly likely to view marriage as a conditional contract. As we shall see later, remarried couples monitor the relationship very closely for they are all too familiar with the signs of deterioration. Their principal strategy for avoiding failure is to maintain a high level of vigilance about this ever-present danger. Second marriages appear to be designed to anticipate rather than deny problems. Remarried people, then, are inclined to embrace, if not exaggerate, the contemporary view of marriage as a difficult and even hazardous undertaking.

SOURCE: Frank F. Furstenberg, Jr., and Graham B. Spanier, *Recycling the Family: Remarriage after Divorce* (Beverly Hills: Sage Publications, 1984), p. 63.

sociologist Lucile Duberman (1977), pointing out that *situational factors* rather than character flaws help explain the somewhat higher divorce rates among remarried persons as compared to first-married persons. "Remarried divorced people face unusual problems—self-doubt, communal skepticism, extra financial burdens, and extraordinary dyadic adjustment—yet most of them rate their marriages 'very happy,' " Duberman emphasizes, "and most of them stay married in spite of the fact that they fear divorce less than those who have never experienced it" (pp. 204–205).

Andrew Cherlin (1978) has proposed that by virtue of its being an "incomplete" institution, lacking the clearly defined societal guidelines of marriage, remarriage has built into it various complexities and strains that increase the risk of a breakup. On the other hand, Furstenberg and Spanier (1984:191–192), while not denying that remarriage creates a much more difficult and less predictable family life that affects couples, children, and extended-kinship ties, take issue with Cherlin's hypothesis. They suggest, instead, that persons who have experienced divorce

in the past "may be less committed to marital continuity for its own sake" and are simply "more averse to remaining in an unhappy marriage or remarriage." In contrast, they emphasize, "Many never-divorced persons . . . have marriages of exceptionally low quality but either would not consider divorce or would consider but reject it as a solution." Furstenberg and Spanier call for further research on ways in which individuals and couples deal creatively with problem-solving in "culturally uncharted situations." They are persuaded that "it is more useful to explore the adaptive mechanisms that remarried couples invent for dealing with their everyday problems than to stress the hazards they are likely to face in returning to married life" (p. 194).

How satisfactory are remarriages? "So far," say sociologists Norval Glenn and Charles Weaver (1977), "divorce and remarriage seem to have been rather effective mechanisms for replacing poor marriages with good ones and for keeping the mean level of marital happiness fairly high" (p. 336). After analyzing data on remarriage and reported happiness, they concluded that "remarriages of divorced persons which do not quickly end in divorce probably are, as a whole, almost as successful as intact first marriages" (p. 331). Of course, the concept "happiness" is subjective, can be difficult to measure, and can mean many things. Glenn and Weaver scored marital happiness according to how respondents answered the question: "Taking all things together, how would you describe your marriage? Would you say your marriage is very happy, pretty happy, or not too happy?"

Another study (Albrecht, 1979) used a comparative approach: how did the remarriage compare in happiness with the first marriage, with the perceived happiness of acquaintances' marriages, and with the happiness the remarried persons had *expected* to find in the new marriages? Respondents tended to rate their remarriages better on all three counts.

Similarly, Furstenberg and Spanier (1984:84) found in their study that "the second marriage usually benefits by comparison to the first. It is as if individuals moved from a dreary, unpleasant job to a better one." The men and women in their sample spoke of now being with the "right person," someone who let them "be themselves," and reported better communication, decision-making, handling of conflict, and division of labor in their second marriages.

In still another study, the researcher focused on "global happiness" rather than on *marital* happiness alone and found indications that overall, "remarried women are *less* happy than women in first marriages" while "remarried men report themselves significantly *more* happy than men in intact first marriages" (White, 1979:869). Divorced women may feel forced into remarriage because of economic circumstances and the difficulties of rearing children alone. Such factors, among others, "suggest the hypothesis that divorced women wanting to remarry are

not in a favorable marriage market, and, to continue the economic analogy, may have to settle for inferior goods," sociologist Lynn White points out. "Divorced men, however, are in a much more favorable market, such that remarriage should be a sign of desire rather than necessity, and of a wide rather than a narrow range of alternatives" (p. 871).

BLENDED FAMILIES

After divorces involving children, remarriage involves not only two *persons* but means the blending of two *families*. "The child of divorced parents who both remarry will have two biological parents, two step-parents, biological siblings, step and half siblings, up to eight grandparents (even more if any grandparents had divorced and remarried) and any number of additional extended relatives through the new spouses of the biological parents," Ahrons (1979:499–500) points out.

When divorced persons combine their families through remarriage, the resultant family is variously called a "reconstituted" family (Duberman, 1975), a "blended" family, a "merged" family, or a "step" family (Roosevelt and Lofas, 1977). The term *step* comes from an old English word meaning "to bereave." A bereaved husband or wife who took a new spouse thereby gave the bereaved children a new parent—a "step" parent.

When reconstituted families were more likely to come about because of the death of a father or mother rather than the parents' divorce, the term *stepparent* made sense, argues Bohannan (1970:119), but it makes less sense now—at least in cases of divorce. In remarriage after divorce, the child still has both biological parents and thus "the stepparent is an addition, not a replacement." The remarriage of one or both parents leaves all parties concerned not only with inade-

REMARRIAGE AFTER THE DEATH OF A SPOUSE

I married a widower who had a 7-year-old boy and a 4-year-old girl. The three of them (father and children) proposed. My "son" said, "Will you marry us?" I willingly became wife and mother with one "I do."

Our first baby was born just before our first anniversary, but before she was born, I had already applied to adopt my husband's two children. This was my way of covering three issues. For one thing, this made all my children full brothers and sisters. In the second place, they would always be mine. I had a terrible fear that if something happened to my husband, someone would take my children away. Most importantly, I felt that in time to come my children would realize how much they meant to me by my making sure they were legally mine.

The greatest joy of my life may well have been the time my oldest daughter asked me if I could love an adopted grandchild. When I said that it wasn't fair to ask me because I have adopted children, she said, "Oh, Mommy, I forgot." Maybe that's the answer to Mrs. Maddox [referring to an earlier article on problems in stepparenting]. In our house we forgot.

Sue Herbach
Delmar, N.Y.

SOURCE: "Letters" department, *The New York Times Magazine,* September 19, 1976, pp. 91–92.

quate kinship terms but also without helpful guidelines for behavior in these new relationships.

Of course, *either* husband or wife may be widowed or may be the parent who has custody of the children after divorce and thus may bring a new spouse into the home. But since traditionally, mothers, more than fathers, have been awarded child custody, a common pattern in remarriage after divorce is the mother/children/stepfather family form. At the same time, the children's biological father is likely to be involved in their lives to some degree—although in some cases he may feel pushed aside. Ruth Roosevelt and Jeannette Lofas (1977), authors of a book on remarriage and steprelationships, speak of this situation:

> When the ex remarries, the parent without custody is presented with the hard fact of a new person in his old place. This other person is his day-to-day replacement in the home with his children. And he didn't even choose the person. At the same time, he still continues to pay out child support.

> It hurts. A father hears his children calling another man Dad. Sometimes he hears them calling himself by his first name rather than Dad. One father wrote a letter to his former wife: "I have lost everything surrounding the relationship. At least let me keep my title and my name. Ask her to call me Dad, not Barry. Please." (p. 165)

Research on blended families has been limited, methodologically flawed, and has yielded inconsistent findings (Esses and Campbell, 1984; Clingempeel et al., 1984). While admittedly complex factors are involved in the relationships that make up such families, research has not supported the fairy-tale fiction that stepparents are cruel

STEPPARENTHOOD IN THE BEGINNING STAGES

Acting on their normal eagerness to be liked, most stepparents reach out to their stepchildren, only to find them rejecting or indifferent. "For two whole years Julie would march in the front door for weekend visits, walk right past me and throw her arms around her father." It is now known that for most children every move toward a stepparent places a child in a loyalty conflict ("If I love my stepfather, have I betrayed my father?"). Furthermore while divorced or widowed adults may be eager to move on, children often struggle for many years with their grief over the breakup of their original family. This original family has been replaced by a single parent family with its intimate parent-child relationship. The stepparent now threatens to dislodge the child once more in order to create a new couple relationship. Unfortunately, all too few stepparents have information about these threats and conflicts, leaving many stepparents straining to make contact, withdrawing in defeat, or alternating between the two.

SOURCE: Patricia L. Papernow, "The Stepfamily Cycle: An Experiential Model of Stepfamily Development, *Family Relations, 33* (July 1984), p. 358.

and unloving nor the generalization that the remarriage of a custodial parent is somehow harmful to children (Ganong and Coleman, 1984). There can be satisfactory remarriages and unsatisfactory remarriages—just as is true of first marriages. And some remarriages may be beneficial to the children involved while others may be detrimental in some way.

Therefore, one team of researchers takes pains to point out that after carefully comparing children in stepfather families with those in natural-parent families, they found that the social-psychological and social characteristics of the two groups indicated no substantial differences associated with the particular family form in which the children lived (Wilson et al., 1975). "The child who is part of a stepfather family may have a predominantly positive, predominantly negative, or mixed experience in that family," say these social scientists, in urging public-policy makers and service agencies not to offer services "to stepfather families (indeed to all

forms of reconstituted families) with a categorical assumption that such families are inevitably inferior to natural-parent families for the well-being of the child" (p. 535; see also Ganong and Coleman, 1984). Many persons who grow up in blended families report positive feelings about their experiences and feelings of affection toward their stepparents (Bernard, 1956). This is not to deny the special problems faced in reconstituted families with their multiple relationships, but it does mean that such problems need not be considered insurmountable (Roosevelt and Lofas, 1977).

We have already seen that divorce is a process and remarriage is a process. Similarly, some family scholars take pains to emphasize that the *formation of a stepfamily* is also a process, involving various stages of development (Papernow, 1984; Mills, 1984). The development of a family consensus on various aspects of life in a blended family takes place gradually. It requires *time* to develop feelings of closeness and to work out rules, boundaries, new rituals, and comfortable roles in the restructured family. "They do not develop instantaneously in first families and they cannot be expected to do so in remarriages," writes Marilyn Ihinger-Tallman (1984:485)

CHAPTER HIGHLIGHTS

Divorce, like marriage, is a *process*, and it involves many aspects: emotional, legal, and economic. Statistics on divorce are often misused and sensationalized, and great care must be taken when assessing divorce trends and projecting the likelihood of eventual marital dissolution. Over the past century, changing attitudes toward divorce appear to be rooted in two basic ideals: (1) a concern for the individual's rights and best interests and (2) a demanding view of marriage, with high expectations for companionship, empathy, affection, and self-actualization. These changing attitudes are reflected in laws, religious rethinking, and actual statistics (5.0 divorces per 1,000 population in 1983, as compared to 0.5 when divorce statistics were first collected, in 1867).

After divorce, the ex-spouses may experience grief and a redefinition of themselves as they take on *new roles* and leave old ones (husband and wife). At the same time, to one degree or another, they must continue their roles as parents, including working out satisfactory child-custody arrangements from a variety of possibilities. Studies of the effects of divorce on the children involved are inconclusive and inconsistent, but one finding has emerged repeatedly: it may be far more distressing for a child to continue living in a conflict-ridden home than to come from a home disrupted by divorce. Some behavioral scientists emphasize that no *one* answer can be given to the question of the impact of divorce on children and suggest research on the multiple issues surrounding the experience of divorce, examining what factors are most troubling to children and why.

After divorce, remarriage is popular—although in recent years, remarriage rates for both divorced and widowed persons have been dropping. This may indicate more caution and more deliberate weighing of costs and rewards before entering a new marriage. Although remarriages are somewhat more likely to end in divorce than are first marriages, those that remain intact are apt to be considered highly satisfactory to the persons involved. Sometimes remarriage involves uniting two families rather than two persons only, thus forming what is variously called the *blended family,* the *merged family,* the *reconstituted family,* or the *step family.* The formation of such a family also needs to be viewed as a process, involving various stages.

REFERENCES

Abbott, Douglas, and Gene H. Brody
1985 "The relationship of child age, gender, and number of children to the marital adjustment of wives." *Journal of Marriage and the Family* 47(February):77–84.

Abrahamson, Mark
1978 *Functionalism.* Englewood Cliffs, NJ: Prentice-Hall.

Acker, Joan
1973 "Women and social stratification: A case of intellectual sexism." *American Journal of Sociology* 78:936–945.

Adams, Bert N.
1968 *Kinship in an Urban Setting.* Chicago: Markham.
1970 "Isolation, function, and beyond: American kinship in the 1960's." *Journal of Marriage and the Family* 32(November):575–597.

Adams, Margaret
1971 "The single woman in today's society: A reappraisal." *The American Journal of Orthopsychiatry* 41:776–786. Reprinted in Arlene Skolnick and Jerome Skolnick (eds.), *Intimacy, Family, and Society,* Boston: Little, Brown, 1974.
1976 *Single Blessedness.* New York: Basic Books.

Ade-Ridder, Linda, and Timothy H. Brubaker
1983 "The quality of long-term marriages." Pp. 21–30 in Timothy H. Brubaker (ed.), *Family Relationships in Later Life.* Beverly Hills, CA: Sage.

Ahrons, Constance
1979 "The binuclear family." *Alternative Lifestyles* 2(November):499–515.
1980 "Divorce: A crisis of family transition and change." *Family Relations* 29(October):533–540.

Aird, John S.
1972 "Population policy and demographic prospects in the People's Republic of China." Bethesda, MD: Center for Population Research. National Institute for Child Health and Human Development.

The Alan Guttmacher Institute
1979 *Abortions and the Poor: Private Morality, Public Responsibility.* New York: The Alan Guttmacher Institute.

Albrecht, Stan L.
1979 "Correlates of marital happiness among the remarried." *Journal of Marriage and the Family* 41(November):857–867.
1980 "Reactions and adjustments to divorce: Differences in the experiences of males and females." *Family Relations* 29(January):59–68.

Aldous, Joan
1978 *Family Careers: Developmental Change in Families.* New York: John Wiley & Sons.
1981 "From dual-earner to dual-career families and back again." *Journal of Family Issues* 2(June):115–125.

Aldridge, Delores P.
1973 "The changing nature of interracial marriage in Georgia: A research note." *Journal of Marriage and the Family* 35:641–642.

Alexander, C. Norman, Jr., and Richard Simpson
1971 "Balance theory and distributive justice." Pp. 69–80 in Herman Turk and Richard Simpson (eds.), *Institutions and Social Exchange.* Indianapolis: Bobbs-Merrill.

Allen, Craig M., and Murray Straus
1980 "Resources, power, and husband-wife violence." Pp. 188–208 in Straus and Hotaling (eds.).

Allen, Suzanne M., and Richard A. Kalish
1984 "Professional women and marriage." *Journal of Marriage and The Family* 46(No. 2, May):375–382.

Altman, Dennis
1971 *Homosexual Oppression and Liberation.* New York: Outerbridge and Lizard. Avon Books edition.

Alzate, Heli
1978 "Sexual behavior of Colombian female university students." *Archives of Sexual Behavior* 7(January):43–54.

Anderson, Stephen A., Candyce S. Russell, and Walter R. Schumm
1983 "Perceived marital quality and family life-cycle categories: A further analysis." *Journal of Marriage and the Family* 45:127–139.

Andrews, Lori B.
1984 "The stork market: The law of the new reproduction technologies." *American Bar Association Journal* 70(August):50–56.

Angrist, Shirley A.
1969 "The study of sex roles." *Journal of Social Issues* 25:215–233.

Appelbaum, Eileen
1981 *Back to Work: Determinants of Women's Successful Re-entry.* Boston: Auburn House.

Arafat, Ibethaj., and Betty Yorburg
1973 "On living together without marriage." *Journal of Sex Research* 9:97–106.

Arizpe, Lourdes
1977 "Women in the informal labor sector: The case of Mexico City. *Signs* 3(Autumn):25–37.

Ashley, Paul P.
1978 *Oh Promise Me But Put It in Writing.* New York: McGraw-Hill.

Atkinson, Maxine P., and Jacqueline Boles
1984 "WASP (Wives as senior partners)." *Journal of Marriage and the Family* 46(November):861–870.

Atkinson, Maxine P., and Becky L. Glass
1985 "Marital age heterogamy and homogamy, 1900 to 1980." *Journal of Marriage and the Family* 47(August):685–691.

Babic, Anne L.
1984 "Flexible retirement: An international survey of public notices." *Aging and Work* 7(1):21–36.

Bach, G., and P. Wyden
1968 *The Intimate Enemy.* New York: Morrow.

Bachrach, Christine A.
1983 "Adoption as a means of family formation: Data from the National Survey of Family Growth." *Journal of Marriage and the Family* 45(November):859–865.

1985 "Characteristics of cohabiting women in the United States: Evidence from the National Survey of Family Growth, Cycle III." Paper presented at the annual meeting of the Population Association of America, Boston, March 27–30, 1985. Summarized in "Digest," *Family Planning Perspectives* 17(July/August, 1985):179–180.

1986 "Adoption plans, adopted children, and adoptive mothers." *Journal of Marriage and the Family* 48(May):243–253.

Bachrach, C. A., and M. C. Horn
1985 "Marriage and first intercourse, marital dissolution and remarriage: United States, 1982." *Advance Data from Vital and Health Statistics,* no. 107.

Bahr, Howard M.
1976 "The kinship role." Pp. 61–79 in F. Ivan Nye (ed.), *Role Structure and Analysis of the Family.* Beverly Hills, CA: Sage.

Bahr, Stephen J.
1983 "Marital dissolution laws: Impact of recent changes for women." *Journal of Family Issues* 4(September):455–466.

Balakrishnan, T. R., Karol Krotki, and Evelyne Lapierre-Adamcyk
1985 "Contraception use in Canada, 1984." *Family Planning Perspectives* 17(September/October):209–215.

Ball, Richard E., and Lynn Robbins
1986 "Marital status and life satisfaction among Black Americans." *Journal of Marriage and the Family* 48(May):389–394.

Balswick, Jack O., and Charles W. Peek
1971 "The inexpressive male: A tragedy of American society." *The Family Coordinator* 20:363–368.

Bane, Mary Jo
1979 "Marital disruption and the lives of children." Pp. 276–286 in Levinger and Moles (eds.).

Barbarin, Oscar, Diane Hughes, and Mark Chesler
1985 Stress, coping, and marital functioning among parents of children with cancer." *Journal of Marriage and the Family* 47(May):473–480.

Bardwick, Judith M.
1973 "Sex, maternity and self-esteem." Paper

read at the National Institute for Health and Human Development and the Center for Population Research Conference on Family and Fertility. June 13–16, Belmont, Elkridge, MD. Mimeographed.

Barker-Benfield, Ben
1972 "The spermatic economy: A nineteenth century view of sexuality." Feminist Studies 1, (1). Reprinted in Michael Gordon (ed.), *The American Family in Social-Historical Perspective.* New York: St. Martin's. Pp. 336–372.

Barnhart, Elizabeth
1975 "Friends and lovers in a lesbian counter-culture community." Pp. 90–115 in Nona Glazer-Malbin (ed.), *Old Family/New Family.* New York: D. Van Nostrand.

Barranti, Chrystal C. Ramirez
1985 "The grandparent/grandchild relationship: Family resource in an era of voluntary bonds." *Family Relations* 34:343–352.

Barron, Milton L.
1972 *The Blending American.* Chicago: Quadrangle.

Bartell, Gilbert
1971 *Group Sex.* New York: Wyden.

Batchelor, Edward, Jr. (ed.)
1980 *Homosexuality and Ethics.* New York: Pilgrim Press.

Bean, Kathleen S.
1985–86 "Grandparent visitation: Can the parent refuse?" *Journal of Family Law* 24(3):393–449.

Beck, Scott H., and Rubye W. Beck
1984 "The formation of extended households during middle age." *Journal of Marriage and the Family* 46(May):277–287.

Becker, Gary S.
1973 "A theory of marriage." *Journal of Political Economy* 81:813–845.

Beckham, Kathryn, and Jeffrey A. Giordano
1986 "Illness and impairment in elderly couples: Implications for marital therapy." *Family Relations* 34(April):257–264.

Beit-Hallahmi, Benjamin, and Albert Rabin
1977 "The Kibbutz as a social experiment and as a child-rearing laboratory," *American Psychologist* vol. 32(July), as reprinted in *Family Factbook* (Chicago: Marquis Academic Media, 1978), pp. 272–281.

Bell, Alan, and Martin Weinberg
1978 *Homosexualities: A study of diversity among men and women.* New York: Simon and Schuster.

Bell, Alan, Martin Weinberg, and Sue Kiefer Hammersmith
1981 *Sexual Preference.* Bloomington: Indiana University Press.

Bell, Robert R.
1966 *Premarital Sex in a Changing Society.* Englewood Cliffs, NJ: Prentice-Hall.
1971 *Social Deviance.* Homewood, IL: Dorsey.
1974 "Married sex: How uninhibited can a woman dare to be?" (with Norman Lobenz). *Redbook* 143(September):176.
1975 "Swinging: Separating the sexual from friendship." Pp. 150–168 in Nona Glazer-Malbin (ed.), *Old Family/New Family.* New York: D. Van Nostrand.

Bell, Robert R., and J. B. Chaskes
1970 "Premarital sexual experience among coeds, 1958–1968." *Journal of Marriage and the Family* 32:81–84.

Belsky, Jay
1985 "Exploring individual differences in marital change across the transition to parenthood: The role of violated expectations." *Journal of Marriage and the Family* 47(November):1037–1044.

Belsky, Jay, Mary Lang, and Michael Rovine
1985 "Stability and change in marriage across the transition to parenthood: A second study." *Journal of Marriage and the Family* 47(November):855–865.

Belsky, Jay, and Michael Rovine
1984 "Social-network contact, family support, and the transition to parenthood." *Journal of Marriage and the Family* 46(May):455–462.

Belsky, Jay, Graham B. Spanier, and Michael Rovine
1983 "Stability and change in marriage across the transition of parenthood." *Journal of Marriage and the Family* 45(August):567–577.

Belsky, Jay, and Laurence D. Steinberg
1978 "The effects of day care: A critical review." *Child Development* 49:929–949.

Bem, Sandra Lipsitz
1975 "Sex-role adaptability: One consequence of psychological androgyny." *Journal of Personality and Social Psychology* 31:634–643.
1976 "Beyond androgyny: Some presumptuous prescriptions for a liberated sexual identity." In A. G. Kaplan and J. P. Beene (eds.), *Beyond Sex Role Stereotypes: Readings Toward a Psychology of Androgyny.* Boston: Little, Brown.

1977 "Psychological androgyny," Pp. 319–324 in Alice G. Sargent, *Beyond Sex Roles.* St. Paul, MN: West Publishing.

1983 "Gender schema theory and its implications for child development: Raising gender-aschematic children in a gender-schematic society." *Signs* 8(4):598–616.

Bengtson, Vern

1973 *The Social Psychology of Aging.* Indianapolis: Bobbs-Merrill.

Bengtson, Vern L., and Lillian Troll

1978 "Youth and their parents: Feedback and intergenerational influence on socialization." Pp. 215–240 in Lerner and Spanier. (eds.).

Bengtson, Vern, and Joan F. Robertson (eds.)

1985 *Grandparenthood.* Beverly Hills, CA: Sage.

Benston, Margaret

1969 "The political economy of women's liberation." *Monthly Rev.* (September):3–4.

Bentler, Peter, and Michael Newcomb

1978 "Longitudinal study of marital success and failure." *Journal of Consulting and Clinical Psychology* 46(5):1053–1070.

Berardo, Felix M.

1967 "Kinship interaction and communications among space-age migrants." *Journal of Marriage and the Family* 29(August):541–554.

1970 "Survivorship and social isolation: The case of the aged widower." *The Family Coordinator* 19:11–25.

Berelson, Bernard

1972 "The value of children: A toxonomical essay." *The Population Council Annual Report—1972.* New York: The Population Council.

1973 "Population growth policy in developed countries." Pp. 145–160 in C. Westoff et al., *Toward the End of Growth: Population in America.* Englewood Cliffs, NJ: Prentice-Hall.

Berger, David, and Morton Wenger

1973 "The ideology of virginity." *Journal of Marriage and the Family* 35:666–676.

Berger, Miriam E.

1971 "Trial marriage: Harnessing the trend constructively." *The Family Coordinator* 20:38–43.

Bernard, Jessie

1956 *Remarriage. A Study of Marriage.* New York: The Dryden Press.

1964 *Academic Women.* University Park: Pennsylvania State University Press.

1966 "Note on educational homogamy in Negro-White and White-Negro marriages." *Journal of Marriage and the Family* 3:274.

1970 "No news, but new ideas." Pp. 3–25 in Paul Bohannan (ed.), *Divorce and After.* Garden City, NY: Doubleday.

1972 *The Future of Marriage.* New York: World.

1974 *The Future of Motherhood.* New York: The Dial Press.

1979 "Foreword," pp. ix–xv in George Levinger and Oliver C. Moles (eds.), *Divorce and Separation: Context, Causes, and Consequences.* New York: Basic Books.

1985 "No-fault—Whose fault?" (A review of Lenore Weitzman, *The Divorce Revolution*), *The Women's Review of Books* 3(November):1,3,4.

Bernard, J. L., and M. L. Bernard

1984 "The abusive male seeking treatment: Jekyll and Hyde." *Family Relations* 33(October):543–547.

Bernard, J. L., S. L. Bernard, and M. L. Bernard

1985 "Courtship violence and sex-typing." *Family Relations* 34(October):573–576.

Berne, Eric

1964 *Games People Play.* New York: Grove.

Besanceney, Paul H.

1970 *Interfaith Marriages: Who and Why.* New Haven, CT: College and University Press.

Bilezikian, Gilbert

1985 *Beyond Sex Roles.* Grand Rapids, MI: Baker Book House.

Billingsley, Andrew

1968 *Black Families in White America.* Englewood Cliffs, NJ: Prentice-Hall.

Bird, Caroline

1979 *The Two-Paycheck Marriage.* New York: Rawson, Wade Publishers.

Blackwell, Elizabeth

1894 *The Human Element in Sex.* London: J. A. Churchill. Excerpt, "On sexual passion in men and women," reprinted in Cott, 1972, pp. 299–303.

Blake, Judith

1979 "Is zero preferred? American attitudes toward childlessness in the 1970's." *Journal of Marriage and the Family* 41(May):245–257.

Blalock, H. M., and P. H. Wilken

1979 *Intergroup Processes: A Micro-Macro Perspective.* New York: Free Press.

Blasi, Joseph R.

1981 "Review of *Gender and Culture: Kibbutz Women Revisited* by Melford E. Spiro,"

Journal of Marriage and the Family 43(May):451–456.

Blau, Peter
1964   *Exchange and Power in Social Life.* New York: Wiley.

Blau, Peter, and Otis Dudley Duncan
1967   *The American Occupational Structure.* New York: Wiley.

Blau, Zena
1973   *Old Age in a Changing Society.* New York: New Viewpoints.

Blood, Robert O., Jr.
1963   "The husband-wife relationship" Pp. 282–305 in Nye and Hoffman, 1963.
1967   *Love Match and Arranged Marriage.* New York: Free Press.
1969   *Marriage.* 2nd ed. New York: Free Press.

Blood, Robert O., Jr., and Donald M. Wolfe
1960   *Husbands and Wives.* New York: Free Press.

Bloom, B.
1963   "Definitional concepts of the crisis concept." *Journal of Consulting Psychology* 27:42.

Bloom, Bernard L., and Konnie R. Kindle
1985   "Demographic factors in the continuing relationship between spouses." *Family Relations* 34(July):375–381.

Bloom, Bernard, Stephen White, and Shirley Asher
1979   "Marital disruption as a stressful life event." Pp. 181–200 in Levinger and Moles (eds.), 1979.

Blumstein, Philip, and Pepper Schwartz
1983   *American Couples: Money, Work, Sex.* New York: William Morrow.

Boak, Arthur
1955   *Manpower Shortage and the Fall of the Roman Empire in the West.* Ann Arbor: University of Michigan Press.

Bock, E. Wilbur, and Irving Webber
1972   "Suicide among the elderly: Isolating widowhood and mitigating alternatives." *Journal of Marriage and the Family* 34:24–31.

Bohannan, Paul (ed.)
1970   *Divorce and After.* Garden City, NY: Doubleday.

Bolig, Rosemary, Peter J. Stein, and Patrick McKenry
1984   "The self-advertisement approach to dating: Male-female differences." *Family Relations* 33(October):587–592.

Booth, Alan, and Lynn White
1980   "Thinking about divorce." *Journal of Marriage and the Family* 42(August):605–616.

Borland, Dolores Cabic
1982   "A cohort analysis approach to the empty-nest syndrome among three ethnic groups of women: A theoretical position." *Journal of Marriage and the Family* 44(February):117–129.

Borman, Kathryn M., Daisy Quarm, and Sarah Gideonse (eds.)
1984   *Women in the Workplace: Effects on Families.* Norwood, NJ: Ablex.

Boserup, Ester
1977   Preface to special issue on "Women and national development." *Signs* 3(Autumn):ix–xiv.

Boswell, John
1980   *Christianity, Social Tolerance, and Homosexuality.* Chicago: University of Chicago Press.

Bott, Elizabeth
1957   *Family and Social Network.* London: Tavistock.

Boulding, Elise
1976   "Familial constraints on women's work roles." *Signs* 1(Spring):95–117.

Bourne, Patricia, and Norma Wikler
1976   "Dual roles and double binds: Women in medical school," Paper presented at the 1976 annual meetings of the American Sociological Association in New York City.

Bowen, William, and T. Aldrich Finegan
1969   *The Economics of Labor Force Participation.* Princeton, NJ: Princeton University Press.

Bower, Donald, and Victor Christopherson
1977   "University student cohabitation: A regional comparison of selected attitudes and behavior." *Journal of Marriage and the Family* 39(August):447–453.

Bozett, Frederick
1980   "Gay fathers: How and why they disclose their homosexuality to their children." *Family Relations* 29(April):173–179.
1981   "Gay fathers: Identity conflict resolution through integrative sanctioning." *Alternative Lifestyles* 4(February):90–107.

Bratt, Carolyn S.
1984   "Incest statutes and the fundamental right of marriage: Is Oedipus free to marry?" *Family Law Quarterly* 18(Fall):257–309.

Brawley, Benjamin
1921   *A Social History of the American Negro.* New York: Macmillan.

Breines, Wini, and Linda Gordon
1983 "The new scholarship on family violence." *Signs* 8(Spring):490–531.

Bremner, William J., and David M. de Kretser
1975 "Contraceptives for males." *Signs* 1(Winter):387–396.

Brenton, Myron
1974 *Friendship*. New York: Stein and Day.

Brickman, Philip (ed.)
1974 *Social Conflict*. Lexington, MA: Heath.

Briggs, Kenneth
1976 "Jews said to ease view on marriage." *The New York Times* (May), p. 29.

Brim, O.
1976 "Theories of the male mid-life crisis." *Counseling Psychologist* 6:2–9.

Bristor, Martha Wingard
1984 "The birth of a handicapped child—A wholistic model for grieving." *Family Relations* 33(January):25–32.

Broderick, Carlfred
1979 *Couples*. New York: Simon and Schuster.

Bronfenbrenner, Urie
1958 "Socialization and social class through time and space." Pp. 400–425 in E. E. Maccoby, T. M. Newcomb, and E. L. Hartley (eds.), *Readings in Social Psychology*, 3d ed. New York: Holt.

Brown, Bruce W.
1980 "Wife-employment, marital equality, and husband-wife violence." Pp. 176–187 in Murray A. Straus and Gerald T. Hotaling (eds.).

Brown, George, and Michael Rutter
1966 "The measurement of family activities and relationships." *Human Relations* 19:241–263.

Brown, Howard
1976 *Familiar Faces, Hidden Lives*. New York: Harcourt Brace Jovanovich.

Brown, Roger
1965 *Social Psychology*. New York: Free Press.

Brownlee, W. Elliot, and Mary M. Brownlee
1976 *Women in the American Economy: A Documentary History, 1675–1929*. New Haven, CT: Yale University Press.

Brubaker, Timothy H.
1983 (ed.) *Family Relationships in Later Life*. Beverly Hills, CA: Sage.
1985 *Later Life Families*. Beverly Hills, CA: Sage.

Buber, Martin
1958 *I and Thou*. New York: Scribner's.

Buckhout, R., et al.
1971 "The war on people: A scenario for population control?" Unpublished manuscript. California State College, Hayward.

Buckley, Walter
1967 *Sociology and Modern Systems Theory*. Englewood Cliffs, NJ: Prentice-Hall.

Bukstel, Lee, Gregory Roeder, Peter Kilmann, James Laughlin, and Wayne Sotile
1978 "Projected extramarital sexual involvement in unmarried college students." *Journal of Marriage and the Family* 40(May):337–340.

Bumpass, Larry, and Ronald Rindfuss
1979 "Children's experience of marital disruption." *American Journal of Sociology* 85:49–65.

Bumpass, Larry L., and Charles F. Westoff
1970 *The Later Years of Childbearing*. Princeton, NJ: Princeton University Press.

Burgess, Ernest W., Harvey Locke, and Mary Thomes
1963 *The Family: From Institution to Companionship*. 3d ed. New York: American.

Burgess, E. W., and P. Wallen
1953 *Engagement and Marriage*. Philadelphia: Lippincott.

Buric, O., and A. Zelevic
1967 "Family authority, marital satisfaction and the social network in Yugoslavia." *Journal of Marriage and the Family* 29:325–336.

Buxembaum, Alva
1973 Women's rights and the class struggle." *Political Affairs* 52:22.

Cain, Glen G.
1966 *Married Women in the Labor Force*. Chicago: University of Chicago Press.

Cain, Leonard, Jr.
1964 "Life course and social structure." In R. E. L. Faris (ed.), *Handbook of Modern Sociology*. Chicago: Rand McNally.

Calhoun, Arthur W.
1919 *A Social History of the American Family*. Volumes 1 and 2. Reprint. New York: Barnes and Noble, 1960.

Calhoun, Lawrence G., and James W. Selby
1980 "Voluntary childlessness, involuntary childlessness, and having children: A study of social perceptions." *Family Relations* 29:181–183.

Campbell, Frederick L., Brenda D. Townes, and Lee Roy Beach
1982 "Motivational bases of childbearing deci-

sions." Pp. 145–159 in Greer Litton Fox (ed.), *The Childbearing Decision.* Beverly Hills, CA: Sage.

Campbell, Helen
1893 *Women Wage Earners.* Reprint. New York: Arno Press, 1972.

Cargan, Leonard, and Matthew Melko
1982 *Singles: Myths and Realities.* Beverly Hills, CA: Sage.

Carlier, Auguste
1867 *Marriage in the United States.* New York: Leypoldt and Holt. Reprint. New York: Arno Press, 1972.

Carns, Donald E.
1969 "Religiosity, premarital sexuality and the American college student." Unpublished doctoral dissertation, Indiana University, Bloomington, IN.
1973 "Talking about sex: Notes on first coitus and the double sexual standard." *Journal of Marriage and the Family* 35:677–688.

Carroll, Kathy (ed.)
1978 *Sexuality and Aging.* Minneapolis: Ebenezer Center for Aging and Human Development.

Carter, Hugh, and Paul C. Glick
1970 *Marriage and Divorce: A Social and Economic Study.* Cambridge, MA: Harvard University Press.

Cazenave, Noel A.
1983 "Black male–black female relationships: The perceptions of 155 middle-class black men." *Family Relations* 32, no. 3(July):341–350.

Centers, R., B. Raven, and A. Rodrigues
1971 "Conjugal power structure: A reexamination." *American Sociological Review* 36:264–278.

Chafetz, Janet Saltzman
1978 *Masculine/Feminine or Human?* 2nd ed. Itasca, IL: F. E. Peacock.

Chen, Xiangming
1985 "The one-child population policy, modernization, and the extended Chinese family." *Journal of Marriage and the Family* 47(February):193–202.

Cherlin, Andrew
1978 "Remarriage as an incomplete institution." *American Journal of Sociology* 84:634–650.
1980 "Postponing marriage: The influence of young women's work expectations." *Journal of Marriage and the Family* 42, no. 2(May):355–365.

Cherlin, Andrew, and Frank F. Furstenberg, Jr.
1986 *The New American Grandparent: A Place*

in the Family, A Life Apart. New York: Basic Books.

Chesler, Phyllis
1985 *Mothers on Trial: The Battle for Children and Custody.* New York: McGraw-Hill.

Chesser, E.
1957 *The Sexual, Marital and Family Relations of English Women.* New York: Ray.

Chinchilla, Norma S.
1977 "Industrialization, monopoly capitalism, and women's work in Guatemala." *Signs* 3(Autumn):38–56.

Chisholm, Shirley
1970 *Unbought and Unbossed.* Boston: Houghton Mifflin.

Christensen, Harold T.
1968 "Children in the family: Relationship of number and spacing to marital success." *Journal of Marriage and the Family* 30:283–289.
1969 "The impact of culture and values." Pp. 155–159 in Carlfred Broderick and Jessie Bernard (eds.), *The Individual, Sex, and Society.* Baltimore: Johns Hopkins.

Christensen, Harold T., and Christina F. Gregg
1970 "Changing sex norms in America and Scandinavia." *Journal of Marriage and the Family* 32:616–627.

Cicirelli, Victor G.
1983 "Adult children and their elderly parents." Pp. 31–46 in Brubaker (ed.).

Cimons, Marlene
1985 "Study says infertility in women 20 to 24 tripled since 1965." L. A. Times–Washington Post News Service report. *Greensboro (NC) News and Record,* February 11, 1985.

Clark, H.
1968 *The Law of Domestic Relations in the United States.* St. Paul, MN: West.

Clatworthy, Nancy Moore
1975 "Living together." Pp. 67–89 in Nona Glazer-Malbin (ed.), *Old Family/New Family.* New York: D. Van Nostrand.

Clayton, Richard R., and Janet L. Bokemeier
1980 "Premarital sex in the seventies." *Journal of Marriage and the Family* 42(November):34–50.

Clayton, Richard, and Harwin Voss
1977 "Shacking up: Cohabitation in the 1970's." *Journal of Marriage and the Family* 39(May):273–283.

Clemens, Audra W., and Leland J. Axelson
1985 "The not-so-empty-nest: The return of the

fledgling adult." *Family Relations* 34(April):259–264.

Clingempeel, W. Glen, Eulalee Brand, and Richard Ievoli
1984 "Stepparent-stepchild relationships in stepmother and stepfather families: A multimethod study." *Family Relations* 33(July): 465–473.

Coale, Ansley J.
1974 "The history of the human population." *Scientific American* 231(September):41–51.

Cohen, Jessica Field
1979 "Male roles in mid-life." *The Family Coordinator* 28(October):465–471.

Cohen, Malcolm S.
1969 "Married women in the labor force: An analysis of participation rates." *Monthly Labor Review* 92(October):31–35.

Cole, Charles Lee
1977 "Cohabitation in social context." Pp. 62–79 in Roger W. Libby and Robert N. Whitehurst (eds.), *Marriage and Alternatives: Exploring Intimate Relationships.* Glenview, IL: Scott, Foresman.

Cole, Cynthia, and Hyman Rodman
1987 "When school-age children care for themselves: Issues for family life educators and parents." *Family Relations* 36(January):92–96.

Coleman, James S.
1966 "Female status and premarital sexual codes." *American Journal of Sociology* 72:217.

Collins, Randall
1971 "A conflict theory of sexual stratification." *Social Problems* 19:3–21.

Connecticut Mutual Life Insurance Company
1981 "The Connecticut Mutual Life Report on American Values in the '80s: The impact of belief." Hartford: Research conducted for Connecticut Mutual by Research and Forecasts Inc.

Coombs, Lolagene C.
1977 "Preferences for sex of children among U.S. couples." *Family Planning Perspectives* 9(November/December):259–265.

Cooper, Pamela, Barbara Cumber, and Robin Hartner
1978 "Decision-making patterns and postdecision adjustment of childfree husbands and wives." *Alternative Lifestyles* 1(February):71–94.

Cornell, Claire Pedrick, and Richard T. Gelles
1982 "Elder abuse: The status of current knowledge." *Family Relations* 31(July):457–465.

Coser, Lewis A.
1956 *The Functions of Social Conflict.* New York: Free Press.

Coser, Rose L. (ed.)
1964 *The Family: Its Structure and Functions.* New York: St. Martin's.

Cott, Nancy F. (ed.)
1972 *Root of Bitterness: Documents of the Social History of American Women.* New York: E. P. Dutton.

Cott, Nancy F.
1977 *The Bonds of Womanhood: "Women's Sphere" in New England, 1780–1835.* New Haven, CT: Yale University Press.

Cottrell, Ann Baker
1973 "Cross-national marriage as an extension of an international life style: A study of Indian-Western couples." *Journal of Marriage and the Family* 35:739–741.

Coverman, Shelley, and Joseph F. Sheley
1986 "Change in men's housework and child-care time, 1965–1975." *Journal of Marriage and the Family* 48(May):413–422.

Cowing, Cedric
1968 "Sex and preaching in the Great Awakening." *American Quarterly* 20:624–644.

Cox, Mary Jane Truesdall, and Lory Cease
1978 "Joint custody." *Family Advocate* 1(Summer):10–13, 42–44.

Cramer, Daniel W., Isaac Schiff, Stephen C. Schoenbaum, Mark Gibson, Serge Belisle, Bruce Albrecht, Robert J. Stillman, Merle J. Berger, Emery Wilson, Bruce V. Stadel, and Machelle Seibel
1985 "Tubal infertility and the intrauterine device." *New England Journal of Medicine* 312(April 11):941–947.

Cramer, J. C.
1980 "Fertility and female employment: Problems of causal direction." *American Sociological Review* (1980):167–190.

Croll, Elisabeth J.
1981 "Women in rural production and reproduction in the Soviet Union, China, Cuba, and Tanzania. Part I, 'Socialist development experiences.' and part II, 'Case studies.'" *Signs* 7(Winter):361–399.

Cromwell, R. E., and D. H. Olson (eds.)
1975 *Power in Families.* New York: Wiley.

Cuber, John, and Peggy Harroff
1965 *Sex and the Significant Americans.* Baltimore: Penguin.

Current Population Reports
(See U.S. Bureau of the Census.)

Cushner, Irvin M.
1986   "Reproductive technologies: New choices, new hopes, new dilemmas." *Family Planning Perspectives* 18(May/June):129–132.

Cutright, Phillips
1971   "Income and family events: Marital stability." *Journal of Marriage and the Family* 33:291–306.

1972a   "The teenage sexual revolution and the myth of an abstinent past." *Family Planning Perspectives* 4(1):24.

1972b   "Illegitimacy in the United States: 1920–1968." Commission on Population Growth and the American Future, Vol. 1: *Demographic and Social Aspects of Population Growth.* Washington, DC: U.S. Government Printing Office.

Cutright, Phillips, and Karen B. Cutright
1973   "Abortion: The court decision and some consequences of a constitutional amendment." Mimeographed. Bloomington: Department of Sociology, Indiana University.

Daling, J. R., N. S. Weiss, B. J. Metch, W. H. Chow, R. M. Soderstrom, D. E. Moore, L. R. Spadoni, and B. V. Stadel
1985   "Primary tubal infertility in relation to the use of an intrauterine device." *New England Journal of Medicine* 312:937–941.

D'Andrade, Roy G.
1966   "Sex differences and cultural institutions." Pp. 174–204 in Eleanor E. Maccoby (ed.), *The Development of Sex Differences,* Stanford, CA: Stanford University Press.

D'Antonio, William V.
1985   "The American Catholic Family: Signs of Cohesion and Polarization." *Journal of Marriage and the Family* 47(May):395–405.

Darity, William A., Jr., and Samuel L. Myers, Jr.
1984   "Does welfare dependency cause female headship? The case of the black family." *Journal of Marriage and the Family* 46(November):765–779.

Davidson, Kenneth M., Ruth Bader Ginsburg, and Herma Hill Kay
1974   *Sex-Based Discrimination: Text, Cases and Materials.* St. Paul, MN: West.

Davis, Elizabeth Gould
1971   *The First Sex.* New York: G. P. Putnam's.

Davis, Kingsley
1941   "Intermarriage in caste societies." *American Anthropologist* 43:376–395.

1960   "Legitimacy and the incest taboo," in Norman Bell and Ezra Vogel (eds.), *A Modern Introduction to the Family.* Glencoe, IL: Free Press.

Davis, Murray S.
1973   *Intimate Relations.* New York: Free Press.

Dean, G., and D. Gurak
1978   "Marital homogamy the second time around." *Journal of Marriage and the Family* 40(August):559–570.

DeLamater, John, and Patricia MacCorquodale
1978   "Premarital contraceptive use: A test of two models." *Journal of Marriage and the Family* 40(May):235–247.

1979   *Premarital Sexuality: Attitudes, Relationships, Behavior.* Madison: University of Wisconsin Press.

Dell, P. F., and A. S. Applebaum
1977   "Trigenerational enmeshment: Unresolved ties of single parents to family of origin." *American Journal of Orthopsychiatry* 47, no. 1:52–59.

DeMaris, Alfred, and Gerald R. Leslie
1984   "Cohabitation with the future spouse: Its influence upon marital satisfaction and communication." *Journal of Marriage and the Family* 46(February):77–84.

deMiranda, Glaura Vasques
1977   "Women's labor force participation in a developing society: The case of Brazil." *Signs* 3(Autumn):261–274.

Demos, John
1972   "Demography and psychology in the historical study of family life: A personal report." Pp. 561–569 in Laslett (ed.).

Denfeld, Duane
1974   "Dropouts from swinging: The marriage counselor as informant." Pp. 260–267 in Smith and Smith (eds.), 1974.

Denfeld, Duane, and Michael Gordon
1970   "The sociology of mate swapping: Or the family that swings together clings together." *Journal of Sex Research* 6(May):85–100.

De Rougemont, Denis
1940   *Love in the Western World.* New York: Harcourt, Brace.

Deutscher, Irwin
1962   "Socialization for postparental life." Pp. 508–523 in Arnold Rose (ed.), *Human Be-*

havior and Social Processes. Boston: Houghton Mifflin.

Dinitz, S., R. Dynes, and A. Clark
  1954 "Preference for male or female children: Traditional or affectional." *Journal of Marriage and Family Living* 16:128–130.

Dizard, Jan
  1968 *Social Change in the Family.* Chicago: Community and Family Study Center, University of Chicago.

Dobash, R. Emerson, and Russell P. Dobash
  1979 *Violence Against Wives: A Case Against the Patriarchy.* New York: Free Press.

Doherty, William J., and Hamilton I. McCubbin (guest eds.)
  1985 Special issue on "The Family and Health Care." *Family Relations* 34, No. 1(January).

Donovan, Patricia
  1986 "New reproductive technologies: Some legal dilemmas." *Family Planning Perspectives* 18(March/April):57–60.

Douglass, Richard L.
  1983 "Domestic neglect and abuse of the elderly: Implications for research and service." *Family Relations* 32(July):395–402.

Dowd, James J.
  1975 "Aging as exchange: A preface to theory." *Journal of Gerontology* 30:584–594.

Drabek, Thomas, William Key, Patricia Erickson, Juanita Crowe
  1975 "The impact of disaster on kin relationships." *Journal of Marriage and the Family* 37(August):481–494.

Draper, Thomas W.
  1981 "On the relationship between welfare and marital stability: A research note." *Journal of Marriage and the Family* 43(May):293–302.

Dressel, Paula, and W. Ray Avant
  1978 "Neogamy and older persons: An examination of alternatives for intimacy in the later years." *Alternative Life Styles* 1(February):13–36.

Driver, Anne Barstow
  1976 "Review essay: Religion." *Signs* 2(Winter):434–442.

Duberman, Lucile
  1975 *The Reconstituted Family.* Chicago: Nelson-Hall.
  1977 *Marriage and Other Alternatives.* 2nd ed. New York: Praeger.

Durkheim, Emile
  1893 *The Division of Labor in Society.* Translated by George Simpson. New York: Free Press edition, 1933.

Duvall, Evelyn M.
  1962 *Family Development.* 2nd edition. Philadelphia: J. B. Lippincott.

Dyer, Everett
  1963 "Parenthood as crisis: A re-study." *Marriage and Family Living* 25:196–201.

Earhart, Eileen, and Michael J. Sporakowski (guest editors)
  1984 Special issue on "The Family with Handicapped Members." *Family Relations* 33, no. 1(January).

Eber, Irene
  1976 "Images of women in recent Chinese fiction: Do women hold up half the sky?" *Signs* 2(Autumn):24–34.

Edleson, Jeffrey L., Zvi Eisikovits, and Edna Guttmann
  1985 "Men who batter women: A critical review of the evidence." *Journal of Family Issues* 6(June):229–247.

Edwards, Carolyn S.
  1981 "The cost of raising a child." *American Demographics* 3(7):24–29.

Edwards, John N., and Janice M. Saunders
  1981 "Coming apart: A model of the marital dissolution decision." *Journal of Marriage and the Family* 43(May):379–389.

Edwards, Margaret
  1985 "But does the new woman really want the new man?" *Working Woman* 10(May):54–58.

Edwards, Sharon R.
  1987 "Adolescent boys and sex: Irresponsible or neglected?" *SIECUS Report* XV (March-April):1-5.

Eekelaar, John, and Sanford Katz (eds.)
  1980 *Marriage and Cohabitation in Contemporary Societies: Areas of Legal, Social, and Ethical Change: An International and Interdisciplinary Study.* Toronto: Butterworths.

Ehrenreich, Barbara, Elizabeth Hess, and Gloria Jacobs
  1982 "A report on the sex crisis." *Ms.,* March:61–64, 87–88.

Ehrenreich, Barbara, and Jane O'Reilly
  1984 "Kate & Allie: Real women as friends." *TV Guide,* November 24, 1984, pp. 6–10.

Ehrhardt, A. A., R. Epstein, and J. Money
1968 "Fetal androgens and female gender identity in the early treated adrogenital syndrome." *Johns Hopkins Medical Journal* 122:160, as cited in Ramey, 1973.

Ehrhardt, Anke
1977 "Gender development." Paper read at the summer program of the Institute for Sex Research, Indiana University, July 28.

Ehrlich, Annette
1976 "The adaptable primates." *Human Behavior* 5(November):25–30.

Ehrmann, Winston
1957 "Some knowns and unknowns in research into human sex behavior." *Marriage and Family Living* 19:16–22.

Einbinder, Michael P.
1973–74 "The legal family—a definitional analysis." *Journal of Family Law* 13:781–802.

Eisler, Rianne Tennenhaus
1977 *Dissolution: No-Fault Divorce, Marriage, and the Future of Women.* New York: McGraw-Hill.

Elder, Glen H., Jr.
1975 "Age differentiation and the life course." Pp. 165–190 in *Annual Review of Sociology*, Vol. 1. Palo Alto, CA: Annual Reviews.

Emerson, Richard M.
1962 "Power-dependence relations." *American Sociological Review* 27:31–41.

Engel, John W.
1984 "Marriage in the People's Republic of China: Analysis of a New Law." *Journal of Marriage and the Family* 46(November):955–961.

Engels, Friedrich
1884 *The Origins of the Family, Private Property and the State.* Chicago: Charles H. Kerr, 1902 edition.

Erlanger, Howard S.
1974 "Social class differences in parents' use of physical punishment." Pp. 150–158 in Steinmetz and Straus (eds.).

Espenshade, Thomas J.
1973 *The Cost of Children in Urban United States.* Population Monograph Series, no. 14. Berkeley: University of California Institute of International Studies.
1984 *Investing in Children: New Estimates of Parental Expenditures.* Washington, DC: The Urban Institute Press.

Esses, Lillian, and Richard Campbell
1984 "Challenges in researching the remarried." *Family Relations* 33(July):415–424.

Etzkowitz, Henry
1971 "The male sister: Sexual separation of labor in society." *Journal of Marriage and the Family* 33:431–434.

Euripides
Hippolytus. Translated by David Grene. Pp. 231–291 in David Grene and Richmond Lattimore (eds.), *Greek Tragedies*, Vol. 1. Chicago: University of Chicago Press.

Everett, William, and Julie Everett
1975 "Childless marriages: A new vocation?" *U.S. Catholic* 40(May):38–39.

Family Life Educator
1982 "Information update: Infertility in men." Vol. 1, no. 2(Winter):10–11.

Family Planning Perspectives
1985a "Portrait of U.S. fertility shows average number of births, family-size differences are shrinking." Digest section. Vol. 17, no. 1(January/February):36–37.
1985b "Sterilizations exceed one million in 1983; vasectomies up sharply." Digest section. Vol. 17, no. 1(January/February):43.

Farber, Bernard
1964 *Family: Organization and Interaction.* San Francisco: Chandler.
1966 *Kinship and Family Organization* (ed.). New York: John Wiley.
1973 *Family and Kinship in Modern Society.* Glenview, IL: Scott, Foresman.

Fasteau, Marc Feigen
1974 *The Male Machine.* New York: McGraw-Hill.

Fawcett, James T. (ed.)
1972 *The Satisfactions and Costs of Children: Theories, Concepts, Methods.* A summary report and proceedings of the Workshop on Assessment of the Satisfactions and Costs of Children, April 27–29. Honolulu: East-West Population Institute.

Feazell, Carann Simpson, Raymond Sanchez Mayers, and Jeanne Deschner
1984 "Services for men who batter: Implications for programs and policies." *Family Relations* 33(April): 217–223.

Feldman, Harold
1971 "The effects of children on the family." Pp. 107–125 in Andree Michel (ed.), *Family Issues of Employed Women in Europe and America.* Leiden, Netherlands: E. J. Brill.
1981 "A comparison of intentional parents and in-

tentionally childless couples." *Journal of Marriage and the Family* 43(August):593–600.

Feldman, Harold, and Margaret Feldman
1973 "The relationship between the family and occupational functioning in a sample of rural women." Ithaca, NY: Department of Human Development and Family Studies, Cornell University.
1975 "The family life cycle: Some suggestions for recycling." *Journal of Marriage and the Family* 37(May):277–284.

Feldman, Saul, and Gerald Theilbar
1972 *Deviant Life Styles: Diversity in American Society.* Boston: Little, Brown.

Feline, Peter Gabriel
1975 *Him/Her/Self: Sex Roles in Modern America.* New York: Harcourt Brace Jovanovich and Mentor Books.

Felstein, Ivor
1970 *Sex in Later Life.* Baltimore: Penguin.

Ferriss, Abbott
1971 *Indicators of Trends in the Status of American Women.* New York: Russell Sage Foundation.

Field, Mark G., and Karin I. Flynn
1970 "Worker, mother, housewife: Soviet woman today." Pp. 257–284 in Georgene H. Seward and Robert C. Williamson (eds.), *Sex Roles in Changing Society.* New York: Random House.

Figes, Eva
1970 *Patriarchal Attitudes.* New York: Stein and Day.

Finkel, Madelon Lubin, and David J. Finkel
1975 "Sexual and contraceptive knowledge, attitudes, and behavior of male adolescents." *Family Planning Perspectives* 7(November/December):256–260.

Finlay, Barbara Agresti
1981 "Sex differences in correlates of abortion attitudes among college students." *Journal of Marriage and the Family* 43(August):571–582.

Fiorenza, Elisabeth Schussler
1983 *In Memory of Her: A Feminist Theological Reconstruction of Christian Origins.* New York: Crossroad.

Firestone, Shulamith
1970 *The Dialectic of Sex.* New York: Morrow.

Fisher, Bruce
1981 *Rebuilding: When Your Relationship Ends.* San Luis Obispo, CA: Impact.

Fitzpatrick, M. Louise
1977 "Review essay: Nursing." *Signs* 2(Summer):818–834.

Fogarty, Michael P., Rhona Rapoport, and Robert N. Rapoport
1971 *Sex, Career, and Family.* Beverly Hills, CA: Sage.

Foote, Nelson
1954 "Sex as play." *Social Problems* 1:159–164.

Forisha, Barbara Lusk
1978 *Sex Roles and Personal Awareness.* Morristown, NJ: General Learning Press.

Fornos, Werner
1985 "Emergency population fund proposed for 12 countries." World Population News Service *Popline* 7(April):1–2.

Forrest, Jacqueline Darroch
1986 "The end of IUD marketing in the United States: What does it mean for American Women?" *Family Planning Perspectives* 18 (March/April):52–57.

Forrest, Jacqueline Darroch, and Stanley K. Henshaw
1983 "What U.S. women think and do about contraception." *Family Planning Perspectives* 15(July/August):157–166.

Forrest, Jacqueline Darroch, Christopher Tietze, and Ellen Sullivan
1978 "Abortion in the United States, 1976-77." Family Planning Perspectives 10(September/October):271–279.

Fortier, Laurie M., and Richard L. Wanlass
1984 "Family crisis following the diagnosis of a handicapped child." *Family Relations* 33(January):13–24.

Fortney, Judith A.
1987 "Contraception for American Women 40 and over." *Family Planning Perspectives* 19(January/February):32–34.

Forward, Susan, and Craig Buck
1978 *Betrayal of Innocence: Incest and Its Devastation.* New York: J. P. Tarcher. Paperback edition, Penguin Books.

Foss, Joyce E.
1980 "The paradoxical nature of family relationships and family conflict." Pp. 115–135 in Straus and Hotaling (eds.).

Fowler, Elizabeth M.
1986 "Older workers filling the labor market." New York Times News Service report, *Greensboro (NC) News and Record,* January 19.

Fox, Greer Litton
1974 "Powerlessness, pragmatics, and resent-

ment: The female response to the male role in contraception." Paper presented at the Groves Conference on Marriage and the Family. Hot Springs, AZ. April. Mimeographed.

1977a " 'Nice girl': Social control of women through a value construct." *Signs* 2(Summer):805–817.

1977b "Sex-role attitudes as predictors of contraceptive use among unmarried university students." *Sex Roles* 3:265–283.

1982 *The Childbearing Decision: Fertility Attitudes and Behavior* (ed.). Beverly Hills, CA: Sage.

Francoeur, Robert T.
1985 "Reproductive technologies: New alternatives and new ethics." *SIECUS Report* 14(September):1–5.

Frankel, Lillian B.
1970 *This Crowded World.* Washington, DC: Population Reference Bureau.

Franklin, Anderson J., and Nancy Boyd-Franklin
1985 "A psychoeducational perspective on black parenting." Pp. 194–210 in McAdoo and McAdoo (eds.).

Franklin, Benjamin
1745 "Advice to a young man on choosing a mistress." In Leonard Labare and Whitfield Bell, Jr. (eds.), *The Papers of Benjamin Franklin,* Vol. 3. New Haven, CT: Yale University Press, 1961.

French Institute of Public Opinion
1961 *Patterns of Sex and Love.* New York: Crown.

Friedan, Betty
1963 *The Feminine Mystique.* New York: Dell.
1981 *The Second Stage.* New York: Summit Books.

Friedl, Ernestine
1975 *Women and Men: An Anthropologist's View.* New York: Holt, Rinehart, and Winston.

Friedlander, Judith
1976 "Comment on Harriet Whitehead's review of *Woman's Evolution.*" *Signs* 2(Winter):501–503.

Friend, Richard A.
1980 "GAYging: Adjustment and the older gay male." *Alternative Lifestyles* 3(May):231–248.

Frieze, Irene Hanson
1983 "Investigating the causes and consequences of marital rape." *Signs* 8(Spring):532–553.

Fromm, Erich
1956 *The Art Of Loving.* New York: Harper & Row.

Bantam Books paperback edition used in citations.

Furstenberg, Frank F., Jr., and Albert G. Crawford
1978 "Family support: Helping teenage mothers to cope." *Family Planning Perspectives* 10(November/December):322–333.

Furstenberg, Frank F., Jr., and Christine Winquist Nord
1985 "Parenting apart: patterns of childrearing after marital disruption." *Journal of Marriage and the Family* 47(November):893–904.

Furstenberg, Frank F., Jr., and Graham B. Spanier
1984 *Recycling the Family: Remarriage after Divorce.* Beverly Hills, CA: Sage.

Gaer, Joseph, and Ben Siegel
1964 *The Puritan Heritage: America's Roots in the Bible.* New York: Mentor Books.

Gagnon, John H., and William Simon
1973 *Sexual Conduct.* Chicago: Aldine.

Galanternick, Mery
1976 "No divorce, but Brazilians find a way." *The New York Times,* August 22, 1976.

Galligan, Richard, and Stephen Bahr
1978 "Economic well-being and marital stability: Implications for income maintenance programs." *Journal of Marriage and the Family* 40(May):283–290.

Gallup Report, The
1985 "Premarital Sex." June, p. 28.

Ganong, Lawrence, and Marilyn Coleman
1984 "The effects of remarriage on children: A review of the empirical literature." *Family Relations* 33(July):389–406.

Gardella, Peter
1985 *Innocent Ecstasy.* New York: Oxford University Press.

Gardner, Richard
1977 *The Parents' Book about Divorce.* New York: Doubleday.

Garland, T. Neal
1972 "The better half? The male in the dual profession family." Pp. 199–215 in Constantina Safilios-Rothschild (ed.), *Toward a Sociology of Women.* Lexington, MA: Xerox College Publishing.

Garrison, Dee
1974 "The tender technicians: The feminization of public librarianship, 1876–1905." Pp. 158–178 in Mary Hartman and Lois Banner (eds.), *Clio's Consciousness Raised.* New York: Harper Colophon Books.

Gebhard, Paul

1966 "Factors in marital orgasm." *Journal of Social Issues* 22:89–95.

1971 "Human sexual behavior: A summary statement." Pp. 206–217 in Donald Marshall and Robert Guggs (eds.), *Human Sexual Behavior*. New York: Basic Books.

1972 "Incidence of overt homosexuality in the United States and Western Europe." Pp. 22–29 in Livingood (ed.), 1972.

1973 "Sex differences in sexual response." *Archives of Sexual Behavior* 2:201–203.

Geiger, H. Kent

1968 *The Family in Soviet Russia*. Cambridge, MA: Harvard University Press.

Geissinger, Shirley

1984 "Adoptive parents' attitudes toward open birth records." *Family Relations* 33(October):579–585.

Gelles, Richard J.

1972 *The Violent Home*. Beverly Hills, CA: Sage.

1973a "An exploratory study of intra-family violence." Unpublished Ph.D. dissertation, University of New Hampshire, Durham, NH.

1973b "Child abuse as psychopathology: A sociological critique and reformulation." *American Journal of Orthopsychiatry* 43:611–621. (Reprinted in Steinmetz and Straus, 1974.)

1979 *Family Violence*. Beverly Hills, CA: Sage.

1980 "Violence in the family: A review of research in the seventies." *Journal of Marriage and the Family* 42(November):143–155.

1982 "Applying research on family violence to clinical practice." *Journal of Marriage and the Family* 44(February):9–20.

1984 "Parental child snatching: A preliminary estimate of the national incidence." *Journal of Marriage and the Family* 46(August):735–739.

Gelles, Richard J., and Claire Pedrick Cornell

1985 *Intimate Violence in Families*. Beverly Hills, CA: Sage.

Gendell, Murray

1963 *Swedish Working Wives*. Totowa, NJ: Bedminster Press.

Genovese, Eugene

1974 *Roll, Jordon, Roll: The World the Slaves Made*. New York: Pantheon.

Gersick, Kelin

1979 "Fathers by choice: Divorced men who receive custody of their children." Pp. 307–323 in Levinger and Moles (eds.).

Gerstel, Naomi

1979 "Marital alternatives and the regulation of sex: Commuter couples as a test case." *Alternative Lifestyles* 2(May):145–176.

Gerstel, Naomi, and Harriet Gross

1984 *Commuter Marriage*. New York: Guilford.

Giles-Sims, Jean

1983 *Wife Battering: A Systems Theory Approach*. New York: Guilford.

1985 "A longitudinal study of battered children of battered wives." *Family Relations* 34(April):205–210.

Gilford, Rosalie

1984 "Contrasts in marital satisfaction throughout old age: An exchange theory analysis." *Journal of Gerontology* 39 (3):325–333.

1986 "Marriages in later life." *Generations* X (Summer):16–20.

Gillespie, Dair L.

1971 "Who has the power? The marital struggle." *Journal of Marriage and the Family* 33:445–458.

Gilmartin, Brian

1974 "Sexual deviance and social networks: A study of social, family, and marital interaction patterns among co-marital sex participants." Pp. 291–323 in Smith and Smith (eds.).

Gilmartin, Brian, and Dave V. Kusisto

1973 "Some personal and social characteristics of mate-sharing swingers." Pp. 146–165 in Roger W. Libby and Robert N. Whitehurst (eds.), *Renovating Marriage*. Danville, CA: Consensus.

Gittelsohn, Roland B.

1980 *Love, Sex, and Marriage: A Jewish View*. New York: Union of American Hebrew Congregations.

Glazer, Nona

1984 "Paid and unpaid work: Contradictions in American women's lives today." Pp. 169–186 in Borman, Quarm, and Gideonse (eds.).

Glazer-Malbin, Nona

1976 "Housework." *Signs* 1(Summer):905–922.

Glenn, Norval D.

1975 "Psychological well-being in the post-parental stage: Some evidence from national surveys." *Journal of Marriage and the Family* 37:105–110.

1979 "Attitude toward premarital, extramarital,

and homosexual relations in the United States in the 1970s." *Journal of Sex Research* (May).

1982 "Interreligious marriage in the United States: Patterns and recent trends." *Journal of Marriage and the Family* 44(August):555–566.

Glenn, Norval D., and Kathryn B. Kramer

1985 "The psychological well-being of adult children of divorce." *Journal of Marriage and the Family* 47(November):905–912.

Glenn, Norval D., and Sara McLanahan

1982 "Children and marital happiness: A further specification of the relationship." *Journal of Marriage and the Family* 44:63–72.

Glenn, Norval D., and Charles Weaver

1977 "The marital happiness of remarried divorced persons." *Journal of Marriage and the Family* 39(May):331–337.

Glick, Paul C.

1977 "Updating the life cycle of the family." *Journal of Marriage and the Family* 39(February):5–13.

1979 "The future of the American family." *Current Population Reports Special Studies,* ser. P-23, no. 78. U.S. Bureau of the Census.

1981 "A demographic picture of black families." Pp. 106–126 in Harriette Pipes McAdoo (ed.), *Black Families*. Beverly Hills, CA: Sage.

1984a "Marriage, divorce, and living arrangements: Prospective changes." *Journal of Family Issues* 5(March):7–26.

1984b "American household structure in transition." *Family Planning Perspectives* 16(September/October):205–211.

Glick, Paul C., and Sung-Ling Lin

1986 "More young adults are living with their parents: Who are they?" *Journal of Marriage and the Family* 48(February):107–112.

Glick, Paul C., and Arthur J. Norton

1977 "Marrying, divorcing, and living together in the U.S. today." *Population Bulletin,* Vol. 32, no. 5. Washington, DC: Population Reference Bureau.

Goetting, Ann

1982 "The six stations of remarriage: Developmental tasks of remarriage after divorce." *Family Relations* 31(April):213–222.

1986 "Parental satisfaction: A review of research." *Journal of Family Issues* 7(March):83–109.

Goffman, Erving

1959 *The Presentation of Self in Everyday Life.* New York: Anchor Books.

1963 *Stigma*. Englewood Cliffs, NJ: Prentice-Hall.

Gold, Rachel Benson, and Barry Nestor

1985 "Public funding of contraceptive, sterilization, and abortion services." *Family Planning Perspectives* 17(January/February): 25–30.

Goldberg, Herb

1976 *The Hazards of Being Male.* Plainview, NY: Nash.

Goldberg, Steven

1974 *The Inevitability of Patriarchy.* Expanded edition. New York: William Morrow.

Goldstein, Diane, and Alan Rosenbaum

1985 "An evaluation of the self-esteem of maritally violent men." *Family Relations* 34(July):425–428.

Goode, William J.

1956 *After Divorce.* Reissued in 1965 as *Women in Divorce.* New York: Free Press.

1959 "The theoretical importance of love." *American Sociological Review* 24:38–47.

1962 "Marital satisfaction and instability: A cross-cultural class analysis of divorce rates." *International Social Science Journal* 14:507–526.

1963 *World Revolution and Family Patterns.* New York: Free Press.

1964 *The Family.* Englewood Cliffs, NJ: Prentice-Hall.

1971 "Force and violence in the family." *Journal of Marriage and the Family* 33:624–636.

Goodman, Mary Ellen, and Alma Beman

1971 "Child's eye-views of life in an urban barrio." Pp. 109–122 in Nathaniel Wagner and Marsha Haug (eds.), *Chicanos: Social and Psychological Perspectives.* St. Louis: C. V. Mosby Co.

Gordis, Robert

1967 *Sex and the Family in the Jewish Tradition.* New York: The Burning Bush.

Gordon, Albert I.

1964 *Intermarriage: Interfaith, Interracial, Interethnic.* Boston: Beacon.

Gordon, Linda, and Paul O'Keefe

1984 "Incest as a form of family violence: Evidence from historical case records." *Journal of Marriage and the Family* 46(February):27–34.

Gordon, Michael

1971 "From an unfortunate necessity to a cult of mutual orgasm." In James Henslin (ed.), *The Sociology of Sex*. New York: Appleton-Century-Crofts.

1978 *The American Family: Past, Present, and Future*. New York: Random House.

1981 "Was Waller ever right? The rating and dating complex reconsidered." *Journal of Marriage and the Family* 43(February):67–76.

Gordon, Michael, and Penelope Shankweiler

1971 "Different equals less: Female sexuality in recent marriage manuals." *Journal of Marriage and the Family* 33:459–465.

Gould, Lois

1972 "X: A fabulous child's story." *Ms.*, December:74–76, 105–106.

1978 *X: A Fabulous Child's Story*. Houston: Daughters Publishing Company.

Gouldner, Alvin

1960 "The norm of reciprocity: A preliminary statement." *American Sociological Review* 25(April):161–178.

Grady, William R., Mark D. Hayward, and Junichi Yagi

1985 "Contraceptive failure in the United States: Estimates from the 1982 National Survey of Family Growth." *Family Planning Perspectives* 18(September/October):200–209.

Graham-Murray, James

1966 *A History of Morals*. London: Library 33 Ltd.

Granovetter, Mark S.

1973 "The strength of weak ties." *American Journal of Sociology* 78(May):1360–1380.

Green, Richard

1974 *Sexual Identity Conflict in Children and Adults*. New York: Basic Books.

Greenblat, Cathy, Peter Stein, and Norman Washburne

1974 *The Marriage Game*. New York: Random House.

Greenwald, Harold

1970 "Marriage as a non-legal voluntary association." Pp. 51–56 in Herbert Otto (ed.), *The Family in Search of a Future*. New York: Appleton-Century Crofts.

Greif, Geoffrey L.

1985a "Single fathers rearing children." *Journal of Marriage and the Family* 47(February):185–191.

1985b *Single Fathers*. Lexington, MA: Lexington Books.

Grimshaw, Allen D.

1970 "Interpreting collective violence: An argument for the importance of social structure." *Annals* 391(September):9–20.

Groat, H. T., and A. G. Neal

1967 "Social psychological correlates of urban fertility." *American Sociological Review* 32:945–959.

Gross, Harriet Engel

1980 "Dual-career couples who live apart: Two types." *Journal of Marriage and the Family*(August):567–576.

Gross, Harriet, Jessie 'Bernard, Alice Dan, Nona Glazer, Judith Lorber, Martha McClintock, Niles Newton, and Alice Rossi

1979 "Considering 'A biosocial perspective on parenting.'" *Signs* 4(Summer):695–717.

Group for the Advancement of Psychiatry (GAP), Committee on Public Education

1973 *Joys and Sorrows of Parenthood*. New York: Scribner.

Gustavus, Susan O., and James R. Henley, Jr.

1971 "Correlates of voluntary childlessness in a select population." *Social Biology* 18:277–284.

Gutman, Herbert

1976 *The Black Family in Slavery and Freedom*. New York: Pantheon.

Guttentag, Marcia, and Helen Bray

1977 "Teachers as mediators of sex-role standards." Pp. 395–411 in Alice G. Sargent (ed.), *Beyond Sex Roles*. St. Paul, MN: West.

Gwartney-Gibbs, Patricia A.

1986 "Institutionalization of premarital cohabitation." *Journal of Marriage and the Family* 48(May):423–434.

Haas, Linda

1980 "Role-sharing couples: A study of egalitarian marriages." *Family Relations* 29(July):289–296.

Hacker, Helen Mayer

1975 "Gender roles from a cross-cultural perspective." Pp. 185–215 in Lucile Duberman, *Gender and Sex in Society*. New York: Praeger.

Hall, Francine S., and Douglas T. Hall

1979 *The Two-Career Couple*. Reading, MA: Addison-Wesley.

Halperin, Sandra

1981 "Abused and non-abused children's perceptions of their mothers, fathers, and siblings: Implications for a comprehensive family treatment plan." *Family Relations* 30(January):89–96.

Hammond, Boone, and Joyce Ladner
1969 "Socialization into sexual behavior in a Negro slum ghetto." Pp. 41–51 in Carlfred Broderick and Jessie Bernard (eds.), *The Individual, Sex, and Society*. Baltimore: Johns Hopkins.

Hanna, Sharon, and Patricia Kain Knaub
1981 "Cohabitation before remarriage." *Alternative Lifestyles* 4(November):507–522.

Hannan, Michael, Nancy Brandon Tuma, and Lyle Groeneveld
1978 "Income and independence effects on marital dissolution: Results from the Seattle and Denver income-maintenance experiments." *American Journal of Sociology* 84:611–633.

Hanson, Shirley M. H., and Frederick W. Bozett (eds.)
1985 *Dimensions of Fatherhood*. Beverly Hills, CA: Sage.

Harriman, Lynda Cooper
1983 "Personal and marital changes accompanying parenthood." *Family Relations* 32(July):387–394.

Harris, Thomas
1967 *I'm OK—You're OK*. New York: Harper & Row and Avon paperback.

Harrison, Algea O.
1985 "The black family's socializing environment: Self-esteem and ethnic attitude among black children." Pp. 174–193 in McAdoo and McAdoo (eds.).

Harrison, James
1978 "Men's roles and men's lives: Review essay." *Signs* 4(Winter):324–336.

Harry, J., and W. B. DeVall
1978 *The Social Organization of Gay Males*. New York: Praeger.

Hass, Paula H.
1972 "Maternal role incompatibility and fertility in Latin America." *Journal of Social Issues* 28(2):111–128.

Hassall, Edward, and Dorothy Madar
1980 "Crisis group therapy with the separated and divorced." *Family Relations* 29(October):591–597.

Hatfield, Elaine, and G. William Walster
1978 *A New Look at Love*. Lanham, MD: University Press of America, Inc.

Hatfield (Walster), Elaine, G. William Walster, and Ellen Berscheid
1978 *Equity: Theory and Research*. Boston: Allyn and Bacon.

Haug, Marie R.
1973 "Social class measurement and women's occupational roles." *Social Forces* 52(September):86–98.

Havens, Elizabeth
1973 "Women, work, and wedlock: A note on female marital patterns in the United States." *American Journal of Sociology* 78:975–981.

Havighurst, Robert J.
1953 *Human Development and Education*. New York: Longmans, Green.

Hayghe, Howard
1984 "Working mothers reach record numbers in 1984." *Monthly Labor Review* 107, no. 12(December):31–34.

Haynes, John M.
1981 *Divorce Mediation: A Practical Guide for Therapists and Counselors*. New York: Springer.

Heaton, Tim B.
1984 "Religious homogamy and marital satisfaction reconsidered." *Journal of Marriage and the Family* 46(August):729–733.

Heckert, Alex, and Jay D. Teachman
1985 "Religious factors in the timing of second births." *Journal of Marriage and the Family* 47(May):361–367.

Heer, David
1958 "Dominance and the working wife." *Social Forces* 36:341–347.
1963 "The measurement and bases of family power: An overview." *Journal of Marriage and the Family* 25:133–139.
1974 "The prevalence of black-white marriage in the United States, 1960 and 1970." *Journal of Marriage and the Family* 36:246–258.

Hendrick, Clyde, and Susan Hendrick
1983 *Liking, Loving, and Relating*. Monterey, CA: Brooks/Cole.

Hennig, Margaret
1973 "Family dynamics for developing positive achievement motivation in women: The successful woman executive." *Annals of the New York Academy of Sciences* 208(March):76–81.

Hennig, Margaret, and Anne Jardim
1977 *The Managerial Woman*. New York: Doubleday.

Henshaw, Stanley K., Nancy J. Binkin, Ellen Baine, and Jack C. Smith
1985 "A portrait of American women who obtain abortions." *Family Planning Perspectives* 17(March/April):90–96.

Henshaw, Stanley K., and Susheela Singh
1986 "Sterilization regret among U.S. couples." *Family Planning Perspectives* 18(September/October):238–240.

Henshel, Anne-Marie
1973 "Swinging: A study of decision making in marriage." *American Journal of Sociology* 78:885–891.

Henslin, James M. (ed.)
1971 *Studies in the Sociology of Sex.* New York: Appleton-Century-Crofts.

Henze, Lura F., and John W. Hudson
1974 "Personal and family characteristics of cohabiting and non-cohabiting college students." *Journal of Marriage and the Family* 36(November):722–727.

Herman, Judith Lewis
1981 *Father-Daughter Incest.* Cambridge, MA: Harvard University Press.

Herzog, Elizabeth
1967 *About the Poor: Some Facts and Some Fictions.* Children's Bureau Publication no. 451. Washington, DC: U.S. Department of Health, Education, and Welfare.

Heschel, Suzannah (ed.)
1983 *On Being a Jewish Feminist.* New York: Schocken Books.

Hess, Beth, and Joan Waring
1978 "Parent and child in later life: Rethinking the relationship." Pp. 241–273 in Lerner and Spanier (eds.).

Hess, Robert, and Judith Torney
1962 "Religion, age and sex in children's perceptions of family authority." *Child Development* 33:781–789.

Hill, Elizabeth A., and Lorraine T. Dorfman
1982 "Reaction of housewives to the retirement of their husbands." *Family Relations* 31(April):195–200.

Hill, Reuben
1949 *Families Under Stress: Adjustment to the Crises of War, Separation, and Reunion.* New York: Harper.
1964 "Methodological issues in family development research." *Family Process* 3:186–206.
1970 *Family Development in Three Generations.* Cambridge, MA: Schenkman.
1978 "Psychosocial consequences of the first birth: A discussion." Pp. 392–401 in Miller and Newman (eds.).

Hill, Reuben, and Roy H. Rodgers
1964 "The developmental approach." Pp. 171–211 in Harold T. Christensen (ed.), *Handbook of Marriage and the Family.* Chicago: Rand McNally.

Hill, Robert, and Lawrence Shackleford
1975 "The black extended family revisited." *The Urban League Review* 1(Fall):18–24. Reprinted in Staples (ed.), 1978.

Hill, Wayne, and John Scanzoni
1982 "An approach for assessing marital decision-making processes." *Journal of Marriage and the Family* 44(November):927–942.

Hiller, Dana V., and William W. Philliber
1978 "The derivation of status benefits from the occupational attainments of working wives." *Journal of Marriage and the Family* 40(February):63–69.
1980 "Necessity, compatibility, and status attainment as factors in the labor-force participation of married women." *Journal of Marriage and the Family* 42(May):347–354.

Himes, Norman
1936 *Medical History of Contraception.* Reprint. New York: Schocken, 1970.

Hirsch, Barbara
1976 *Living Together: A Guide to the Law for Unmarried Couples.* Boston: Houghton Mifflin.

Hirschhorn, L.
1977 "Social policy and the life cycle: A developmental perspective." *Social Service Review* 51:434–450.

Hobbs, Daniel F., Jr.
1965 "Parenthood as crisis: A third study." *Journal of Marriage and the Family* 27(August):367–372.
1968 "Transition to parenthood: A replication and an extension." *Journal of Marriage and the Family* 30(August):413–417.

Hobbs, Daniel F., Jr., and Sue Peck (Cole)
1976 "Transition to parenthood: A decade replication." *Journal of Marriage and the Family* 38(November):723–731.

Hobbs, Daniel F., Jr., and Jane Maynard Wimbish
1977 "Transition to parenthood by black couples." *Journal of Marriage and the Family* 39(November):677–689.

Hoffman, Lois Wladis
1972a "A psychological perspective on the value of children to parents: Concepts and measures." In Fawcett (ed.), 1972.
1972b "Early childhood experiences and women's achievement motive." *Journal of Social Issues* 28(2):129–155.
1973 "The professional woman as mother." *An-*

nals of the New York Academy of Sciences 208(March):211–217.

1974   "Effects on child." Pp. 126–166 in Hoffman and Nye, 1974.

1978   "Effects of the first child on the woman's role." Pp. 340–367 in Miller and Newman (eds.).

Hoffman, Lois Wladis, and Martin L. Hoffman

1973   "The value of children to parents." Pp. 19–76 in James T. Fawcett (ed.), *Psychological Perspectives on Population.* New York: Basic Books.

Hoffman, Lois Wladis, and Jean Denby Manis

1978   "Influences of children on marital interaction and parental satisfaction and dissatisfaction." Pp. 165–213 in Lerner and Spanier (eds.).

1979   "The value of children in the United States: A new approach to the study of fertility." *Journal of Marriage and the Family* 41(August).

Hoffman, Lois Wladis, and F. Ivan Nye

1974   *Working Mothers.* San Francisco: Jossey-Bass.

Hoffman, Martin L.

1963   "Personality, family structure, and social class as antecedents of parental power assertion." *Child Development* 34:869–884.

Hoffman, Susan R., and Ronald F. Levant

1985   "A comparison of childfree and child-anticipated married couples." *Family Relations* 34(April):197–203.

Hogan, Dennis P., Nan Marie Astone, and Evelyn M. Kitagawa

1985   "Social and environmental factors influencing contraceptive use among black adolescents." *Family Planning Perspectives* 17(July/August):165–169.

Holmstrom, Lynda Lytle

1972   *The Two-Career Family.* Cambridge, MA: Schenkman.

Holter, Harriet

1970   *Sex Roles and Social Structure.* Oslo, Norway: Universitetsforlaget.

Homans, George C.

1961   *Social Behavior: Its Elementary Forms.* New York: Harcourt, Brace, and World.

Hong, Lawrence

1976   "The role of women in the People's Republic of China: Legacy and change." *Social Problems* 23(June):545–557.

Hooker, Evelyn

1965   "The homosexual community." Pp. 167–184 in John Gagnon and William Simon (eds.), *Sexual Deviance.* New York: Harper & Row, 1967. Originally published in *Perspectives in Psychopathology.* New York: Oxford University Press, 1965.

Horne, Jo

1985   *Caregiving: Helping an Aging Loved One.* Washington, DC: American Association of Retired Persons and Scott, Foresman.

Hornung, Carlton, and B. Claire McCullough

1981   "Status relationships in dual-employment marriages: Consequences for psychological well-being." *Journal of Marriage and the Family* 43(February):125–141.

Hornung, Carlton, B. Claire McCullough, and Taichi Sugimoto

1981   "Status relationships in marriage: Risk factors in spouse abuse." *Journal of Marriage and the Family* 43(August):675–692.

Horowitz, Amy

1985   "Sons and daughters as caregivers to older parents: Differences in role performance and consequences." *The Gerontologist* 25(December):612–617.

Hotvedt, Mary, and Jane Barclay Mandel

1982   "Children of lesbian mothers." Pp. 275–285 in Paul et al.

Hoult, Thomas Ford, Lura Henze, and John Hudson

1978   *Courtship and Marriage in America.* Boston: Little, Brown.

Houseknecht, Sharon K.

1979   "Childlessness and marital adjustment." *Journal of Marriage and the Family* 41(May):259–265.

1981   "Review of Jean E. Veevers, *Childless by Choice.*" *Journal of Marriage and the Family* 43(August):759–761.

1982   "Voluntary childlessness in the 1980's: A significant increase?" *Marriage and Family Review* 5(2):51–69.

Houseknecht, Sharon K., and Anne S. Macke

1981   "Combining marriage and career: The marital adjustment of professional women." *Journal of Marriage and the Family* 43(August):651–661.

Huang, Lucy Jen

1982   "Planned fertility of one-couple/one-child policy in the People's Republic of China." *Journal of Marriage and the Family* 44(August):775–784.

Humanae Vitae: Pope Paul's Encyclical on Birth Control

1968   St. Louis: Religious Information Bureau

of the Knights of Columbus, Pamphlet No. 69.

Hunter, Gertrude
    1973 "Pediatrician." In *Successful Women in the Sciences: An Analysis of Determinants.* Special issue of the *Annals of the New York Academy of Sciences* 208(March):37–40.

Ickes, William, Brian Shermer, and Jeff Steeno
    1979 "Sex and sex-role influences in same-sex dyads." *Social Psychology Quarterly* 42(December):373–385.

Ihara, Toni, and Ralph Warner
    1979 "Making illegitimacy legitimate." *Ms.,* April:92–93.

Ihinger-Tallman, Marilyn
    1984 "Epilogue." *Family Relations* (special issue on remarriage and stepparenting) 33(July): 483–487.

Jacques, Jeffrey, and Karen Chason
    1978 "Cohabitation: A test of reference group theory among black and white college students." *Journal of Comparative Family Studies* 9(Summer):147–165.

Jedlicka, Davor
    1980 "Formal mate selection networks in the United States." *Family Relations* 29(April):199–203.

Jennings (Walstedt), Joyce
    1978 "Reform of women's roles and family structures in the recent history of China." *Journal of Marriage and the Family* 40(May):379–392.

Jennings, Theodore
    1977 "Homosexuality and the Christian faith." *The Christian Century* 94(February 16).

Jensen, Mehri Samandari
    1974 "Role differentiation in female homosexual quasi-marital unions." *Journal of Marriage and the Family* 36:360–367.

Joe, T., and P. Yu
    1984 *The "Flip Side" of Black Families Headed by Women: The Economic Status of Black Men.* Washington, DC: The Center for the Study of Social Policy.

Jones, Elise F., Jacqueline Darroch Forrest, Noreen Goldman, Stanley Henshaw, Richard Lincoln, Jeannie I. Rosoff, Charles F. Westoff, and Deirdre Wulf
    1985 "Teenage pregnancy in developed countries: Determinants and policy implications." *Family Planning Perspectives* 17(March/April):53–63.

Jurich, Anthony P., and Julie A. Jurich
    1974 "The effect of cognitive moral development

upon the selection of premarital sexual standards." *Journal of Marriage and the Family* 36(November):736–741.

Kaberry, Phyllis M.
    1953 *Women of the Grassfields.* London: Her Majesty's Stationery Office.

Kadushin, Alfred
    1970 "Single parent adoptions; An overview and some relevant research." *Social Service Review* 44(3).

Kalmuss, Debra S., and Murray A. Straus
    1982 "Wife's marital dependency and wife abuse." *Journal of Marriage and the Family* 44(May):277–286.

Kanowitz, Leo
    1973 *Sex Roles in Law and Society.* Albuquerque: University of New Mexico Press.

Kanter, Rosabeth Moss
    1977 *Work and Family in the United States.* New York: Russell Sage Foundation.

Kantner, John F., and Melvin Zelnik
    1972 "Sexual experience of young unmarried women in the United States." *Family Planning Perspectives* 5(Winter):21–35.

Kar, S. B.
    1971 "Individual aspirations as related to early and late acceptance of contraception." *The Journal of Social Psychology* 83:235–245.

Kaslow, Florence W.
    1984 "Divorce mediation and its emotional impact on the couple and their children." *The American Journal of Family Therapy* 12(3):58–66.

Katy, Barbara J.
    1972 "Cooling motherhood." *National Observer,* December 20.

Katzenstein, Alfred
    1970 "Male and female in the German Democratic Republic." In Georgene H. Seward and Robert C. Williamson (eds.), *Sex Roles in Changing Society.* New York: Random House.

Kelley, Harold H.
    1979 *Personal Relationships: Their Structures and Processes.* Hillsdale, NJ: Lawrence Erlbaum.

Kelley, H. H., and D. P. Schenitzki
    1972 "Bargaining." In C. G. McClintock (ed.), *Experimental Social Psychology.* New York: Holt.

Kelley, H. H., and A. Stahelski
    1970 "Social interaction basis of cooperators' and competitors' beliefs about others." *Journal*

of Personality and Social Psychology 16:66–91.

Kelly, Maria Patricia Fernandez
1981 "Development and the Sexual Division of Labor: An Introduction." *Signs,* Vol 7:268–278.

Kempe, C. Henry
1971 "Pediatric implications of the battered baby syndrome." *Archives of Disease in Children* 46:28–37.

Kempe, C. Henry, Frederic N. Silverman, Brandt F. Steele, William Droegemueller, and Henry K. Silver
1962 "The battered child syndrome." *Journal of the American Medical Association* 181(July):107–112.

Kenkel, William F.
1985 "The desire for voluntary childlessness among low-income youth." *Journal of Marriage and the Family* 47(May):509–512.

Kennedy, David M.
1970 *Birth Control in America: The Career of Margaret Sanger.* New Haven, CT: Yale University Press.

Kephart, William
1964 "Legal and procedural aspects of marriage and divorce." Pp. 944–968 in Harold T. Christensen (ed.), *Handbook of Marriage and the Family.* Chicago: Rand McNally.
1977 *The Family, Society, and the Individual.* 4th ed. Boston: Houghton Mifflin.

Kerckhoff, Alan C.
1972 *Socialization and Social Class.* Englewood Cliffs, NJ: Prentice-Hall.

Kim, Choong Soon
1974 "The Yon' jul-hon or Chain-String form of marriage arrangement in Korea." *Journal of Marriage and the Family* 36(August):575–579.

Kinderknecht, Cheryl
1986 "In home social work with abused or neglected elderly: An experiential guide to assessment and treatment." *Journal of Gerontological Social Work* 9(Spring):29–42.

King, Karl, Jack O. Balswick, and Ira E. Robinson
1977 "The continuing premarital sexual revolution among college females." *Journal of Marriage and the Family* 39(August):455–459.

Kinsey, Alfred C., W. B. Pomeroy, and C. E. Martin
1948 *Sexual Behavior in the Human Male.* Philadelphia: Saunders.

Kinsey, A. C., W. B. Pomeroy, C. E. Martin, and P. H. Gebhard
1953 *Sexual Behavior in the Human Female.* Philadelphia: Saunders. New York: Pocket Books paperback edition.

Kirkendall, Lester
1968 "Understanding the problems of the male virgin." Pp. 123–129 in Isadore Rubin and Lester Kirkendall (eds.), *Sex in the Adolescent Years.* New York: Association.

Kirschner, Betty Frankle, and Laurel Richardson Walum
1978 "Two-location families: Married singles." *Alternative Life-Styles* 1(November):513–525.

Kitson, Gay C.
1982 "Attachment to the spouse in divorce: A scale and its application." *Journal of Marriage and the Family* 44(May):379–393.

Kivett, Vira R.
1985 "Grandfathers and grandchildren: Patterns of association, helping and psychological closeness." *Family Relations* 34(October):565–571.

Klatzky, Sheila R.
1972 *Patterns of Contact with Relatives.* Washington, DC: American Sociological Association.

Klaus, Marshall H., and John H. Kennell
1978 "Parent-to-infant attachment." Pp. 5–29 in Joseph Stevens, Jr., and Marilyn Matthews (eds.), *Mother/Child, Father/Child Relationships.* Washington, DC: National Association for the Education of Young Children.

Kliman, Deborah S., and Carol Vukelich
1985 "Mothers and fathers: Expectations for infants." *Family Relations* 34(July):305–313.

Klineberg, O.
1964 *The Human Dimension in International Relations.* New York: Holt.

Kobrin, Frances
1976 "The primary individual and the family: Changes in living arrangements in the United States since 1940." *Journal of Marriage and Family* 38(May):233–239.

Kohen, Janet, Carol A. Brown, and Roslyn Feldberg
1979 "Divorced mothers: The costs and benefits of female family control." Pp. 228–245 in Levinger and Moles (eds.).

Kohlberg, Lawrence
1966 "A cognitive developmental analysis of children's sex-role concepts and attitudes." In E. E. Maccoby (ed.), *The Development of*

Sex Differences. Stanford, CA: Stanford University Press.

Kohn, Melvin L.
1969 *Class and Conformity: A Study in Values.* Homewood, IL: Dorsey.

Kolbenschlag, Michael
1976 "Dr. Estelle Ramey: Reclaiming the feminine legacy." *Human Behavior* 5(July):24–27.

Koller, Marvin
1974 *Families: A Multigenerational Approach.* New York: McGraw-Hill.

Komarovsky, Mirra
1962 *Blue-Collar Marriage.* New York: Random House.

Korman, Sheila K.
1983 "Nontraditional dating behavior: date-initiation and date expense-sharing among feminists and nonfeminists." *Family Relations* 32(October):575–581.

Korpivaara, Ari
1982 "Play groups for Dads." *Ms.,* February:52–54.

Kowal, Katherine A., and Karen Maitland Schilling
1985 "Adoption through the eyes of adult adoptees." *American Journal of Orthopsychiatry* 55(July):354–362.

Kraditor, Aileen S.
1968 *Up From the Pedestal.* Chicago: Quadrangle Books.

Krain, Mark, Drew Cannon, and Jeffery Bagford
1977 "Rating-dating or simply prestige homogamy? Data on dating in the Greek System on a midwestern campus." *Journal of Marriage and the Family* 39(November):663–674.

Krantzler, Mel
1973 *Creative Divorce.* New York: Evans, New American Library Signet paperback edition.

Krause, Harry D.
1971 *Illegitimacy: Law and Social Policy.* Indianapolis: Bobbs-Merrill.

Krauskopf, Joan M.
1977 "Partnership marriage: Legal reforms needed." Pp. 93–121 in Jane Roberts Chapman and Margaret Gates (eds.), *Women into Wives: The Legal and Economic Impact of Marriage.* Beverly Hills, CA: Sage.

Kriesberg, Louis
1973 *The Sociology of Social Conflicts.* Englewood Cliffs, NJ: Prentice-Hall.

Kristeva, Julia
1975 "On the women of China." *Signs* 1(Autumn):57–81.

Kübler-Ross, Elisabeth
1969 *On Death and Dying.* New York: Macmillan.

Kutner, Nancy, and Donna Brogan
1974 "An investigation of sex-related slang vocabulary and sex-role orientation among male and female university students." *Journal of Marriage and the Family* 36:474–484.

Kutner, Nancy, and Richard Levinson
1976 "The toy salesperson: A potential gatekeeper for change in sex-role definitions." Paper presented at the annual meetings of the American Sociological Association, New York, August.

LaFree, Gary
1974 "Independence among the Igbo women of West Africa." Unpublished paper, department of sociology, Indiana University, Bloomington, IN.

Lamb, Michael E.
1975 "Fathers: Forgotten contributors to child development." *Human Development* 18:245–266.
1976 (ed.) *The Role of the Father in Child Development.* New York: Wiley.
1982 "Maternal employment and child development: A review." In Michael E. Lamb (ed.) *Nontraditional Families: Parenting and Child Development.* Hillsdale, NJ: Erlbaum.
1984 "Fathers, mothers, and child care in the 1980's. Family influences on child development." Pp. 61–88 in Borman, Quarm, and Gideonse (eds.).

Lamb, Michael E., Joseph H. Pleck, and James A. Levine
1986 "Effects of paternal involvement on fathers and mothers." *Marriage and Family Review* 9(Winter, nos.3/4):67–83.

Lamb, Michael E., and Abraham Sagi (eds.)
1983 *Fatherhood and Social Policy.* Hillsdale, NJ: Lawrence Erlbaum.

Lamm, Maurice
1980 *The Jewish Way in Love and Marriage.* San Francisco: Harper & Row.

Lamphere, Louise
1977 "Anthropology." *Signs* 2(Spring):612–627.

Langley, Roger, and Richard C. Levy
1977 *Wife Beating: The Silent Crisis.* New York: E. P. Dutton.

LaRossa, Ralph
1980 "And we haven't had any problems since: Conjugal Violence and the politics of marriage." Pp. 157–175 in Straus and Hotaling (eds.).

Larson, Jeffry H.

1984 "The effect of husband's unemployment on marital and family relations in blue-collar families." *Family Relations* 33(October):503–511.

Larson, Paul C.

1982 "Gay male relationships." Pp. 219–232 in Paul et. al., eds.

Lasch, Christopher

1973 "Marriage in the middle ages." *The Columbia Forum* 2(Fall).

Laslett, Peter (ed., with the assistance of Richard Wall)

1972 *Household and Family in Past Time.* London and New York: Cambridge University Press (second impression 1974).

Laws, Judith Long, and Pepper Schwartz

1977 *Sexual Scripts: The Social Construction of Female Sexuality.* Hinsdale, IL: Dryden Press.

Leacock, Eleanor

1976 "Comment on Harriet Whitehead's review of *Woman's Evolution.*" *Signs* 2(Winter):504–507.

1977 "Review of *Toward an Anthropology of Women,* ed. by Rayna Reiter." In *Signs* 3(Winter):495–497.

Lederer, W. J., and D. D. Jackson

1968 *The Mirages of Marriage.* New York: Norton.

Lee, Gary R.

1977 *Family Structure and Interaction.* Philadelphia: Lippincott.

1978 "Marriage and morale in later life." *Journal of Marriage and the Family* 40(February):131–139.

1980 "Kinship in the seventies: A decade review of research and theory." *Journal of Marriage and the Family* 42(November):193–204.

Leigh, Geoffrey K.

1982 "Kinship interaction over the family life span." *Journal of Marriage and the Family* 44(February):197–208.

LeMasters, E. E.

1957 "Parenthood as crisis." *Marriage and Family Living* 19:352–355.

1975 *Blue-Collar Aristocrats.* Madison: University of Wisconsin Press.

Lenz, Elinor

1981 *Once My Child ... Now My Friend.* New York: Warner Books.

Lerner, Gerda (ed.)

1972 *Black Women in White America.* New York: Random House.

Lerner, Richard, and Graham Spanier (eds.)

1978 *Child Influences on Marital and Family Interaction: A Life-Span Perspective.* New York: Academic Press.

Lever, Janet

1978 "Sex differences in the complexity of children's play." *American Sociological Review* 43(August):471–483.

Levine, Donald, Ellwood Carter, and Eleanor Miller Gorman

1976 "Simmel's influence on American sociology. Part I." *American Journal of Sociology* 81:813–845.

Levine, Robert A.

1970 "Sex roles and economic change in Africa." Pp. 174–180 in John Middleton (ed.), *Black Africa.* New York: Macmillan.

Levinger, George

1966 "Physical abuse among applicants for divorce," an excerpt from "Source of marital satisfaction among applicants for divorce." *American Journal of Orthopsychiatry* 36(October), as reprinted in Steinmetz and Straus, 1974, pp. 85–88.

1979 "A social psychological perspective on marital dissolution." Pp. 37–60 in Levinger and Moles (eds.).

Levinger, George, and Oliver C. Moles (eds.)

1979 *Divorce and Separation: Context, Causes, and Consequences.* New York: Basic Books.

Levi-Strauss, Claude

1949 "The principle of reciprocity." Chapter 5 of *Les Structures Elementaires de la Parente.* Presses Universitaires de France. Abridged and translated by Rose L. Coser and Grace Frazer. Pp. 61–70 in Lewis Coser and Bernard Rosenberg (eds.), *Sociological Theory,* 5th ed. New York: Macmillan, 1982.

1956 "The family." Pp. 261–285 in Harry L. Shapiro (ed.), *Man, Culture, and Society.* New York: Oxford.

Lewin, Bo

1982 "Unmarried Cohabitation: A marriage form in a changing society." *Journal of Marriage and the Family* (August):763–773.

Lewin, Eller, and Terrie Lyons

1982 "Everything in its place: The co-existence of lesbianism and motherhood." Pp. 249–273 in Paul et. al.

Lewis, Diane K.

1975 "The black family: Socialization and sex roles." *Phylon* 36(September):221–237.

1977 "A response to inequality: Black women, racism, and sexism." *Signs* 3(Winter):339–361.

1978 "Reply to Bernstein's comment." *Signs* 3(Spring):736–737.

Lewis, Lionel, and Dennis Brissett

1967 "Sex as work: A study of avocational counseling." *Social Problems* 15(Summer):8–18.

Lewis, Oscar

1951 *Life in a Mexican Village: Tepoztlan Restudied.* Urbana: University of Illinois Press.

1968 *A Study of Slum Culture.* New York: Random House.

Lewis, Robert, Phillip Freneau, and Craig Roberts

1979 "Fathers and the postparental transition." *Family Coordinator* 28(October):514–520.

Lewis, Robert A., Ellen Kozac, Robert Milardo, and Wayne Grosnick

1981 "Commitment in same-sex love relationships. *Alternative Life-Styles* 4(February):22–42.

Lewis, Robert A., and Robert E. Salt (eds.)

1985 *Men in Families.* Beverly Hills, CA: Sage.

Lewis, Sasha Gregory

1979 *Sunday's Women: A Report on Lesbian Life Today.* Boston: Beacon Press.

Libby, Roger W.

1977a "Creative singlehood as a sexual lifestyle: Beyond marriage as a rite of passage." Pp. 37–61 in Robert W. Libby and Robert N. Whitehurst (eds.), *Marriage and Alternatives: Exploring Intimate Relationships.* Glenview, IL: Scott, Foresman.

1977b "Extramarital and comarital sex: A critique of the literature." Pp. 80–111 in Roger W. Libby and Robert N. Whitehurst (eds.), *Marriage and Alternatives: Exploring Intimate Relationships,* Glenview, IL: Scott, Foresman.

Libby, Roger W., and John E. Carlson

1973 "A theoretical framework for premarital sexual decisions in the dyad." *Archives of Sexual Behavior* 2:365–378.

Lieberman, Mendel, and Marion Hardie

1981 *Resolving Family and Other Conflicts: Everybody Wins.* Santa Cruz, CA: Unity Press.

Liebow, Elliot

1967 *Tally's Corner: A Study of Negro Street-corner Men.* Boston: Little, Brown.

Lindsey, Ben B.

1926 "The companionate marriage." *Redbook,* October.

1927 "The companionate marriage." *Redbook,* March.

Lindsey, Ben, and Wainwright Evans

1927 *The Companionate Marriage.* New York: Liveright.

Lindsey, Karen

1981 *Friends as Family.* Boston: Beacon Press.

Linner, Birgitta

1966 "Sexual morality and sexual reality—the Scandinavian approach." *American Journal of Orthopsychiatry* 36:686–693.

1967 *Sex and Society in Sweden.* New York: Pantheon.

Lipman-Blumen, Jean

1984 *Gender Roles and Power.* Englewood Cliffs, NJ: Prentice-Hall.

Litwak, Eugene

1960 "Occupational mobility and extended family cohesion." *American Sociological Review* 25(February):9–21.

Liu, William T., I. W. Hutchinson, and L. K. Hong

1973 "Conjugal power and decision making: A methodological note on cross-culture study of the family." *American Journal of Sociology* 79:84–98.

Livingood, John M. (ed.)

1972 *National Institute of Mental Health Task Force on Homosexuality: Final Report and Background Papers.* Rockville, MD.: National Institute of Mental Health.

Locke, Harvey J.

1968 *Predicting Adjustment in Marriage: A Comparison of a Divorced and a Happily Married Group.* New York: Greenwood.

Locksley, Anne

1980 "On the effects of wives' employment on marital adjustment and companionship." *Journal of Marriage and the Family* 42(May):337–346.

Loether, Herman

1964 "The meaning of work and adjustment to retirement." Pp. 517–525 in A. B. Shostak and W. Gomberg (eds.), *Blue-Collar World.* Englewood Cliffs, NJ: Prentice-Hall.

1967 *Problems of Aging.* Belmont, CA: Dickenson.

Longfellow, Cynthia

1979 "Divorce in context: Its impact on children." Pp. 287–306 in Levinger and Moles (eds.).

Lopata, Helena Znaniecki
1973a *Widowhood in an American City.* Cambridge, MA: Schenkman.
1973b "Self-identity in marriage and widowhood." *The Sociological Quarterly* 14(Summer):407–418.
1979 *Women as Widows: Support Systems.* New York: Elsevier North Holland.

Lott, J., and B. E. Lott
1963 *Negro and White Youth.* New York: Holt.

Louis Harris and Associates
1981 *The General Mills American Family Report, 1980–81: Families at Work—Strengths and Strains.* Minneapolis: General Mills, Inc.

Lowenthall, Marjorie Fiske, and Clayton Haven
1968 "Interaction and adaptation: Intimacy as a critical variable." *American Sociological Review* 33:20–30.

Lu, Xiao
1984 "China: feudal attitudes, party control and half the sky." Pp. 151–156 in Robin Morgan, ed., *Sisterhood Is Global.* Garden City, NY: Anchor Press/Doubleday.

Luckey, Eleanore, and Gilbert Nass
1969 "A comparison of sexual attitudes and behavior in an international sample." *Journal of Marriage and the Family* 31:364–379.

Luepnitz, Deborah
1979 "Which aspects of divorce affect children?" *The Family Coordinator* 28(January):79–85.

Luker, Kristin
1975 *Taking Chances.* Berkeley: University of California Press.
1984 *Abortion and the Politics of Motherhood.* Berkeley: University of California Press.

Lyness, Judith, Milton Lipetz, and Keith Davis
1972 "Living together: An alternative to marriage." *Journal of Marriage and the Family* 34:305–311.

McAdoo, Harriette Pipes
1978 "The impact of extended family variables upon the upward mobility of black families." Summary report of research sponsored by the Office of Child Development. Department of Health, Education, and Welfare, Grant no. 90-C-631(1). Washington, DC: Howard University.
1981a (ed.) *Black Families.* Beverly Hills, CA: Sage.
1981b "Patterns of upward mobility in black families." Pp. 155–169 in McAdoo (ed.), *Black Families.*

1982 "Stress absorbing systems in black families." *Family Relations* 31(October):479–488.
1985 "Racial attitude and self-concept of young black children over time." Pp. 213–242 in McAdoo and McAdoo (eds.), *Black Children.*

McAdoo, Harriette Pipes, and John Lewis McAdoo (eds.)
1985 *Black Children: Social, Educational, and Parental Environments.* Beverly Hills, CA: Sage.

McAdoo, John Lewis
1986 "A black perspective on the father's role in child development." *Marriage and Family Review* 9(Winter, 1985/86):117–133.

McCall, Michal M.
1966 "Courtship as social exchange." Pp. 190–210 in Bernard Farber (ed.), *Kinship and Family Organization.* New York: John Wiley.

Macciocchi, Maria
1972 *Daily Life in Revolutionary China.* New York: Monthly Review Press.

McClelland, David C.
1961 *The Achieving Society.* Princeton, NJ: D. Van Nostrand.

Maccoby, Eleanor Emmons, and Carol Nay Jacklin
1974 *The Psychology of Sex Differences.* Stanford, CA: Stanford University Press.

MacCorquodale, Patricia L.
1984 "Gender roles and premarital contraception." *Journal of Marriage and the Family* 46(February):57–63.

McDonald, Gerald W.
1980 "Family power: the assessment of a decade of theory and research, 1970–1979." *Journal of Marriage and the Family* 42(November):111–124.

Mace, David, and Vera Mace
1981 "What is marriage beyond living together? Some Quaker reactions to cohabitation." *Family Relations* 30(January):17–20.

Mack, Phyllis
1984 "Choosing single motherhood." *Ms.,* November:58–64.

McKinley, Donald Gilbert
1964 *Social Class and Family Life.* New York: Free Press.

Macklin, Eleanor
1972 "Heterosexual cohabitation among unmarried college students." *Non-traditional Family Forms in the 1970's.* (Reprint of a special issue of *The Family Coordinator,* October,

1972). Minneapolis: National Council on Family Relations, pp. 95–104.

1978 "Non-marital heterosexual cohabitation: a review of research." *Marriage and Family Review* 1(March/April):1–12.

1980 "Nontraditional family forms: a decade of research." *Journal of Marriage and the Family* 42(November):175–192.

McLanahan, Sarah, Nancy Wedemeyer, and Tina Adelberg
1981 "Network structure, social support, and psychological well-being in the single-parent family." *Journal of Marriage and the Family* 43(August):601–612.

McNeill, John J.
1976 *The Church and the Homosexual.* Kansas City, KS: Sheed Andrews and McMeel.

Maddox, George
1970 "Themes and issues in sociological theories of human aging." *Human Development* 13:17–27.

Mainardi, Pat
1970 "The politics of housework." Pp. 447–454 in Robin Morgan (ed.) *Sisterhood Is Powerful.* New York: Vintage.

Malcolm X
1964 *The Autobiography of Malcolm X.* New York: Grove.

Malinowski, Bronislaw
1930 "Parenthood, the basis of social structure." In V. F. Calverton and S. D. Schmalhausen (eds.), *The New Generation.* New York: Macauley. Reprinted in Rose L. Coser (ed.), *The Family: Its Structures and Functions,* New York: St. Martin's, 1964, pp. 3–19.

Mamonova, Tatyana (ed.)
1984 *Women and Russia: Feminist Writings from the Soviet Union.* Boston: Beacon Press.

Marciano, Teresa Donati
1978 "Male pressure in the decision to remain childfree." *Alternative Lifestyles* 1(February):95–112.

Maret, Elizabeth, and Barbara Finlay
1984 "The distribution of household labor among women in dual-earner families." *Journal of Marriage and the Family* 46(May):357–364.

Marindin, Hope (ed.)
1985 *The Handbook for Single Adoptive Parents,* Rev. ed. Chevy Chase, MD: Committee for Single Adoptive Parents.

Marion, Marian
1982 "Primary prevention of child abuse: The role

of the family life educator." *Family Relations* 31(October):575–582.

Markle, Gerald E.
1973 "Sexism and the sex ratio." Paper read at the annual meeting of the American Sociological Association, New York, August.

1974 "Sex ratio at birth: Values, variance and some determinants." *Demography* 11:131–142.

Martin, Del, and Phyllis Lyon
1972 *Lesbian/Woman.* New York: Basic Books.

Martin, Del, and Paul Moriah
1972 "Homosexual Love—woman to woman, man to man." Pp. 120–134 in Herbert Otto, *Love Today.* New York: Association.

Martin, Elmer, and Joanne Mitchell Martin
1978 *The Black Extended Family.* Chicago: University of Chicago Press.

Martin, Ralph G.
1969 *Jennie: The Life of Lady Randolph Churchill.* Englewood Cliffs, NJ: Prentice-Hall.

Maslow, Abraham H.
1970 *Motivation and Personality.* New York: Harper & Row.

Masters, William, and Virginia Johnson
1966 *Human Sexual Response.* Boston: Little, Brown.

1973 "Why 'working at' sex doesn't work." *Redbook,* April:87.

1979 *Homosexuality in Perspective.* Boston: Little, Brown.

Mattessich, Paul
1978 "The family life cycle and three forms of social participation." Unpublished manuscript, University of Minnesota. Mimeographed.

Matthews, Sarah
1979 *The Social World of Old Women: Management of Self-Identity.* Beverly Hills, CA: Sage.

Mayer, Egon
1983 *Children of Intermarriage: A Study in Patterns of Identification and Family Life.* New York: The American Jewish Committee.

Mayer, Egon, and Carl Sheingold
1979 *Intermarriage and the Jewish Future: A National Study in Summary.* New York: The American Jewish Committee.

Mead, Margaret
1935 *Sex and Temperament.* New York: Morrow.

1966 "Marriage in two steps." *Redbook,* July:48–49.

1968 "A continuing dialogue on marriage." *Redbook*, April:44.

Melli, Marygold S.
1986 "The changing legal status of the single parent." *Family Relations* 35(January):31–35.

Melton, Willie, and Darwin L. Thomas
1976 "Instrumental and expressive values in mate selection of black and white college students." *Journal of Marriage and the Family* 38(August):509–517.

Meltzer, Bernard N.
1967 "Mead's social psychology." Pp. 5–24 in Jerome G. Manis and Bernard N. Meltzer (eds.), *Symbolic Interaction: A Reader in Social Psychology*. Boston: Allyn and Bacon.

Meltzer, Bernard N., John W. Petras, and Larry T. Reynolds
1975 *Symbolic Interactionism: Genesis, Varieties and Criticism*. Boston: Routledge and Kegan Paul.

Mendes, H.
1975 "Parental experiences of single fathers." Ph.D. dissertation. University of California at Los Angeles.

Mendola, Mary
1980 *The Mendola Report: A New Look at Gay Couples*. New York: Crown.

Mernissi, Fatima
1975 *Beyond the Veil: Male-Female Dynamics in a Modern Muslim Society*. New York: Schenkman.

Merton, Robert K.
1941 "Intermarriage and the social structure: fact and theory." *Psychiatry* 4:361–374.

Meyer, J., and B. Sobieszek
1972 "Effect of a child's sex on adult interpretations of its behavior." *Developmental Psychology* 6:42–48.

Middleton, Russell
1962 "A deviant case: Brother-sister and father-daughter marriage in Ancient Egypt. *American Sociological Review* 27:603–611.

Mill, John Stuart
1869 "The subjection of women." Reprinted in John Stuart Mill and Harriet Taylor Mill, *Essays on Sex Equality*, edited by Alice Rossi. Chicago: University of Chicago Press, 1970, pp. 125–242.

Miller, Arthur A.
1970 "Reactions of friends to divorce." Pp. 56–77 in Paul Bohannan (ed.), *Divorce and After*. Garden City, NY: Doubleday.

Miller, Brent, and Donna Sollie
1980 "Normal stress during the transition to parenthood." *Family Relations* 29(October):459–465.

Miller, Brian
1978 "Adult sexual resocialization: Adjustments toward a stigmatized identity." *Alternative Lifestyles* 1(May): 207–234.
1979 "Gay fathers and their children." *The Family Coordinator* 28(October):544–552.

Miller, Daniel, and Guy Swanson
1958 *The Changing American Parent: A Study in the Detroit Area*. New York: Wiley.

Miller, Howard L., and Paul S. Siegel
1972 *Loving: A Psychological Approach*. New York: Wiley.

Miller, Sherod, Elam Nunnally, and Daniel Wackman
1975 *Alive and Aware: Improving Communication in Relationships*. Minneapolis: Interpersonal Communications Programs.

Miller, Sherod, Daniel Wackman, Elam Nunnally, and Carol Saline
1982 *Straight Talk*. New York: Rawson, Wade Publishers, Inc. Also Signet paperback edition.

Miller, Warren B.
1973 "Psychological vulnerability to unwanted pregnancy." *Family Planning Perspectives* 5(Fall):199–201.

Miller, Warren B., and Lucile F. Newman (eds.)
1978 *The First Child and Family Formation*. Chapel Hill, NC: Carolina Population Center, University of North Carolina.

Mills, David
1984 "A model for stepfamily development." *Family Relations* 33(July):365–372.

Milton, John
1820 *The Doctrine and Discipline of Divorce*. London: Sherwood, Neely, and Jones. Reprint of pamphlet originally published in 1643.

Minnegerode, Fred, and Marcy Adelman
1978 "Elderly homosexual women and men: Report on a pilot study." *The Family Coordinator* 27(October):451–456.

Mirandé, Alfredo
1977 "The Chicano family: A reanalysis of conflicting views." *Journal of Marriage and the Family* 39(November):747–756.

Mitchell, Juliet
1971 *Woman's Estate*. New York: Pantheon.

Mochizuki, Takashi
1981 "Changing pattern of mate selection." *Jour-

nal of Comparative Family Studies XII, no. 3(Summer):317–328.

Model, Suzanne
1981 "Housework by husbands: Determinants and implications." *Journal of Family Issues* 2(June):225–237.

Moghissi, K. S.
1978 *Infertility.* Kansas City, MO: American Academy of Family Physicians.

Moles, Oliver C.
1979 "Public welfare payments and marital dissolution: A review of recent studies." Pp. 167–180 in George Levinger and Oliver C. Moles (eds.), *Divorce and Separation: Context, Causes, and Consequences.* New York: Basic Books.

Mollenkott, Virginia Ramey
1977 *Women, Men, and the Bible.* Nashville, TN: Abingdon.

Monahan, Thomas P.
1973 "Marriage across racial lines in Indiana." *Journal of Marriage and the Family* 35:632–640.

Money, John, and Anke A. Ehrhardt
1972 *Man and Woman, Boy and Girl.* Baltimore: The Johns Hopkins University Press. (Mentor paperback edition used in citations in this book.)

Money, John, and Patricia Tucker
1975 *Sexual Signatures: On Being a Man or a Woman.* Boston: Little, Brown.

Montgomery, Barbara M.
1981 "The form and function of quality communication in marriage." *Family Relations* 30(January):21–30.

Monthly Vital Statistics Reports
See U.S. Department of Health and Human Services.

Mooney, Elizabeth C.
1979 "I asked my daughter why she lives like she does." *Washington Post,* May 6.

Moore, Kristin
1978 "Teenage childbirth and welfare dependency." *Family Planning Perspectives* 10(July/August):233–235.

Moore, Patricia
1974 "Interview with Art and Irene Siegle." *Chicago Daily News,* May 26.

Morgan, Edmund S.
1966 *The Puritan Family.* New York: Harper & Row.

Morgan, Robin (ed.)
1970 *Sisterhood Is Powerful.* New York: Vintage.

1984 *Sisterhood Is Global.* Garden City, NY: Anchor Press/Doubleday.

Mortimer, Jeylan T., and Glorian Sorensen
1984 "Men, women, work, and family." Pp. 139–167 in Borman, Quarm, and Gideonse (eds.).

Moses, Yolanda T.
1985 "Black American women and work: Historical and contemporary strategies for empowerment, II." *Women's Studies International Forum* 8 (4):351–359.

Mosher, William D., and Christine A. Bachrach
1982 "Childlessness in the United States: Estimates from the National Survey of Family Growth." *Journal of Family Issues* 3 (4):517–543.

Mosher, William D., and Gerry E. Hendershot
1984 "Religious affiliation and the fertility of married couples." *Journal of Marriage and the Family* 46(August):671–677.

Mueller, Eva
1972 "Economic cost and value of children: Conceptualization and measurement." In Fawcett (ed.), 1972.

Mueller, Samuel A.
1971 "The new triple melting pot: Herberg revisited." *Review of Religous Research* 13:18–33.

Mulvihill, J. J., M. M. Tumin, and L. A. Curtis
1969 *Crimes of Violence.* Staff report to the National Commission on the Causes and Prevention of Violence.

Murdock, George P.
1949 *Social Structure.* New York: Macmillan.

Murillo, Nathan
1971 "The Mexican American family." Pp. 97–108 in N. N. Wagner and M. J. Haug (eds.), *Chicanos: Social and Psychological Perspectives.* St. Louis: Mosby.

Murphy, Patrick E., and William A. Staples
1979 "A modernized family life cycle." *Journal of Consumer Research* (June).

Murstein, Bernard L.
1980 "Mate selection in the seventies." *Decade Review: Family Research 1970–1979.* Special reprint of November issue of *Journal of Marriage and the Family* 42:51–66.

Myricks, Noel
1980 " 'Palimony': The impact of Marvin v. Marvin." *Family Relations* 29:210–215.

Nagi, Saad Z.
1977 *Child Maltreatment in the United States.* New York: Columbia University Press.

National Alliance for Optional Parenthood
1978 "Are you kidding yourself?" Pamphlet on teenage pregnancy.

National Center for Health Statistics
See U.S. Department of Health and Human Services.

National Commission for Employment Policy
1985 *Older Worker Employment Comes of Age: Practice and Potential.* Washington, DC: National Commission for Employment Policy (NECP).

Nazzari, Muriel
1983 "The 'woman question' in Cuba: An analysis of material constraints on its solution." *Signs* 9(Winter):246–263.

Nelson, James B.
1978 *Embodiment: An Approach to Sexuality and Christian Theology.* Minneapolis: Augsburg.

Nelson, Mary
1984 "Conceiving in 1984: The high-tech baby boom." *Family Life Educator* 2(Summer):4–8.

Neugarten, Bernice L.
1968 "The awareness of middle age." Pp. 93–98 in Bernice L. Neugarten (ed.), *Middle Age and Aging: A Reader in Social Psychology.* Chicago: University of Chicago Press.
1979 "Time, age, and the life cycle." *American Journal of Psychiatry* 136(July):887–894.

Neugarten, Bernice L., and Dail A. Neugarten
1987 "The Changing Meanings of Age." *Psychology Today* 21(May):29–33.

Newcomb, Michael, and Peter Bentler
1980 "Cohabitation before marriage: A comparison of married couples who did and did not cohabit." *Alternative Lifestyles* 3(February):65–85.

Nielsen, Joyce McCarl
1978 *Sex in Society: Perspectives on Stratification.* Belmont, CA: Wadsworth.

Nisbet, Robert A.
1970 *The Social Bond.* New York: Knopf.

Noble, Jeanne L.
1966 "The American Negro woman." Pp. 522–547 in John P. Davis (ed.) *The American Negro Reference Book.* Englewood Cliffs, NJ: Prentice-Hall.

Nock, Stephen L.
1979 "The family life cycle: Empirical or conceptual tool?" *Journal of Marriage and the Family* 41 (February):15–26.

Norton, Arthur J.
1983 "Family life cycle: 1980." *Journal of Marriage and the Family* 45(May):267–275.

Norton, Arthur J., and Paul C. Glick
1979 "Marital instability in America: Past, present, and future." Pp. 6–19 in Levinger and Moles (eds.).
1986 "One parent families: A social and economic profile." *Family Relations* 35(January):9–17.

Norwood, Janet L.
1982 "The female-male earnings gap: A review of employment and earnings issues." U.S. Department of Labor, Bureau of Labor Statistics Report 673 (September).

Nunnally, Jum C.
1972 "Major issues, measurement methods, and research strategies for investigating the effects of children on parents. In Fawcett (ed.), 1972.

Nye, F. Ivan
1963 "Marital interaction." Pp. 263–281 in Nye and Hoffman (eds.), 1963.
1974a "Sociocultural context." Pp. 1–31 in Hoffman and Nye (eds.), 1974.
1974b "Husband-wife relationship." Pp. 186–206 in Hoffman and Nye (eds.), 1974.

Nye, F. Ivan, and Lois W. Hoffman
1963 *The Employed Mother in America.* Chicago: Rand McNally.

Oakley, Ann
1974a *Women's Work: The Housewife, Past and Present.* New York: Pantheon. (Vintage paperback edition used in citations.)
1974b *The Sociology of Housework.* New York: Pantheon Books.
1981 *Subject Women.* New York: Pantheon Books.

O'Brien, John
1971 "Violence in divorce-prone families." *Journal of Marriage and the Family* 33:692–698.

Olson, D., and C. Rabunsky
1972 "Validity of four measures of family power." *Journal of Marriage and the Family* 34:224–234.

Olson, Lawrence
1983 *Costs of Children.* Lexington, MA: Lexington Books.

O'Malia, Ned
1982 "Charlie's shower—celebrating the expectant father." *Ms.,* February:48–49.

O'Neill, Nena, and George O'Neill
1970 "Patterns in group sexual activity." *Journal of Sex Research* 6(2):101–112.
1972 *Open Marriage*. New York: Evans. Avon paperback edition.

O'Neill, William L.
1967 *Divorce in the Progressive Era*. New Haven, CT. Yale University Press.

Oppenheimer, Valerie K.
1977 "The sociology of women's economic role in the family." *American Sociological Review* 42(June):387–406.

Orden, Susan, and Norman Bradburn
1969 "Working wives and marriage happiness." *American Journal of Sociology* 74:392–407.

Orthner, Dennis, Terry Brown, and Dennis Ferguson
1976 "Single-parent fatherhood: An emerging lifestyle." *The Family Coordinator* 25(October):429–437.

Orthner, Dennis, and Ken Lewis
1979 "Evidence of single-father competence in childrearing." *Family Law Quarterly* XIII(Spring):27–47.

Ovid
Metamorphoses. Translated by Mary M. Innes. Baltimore: Penguin, 1955.

Pagelow, Mildred Daley
1976 "Lesbian mothers." Paper presented at the annual meetings of the American Sociological Association, New York, August 31.
1981 *Woman-Battering*. Beverly Hills, CA: Sage.

Pala, Achola O.
1977 "Definitions of women and development: An African perspective." *Signs* 3(Autumn):9–13.

Palmore, Erdman
1968 "The effects of aging on activities and attitudes." *The Gerontologist* 8(Winter):259–263.
1970 (ed.) *Normal Aging: Reports from the Duke Longitudinal Study 1955–1969*. Durham, NC: Duke University Press.

Papanek, Hanna
1977 "Development planning for women." *Signs* 3(Autumn):14–21.

Papernow, Patricia L.
1984 "The stepfamily cycle: An experiential model of stepfamily development." *Family Relations* 33(July):355–363.

Parron, Eugenia, and Lillian E. Troll
1978 "Golden wedding couples: Effects of retirement on intimacy in long-standing marriages." *Alternative Lifestyles* 1(November):447–464.

Parsons, Talcott
1942 "Age and sex in the social structure." *American Sociological Review* 7:604–606.
1943 "The kinship system of the contemporary United States." *American Anthropologist* 45:22–38.
1951 *The Social System*. New York: Free Press.
1954 "The incest taboo in relation to the social structure." *The British Journal of Sociology* V:101–117. Reprinted in Rose L. Coser (ed.), *The Family: Its Structure and Functions*. New York: St. Martin's Press, 1964.
1955 "The American family: Its relation to personality and to social structure." In T. Parsons and R. F. Bales (eds.), *Family, Socialization and Interaction Process*. New York: Free Press.

Parsons, Talcott, and Robert F. Bales (eds.)
1955 *Family, Socialization and Interaction Process*. New York: Free Press.

Paul, William, James Weinrich, John Gonsiorek, and Mary Hotvedt (eds.)
1982 *Homosexuality: Social, Psychological, and Biological Issues*. Beverly Hills, CA: Sage.

Pearlin, Leonard
1972 *Class Context and Family Relations: A Cross-National Study*. Boston: Little, Brown.

Peck, Ellen
1971 *The Baby Trap*. New York: Bernard Geis.

Peplau, Letitia, and Hortensia Amaro
1982 "Understanding lesbian relationships." Pp. 233–247 in William Paul et al. (eds.).

Peterman, Dan, Carl Ridley, and Scott Anderson
1974 "A comparison of cohabiting and noncohabiting college students." *Journal of Marriage and the Family* 36(May):344–354.

Peters, Marie Ferguson
1985 "Racial socialization of young black children." Pp. 159–173 in McAdoo and McAdoo (eds.), *Black Children*.

Peterson, Candida C., and James L. Peterson
1973 "Preference for sex of offspring as a measure of change in sex attitudes." *Psychology* 10(August):3–5.

Peterson, Nancy L.
1981 *Our Lives for Ourselves: Women Who Have Never Married*. New York: G. P. Putnam's Sons. Republished under the title, *The Ever-Single Woman*. New York: Quill, 1982.

Pettigrew, Thomas
1964   *A Profile of the Negro American.* Princeton, NJ: D. Van Nostrand.

Philliber, William W., and Dana V. Hiller
1978   "The implication of wife's occupational attainment for husband's class identification." *Sociological Quarterly* 19(Autumn):450–458.

Piddington, Ralph
1965   "A study of French Canadian kinship." *International Journal of Comparative Sociology* 12 (1). Reprinted in C. C. Harris (ed.), *Readings in Kinship in Urban Society.* New York: Pergamon, 1970:71–98.

Pineo, Peter C.
1961   "Disenchantment in the later years of marriage." *Marriage and Family Living* 23:3–11.

Plateris, Alexander A.
1979   "Divorces by marriage cohort." *Vital and Health Statistics,* ser. 21, no. 34 (August). Washington, DC: National Center for Health Statistics.
1981   "Duration of Marriage before Divorce: United States." *Vital and Health Statistics,* ser. 21, no. 38. Hyattsville, MD: National Center for Health Statistics, Public Health Service.

Pleck, Joseph H.
1985   *Working Wives, Wives, Working Husbands.* Beverly Hills, CA: Sage.

Pleck, Joseph, and Jack Sawyer (eds.)
1974   *Men and Masculinity.* Englewood Cliffs, NJ: Prentice-Hall.

Poertner, John
1986   "Estimating the incidence of abused older persons." *Journal of Gerontological Social Work* 9(Spring):3–15.

Poffenberger, T.
1969   "Husband-wife communication and motivational aspects of population control in an Indian village." Monograph ser. no. 10(December). New Delhi: Central Family Planning Institute.

Pogrebin, Bertrand B.
1972   "How does it feel to be the husband of . . . ?" *Ms.* (September). Reprinted in *Scenes from Life,* Judy Blankenship (ed.), pp. 385–388. Boston: Little, Brown, 1976.

Pogrebin, Letty Cottin
1982   "Big changes in parenting." *Ms.,* February:41–46.

Polonko, Karen
1979   "Accounting for the conditions of voluntary childlessness." Ph.D. dissertation, Indiana University, Bloomington.

Polonko, Karen, John Scanzoni, and Jay Teachman
1982   "Childlessness and marital satisfaction: A further assessment." *Journal of Family Issues* 3(December):545–573.

Pomeroy, Wardell B.
1972   *Dr. Kinsey and the Institute for Sex Research.* New York: Harper & Row.

Pomroy, Martha
1980   *What Every Woman Needs to Know about the Law.* Garden City, NY: Doubleday.

Ponse, Barbara
1978   *Identities in the Lesbian World.* Westport, CT: Greenwood Press.

Population Institute, The
1982   *The Population Institute Annual Report.* Washington, DC: The Population Institute. December.

Porter, Nancy L., and F. Scott Christopher
1984   "Infertility: Towards an awareness of a need among family life practitioners." *Family Relations* 33(April):309–315.

Powers, Edward A., and Gordon L. Bultena
1976   "Sex differences in intimate friendships of old age." *Journal of Marriage and the Family* 38(November):739–747.

Powers, Jeanne Audrey
1976   "Rituals with the divorced." Pp. 73–96 in *Ritual in a New Day.* Nashville: Abingdon.

Prager, Emily
1979   "Roommates, but not lovers." *Ms.,* April:16–19.

Presser, Harriet B., and Larry L. Bumpass
1972   "The acceptability of contraceptive sterilization among U.S. couples: 1970." *Family Planning Perspectives* 4(October):18–26.

Price-Bonham, Sharon, and Jack O. Balswick
1980   "The noninstitutions": Divorce, desertion, and remarriage." *Journal of Marriage and the Family* 42(November):225–238.

Pryor, Edward, Jr.
1972   "Rhode Island family structure: 1875 and 1960." In Laslett, 1972.

Queen, Stuart, and Robert Habenstein
1974   *The Family in Various Cultures,* 4th ed. Philadelphia: Lippincott.

Rabin, Albert I.
1970   "The sexes: Ideology and reality in the Israeli kibbutz." In Georgene H. Seward and

Robert C. Williamson (eds.), *Sex Roles in a Changing Society*. New York: Random House, pp. 285–307.

Rabin, Albert I., and Benjamin Beit-Hallahmi
1982 *Twenty Years Later: Kibbutz Children Grown Up*. New York: Springer.

Rabkin, Leslie, and Melford Spiro
1970 "Postscript: The kibbutz in 1970." Chap. 9 in Melford Spiro, *Kibbutz: Venture in Utopia*. New York: Schocken.

Rains, Prudence
1971 *Becoming an Unwed Mother*. Chicago: Aldine.

Rainwater, Lee
1960 *And the Poor Get Children*. Chicago: Quadrangle.
1964 "Marital sexuality in four 'cultures of poverty' " *Journal of Marriage and the Family* 26(November):457–466.
1965 *Family Design: Marital Sexuality, Family Size, and Contraception*. Chicago: Aldine.
1966a "Sex in the culture of poverty." *Journal of Social Issues* 22(April), as reprinted in a later version in Carlfred Broderick and Jessie Bernard, *The Individual, Sex and Society*. Baltimore: Johns Hopkins, 1969. Pp. 129–140.
1966b "Crucible of identity: The Negro lower-class family." *Daedalus* 95(Winter):172–216.
1970 *Behind Ghetto Walls*. Chicago: Aldine.

Ramey, Estelle
1973 "Sex hormones and executive ability." *Annals of the New York Academy of Sciences* 208(March 15):237–245.

Rank, Mark
1981 "The transition to marriage: A comparison of cohabiting and dating relationships ending in marriage or divorce." *Alternative Lifestyles* 4(November):487–506.

Rank, Mark R., and Craig W. LeCroy
1983 "Toward a multiple perspective in family theory and practice: The case of social exchange theory, symbolic interactionism, conflict theory." *Family Relations* 32(July):441–448.

Raphael, Sharon M., and Mina K. Robinson
1980 "The older lesbian," *Alternative Lifestyles* 3(May):207–229.

Rapoport, Rhona
1963 "Normal crises, family structures and mental health." *Family Process* 2(March):68–80.

Rapoport, Rhona, Robert Rapoport, Ziona Strelitz, and Stephen Kew
1977 *Fathers, Mothers and Society: Towards New Alliances*. New York: Basic Books.

Raschke, Helen, and Vernon Raschke
1979 "Family conflict and children's self-concepts: A comparison of intact and single-parent families." *Journal of Marriage and the Family* 41(May):367–374.

Rawlings, Stephen
1978 "Perspectives on American husbands and wives." *Current Population Reports: Special Studies*, ser. P-23, no. 77. Washington, DC: U.S. Bureau of the Census, 1978.

Redford, Myron H., Gordon W. Duncan, and Denis J. Prager (eds.)
1974 *The Condom: Increasing Utilization in the United States*. San Francisco: San Francisco Press.

Reed, Evelyn
1975 *Woman's Evolution: From Matriarchal Clan to Patriarchal Family*. New York: Pathfinder Press.

Rehwinkel, Alfred M.
1959 *Planned Parenthood*. St. Louis: Concordia.

Reiss, Ira L.
1960a *Premarital Sexual Standards in America*. New York: Free Press.
1960b "Toward a sociology of the heterosexual love relationship." *Journal of Marriage and Family Living* 22(May):139–155.
1967a "Some comments on premarital sexual permissiveness." *American Journal of Sociology* 72:558–559.
1967b *The Social Context of Premarital Sexual Permissiveness*. New York: Holt.
1972 "Premarital sexuality: Past, present, and future." Pp. 167–188 in Ira L. Reiss (ed.), *Readings on the Family System*. New York: Holt.
1973 "The role of sexuality in the study of family and fertility." Paper presented at the conference "Family and Fertility," sponsored by the Center for Population Research and the National Institute for Child Health and Human Development, June 13–16, Belmont, Elkridge, Maryland. Mimeographed.

Reiss, Ira L., Ronald E. Anderson, and G. C. Sponaugle
1980 "Multivariate Model of the Determinants of Extramarital Permissiveness." *Journal of*

Marriage and the Family 42(May):395–411.

Reiss, Ira L., Albert Banwart, and Harry Foreman
1975 "Premarital contraceptive usage: A study and some theoretical explorations." *Journal of Marriage and the Family* 37(August):619–630.

Rempel, Judith
1985 "Childless Elderly: What Are They Missing?" *Journal of Marriage and the Family* 47(May):343–348.

Renne, Karen
1970 "Correlates of dissatisfaction in marriage." *Journal of Marriage and the Family* 32:54–67.

Rheinstein, Max
1972 *Marriage, Stability, Divorce, and the Law.* Chicago: University of Chicago Press.

Rich, Adrienne
1976 *Of Woman Born: Motherhood as Experience and Institution.* New York: Norton.

Richer, Stephen
1968 "The economics of child rearing." *Journal of Marriage and the Family* 30:462–466.

Richman, Judith
1977 "Bargaining for sex and status: The dating service and sex-role change." Pp. 158–165 in Peter J. Stein, Judith Richman, and Natalie Hannon (eds.), *The Family: Functions, Conflicts, and Symbols.* Reading, MA: Addison-Wesley.

Ricks, Shirley S.
1985 "Father-infant interactions: A review of empirical research." *Family Relations,* 34(October):505–511.

Ridley, Carl, Dan Peterman, and Arthur Avery
1978 "Cohabitation: Does it make for a better marriage?" *The Family Coordinator* 27(April):129–136.

Riley, Matilda White
1983 "The family in an aging society." *Journal of Family Issues* 4(September):439–454.

Riley, Matilda White, and Anne Foner, in association with M. Moore, B. Hess, and B. Roth
1968 *Aging and Society,* Vol. 1. New York: Russell Sage.

Risman, Barbara J.
1986 "Can men 'mother'? Life as a single father." *Family Relations* 35(January):95–102.

Risman, Barbara, Charles Hill, Zick Rubin, and Letitia Anne Peplau
1981 "Living together in college: Implications for courtship." *Journal of Marriage and the Family* 43(February):77–83.

Rivers, Ulysses J.
1986 "Black Women: Their struggle to find a lasting love." *USA Today,* May 29, p. 5D.

Rivlin, Lilly
1979 "Choosing to have a baby on your own." *Ms.,* April:68–70, 91–94.

Roberts, Helene
1977 "The exquisite slave: The role of clothes in the making of the Victorian woman." *Signs* 2(Spring):554–569.

Robertson, Joan
1977 "Grandmotherhood: A study of role conceptions." *Journal of Marriage and the Family* 39(February):165–174.

1978 "Women in midlife: Crises, reverberations, and support networks." *The Family Coordinator* 27(October):375–382.

Robins, Lee, and Miroda Tomanec
1962 "Closeness to blood relatives outside the immediate family." *Marriage and Family Living* 24(November):340–346. Reprinted in Farber, 1966.

Robinson, Ira E., and Davor Jedlicka
1982 "Change in sexual attitudes and behavior of college students from 1965 to 1980: A research note." *Journal of Marriage and the Family* 44(February):237–240.

Rodgers, Roy H.
1964 "Toward a theory of family development." *Journal of Marriage and the Family* 26:262–270.

1973 *Family Interaction and Transaction: The Developmental Approach.* Englewood Cliffs, NJ: Prentice-Hall.

Rodgers, Roy H., and Gail Witney
1981 "The family cycle in twentieth century Canada." *Journal of Marriage and the Family* 43(August):727–740.

Rodman, Hyman
1967 "Marital power in France, Greece, Yugoslavia and the United States: A cross-national discussion." *Journal of Marriage and the Family* 29:320–324.

1972 "Marital power and the theory of resources in cultural context." *Journal of Comparative Family Studies* 3:50–67.

Rodman, Hyman, David J. Pratto, and Rosemary Smith Nelson
1985 "Child care arrangements and children's functioning: A comparison of self-care and

adult-care children." *Developmental Psychology* 21 (3):413–418.

Rohrlich-Leavitt, Ruby
1976 "Comment on Harriet Whitehead's review of *Woman's Evolution.*" *Signs* 2(Winter):498–500.

Rollins, Boyd, and Harold Feldman
1970 "Marital satisfaction over the family life cycle." *Journal of Marriage and the Family* 26:20–28.

Rollins, Boyd, and Richard Galligan
1978 "The developing child and marital satisfaction." Pp. 71–105 in Lerner and Spanier (eds.).

Roosevelt, Ruth, and Jeannette Lofas
1977 *Living in Step: A Remarriage Manual for Parents and Children.* New York: McGraw-Hill.

Rosaldo, Michelle Zimbalist
1974 "Woman, culture, and society: A theoretical overview." Pp. 17–42 in Michelle Zimbalist Rosaldo and Louise Lamphere (eds.), *Woman, Culture and Society.* Stanford, CA: Stanford University Press.

Rosaldo, Michelle Zimbalist, and Louise Lamphere (eds.)
1974 *Woman, Culture, and Society.* Stanford, CA: Stanford University Press.

Rosenberg, Bernard, and Joseph Bensman
1968 "Sexual patterns in three ethnic subcultures of an American underclass." *Annals of the American Academy of Political and Social Science* 376:61–75.

Rosenthal, Carolyn J.
1985 "Kinkeeping in the familial division of labor." *Journal of Marriage and the Family* 47(November):965–974.

Rosenthal, Kristine, and Harry Keshet
1978 "The impact of childcare responsibilities on part-time or single fathers." *Alternative Lifestyles* (November):465–491.

Rosenthal, Lois
1983 *Partnering.* Cincinnati: Writer's Digest Books.

Rosoff, Jeannie I.
1985 Editorial: "An interlocking agenda." *Family Planning Perspectives* 17(May/June):100.

Rosow, Irving
1973 *Socialization to Old Age.* Berkeley: University of California Press.

Rossi, Alice
1964 "Equality between the sexes: An immodest proposal." Pp. 98–143 in R. J. Lifton (ed.), *The Woman in America.* Boston: Beacon Press Daedalus Library.

1965 "Barriers to the career choice of engineering, medicine, or science among American women." Pp. 51–127 in Jacquelyn Mattfield and Carol Van Aken (eds.), *Women and the Scientific Professions.* Cambridge, MA: M.I.T. Press.

1968 "Transition to parenthood." *Journal of Marriage and the Family* 30:26–39.

1973a "Sexuality and gender roles." Lecture given in the human sexuality unit of the Year II Program in Psychiatry and Behavioral Sciences, The Johns Hopkins University School of Medicine, February 2. Revised version. Mimeographed.

1973b (ed.) *The Feminist Papers.* New York: Columbia University Press.

1977 "A biosocial perspective on parenting." *Daedalus* 106(Spring):1–31.

1980 "Life-span theories and women's lives." *Signs* 6(Autumn):4–32.

1985 *Gender and the Life Course.* New York: Aldine.

Rossi, Peter
1961 In Philip Ennis, ed. *Seven Questions about the Profession of Librarianship.* Chicago: University of Chicago Press. (Quoted in Dee Garison, "The Tender Technicians: The Feminization of Public Librarianship, 1976–1905," pp. 158–178 in Mary Hartman and Lois W. Banner, eds., *Clio's Consciousness Raised.* New York: Harper Colophon Books, 1974.)

Rowbotham, Sheila
1972 *Women, Resistance and Revolution.* New York: Pantheon.

Rubin, Lillian Breslow
1976 *Worlds of Pain: Life in the Working-Class Family.* New York: Basic Books.

1979 *Women of a Certain Age: The Midlife Search for Self.* New York: Harper & Row.

1983 *Intimate Strangers: Men and Women Together.* New York: Harper & Row.

Rubin, Zick
1973 *Liking and Loving.* New York: Holt.

Ruether, Rosemary Radford
1983 *Sexism and God-Talk: Toward a Feminist Theology.* Boston: Beacon Press.

Ruether, Rosemary Radford, and Eleanor McLaughlin
1979 *Women of Spirit: Female Leadership in the*

Jewish and Christian Traditions. New York: Simon and Schuster.

Rugoff, Milton
1971 *Prudery and Passion.* New York: Putnam.

Russell, Bertrand
1929 *Marriage and Morals.*

Russell, Candyce Smith
1974 "Transition to parenthood: Problems and gratifications." *Journal of Marriage and the Family* 36(May):294.

Russell, Diana E. H.
1982 *Rape in Marriage.* New York: Macmillan.

Ryder, Norman
1973 "Contraceptive failure in the United States." *Family Planning Perspectives* 5(Summer): 133–142.

Ryder, Norman, and Charles Westoff
1971 *Reproduction in the United States, 1965.* Princeton, NJ: Princeton University Press.

Ryder, Robert G.
1970 "Dimensions of early marriage." *Family Process* 9(March):51–68.
1973 "Longitudinal data relating marriage satisfaction and having a child." *Journal of Marriage and the Family* 35:604–606.

Safa, Helen I.
1971 "The matrifocal family in the black ghetto: Sign of pathology or pattern of survival?" Pp. 35–59 in Charles O. Crawford (ed.), *Health and the Family: A Medical-Sociological Analysis.* New York: Macmillan.

Safilios-Rothschild, Constantina
1967 "A comparison of power structure and marital satisfaction in urban Greek and French families." *Journal of Marriage and the Family* 29:345–352.
1969 "Family sociology or wives' family sociology? A cross-cultural examination of decision making." *Journal of Marriage and the Family* 31:290–301.
1970 "The study of family power structure: A review 1960–1969." *Journal of Marriage and the Family* 32:539–552.

St. George, George
1973 *Our Soviet Sister.* Washington, DC: Luce.

Salas, Rafael M.
1985 "The state of world population, 1985: Population and Women." World Population News Service, *Popline* 7(July):4–5.

Salts, C. J.
1979 "Divorce Process: Integration and Theory." *Journal of Divorce* 2(Spring):233–240.

Sanday, Peggy R.
1973 "Toward a theory of the status of women." *American Anthropologist* 75:1682–1700.

Satir, Virginia
1967 "Marriage as a statutory five-year renewable contract." Paper presented at the annual convention of the American Psychological Association, Washington, DC, September 1.

Saunders, Janice Miller, and John N. Edwards
1984 "Extramarital sexuality: A predictive model of permissive attitudes." *Journal of Marriage and the Family* 46(November):825–835.

Sawin, Margaret M.
1982 *Hope for Families.* New York: William H. Sadlier.

Scanzoni, John
1965 "A note on the sufficiency of wife responses in family research." *Pacific Sociological Review*(Fall):109–115.
1970 *Opportunity and the Family.* New York: Free Press.
1972 *Sexual Bargaining: Power Politics in the American Marriage.* Englewood Cliffs, NJ: Prentice-Hall. (2d edition, Chicago: University of Chicago Press, 1982.)
1975a "Sex roles, economic factors, and marital solidarity in black and white marriages." *Journal of Marriage and the Family* 37:130–145.
1975b *Sex Roles, Life Styles, and Childbearing: Changing Patterns in Marriage and Family.* New York: Free Press.
1975c "Change in gender roles." Unpublished student study. Department of Sociology, Indiana University, Bloomington.
1977 *The Black Family in Modern Society: Patterns of Stability and Security.* Chicago: University of Chicago Press (enlarged edition).
1978 *Sex Roles, Women's Work, and Marital Conflict.* Lexington, MA: Lexington Books, D. C. Heath.
1979a "Strategies for changing male family roles: Research and practice implications." *The Family Coordinator* 28(October):435–442.
1979b "Social processes and power in families." In Wesley R. Burr, Reuben Hill, F. Ivan Nye, and Ira L. Reiss (eds.), *Contemporary Theories About the Family,* Vol. 1. New York: Free Press.
1979c "A historical perspective on husband-wife

bargaining power and marital dissolution." Pp. 20–36 in Levinger and Moles (eds.).

1980 "Contemporary marriage types: A research note." *Journal of Family Issues* 1(March): 125–140.

1983a "Changing gender roles and redefinitions of family development." Paper presented at a thematic session of the annual meetings of the American Sociological Association, August 1983; Detroit, MI.

1983b *Shaping Tomorrow's Family: Theory and Policy for the 21st Century.* Beverly Hills, CA: Sage.

1985 "Black parental values and expectations of children's occupational and educational success." Pp. 113–122 in Harriette Pipes McAdoo and John Lewis McAdoo (eds.), *Black Children.* Beverly Hills, CA: Sage.

Scanzoni, John, and Greer Litton Fox

1980 "Sex roles, family and society: The seventies and beyond." *Journal of Marriage and the Family* 42(November):20–33.

Scanzoni, John, and Maximiliane Szinovacz

1980 *Family Decision-Making: A Developmental Sex Role Model.* Beverly Hills, CA: Sage.

Scanzoni, Letha Dawson, and Nancy A. Hardesty

1986 *All We're Meant to be: Biblical Feminism for Today,* revised edition. Nashville, TN: Abingdon.

Scanzoni, Letha, and Virginia Ramey Mollenkott

1978 *Is the Homosexual My Neighbor? Another Christian View.* San Francisco: Harper & Row.

Schäfer, Siegrid

1977 "Sociosexual behavior in male and female homosexuals: A study in sex differences." *Archives of Sexual Behavior* 6(September):355–364.

Schelling, T. C., and M. H. Halperin

1961 *Strategy and Arms Control.* New York: Twentieth Century Fund.

Schlesinger, Yatta

1977 "Sex roles and social change in the kibbutz." *Journal of Marriage and the Family* 39(November):771–779.

Schmidt, Gunter, and Volkmar Sigusch

1970 "Sex differences in responses to psychosexual stimulation by films and slides." *The Journal of Sex Research* 6:268–283.

1972 "Changes in sexual behavior among young males and females between 1960–1970." *Archives of Sexual Behavior* 2:27–45.

1973 "Women's sexual arousal." Pp. 117–143 in Joseph Zubin and John Money (eds.), *Contemporary Sexual Behavior: Critical Issues in the 1970's.* Baltimore: Johns Hopkins.

Schmidt, G., V. Sigusch, and S. Schäfer

1973 "Responses to reading erotic stories: Male-female differences." *Archives of Sexual Behavior* 2(June):181–199.

Schneider, David

1968 *American Kinship: A Cultural Account.* Englewood Cliffs, NJ: Prentice-Hall.

Schoenmaker, Adrian, and Davis Radosevich

1976 "Men nursing students: How they perceive their situation." *Nursing Outlook* 24(1976): 298–303. Cited in *Signs* (Summer):1977, p. 831.

Schram, Rosalyn Weinman

1979 "Marital satisfaction over the family life cycle: A critique and proposal." *Journal of Marriage and the Family* 41(February):7–12.

Schulz, David A.

1969 *Coming Up Black.* Englewood Cliffs, NJ: Prentice-Hall.

Scott, Hilda

1974 *Does Socialism Liberate Women?* Boston: Beacon Press.

Scott, Jean Pearson

1979 "Single rural elders: A comparison of dimensions of life satisfaction." *Alternative Lifestyles* 2(August):359–378.

Scott, John Finley

1965 "The American college sorority: Its role in class and ethnic endogamy." *American Sociological Review* 30:514–527.

Scroggs, Robin

1983 *The New Testament and Homosexuality.* Philadelphia: Fortress Press.

Seaman, Barbara

1972 *Free and Female.* New York: Coward, McCann and Geoghegan.

Sears, Robert, Eleanor E. Maccoby, and Harry Levin

1957 *Patterns of Child Rearing.* Evanston, IL: Row, Peterson.

Secord, Paul F., and Kenneth Ghee

1986 "Implications of the black marriage market for marital conflict." *Journal of Family Issues* 7(March):21–30.

Sedugin, P.

1973 *New Soviet Legislation on Marriage and the Family.* Moscow: Progress Publishers.

Seeley, John R., R. Alexander Sim, and Elizabeth W. Loosley

1956 *Crestwood Heights.* New York: Basic Books.

Segal, Sheldon J.

1972 "Contraceptive research: A male chauvinist plot?" *Family Planning Perspectives* 4(July):21–25.

Seidenberg, Robert

1970 *Marriage between Equals.* First published as *Marriage in Life and Literature.* New York: Philosophical Library. Doubleday, Anchor Press edition, 1973.

Seltman, Charles

1956 *Women in Antiquity.* London: Thames and Hudson.

Sengstock, Mary C., and Sara Barrett

1986 "Elderly victims of family abuse, neglect, and maltreatment: Can legal assistance help?" *Journal of Gerontological Social Work* 9(Spring):43–61.

Shack-Marquez, Janice

1984 "Earnings differences between men and women: An introductory note." *Monthly Labor Review* 107, no. 6(June):15–16.

Shah, Farida, and Melvin Zelnik

1981 "Parent and peer influence on sexual behavior, contraceptive use, and pregnancy experience of young women." *Journal of Marriage and the Family* 43(May):339–348.

Shanas, Ethel

1972 "Adjustment to retirement: Substitution or accommodation?" in Frances Carp (ed.), *Retirement.* New York: Behavioral Publications.

1979 "Social myth as hypothesis: The case of the family relations of old people." *The Gerontologist* 19(February):3–9.

Shannon, T. W.

1917 *Eugenics: The Laws of Sex Life and Heredity.* Marietta, OH: Mullikin. Replica edition. Garden City, NY: Doubleday, 1970.

Shearer, Lloyd

1986 "Dr. George Hatem and Prostitution in China." *Parade,* June 22:14–15.

Shedd, Charlie W.

1968 *The Stork is Dead.* Waco, TX: Word.

Shenker, Israel

1976 "Smithsonian urges public to dig at the family tree." *The New York Times,* June 17.

Sheppard, Harold, and Neal Herrick

1972 *Where Have All the Robots Gone? Worker Dissatisfaction in the 1970's.* New York: Free Press.

Shideler, Mary McDermott

1971 "An amicable divorce." *The Christian Century,* May 5.

Shorter, Edward

1977 *The Making of the Modern Family.* New York: Basic Books.

Shulman, Norman

1975 "Life-cycle variations in patterns of close relationships." *Journal of Marriage and the Family* 37(November):813–821.

Sickels, Robert J.

1972 *Race, Marriage and the Law.* Albuquerque: University of New Mexico Press.

Sidel, Ruth

1972 *Women and Child Care in China.* New York: Hill and Wang. Baltimore: Penguin.

SIECUS (Sex Information and Education Council of the United States)

1970 *Sexuality and Man.* New York: Scribner's Sons.

Siegel, Sidney, and Lawrence Fouraker

1960 *Bargaining and Group Decision Making.* New York: McGraw-Hill.

Silberman, Charles

1985 *A Certain People: American Jews and Their Lives Today.* New York: Summit Books.

Silka, Linda, and Sara Kiesler

1977 "Couples who choose to remain childless." *Family Planning Perspectives* 9(January/February):16–25.

Silverman, Phyllis

1972 "Widowhood and preventive intervention." *The Family Coordinator* 21(January):95–102.

Silverstein, Arthur J.

1972–73 "Comment: Constitutional aspects of the homosexual's right to a marriage license." *Journal of Family Law* 12:607–634.

Silverstein, Charles

1981 *Man to Man: Gay Couples in America.* New York: Morrow.

Simmel, Georg

1950 *The Sociology of Georg Simmel.* Translated and edited by Kurt H. Wolff. New York: Free Press.

1955 *Conflict and the Web of Group-Affiliations.* Translated by Kurt H. Wolff and Reinhard Bendix. New York: Free Press.

Simon, W., A. S. Berger, and J. H. Gagnon

1972 "Beyond anxiety and fantasy: The coital experiences of college youth." *Journal of Youth and Adolescence* 1:203–222.

Simon, William, and John Gagnon

1969 "On psychosexual development." Pp. 733–752 in D. A. Goslin (ed.), *Handbook of So-*

cialization Theory and Research. Chicago: Rand McNally.

Simpson, Joanne
1973 "Meteorologist." *Annals of the New York Academy of Sciences.* 208(March 15):41–46. (Special issue, "Successful women in the sciences: An analysis of determinants.")

Singh, B. K.
1980 "Trends in attitudes toward premarital sexual relations." *Journal of Marriage and the Family* 42(May):387–393.

Skinner, Denise A.
1980 "Dual-career family stress and coping: A literature review." *Family Relations* 29(October):473–480.

Skipper, James K., Jr., and Gilbert Nass
1966 "Dating behavior: A framework for analysis and an illustration." *Journal of Marriage and the Family* 28(November):412–420.

Sklar, J., and B. Berkov
1974 "Abortion, illegitimacy and the American birth rate." *Science* 185:909. Also see summary, "Legal abortion reduces out-of-wedlock births." *Family Planning Perspectives* 7(January/February, 1975):11–12.

Skolnick, Arlene
1973 *The Intimate Environment.* Boston: Little, Brown.

Slocum, Walter L.
1966 *Occupational Careers.* Chicago: Aldine.

Smith, Daniel Scott
1973 "The dating of the American sexual revolution: Evidence and interpretation." Pp. 321–335 in Michael Gordon (ed.), *The American Family in Social-Historical Perspective.* New York: St. Martin's.

Smith, Drake S.
1985 "Wife employment and marital adjustment: A cumulation of results." *Family Relations* 34(October):483–490.

Smith, Eleanor
1985 "Black American women and work: A historical review—1619–1920." *Women's Studies International Forum* 8(4):343–349.

Smith, Harold E.
1965 "Family interaction patterns of the aged: A review." Pp. 143–161 in Arnold Rose and Warren Peterson (eds.), *Older People and Their Social World.* Philadelphia: Davis.

Smith, James, and Lynn Smith
1970 "Co-marital sex and the sexual freedom movement." *Journal of Sex Research* 6(2):131–142.

1974 (eds.) *Beyond Monogamy.* Baltimore: Johns Hopkins.

Smith, Lynn, and James Smith
1973 "Co-marital sex: The incorporation of extramarital sex into the marriage relationship." In J. Zubin and J. Money (eds.), *Critical Issues in Contemporary Sexual Behavior.* Baltimore: Johns Hopkins. (Reprinted in Smith and Smith, 1974.)

Smith, Michael J.
1980 "The social consequences of single parenthood: A longitudinal perspective." *Family Relations* 29(January):75–81.

Sobol, Michael P., and Jeanette Cardiff
1983 "A sociopsychological investigation of adult adoptees' search for birth parents." *Family Relations* 32(October):477–483.

Sonenblick, Jerry, with Martha Sowerwine
1981 *The Legality of Love,* New York: Jove.

Spanier, Graham B.
1976 "Formal and informal sex education as determinants of premarital sexual behavior." *Archives of Sexual Behavior* 5(January):39–67.

1983 "Married and unmarried cohabitation in the United States: 1980." *Journal of Marriage and the Family* 45(May):277–288.

Spanier, Graham B., and Robert F. Casto
1979 "Adjustment to separation and divorce: A qualitative analysis." Pp. 211–227 in Levinger and Moles (eds.), 1979.

Spanier, Graham B., and Frank F. Furstenberg, Jr.
1984 *Recycling the Family: Remarriage After Divorce.* Beverly Hills, CA: Sage.

Spanier, Graham B., and Paul C. Glick
1980a "The life cycle of American families: An expanded analysis," *Journal of Family History* 5(Spring):97–111.

1980b "Mate selection differentials between whites and blacks in the United States." *Social Forces* 58(3):707–725.

Spanier, Graham B., and Robert A. Lewis
1980 "Marital quality: A review of the seventies." *Journal and the Family* 42(November):96–110.

Spanier, Graham B., Robert A. Lewis, and Charles L. Cole
1975 "Marital adjustment over the family life cycle: The issue of curvilinearity." *Journal of Marriage and the Family* 37(May):263–275.

Spanier, Graham B., and Randie L. Margolis
1983 "Marital separation and extramarital sexual

behavior." *The Journal of Sex Research* 19(February):23–48.

Spanier, Graham, and William Sauer
1979 "An empirical evaluation of the family life cycle." *Journal of Marriage and the Family* 41(February):27–38.

Spanier, Graham B., and Linda Thompson
1984 *Parting: The Aftermath of Separation and Divorce.* Beverly Hills, CA: Sage.

Spiro, Melford E.
1965 *Children of the Kibbutz.* New York: Schocken.
1970 *Kibbutz: Venture in Utopia.* New York: Schocken.

Spitze, G. D., and J. L. Spaeth
1979 "Employment among married female college graduates." *Social Science Research* 8:184–199.

Spitze, Glenna D., and Linda J. Waite
1981 "Wives' employment: The role of husbands' perceived attitudes." *Journal of Marriage and the Family* 43(February):117–124.

Spreitzer, Elmer, and Lawrence Riley
1974 "Factors associated with singlehood." *Journal of Marriage and the Family* 36:533–542.

Sprey, Jetse
1971 "On the management of conflict in families." *Journal of Marriage and the Family* 33:722–732.

Stack, Carol B., Mina D. Caulfield, Valerie Estes, Susan Landes, Karen Larson, Pamela Johnson, Juliet Rake, and Judith Shirek
1975 "Anthropology." *Signs* 1(Autumn):147–159.

Stafford, Rebecca, Elaine Backman, and Pamela diBona
1977 "The division of labor among cohabiting and married couples." *Journal of Marriage and the Family* 39(February):43–57.

Stainton, M. Colleen
1985 "The fetus: A growing member of the family." *Family Relations* 34(July):321–326.

Stannard, Una
1977 *Mrs. Man.* San Francisco: Germainbooks.

Staples, Robert
1973 "The black dating game." *Essence,* October:92–96. Reprinted in Staples, 1978. Pp. 64–67.
1978 *The Black Family: Essays and Studies* (ed.). 2d edition. Belmont, CA: Wadsworth.

1981a *The World of Black Singles: Changing Patterns of Male/Female Relations.* Westport, CT: Greenwood Press.
1981b "Race and marital status: An overview." Pp. 173–175 in McAdoo (ed.), *Black Families.*
1985 "Changes in black family structure: The conflict between family ideology and structural conditions." *Journal of Marriage and the Family* 47(November):1005–1013.

Stein, Peter
1976 *Single.* Englewood Cliffs, NJ: Prentice-Hall.

Steinmann, Anne, D. J. Fox, and R. Farkas
1968 "Male and female perceptions of male sex roles." Pp. 421–422 in *Proceedings of the American Psychological Association.*

Steinmetz, Suzanne K.
1977 *The Cycle of Violence: Assertive, Aggressive, and Abusive Family Interaction.* New York: Praeger.
1978 "Violence between family members." *Marriage and the Family Review,* Vol. 1, no. 3(May/June):1–16.

Steinmetz, Suzanne K., and Deborah J. Amsden
1983 "Dependent elders, family stress, and abuse," Pp. 173–192 in Timothy H. Brubaker (ed.), *Family Relationships in Later Life.* Beverly Hills, CA: Sage.

Steinmetz, Suzanne, and Murray Straus
1973 "The family as a cradle of violence." *Society* 10(September–October):50–58.
1974 (eds.), *Violence in the Family.* New York: Dodd, Mead.

Stember, Charles H.
1966 *Jews in the Mind of America.* New York: Basic Books.

Stephens, William
1963 *The Family in Cross-Cultural Perspective.* New York: Holt.

Stevens, Evelyn P.
1973 "Marianismo: The other face of machismo in Latin America." In A. Pescatello (ed.), *Female and Male in Latin America.* Pittsburgh: University of Pittsburgh Press.

Stinnett, Nick, Linda M. Carter, and James Montgomery
1972 "Older persons' perception of their marriages." *Journal of Marriage and the Family* 34:665–670.

Stoler, Ann
1977 "Class structure and female autonomy in rural Java." *Signs* 3(Autumn):74–89.

Stoller, Eleanor Palo
1983 "Parental caregiving by adult children." *Journal of Marriage and the Family* 45:851–858.

Stoller, Frederick
1970 "The intimate network of families as a new structure." Pp. 145–159 in Herbert Otto (ed.), *The Family in Search of a Future.* New York: Appleton-Century-Crofts.

Straus, Murray A.
1971 "Some social antecedents of physical punishment: A linkage theory interpretation. *Journal of Marriage and the Family* 33:658–663.

1973 "A general systems theory approach to a theory of violence between family members." *Social Science Information* 12:105–125.

1974a "Foreword." Pp. 13–17 in Richard J. Gelles, ed., *The Violent Home.* Beverly Hills, CA: Sage.

1974b "Leveling, civility, and violence in the family." *Journal of Marriage and the Family* 36:13–29.

1977 "Sexual inequality, cultural norms, and wife-beating." Pp. 59–77 jn Jane Roberts Chapman and Margaret Gates (eds.), *Women into Wives: The Legal and Economic Impact of Marriage.* Beverly Hills, CA: Sage.

1979 "Measuring intrafamily conflict and violence: The conflict tactics (CT) scales." *Journal of Marriage and the Family* 41:75–88.

1980a "Wife-beating: How common and why?" Pp. 23–36 in Straus and Hotaling (eds.).

1980b "Sexual inequality and wife beating." Pp. 86–93 in Straus and Hotaling (eds.).

Straus, Murray A., Richard J. Gelles, and Suzanne K. Steinmetz
1980 *Behind Closed Doors: Violence in the American Family.* Garden City, NY: Anchor Press/Doubleday. Anchor Books paperback edition.

Straus, Murray A., and Gerald T. Hotaling (eds.)
1980 *The Social Causes of Husband-Wife Violence.* Minneapolis: University of Minnesota Press.

Strauss, Anselm (ed.)
1956 *The Social Psychology of George Herbert Mead: Selected Writings of an American Pragmatist.* Chicago: University of Chicago Press.

Straver, Cees J.
1981 "Unmarried couples: Different from marriage?" *Alternative Lifestyles* 4(February):43–74.

Streib, Gordon F.
1978 "An alternative family form for older persons: Need for social context." *Family Coordinator* 27(October):413–420.

Streib, Gordon F., and Rubye Wilkerson Beck
1980 "Older families: A decade review." *Journal of Marriage and the Family* 42(November):205–224.

Streib, Gordon F., and Mary Anne Hilker
1980 "The cooperative 'family': An alternative lifestyle for the elderly." *Alternative Lifestyles* 3(May):167–184.

Strobel, Margaret
1982 "African women." *Signs* Vol. 8, no. 1:109–131(autumn).

Strube, Michael J., and Linda S. Barbour
1983 "The decision to leave an abusive relationship: Economic dependence and psychological commitment." *Journal of Marriage and the Family* 45(November):785–793.

1984 "Factors related to the decision to leave an abusive relationship." *Journal of Marriage and the Family* 46(November):837–844.

Stryker, Sheldon
1964 "The interactional and situational approaches." Pp. 125–170 in Harold T. Christensen (ed.), *Handbook of Marriage and the Family.* Chicago: Rand McNally.

Stump, Al
1974 "Another oppressed minority is heard from." *TV Guide,* July 27.

Sullerot, Evelyne
1971 *Women, Society and Change.* Translated from the French by Margaret Scotford Archer. New York: McGraw-Hill.

Sussman, Marvin B.
1966 "Theoretical bases for an urban kinship network system." Cleveland: Case-Western Reserve University. Mimeographed.

Sussman, Marvin B., and Lee Burchinal
1962 "Kin family network, unheralded structure in current conceptualization of family functioning." *Marriage and Family Living.* 24:231–240.

Sussman, Marvin B., Judith N. Cates, and David T. Smith
1970 *The Family and Inheritance.* New York: Russell Sage.

Sweet, James A.
1982 "Work and Fertility." Pp. 197–218 in Greer Litton Fox (ed.), *The Childbearing Decision.* Beverly Hills, CA: Sage.

Swidler, Ann
1980 "Love and adulthood in American culture." Pp. 120–147 in Neil Smelser and Erik Erikson (eds.), *Themes of Work and Love in Adulthood.* Cambridge, MA: Harvard University Press.

Symonds, Carolyn
1971 "Sexual mate-swapping: Violation of norms and reconciliation of guilt." Pp. 81–109 in James Henslin (ed.), *Studies in the Sociology of Sex.* New York: Appleton-Century-Crofts.

Talmon, Yonina
1972 *Family and Community in the Kibbutz.* Cambridge, MA: Harvard University Press.

Tanfer, Koray, and Marjorie C. Horn
1985a "Contraceptive use, pregnancy and fertility patterns among single American women in their 20s." *Family Planning Perspectives* 17(January/February):10–19.
1985b "Nonmarital cohabitation among young women: Findings from a national survey." Paper presented at the annual meeting of the Population Association of America. Boston, March 27–30, 1985. Summarized in "Digest," *Family Planning Perspectives* 17(July/August):179–180.

Tanner, Donna
1978 *The Lesbian Couple.* Lexington, MA: Lexington Books, D. C. Heath.

Targ, Dena
1979 "Toward a reassessment of women's experience at middle age." *The Family Coordinator* 28(July):377–382.

Tavris, Carol, and Carole Offir
1977 *The Longest War: Sex Differences in Perspective.* New York: Harcourt Brace Jovanovich.

Taylor, Dalmas A.
1968 "The development of interpersonal relationships: Social penetration processes." *The Journal of Social Psychology* 75:79–90.

Taylor, Dalmas, Irwin Altman, and Richard Sorrentino
1969 "Interpersonal exchange as a function of rewards and costs and situational factors: Expectancy confirmation-disconfirmation." *Journal of Experimental Social Psychology* 5:324–339.

Taylor, Jeremy
1650 *The Rule and Exercises of Holy Living.*

Taylor, Robert Joseph
1986 "Receipt of support from family among black Americans: Demographic and familial differences." *Journal of Marriage and the Family* 48(February):67–77.

Terman, L. M.
1938 *Psychological Factors in Marital Happiness.* New York: McGraw-Hill.

Thibaut, J. W., and H. H. Kelley
1959 *The Social Psychology of Groups.* New York: Wiley.

Thomas, W. I.
1923 *The Unadjusted Girl.* Boston: Little, Brown.
1928 *The Child in America.* New York: Knopf.

Thompson, Anthony Peter
1983 "Extramarital sex: A review of the research literature." *Journal of Sex Research* 19(February):1–22.
1984 "Emotional and sexual components of extramarital relations." *Journal of Marriage and the Family* 46(February):35–42.

Thompson, Linda, and Graham B. Spanier
1978 "Influence of parents, peers, and partners on the contraceptive use of college men and women." *Journal of Marriage and the Family* 40(August):481–492.

Thomson, Elizabeth
1980 "The value of employment to mothers of young children." *Journal of Marriage and the Family* 42(August):551–566.

Tietze, Christopher
1973 "Two years' experience with a liberal abortion law: Its impact on fertility trends in New York City." *Family Planning Perspectives* 5(Winter):36–41.
1975 "The effect of legalization of abortion on population growth and public health." *Family Planning Perspectives* 7(May/June):123–127.

Titus, Sandra L.
1976 "Family photographs and transition to parenthood." *Journal of Marriage and the Family* 38(August):525–530.

Toby, Jackson
1966 "Violence and the masculine ideal: Some qualitative data." Pp. 20–27 in Marvin Wolfgang (ed.), *Patterns of Violence: The Annals*

of the American Academy of Political and Social Science 364(March).

Tomasson, R. F.
1970 Sweden: Prototype of Modern Society. New York: Random House.

Toney, Michael, Banu Golesorkhi, and William F. Stinner
1985 "Residence exposure and fertility expectations of young Mormon and non-Mormon women in Utah." Journal of Marriage and the Family 47(May):459–465.

Trible, Phyllis
1978 God and the Rhetoric of Sexuality. Philadelphia: Fortress Press.

Trimberger, Rosemary, and Michael J. MacLean
1982 "Maternal employment: The child's perspective." Journal of Marriage and the Family 44(May):469–475.

Troll, Lillian
1971 "The family of later life: A decade review." Journal of Marriage and the Family 33(May):263–290.
1983 "Grandparents: The family watchdogs." Pp. 63–74 in Brubaker (ed.).

Trost, Jan
1974 "This family life cycle—an impossible concept?" International Journal of Sociology and the Family 4(Spring):37–47.
1977 "The family life cycle—a problematic concept." Pp. 467–481 in Jean Cuisenieu (ed.), The Family Cycle in European Societies. Mouton: The Hague.
1981 "Cohabitation in Nordic Countries." Alternative Lifestyles 4(November):401–427.

Truzzi, Marcello (ed.)
1971 Sociology: The Classic Statements. New York: Random House.

Turk, J. L., and N. W. Bell
1972 "Measuring power in families." Journal of Marriage and the Family 34:215–223.

Turner, Ralph H.
1970 Family Interaction. New York: Wiley.

Twiss, Harold L. (ed.)
1978 Homosexuality and the Christian Faith: A Symposium. Valley Forge, PA: Judson Press.

Tyler, Alice Felt
1944 Freedom's Ferment. Minneapolis: University of Minnesota Press. New York: Harper Torchbooks reprint, 1962.

Udry, T. Richard
1981 "Marital alternatives and marital disrup-

tion." Journal of Marriage and the Family 43(November):889–897.

Ulbrich, Patricia, and Joan Huber
1981 "Observing parental violence: Distribution and effects." Journal of Marriage and the Family 43(August):623–631.

U.S. Bureau of the Census
1973 Census of the Population, 1970: Age at First Marriage. Final Report PC(2)-4D.
1974 Current Population Reports, ser. P-23, no. 49.
1979 Current Population Reports, ser. P-60, no. 118. "Money Income in 1977 of Families and Persons in the United States."
1983 Current Population Reports, ser. P-23, no. 129. "Child Care Arrangements of Working Mothers: June, 1982."
1983 Current Population Reports, ser. P-23, no. 130. "Population Profile of the United States, 1982."
1983 Special Demographic Analyses, CDS-80-8. American Women: Three Decades of Change.
1983 Special Demographic Analyses, CDS-80-9. Wives Who Earn More than Their Husbands.
1983 Special Publication PIO/POP-83-1. America's Black Population: 1970–1982, A Statistical View.
1984 Current Population Reports, ser. P-20, no. 388. "Household and Family Characteristics: March, 1983."
1984 Current Population Reports, ser. P-20, no. 389. "Marital Status and Living Arrangements: March, 1983."
1984 Current Population Reports, ser. P-20, no. 391. "Households, Families, Marital Status, and Living Arrangements: March, 1984" (Advance Report).
1984 Current Population Reports, ser. P-23, no. 133. "Earnings in 1981 of Married-Couple Families, by Selected Characteristics of Husbands and Wives."
1984 Current Population Reports, ser. P-23, no. 138. "Demographic and Socioeconomic Aspects of Aging in the United States."
1984 Current Population Reports, ser. P-60, no. 142. "Money Income of Households, Families, and Persons in the United States: 1982."
1984 Current Population Reports, ser. P-60, no.

144. "Characteristics of the Population below the Poverty Level: 1982."

1984   *Statistical Abstract of the United States: 1985.* 105th edition, December.

1986   *Current Population Reports,* ser. P-20, no. 410. "Marital Status and Living Arrangements: March, 1985." (November)

1986   *Current Population Reports,* ser. P-20, no. 411. "Household and Family Characteristics: March, 1985." (September)

1986   *Current Population Reports,* ser. P-20, no. 412. "Households, Families, Marital Status, and Living Arrangements: March, 1986 (Advance Report)." (November)

U.S. Department of Health and Human Services: Children's Bureau, National Center on Child Abuse and Neglect

1980   *Sexual Abuse of Children: Selected Readings.*

U.S. Department of Health and Human Services *(formerly U.S. Department of Health, Education, and Welfare): National Center for Health Statistics*

1973   *100 Years of Marriage and Divorce Statistics, 1867–1967,* ser. 21, no. 24.

1974   *Monthly Vital Statistics Report,* Vol. 22, no. 13. "Annual Summary for the United States, 1973: Births, Deaths, Marriages, and Divorces."

1975   *Monthly Vital Statistics Report,* Vol. 23, no. 12.

1979   *Monthly Vital Statistics Report,* Vol. 27, no. 13. "Annual Summary for the United States, 1978."

1983   *Monthly Vital Statistics Report,* Vol. 32, no. 9, Supplement. "Advance Report of Final Natality Statistics, 1981."

1984   *Monthly Vital Statistics Report,* Vol. 32, no. 11, Supplement. "Advance Report of Final Marriage Statistics, 1981."

1984   *Monthly Vital Statistics Report,* Vol. 32, no. 13. "Annual Summary of Births, Deaths, Marriages, and Divorces: United States, 1983."

1984   *Monthly Vital Statistics Report,* Vol. 33, no. 6, Supplement. "Advance Report of Final Natality Statistics, 1982."

1985   *Monthly Vital Statistics Report,* Vol. 33, no. 11, Supplement. "Advance Report of Final Divorce Statistics."

1985   *Advance Data from Vital and Health Statistics,* no. 104. William D. Mosher and William

F. Pratt, "Fecundity and Infertility in the United States, 1965–82."

1985   *Data from the National Health Survey,* ser. 10, no. 147. "Health Characteristics According to Family and Personal Income: United States."

U.S. Department of Labor

1970   *Dual Careers: A Longitudinal Study of the Labor Market Experience of Women,* Vol. 1. Manpower Research Monograph no. 21.

1973   *Dual Careers,* Vol. 2. Manpower Research Monograph no. 21.

U.S. Senate Special Committee on Aging

1985   *America in Transition: An Aging Society,* 1984–85 edition.

Valentine, Deborah, and Tim Cash

1986   "A definitional discussion of elder maltreatment." *Journal of Gerontological Social Work* (Spring) 9:17–28.

Van Buren, Abigail

1978   "Dear Abby" syndicated column. *Greensboro (NC) Record,* October 25, 1978.

Vanderkooi, Lois, and Jessica Pearson

1983   "Mediating divorce disputes: Mediator behaviors, styles, and roles." *Family Relations* 32(October):557–566.

Varni, Charles A.

1973   "Contexts of conversion: The case of swinging." Pp. 166–181 in Roger W. Libby and Robert N. Whitehurst (eds.), *Renovating Marriage.* Danville, CA: Consensus.

Vaughan, Denton, and Gerald Sparer

1974   "Ethnic group and welfare status of women sterilized in federally funded family planning programs, 1972." *Family Planning Perspectives* 6(Fall):224–229.

Vaughan, Diane

1979   "Uncoupling: The process of moving from one lifestyle to another." *Alternative Lifestyles* 2(November):415–442.

Veevers, Jean E.

1972   "Factors in the incidence of childlessness in Canada: An analysis of census data." *Social Biology* 19:266–274.

1973a   "Voluntarily childless wives: An exploratory study." *Sociology and Social Research* 57(April):356–366.

1973b   "The child-free alternative: Rejection of the motherhood mystique." Pp. 183–199 in Maryles Stephenson (ed.), *Women in Canada.* Toronto: New Press.

1974 "The life style of voluntarily childless couples." In Lyle Larson (ed.), *The Canadian Family in Comparative Perspective*. Toronto: Prentice-Hall.

1979 "Voluntary childlessness: a review of issues and evidence." *Marriage and Family Review* 2:1–26.

1980 *Childless by Choice*. Toronto, Canada: Butterworths.

Ventura, S. J.

1982 "Trends in first births to older mothers, 1970–1979." *Monthly Vital Statistics Report*. National Center for Health Statistics, Vol. 31, no. 2.

Vera, Hernan, Donna H. Berardo, and Felix M. Berardo

1985 "Age heterogamy in marriage." *Journal of Marriage and the Family* 47(August):553–566.

Vinick, Barbara

1978 "Remarriage in old age." *The Family Coordinator* 27(October):359–363.

Vogel, Ezra

1963 *Japan's New Middle Class*. Berkeley: University of California Press.

Wahlroos, Sven

1974 *Family Communication*. New York: Macmillan. (Signet paperback used in citations.)

Walker, Lenore E.

1979 *The Battered Woman*. New York: Harper & Row.

1984 *The Battered Woman Syndrome*. New York: Springer.

Wallace, Michele

1979 *Black Macho and the Myth of the Superwoman*. New York: Dial Press.

Wallace, Phyllis A.

1980 *Black Women in the Labor Force*. Cambridge, MA: The M.I.T. Press.

Wallace, Walter L. (ed.)

1969 *Sociological Theory*. Chicago: Aldine.

Waller, Willard

1930 *The Old Love and the New*. Reprint edition. Carbondale: Southern Illinois University Press, 1967.

1937 "The rating-dating complex." *American Sociological Review* 2(October):727–735.

1938 *The Family*. Reprint edition, revised by Reuben Hill. New York: Dryden Press, 1951.

Walshok, Mary Lindenstein

1971 "The emergence of middle-class deviant subcultures: The case of swingers." *Social Problems* 18:488–495.

1973 "Sex role typing and feminine sexuality." Paper presented at the annual meetings of the American Sociological Association, New York, August 30.

Walstedt, Joyce Jennings (see Jennings, Joyce)

(Walster) Elaine Hatfield, and G. William Walster (see Hatfield and Walster, 1978)

(Walster) Elaine Hatfield, G. William Walster, and Ellen Berscheid (see Hatfield et al., 1978)

Walters, James, and Lynda Henly Walters

1980 "Parent-child relationships: A review, 1970–1979." *Journal of Marriage and the Family* 42(November):80–95.

Washington, Joseph R.

1970 *Marriage in Black and White*. Boston: Beacon.

Watkins, Harriet, and Marilyn Bradbard

1982 "Child maltreatment: An overview with suggestions for intervention and research." *Family Relations* 31(July):323–333.

Watt, Ian

1957 *The Rise of the Novel*. Berkeley: University of California Press.

Weinberg, George

1972 *Society and the Healthy Homosexual*. New York: St. Martin's. Garden City, NY: Doubleday Anchor Press edition, 1973.

Weinberg, Martin, and Colin Williams

1974 *Male Homosexuals*. New York: Oxford.

1975 "Gay baths and the social organization of impersonal sex." *Social Problems* 23(December):124–136.

Weis, David L., and Michael Slosnerick

1981 "Attitudes toward sexual and nonsexual extramarital involvements among a sample of college students." *Journal of Marriage and the Family* 43(May):349–358.

Weisberg, D. Kelly

1975 "Alternative family structures and the law." *The Family Coordinator* 24(October):549–559.

Weiss, Henry Walter

1984 "On gay fathers." *SIECUS Report* XII, no. 3(January):7–8.

Weiss, Robert S.

1975 *Marital Separation*. New York: Basic Books.

1979a *Going It Alone: The Family Life and Social Situation of the Single Parent*. New York: Basic Books.

1979b "Issues in the adjudication of custody when parents separate." Pp. 324–336 in Levinger and Moles (eds.).

Weisstein, Naomi
1971 "Psychology constructs the female, or the fantasy life of the male psychologist." Pp. 143–159 in Edith Hoshino Altback (ed.), *From Feminism to Liberation.* Cambridge, MA: Schenkman.

Weitz, Shirley
1977 *Sex Roles: Biological, Psychological, and Social Foundations.* New York: Oxford University Press.

Weitzman, Lenore J.
1974 "Legal regulation of marriage: Tradition and change." *California Law Review* 62(July/September):1169–1288.
1981 *The Marriage Contract: A Guide to Living with Lovers and Spouses.* New York: Free Press.
1985 *The Divorce Revolution: The Unexpected Social and Economic Consequences for Women and Children in America.* New York: Free Press.

Weitzman, Lenore J., and Ruth B. Dixon
1976 "Alimony: A quest for justice in changing times." Paper read at the annual meetings of the American Sociological Association, New York, August. Final version in *Family Law Quarterly,* Fall, 1980.
1979 "Child custody awards: Legal standards and empirical patterns for child custody, support, and visitation after divorce." *UCD Law Review* 12(Summer):473–521.

Weitzman, Lenore, Carol Dixon, Joyce Adair Bird, Neil McGinn, and Dena Robertson
1978 "Contracts for intimate relationships: A study of contracts before, within, and in lieu of legal marriage." *Alternative Lifestyles* 1(August):303–378.

Welter, Barbara
1966 "The cult of true womanhood: 1820–1860." *American Quarterly* 18:151–174.

Wentowski, Gloria J.
1985 "Older women's perceptions of great-grandmotherhood: A research note." *The Gerontologist* 25(December):593–596.

Westoff, Charles F.
1972 "The modernization of U.S. contraceptive practice." *Family Planning Perspectives* 4(July):9–12.

1974 "The populations of the developed countries." *Scientific American* 231(September):109–120.

Westoff, Charles, and Elise Jones
1977 "The secularization of U.S. Catholic birth control practices." *Family Planning Perspectives* 9(September/October):203–207.
1979a "The end of 'Catholic' fertility." *Demography* 16(May):209–217.
1979b "Patterns of aggregate and individual changes in contraceptive practice." National Center for Health Statistics, *Vital and Health Statistics,* ser. 3, no. 17.

Westoff, Charles, and James McCarthy
1979 "Sterilization in the United States." *Family Planning Perspectives* 11(May/June):147–152.

Westoff, Charles F., R. G. Potter, and P. C. Sagi
1963 *The Third Child.* Princeton, NJ: Princeton University Press.

Westoff, Charles F., and R. H. Potvin
1967 *College Women and Fertility Values.* Princeton, NJ: Princeton University Press.

Westoff, Charles, and Norman Ryder
1977 *The Contraceptive Revolution.* Princeton, NJ: Princeton University Press.

Westoff, Leslie Aldridge, and Charles F. Westoff
1971 *From Now to Zero: Fertility, Contraception, and Abortion in America.* Boston: Little, Brown.

White, Lynn
1979 "Sex differentials in the effect of remarriage on global happiness." *Journal of Marriage and the Family* 41(November):869–876.

White, Mervin, and Carolyn Wells
1973 "Student attitudes toward alternate marriage forms." Pp. 280–295 in Roger Libby and Robert Whitehurst (eds.), *Renovating Marriage.* Danville, CA: Consensus Publishers.

White, Ralph
1966 "Misperception as a cause of two world wars." *Journal of Social Issues* 22:1–19.

Whitehead, Harriet
1976a "Review of *Woman's Evolution* by Evelyn Reed." *Signs* 1 (Spring):746–748.
1976b "A reply." *Signs* 2 (Winter):508–511.

Whitehurst, Robert
1974a "Sex role equality and changing meanings of cohabitation." Unpublished manuscript. University of Windsor.

1974b "Violence in husband-wife interaction."
Pp. 75–82 in Steinmetz and Straus (eds.),
1974.

Wilkie, Jane Riblett
1981 "The trend toward delayed parenthood."
Journal of Marriage and the Family
43(August):583–591.

Williams, J. Allen, Jr., and Robert Stockton
1973 "Black family structures and functions:
An empirical examination of some suggestions made by Billingsley." *Journal of Marriage and the Family* 33(February):39–
49.

Williamson, Nancy E.
1976 *Sons or Daughters: A Cross-Cultural Survey of Parental Preferences.* Beverly Hills,
CA: Sage.

**Wilson, Kenneth, Louis Zurcher, Diana Claire Mc-
Adams, and Russell L. Curtis**
1975 "Stepfathers and stepchildren: An exploratory analysis from two national surveys."
Journal of Marriage and the Family 37 (August):526–536.

Winch, Robert
1962 *Identification and Its Familial Determinants.* Indianapolis: Bobbs-Merrill.

Winch, Robert, and Margaret Gordon
1974 *Familial Structure and Function as Influence.* Lexington, MA: D. C. Heath, Lexington
Books.

Wineberg, H., and J. McCarthy
1986 "Differential fertility in the U.S.: 1980."
Journal of Biosocial Science 18:311.

Winter, David
1973 *The Power Motive.* New York: Free Press.

Wirth, Louis
1938 "Urbanism as a way of life." *American Journal of Sociology* 44:1–24.

Wishik, Heather Ruth
1986 "Economics of divorce: An exploratory
study." *Family Law Quarterly* XX(Spring):
79–107.

Wolfe, Linda
1981 *The Cosmo Report: Women and Sex in the
80s.* New York: Arbor House.

Wolins, Martin
1983 "The gender dilemma in social welfare: Who
cares for children?" Pp. 113–128 in Lamb
and Sagi (eds.).

Wollstonecraft, Mary
1792 *A Vindication of the Rights of Woman.* Re-

print edition, edited by Charles W. Hagel-
man, Jr. New York: Norton, 1967.

Wood, Vivian, and Joan Robertson
1978 "Friendship and kinship interaction: Differential effect on the morale of the elderly."
Journal of Marriage and the Family
40(May):367–375.

Woods, Richard
1978 *Another Kind of Love: Homosexuality and
Spirituality.* Garden City, NY: Doubleday
Image Books.

Woolley, Persia
1978 "Shared custody." *Family Advocate*
1(Summer):6–9, 33–34.

Worthy, Morgan, Albert Gary, and Gay Kahn
1969 "Self-disclosure as an exchange process."
*Journal of Personality and Social Psychol-
ogy* 13:59–63.

Wright, Gerald C., Jr., and Dorothy M. Stetson
1978 "The impact of no-fault divorce law reform
on divorce in American states." *Journal of
Marriage and the Family* 40(August):575–
580.

Wu, Tson-Shien
1972 "The value of children or boy preference?"
In Fawcett (ed.), 1972.

Yankelovich, Daniel
1974 "The meaning of work." Pp. 19–48 in J. M.
Rosow (ed.), *The Worker and the Job.* Englewood Cliffs, NJ: Prentice-Hall.
1981 *New Rules.* New York: Random House. Bantam paperback edition used in citations.

Ybarra, Lea
1982 "When wives work: The impact on the Chicano family." *Journal of Marriage and the
Family* 44(February):169–178.

Yllo, Kersti Alice
1978 "Nonmarital cohabitation: Beyond the college campus." *Alternative Lifestyles*
1(February):37–54.

Yoder, John Howard
1974 "Singleness in ethical and pastoral perspective." Mimeographed. Elkhart, IN: Associated Mennonite Biblical Seminaries.

Yogev, Sara
1981 "Do professional women have egalitarian
marital relationships?" *Journal of Marriage
and the Family* 43(November):865–871.

Young, James, and Muriel Hamilton
1978 "Paternal behavior: Implications for childrearing practice." Pp. 135–145 in Joseph

Stevens, Jr., and Marilyn Mathews (eds.), *Mother/Child, Father/Child Relationships.* Washington, DC: National Association for the Education of Young Children.

Zelnik, Melvin, and John F. Kantner

1977 "Sexual and contraceptive experience of young unmarried women in the United States, 1976 and 1971." *Family Planning Perspectives* 9(March/April):55–71.

1978 "Contraceptive patterns and premarital pregnancy among women aged 15–19 in 1976." *Family Planning Perspectives* 10(May/June):135–142.

1980 "Sexual activity, contraceptive use and pregnancy among Metropolitan-area teenagers: 1971–1979." *Family Planning Perspectives* 12(September/October):230–237.

Zelnik, Melvin, John F. Kantner, and Kathleen Ford

1981 *Sex and Pregnancy in Adolescence.* Beverly Hills, CA: Sage.

Zetkin, Clara

1934 *Lenin on the Woman Question.* New York: International Publishers.

Zimmerman, Shirley L.

1982 "Alternatives in human reproduction for involuntarily childless couples." *Family Relations* 31(April):233–241.

1986 "Adult day care: Correlates of its coping effects for families of an elderly disabled member." *Family Relations* 35(April):305–311.

Zube, Margaret

1982 "Changing behavior and outlook of aging men and women: Implications for marriage in the middle and later years." *Family Relations* 31(January):147–156.

ACKNOWLEDGMENTS

Addison-Wesley
Reprinted from *A New Look at Love* by Elaine Hatfield and G. William Walster, copyright © 1978 by Elaine Hatfield and G. William Walster. By permission of Addison-Wesley Publishing Company, Inc., Reading, Massachusetts and the authors.

Agence-France Press
"Zulu Chief Orders Test for Virginity," © 1979.

Aldine Publishing Co.
Gagnon, John H., and William Simon, *Sexual Conduct.* Copyright © 1973 by John H. Gagnon and William Simon. Reprinted by permission of the authors and the publisher, Aldine de Gruyter, New York.

Alternative Lifestyles
Ahrons, Constance, "The Binuclear Family," copyright © 1979 *Alternative Lifestyles.* Reprinted by permission of Human Sciences Press, publisher, New York.

Gerstel, Naomi, "Marital Alternatives and the Regulation of Sex," copyright © 1979 *Alternative Lifestyles.* Reprinted by permission of Human Sciences Press, publisher, New York.

Kirschner, Betty Frankle, and Laurel Richardson Walum, "Two-Location Families," copyright © 1978 *Alternative Lifestyles.* Reprinted by permission of Human Sciences Press, publisher, New York.

Newcomb, Michael, and Peter Bentler, "Cohabitation before Marriage," copyright © 1980 *Alternative Lifestyles.* Reprinted by permission of Human Sciences Press, publisher, New York.

Rosenthal, Kristine, and Harry Keshet, "The Impact of Childcare Responsibilities on Part-Time or Single Fathers," copyright © 1978 *Alternative Lifestyles.* Reprinted by permission of Human Sciences Press, publisher, New York.

Weitzman, Lenore et al., "Contracts for Intimate Relationships," copyright © 1978 *Alternative Lifestyles.* Reprinted by permission of Human Sciences Press, publisher, New York.

Yllo, Alice Kersti, "Nonmarital Cohabitation," copyright © 1978 *Alternative Lifestyles.* Reprinted by permission of Human Sciences Press, publisher, New York.

American Academy of Political and Social Science
Rosenberg, Bernard, and Joseph Bensman, "Sexual Patterns in Three Ethnic Subcultures of an American Underclass," *The Annals* of the American Academy of Political and Social Science, vol. 376. © 1968.

American Anthropologist
Sanday, Peggy R., "Toward a Theory of the Status of Women." Reproduced by permission of the American Anthropological Association from *American Anthropologist,* volume 75, number 5, 1973. Not for further reproduction.

American Bar Association
Cox, Mary Jane Truesdall, and Lory Cease, "Joint Custody," *Family Advocate,* vol. 1, published by the American Bar Association, Family Law Section. Copyright © 1978, American Bar Association, reprinted by permission.

American Jewish Committee
Mayer, Egon, and Carl Sheingold, *Intermarriage and the Jewish Future: A National Study in Summary.* Copyright © 1979 The American Jewish Committee. All rights reserved.

American Journal of Orthopsychiatry
Kowal, Katherine, and Karen Maitland Schilling, "Adoption through the Eyes of Adult Adoptees," *American Journal of Orthopsychiatry* 55. Copyright © 1985 the American Orthopsychiatric Association, Inc. Reproduced by permission.

The American Journal of Psychiatry
Neugarten, Bernice L., "Time, Age and the Life Cycle," *The American Journal of Psychiatry.* Copyright © 1979, the American Psychiatric Association. Reprinted by permission.

American Sociological Association
From "Lesbian Mothers" by Mildred Pagelow. Paper presented at the annual meeting of the American Sociological Association, New York, August 1976.

Associated Press
Permission was granted by the Associated Press for "101-Year-Old Bachelor to Wed," "Russian Women Change, but the Menfolks Don't" "Family Imprisons Woman 29 Years over Love Affair," "10-Year-Old Is Mother of Twins," "4-Month-Old Attends College Classes," "Cooking Couples Bring Changes to the Kitchen," "Husband Raises Roof over Divorce," "Hysterectomy Doesn't Bar Pregnancy," "5 Billionth Baby Due Today," "Surrogate Motherhood: A Special Case," "Eighth-Grade Dropout Saw Children Educated," "Death of 80-Year-Old Woman Goes Unnoticed for Four Years," "At Age 103, Man Ties Knot with 84-Year Old," and "Love's Labour's Lost and Found."

Basic Books, Inc.
Reprinted from *Single Blessedness* by Margaret Adams, © 1976, by permission.

Reprinted from "Marital Disruption and the Lives of Children," by Mary Jo Bane in *Divorce and Separation* by Levinger and Moles (eds.), © 1979, by permission.

Reprinted from "The Value of Children to Parents" by Lois Wladis Hoffman and Martin L. Hoffman in *Psychology Perspectives on Population* by James T. Fawcett (ed.), © 1973, by permission.

Reprinted from "Divorced Mothers," by Janet Kohen, Carol A. Brown, and Roslyn Feldberg in *Divorce and Separation* by Levinger and Moles (eds.), © 1979, by permission.

Reprinted from *Fathers, Mothers and Society* by Rhona Rapoport, Robert Rapoport, Ziona Strelitz, and Stephen Kew. Copyright © 1977 by Institute of Family and Environmental Research. Reprinted by permission of the authors and Basic Books, Inc., publishers.

Reprinted from *Worlds of Pain* by Lillian Rubin, © 1976, by permission.

Reprinted from *The Making of the Modern Family* by Edward Shorter, © 1977, by permission

Reprinted from *Marital Separation* by Robert S. Weiss, © 1977, by permission.

Reprinted from "Issues in the Adjudication of Custody When Parents Separate," by Robert S. Weiss in *Divorce and Separation* by Levinger and Moles (eds.), © 1979, by permission.

Beacon Press
From *Sunday's Women* by Sasha Gregory Lewis. Copyright © 1979 by Sasha Gregory Lewis. Reprinted by permission of Beacon Press.

Berkley Publishing Group
From *The Legality of Love.* Copyright © Jerry Sonnenblick, attorney, and Martha Sowerine. Reprinted by permission of the Berkley Publishing Group.

California Law Review
Laslett, Peter, "Mean Household Size in England Since the 16th Century," in *Household and Fam-*

ily in Past Time by Peter Laslett and R. Wall. Copyright © 1972, Cambridge University Press, reprinted with permission.

Weitzman, Lenore J., "Legal Regulation of Marriage: Tradition and Change." Copyright © 1974, California Law Review, Inc., reprinted by permission. Cambridge University Press.

Columbia University Press
Nagi, Saad, *Child Maltreatment in the United States.* Copyright © 1977, Columbia University Press, reprinted by permission.

Concordia Publishing House
Adapted from *Planned Parenthood* by Alfred M. Rehwinkel. Copyright © 1959 by Concordia Publishing House, reprinted by permission.

The Dial Press
Excerpt from the book *The Future of Motherhood* by Jessie Bernard. Copyright © 1974 by Jessie Bernard. Reprinted by permission of The Dial Press.

Dorsey Press
Kohn, Melvin, *Class and Conformity: A Study in Values.* Copyright © 1969, Dorsey Press, reprinted by permission.

Dutton and Company, Inc.
From *Homosexual Oppression and Liberation* by Dennis Altman. Copyright © 1971 by Dennis Altman. Reprinted by permission of the publisher, E. P. Dutton, a division of NAL Penguin, Inc.

Family Planning Perspectives
"American Adults' Approval of Legal Abortion Has Remained Virtually Unchanged Since 1972," reprinted with permission from *Family Planning Perspectives,* vol. 17, 1985.

Balakrishnan, T. R., Karol Drotki, and Evelyne Lapierre-Adamcyk, "Contraceptive Use in Canada, 1984," reprinted with permission from *Family Planning Perspectives,* vol. 17, 1985, and with permission of T. R. Balakrishnan.

Finkel, Madelon Lubin, and David J. Finkel, "Sexual and Contraceptive Knowledge, Attitudes, and Behavior of Male Adolescents," reprinted with permission from *Family Planning Perspectives,* vol. 7, no. 6, 1975, and with permission of Madelon Lubin Finkel.

Forrest, Jacqueline D., and Stanley K. Henshaw, "What U.S. Women Think and Do about Contraception," reprinted with permission from *Family Planning Perspectives,* vol. 15, no. 4, 1983.

Glick, Paul C., "American Household Structure in Transition," reprinted with permission from *Family Planning Perspectives,* vol. 15, no. 5, 1984, and with permission of Paul C. Glick.

Henshaw, Stanley K., Nancy J. Binkin, Ellen Blaine, and Jack C. Smith, "A Portrait of American Women Who Obtain Abortions," reprinted with permission from *Family Planning Perspectives,* vol. 17, 1985.

Miller, Warren B., "Psychological Vulnerability to Unwanted Pregnancy," reprinted with permission from *Family Planning Perspectives,* vol. 5, 1973, and with permission of Warren B. Miller.

The Free Press
Adapted with permission of The Free Press, a division of Macmillan, Inc., from *Husbands and Wives* by Robert O. Blood and Donald M. Wolfe. Copyright © 1960 by The Free Press.

Reprinted with permission of The Free Press, a division of Macmillan, Inc., from *The Function of Social Conflict* by Lewis A. Coser. Copyright 1956 by The Free Press, renewed 1984 by Lewis A. Coser.

Adapted with permission of The Free Press, a division of Macmillan, Inc., from *Opportunity and the Family* by John Scanzoni. Copyright © 1970 by The Free Press.

Adapted with permission of The Free Press, a division of Macmillan, Inc., from *Sex Roles, Life Styles and Child Bearing* by John Scanzoni. Copyright © 1975 by The Free Press.

Reprinted with permission of The Free Press, a division of Macmillan, Inc. From *The Marriage Contract: Spouses, Lovers and the Law* by Lenore J. Weitzman. Copyright © 1981 by Lenore J. Weitzman.

Adapted with permission of The Free Press, a division of Macmillan, Inc., from *The Divorce Revo-*

lution: The Unexpected Social and Economic Consequences for Women and Children in America by Lenore J. Weitzman. Copyright © 1985 by Dr. Lenore J. Weitzman.

The Gerontologist
Horowitz, Amy, "Sons and Daughters as Caregivers to Older Parents." Reprinted by permission from *The Gerontologist* 25 (December 1985): 612–617.

Greenwood Press, Inc.
Reprinted from *The World of Black Singles* by Robert Staples, by permission of the author and the publisher, Greenwood Press, Inc., Westport, Connecticut. Copyright © 1981 by Robert Staples.

Allan Guttmacher Institute
Abortions and the Poor: Private Morality, Public Responsibility, published by the Allan Guttmacher Institute, New York, 1979, reprinted with permission.

G. K. Hall and Company
Chambers-Schiller, Lee, "The Single Woman: Family and Vocation among Nineteenth-Century Reformers," in *Woman's Being, Woman's Place: Female Identity and Vocation in American History* by Mary Kelly. Copyright © 1979 by G. K. Hall, and reprinted with permission of Twayne Publishers, a division of G. K. Hall and Company, Boston.

Harcourt Brace Jovanovich, Inc.
From *Familiar Faces, Hidden Lives* by Howard Brown, copyright © 1976 by the Estate of Howard J. Brown. Reprinted by permission of Harcourt Brace Jovanovich, Inc.

Harper & Row, Publishers, Inc.
Brief excerpt from *Motivation and Personality*, 2nd edition, by Abraham H. Maslow. Copyright © 1970 by Abraham H. Maslow. Reprinted by permission of Harper & Row, Publishers, Inc.

Abridged and adapted from pp. 7–8, 179–180, 182, 197–198, and 207 in *Women of a Certain Age* by Lillian B. Rubin. Copyright © 1979 by Lillian B. Rubin. Reprinted by permission of Harper & Row, Publishers, Inc.

Brief excerpt from *The Family in Various Cultures*, 4th edition, by Stuart Queen and Robert Habenstein. Copyright © 1974 by J. B. Lippincott. Reprinted by permission of Harper & Row, Publishers, Inc.

Harvard University Press
Herman, Judith, *Father-Daughter Incest*, 1981. Reprinted by permission of Harvard University Press.

Swidler, Ann, "Love and Adulthood in American Culture," in *Themes of Work and Love in Adulthood* by Neil J. Smelser and Erik H. Erikson, 1980. Reprinted by permission of Harvard University Press.

Holt, Rinehart and Winston, Inc.
From *Women and Men: An Anthropologist's View* by Ernestine Friedl. Copyright © 1975 by Holt, Rinehart and Winston, Inc. Reprinted by permission of Holt, Rinehart and Winston, Inc.

From *Liking and Loving: An Invitation to Social Psychology* by Zick Rubin. Copyright © 1973 by Holt, Rinehart and Winston, Inc., reprinted by permission of CBS College Publishing.

Houghton Mifflin Company
From *Unbought and Unbossed* by Shirley Chisholm, published by Houghton Mifflin Company. Copyright © 1970 by Shirley Chisholm. Reprinted by permission.

From *Economics and the Public Purpose* by John Kenneth Galbraith, published by Houghton Mifflin Company. Copyright © 1973 by John Kenneth Galbraith. Reprinted by permission.

From *Living Together: A Guide to the Law for Unmarried Couples* by Barbara Hirsch. Copyright © 1976 by Barbara Hirsch. Reprinted by permission of Houghton Mifflin Company.

Kinsey Institute for Research in Sex, Gender and Reproduction, Inc.
From Alfred C. Kinsey, Wardell B. Pomeroy, Clyde E. Martin, and Paul C. Gebhard, *Sexual Behavior*

in the Human Female, published in 1962 by W. B. Saunders and Company. Reprinted by permission.

Lexington Books
From *The Lesbian Couple* by Donna Tanner. Copyright © 1978, D. C. Heath and Company. Reprinted with permission of the publisher, Lexington Books, D. C. Heath and Company, Lexington, Mass.

Liveright Publishing Corporation
From *The Old Love and the New* (1930) by Willard Waller, reprinted 1967 by Southern Illinois University Press. Reprinted by permission of Liveright Publishing Corporation, publisher.

Los-Angeles Times-Washington Post News Service
Permission was granted by the Los Angeles Times-Washington Post News Service for "Reported Syphilis Cases Show Sharp Decline" and "China Relaxing Standard of One-Child per Family."

McGraw-Hill Book Company
Green, Maureen. *Fathering: A New Look at the Art of Being a Father.* Copyright © 1977. Reprinted by permission of McGraw-Hill Book Company.

Pogrebin, Letty Cottin. *Family Politics: Love and Power on an Intimate Frontier.* McGraw-Hill Book Company, 1983. By permission of the author.

Siegel, Sidney, and Lawrence Fouraker, *Bargaining and Group Decision-Making.* Copyright © 1960, McGraw Hill Book Company, reprinted by permission.

Macmillan Publishing Company
Reprinted with permission of Macmillan Publishing Company from *The Economics of Being a Woman* by Dee Dee Ahern and Betsy Bliss. Copyright © 1976 by Dee Dee Ahern and Betsy Bliss.

Reprinted with permission of Macmillan Publishing Company from "The Principle of Reciprocity" by Claude Levi-Strauss in *Les Structures Elementaires de la Parente,* abridged and translated by Rose L. Coser and Grace Frazer in *Sociological*

Theory, 5th edition, by Lewis Coser and Bernard Rosenberg. Copyright © 1982 by the Macmillan Publishing Company.

Reprinted with permission of Macmillan Publishing Company from "The Matrifocal Family in the Black Ghetto: Sign of Pathology or Pattern of Survival" by Helen Safa in *Health and the Family: A Medical-Sociological Analysis* by Charles O. Crawford. Copyright © 1971 by Charles O. Crawford.

Reprinted with permission of Macmillan Publishing Company from *Family Communication* by Sven Wahlroos. Copyright © 1974 by Sven Wahlroos.

Manson Western Corporation
From Annette Ehrlich, "The Adaptable Primates," *Human Behavior* (November 1976). Copyright © 1976 by *Human Behavior.* Reprinted by permission of the publisher, Manson Western Corporation, Los Angeles.

The Michie Company
Reprinted from *Illegitimacy: Law and Social Policy* by Henry Krause, with permission of the Michie Company.

William Morrow and Company, Inc.
Blumstein, Philip, and Pepper Schwartz, *American Couples.* Copyright © 1983 by Philip Blumstein and Pepper Schwartz. Reprinted by permission of William Morrow and Company, Inc.

Ms. Magazine
Permission was granted by the authors for Meg Campbell "On Having a Second Child," September 1984; Frances Cerra "Live-in Child Care," August 1985; Barbara Ehrenreich, Elizabeth Hess and Gloria Jacobs "A Report on the Sex Crisis," March 1982; Lois Gould, "A Fabulous Child's Story," copyright © 1972, December 1972; Carol Kleiman, "My Home Is Not Broken, It Works," November 1984; Phyllis Mack, "Choosing Single Motherhood," November 1984; Bertrand P. Pogrebin, "How Does It Feel to Be the Husband of . . . ?" September 1972; Letty Cottin Pogrebin, "Big Changes in Parenting," February 1982; Beverly

Stephen, "Rites of Independence," November 1984; Lindsy Van Gelder, "Love among the Classifieds," August 1983, and "Marriage as a Restricted Club," February 1984; Cynthia Werthamer, "Guess Who's Buying Condoms," July 1986.

National Catholic Reporter
"Annulments: 15,000 % Increase in 15 Years." Reprinted with permission of the *National Catholic Reporter,* Kansas City, Mo.

National Council on Family Relations
Ahrons, Constance, "Divorce: A Crisis of Family Transition and Change," *Family Relations.* Copyright © 1984 by the National Council on Family Relations. Reprinted by permission.

Atkinson, Maxine, and Becky L. Glass, "Marital Age Heterogamy and Homogamy, 1900–1980," *Journal of Marriage and the Family.* Copyright © 1985 by the National Council on Family Relations. Reprinted by permission.

Atkinson, Maxine, and Jacqueline Boles, "WASP (Wives as Senior Partners)," *Journal of Marriage and the Family.* Copyright © 1984 by the National Council on Family Relations. Reprinted by permission.

Balswick, Jack, and Charles Peek, "The Inexpressive Male," *The Family Coordinator.* Copyright © 1971 by the National Council on Family Relations. Reprinted by permission.

Barranti, Chrystal Ramirez, "The Grandparent/Grandchild Relationship: Family Resource in an Era of Voluntary Bonds," *Family Relations.* Copyright © 1985 by the National Council on Family Relations. Reprinted by permission.

Berger, David G., and Morton G. Wenger, "The Ideology of Virginity," *Journal of Marriage and the Family.* Copyright © 1973 by the National Council on Family Relations. Reprinted by permission.

Bolig, Rosemary, Peter Stein and Patrick McKenry, "The Self-Advertisement Approach to Dating," *Family Relations.* Copyright © 1984 by the National Council on Family Relations. Reprinted by permission.

Bozett, Frederick, "Gay Fathers: How and Why They Disclose Their Homosexuality to Their Children," *Family Relations.* Copyright © 1980 by the National Council on Family Relations. Reprinted by permission.

Carns, Donald, "Talking About Sex: Notes on First Coitus and the Double Sexual Standard," *Journal of Marriage and the Family.* Copyright © 1973 by the National Council on Family Relations. Reprinted by permission.

DeMaris, Alfred, and Gerald Leslie, "Cohabitation with the Future Spouse," *Journal of Marriage and the Family.* Copyright © 1984 by the National Council on Family Relations. Reprinted by permission.

Edwards, John N., and Janice M. Saunders, "Coming Apart: A Model of the Marital Dissolution Decision," *Journal of Marriage and the Family.* Copyright © 1981 by the National Council on Family Relations. Reprinted by permission.

Gillespie, Dair, "Who Has the Power? The Marital Struggle," *Journal of Marriage and the Family.* Copyright © 1971 by the National Council on Family Relations. Reprinted by permission.

Glenn, Norval, and Charles Weaver, "The Marital Happiness of Remarried Divorced Persons," *Journal of Marriage and the Family.* Copyright © 1977. Reprinted by permission.

Gordon, Linda, and Paul O'Keefe, "Incest as a Form of Family Violence," *Journal of Marriage and the Family.* Copyright © 1984 by the National Council on Family Relations. Reprinted by permission.

Gordon, Michael, "Was Waller Ever Right? The Rating and Dating Complex Reconsidered," *Journal of Marriage and the Family.* Copyright © 1981 by the National Council on Family Relations. Reprinted by permission.

Gordon, Michael, and Penelope Shankweiler, "Different Equals Less," *Journal of Marriage and the Family.* Copyright © 1971 by the National Council on Family Relations. Reprinted by permission.

Hawke, Sharryl, and David Knox, "The One-Child Family," *The Family Coordinator.* Copyright ©

1978 by the National Council on Family Relations. Reprinted by permission.

Robertson, Joan, "Grandmotherhood: A Study of Role Conceptions," *Journal of Marriage and the Family*. Copyright © 1977 by the National Council on Family Relations. Reprinted by permission.

Robertson, Joan, "Women in Midlife Crises, Reverberations, and Support Networks," *The Family Coordinator*. Copyright © 1978 by the National Council on Family Relations. Reprinted by permission.

Robinson, Ira E., and Davor Jedlicka, "Change in Sexual Attitudes and Behavior in College Students from 1965 to 1980: A Research Note," *Journal of Marriage and the Family*. Copyright © 1985 by the National Council on Family Relations. Reprinted by permission.

Rossi, Alice, "Transition to Parenthood," *Journal of Marriage and the Family*. Copyright © 1968 by the National Council on Family Relations. Reprinted by permission.

Russell, Candyce Smith, "Transition to Parenthood: Problems and Gratifications," *Journal of Marriage and the Family*. Copyright © 1974 by the National Council on Family Relations. Reprinted by permission.

Safilios-Rothschild, Constantina, "The Study of Family Power Structure: A Review, 1960–1969," *Journal of Marriage and the Family*. Copyright © 1970 by the National Council on Family Relations. Reprinted by permission.

Skipper, James K., Jr., and Gilbert Nass, "Dating Behavior: A Framework for Analysis and an Illustration," *Journal of Marriage and the Family*. Copyright © 1966 by the National Council on Family Relations. Reprinted by permission.

Sobol, Michael, and Jeanette Cardiff, "A Sociopsychological Investigation of Adult Adoptees' Search for Birth Parents," *Family Relations*. Copyright © 1983 by the National Council on Family Relations. Reprinted by permission.

Staples, Robert, "Changes in Black Family Structure: The Conflict between Family Ideology and Structural Conditions," *Journal of Marriage and the Family*. Copyright © 1985 by the National Council on Family Relations. Reprinted by permission.

Straus, Murray, "Leveling, Civility, and Violence in the Family," *Journal of Marriage and the Family*. Copyright © 1974 by the National Council on Family Relations. Reprinted by permission.

Vinick, Barbara H., "Remarriage in Old Age," *The Family Coordinator*. Copyright © 1978 by the National Council on Family Relations. Reprinted by permission.

Voeller, Bruce, and James Walters (interviewer), "Gay Fathers," *The Family Coordinator*. Copyright © 1978 by the National Council on Family Relations. Reprinted by permission.

Walstedt, Joyce Jennings, "Reform of Women's Roles and Family Structures in the Recent History of China," *Journal of Marriage and the Family*. Copyright © 1978 by the National Council on Family Relations. Reprinted by permission.

White, Lynn, "Sex Differentials in the Effect of Remarriage on Global Happiness," *Journal of Marriage and the Family*. Copyright © 1979 by the National Council on Family Relations. Reprinted by permission.

Wilson Kenneth, Louise Zurcher, Diana Claire MacAdams, and Russell L. Curtis, "Stepfathers and Stepchildren: An Exploratory Analysis from Two National Surveys," *Journal of Marriage and the Family*. Copyright © 1975 by the National Council on Family Relations. Reprinted by permission.

Wood, Vivian, and Joan Robertson, "Friendship and Kinship Interaction: Differential Effect on the Morale of the Elderly," *Journal of Marriage and the Family*. Copyright © 1978 by the National Council on Family Relations. Reprinted by permission.

Ybarra, Lea, "When Wives Don't Work: The Impact on the Chicano Family," *Journal of Marriage and the Family*. Copyright © 1982 by the National Council on Family Relations. Reprinted by permission.

National Family Life Education Network
Excerpt from "Better Housing Options for the Elderly," reprinted with permission from *Family*

Life Educator, vol. 2, (Summer 1983), published by the National Family Education Network, Santa Cruz, CA.

Excerpt from "Good Reasons to Choose Abstinence," reprinted with permission from *Family Life Educator,* vol. 3, no. 1 (Fall 1984), published by the National Family Education Network, Santa Cruz, CA.

National Organization for Women

"Childbearing: A Patriotic Duty?" *National NOW Times,* January/February 1985. Copyright © National Organization for Women, used by permission.

"Professional Licenses Ruled Marital Property in New York," *National NOW Times,* December/January 1986. Copyright © National Organization for Women, used by permission.

National Urban League

Quotes from Hill, Robert, and Lawrence Shackleford, "The Black Extended Family Revisited," *Urban League Review* 1 (Fall 1975). Reprinted with permission of the National Urban League.

New Directions for Women

Excerpt from Kemper, Jean, "Prime Time," *New Directions for Women* 14 (March/April 1985). Reprinted by permission of New Directions for Women, Englewood, NJ.

New York Academy of Sciences

Permission granted by the New York Academy of Sciences and the author for "Family Dynamics for Developing Positive Achievement Motivation in Women: The Successful Woman Executive," by Margaret Henning from *Annals of the New York Academy of Sciences,* 208 (March 1973).

Permission granted by the New York Academy of Sciences and the author for "The Professional Woman as Mother," by Lois Wladis Hoffman from *Annals of the New York Academy of Sciences* 208 (March 1973).

Permission granted by the New York Academy of Sciences and the author for "Pediatrician," by Gertrude Hunter from *Annals of the New York Academy of Sciences* 208 (March 1973).

Permission granted by the New York Academy of Sciences and the author for "Sex Hormones and Executive Ability," by Estelle Ramey from *Annals of the New York Academy of Sciences* 208 (March 1973).

New York Times

Atlas, James, "Alice Entertained the Wives," copyright © 1979 by the New York Times Company. Reprinted by permission.

Briggs, Kenneth, "Jews Said to Ease View on Marriage," copyright © 1976 by the New York Times Company. Reprinted by permission.

Compa, Lance, "The Faithful Desperado," copyright © 1985 by the New York Times Company. Reprinted by permission.

Freudenheim, Milt, "Business and Health: Help in Caring for the Elderly," copyright © 1986 by the New York Times Company. Reprinted by permission.

Herbach, Sue, "Letters," copyright © 1976 by the New York Times Company. Reprinted by permission.

Meyers, William, "Child Care Finds a Champion in the Corporation," copyright © 1985 by the New York Times Company. Reprinted by permission.

North America Syndicate, Inc.

To Your Good Health by Paul G. Donohue, M.D. © Field Enterprises, Inc., March 20, 1980, by permission of North America Syndicate, Inc.

W. W. Norton and Company, Inc.

Quotes from *Of Woman Born, Motherhood as Experience and Institution* by Adrienne Rich is reprinted by permission of W. W. Norton and Company, Inc. Copyright © 1976 by W. W. Norton and Company, Inc.

Parade

Gordon, Barbara, "How to Share Life with a Famous Wife," *Parade,* April 21, 1985. Reprinted by permission of the author.

Totenberg, Nina, "How to Write a Marriage Contract," *Parade,* Dec. 16, 1984. Reprinted by permission of the author, legal affairs correspondent for National Public Radio.

Wallace, Irving, David Wallechinsky, and Amy Wallace, "Man Arrested for Topless Bathing," *Parade,* Oct. 3, 1982, from *Significa.* Reprinted by permission of the authors.

Plenum Press
Schäfer, Siegrid, "Sociosexual Behavior in Male and Female Homosexuals," from *Archives of Sexual Behavior,* 6, 1977.

Schmidt, Gunter, and Volkmar Sigusch, "Changes in Sexual Behavior among Young Males and Females between 1960 and 1970," From *Archives of Sexual Behavior,* 2, 1972.

Schmidt, Gunter, Volkmar Sigusch, and Siegrid Schäfer, "Responses to Reading Erotic Stories," from *Archives of Sexual Behavior,* 3, 1973.

Prentice-Hall
Buckley, Walter, *Sociology and Modern Systems Theory,* © 1967. Reprinted by permission of Prentice-Hall, Inc., Englewood Cliffs, NJ.

Kerckhoff, Alan C., *Socialization and Social Class,* © 1972. Reprinted by permission of Prentice-Hall, Inc., Englewood Cliffs, NJ.

Lipmen-Blumen, Jean, *Gender Roles and Power,* © 1984. Reprinted by permission of Prentice-Hall, Inc., Englewood Cliffs, NJ.

Stein, Peter J., *Single.* Copyright © 1976 by the author, professor of sociology, William Paterson College. Reprinted with permission.

Stoller, Frederick. "The Intimate Network of Families as a New Structure," pp. 145–159 in *The Family in Search of a Future,* by Herbert Otto (ed.). © 1970. Reprinted by permission of Prentice-Hall, Inc., Englewood Cliffs, NJ.

Random House, Inc.
Richman, Judith, "Bargaining for Sex and Status: The Dating Service and Sex-Role Change," pp. 158–165 in Peter J. Stein, Judith Richman, and Natalie Hannon (eds.), *The Family: Functions, Conflicts and Symbols.* Copyright © 1977. Reprinted by permission of Random House, Inc.

Rose, Phyllis. *Parallel Lives: Five Victorian Marriages.* Reprinted by permission of Alfred A. Knopf, division of Random House, Inc.

Tomasson, Richard F. *Sweden: Prototype of Modern Society.* Copyright © 1970. Reprinted by permission of Random House, Inc.

Yankelovich, Daniel. *New Rules.* Copyright © 1981. Reprinted by permission of Random House, Inc.

Redbook
Booker, Marion, "A Young Mother's Story: Pink is from Mama," *Redbook,* October 1969.

Sage Publications, Inc.
Cicirelli, Victor, "Adult Children and their Elderly Parents," pp. 31–46 in *Family Relationships in Later Life,* by Timothy H. Brubaker (ed.). Copyright © 1983. Reprinted by permission.

Furstenberg, Frank, Jr., and Graham B. Spanier, *Recycling the Family: Remarriage after Divorce.* Copyright © 1984. Reprinted by permission.

Gelles, Richard, *Family Violence.* Copyright © 1979. Reprinted by permission.

Gelles, Richard J., and Claire P. Cornell, *Intimate Violence in Families.* Copyright © 1985. Reprinted by permission.

Glick, Paul C., "Marriage, Divorce and Living Arrangements," *Journal of Family Issues,* vol. 5, (March 1984), p. 6, copyright © 1984. Reprinted by permission of Sage Publications.

McAdoo, Harriette Pipes, "Patterns of Upward Mobility in Black Families," pp. 155–169 in *Black Families* by Harriette Pipes McAdoo (ed.). Copyright © 1981. Reprinted by permission.

Matthews, Sarah, *The Social World of Old Women: Management of Self-Identity.* Copyright © 1979. Reprinted by permission.

Peters, Marie Ferguson, "Racial Socialization of Young Black Children," pp. 159–173 in *Black Children: Social, Educational and Parental Environments* by Harriette Pipes McAdoo and John Lewis McAdoo (eds.). Copyright © 1985. Reprinted by permission.

Riley, Matilda White, "The Family in an Aging Society," *Journal of Family Issues* 4 (September 1983), pp. 439–454. Copyright © 1983. Reprinted by permission.

Spanier, Graham, and Linda Thompson, *Parting: The Aftermath of Divorce.* Copyright © 1984. Reprinted by permission.

Staples, Robert, "Race and Marital Status: An Overview," pp. 173–175 in *Black Families* by Harriette Pipes McAdoo (ed.). Copyright © 1981. Reprinted by permission.

Zelnick, Melvin, John Kantner, and Kathleen Ford, *Sex and Pregnancy in Adolescence.* Copyright © 1981. Reprinted by permission.

Scientific American
Excerpt from "The History of the Human Population" by Ansley J. Coale. Copyright © 1974 by Scientific American, Inc. All rights reserved.

Senior Action in a Gay Environment
"The Homosexual Community Caring for Its Older Adults," from a brochure by SAGE: Senior Action in a Gay Environment, New York. Reprinted by permission.

Simon and Schuster
Bell, Alan P., and Martin S. Weinberg, *Homosexualities: A Study of Diversity among Men and Women.* Copyright © 1978 by Alan P. Bell and Martin S. Weinberg. Reprinted by permission of Simon and Schuster, Inc.

Friedan, Betty, *The Second Stage.* Copyright © 1981 by Betty Friedan. Reprinted by permission of Summit Books, a division of Simon and Schuster.

Stanford University Press
Reprinted from Roy G. Andrade, "Sex Differences and Cultural Institutions," in *The Development of Sex Differences,* edited by Eleanor E. Maccoby with the permission of the publishers, Stanford University Press. Copyright © 1966 by the Board of Trustees of the Leland Stanford Junior University.

Stein and Day
Roosevelt, Ruth, and Jeannette Lofas, *Living in Step.* Copyright © 1976 by the authors. Reprinted with permission of Stein and Day Publishers.

Starr, Bernard D., and Marcella Baker Weiner, *The Starr-Weiner Report on Sex and Sexuality in the Mature Years.* Copyright © 1981 by the authors. Reprinted with permission of Stein and Day Publishers.

Jeremy Tarcher, Inc.
Excerpt from *Betrayal of Innocence,* copyright © 1978 by the authors, Susan Forward and Craig Buck. Reprinted by permission of Jeremy Tarcher, Inc.

University of Chicago Press
Reprinted from "Gender Schema Theory and its Implications for Child Development," by Sandra Bem, *Signs,* by permission of the University of Chicago Press, copyright © 1983.

Reprinted from "Preface to Special Issue on Women and National Development," by Esther Boserup, *Signs,* by permission of the University of Chicago Press, copyright © 1977.

Reprinted from "Women in Rural Production and Reproduction in the Soviet Union, China, Cuba, and Tanzania." Part I, "Socialist Development Experiences," and Part II, "Case Studies," by Elisabeth Croll, *Signs,* by permission of the University of Chicago Press, copyright © 1981.

Reprinted from "Images of Women in Recent Chinese Fiction," by Irene Eber, *Signs,* by permission of the University of Chicago Press, copyright © 1976.

Reprinted from *The Black Extended Family,* by Elmer Martin and Joanne Mitchell Martin. Copyright © 1978. Reprinted by permission of the University of Chicago Press.

Reprinted from "The 'Woman Question' in Cuba," by Muriel Nazzari, *Signs,* by permission of the University of Chicago Press, copyright © 1983.

Reprinted from *Marriage Stability, Divorce and the Law,* by Max Rheinstein. Copyright © 1972. Reprinted by permission of the University of Chicago Press.

Reprinted from "Life-Span Theories and Women's Lives," by Alice Rossi, *Signs,* by permission of the University of Chicago Press, copyright © 1980.

Reprinted from "Migrants and Women Who Wait," by Harriet Sibisi, *Signs,* by permission of the University of Chicago Press, copyright © 1977.

Reprinted from *The Black Family in Modern Society,* by John Scanzoni. Copyright © 1977. Reprinted by permission of the University of Chicago Press.

Universitetsforlaget

Holter, Harriet, *Sex Roles and Social Structure.* By permission of Universitetsforlaget, AS, Oslo.

University of North Carolina Press

Haug, Marie R., "Social Class Measurement and Women's Occupational Roles," *Social Forces* 52. Copyright © University of North Carolina Press.

Warner Books, Inc.

From *Once My Child…Now My Friend,* by Elinor Lenz. Copyright © 1981 by Elinor Lenz. By permission of Warner Books, Inc.

Washington Post

Mooney, Elizabeth C., "I Asked My Daughter Why She Lives Like She Does." Copyright © 1979 The Washington Post.

West Publishing Company

Excerpt from *Sex-Based Discrimination* by Kenneth Davidson, Ruth B. Ginsburg, and Herma H. Kay, reprinted with permission of West Publishing Company.

John Wiley & Sons

McCall, Michal M., "Courtship as Social Exchange," pp. 190–210 in *Kinship and Family Organization* by Bernard Farber (ed.). © 1966. Reprinted by permission of John Wiley & Sons.

Miller, Howard, and Paul Siegel. *Loving: A Psychological Approach.* © 1972. Reprinted by permission of John Wiley & Sons.

Turner, Ralph. *Family Interaction.* © 1970. Reprinted by permission of John Wiley & Sons.

Workman Publishing Company, Inc.

Kavanaugh, Dorriet. *Listen to Us: The Children's Express Report.* Copyright © 1978 by Dorriet Kavanaugh. Reprinted with permission.

World Population News Service

Salas, Rafael M., "The State of World Population, 1985: Population and Women," *Popline 7* (July 1985).

Peter H. Wyden, Inc.

Harrison-Ross, Phyllis, and Barbara Wyden, *The Black Child: A Parent's Guide to Raising Happy and Healthy Children.* Copyright © 1973 Barbara Wyden.

Yale University Press

Cott, Nancy F., *The Bonds of Womanhood.* Reprinted by permission of Yale University Press.

O'Neill, William L., *Divorce in the Progressive Era.* Reprinted by permission of Yale University Press.

CREDITS FOR PART-OPENING PHOTOS

One   Ossip Zadkine, *Le Brillant Silence.* Denver Art Museum, Denver, Colorado

Two   Elie Nadelman, *Standing Male Nude.* Collection, E. Jan Nadelman, photo Geoffrey Clements.
and
Elie Nadelman, *Standing Female Nude.* Collection, The Museum of Modern Art, New York; Aristide Maillol Fund.

Three   Elie Nadelman, *Tango,* Collection, School of American Ballet, photo by R. V. Smutný courtesy of Eakins Press Foundation.

Four   Alexander Archipenko, *Walking Woman.* Collection, Mrs. Frances Archipenko Gray, photo courtesy Perls Galleries, New York.

Five   Constantin Brancusi, *The Kiss.* Philadelphia Museum of Art; Louise and Walter Arensberg Collection.

Six   Henry Moore. *Family Group.* Collection, The Museum of Modern Art, New York; A. Conger Goodyear Fund.

CREDITS FOR CHAPTER-OPENING PHOTOS

1   Mark Antman/The Image Works
2   Lew Merrim/Monkmeyer Press Photo Service
3   Photo by Arthur Tress/Photo Researchers, Inc.
4   © Beryl Goldberg
5   © Henri Cartier-Bresson/Magnum
6   Kenneth Karp
7   David S. Strickler/The Picture Cube
8   © Michal Heron 1981/Woodfin Camp & Associates
9   Photo by Ellis Herwig/Stock, Boston
10 Alan Carey/The Image Works
11 © Joel Gordon 1981
12 © Suzanne Szasz/Photo Researchers, Inc.
13 © 1984 Nancy Durrell McKenna/Photo Researchers, Inc.
14 Irene Bayer/Monkmeyer Press Photo Service
15 © 1985 Chuck Fishman/Woodfin Camp & Associates
16 © 1986 Bill Aron/Photo Researchers, Inc.
17 © 1976 Joel Gordon

N·A·M·E I·N·D·E·X

S·U·B·J·E·C·T I·N·D·E·X